Claudia Mickel-Keller

Sex Segregation in the Workplace

Trends, Explanations, Remedies

Barbara F. Reskin, *Editor*

Committee on Women's Employment and Related Social Issues

Commission on Behavioral and Social Sciences and Education

National Research Council

NATIONAL ACADEMY PRESS
Washington, D.C. 1984

NATIONAL ACADEMY PRESS   2101 CONSTITUTION AVENUE, NW   WASHINGTON, DC 20418

Library of Congress Cataloging in Publication Data
Main entry under title:

Sex segregation in the workplace.

   Revised versions of papers originally presented
at a workshop held in May 1982.
      1.   Sex discrimination in employment—United States—
Congresses.   2.   Sex discrimination against women—
United States—Congresses. I. Reskin, Barbara F.
II. National Research Council (U.S.). Committee on
Women's Employment and Related Social Issues.
HD6060.5.U5S475   1984   331.4'133'0973   84-8342

ISBN 0-309-03445-0

Printed in the United States of America

Committee on Women's Employment and Related Social Issues

Contributors

JAMES N. BARON, School of Business, Stanford University

ANDREA H. BELLER, Department of Family and Consumer Economics, University of Illinois

SUE E. BERRYMAN, The Rand Corporation, Santa Monica, California

WILLIAM T. BIELBY, Department of Sociology, University of California, Santa Barbara

FRANCINE D. BLAU, Department of Economics and Institute of Industrial and Labor Relations, University of Illinois

MARY C. BRINTON, Department of Sociology, University of Washington

PAMELA S. CAIN, Department of Sociology, Hunter College

MARY CORCORAN, Department of Political Science and Institute for Social Research, University of Michigan

GREG J. DUNCAN, Department of Economics and Institute for Social Research, University of Michigan

KEE-OK KIM HAN, Department of Family and Consumer Economics, University of Illinois

SHARON L. HARLAN, Center for Research on Women, Wellesley College

MARYELLEN R. KELLEY, College of Management, University of Massachusetts, Boston

MARGARET MOONEY MARINI, Department of Sociology and Anthropology, Vanderbilt University

KAREN OPPENHEIM MASON, Department of Sociology and Population Studies Center, University of Michigan

BRIGID O'FARRELL, Center for Research on Women, Wellesley College

MICHAEL PONZA, Department of Economics, University of Michigan

BARBARA F. RESKIN, Department of Sociology, University of Michigan

PATRICIA A. ROOS, Department of Sociology, State University of New York, Stony Brook

RACHEL A. ROSENFELD, Department of Sociology and Carolina Population Center, University of North Carolina

MYRA H. STROBER, Center for Research on Women and School of Education, Stanford University

LINDA J. WAITE, The Rand Corporation, Santa Monica, California

WENDY C. WOLF, Public/Private Ventures, Philadelphia

Contents

v

Preface

The segregation of the sexes into different occupations, industries, and (within firms) specific jobs is one of the most stable and striking features of the American workplace. Although the sexes have become increasingly similar in their likelihood of employment outside the home, within the workplace women and men differ dramatically in the kinds of jobs they hold. Sex segregation is problematic for several reasons. Most importantly, it promotes and sustains the wage gap between the sexes. Barring substantial changes in the ways that jobs are evaluated and wages set, women's prospects for economic parity will depend on their migration into mainstream "male" jobs, away from the many low-paying jobs most frequently held by women.

In view of the pervasiveness of segregation and its adverse consequences for women, in 1981 several groups sponsored an examination of sex segregation in the workplace by the Committee on Women's Employment and Related Social Issues of the National Research Council. The sponsors are the U.S. Department of Education, the Employment and Training Administration of the U.S. Department of Labor, and the Carnegie Corporation of New York.

The committee's mandate was twofold: to convene a major interdisciplinary workshop on job segregation and to prepare a state-of-the-art report on the topic. The two-day workshop, held in May 1982, brought together two dozen scholars. This volume includes revised versions of several papers presented there and the remarks of commentators, along with three papers the committee subsequently commissioned. These papers served as a resource to the committee in preparing its final report, *Women's Work, Men's Work: Segregation on the Job*, and stand as a companion to that volume.

The purposes of the workshop were to bring together scholars from several disciplines to review the evidence for various theoretical explanations for segregation and to report empirical research they were conducting that would enlarge our understanding of its extent, form, and causes. For this reason some of the papers, and thus the chapters in this volume, primarily review the literature (Blau, Marini and Brinton, Roos and Reskin, and O'Farrell and Harlan), while others offer up-to-date empirical findings (Beller, Bielby and Baron, Beller and Han, Rosenfeld, and Waite and Berryman). Two papers combine the presentation of original research with either a critical review of a theoretical perspective (Corcoran, Duncan, and Ponza) or the presentation of a new theoretical approach (Strober).

Many of the authors of this volume thank colleagues or assistants for their help. The workshop at which most of these chapters and comments were first presented and this volume also benefited from the work of several people, to whom I express my appreciation. As study director of the committee, Barbara F. Reskin was a valuable intellectual resource and an able manager of our work. Marie A. Matthews, administrative assistant to the committee, was indispensable in organizing the workshop. The members of the Committee on Women's Employment and Related Social Issues and Heidi I. Hartmann, as associate executive director of the Commission on Behavioral and Social Sciences and Education, helped identify workshop participants, participated in the workshop, and refereed papers for inclusion in this volume. Christine L. McShane, editor for the commission, worked with the authors and the National Academy Press in producing it. This volume would not exist without the behind-the-scene contributions of these people, and I thank them warmly.

ALICE S. ILCHMAN, Chair
Committee on Women's Employment and Related Social Issues

Sex Segregation in the Workplace

Trends, Explanations, Remedies

1 Introduction

BARBARA F. RESKIN

The concept of segregation was first brought to public attention in the United States to describe the enforced separation of black and white children in different schools. Although strictly speaking segregation denotes physical separation, it typically involves an institutionalized form of social distance between dominant and subordinate groups (Kuper, 1968:144). Certainly racial segregation in this country entailed more than physical separation; not only did it reflect the belief that black children were not fit to associate with white children, but it also made other forms of unequal treatment possible.

Years of litigation, protests, and busing have brought the concept of segregation into the public vocabulary and persuaded most Americans of the existence of racial segregation in schools and neighborhoods. At the same time, these activities have probably helped to associate the idea of segregation with *race* discrimination. But our society, like most others, segregates its members on the basis of characteristics other than race;

I wish to express my thanks to my friend and colleague, Lowell L. Hargens, for his help in reading and discussing the papers in this volume.

age, sex, and social class are the most common. Because most of these forms of segregation mirror social norms about the appropriate and "natural" relations between groups (just as prior to the 1954 *Brown* decision many people defined race segregation as natural and appropriate) and because of their very pervasiveness, these forms of separation are not readily thought of as segregation. We take for granted, for example, that children will be separated into age-based groups at school and that they will spend their days apart from most adults. Indeed, it is when the accepted patterns of segregation vary that we notice—for example, more than one or two adults on a school playground during recess or children in work settings.

The segregation of the sexes in some spheres is at least as common as that of children from adults. Yet it is often not visible for two reasons. First, cultural expectations, which structure our perceptions of the world, take for granted that most adults live intimately with a member of the opposite sex. Because such intimacy is at odds with the model of physical separation implied by the paradigmatic case of racial segregation, it masks the existence of sex segregation. Second, the presence of women and men publicly carrying out a variety of activities together supports the impression of sex integration. Superficially these two phenomena appear to invalidate any claim that the sexes are segregated.

Our interest in this volume centers on the segregation of women and men at work, regardless of whether the sexes are substantially segregated in most parts of their lives. In that context, work can be characterized as sex segregated in three ways. First, norms that relegate the sexes to separate spheres (Welter, 1966; Bloch, 1978)—women to the home and men to the public sector—necessarily imply their physical separation. For example, domestic workers in the private sphere, whether they are unpaid or paid, carry out their duties in a female environment, pursuing one of the most segregated jobs. Second, many paid employees work in exclusively one-sex settings. Whole industries are dominated by men; metal and coal mining, fisheries, horticultural services, logging, construction, and railroads were all more than 90 percent male in 1980 (Bureau of Labor Statistics, 1981:Table 30). Although there are no industries so overwhelmingly female, in part because in even the most female-intensive industries men hold managerial posts, women constitute more than three-quarters of all workers in several industries, including direct sales, employment agencies, convalescent institutions, libraries, and apparel and fabricated textile manufacturing. In 1980 over 32 million workers were employed in industries whose work forces were at least 80 percent male or female, and slightly more than this number—11 million women and 22 million men—worked in detailed census occupations in which at least 90 percent of the incumbents were of their own sex.[1] In ad-

dition, even within integrated industries, firms may employ only men or only women (see Bielby and Baron, in this volume). Clearly, then, a substantial proportion of American workers are physically segregated from the opposite sex.

If we extend the meaning of segregation beyond physical separation to encompass functional separation, the workplace is segregated in a third way, with a division of labor by sex the rule. Furthermore, the practice of employing women and men to do different jobs within the same work setting is often accompanied by the institutionalized social distance that segregation frequently entails. This social distance is marked by differential access to authority (Wolf and Fligstein, 1979), unequal wages (Treiman and Hartmann, 1981), separate job ladders, and exclusionary practices restricting mobility between positions labeled "male" and "female" (Roos and Reskin, in this volume). Hospitals are a good example. As outsiders, we notice female and male employees interacting in various ways—talking or joking together in the corridors or wards, working side by side over patients in examining and operating rooms, often similarly dressed in lab coats or scrub suits. Yet nurses, technicians, clerical workers, and food service workers are overwhelmingly female, while doctors, administrators, and orderlies are predominantly male. Ironically, it is the functional segregation of the sexes into different jobs that renders them interdependent and ensures their physical integration. It should be recognized, too, that the physical integration we observe is preceded, at least for technical and professional staff, by separate training programs in which the sexes are physically segregated. This separation may help prepare them for the unequal status and rewards they experience when as

---

[1] The Census Bureau categorizes occupations at varying levels of detail. In 1980 the classification referred to as "detailed" included 503 occupations. The number of workers in industries that were at least 80 percent female was computed from Bureau of Labor Statistics (1981:Table 30). The number of workers in occupations that were at least 90 percent members of the incumbent's sex was computed from Bureau of the Census data (1983:Table 1).

workers they are physically integrated.

Having shown how the concept of segregation applies to women's positions in the workplace, we must now ask why an inquiry into sex segregation in the world of work is necessary. Since dividing work on the basis of sex is customary in the home, why not in the workplace? To answer this question, let's return to the discussion of the consequences of segregating black and white schoolchildren. Beyond its stigmatizing effects, differentiating and separating people are often accompanied by differential treatment. Just as the segregated schools to which black children were sent were inferior to white children's schools (Kluger, 1975), the jobs that women hold provide rewards that are inferior to those that "male" jobs offer.

Foremost is the effect of segregation on women's wages. The more "female" an occupation is, the less it typically pays (Rytina, 1982). Between 35 and 40 percent of the well-documented wage gap between female and male full-time workers can be attributed to their segregation into different detailed occupational categories (Treiman and Hartmann, 1981). The additional segregation of women and men in the same occupations into different jobs explains even more of the differential. The wage loss associated with working in female-dominated occupations has especially adverse consequences for women who are the sole supporters of their families. Ehrenreich and Stallard (1982) commented that it is not the absence of a man in a household but the absence of a male salary that pushes working women into poverty; more precisely, it is the absence of the salary levels that male-dominated jobs provide. For women who support families on their own, segregation may mean poverty.

These facts—the pervasiveness of sex segregation and its economic implications for women—pose important scholarly and policy questions. What are the current levels of segregation, and what are the prospects for the decade ahead? Why is work so overwhelmingly sex typed? What kinds of remedies might reduce segregation levels? It is these questions to which the papers in this volume provide answers. The remainder of this chapter is an overview of their themes.

EXTENT, TRENDS, AND PROJECTIONS FOR THE FUTURE

From its emergence as a major institution in the nineteenth century, the U.S. labor force has been highly segregated by sex. Most occupations were so dominated by one sex that for decades the Census Bureau changed gender-discrepant responses for certain occupations on the assumption that they represented coding errors (Conk, 1981). Empirical studies assessing the extent of occupational segregation have consistently confirmed high levels of segregation (Gross, 1968; Blau and Hendricks, 1979; Lloyd and Niemi, 1979; Williams, 1979; England, 1981). Despite dramatic changes in both the composition of the labor force and the occupational structure, segregation levels have been extraordinarily stable throughout the twentieth century. This raises several questions. First, have social and normative changes in the 1970s or the existence or enforcement of antidiscrimination laws led to appreciable declines in segregation? What are the prospects for the remainder of this decade? How much segregation within specific employment settings is masked by aggregate estimates based on data for occupations? What can we learn if we go beyond the static pictures that occupational distributions yield to look at workers' job histories?

The papers on the extent of and trends in segregation in Part I of this volume illuminate these questions. In Chapter 2, Andrea H. Beller provides new and encouraging evidence regarding trends in aggregate segregation levels since 1970. Using Current Population Survey data for the period between 1971 and 1981, she documents a 10 percent decline in the segregation index. Unlike most of the previous research, she provides separate analyses for nonwhites and whites that show more rapid declines among nonwhites. Especially telling are results that reveal particular progress within professional occupations for whites (but not nonwhites), an outcome that Beller argues is linked to desegregation in college majors.

It is well known that the more closely one is able to look into the workplace, the more segregation one will observe. Thus, segregation indices computed for the 11 major census occupational groupings show considerably less segregation than do indices computed for detailed occupational categories. However, researchers have not had data sets that permit them to assess segregation levels within firms for a large number of establishments. William T. Bielby and James N. Baron's work (Chapter 3) is an important exception. They examined U.S. Employment Service data for almost 400 California firms employing more than 60,000 workers to address several issues previously beyond the reach of scholars. The result is a set of striking and disturbing findings. For example, over half the firms were totally sex segregated: not a single job title was held by both men and women. Furthermore, across all firms, the proportion of workers who held nominally integrated jobs (i.e., jobs held by both men and women in a firm) was only 10 percent. An analysis of the small number of firms that were minimally integrated permitted the authors to identify mechanisms that support segregation in different types of establishments. These findings contribute to our understanding of the organizational bases of sex segregation.

It is also possible to get beyond aggregated occupational data by tracking workers' patterns of movement between segregated and integrated jobs. Rachel A. Rosenfeld's research employs such an approach. In Chapter 4, Rosenfeld estimates the amount of such mobility between sex-typical and sex-atypical occupations and then investigates its determinants. Of considerable interest are results broken down by race that show the proportions of women and men who moved between occupations in which members of their sex were a majority and those in which they were a minority. Rosenfeld's subsequent examination of the wage and prestige consequences of different types of moves points to factors that may prompt workers to enter and leave sex-atypical work. Also important are analyses showing (1) how workers' personal characteristics are linked to an occupation's sex type and (2) what characteristics are associated with an individual's breaking an occupation's sex barrier. Specific findings, such as the absence of any effect of family responsibilities on the type of move a worker makes, bear on theories that seek to explain segregation.

In commenting on the first three chapters in Part I, Pamela S. Cain notes in Chapter 5 some apparent contradictions between them and offers a resolution. She also reminds the reader of the inherent limitations that available tools and data place on studying sex segregation.

In the final chapter in Part I, Andrea H. Beller and Kee-ok Kim Han use trend data to project the level of occupational segregation at the end of the decade (Chapter 6). They use several models to generate a set of projections. Of particular relevance to policy makers are the results for models based on optimistic, intermediate, and conservative assumptions about the rate of decline, which could reflect such factors as whether affirmative action regulations are enforced. Under the most optimistic assumption, segregation would decline markedly, but the models that Beller and Han judge to be more realistic predict only modest declines. Social policy must be guided by what is likely to happen in both the presence and absence of deliberate interventions to reduce segregation. Their paper provides such information and draws its implications for policy.

EXPLAINING SEGREGATION

The chapters in Part II grapple with the controversial and difficult question of why gender is linked to the work people do. Individually, each summarizes and weighs the empirical evidence associated with a particular explanatory orientation. Jointly, they provide both a sound foundation and an agenda for needed research.

Francine D. Blau's paper on labor market discrimination and occupational segregation (Chapter 7) is one of three that consider economic approaches to sex segregation. The economics literature on discrimination has concentrated on the role of discrimination in the wage differential between the sexes (see Blinder, 1973; Osterman, 1979; Cabral et al., 1981), but very little has been published specifically on the role of labor market discrimination in maintaining sex segregation. Focusing on this question, Blau critically appraises the utility of several general theories of discrimination, including those invoking taste, overcrowding, monopsony, statistical discrimination, and dual labor markets as well as the human capital alternative. Having laid out the theoretical alternatives, Blau evaluates the empirical evidence on the extent to which discrimination contributes to segregation. In doing so she details the difficulties in trying to measure discrimination and emphasizes the need for research that can distinguish between the various alternatives.

In Chapter 8, economist Myra H. Strober rejects existing theories of discrimination as inadequate to explain how occupations get assigned to one sex or the other and what contributes to stability or change in these gender designations. Exploiting ideas from existing theories, she proposes a provocative new "general theory" to explain both occupational segregation and wage differentials. The argument claims that the labor market behavior of men—employees and workers—is governed by their desire to maintain patriarchal privilege in the home and that pursuing this goal gives rise to both segregation and lower wages for women. Historical data on shifts in the gender label of public school teaching illustrate the theory.

In a close analysis of Strober's theory (Chapter 9), Karen Oppenheim Mason takes issue with certain assumptions as empirically unsupported. Mason disputes Strober's claim that existing ideas cannot adequately explain segregation and offers a set of theoretical approaches that she contends account for the persistence of segregation.

It has been suggested that the concentration of women in certain occupations reflects their own preferences, which in turn stem either from beliefs that these occupations are compatible with women's domestic roles or from a socialization process that predisposes them toward certain kinds of work. Each alternative has stimulated large bodies of research. Mary Corcoran, Greg J. Duncan, and Michael Ponza review in Chapter 10 the human capital explanation that attributes segregation to women's desire to find jobs that do not conflict with their domestic obligations. They put this explanation to a test with evidence from other research and their own current work. The authors present results from their analysis of data from the Panel Study of Income Dynamics on the duration of work experience, part-time work, and occupational sex composition that challenge predictions based on the human capital approach. Of special interest are analyses that cast doubt on the human capital assumption that skill depreciation and concomitant wage losses associated with time out of the labor force prompt women to eschew certain occupations. Their findings represent an important contribution to the development of a body of knowledge regarding how familial roles influence women's occupational outcomes.

Margaret Mooney Marini and Mary C. Brinton provide in Chapter 11 a comprehensive synthetic review of the massive literature that links sex typing in socialization to occupational choice. Their review covers research on (1) the existence of sex differences in occupational preferences, knowledge, skills, and traits and (2) whether observed differences result from sex-role socialization within families, schools, and the mass media. Because of the direct link between education and occupational options, they pay special attention to education in general and mathematics and science education in particular. This chapter, which ultimately draws conclusions about the effects of sex typing on segregation, is an important resource for researchers.

In response to Marini and Brinton, Wendy C. Wolf cautions that, in view of the multitude of factors implicated by the occupational socialization literature, the outcomes of any particular intervention attempts are unpredictable (Chapter 12). She reminds the reader that most of the literature reviewed by Marini and Brinton deals with differences between the sexes before they enter the labor market. She points out that the constraining effects of such factors may decline for adult women who face the economic realities of earning adequate wages.

In Chapter 13, Patricia A. Roos and Barbara F. Reskin draw on labor market theories to develop a framework in which a variety of institutional barriers to sex integration are examined. They focus on formal procedures within establishments and the organization of labor markets that discourage or exclude workers from entering jobs that have been defined as belonging to the other sex. They consider, in turn, barriers to job training (including apprenticeships), barriers to entry-level positions, and structural barriers that limit women's promotion into and retention in sex-atypical jobs. They cite a wide variety of studies that show how these barriers perpetuate the segregation of the sexes.

In commenting on this paper (Chapter 14), Maryellen R. Kelley points to limita-

tions in the research that Roos and Reskin review and questions the omission of the effects of such factors as job design and evaluation. Noting that little is known about how women are channelled into sex-typed career paths, she calls for research on this topic.

REDUCING SEGREGATION

Policy makers will find the chapters in Part III on the effectiveness of interventions to reduce segregation especially useful. In Chapter 15, Brigid O'Farrell and Sharon L. Harlan examine the impacts of various interventions on the basis of an extensive reading of case studies. From these data they draw some general conclusions about what kinds of intervention succeed and the conditions under which they work best. They point out, for example, that, to increase women's representation in male-labeled jobs, companies had to modify certain personnel practices, such as recruitment procedures, seniority systems, required qualifications, and job training.

In contrast to O'Farrell and Harlan's survey of workplace-based remedies, Linda J. Waite and Sue E. Berryman evaluate the effectiveness of a single program, the Comprehensive Employment and Training Act (CETA), for several employment outcomes of black, white, and Hispanic women and men (Chapter 16). Their statistical analyses fail to show effects of race or Hispanic ethnicity but do show sex differences in program assignment consistent with sex segregation. Two especially interesting analyses address CETA's ability to foster desegregation. The first examines the link between the sex label of participants' pre-CETA jobs and their CETA placements, and the second looks at CETA's record in meeting participants' preferences for sex-atypical assignments. However, the data Waite and Berryman use were collected prior to 1978, when CETA reauthorization legislation made sex equity an explicit program goal, as Wendy Wolf notes in her commentary (Chapter 17).

Post-1978 evaluations might yield a different picture.

CONCLUSION

In recapping the papers in this volume, Francine D. Blau integrates several recurring themes (Chapter 18). She points to the variety of ways that federal activities may help reduce or sustain sex segregation. Blau reminds readers that economic parity is not a necessary consequence of occupational desegregation. On the basis of the papers in this volume, however, it seems unlikely that we shall have to cope with that concern in the near future. It is to be hoped that the publication of these papers will help move us closer toward that goal.

REFERENCES

Blau, Francine D., and Wallace E. Hendricks
1979   Occupational segregation by sex: trends and prospects. *Journal of Human Resources* 14(2):197-210.

Blinder, Alan S.
1973   Wage discrimination: reduced form and structural estimates. *Journal of Human Resources* 8(Fall):436-55.

Bloch, Ruth H.
1978   American feminine ideals in transition: the rise of the moral mother, 1785-1815. *Feminist Studies* 4(June):101-26.

Bureau of the Census
1983   *Detailed Occupations and Years of School Completed by Age, for the Civilian Labor Force by Sex, Race, and Spanish Origin: 1980.* Washington, D.C.: U.S. Department of Commerce.

Bureau of Labor Statistics
1981   *Employment and Unemployment: A Report on 1980.* Washington, D.C.: U.S. Department of Labor.

Cabral, Robert, Marianne A. Ferber, and Carole A. Green
1981   Men and women in fiduciary institutions: a study of sex differences in career development. *Review of Economics and Statistics* 63(November):573-80.

Conk, Margo A.
1981   Accuracy, efficiency and bias: the interpretation of women's work in the U.S. Census of Occupations, 1890-1940. *Historical Methods* 1(Spring):65-72.

Duncan, Otis Dudley, and Beverly Duncan
1955   A methodological analysis of segregation indices. *American Sociological Review* 20:200-17.

Ehrenreich, Barbara, and Karin Stallard
1982   The nouveau poor. *Ms. Magazine* 11(August):217-24.

England, Paula
1981   Assessing trends in occupational sex segregation, 1900-1976. Pp. 273-95 in Ivar Berg (ed.), *Sociological Perspectives on Labor Markets.* New York: Academic Press.

Gross, Edward
1968   Plus ca change . . .? The sexual structure of occupations over time. *Social Problems* 16:198-208.

Kluger, Richard
1975   *Simple Justice.* New York: Random House.

Kuper, Leo
1968   Segregation. Pp. 144-150 in David L. Sills (ed.), *International Encyclopedia of the Social Sciences* 14. New York: Macmillan.

Lloyd, Cynthia B., and Beth T. Niemi
1979   *The Economics of Sex Differentials.* New York: Columbia University Press.

Osterman, Paul
1979   Sex discrimination in professional employment: a case study. *Industrial and Labor Relations Review* 32(July):451-64.

Rytina, Nancy F.
1982   Earnings of men and women: a look at specific occupations. *Monthly Labor Review* 105 (April):25-31.

Treiman, Donald J., and Heidi Hartmann (eds.)
1981   *Women, Work, and Wages: Equal Pay for Jobs of Equal Value.* Washington, D.C.: National Academy Press.

Welter, Barbara
1966   The cult of true womanhood. *American Quarterly* 18(Summer):151-74.

Williams, Gregory
1979   The changing U.S. labor force and occupational differentiation by sex. *Demography* 16:73-88.

Wolf, Wendy C., and Neil D. Fligstein
1979   Sex and authority in the workplace. *American Sociological Review* 44(April):235-52.

Part I
Extent, Trends, and
Projections for the Future

2 Trends in Occupational Segregation by Sex and Race, 1960-1981

ANDREA H. BELLER

Interest among economists in occupational sex segregation stems from the fairly well established relationship between the sex differential in earnings and women's concentration in a small number of occupations. It also stems from a family-based analysis of women's roles, although this connection continues to be controversial. Such an analysis says that because of their family roles, women invest less in market-oriented human capital than men do (Becker, 1981), and this includes choosing traditionally female occupations (Polachek, 1979). Recent empirical studies tend to refute this explanation of sex differences in occupational choices (Beller, 1982b; Corcoran and Duncan, 1979; England, 1982). While untangling the causes of occupational sex segregation has proved an ambitious challenge, measuring its trends is no less difficult.

This paper assesses the trends in occupational segregation of the sexes during the 1970s and compares them with those of the 1960s. A number of studies have examined changes in occupational segregation between census years: 1900-1960 (Gross, 1968), 1950-1970 (Blau and Hendricks, 1979), 1960-1970 (*Economic Report of the President*,

1973), and 1950-1970 among professional occupations (Fuchs, 1975). Using the index of segregation from the Duncan Index (Duncan and Duncan, 1955), these studies concur in the relative lack of change noted in occupational segregation through 1960 and the small decline during the 1960s. (The decline of sex segregation in the professional occupations during the 1960s was somewhat greater than that for all occupations.)

With the strengthening of equal employment opportunity (EEO) legislation and the promulgation of equal educational opportunity legislation in 1972, one might have anticipated an accelerated decline in occupational segregation during the 1970s. Moreover, there is a general perception that many women are becoming increasingly oriented toward nontraditional family roles and nontraditional jobs in the workplace.[1] Surprisingly, the index of segregation remained unchanged through 1976 or 1977, according to two recent works (Lloyd and Niemi, 1979;

---

[1] See, for example, Cherlin and Walters (1981) and Mason et al. (1976).

U.S. Commission on Civil Rights, 1978). The segregation indexes computed by these studies (as well as by Blau and Hendricks and by Fuchs) are presented in Appendix B, Table B-l. But findings from other studies seem to conflict with these reports of no change. Beller (1982b) showed that EEO laws reduced occupational segregation by 1974 and that EEO laws combined with equal educational opportunity legislation increased the effects of years of college completed on women's entry into nontraditional occupations between 1971 and 1977, especially among new entrants (Beller, 1982a). The reason these studies detected no change is a lack of comparability between the two data sets they used to compute the segregation indexes. In fact, I have found that the index of segregation declined from 68.32 in 1972 to 64.65 in 1977 and 61.66 in 1981, a rate of decline almost three times as large as that during the 1960s.

In the next section, the trends in occupational segregation from 1971 to 1981 are documented and compared with those of the 1960s. Trends in segregation among all occupations, among professional occupations, and among college majors are discussed. An analysis of cohort differences in occupational segregation during the 1970s follows. I then compare and contrast changes in the sex composition of detailed occupations during the 1960s and the 1970s. Finally, race differences in trends in occupational segregation are presented.

MEASUREMENT AND DATA

Trends in occupational segregation are commonly measured by the index of segregation (Duncan and Duncan, 1955). The index is defined as follows:

$$S_t = \frac{1}{2} \sum_i \left| m_{it} - f_{it} \right|,$$

where m_{it} = the percentage of the male labor force employed in occupation i in year

t, and f_{it} = the percentage of the female labor force employed in occupation i in year t. The index may take on a value between 0 and 100, where zero represents perfect integration and 100 represents complete segregation. The number tells the proportion of women (or men) that would have to be redistributed among occupations for the occupational distribution to reach complete equality between the sexes.

The index of segregation has two components, labeled the mix effect and the composition effect by Blau and Hendricks (1979). The value of the index depends on both the relative size of various occupations and the sex composition within occupations.[2] Changes in the index thus derive from two sources: changes in the occupational distribution and changes in the entry of the sexes into various occupations. (It also depends on the interaction of the two.) These changes may be in reinforcing or opposing directions. Signs of progress within occupations, for example, could be masked by unusual growth in occupations that are predominantly single sex. A standardization procedure can be used to determine the influence of each of these two effects. For example, to determine the effect of changes in the sex composition within occupations on the changes in the segregation index from year $t - 1$ to year t, the index of segregation for year t can be computed standardizing the size of occupations to year $t - 1$. Thus, the employment standardized index of segregation holds constant the distribution of employment across occupations (occupational mix) and enables one

---

[2] The value of the index may also depend on the degree of aggregation of the occupations. Typically, the greater the degree of aggregation, i.e., the fewer the occupations, the lower the level of measured segregation. For this reason, in comparing indexes over time, one should use the same number of occupations at the same degree of aggregation. This methodological issue is discussed in England (1981).

to observe the effects of changes in the sex composition within occupations alone.[3]

Similarly, to observe the effects of changes in the occupational structure alone, the proportion standardized index of segregation can be computed holding constant the sex composition at year $t - 1$ and using the employment distribution of year t. (Standardizing by the size of occupations in year $t - 1$ arbitrarily assigns the interaction term in one direction. Standardizing by the size of occupations in year t would assign the interaction term in the other direction.) These standardization procedures can also be applied to a given year to determine how the index of subgroup j differs from that of the population as a whole. This allows us to decompose the index of the subgroup into the effects of occupational mix and sex composition. For example, by standardizing the segregation index of the youngest cohort to the occupational mix of the whole labor force, it can be seen how the sex composition within occupations for the youngest cohort differs from that of the rest of the labor force.

To assess trends in occupational segregation during the 1970s, I used data from the Current Population Survey (CPS) conducted monthly by the U.S. Bureau of the Census. Data for the years 1971-1974 and 1977 used for the detailed analyses presented in this paper come from the March Annual Demographic Files (ADF) of the CPS. The ADF data are supplemented here with more recent data from the Bureau of Labor Statistics' (BLS) annual averages (AA), tab-

ulated by the BLS from the monthly CPS.[4] More detail on these sources and on issues of comparability and the choice of occupations included in the sample are discussed in Appendix A. As discussed there, the CPS occupational data collected during the 1970s are not comparable to the 1970 census data even though the same occupation codes are used, because the Census Bureau changed its method of assigning individuals to occupations in December 1971. Hence, statistics based on these two sources should not be compared. Although their reliability differs (see Appendix A), I make some comparisons between the two different sources of CPS data in order to include 1981 data in the analysis. The 1960 and 1970 census occupational data are used to show trends during the 1960s; these data were made comparable by the Census Bureau's recoding of the 1960 data according to the 1970 occupation codes (U.S. Bureau of the Census, 1972).

TRENDS IN OCCUPATIONAL SEGREGATION, 1960-1981

Occupational segregation of the sexes declined continuously during the 1970s at a

---

[3] The employment standardized index of segregation is defined as follows:

$$S_{it}^* = \frac{1}{2}\sum_i \left| m_{it}^* - f_{it}^* \right|,$$

where $m_{it}^* = (M_{it}/T_{it})\,(T_{it-1})\,(100)/\sum_i (M_{it}/T_{it})\,(T_{it-1})$, $f_{it}^* = (F_{it}/T_{it})\,(T_{it-1})\,(100)/\sum_i (F_{it}/T_{it})\,(T_{it-1})$, F_{it} = the number of females in occupation i in year t, M_{it} = the number of males in occupation i in year t, and T_{it} = $F_{it} + M_{it}$ = total employment in occupation i in year t.

[4] Data on occupations for 1971-1974 and 1977 come from the 1972-1975 and 1978 Annual Demographic Files, which are available on public-use computer tapes. These files contain considerable demographic detail, making it possible to cross-classify occupation by such characteristics as labor market experience, which is done later in this paper. These were the only years for which I had these data at the time of this writing. To incorporate more recent data than 1977, I obtained from the BLS unpublished tabulations of annual averages (AA) for 1981; to ascertain comparability between the AA and the ADF data, I also obtained these tabulations for 1977 and for 1972, the earliest year for which they are available. (The cooperation of Elizabeth Waldman and Jack Bregger of the BLS, who made these data available expeditiously, is gratefully acknowledged.) These data are not cross-classified by demographic characteristics. Thus, while overall trends can be assessed through 1981, cohort trends can be assessed only through 1977.

rate that exceeded the decline during the 1960s. The index of segregation declined from 68.32 in 1972 to 61.66 in 1981, according to the BLS AA data. According to the ADF, it declined from 68.14 in 1971 to 64.15 in 1977, and the decline occurred continuously over the intervening years. These indexes, which are computed over a common group of 262 three-digit census occupations, appear in Table 2-1, lines 2 and 3. For comparison purposes, indexes of segregation for 1960 and 1970 computed from the decennial census over the same 262 occupations are included. According to Census Bureau data, the index declined from 68.69 in 1960 to 65.90 in 1970.

As pointed out earlier, the index levels are not comparable across data sets, but trends in one data set should be comparable to trends in the other as long as comparability has been established within each data set. Between 1972 and 1981 the index of segregation declined at an average annual rate nearly three times as high as during the 1960s, i.e., -0.74 compared with -0.28. These figures appear in the bottom part of Table 2-1. The annual rate of decline in the segregation index appears to have accelerated slightly in the mid-1970s and to have remained steady through 1981.

To decompose the change in the segregation index during the 1970s, I have standardized it to the employment mix at the beginning of the decade. As mentioned above, we want to make comparisons only within a data set, so we standardize the Cen-

TABLE 2-1   Segregation Indexes, 1960-1981, All Occupations

	Census		CPS					
	1960	1970	1971	1972	1973	1974	1977	1981
	Index Level							
Unstandardized								
Census	68.69	65.90	—	—	—	—	—	—
Annual Demographic File (ADF)	—	—	68.14	67.36	67.09	66.39	64.15	—
Annual Averages (AA)	—	—	—	68.32	—	—	64.65	61.66
Employment Standardized								
Census (1970)	68.06	65.90	—	—	—	—	—	—
ADF (1972)	—	—	67.99	67.36	66.97	66.64	64.49	—
AA (1972)	—	—	—	68.32	—	—	65.18	62.88

	Change in Index					
	Average Annual Rate of Change					Total Change
Unstandardized	1960-1970	1971-1974	1974-1977	1977-1981	1972-1981	1972-1981
Census	-0.28	—	—	—	—	—
ADF	—	-0.58	-0.75	—	—	—
AA	—	—	—	-0.75	-0.74	-6.66
Employment Standardized						
Census (1970)	-0.22	—	—	—	—	—
ADF (1972)	—	-0.45	-0.72	—	—	—
AA (1972)	—	—	—	-0.56	-0.60	-5.44

NOTE: These indexes are based on a common group of 262 three-digit census occupations.

SOURCE: U.S. Commerce Department, Bureau of the Census, *U.S. Census of Population: 1970, Detailed Characteristics*, Final Report PC(1)-D1, U.S. Summary (Washington, D.C.: U.S. Government Printing Office, 1973), Table 221; Annual Demographic Files of Current Population Survey, 1972-1975 and 1978, computer tapes; and Bureau of Labor Statistics, annual averages of monthly Current Population Surveys, 1972, 1977, and 1981, unpublished tabulations.

sus Bureau data to 1970 and the ADF and AA data to 1972. Employment standardized indexes reveal the amount of the change in segregation that is due to changes in sex composition within occupations of a fixed size, the composition effects. As shown in Table 2-1, the employment standardized segregation index declined from 68.32 in 1972 to 62.88 in 1981, or by almost as much as the unstandardized index declined. Thus, most of the decline in the segregation index during the 1970s was due to changes in the sex composition within occupations, but the employment distribution also shifted slightly toward a less segregated work force.

Professional occupations continued during the 1970s to be less segregated than the work force as a whole and to experience a somewhat larger decline in segregation. The segregation index for 59 professional occupations declined from 59.44 in 1972 to 50.55 in 1981, according to the annual averages data. This yields an average annual rate of decline of nearly 1 percentage point, 0.99. Since these occupations are composed primarily of individuals with a college degree, it is instructive to examine an index of segregation for earned bachelor's degrees conferred on men and women by field of study. These data, published annually by the National Center for Education Statistics (NCES), are based on the distribution of all degrees granted by all accredited degree-granting institutions in the United States during a specific academic year.[5] The segregation index computed over college majors declined

from 46.08 in 1969 to 35.62 in 1978. The average annual rate of decline in this index is 1.16 per year.[6] Thus, segregation by field of study among bachelor's degree recipients declined rapidly during the 1970s, followed by the professional occupations, and, finally, the work force as a whole.

COHORT DIFFERENCES IN OCCUPATIONAL SEGREGATION, 1971-1977

Was the decline in occupational segregation by sex during the 1970s distributed throughout the labor force or concentrated in groups most able to take advantage of improved access to nontraditional jobs and opportunities for advancement? Beller (1982a) found the effect of equal employment opportunity legislation between 1971 and 1977 to be largest among college-educated new and recent entrants into the labor market. That is, compared to 1971, the chances of women with 1-10 years of potential labor market experience (new entrants) in 1977 or with 7-16 years (recent entrants) finding employment in a nontraditional occupation increased more than for older cohorts in 1977. Recent entrants in 1977, who were new entrants in 1971, found increased opportunities to move into nontraditional occupations as they aged over this period.

To examine changes in occupational segregation by cohort, I stratified the labor force by potential work experience, defined as Age − Education − 6, as in this previous study. Using the ADF data for 1971 and 1977, I stratified women and men into groups with the following years of experience (EXPER): 1-10, 7-16, and 11-40+. I believe that new and recent labor market entrants are best able to benefit from improved opportunities, and I hypothesize that young

---

[5] These data are taken from National Center for Education Statistics, *Projections of Education Statistics to 1988-89*, by Martin M. Frankel and Debra E. Gerald, April 1980. The original sources for the major portion of these data are the annual NCES reports on *Earned Degrees Conferred*. Further information came from ". . . education and professional associations, experts in other academic areas, and other agencies in the federal government . . ." (as cited in NCES, April 1980, p. 49). The numbers in this report differ slightly from the ones for the same year published in *Earned Degrees Conferred*.

---

[6] The index of segregation did not decline for postgraduate degrees; however, it is at a lower level than for bachelor's degrees (Beller and Han, in press).

cohorts will show greater changes than older cohorts. If access to nontraditional occupations increases, new entrants will have more opportunities to enter the occupational structure at preferred points than older cohorts with the same education. Since adjustments in education can only occur with some lag, new entrants also have the greatest opportunities to acquire more education and to alter their field of study in response to perceptions of improved opportunities in the labor market. In general, the educational attainment of younger cohorts of women is higher than of older cohorts, and women are increasingly likely to obtain additional degrees at all degree levels (Beller and Han, 1984). Recent entrants in the early stages of their careers can take advantage of new opportunities for advancement.[7] Thus, I compared new entrants into the labor market (EXPER = 1-10) with the rest of the labor force (EXPER = 11-40+), new entrants in 1971 with new entrants in 1977, and new entrants in 1971 (EXPER = 1-10) with themselves 6 years later in 1977 (EXPER = 7-16). We can see how segregated the youngest cohort is compared with the rest of the labor force, how segregated the entering cohort is at the beginning compared with the mid-1970s, and how much change in occupational segregation the 1971 entering cohort experienced as it aged.

The segregation indexes for these experience cohorts appear in Table 2-2. The youngest cohort is less segregated than the remainder of the labor force in both 1971 and 1977, and segregation declined for all

TABLE 2-2   Segregation Indexes by Experience Cohort

Experience Cohort	1971	1977	Change 1971-1977
Unstandardized			
1-10	67.47	62.51	−4.96
7-16	69.94	64.03	−5.91
11-40+	69.36	66.31	−3.05
Standardized to Employment of Whole Labor Force			
1-10	67.44	61.96	−5.48
7-16	69.07	64.89	−4.18
11-40+	69.13	66.65	−2.48
Standardized to Proportions of Whole Labor Force			
1-10	67.78	64.35	−3.43
7-16	68.54	63.93	−4.61
11-40+	67.84	63.69	−4.15

NOTE: The indexes are computed on the basis of 258 occupations. Occupations with no employment in any experience cohort were dropped from all groups.

SOURCE: Current Population Survey, Annual Demographic Files, computer tapes.

groups over this period. The differential between the youngest cohort and the rest of the labor force widened over time, however, as segregation decreased more rapidly in the youngest cohort as hypothesized. The segregation index for this group (EXPER = 1-10) declined from 67.47 in 1971 to 62.51 in 1977, or by 0.83 percentage points per year, while the index for the remainder of the labor force (EXPER = 11-40+) declined from 69.36 to 66.31, or by 0.51 points per year. During this period the decline is greatest not for the youngest cohort but for the group with 7-16 years of potential work experience. For this group (EXPER = 7-16) the segregation index declined from 69.94 in 1971 to 64.03 in 1977, or by 0.99 points per year. If we follow the entering cohort in 1971 for 6 years to 1977 (EXPER = 7-16), we find that the segregation index declined within this cohort by 3.44 percentage points from 67.47 to 64.03, or by 0.57 points per year. The entering cohort in 1971 became less segregated as it aged through 1977

---

[7] While these arguments and data strongly suggest that the results should be stronger for young cohorts, a potential bias in our results exists in that the sex difference in actual experience probably widens with potential experience. Thus, stronger results for younger cohorts might be related to the actual versus potential experience issue. In the absence of comparable cohort data prior to 1971, it wasn't possible to assess the effect of such a potential bias.

when the entering cohort is less segregated than in 1971. This implies that each entering cohort is less segregated than in the past and experiences a greater decline in segregation as it ages.

To decompose these cohort changes in occupational segregation, I standardized each subgroup to the whole labor force in each year. To determine how segregated this group would be if it had the same occupational mix as the labor force as a whole but maintained its own sex composition within occupations, I standardized the segregation index to the occupational mix of the whole (employment standardized). To determine how segregated this group would be if it had the same sex composition within occupations as the whole but its own occupational mix, I standardized to the sex composition within occupations of the whole (proportion standardized).

As it turns out, the occupational mix is quite similar across cohorts; the employment standardized indexes are nearly identical to the unstandardized indexes. What this implies is that, while the occupational distribution does not differ between older and younger generations as a whole, the sex composition within occupations differs substantially between recent and older cohorts. Thus, for example, while approximately the same proportion of the youngest and the older cohorts are accountants, a higher proportion of youthful than of older accountants are women. The proportion standardized indexes for 1977 show that the youngest cohort (EXPER = 1-10) would be much more segregated if it had the same sex composition within occupations as the labor force as a whole (64.35 compared to the actual 62.51); symmetrically, the remainder of the labor force would be less segregated if it had the sex composition of the whole (63.69 compared to the actual 66.31). Although as a group new entrants have the same occupational distribution as everyone else, new female entrants (as well as new male entrants) are in different occupations than their older counterparts.

MAJOR COMPONENTS OF CHANGE IN THE OVERALL INDEX, 1972-1981

The specific detailed occupations contributing the largest amounts to the decline in the index of segregation between 1972 and 1981 based on the AA data are the following: accountants; elementary school teachers; bank officers and financial managers; sales clerks, retail trade; secretaries, not elsewhere classified (n.e.c.); telephone operators; typists; sewers and stitchers; delivery and route workers; janitors and sextons; cooks, except private household; child care workers, private household; and maids and servants, private household.

Any difference in contribution can be due to either a change in the size of a segregated occupation or a change in the sex composition within an occupation. Two of the traditionally female occupations, private household maids and servants and sewers and stitchers, showed a large decrease in size over the period. Each of these declines took over 1 percentage point off of the segregation index in 1981. Other traditionally female occupations that decreased in size are telephone operators and private household child care workers. One traditionally male occupation, delivery and route workers, also decreased in size over the period. Although the numbers of secretaries, n.e.c., and elementary school teachers increased between 1972 and 1981, the proportion of the female labor force that crowded into these traditionally female occupations declined from 9.2 to 8.7 percent and from 3.6 to 2.8 percent, respectively. A smaller proportion of the female labor force crowded into the constant-sized female occupations of retail sales clerk and typist in 1981 than in 1972, 4.2 percent as opposed to 5.4 percent, and 2.4 percent as opposed to 3.3 percent, respectively. But the female share in these occupations did not decline. Women also entered three rapidly growing traditionally male occupations: accountants, bank officers and financial managers, and janitors and sextons. The female share in these occupations increased from 21.7 to 38.5 percent among accountants, from 18.7 to 37.4 among bank officers, and from 10.5 to 19.0 among janitors. Cooks is a rapidly growing occupation that men are entering in greater numbers than previously; the percentage of females in this occupation declined from 62.4 to 52.3 percent over this period.

The segregation index declined despite the fact that some occupations contributed more to segregation in 1981 than in 1972. The occupations that contributed more to the index are primarily rapidly growing female occupations. The largest increases came from registered nurses; office managers, n.e.c.; bank tellers; computer and peripheral equipment operators; and miscellaneous clerical workers. Nurses and bank tellers are both rapidly growing predominantly female occupations. The field of miscellaneous clerical workers is both growing and becoming increasingly female as are the fields of office managers and computer and peripheral equipment operators.

Changes in segregation during the 1970s may be summarized as follows. While women continued to enter some of the traditionally female occupations in large numbers, such as registered nurses, they decreased their rate of entry into others, such as secretaries. While many nontraditional occupations became slightly less male dominated, large declines in segregation occurred in only a few, e.g., accountants. Also contributing to a decline in segregation were the dramatic declines in the size of the traditionally female occupations of sewers and stitchers and telephone operators, presumably the first due to a declining industry and the second to rapid mechanization, eliminating the need for as many telephone operators. These changes suggest that women are working in many different nontraditional places in the labor force, changes which bear a closer look.

CHANGES IN THE SEX COMPOSITION OF OCCUPATIONS, 1960-1977

This section examines changes in the sex composition of size-standardized occupations, assuming that all are of equal size. It also summarizes material presented in greater detail in Beller (1981). Occupations are categorized according to their sex label and broad occupational group. Changes in the sex composition of detailed occupations during the 1960s are contrasted with changes between 1971 and 1977. These analyses are based on data for 262 occupations from the decennial censuses and the ADF and focus exclusively on changes in the sex composition within occupations, a variable amenable to alteration through public policy.

Each detailed occupation is assigned a sex label defined by deviations in its sex composition of ±.05 from that of the labor force as a whole. According to this definition, occupations are categorized as male if in 1960 the percentage of males equaled or exceeded .722; in 1970, .669; in 1971, .668; and in 1977, .640. Table 2-3 shows the number and percentage of occupations that are male, female, and integrated in each year.[8] Although a majority of occupations continue to be male dominated, the percentage declined during the 1970s, though it had increased during the 1960s; a number of occupations changed from male to integrated, while the percentage that was female remained unchanged.

A comparison of changes in women's share of employment by occupation from 1971 to

---

[8] Although the choice of the value ±.05 is somewhat arbitrary, it has little effect on substantive conclusions in this paper. It simply affects how wide a segment of the occupational distribution we choose to call integrated.

TABLE 2-3   Sex Label of Detailed Occupations

Sex Label[a]	Census		CPS	
	1960	1970	1971	1977
Male	159	165	157	140
Integrated	17	19	15	32
Female	86	78	90	90
Total	262	262	262	262
	Percentage			
Male	60.7	63.0	59.9	53.4
Integrated	6.5	7.3	5.7	12.2
Female	32.8	29.8	34.4	34.4
Total	100.0	100.0	100.0	100.0

[a] Defined relative to the sex composition of the labor force in the year given.
SOURCE: U.S. Bureau of the Census, *U.S. Census of Population: 1960*. Final Report PC(2)-7A. Subject Reports. Occupational Characteristics. (Washington, D.C.: U.S. Government Printing Office, 1963), Table 1; U.S. Bureau of the Census, *U.S. Census of Population: 1970*. Final Report PC(2)-7A. Subject Reports. Occupational Characteristics. (Washington, D.C.: U.S. Government Printing Office, 1973), Table 1; 1972 and 1978 Current Population Survey, Annual Demographic Files, computer tapes.

1977 with those from 1960 to 1970 reveals the following. Women's share of employment increased absolutely in a majority of occupations in both periods: in 77 percent of occupations between 1960 and 1970 and in 71 percent between 1971 and 1977. But women's share of employment relative to their share of the labor force increased in many more occupations during the 1970s than during the 1960s: in 45 percent of occupations between 1971 and 1977 as compared to 26 percent between 1960 and 1970. Women's relative share in male occupations also increased much more widely during the 1970s: in 46 percent of male occupations compared to 25 percent during the 1960s. These changes were most pronounced among the white-collar occupations, especially professional and managerial, and little or no change occurred among the blue-collar occupations. Women's share continued to grow both absolutely and relatively in the already predominantly female clerical occupations.

I have also examined the magnitude of change in the sex composition of the average occupation. Between 1960 and 1970 the average occupation became 2.8 percent relatively *more* male, while between 1971 and 1977 it became 0.6 percent relatively *less* male. Thus, while women had become more occupationally concentrated during the 1960s, they began entering nontraditional occupations at a greater rate than the labor force as a whole during the 1970s. Male occupations also became relatively *more* male on average during the 1960s in every broad occupational category with the exception of clerical. In the 1970s, with the exception of crafts and operatives, in every broad occupational category male occupations became relatively *less* male. For example, the average male managerial occupation, which became 2.5 percent *more* male during the 1960s, became 4.9 percent *less* male between 1971 and 1977.

In summary, the contrast in changes in the sex composition of occupations between the 1960s and 1970s shows that a new pattern of female entry has emerged. Rather than continue to crowd into a limited subset of occupations, women are entering a wide variety of nontraditional occupations. These changes are most prominent at the white-collar level, especially among professional and managerial occupations. But little such change appeared for the blue-collar occupations.

TABLE 2-4   Sex Segregation Indexes for All Occupations and Professional Occupations by Race

	All Occupations			Professional Occupations		
	1972	1977	1981	1972	1977	1981
	Index Level					
Unstandardized						
White	68.39	64.96	62.08	60.05	54.68	50.75
Nonwhite	68.00	63.29	59.39	51.58	49.95	48.88
Employment Standardized to 1972						
White	68.39	65.35	63.07	60.05	55.20	50.89
Nonwhite	68.00	65.43	63.52	51.58	48.58	50.59
	Change in Index, 1972-1981					
Unstandardized	*Annual Average*	*Total*		*Annual Average*	*Total*	
White	−0.70	−6.31		−1.03	−9.30	
Nonwhite	−0.96	−8.61		−0.30	−2.70	
Employment Standardized to 1972						
White	−0.59	−5.32		−1.02	−9.16	
Nonwhite	−0.50	−4.48		−0.11	−0.99	

NOTE: These indexes are based on a common group of 262 three-digit census occupations of which 59 are professional occupations.

SOURCE: U.S. Bureau of Labor Statistics, annual averages of monthly Current Population Survey, 1972, 1977, and 1981, unpublished tabulations.

TRENDS IN THE SEX SEGREGATION OF OCCUPATIONS BY RACE, 1972-1981

Occupational segregation by sex declined continuously for both whites and nonwhites between 1972 and 1981. While the index of segregation was approximately the same for both races in 1972—68.39 for whites and 68.00 for nonwhites—it declined relatively faster for nonwhites during the 1970s. For whites it declined to 62.08 in 1981, while for nonwhites it declined to 59.39. These indexes appear in Table 2-4. The figures in the bottom part of this table show the average annual rate of decline in the index of segregation between 1972 and 1981, 0.96 for nonwhites compared to 0.70 for whites.[9]

To identify the portion of the overall change attributable to changes in the sex compo-

sition within occupations, the indexes were standardized to the occupational distribution of employment in the initial year, 1972. By contrast to the unstandardized indexes, the standardized indexes, shown in Table 2-1, declined slightly more for whites than for nonwhites, from 68.39 to 63.07 for whites and from 68.00 to 63.52 for nonwhites. Thus, the greater decline for nonwhites than whites in the unstandardized index can be attributed to shifts in the nonwhite occupational distribution from heavily single-sex occupations toward less segregated ones. As a matter of fact, nearly one-half of the decline in sex segregation among nonwhites was due to such changes in their occupational distribution (−4.13) toward less segregated occupations as compared with changes in their sex composition within size-standardized occupations (−4.48). I conclude that changes in the sex composition within occupations was about the same for both races over the decade, but the occupational distribution of nonwhites also shifted toward less sex segregation.

_____

[9] Although in this sample many occupations contain only a few nonwhites, the level of the segregation indexes changes very little when occupations with fewer than 10 nonwhites are excluded from the computations.

The picture for professional occupations contrasts dramatically. On the one hand, while the levels of the segregation indexes are lower for both races for professional than for all occupations in 1972, these indexes are much lower for nonwhites. As shown in the second panel of Table 2-4, the 1972 segregation index was 60.05 for white professionals and 51.58 for nonwhite professionals in contrast to 68.39 and 68.00, respectively, for all occupations. On the other hand, nonwhites experienced little decline in sex segregation among professional occupations during the 1970s, while whites experienced larger declines than among all occupations. By the end of the decade, white professionals had become slightly less sex segregated than nonwhite professionals had been at the beginning of the decade—an index value of 50.75 compared to 51.58—while nonwhites had become somewhat less segregated—an index value of 48.88. The annual average rate of decline in the segregation indexes for professional occupations over the decade was 1.03 for whites and 0.30 for nonwhites, in contrast to 0.70 and 0.96, respectively, for all occupations. According to the employment standardized indexes, this entire decline for whites resulted from changes in their sex composition within occupations (1.02), while for nonwhites most of this decline came from shifts in their occupational distribution toward less (nonwhite) sex-segregated professional occupations (0.11).

The question naturally arises as to what proportion of each racial group constitutes the professional occupations. In 1972, 14 percent of white men and 15 percent of white women were in professional occupations, while only 8 percent of nonwhite men and 11 percent of nonwhite women were. By 1981 the proportions had risen for all groups, with the largest increase occurring for nonwhite women to 15 percent, the next largest increase for nonwhite men to 11 percent, and identical increases for whites of both sexes to 16 percent for men and 17 percent for women. These percentages reflect growth

rates of professional employment of 90 percent for nonwhite women, 69 percent for nonwhite men, 54 percent for white women, and 26 percent for white men. Nevertheless, professional occupations still comprised a smaller proportion of nonwhite than white employment in 1981.

If sex segregation declined as much for nonwhites as for whites over all occupations but not among professional occupations, then most change among nonwhites must have occurred at other levels of the occupational distribution.

MAJOR COMPONENTS OF CHANGE IN THE OVERALL INDEX BY RACE

The occupations contributing the most to decreasing the segregation index among nonwhites between 1972 and 1981 differ considerably from the ones for whites, although some similarities exist. The occupations that contributed the most to declines in the index of sex segregation among nonwhites only are primarily laborer and service worker occupations. Frequently, they are typically male occupations that declined in size over this period and in which nonwhites are represented disproportionately. The larger decline for nonwhites than for whites in the index of segregation over all occupations can be traced to this source. The specific detailed occupations taking over one-half a percentage point off the segregation index for nonwhites only between 1972 and 1981 are the following: storekeepers and stock clerks; clothing ironers and pressers; construction laborers, except carpenters' helpers; freight and material handlers; gardeners and groundskeepers, except farm; miscellaneous laborers; unspecified laborers; farm laborers, wage workers; chambermaids and maids, except private household; cleaners and charwomen; nursing aids, orderlies, and attendants; and practical nurses. Among these, nearly all laborer occupations declined in size, while nearly all service worker occupations increased in size. Nonwhite women increased their share of store-keeper jobs from 20 to 41 percent between 1972 and 1981.

The segregation index declined for both races because of the dramatic decline in the size of the private household maids and servants occupation, but the decline was much greater for nonwhites. The decline in the number of nonwhite females in this occupation took an exceptional 8.04 percentage points off the segregation index for nonwhites.

The specific detailed occupations contributing the largest amounts to the decline in the index of segregation among whites between 1972 and 1981 are mostly the same as for the whole population presented earlier. Nevertheless, some occupations contributed to the decline in the index for whites only: bookkeepers, garage workers and gas station attendants, waiters and waitresses, and hairdressers and cosmetologists. Although the number of whites employed as bookkeepers increased between 1972 and 1981, the proportion of the white female labor force that crowded into this traditionally female occupation declined from 5.2 to 4.6 percent. While men entered the two expanding traditionally female occupations—waiters and waitresses, and hairdressers and cosmetologists—at an increasing rate over this period, the male share of white employment increased from 7.2 percent to 9.2 percent in the former and from 9.2 to 11.1 percent in the latter. The traditionally male occupation of garage workers and gas station attendants showed a decline in size over the period.

Comparable declines in segregation for whites and nonwhites occurred for the following occupations: the clerical occupation, telephone operators; the operative occupation, sewers and stitchers; the laborer occupation, delivery and route workers; and the three service worker occupations, janitors and sextons, cooks (except private household), and child care workers (private household). By contrast, sex segregation

among whites also declined among the following white-collar occupations: accountants; elementary school teachers; bank officers and financial managers; sales clerks, retail trade; bookkeepers; secretaries, n.e.c.; and typists. Two of these occupations—bookkeepers and secretaries, n.e.c.—actually became more segregated among nonwhites because women but not men entered these fields.

The occupations that contributed more in 1981 than in 1972 to the segregation index for whites are identical to those for the population as a whole reported earlier. Occupations that became more segregated among nonwhites only include bookkeepers; secretaries, n.e.c.; investigators and estimators, n.e.c.; statistical clerks; electricians; and assemblers. These were all sex-segregated occupations in which the numbers of nonwhites employed grew. The typically female occupations among them also became increasingly female. While the number of electricians grew rapidly, the female share of nonwhite employment increased from 0 in 1972 to 3.9 percent in 1981. Contributing toward increasing the segregation index by comparable amounts for both races are registered nurses, bank tellers, computer and peripheral equipment operators, and miscellaneous clerical workers.

In summary, much of the decline in occupational segregation by sex during the 1970s occurred for both races; however, major differences exist. The major exodus of nonwhite females from the occupation of private household maids and servants and the decline in size of a number of laborer occupations in which nonwhite males dominated shifted the nonwhite occupational distribution toward a greater reduction in occupational sex segregation during the 1970s than for whites. On the other hand, white women reduced their rate of entry into a number of traditionally female white-collar occupations that nonwhite women continued to enter, and white women increased their entry into a number of traditionally male white-collar occupations more than nonwhite women did.

CONCLUSION

Occupational segregation of the sexes diminished significantly during the 1970s, as measured by the index of segregation. Most of the decline was due to changes in the sex composition of traditionally male occupations, particularly at the professional and managerial levels. Declines in segregation among new and recent job market entrants were greater than for the rest of the labor force. While nonwhites experienced a greater decline in occupational sex segregation than whites over the decade, about the same amount was due to changes in the sex composition of traditionally male occupations. The marked declines in sex segregation in professional occupations apparent among whites did not hold for nonwhites, but nonwhite professionals were much less segregated than white professionals at the start of the decade. Continued declines in occupational segregation by sex depend on the apparent momentum for change continuing into the next decade.

ACKNOWLEDGMENTS

This research was supported in part by funds from the University of Illinois at Urbana-Champaign, Research Board. Helpful comments on an earlier draft were provided by Marianne Ferber, Victor Fuchs, Barbara Reskin, and several reviewers. Excellent research assistance was provided by Kee-ok Kim Han. Computational assistance by John Boyd and Alex Kwok is gratefully acknowledged.

APPENDIX A

Data Sources

To assess trends in occupational segregation for intercensal years, a data set other than the decennial census must be selected. The monthly Current Population Survey (CPS) collects detailed three-digit census occupation data from a random cluster sample of (initially around 50,000) around 60,000 households (1/1500) designed to represent the civilian noninstitutional population of the United States. Two sources provide detailed occupational data from this survey. The first is the Bureau of the Census's March Annual Demographic Files (ADF), available on public-use tapes since 1968. The question on "longest job held last year" should provide reasonably reliable estimates of the previous year's occupational distribution. The second is the monthly statistics compiled by the Census Bureau for the Bureau of Labor Statistics (BLS) from which the latter compute, and since 1974 publish in *Employment and Earnings*, the annual averages (AA). AA data were used in the two studies referred to in the text (Lloyd and Niemi and U.S. Commission on Civil Rights), which computed segregation indexes for more recent data than the 1970 census. Unpublished tabulations of AA, which include data for smaller occupations than the published data (50,000 incumbents), are available directly from the BLS for 1972 on.

In comparing the CPS with the decennial census, the primary disadvantage of the CPS is its smaller sample size. The AA data are somewhat more reliable on these grounds than the ADF data. For total labor force data other than agricultural employment and unemployment, the sampling error of the annual averages is 0.67 times the sampling error of the monthly data (*Employment and Earnings*, May 1982, Table J). To improve reliability, the smallest occupations should be excluded. For purposes of this paper, all tabulations excluded occupations with fewer than 25 survey respondents in either the 1975 or the 1978 ADF data set (representing occupations with fewer than approximately 40,000 incumbents). Out of the 441 detailed three-digit 1970 census occupations, this left 267 in 1974 and 280 in 1977, 262 of which are common to both years. All tabulations in this paper include only those 262 occupations, or fewer where noted.

Comparability of Data

In attempting to assess trends in occupational data over time, two comparability problems arise, depending on the period of interest. The first is changes in the Census Bureau's occupation codes with each decennial census. A variety of techniques for dealing with this problem are discussed in England (1981). The 1960 census data were recoded according to the 1970 census codes by John A. Priebe (U.S. Bureau of the Census, 1972). These data are published in U.S. Bureau of the Census (1973, Table 221); the 1960 and 1970 census data in this paper, as well as in Blau and Hendricks (1979), come from this source. The 1980 census used a substantially revised set of occupation codes, and thus its occupation data will not be comparable to earlier census occupation data unless the Census Bureau double codes them with the 1970 and 1980 occupation codes.

Another comparability problem arose in that the segregation indexes computed using the CPS data were inconsistent with the one computed using the 1970 census data despite the fact that both used 1970 census codes. In an attempt to find out why, the following information was discovered. In

December 1971 a question eliciting information on major activities or duties was added to the monthly CPS in order to determine more precisely the occupational classification of individuals. According to the BLS (*Employment and Earnings*, January 1979, p. 207), "this change resulted in several dramatic occupational shifts, particularly from managers and administrators to other groups. Thus, meaningful comparisons of occupational levels cannot always be made for 1972 and subsequent years with earlier periods." For this reason, the 1970 census data are not comparable with the CPS data after 1971. The two studies that found no change in segregation in the 1970s relied on such a comparison. The earliest comparable data would be from the 1972 ADF on the longest job held last year, 1971. For these reasons, presented here are census data for 1960 and 1970 comparisons; data from the ADF for 1971-1974 and 1977, the years for which we have the data tapes; and the unpublished annual averages data for 1972, 1977, and 1981 for more recent data. It was found that the computations based on the ADF and the AA data sets are quite similar, although individual occupations can differ. To include data as current as 1981, comparisons across these two data sources were sometimes made, although their reliability differs. Additional comparability problems will arise when the CPS converts to the new 1980 occupation codes, beginning with the 1982 data.

APPENDIX B

TABLE B-1   Indexes of Segregation From Other Studies

	Census		CPS[a]		Projected
	1960	1970	1976	1977	1985
All Occupations					
Blau and Hendricks (1979) (N = 280)	68.33	65.77	—	—	60.10
Lloyd and Niemi (1979) (N = 236)	—	64.5	—	64.3	—
U.S. Commission on Civil Rights (1978) (N = 441)	—	65.8	66.1	—	—
Professional Occupations					
Fuchs (1975) (N = 33)					
Unstandardized	66.2	59.2	—	—	—
Standardized to 1960	66.2	62.7	—	—	—

[a] Computed from the BLS's AA data.

TABLE B-2   Percentage of Occupations With Changes in Sex Label by Initial Sex Label and Period

	1960-1970	1971-1977	1971-1974	1974-1977
All	9.5	11.1	11.5	11.1
Male	3.1	10.8	8.9	7.5
Integrated	53.0	33.3	53.3	37.5
Female	12.8	7.8	8.9	9.9

SOURCE: Same as for Table 2-3.

REFERENCES

Becker, Gary S.
1981   *A Treatise on the Family*. Cambridge, Mass.: Harvard University Press.

Beller, Andrea H.
1981   "Changes in the Sex Composition of U.S. Occupations, 1960-77." Unpublished paper.

1982a   "The Impact of Equal Opportunity Policy on Sex Differentials in Earnings and Occupations." *The American Economic Review, Papers and Proceedings* (May):171-75.

1982b   "Occupational Segregation by Sex: Determinants and Changes." *The Journal of Human Resources* 17 (Summer):371-92.

Beller, Andrea H., and Kee-ok Kim Han
1984   "Trends in Major Fields of Study Among Women in Higher Education." In Kathryn Rettig and Mohamed Abdel-Ghany, eds., *Economic Decisions of Families: Security for the Elderly and Labor Force Participation of Women*. Washington, D.C.: American Home Economics Association.

Blau, Francine D., and Wallace E. Hendricks
1979   "Occupational Segregation by Sex: Trends and Prospects." *The Journal of Human Resources* 14 (Spring):197-210.

Cherlin, Andrew, and Pamela B. Walters
1981   "Trends in United States Men's and Women's Sex-Role Attitudes: 1972 to 1978." *American Sociological Review* 46 (August):453-60.

Corcoran, Mary, and Gregory J. Duncan
1979   "Work History, Labor Force Attachment, and Earnings Differences Between the Races and Sexes." *The Journal of Human Resources* 14 (Winter):3-20.

Duncan, Gus Dudley, and Beverly Duncan
1955   "A Methodological Analysis of Segregation Indexes." *American Sociological Review* 20 (April):210-17.

Economic Report of the President
1973   Washington, D.C.: U.S. Government Printing Office, pp. 155-59.

England, Paula
1981   "Assessing Trends in Occupational Sex Segregation, 1900-1976." Pp. 273-95 in Ivar Berg, ed., *Sociological Perspectives on Labor Markets*. New York: Academic Press.

1982   "The Failure of Human Capital Theory to Explain Occupational Sex Segregation." *The Journal of Human Resources* 17 (Summer): 358-70.

Fuchs, Victor R.
1975   "A Note on Sex Segregation in Professional Occupations." *Explorations in Economic Research* 2 (Winter):105-11.

Gross, Edward
1968   "Plus ca change . . .? The Sexual Structure of Occupations Over Time." *Social Problems* 16 (Fall):198-208.

Lloyd, Cynthia, and Beth Niemi
1979   *The Economics of Sex Differentials*. New York: Columbia University Press.

Mason, Karen D., et al.
1976   "Changes in U.S. Women's Sex-Role Attitudes, 1964-1974." *American Sociological Review* 41 (August):573-96.

Polachek, Solomon W.
1979   "Occupational Segregation Among Women: Theory, Evidence and a Prognosis." Pp. 137-157 in Cynthia B. Lloyd et al., eds., *Women in the Labor Market*. New York: Columbia University Press.

U.S. Bureau of the Census
1963   *Census of Population: 1960*. Subject Reports. Final Report PC(2)-7A. Occupational Characteristics. Washington, D.C.: U.S. Government Printing Office.

1972   "1970 Occupation and Industry Classification Systems in Terms of their 1960 Occupation and Industry Elements," by John A. Priebe. Technical Papers, No. 26.

1973a   *Census of Population: 1970, Detailed Characteristics*. Final Report PC(1)-D1. U.S. Summary. Washington, D.C.: U.S. Government Printing Office, Table 221.

1973b   *Census of Population: 1970*. Subject Reports. Final Report PC(2)-7A. Occupational Characteristics. Washington, D.C.: U.S. Government Printing Office.

U.S. Commission on Civil Rights
1978   *Social Indicators of Equality for Minorities and Women*. August.

U.S. Department of Labor, Bureau of Labor Statistics
1979   *Employment and Earnings* 26(1):207.
1980   *Employment and Training Report of the President*. Employment and Training Administration.
1982a   *Employment and Earnings* 29(5):Table J.

1982b   *Labor Force Statistics Derived from the Current Population Survey: A Databook* 1 (Bulletin 2096):Table C-23.
U.S. National Center for Education Statistics
1980   *Projections of Education Statistics to 1988-89*. April.

3 A Woman's Place Is With Other Women: Sex Segregation Within Organizations

WILLIAM T. BIELBY *and*
JAMES N. BARON

Sex segregation in the workplace is one of the most visible signs of social inequality. In almost every work setting, it is unusual to see men and women working at the same job. When they do, they typically perform different tasks, with unequal levels of responsibility and authority. Even when job tasks are virtually identical, it is not uncommon to find men and women allocated to distinct job classifications within an organization.

Even women working full time, year round are paid less than men. While the earnings gap is partly due to unequal access to high wage firms and to unequal pay for comparable work, a substantial portion is due to differences in pay scales for job classifications filled by men and those filled by women (Bridges and Berk, 1974; Halaby, 1979; Treiman and Hartmann, 1981). Sex segregation has social-psychological consequences as well. For example, groups with limited opportunities for advancement may respond with psychological disengagement from the firm, lowered career aspirations, and an increasingly narrow, instrumental orientation toward work (Kanter, 1977b).

In short, sex-segregated workplaces affect us personally. Social structures that generate gender segregation are of great concern to social scientists, and the inequities that segregation engenders are obviously relevant to social policy. Yet sociologists know surprisingly little about job segregation by sex. Most of what we have learned concerns segregation among occupations. For example, we know that equalizing the detailed (census 3-digit) occupational distribution for men versus women would require moving roughly 60 percent of women working outside the home across occupational categories, and this has changed very little since 1900 (Gross, 1968; Blau and Hendricks, 1978; Williams, 1979; England, 1981a). We are also learning more about how men and women make occupational choices (Bielby, 1978; Marini, 1978, 1980). Empirical research on job segregation across organizational settings, however, is quite sparse.

Accordingly, this paper examines sex segregation in the workplace, utilizing data describing work arrangements in nearly 400 establishments across a wide range of industrial and institutional settings. We distinguish situations in which employers place men and women in the same job classifi-

cation from those in which job titles segregate the sexes within establishments.

Our study could be viewed as a straightforward job-level disaggregation of findings
regarding occupational sex segregation. Those
studies acknowledge that considerable segregation may exist even within detailed occupational categories. Our measures and
methods parallel such studies, and our findings confirm their speculations about pervasive segregation within occupations.
However, our aim is not merely to reveal
hidden segregation among jobs within firms.
Rather, since sex segregation is accomplished in organizations and is affected by
technical, administrative, and social exigencies of the workplace, it is important to examine how organizational structures and
processes produce sex segregation.

Our research does not consider how men's
and women's occupational choices, labor force
participation, and human capital investments affect the sex composition of the
workplace (for contrasting interpretations,
see England, 1982, and Polachek, 1979). Nor
are we investigating the demand side in the
economist's sense of the term, since we have
no information on the productivities of different classes of workers and the wages employers are willing to offer them (cf. Blau,
1977). Rather, the intersection of labor supply and demand enters into our analysis indirectly, since occupational composition and
skill mix of the firm are examined as determinants of sex segregation. However, if jobs
in most establishments are highly segregated by sex — even across firms differing
dramatically in their production functions
and cost structures — then it seems unlikely
that marginal adjustments of supply and demand account for distinct job assignments
of men and women (for a similar view, see
Blau and Jusenius, 1976).

WHY ARE SOME FIRMS MORE SEGREGATED THAN OTHERS?

Diverse explanations of sex segregation
have been reviewed thoroughly by others

(e.g., Blau and Jusenius, 1976; England,
1981b). Much more has been written, however, about why employers treat men and
women differently than about the extent to
which they do so. The sparse literature addressing why some firms are more segregated than others falls into three categories:
institutional accounts, explanations based on
tastes for discrimination, and human capital
market models.

Institutional accounts stress how statistical discrimination in hiring and allocating
employees places men and women in distinct career trajectories. Men tend to enter
internal labor markets in which they can
expect an orderly progression through successively more attractive jobs, insulated from
competition outside the firm. This increases
organizational loyalty, decreases costly
worker turnover, and allows employers to
recoup investments in firm-specific training
(Doeringer and Piore, 1971). Women are
perceived to have weaker commitments both
to specific firms and to paid employment in
general and are thus allocated to jobs with
low turnover costs and limited opportunity
for security and advancement (Bielby and
Baron, 1982). Not all firms, however, require specifically trained workers or have
internal labor markets. Therefore, if sex biases
in allocating workers to job ladders were the
only basis for segregating men and women,
one would expect less segregation in firms
lacking institutionalized employment arrangements — particularly small, labor-intensive, entrepreneurial firms in the so-called
economic periphery (Averitt, 1968).

This is certainly not the only mechanism
placing men and women in distinct job classifications, and perhaps a more reasonable
hypothesis is that the process of segregation
differs according to an organization's administrative arrangements and location within
the economy. For example, small manufacturing, service, and retail establishments
typically rely on an unskilled secondary labor market and use simple hierarchy or entrepreneurial despotism to control workers
(Edwards, 1979).

These enterprises might apply one of several strategies in allocating men and women to jobs. Highly trained line workers with job- and firm-specific skills typically are not employed in such establishments, nor are highly rationalized personnel and job classification procedures utilized. Thus, these firms might provide precisely the work contexts in which men and women who lack credentials for more desirable employment work together within broadly defined job categories. Furthermore, if employers must sacrifice profits in order to discriminate, they must be able to afford the costs of their policies. Marginal firms with weak competitive positions can least afford these costs and have an economic incentive to ignore sex in hiring and allocating workers (Arrow, 1973).

In the absence, however, of institutionalized procedures for hiring and allocating workers, male employers in the economic periphery may have more discretion to implement tastes for discrimination, which can reflect their own preferences or those of their employees or even their clients. In the most extreme case, patriarchal control strategies would exclude women from the workplace entirely. Such arrangements should be most prevalent in organizational niches that are protected from competitive pressures (e.g., through satellite linkages with larger firms) or where preferences for a segregated work force are so widely held within an industry or area that they have the force of customary law constraining market forces (Doeringer and Piore, 1971:22-27).

If labor supply and technical requisites determine the distribution of men and women across job categories, then a firm's mix of occupations and skills should largely account for its tendencies to segregate men from women. According to such human capital models, workers expecting intermittent labor force participation (primarily women) choose to enter occupations in which job skills do not atrophy from nonuse (Polachek, 1979). Indeed, if jobs with the highest turnover costs are also those in which skills atrophy most quickly, then extreme segregation can reflect maxi-mizing behavior by both workers and employers. That is, firms will assign men and women to the same job titles only under specific, and rare, circumstances: (a) when there is an available labor pool composed of men and women and (b) when employers perceive that the costs of employing men and women roughly are the same.

To summarize, certain analysts argue that gender segregation at work is caused by administrative arrangements for hiring, allocating, and controlling employees. Others emphasize the impact of tastes or prejudices, while still others claim that sex segregation reflects rational decisions regarding human capital investments on the part of workers and employers. Perhaps because segregation is such a natural attribute of most work situations, little has been written about the conditions under which it does not occur.

Our empirical analysis is guided by several general hypotheses. First, institutional accounts suggest that less segregated firms lack the administrative apparatus to differentiate workers by sex and cannot afford the costs of implementing employers' tastes for a segregated work force. Second, neoclassical accounts, grounded in notions of technical efficiency, suggest that desegregated organizations do not rely heavily on firm-specific skills but employ workers in occupations that are attractive to both men and women and for which both sexes are eligible. Of course, each of the mechanisms summarized above might operate but within specific organizational settings. Consequently, we examine the heterogeneity among highly segregated establishments to see if there are alternate strategies by which employers achieve the same result: distinct job assignments for men and women.

DATA AND METHODS

We analyzed data on work arrangements in hundreds of economic establishments studied in California between 1959 and 1979 by the California Occupational Analysis Field Center of the U.S. Employment Service. These data, used primarily in preparing the *Dictionary of Occupational Titles* (DOT), and procedures for collecting them are described in U.S. Department of Labor (1972). Our unit of analysis is the *establishment*, the "physical location where business is conducted or where services or industrial operations are performed" (U.S. Bureau of the Census, 1976:iv). Industrial characteristics serve as contextual factors, and suborganizational information about workers and jobs has been aggregated to characterize each enterprise. The majority of the establishments are firms; others are branches, regional divisions, subsidiaries, and production sites. Since we focused on work sites rather than firms, corporate headquarters of multiplant organizations are typically not included in our data. Corporations often direct initial desegregation efforts at headquarter managerial and office work (Shaeffer and Lynton, 1979), and progress toward equal employment opportunity (EEO) goals in these areas will not be reflected in our results.

The Sample

No well-defined sampling frame guides the Employment Service's selection of enterprises to study, but they try to represent the diversity of activities carried out within any industry (Miller et al., 1980). The California Field Center tended to study those industries that are regionally concentrated in the state, so our sample of establishments includes, for example, firms engaged in agriculture, aircraft manufacturing, banking, fishing, and motion picture production but not automobile or furniture manufacturing. While our sample provides a reasonable representation of the composition of establishments *within* industries,[1] the actual industries studied are not fully representative of economic activities in California. Most importantly, manufacturing establishments

are overrepresented in the sample. Major California industries not represented in our sample include construction trades, trucking, apparel and general merchandise retail trade (department stores), and insurance carriers. The first two industries are male dominated and highly segregated; the latter two employ many women and may be less segregated. While these data do not characterize a distinct population, they do reflect a diversity of work arrangements across a broad range of industrial and organizational contexts. In our view they provide invaluable comparative evidence regarding how administrative, technical, and environmental contingencies in organizations affect the structuring of work.

The data collected and coded for our project include 742 observations in over 500 distinct enterprises. About one-fifth of the establishments were visited more than once by Employment Service analysts. The most recent analysis was used for firms with follow-up data. Since some of the information used to characterize organizational attributes, however, was derived from narrative reports (described below), precedence was given to complete observations that also possessed a contemporaneous narrative report, even if a more recent follow-up analysis, lacking a narrative, had occurred.

To ensure comparability, analyses restricted to the firm's productive component or some other subset of jobs or departments were omitted, since they do not accurately characterize an entire work site. This restriction reduces the sample of establishments to 415. The sex composition of jobs was not reported for 22 of these firms, reducing the sample size for analyses reported in this paper to 393.[2] Of these, about 26

---

[1] Reweighting our observations according to published data on the size distribution of establishments within California's industries has virtually no effect on the distribution of organizational attributes in our sample.

[2] Job composition was not enumerated by sex after 1977-1978, apparently because of increasing resistance from establishments approached by the Employment Service. Unfortunately, this occurred when the California Field Center was studying agricultural establishments; therefore, 7 of the 22 observations lacking information on sex composition are in agriculture.

percent are plants, franchises, or production sites within some larger entity (though not necessarily corporations); 10 percent are administrative divisions, regions, or branches of larger companies; 3 percent are subsidiaries (distinct firms owned by another firm); and 61 percent are independent businesses.[3] Over half, 54 percent of these establishments were studied between 1968 and 1971, and 76 percent were visited by the Employment Service between 1965 and 1973. The 393 establishments in our sample employ nearly 47,000 men and over 14,000 women.[4]

The Documents

This paper uses two types of data obtained from the records of the California Occupational Analysis Field Center. *Staffing Sched-* *ules* supply, in essence, a complete organizational division of labor for the plant or firm in which job titles are analyzed. *Face Sheets* provide identifying information about the establishment and analysis. After assigning the firm to one or more categories of the Standard Industrial Classification (SIC), the Employment Service classifies the enterprise by its primary product(s) and supplies information about any unique or noteworthy characteristics of the firm, such as its jobs and processes. *Narrative reports* prepared for many establishments include information on some or all of the following: history and purpose of establishment; environmental conditions; operations and activities (departmentation, workflow, processes or services); personnel policies and practices; recent job restructuring; effects of automation on personnel and operations; and optional sections dealing with such topics as the product market and relations with government, the community, or other firms.

Operationalization

Staffing schedules, face sheets, and narrative reports were used to measure various environmental, organizational, and technical attributes of establishments as well as the composition of occupations and skills employed in each enterprise. Operationalizations are summarized in Table 3-1, which also reports descriptive statistics for variables used in our analysis. Organizational scale is measured by the natural logarithm of the number of employees, and positional specialization is measured by the logarithm of median job size. The latter measure is computed across workers, so a median of 10 indicates that one-half of the workers are in establishment job titles with 10 or more incumbents—as opposed to half the jobs containing 10 or more workers. This measure indexes the degree to which establishments "massify" the work force by assigning many workers to the same job title. Consequently, low scores correspond to high levels of spe-

---

[3] In practice, it sometimes was difficult to determine precisely if establishments studied by the Employment Service were autonomous firms or productive or administrative units within larger companies. When our materials indicated an owner or president, we assumed the enterprise was autonomous, owner-operated, unless other information indicated to the contrary. When the top position had such titles as plant superintendent, plant manager, general manager we assumed the enterprise was a subdivision of a larger firm, unless background information suggested otherwise. Anomalous cases were referred for clarification to the Employment Service analysts who conducted the original studies. Confidentiality restrictions precluded access to establishments' identities, preventing us from resolving such ambiguities directly.

[4] The disproportionate share of manufacturing establishments in our sample accounts for the underrepresentation of women workers. Nevertheless, the range of industries covered represents nearly every work context in which women labor. One important exception: The Employment Service tends to analyze branch plants and to overlook corporate headquarters. Therefore, virtually every kind of nonmanual work performed by women is represented in our study, but, unfortunately, we have no instances of such work done at the headquarter offices of large corporations. Evidence from the early 1970s suggests that efforts to desegregate nonmanual work occurred first in such contexts (Shaeffer and Lynton, 1979).

TABLE 3-1   Descriptive Statistics and Operationalizations of Organizational Attributes (N = 393)

Variable (range)	Mean	Standard Deviation	N	Description
Establishment Scale and Specialization				
Log establishment size (.69–8.97)	3.67	1.48	393	Natural log of number of employees in establishment.
Log specialization (0–6.49)	1.12	1.03	368	Natural log of median job size (see text).
Manufacturing Industry (0–1)	.63	—	393	One or more of establishment's standard industrial classification designations is in the manufacturing industry.
Economic Sector				
Core (0–1)	.38	—	393	See text.
Ambiguous (0–1)	.41	—	393	See text.
Periphery (0–1)	.21	—	393	See text.
Social Organization				
Log fragmentation (−1.10–1.39)	.14	.28	360	Natural log of ratio of establishment job titles to unique *DOT* titles.
Union or bidding arrangements (0–1)	.25	—	393	1 = some or all employees unionized or covered by formal bidding arrangements.
Proportion women (.00–1.00)	.32	.26	393	Proportion of female employees.
Occupational and Skill Composition				
Proportion production workers (.00–1.00)	.56	.33	380	Proportion of workers with *DOT* codes denoting production occupations.
Proportion clerical and sales workers (.00–1.00)	.20	.23	379	Proportion of workers with *DOT* codes denoting clerical and sales occupations.
Proportion service workers (.00–1.00)	.08	.21	379	Proportion of workers with *DOT* codes denoting service occupations.
Proportion professional, managerial, technical workers (.00–1.00)	.16	.20	379	Proportion of workers with *DOT* codes denoting professional, managerial, or technical occupations.
Average complexity: data (0–5.71)	1.92	1.09	336	Mean of ratings indicating complexity of workers' involvement with data.
Average complexity: people (0–8.00)	1.27	1.11	336	Mean of ratings indicating complexity of workers' involvement with people.
Average technical skills (−2.19–3.08)	−0.01	1.00	379	Mean of standardized ratings of production workers' technical skill (see text).
Skill specificity (.00–.99)	.51	.27	173	Proportion of workers in nonentry-level jobs.
Sex Segregation (12.5–100)	93.4	13.8	393	Index of dissimilarity computed across job titles. 100 = all male, all female, or completely segregated.

cialization.[5] One way to segregate workers is to place each worker in a unique job category; therefore, we expect greater sex seg-regation in more specialized establishments. We failed to detect any net differences in relationships between sex segregation

[5] This measure correlated −.87 with Gibbs and Poston's (1975) "M4" index of distributive differentiation, describing the evenness of the distribution of workers across positions. Functional (horizontal) differentiation of departments is reflected in our criteria for assigning establishments to economic sectors (see below). Structural differentiation — the proliferation of work roles — is almost completely determined by organizational scale; the correlation between the number of employees and the number of job titles is .92 when both are measured in a logarithmic metric. Consequently, while such differentiation may mediate the effects of scale, it is unlikely to affect work arrangements independently.

across 6 industrial sectors: manufacturing, state, services, social overhead capital, agriculture, and trade. We distinguish manufacturing from nonmanufacturing, however, to assess indirectly whether physical demands of work account for patterns of sex segregation.

We argued above that organizations confront different incentives to segregate depending on their niche within the economy and their size, structure, and technology. These differences in organizational forms and environments capture distinctive locations within the economy—what some institutionalists and Marxists have called *sectors* or *segments*. In certain respects, these are the organizational equivalent of "classes"; that is, actors presumed to share certain interests and attributes by virtue of their common market positions. Core firms are typically large, differentiated, use automated technologies, produce multiple products, are unionized, and are linked to larger organizational entities. Their environments are characterized by interorganizational dependence within key industrial sectors, and these establishments tend to be dominant actors in their milieux. In contrast, the economic periphery is composed of small, undifferentiated enterprises, typically operating in highly competitive markets in industries other than manufacturing. This congruence of organizational form and environment does not characterize all firms; the 161 establishments allocated to the ambiguous sector include those in small-scale manufacturing and many nonmanufacturing firms in less vulnerable situations with regard to their environments. The measures and procedures underlying this sectoral classification scheme are discussed in detail by Baron (1982:Chapter IV).

Radical accounts of workplace relations suggest that three aspects of an establishment's social organization should be associated with its level of sex segregation. Fragmentation is measured by the logged ratio of job titles in the establishment to unique 6-digit DOT titles assigned by the Employment Service analyst.[6] It measures the degree to which the organization differentiates its work force administratively beyond what might be expected from a breakdown of detailed occupational functions (Braverman, 1974:70-83; Edwards, 1979). Fragmentation is one strategy for segregating male and female workers who perform similar job tasks; that is, separate names are attached to men's and women's work. Other facets of the social organization of workplaces are measured by a dummy variable that denotes the presence of unions or formalized bidding arrangements, covering some or all workers, and the sex ratio, the percentage of workers who are female. Unions and formal bidding arrangements are an institutional arrangement that may constrain employers' (and male employees') ability to indulge tastes for discrimination. Some argue, however, that unions can exacerbate gender inequalities (e.g., Milkman, 1980; Baron and Bielby, 1982). Finally, tokenism—a highly unbalanced sex ratio—can facilitate the segregation of women or men into one or two separate job titles, while a more balanced work force may be more difficult to segregate (Kanter, 1977a).

The occupational composition of each enterprise was computed from the DOT occupational codes corresponding to each job title.[7] We measured the distributions of workers across the following broad categories: professional, managerial, and tech-

---

[6] In many firms, not every job title was mapped to a DOT title by the Employment Service analyst. The fragmentation measure was computed only for firms in which both 90 percent of the jobs and 90 percent of the workers were assigned a 6-digit DOT code (see Baron, 1982: Chapter VI). Six-digit DOT codes do not correspond to unique titles in the DOT, but more detailed classification is possible only for those jobs assigned to occupational categories according to the fourth edition classification scheme.

[7] Establishments in which less than 75 percent of the workers could be assigned a DOT code were treated as missing data on this outcome.

nical; clerical and sales; service — domestic, business, personal — and production, including extractive and transportation occupations. Levels of informational and interpersonal skill were measured by the mean of ratings indicating the complexity of workers' involvements with data and people, respectively.[8]

The measures of technical skills used depended on the edition of the DOT used in the analysis of an establishment. Production occupations were classified as skilled, semiskilled, or unskilled in the second edition, and we assigned values of 2, 1, and 0 to these categories, respectively. Ratings of workers' involvements with "things" began with the third edition. Average ratings were computed for each establishment's labor force using either the measure based on second edition DOT codes or the one based on subsequent versions of the DOT. Each establishment's score was then normalized relative to all others sharing the same version of the skill measure. That is, each enterprise's level of technical complexity is measured relative to other organizations incorporating the same version of the DOT occupational classification.[9] Finally, the level of firm-specific skills was assessed indirectly by the proportion of workers in "line" de-

partments who were not in entry-level jobs, as indicated on the staffing schedule.[10]

The index of dissimilarity measures the percentage of workers of one sex that would have to be moved to new job classifications in order to equalize the job distribution of workers by sex (Duncan and Duncan, 1955). It equals zero when the percentage distributions of men and women across job categories are identical, and it equals 100 when no men and women work in the same job.[11]

The Analysis

We first describe the distribution of establishments by level of sex segregation. Then we examine the organizational attributes that distinguish propensities to segregate. The relative contribution of social, administrative, and technical attributes to patterns of segregation may suggest mechanisms that account for those results, but we do not expect conclusive results from cross-sectional findings. Accordingly, these analyses are supplemented in two ways. First, we examine specific cases for which qualitative information exists on the hiring and alloca-

---

[8] This information, when available, was coded from job analyses pertaining to each position in the firm. Otherwise, it was obtained from 6-digit DOT occupational codes listed on staffing schedules. Third edition DOT ratings of 7 or 8 for relations with data were recoded to 6 to conform to the fourth edition rating scheme. Mean ratings for each establishment were computed only if: (a) at least half the jobs and workers in line departments could be characterized on the data and people dimensions; (b) at least half of the jobs and workers in other departments could be characterized; and (c) no more than 10 percent of the establishment labor force was missing data on these variables. Finally, scale values were inverted so that large values correspond to high levels of involvement with data and people.

[9] The mean level of technical skills was computed from third or fourth edition ratings (from job analyses or DOT codes), subject to the same restrictions described in footnote 7. Third edition codes of 8 were recoded to 7 to conform to the fourth edition rating

scheme. Mean ratings were computed from second edition codes only if: (a) detailed occupational codes existed for at least 75 percent of the employees in the enterprise and (b) at least 25 percent of the workers were in production jobs. Preference was given to third edition data for establishments that contained jobs analyzed in terms of both second and third edition DOT procedures.

[10] Workers in nonproduction departments were excluded because the Employment Service did not always collect information denoting entry-level jobs in those departments. The measure was not computed for establishments with less than 15 percent of their labor force in production-related departments. We also eliminated observations in which any department had no entry-level workers, or in which certain traditionally entry-level occupations occurred—e.g., janitor, receptionist—but none was coded as such. Given these restrictions, a measure of skill specificity is available for less than half of our observations.

[11] We consider all-male and all-female establishments to be perfectly segregated and assign a value of 100 to the index of dissimilarity. However, in analyses reported below, these enterprises are considered separately.

TABLE 3-2   Distribution of Establishments and Workers by Level of Segregation (N = 393)

(1) Segregation Index	(2) Number of Establishments	(3) Percentage of Establishments	(4) Cumulative Percentage of Establishments	(5) Median Establishment Size	(6) Number of Workers	(7) Percentage of Workers	(8) Cumulative Percentage of Workers
0–9	0	0.0	0.0	—	0	0.0	0.0
10–19	1	0.3	0.3	30	30	0.0	0.0
20–29	2	0.5	0.8	94.5	189	0.3	0.4
30–39	4	1.0	1.8	64	457	0.7	1.1
40–49	2	0.5	2.3	25.5	51	0.1	1.2
50–59	7	1.8	4.1	11	186	0.3	1.5
60–69	13	3.3	7.4	28	540	0.9	2.4
70–79	18	4.6	12.0	29.5	3,746	6.1	8.5
80–89	27	6.9	18.8	57	2,281	3.7	12.2
90–96	35	8.9	27.7	72	7,260	11.9	24.2
96–99.99	52	13.2	40.9	195	26,587	43.6	67.8
100	202[a]	51.4	92.3	25	19,250	31.6	99.4
All male	21	5.3	97.7	7	322	0.5	99.9
All female	9	2.3	100	5	51	0.1	100
TOTAL	393	100	—	36	60,950	100	—

[a] Subsequent tables report 201 completely segregated establishments. After completing our analyses, however, we discovered 1 establishment for which the sole integrated job was in fact due to a coding error.

tion of women. Second, we examine the subset of organizations for which longitudinal information is available in order to learn (1) the extent to which patterns of sex segregation change over time and (2) the organizational circumstances under which gender segregation increases, decreases, or remains constant. The concluding section addresses implications of our findings for policies aimed at equalizing job experiences and attainments of men and women.

RESULTS

Descriptive Statistics

Table 3-2 presents a remarkable story: Most establishments are either completely segregated or nearly so. Less than one-fifth of the establishments have segregation indices lower than 90, and they employ less than one-eighth of the workers in our sample. Over one-half of the establishments are completely segregated, and over three-quarters of the workers are in organizations having indices between 96 and 100. Indeed,

only 10 percent of the nearly 61,000 workers are in establishment job titles that have both men and women assigned to them. Even among the 162 establishments having some men and women in the same job titles, the mean segregation index is 84.1. In short, the workplace is substantially more segregated by sex than is suggested by studies that aggregate work force composition across establishments and into 3-digit occupational categories.[12]

One way to segregate male and female workers is to employ either men or women exclusively in an establishment. The 21 establishments without female workers, listed by establishment size in Table 3-3, are al-

[12] Of course, statistics on the distribution of workers in our sample are not representative of the California labor force, since establishments, not workers, were sampled. Nevertheless, these results show that there are very few work contexts in which men and women are assigned to the same job titles, and results reported below suggest that even the least segregated enterprises are seldom examples of workplace equity between the sexes.

TABLE 3-3 Organizational Attributes of Establishments That Employ Only Males or Only Females

Products or Activities	Sector[a]	Industry[b]	Employees	Job Titles	Job Titles per DOT	Median Job Size	Occupational Composition: Percentage in				Physical Demands Exclude Women[d]	Comments
							Production	Clerical & Sales	PTM[c]	Service		
Establishments With No Female Workers												
Flight instruction	P	SOC	2	1	.5	2.0	0	0	100	0	NA	
Food products	A	MFG	3	3	1.0	1.0	80	20	0	0	Y	
Glass products	A	MFG	3	2	.67	1.2	100	0	0	0	NA	
Stonework	A	MFG	3	3	1.0	1.0	100	0	0	0	NA	
Stonework	A	MFG	4	4	1.0	1.0	75	0	25	0	NA	
Stonework	P	TRADE	4	2	1.0	2.0	100	0	0	0	NA	
Sports equipment	A	MFG	4	3	1.0	1.0	75	0	25	0	NA	
Wallpaper	A	MFG	4	2	0.5	2.0	50	0	50	0	N	
Canning	A	MFG	6	4	0.8	1.0	67	0	33	0	N	
Plastics	A	MFG	7	3	1.0	2.3	100	0	0	0	Y	Subsidiary of a large chemical company.
Crop dusting	P	AG	7	6	NA	1.0	50	0	50	0	N	
Pens and pencils	A	MFG	8	5	0.8	2.0	75	0	25	0	NA	
Sports equipment	A	MFG	8	3	0.5	2.7	75	0	25	0	NA	
Fish hatchery	A	AG	10	2	1.0	4.2	100	0	0	0	Y	
Dairy products	A	MFG	11	9	0.9	1.0	77	13	9	0	Y	Branch of large dairy.
Laundry	P	SERV	17	10	NA	2.0	NA	NA	NA	NA	N	
Fertilizer	A	MFG	17	7	1.0	3.0	71	23	6	0	NA	
Brick & tile	A	MFG	36	14	1.1	3.0	94	3	3	0	Y	Branch plant of larger company.
Water transportation	A	SOC	46	7	1.0	10.0	52	0	48	0	NA	Subsidiary of larger company.
Golf course	A	STATE, SERV	56	9	1.0	18.4	43	0	4	54	NA	City-owned.
Wire	C	MFG	66	21	1.3	4.0	92	0	8	0	Y	Production plant of larger company.

							Establishments With No Male Workers					
Domestic service	P	SERV	2	2	1.0	1.0	0	0	50	50	—	Licensed foster mother who employs a housekeeper.
Real estate rentals	P	SOC	2	2	1.0	1.0	0	100	0	0	—	
Real estate escrow	P	SOC	2	2	1.0	1.0	0	25	75	0	—	
Business services	P	SERV	3	2	NA	1.2	NA	NA	NA	NA	—	Female labor contractor of office services.
Confection	A	MFG	5	5	1.0	1.0	100	0	0	0	—	Female-owned.
Hairpieces	A	MFG	5	4	1.0	1.0	60	20	0	20	—	Female-owned.
Real estate escrow	P	SOC	6	4	1.0	1.5	0	50	0	50	—	Female owner-manager.
Library	P	STATE, SOC	10	5	1.7	2.3	0	20	0	80	—	Library branch of veterans' hospital; civil service.
Business services	P	SERV	16	2	1.0	7.5	0	20	0	80	—	Female-owned telephone answering service.

[a] P = periphery; A = ambiguous; C = core.

[b] SOC = social overhead capital; MFG = manufacturing; AG = agriculture; SERV = service.

[c] PTM = professional, technical, and managerial occupations.

[d] NA = information not available; Y = yes; N = no.

most entirely small manufacturing operations in which most workers are in production jobs. Only 1 of the 9 all-female
establishments listed in Table 3-3 has more
than 10 employees, and only 2 employ women
in manufacturing. The typical all-female establishment provides services and does not
utilize the technical skills of blue-collar
workers.[13]

While extreme sex segregation is pervasive, hiring policies that exclude one sex
entirely are utilized only by establishments
engaged in marginal economic activities on
a very small scale. Only 5 of the all-male
establishments are branches of larger companies, and 4 of those cite physical demands
of work as the reason for excluding women.
It seems that autonomous employers operating small firms need no explicit rationale
for excluding female workers; they can unilaterally exercise their preferences for an all-
male work force.

The strong association between organizational scale and segregation is documented in the first line of Table 3-4. The
table reports mean levels of various organizational attributes across 6 categories of
sex segregation: moderate ($\Delta \leq 75$); high ($75
< \Delta \leq 90$); very high ($90 < \Delta < 100$); com-
plete segregation ($\Delta = 100$); exclusive employment of males; and exclusive employment of females. Excluding the 9
establishments employing only women, column 7 reports the proportion of variance in
each organizational attribute occurring across
categories of segregation.[14] Establishments
that exclude men or women are the smallest
on average, followed by those that are com-

pletely segregated. Moderately segregated
enterprises are larger still, followed by highly
and almost perfectly segregated ones (antil-
ogs of the means are 4, 9, 27, 30, 67, and
159 employees, respectively). Among the
384 establishments employing men, 30 percent of the variance in log size occurs across
the 5 segregation categories.

This strong association between organizational scale and segregation persists in
multivariate analyses (see below) and seems
to involve the changing mix of employer discretion versus the impersonal rule of bur-
eacratic procedures as organizations grow.
For example, employers operating on a very
small scale may exercise tastes for discrimination by excluding women altogether.
However, as tasks become increasingly differentiated and specialized clerical roles are
introduced, inexpensive female labor can be
utilized in segregated job classifications.
However, not all small establishments differentiate job tasks to the same degree, and
some allocate both men and women to
broadly defined job classifications. Continued expansion leads to the implementation
of rationalized, bureaucratic personnel procedures in nearly all firms. Mechanisms segregating the sexes become institutionalized,
and in large establishments men and women
are almost always assigned to separate job
families.

Other organizational attributes listed in
Table 3-4 are moderately associated with
segregation levels. Means for each variable
listed in Table 3-4 differ monotonically across
categories of moderate, high, and very high
segregation. Indeed, the characteristics most
strongly associated with segregation — core
sectoral location, specialization, and fragmentation — are also highly correlated with

---

[13] There are 13 establishments with just 1 male worker,
and these are quite similar to those listed in Table 3-
3. The largest has 22 employees and 9 have 5 workers
or less. The 60 firms with just 1 female employee are
concentrated in small-scale manufacturing and social
overhead capital industries. Only 1 has more than 30
employees.

[14] Total exclusion of males is not only rare but also

seems to reflect processes qualitatively different from
those that exclude or segregate women. Accordingly,
we exclude the 9 all female establishments from the
multivariate analyses reported below and from the variance explained computations reported in Table 3-4.

TABLE 3-4 Means of Organizational Attributes by Level of Sex Segregation

Variable	Level of Sex Segregation (Δ)						
	(1) $\Delta \leq 75$ (N = 42)	(2) $75 < \Delta \leq 90$ (N = 40)	(3) $90 < \Delta < 100$ (N = 80)	(4) $\Delta = 100$ (N = 201)	(5) All Male (N = 21)	(6) All Female (N = 9)	η^2 Columns (1)–(5) (N = 384)
Log size	3.40	4.20	5.07	3.31	2.17	1.47	.30
Log specialization	1.34	1.40	1.72	.87	.74	.39	.12
	$(1.52)^a$	(1.12)	(.93)	(1.14)	(1.64)		$(.03)^b$
Manufacturing industry	.45	.68	.76	.62	.67	.22	.03
	(.46)	(.66)	(.71)	(.63)	(.71)		(.02)
Core sector	.17	.50	.78	.29	.05	.00	.21
	(.23)	(.40)	(.49)	(.37)	(.35)		(.02)
Ambiguous sector	.52	.42	.21	.45	.71	.22	.06
	(.50)	(.47)	(.33)	(.41)	(.58)		(.01)
Periphery sector	.31	.08	.01	.26	.24	.88	.08
	(.27)	(.13)	(.18)	(.21)	(.05)		(.02)
Log fragmentation	.09	.21	.33	.10	−.14	.06	.16
	(.12)	(.16)	(.20)	(.13)	(.00)		(.02)
Union/bidding arrangements	.05	.30	.46	.22	.14	.00	.08
	(.09)	(.23)	(.28)	(.28)	(.35)		(.02)
Proportion women	.44	.42	.34	.28	.00	1.00	—
Proportion production workers	.44	.55	.61	.56	.74	.20	.04
	(.45)	(.54)	(.56)	(.56)	(.80)		(.04)
Proportion clerical & sales workers	.28	.20	.17	.20	.02	.39	.05
	(.27)	(.21)	(.21)	(.19)	(−.02)		(.06)
Proportion service workers	.06	.08	.09	.07	.03	.33	.00
	(.07)	(.08)	(.09)	(.08)	(.03)		(.00)
Proportion PTM^c workers	.22	.17	.11	.16	.21	.33	.03
	(.21)	(.18)	(.14)	(.16)	(.19)		(.01)
Average complexity: data	2.24	1.88	1.73	1.95	1.66	2.36	.02
	(2.23)	(1.89)	(1.77)	(1.94)	(1.62)		(.02)
Average complexity: people	1.64	1.05	.91	1.36	1.41	1.50	.04
	(1.58)	(1.14)	(1.17)	(1.28)	(1.15)		(.07)
Average technical skills	−.37	−.04	.12	.02	.30	−.96	.02
	(−.34)	(−.09)	(−.02)	(.05)	(.48)		(.04)
Skill specificity	.43	.48	.52	.50	.53	.31	.01
	(.57)	(.52)	(.48)	(.50)	(.47)		(.00)

^{a} Entries in parentheses for columns (1)–(5) are means adjusted for linear association with size.

^{b} Entries in parentheses in right-most column are the increments to explained variance due to segregation categories, net of size.

^{c} Professional, technical, and managerial.

log size, suggesting that the pattern of means in the table may simply reflect concomitants of organizational scale. Therefore, we also control for each attribute's linear relationship with log size (coefficients in parentheses).[15]

While controlling for size weakens most relationships in Table 3-4, the general pattern of coefficients across categories of seg-

[15] Specifically, each attribute was regressed on log size and binary variables representing segregation level, and adjusted means were computed at the average value of log size. The value reported in parentheses below the zero-order eta-squared for each attribute "y" is the increase in explained variance when variables denoting segregation group are added to the regression of y on log size.

regation is unchanged in many instances. Net of size, segregation is most strongly associated with the level of interpersonal skills and the proportion of clerical and sales workers in the enterprise. The former variable seems to differentiate moderately integrated establishments engaged in personal services from all others, and the latter differentiates all-male establishments, with virtually no clerical component, from those with a significant fraction of the work force engaged in clerical duties.

In sum, work settings in our sample approach complete gender segregation, and descriptive statistics suggest two mechanisms that may contribute to patterns of segregation: one reflecting the impact of administrative structures and personnel procedures that vary with organizational scale and the other pertaining to the occupational composition and skill level of establishments that rely primarily on nonmanual tasks typically done by women. The analyses reported below examine those mechanisms in greater detail.

Multivariate Analyses

Standardized coefficients for discriminant analyses reported in Table 3-5 indicate the organizational attributes that best differentiate establishments according to levels of sex segregation. The first function defines the linear composite of organizational attributes that differs most among segregation categories, relative to variation within categories. The second function extracts an additional dimension differentiating among segregation categories and is uncorrelated with the first function. The standardized weights index the relative importance of each attribute in distinguishing among categories of segregation, and the group means locate the segregation categories along each composite dimension.[16] The analyses reported

in the first two columns include the 21 all-male establishments; accordingly, the variable measuring organizational sex ratios (proportion women) is excluded from that discriminant analysis. The other results are based on the 363 establishments that employ both men and women. Standardized weights are computed by scaling both the linear composite function and the organizational attributes to unit variances. Coefficients were computed from a canonical correlation analysis applied to a pairwise-deletion correlation matrix with binary variables denoting group membership. Category means on the discriminant function are metric coefficients for those binary variables.

Organizational scale clearly dominates the results. Log size has a standardized loading of .79 on the first function and is correlated .89 with the linear composite. Consequently, the group means convey the same message as Table 3-4: Scale accounts for most of the association between organizational attributes and segregation.

The second discriminant function differentiates the 42 moderately integrated enterprises and the 21 all-male ones from other establishments, the overwhelming majority of which have segregation indices between 90 and 100. The function apparently reflects the impact of institutionalized personnel procedures and occupational composition. Formal bidding procedures for job advancement, combined with a work force occupying specialized, nonentry jobs, apparently inhibit the assignment of men and women to the same job classification, in some cases facilitating the exclusion of women employees altogether. This can occur when men and women are assigned to separate

---

[16] Discriminant analysis rests on distributional assumptions of within-group multinormality that are clearly

not met in our data. We are, however, not making inferences to a larger population, so significance tests are not appropriate for our analyses. We are reporting descriptive statistics about group differences, scaling levels of segregation to maximize the correlation with a linear combination of organizational attributes.

TABLE 3-5 Discriminant Analyses Relating Level of Sex Segregation to Organizational Attributes

Variable	Including Establishments With Only Male Workers (N = 384) Standardized Weights		Excluding Establishments With Only Male Workers (N = 363) Standardized Weights	
	1st Function	2nd Function	1st Function	2nd Function
Log size	.79	.02	.74	.20
	(.89)[a]	(−.01)	(.87)	(−.02)
Log specialization	−.33	.36	−.22	−.68
	(.48)	(−.23)	(.52)	(−.37)
Core sector	.37	−.03	.33	−.06
	(.72)	(.32)	(.72)	(.26)
Ambiguous sector	.07	−.23	.07	−.29
	(−.40)	(−.09)	(−.34)	(−.20)
Log fragmentation	.24	−.15	.21	.00
	(.66)	(−.04)	(.59)	(.09)
Union/bidding arrangements	.00	.53	.14	.32
	(.40)	(.45)	(.42)	(.37)
Proportion women	—	—	.35	−.55
			(.14)	(−.67)
Proportion production workers	.27	.21	−.14	−.06
	(.02)	(.59)	(.16)	(.34)
Proportion clerical and sales workers	.15	−.36	.16	−.20
	(.08)	(−.65)	(−.12)	(−.30)
Proportion PTM[b] workers	−.09	−.01	.05	−.34
	(−.21)	(−.24)	(−.18)	(−.31)
Average complexity: data	−.11	−.49	−.27	−.27
	(−.09)	(−.39)	(−.18)	(−.23)
Average complexity: people	−.07	.25	−.05	.21
	(−.29)	(−.30)	(−.34)	(−.20)
Average technical skills	.05	.03	.12	−.03
	(.03)	(.47)	(.11)	(.35)
Skill specificity	.06	.49	.08	.23
	(−.04)	(.35)	(.08)	(.28)
Segregation Group Means on Discriminant Function				
Moderate (N = 42)	0.00	0.00	0.00	0.00
High (N = 40)	1.43	2.23	1.36	1.36
Very high (N = 80)	2.19	2.98	2.37	2.71
Complete (N = 201)	0.19	2.64	−0.01	2.98
All male (N = 21)	−1.76	4.52	—	—
Canonical correlation	.610	.309	.584	.345

[a] Correlations between composite function and organizational attributes appear in parentheses.

[b] Professional, technical, and managerial.

entry classifications and department-spe-cific seniority systems keep women from transferring into male career lines (Shaeffer and Lynton, 1979). Net of these tendencies, similar consequences occur when the cler-ical and sales component is small and few workers have complex informational tasks.[17]

In other words, establishments in which most workers perform nonmanual tasks tend to have the occupational composition, task requirements, nonunion environment, and unspecialized job structures that facilitate a modicum of parity in work arrangements by sex. Indeed, 9 of the 16 least segregated firms have no workers in production occu-pations and 2 others have less than 10 per-cent in such roles (see Table 3-6). In con-trast, most all-male establishments are engaged in manufacturing activities and em-ploy most of their workers in production roles (see Table 3-3). Note that economic sector dominates neither discriminant func-tion. Thus, organizational arrangements as-sociated with sectoral location — not sector per se — affect sex segregation.

While the discriminant analyses seem to support institutionalist accounts of sex seg-regation, a more parsimonious explanation may account for the results on the second function: It is easier to segregate women when they are a minority of the work force, regardless of administrative arrangements. Relative group size is often a crucial basis

of solidarity and power (Simmel, [1923] 1950; Kanter, 1977a), but our analyses provide only partial support for the relative numbers hy-pothesis. Since sex composition defined membership in 1 of the 5 segregation groups (all-male), it was inappropriate to include that item in the discriminant analysis. Nevertheless, the second discriminant func-tion should be highly correlated with pro-portion women if the measures loading highly on it are simply proxies for organizational sex ratios. The correlation, however, ranges from −.27 and −.32 depending on how missing values are treated, about half the size of the correlations between the second function and occupational composition. Therefore, it appears that technical and ad-ministrative concomitants of production work are more important than relative numbers in differentiating levels of segregation.

On the other hand, sex ratios do figure more prominently in the discriminant anal-ysis restricted to the 363 establishments that employ men and women. According to Table 3-5, the first dimension remains dominated by organizational scale, but specialization and sex ratios clearly define the second factor: Segregation increases monotonically as or-ganizations become more specialized and less dependent on female personnel. Unfortu-nately, the 2 discriminant analyses are not directly comparable, since the latter differ-entiates among segregation levels condi-tional upon a mixed work force, while the distinction between all-male establishments and others is prominent in the former anal-ysis.

In short, there apparently is some strength in relative numbers, but that strength can be offset by countervailing organizational ar-rangements. Union contracts and formal bidding procedures, positional specializa-tion of the work force, reliance on firm-spe-cific skills, and manual job tasks facilitate employer strategies that either keep women out of the establishment completely or con-fine them in segregated job classifications.

---

[17] Since the 4 variables characterizing occupational composition sum to 100 percent, coefficients depend on which of the 4 is omitted. When the proportion of workers in production occupations is omitted, the coef-ficients are −.49, −.13, and −.14 for clerical and sales; service; and professional, technical, and mana-gerial, respectively. Of course, zero-order correlations between the discriminant function and the measures of occupational composition are not affected by alter-native choices for the omitted variable. Percent service correlates −.01 with the second discriminant function. The second function correlates most highly with the percentage of clerical and sales workers (−.65) and the proportion of production workers (.59).

Deviant Cases: Moderately Desegregated Establishments

The foregoing analyses discriminate very segregated organizations from segregated ones, but we must not lose sight of the fact that there is very little variance to explain. Less than one-eighth of the establishments in our study are even moderately integrated (using a generous definition of moderation), and the remaining, highly segregated organizations display virtually every possible configuration of organizational form and environment. The completely segregated establishments include huge bureaucracies that dominate their industrial environments, as well as small entrepreneurial firms at the economic margins. These enterprises are public and private, in manufacturing and nonmanufacturing; some employ women almost exclusively, while women have only a token presence in others. Indeed, an unsegregated work force is so rare that it is worthwhile examining commonalities among the few aberrant enterprises that do assign men and women to the same job classifications.

The top panel of Table 3-6 lists organizational attributes of the 16 establishments with indices of dissimilarity less than 60. Examining them on a case by case basis revealed some regularities not detected in the statistical analyses. First, we discovered that small enterprises with just one mixed job classification typically have indices substantially less than 100. That is, small establishments that employ men and women can appear moderately desegregated, but that desegregation can be nominal. The most extreme instances in Table 3-6 are the retail bookstore and pet store, each employing just one woman—a sales clerk: Their indices are 37.5 and 50, respectively. Accordingly, sex segregation appears bimodally distributed among small firms. Of the 234 establishments with fewer than 50 employees, 173 are completely segregated. But the median

segregation index among the other 61 is 75. Ten of the 16 establishments in Table 3-6 have relatively low segregation indices simply by virtue of having one job title in which a few men and women are employed.

Two real estate firms listed in Table 3-6 have men and women in integrated job titles but segregate them locationally. The third least segregated enterprise in our sample is a real estate management firm whose 23 male and 126 female apartment managers work and live in 149 different buildings, while the managers and officers of the escrow service are dispersed across field offices throughout a large metropolitan area. In both instances, men and women have the same rank and may have similar responsibilities, but within each of the individual workplaces there is perfect or near-perfect segregation.

Another source of integrated job classifications is the sex-linked practices in dealing with clients, accounting for low segregation indices in 4 other establishments. In 2 residential children's camps and an institution providing educational therapy, male counselors supervise boys and female counselors supervise girls. Another example is a language school, the second least segregated establishment in our sample, in which "it is deemed necessary that [students] be taught by both men and women as they are likely to need to communicate with each sex when using their language" (Narrative report 1712, 1970). Gender role ideologies have historically played an important part in creating and sustaining inequities against women in the teaching professions (Tyack and Strober, 1981). These educational establishments show that cultural definitions of men's and women's work — and responsibilities for socializing the next generation — can demarcate responsibilities by sex even within detailed organizational positions.

Integrated work forces are utilized in several establishments under circumstances that corroborate neoclassical accounts of sex segregation (Polachek, 1979). Real estate sales

TABLE 3-6 Occupational Attributes of the Least Segregated and Largest Establishments

Entry No.	Products or Activities	Sector[a]	Industry[b]	Total Employees	Female Employees	Segregation Index	Job Titles
		Sixteen Least-Segregated Establishments					
1	Citrus	P	Agriculture	30	14	12.5	3
2	Language schools	A	SOC	20	9	23.2	6
3	Real estate management	A	SOC	169	137	28.1	9
4	Real estate	P	SOC	23	6	33.3	5
5	Real estate escrow	A	SOC	105	95	36.3	12
6	Real estate	A	SOC	320	128	37.0	63
7	Retail books	P	Trade	9	1	37.5	4
8	Children's camps	P	Services	10	5	40.0	5
9	Tomatoes	P	Agriculture	41	23	42.3	6
10	Real estate	P	SOC	9	7	50.0	2
11	Retail pets	P	Trade	3	1	50.0	2
12	Scientific instruments	A	Manufacturing	8	2	50.0	5
13	Educational therapy	A	SOC	98	57	53.6	35
14	Plumbing supplies	A	Manufacturing	11	2	55.6	7
15	Garments	A	Manufacturing	14	7	57.1	8
16	Children's camps	A	Services	43	17	57.7	24
		Eleven Largest Establishments					
17	Mining and quarrying	C	Manufacturing	825	18	99.5	204
18	Bakery products	C	Manufacturing	886	268	96.3	60
19	Printing and publishing	C	Manufacturing	985	236	100.0	148
20	Sugar refining	C	Manufacturing	1277	82	99.0	337
21	Thoroughbred racing	C	Services	1464	49	96.1	83
22	Ordnance	C	Manufacturing	1727	967	99.2	129
23	Banking	C	SOC	2340	1384	79.2	346
24	Thoroughbred racing	C	Services	2845	59	99.5	83
25	Airline	C	SOC	2987	661	90.0	252
26	Telephone	C	SOC	6874	369	99.2	78
27	Naval shipyards	C	State, Manufacturing	7825	334	100.0	615

[a] P = periphery; A = ambiguous; C = core.
[b] SOC = social overhead capital.

is a vocation for which reentry costs to employees and turnover costs to employers are minimal. Consequently, one would expect an abundant supply of and demand for qualified female workers for these positions. At the same time, real estate sales can be sufficiently lucrative—especially in California—to attract males as well. Further, because salespersons work primarily outside the office, there should be fewer costs associated with employee tastes for discrimi-

nation. If market forces, however, account for the disproportionate share of real estate firms among the moderately integrated establishments, they cannot account for 4 of the other 5 real estate enterprises that completely segregate men and women in otherwise similar market and organizational circumstances.

Similarly, it is not surprising to find integrated work forces engaged in harvesting of fruits and vegetables. There is an ample

TABLE 3-6 (Continued)

Entry No.	Job Titles per *DOT*	Median Job Size	Occupational Composition: Percentage in				Comments
			Production	Clerical Sales	PTM[c]	Service	
				Sixteen Least-Segregated Establishments			
1	1.0	13.5	100	0	0	0	Picker—14M, 14F.
2	0.9	6.2	0	8	92	0	Language teachers—6M, 6F; department head—3M, 2F.
3	1.1	67.9	0	7	93	0	Apt. manager—23M, 126F.
4	0.5	6.8	0	76	24	0	Salesmen—13M, 4F.
5	1.8	25.5	0	22	78	0	Escrow manager—4M, 24F; escrow officer—3M, 32F.
6	1.4	59.1	8	82	10	1	Salesman—130M, 80F.
7	1.0	2.2	0	78	22	0	Sales clerk—5M, 1F.
8	1.0	1.8	0	0	70	30	Counselor—3M, 3F.
9	1.0	11.4	100	0	0	0	Worker—11M, 12F.
10	1.0	4.1	0	94	5	0	Salesman—1M, 7F.
11	1.0	1.2	0	67	0	33	Salesperson—1M, 1F.
12	1.0	1.0	62	12	25	0	Instrument maker—3M, 1F.
13	1.3	2.0	0	17	80	3	Psychologist—3M, 2F; therapist—13M, 25F; camp counselor—4M, 3F.
14	0.8	1.0	57	25	18	0	Assembler—4M, 1F.
15	1.3	2.0	86	0	14	0	Four women in 3 integrated production jobs.
16	1.4	2.0	9	5	70	16	Counselor—11M, 11F.
				Eleven Largest Establishments			
17	1.9	8.0	79	6	14	1	No women placed in production jobs due to nature of work.
18	1.4	61.2	35	54	3	8	
19	1.4	18.0	79	13	5	3	Women mostly in clerical and bindery classifications.
20	2.4	NA	75	10	11	4	Eleven women in 3 integrated quality control classifications; none in production.
21	1.3	111.5	15	60	7	18	Women mostly in clerical classifications.
22	1.4	102.6	84	6	8	2	See text.
23	3.2	15.0	0	68	30	2	Company policy to place women in other than routine clerical positions. Several integrated officer and manager jobs.
24	1.3	268.3	8	33	25	34	Women mostly in clerical classifications.
25	NA	111.7	NA	NA	NA	NA	Women employed only in clerical, stewardess, and ticket agent classifications.
26	1.6	157.5	74	26	1	0	Women employed without restriction except in jobs requiring lifting 25 pounds or more.
27	2.1	69.2	77	8	15	0	No women assigned to production classifications due to vigorous requirements of various crafts.

[c] PTM = professional, technical, and managerial occupations.

supply of male and female workers who are ill prepared for most other types of employment, and employers bear none of the training costs (Thomas, 1980). Nevertheless, Thomas's study suggests that the two agricultural establishments in our sample may be atypical. He found that men in lettuce harvesting are typically assigned to higher paid piece-rate jobs, while women are concentrated in hourly crews. Unfortunately, we have no evidence of the generalizability of his or our findings, since the sex composition of jobs was not compiled for the Employment Service's more recent analyses of agricultural work.

In sum, no single dimension of desegregation emerges from our analysis of "deviant" organizations. Instead, we found 4 qualitatively different but sometimes overlapping sets of circumstances that contribute to a desegregated workforce: (1) nominal desegregation of a single job title in a very small firm; (2) spatial segregation across work sites of male and female workers assigned to the same job classification; (3) sex-linked desegregation of jobs like camp counselor, which employ men and women, but toward different ends; and (4) market desegregation that occurs when a mixed labor pool is available to employers who perceive that training and turnover costs are identical for male and female workers. Moderate desegregation occurs rarely in the work contexts we have examined, and, when it does occur, it is typically of the nominal variety.

Large Establishments and Bureaucratic Segregation

Almost all large establishments are highly segregated, and most have written rules governing the hiring and allocation of workers. Consequently, if bureaucratic control strategies segregate men from women (Edwards, 1979), this should be most apparent in the largest establishments. The bottom panel of Table 3-6 lists attributes of the 11 establishments in our sample employing more than 800 workers. Case materials provide insight into administrative roles and procedures that support sex segregation.

All but one of these establishments segregate employees almost perfectly by sex, and narrative information available for 7 of them suggests that this total segregation is accomplished largely through bureaucratic rules and procedures. Possibly the most important factor, particularly in manufacturing establishments, is the existence of legal restrictions on the weight that women may lift. California law specified until 1970 that "no female employee should be requested or permitted to lift any object weighing 50 pounds or over," and regulations enforced by the state's Industrial Welfare Commission further restricted the maximum to 25 pounds. In 1970 a federal court ruled that this law conflicted with Title VII of the Civil Rights Act (*Utility Workers' Union of America* vs. *Southern California Edison* [69-543]).

References to these restrictions occur re-

peatedly in both narrative reports and job analyses. For example, the Naval shipyard in Table 3-6 assigns no women to production jobs due to "vigorous requirements of various crafts" (Narrative report 3, 1965), and the mining enterprise followed the same policy due to the "nature of work" (Narrative report 1800, 1971). A company providing telephone service to a large metropolitan area states that it was company policy to employ women "without restriction" except in jobs requiring lifting 25 pounds or more, yet the segregation index was 99.2 (Narrative report 100, 1965).

The ordnance plant, studied in 1970, employed 555 females as assemblers and 243 males as production workers. Each is an entry job, and both were mapped to the same detailed DOT occupational category by the Employment Service analyst.[18] According to the job analysis, these jobs differ primarily in that male "workers" lift 25 to 40 pounds, but female "assemblers" lift 5 to 20 pounds.

Weight restrictions are not mentioned explicitly in the narrative for the printing establishment in Table 3-6 (one of the largest in the western U.S. in 1968), but as in nearly all other manufacturing plants, the only production activities assigned to women are light assembly tasks. Most production tasks in this establishment are done by skilled craftsmen. The union contract establishes procedures for hiring and apprenticeship, and it seems reasonable to conclude that the union plays a substantial role in enforcing sex segregation in this plant. A narrative report prepared in 1966 for one of the two race tracks provides evidence of that role in another organizational context: Union dispatching policies explicitly exclude women from the job of parimutuel clerk (Narrative report 1536). No report was prepared for the other track in the same area, but pre-

---

[18] In other words, at the *occupational* level, entry-level production work has a relatively balanced sex ratio in this firm.

sumably it falls under the jurisdiction of the same union. Of course, these industries might have been sex-segregated long before they were unionized. That is, unions may be perpetuating gender-based inequalities rather than creating them.

Lifting restrictions and union contracts cannot account for all sex segregation in large establishments, because segregation is equally pervasive in large, nonunion establishments outside manufacturing. Indeed, in most firms — including all but 1 of the 11 in the bottom panel of Table 3-6 — nonproduction jobs are as segregated as production jobs, if not more so. While this situation primarily reflects distinctions between male managers and female clerical workers, it is also true that the few male clerical workers and female managers in our sample of establishments are hardly ever assigned to job classifications with workers of the opposite sex.

One notable exception is the bank studied in 1968, which employs more women than any other establishment in our sample. The bank claimed it had recently initiated a program to hire and promote women into officer classifications (Narrative report 415, 1968). The staffing schedule supports this claim: In 1968, women comprised 7 of 81 vice presidents, 18 of 108 assistant vice presidents, 16 of 49 management trainees, and 29 of 118 operations officers. While females were used exclusively in routine data processing jobs like keypunch operator, 10 of 23 systems analysts were women.

In one sense the bank's efforts are only noteworthy when contrasted against the uniformly high levels of segregation in other comparable large establishments: Fully equalizing the job distribution by sex would still require reclassifying 80 percent of this bank's female employees. Most managerial and professional positions remained exclusively male, while few men were employed in routine clerical duties. An organization's demography, history, technology, and labor supply, however, constrain the degree to which its work force composition can change

in a short period of time. This is especially true of large bureaucracies employing many workers in nonentry jobs. As long as seniority and accrued skills remain important bases for advancement in such contexts, workplace equity cannot happen overnight: The existing stratification regime favoring males essentially guarantees more workplace inequality in the short run, just as reduction of childbearing to below replacement levels would not immediately eliminate population growth in a society.

This particular bank's egalitarian policies toward women seem to have overcome bureaucratic inertia because they were implemented during a time of extraordinary organizational growth and change. When analyzed in 1968, the bank was described as one of the "largest and fastest growing business concerns in the nation" (Narrative report 415, 1968). Employment increased nearly 50 percent between 1961 and 1968, when the bank was automating its data processing operation and establishing regional offices and branch banks throughout southern California. Growth and technological change appear to be directly responsible for the desegregation of several management, administrative, and data processing job classifications in this firm. Its atypical experience demonstrates that the segregation observed in other large establishments is not inevitable.[19] These jobs, however, may have

---

[19] Other data gathered in California by the Employment Service corroborate this. They studied about 30 other establishments with more than 800 employees not included in our analysis because of incomplete coverage of some aspect of their operations. Of these, only 3 were moderately desegregated: a university campus ($\Delta = 70.5$), a unified school district ($\Delta = 76.5$), and an insurance company ($\Delta = 77.2$). Among large bureaucracies, assignment of both sexes to the same job titles occurs most often in social overhead capital organizations—firms in health, education, and welfare services, transportation, utilities, finance, insurance, and real estate industries. But the banking and finance industry is not uniformly desegregated. Of the 5 other establishments in our sample engaged in such activities, 3 were completely segregated, 1 was nearly so ($\Delta = 93.3$), and 1 was moderately integrated ($\Delta = 73.7$).

TABLE 3-7   Descriptive Statistics for Longitudinal Sample (N = 75)

| | Time 1 | | Time 2 | |
Variable	Mean	Standard Deviation	Mean	Standard Deviation
Log size	4.26	1.21	4.38	1.21
Log specialization	1.37	0.99	1.48	1.03
Manufacturing industry	.79	—	—	—
Core sector	.61	—	—	—
Ambiguous sector	.32	—	—	—
Periphery sector	.07	—	—	—
Log fragmentation	.18	.20	.17	.19
Union/bidding arrangements	.37	—	.39	—
Proportion women	.29	.25	.29	.24
Proportion production workers	.64	.30	.62	.29
Proportion clerical and sales workers	.16	.17	.18	.18
Proportion service workers	.08	.22	.09	.22
Proportion PTM[a] workers	.10	.12	.11	.11

[a] Professional, technical, and managerial.

been integrated precisely because they were new; it may take several years for the sex label of a new line of work to become established.

Longitudinal Analyses: The Permanence of Sex Segregation

Seventy-five of the 393 establishments in our sample were studied more than once. The average interval between visits was about 5 years, with a range of 2 to 12 years. The size composition of the follow-up sample is very consistent with the age and size-specific establishment mortality rates reported by Birch (1979). While moderately large, older enterprises were slightly more likely to be revisited, we detected no other systematic biases in the Employment Service's choice of establishments for follow-up analyses (for details see Baron, 1982, Chapter VII).

Descriptive statistics for the 75 establishments are reported in Table 3-7.[20] Estab-

[20] Several establishments were studied more than twice by the Employment Service. In those instances, we selected the pair for which the interval between analyses was closest to 5 years. Consequently, analyses for 16 of the establishments in the longitudinal analyses do not include the one selected for the cross-sectional sample of 393 observations.

lishments selected for restudy were slightly larger on average and more concentrated in manufacturing; other differences between descriptive statistics for these observations and those for the entire sample reflect concomitants of organizational scale (cf. Tables 3-1 and 3-7). In most instances, the temporal data describe changes between the mid-1960s and the early 1970s — the period immediately following passage of Title VII of the Civil Rights Act of 1964. Most establishments expanded employment between analyses; the labor force was stable in just 6 cases and was reduced in 25 establishments.

As Table 3-8 shows, neither legislation nor organizational change effected much change in sex segregation in the late 1960s and early 1970s. Two-thirds of the establishments remained all-male, completely segregated, or almost fully segregated (see the 9 cells in the bottom-right corner of the table). Indeed, much of the change in Table 3-8 reflects very small differences in segregation indices.

Table 3-9 lists characteristics of the 18 establishments for which the segregation index changed by at least 5 points. Only a few attributes differed systematically between the 11 organizations that became less segregated, between the 7 that became more segregated, and between the 57 in which

TABLE 3-8   Segregation Levels Over Time (N = 75)

Segregation: Time 1	Segregation: Time 2					
	Mod	High	Very High	Complete	All Male	Total
Moderate (Δ ≤ 75)	1	—	—	—	—	1 (1%)
High (75 < Δ < 90)	3	2	2	2	—	9 (12%)
Very high (90 < Δ < 100)	1	4	15	3	—	23 (31%)
Complete (Δ = 100)	—	4	5	29	2	40 (53%)
All male	—	—	—	1	1	2 (3%)
TOTAL	5 (7%)	10 (13%)	23 (29%)	34 (47%)	3 (4%)	75 (100%)

sex segregation remained virtually constant. Unionized establishments and those with formal bidding arrangements tended not to change from their high levels of segregation, nor did those in which women comprised a small minority of the work force. Organizations that partially desegregated were typically in small-scale manufacturing or were providers of personal and social services.

Most declines in segregation are attributable to a nominal change in the composition of 1 or 2 jobs rather than a major change in personnel practices. For example, 2 male checkers were hired by a large-chain supermarket, a male operator was hired by a firm providing mobile telephone service, and a woman was hired to work as a lens finisher in a firm manufacturing contact lenses. The "integrated" title of chip girl in the poker cardroom is completely segregated by shift; apparently, only males work in the early morning hours.[21] A company that manufactured silkscreened wall coverings hired 4 female inspectors, but continued to discriminate statistically, hiring women only as inspectors, paint mixers, and clericals "due to occasional job requirements of lifting heavy

reels of paper" in the other production work (Narrative report 1476, 1970). Only a manufacturer of kitchen ranges displays a deliberate effort to desegregate its work force. Only 2 women were employed in production departments in 1966. As in the case of the bank described earlier, organizational growth appears to have facilitated gender parity. By 1970 the work force of this manufacturing firm had more than doubled, and women worked alongside men in 14 entry-level jobs in the assembly department, reducing the segregation index from 99.5 to 78.8. Nevertheless, as in the bank, employment in several other nonadministrative departments remained restricted to males in 1970.

The 7 establishments that became more segregated over time were all highly segregated initially, and typically the segregation of only 1 job produced most or all of the change. In several instances, increased segregation took place in the context of organizational retrenchment or consolidation. But in no case was there any evidence that increased segregation resulted from deliberate employer strategy to manipulate the sex composition of jobs. Given the high initial levels of segregation, the small increases in the index could easily be attributable to random perturbations in labor supply and demand.

---

[21] The apparent integration of the chip girl position may simply reflect a typographical error on the 1970 staffing schedule. If so, the establishment was perfectly segregated in 1966 and 1970.

TABLE 3-9   Attributes of Establishments With Increasing or Decreasing Levels of Sex Segregation

Entry No.	Products or Activities	Year T1–T2	Sector[a]	Industry[b]	Number of Employees T1–T2	Number of Females T1–T2	Segregation Index T1–T2
		Establishments With Decreasing Segregation					
1	Supermarkets	1961–1967	A	Trade	56–49	16–12	100.0–94.6
2	Optical goods	1965–1968	C	Manufacturing	42–44	18–21	77.8–69.6
3	Mental health facilities	1966–1970	A	SOC	149–145	124–118	96.0–86.4
4	Wall coverings	1965–1970	C	Manufacturing	139–142	12–26	96.1–85.8
5	Mobile telephone service	1966–1971	P	SOC	15–30	13–21	100.0–88.9
6	Clay products	1964–1971	A	Manufacturing	20–35	3–11	100.0–87.5
7	Poker cardrooms	1966–1970	A	Services	149–190	97–66	100.0–87.1
8	Optical goods	1965–1968	A	Manufacturing	9–10	3–3	100.0–85.7
9	Kitchen ranges	1966–1970	C	Manufacturing	198–438	8–32	99.5–78.8
10	Wigs	1965–1971	A	Manufacturing	11–11	10–6	90.0–63.3
11	Wall coverings	1965–1970	C	Manufacturing	27–54	6–17	95.2–67.9
		Establishments With Increasing Segregation					
12	Trophies	1961–1971	C	Manufacturing	75–58	29–33	86.6–92.0
13	Electronic instruments	1967–1970	C	Manufacturing	95–49	20–11	84.0–89.5
14	Pottery	1960–1968	C	Manufacturing	309–535	137–294	92.7–99.2
15	Musical instruments	1960–1970	C	Manufacturing	164–173	10–4	89.0–95.9
16	Ceramic tiles	1971–1977	A	Manufacturing	21–42	9–18	91.7–100.0
17	Securities exchange	1960–1968	A	SOC	60–55	42–21	80.1–100.0
18	Garments	1960–1970	A	Manufacturing	25–26	16–17	77.8–100.0

[a] P = periphery; A = ambiguous; C = core.
[b] SOC = social overhead capital.

In sum, changes in organizational forms and environments and shifting labor supply and demand had little effect on sex segregation in the late 1960s and early 1970s.[22] In most of the establishments we examined, the consistently high levels of segregation are probably due to long-standing policies for hiring and allocating workers, perhaps reflecting industrywide practices predating the establishment itself. Neither a changing political and legal climate nor an influx of women workers in the late 1960s affected definitions of women's work within this sample of work organizations, especially in large, unionized establishments with institutionalized procedures governing hiring and advancement.

DISCUSSION

In most establishments, few job classifications are staffed by both men and women. Indeed, complete segregation was the norm in establishments studied in California by the U.S. Employment Service between 1959 and 1979, and segregation levels were virtually constant in these organizations during

[22] Nineteen establishments were visited 3 or more times by the Employment Service. Seven were perfectly segregated at each visit, and segregation decreased between analyses in only 1 establishment. In short, there is no evidence of a secular trend in job segregation by sex between 1959 and 1979.

TABLE 3-9 (Continued)

Entry No.	Title	If segregation due mostly to one title:				Comments
		T1		T2		
		Number of Males	Number of Females	Number of Males	Number of Females	
		Establishments With Decreasing Segregation				
1	Checker	0	10	2	5	Managerial promotion track for box boy but not for checker.
2	Several	–	–	–	–	Integration of 2 lens grinding jobs.
3	Several	–	–	–	–	Integration of kitchen helper (initially male) and head nurse (initially female) titles.
4	Several	–	–	–	–	Integration of 2 inspector titles (initially male).
5	Operator	0	10	1	9	
6	Press operator	2	0	3	2	
7	Chip girl	0	35	16	18	Chip girl title segregated by shifts.
8	Finisher	2	0	1	1	
9	Several	–	–	–	–	Desegregated 14 of 19 jobs in assembly department; 7 of 8 other departments completely segregated.
10	Ventilator	0	3	1	3	
11	Several	–	–	–	–	Integration of 1 nonproduction and 3 production jobs; 23 of 28 jobs still segregated in 1970.
		Establishments With Increasing Segregation				
12	Several	–	–	–	–	Discontinued jewelry manufacturing, eliminating 2 integrated jobs.
13	Assembler	10	13	3	8	Decline in production between 1967 and 1970.
14	Packer	5	5	0	8	
15	Assembler	3	3	5	0	
16	Kiln loader	1	1	8	0	Kiln loader only integrated job in 1971.
17	Tabulation clerk	6	5	0	0	Data processing operation consolidated as separate subsidiary between 1960 and 1968.
18	Sewing machine operator	1	3	0	3	Administrative jobs not included in staffing schedule for 1970.

the late 1960s and early 1970s. When balanced sex ratios did occur, they almost always reflected just 1 or 2 integrated job titles within an establishment.

Multivariate analyses revealed that organizational scale is strongly associated with levels of sex segregation. Small enterprises are either completely segregated or trivially desegregated; larger enterprises tend to have almost all workers in segregated jobs. Union contracts and formal bidding procedures, positional specialization, reliance on trained nonentry personnel, and manual job tasks facilitate a division of labor segregated by sex, while women are less extensively segregated when they comprise more than a small minority of the work force.

Institutional arrangements that prevail in core firms — rather than sectoral location per se — shape sex segregation, and they are most visible in the largest establishments in our sample. Many had sex-specific policies for allocating workers, oftentimes sanctioned by collective bargaining agreements. In manufacturing establishments, legal restrictions on physical demands of women's work typically rationalized complete sex segregation among production jobs, even when lifting was only required infrequently. Establishments in the economic core also specialize skills and fragment job tasks more than other enterprises, and these aspects of bureaucracy are not gender-neutral.

Of course, most women are not employed

in such manufacturing contexts. Less than one-quarter of all women workers are in manufacturing enterprises with 50 or more employees, and one-half the females in non-manufacturing industries work in establishments with fewer than 50 employees.[23] Even small organizations outside of manufacturing, however, are highly segregated. Of the 100 nonmanufacturing establishments in our sample having fewer than 50 employees, 73 were perfectly segregated, and women employed in those establishments are more likely to be segregated through the patriarchical actions of an entrepreneur or supervisor than by institutionalized bureaucratic rules and procedures. In short, there is equifinality in sex segregation of the workplace. Personal and patriarchal control prevails in small establishments, bureaucratic structures segregate men and women in large nonmanufacturing enterprises, and technical control excludes women from many production jobs within the manufacturing sector.

Do these findings imply that sex segregation is immutable? We detected little change in segregation indices, even among firms analyzed after court decisions in 1971 struck down California's restrictions on women's lifting.[24] In 1968, affirmative action goals and timetables were required of firms holding federal contracts, yet establishments in our sample covered by this order

were no less segregated than others (see also Salancik, 1979).

Nevertheless, we can point to some extraordinary circumstances under which desegregation did occur. As noted above, one bank and a manufacturing enterprise integrated a number of nonclerical jobs during a time of rapid growth or technological change or both, before there was any substantial government pressure to change personnel policies regarding minorities. Short of these fortuitous and idiosyncratic circumstances, large and systematic reductions in gender segregation seem unlikely to occur in the absence of fundamental shocks to the social system. For example, during World War II, employers faced extreme labor shortages. California's Industrial Welfare Commission granted 60 permits that exempted women from its 25-pound restriction on lifting, allowing 4,539 women workers to enter production jobs formerly closed to them.[25] Thus, unusual extraorganizational circumstances forced employers to reject long-standing practices based ostensibly on physiological differences between the sexes. Nevertheless, after the war these women were demobilized as rapidly as they had been integrated into the work force. The procedures for obtaining exemptions from the state labor code remained in effect but were barely utilized, and until 1971 the code rationalized sex segregation of production jobs in manufacturing.

To the extent that our results are generalizable, two policy implications of our study are clear. First, sex segregation will undoubtedly persist if policy makers adopt a laissez faire stance. Neither demographic trends, nor technological changes, nor bureaucratic imperatives are natural forces that lead to balanced sex ratios within jobs or firms. Second, policy intervention is un-

---

[23] Figures are based on the 1967 *Technological Advance in an Expanding Economy* survey by the University of Michigan's Institute for Social Research (Mueller et al., 1969). Of 766 women working outside the home, 560 were employed in nonmanufacturing industries, and 282 of those were in establishments with fewer than 50 employees. Since then, the female work force has become even less concentrated in manufacturing, although there may have been a shift toward employment in larger establishments.

[24] Of 46 establishments analyzed between 1972 and 1979, 26 were completely segregated. Eleven had segregation indices less than 75, but 5 were real estate enterprises studied by the Employment Service in 1973. Levels of segregation remained uniformly high in manufacturing establishments studied after 1971.

[25] Personal communication, Margaret Miller, Executive Officer, California Industrial Welfare Commission.

likely to make matters worse — most establishments are about as segregated as they can possibly be. While there may be political or economic incentives for focusing on certain kinds of work contexts, policy efforts could justifiably be directed at almost any area of economic activity, since almost all establishments are equally segregated.

Our findings also suggest some strategies for attacking sex segregation. First, policies that segregate men and women are most visible in large organizations. They are documented in written contracts, rules, job definitions, and procedures; they do not exist solely in subjective tastes of employers, employees, and clients. Large firms are often subject to public scrutiny, and their greater dependence on government contracts and regulations makes them susceptible to policy interventions (Salancik, 1979). They are also more likely to have slack resources with which to absorb the costs of social change. In short, it seems reasonable first to redress visible and easily identifiable mechanisms of sex segregation in organizations that are vulnerable to outside pressures, even if only a fraction of all women work in such establishments.

Second, interventions seem more likely to succeed in organizations that already have a sizable female work force. Sex ratios affect the balance of power among organizational constituents (Kanter, 1977a), and our results show that, as women comprise a larger percentage of an organization's labor force, employers seem less likely to segregate them. Changing the sex composition of jobs will require modifying organizations' rules for advancement through internal labor markets. Such changes are easier to accomplish when female workers command firm-specific experience. In short, segregation seems likely to persist in the absence of severe external pressures on the organization. Furthermore, the technical and political viability of efforts to abate the sexual division of labor depends on the existence of a constituency inside. The presence of a visible contingent of minority employees within an organization — even at the lowest ranks — may facilitate efforts to desegregate work.

Efforts to impose workplace equity in the absence of such a constituency might actually backfire. "Tokens" or "solos" can solidify resistance by male workers and demoralize those who should champion and benefit from equal employment opportunity programs (Kanter, 1977a; Northcraft and Martin, 1981). This underscores once again the limits of laissez faire approaches, since nearly all of the natural desegregation we observed in our sample involved tokenism.

Our recommendations are based on statistical associations rather than examinations of specific policy interventions. Nevertheless, recent surveys of attempts to reduce sex segregation do document the effectiveness of the organizational strategies we have suggested (Shaeffer and Lynton, 1979; O'Farrell and Harlan, 1982). One conclusion cannot be disputed: Doing nothing guarantees persistent sex segregation in all areas of economic activity. Although not the focus of this study, we repeatedly encountered instances of sex segregation of jobs leading to gender-specific promotion lines — an orderly progression through jobs of successively greater authority and responsibility for men and dead-end careers for women. The pervasive sex segregation across organizational and institutional contexts that our study has documented almost certainly accounts for the substantial sex differences revealed by individual-level analyses of work inequalities (e.g., Baron and Bielby, 1982; Bielby and Baron, 1982; Wolf and Fligstein, 1979).

The degree and persistence of sex segregation leave us somewhat pessimistic about prospects for rapid or extensive change. On the other hand, by documenting the impact of organizational structures and dynamics on the sexual division of labor — and by underscoring the pervasiveness of gender segregation — we hope to facilitate more informed research efforts and policy interventions in the future.

ACKNOWLEDGMENTS

The authors were supported in part by a grant from the National Science Foundation (SES 79-24905). We gratefully acknowledge the cooperation and assistance of the California Occupational Analysis Field Center. Our thanks go to Isabelle M. Allain, Hallie Anderson, and Kelly Moreno who assisted in this research, and to Trina Miller who processed many versions of this manuscript. We are indebted to our many colleagues who have influenced our thinking on sex segregation and have commented on earlier versions of this report, especially to Donald J. Treiman and Karen O. Mason for their detailed suggestions.

REFERENCES

Arrow, Kenneth
1973   "The theory of discrimination," Pp. 3-33 in Orley Ashenfelter and Albert Rees (eds.), Discrimination in Labor Markets. Princeton, N.J.: Princeton University Press.

Averitt, Robert
1968   The Dual Economy. New York: Horton.

Baron, James
1982   Economic Segmentation and the Organization of Work. Unpublished Ph.D. dissertation, University of California, Santa Barbara.

Baron, James, and William Bielby
1982   "Workers and machines: dimensions and determinants of technical relations in the workplace." American Sociological Review 47:175-188.

Bielby, Denise
1978   "Career sex-atypicality and career involvement of college educated women: baseline evidence from the 1960's." Sociology of Education 51 (January):7-28.

Bielby, William, and James Baron
1982   "Organizations, technology, and worker attachment to the firm." In Donald J. Treiman and Robert V. Robinson (eds.), Research in Social Stratification and Mobility, Vol. II. Greenwich, Conn.: JAI Press.

Birch, David
1979   The Job Generation Process. Cambridge, Mass.: MIT Program on Neighborhood and Regional Change.

Blau, Francine
1977   Equal Pay in the Office. Lexington, Mass.: Lexington Books.

Blau, Francine, and Wallace Hendricks
1978   "Occupational segregation by sex: trends and prospects." Journal of Human Resources 14 (2):197-210.

Blau, Francine, and Carol Jusenius
1976   "Economists' approaches to sex segregation in the labor market: an appraisal." Pp. 181-99 in Martha Blaxall and Barbara Reagan (eds.), Women and the Workplace: The Implications of Occupational Segregation. Chicago: University of Chicago Press.

Braverman, Harry
1974   Labor and Monopoly Capital. New York: Monthly Review Press.

Bridges, William, and Richard Berk
1974   "Determinants of white-collar income: an evaluation of equal pay for equal work." Social Science Research 3:211-34.

Doeringer, Peter, and Michael Piore
1971   Internal Labor Markets and Manpower Analysis. Lexington, Mass.: D. C. Heath.

Duncan, Otis, and Beverly Duncan
1955   "A methodological analysis of segregation indexes." American Sociological Review 20:210-17.

Edwards, Richard
1979   Contested Terrain. The Transformation of the Workplace in America. New York: Basic Books.

England, Paula
1981a   "Assessing trends in occupational sex segregation, 1900-1976." Pp. 273-95 in Ivar Berg (ed.), Sociological Perspectives on Labor Markets. New York: Academic Press.

1981b   "Explanations of occupational sex segregation: an interdisciplinary review." Unpublished manuscript, University of Texas at Dallas (January).

1982   "The failure of human capital theory to explain occupational sex segregation." Journal of Human Resources 17:358-70.

Gibbs, Jack, and Dudley Poston, Jr.
1975   "The division of labor: conceptualization and related measures." Social Forces 53:468-76.

Gross, Edward
1968   "Plus ca change . . . ? The sexual structure of occupations over time." Social Problems 16:198-208.

Halaby, Charles
1979   "Job-specific sex differences in organizational reward attainment: wage discrimination vs. rank segregation." Social Forces 58 (September): 108-127.

Kanter, Rosabeth
1977a   "Some effects of proportions on group life: skewed sex ratios and responses to token women." American Journal of Sociology 82:965-90.

1977b   Men and Women of the Corporation. New York: Harper & Row.

Marini, Margaret
1980   "Sex differences in the process of occupational attainment: a closer look." Social Science Research 9:307-61.

1978 "Sex differences in the determination of adolescent aspirations: a review of research." Sex Roles 4:723-53.

Milkman, Ruth
1980 "Organizing the sexual division of labor: historical perspectives on women's work and the American labor movement." Socialist Review 49:95-150.

Miller, Ann R., Donald J. Treiman, Pamela S. Cain, and Patricia A. Roos
1980 Work, Jobs, and Occupations: A Critical Review of the Dictionary of Occupational Titles. Washington D.C.: National Academy Press.

Mueller, Eva, Judith Hybels, Jay Schmiedeskamp, John Sonquist, and Charles Staelin
1969 Technological Advance in an Expanding Economy. Ann Arbor, Mich.: Institute for Social Research, University of Michigan.

Northcraft, Gregory, and Joanne Martin
1981 "Double jeopardy: why some women and minorities object to affirmative action programs." Research paper 599, Graduate School of Business, Stanford University.

O'Farrell, Brigid, and Sharon Harlan
1982 "Job integration strategies: today's programs and tomorrow's needs." Paper presented at the National Research Council's Workshop on Job Segregation by Sex, May, Washington, D.C.

Polachek, Solomon
1979 "Occupational segregation among women: theory, evidence, and a prognosis." Pp. 137-57 in Cynthia B. Lloyd, Emily S. Andrews, and Curtis L. Gilroy (eds.), Women in the Labor Market. New York: Columbia University Press.

Salancik, Gerald
1979 "Interorganizational dependence and responsiveness to affirmative action: the case of women and defense contractors." Academy of Management Journal 22:375-94.

Shaeffer, Ruth Gilbert, and Edith F. Lynton
1979 Corporate Experiences in Improving Women's Job Opportunities. New York: The Conference Board.

Simmel, George
1950 "Quantitative aspects of the group." Pp. 87-177 in Kurt H. Wolff (ed.), The Sociology of George Simmel. New York: Free Press. Originally published in 1923.

Thomas, Robert
1980 "The social organization of industrial agriculture." Paper presented at the 1980 meeting of the American Sociological Association, New York.

Treiman, Donald J., and Heidi I. Hartmann (eds.)
1981 Women, Work and Wages: Equal Pay for Jobs of Equal Value. Washington, D.C.: National Academy Press.

Tyack, David, and Myra Strober
1981 "Jobs and gender: a history of the structuring of educational employment by sex." Pp. 131-52 in Patricia Schmuck and W. W. Charters (eds.), Educational Policy and Management: Sex Differentials. New York: Academic Press.

U.S. Bureau of the Census
1976 County Business Patterns, United States Summary. Washington, D.C.: U.S. Government Printing Office.

U.S. Department of Labor
1972 Handbook for Analyzing Jobs. Manpower Administration. Washington, D.C.: U.S. Government Printing Office.

Williams, Gregory
1979 "The changing U.S. labor force and occupational differentiation by sex." Demography 16:73-88.

Wolf, Wendy C., and Neil D. Fligstein
1979 "Sex and authority in the workplace: the causes of sexual inequality." American Sociological Review 44:232-52.

4 Job Changing and Occupational Sex Segregation: Sex and Race Comparisons

RACHEL A. ROSENFELD

The U.S. occupational structure is and has been extremely sex segregated (see Beller, in this volume). The extent and stability of such sex segregation prevents most individuals from considering possible mobility between sex-typical and atypical occupations. Such mobility does, however, occur. World War II was a dramatic example of a situation where many women changed from typically female to typically male jobs. Even under less extreme circumstances, the sex composition of a person's occupation is not a constant throughout one's work life, as will be shown here and as others have demonstrated (Wolf and Rosenfeld, 1978; England, 1982b; Corcoran et al., in this volume; Jusenius, 1975; Sociology of Work and Occupations, vol. 9, number 3, 1982). Using 1973 data on job changers, this paper will focus on change in occupational sex composition that people experience with a change in employer. It will describe the movement by black and white women and men[1] among occupations with different sex compositions and will predict movement to or from sex-atypical occupations using a range of individual and job history variables.

EXPLANATIONS OF SEX SEGREGATION

Explanations for why women end up in typically and predominantly female occupations vary depending on whether the explanations focus on labor supply or labor demand. Both types of explanations usually fail to consider that a person might break through the sex segregation barrier.

Labor Supply Explanations

Labor supply arguments about sex segregation often give the impression that a person makes a once-in-a-lifetime and usually sex-typical occupational choice. Socialization explanations, one type of supply side argument, suggest that women are socialized to plan for

---

[1] There are, of course, other ethnic groups whose occupational sex segregation would be interesting and useful to study. One might like, for example, to follow Malveaux's (1982) lead and look at the position of Hispanics and their mobility. The data set used here, however, identifies race/ethnicity only as white, black, and other. The other group is extremely small and probably quite heterogeneous. In what follows, those identified as other are dropped from the analysis, leaving comparisons between blacks and whites.

and enter occupations that society considers appropriate for women, while men are socialized to choose from a wider range of suitably male occupations. Consistent with this explanation is the evidence of students' early expectations of and aspirations for sex-typical occupations (see Marini and Brinton, in this volume, for a review of this literature). Human capital explanations of sex segregation, another supply side argument, see the choice and preparation for a sex-typical occupation as part of economically rational planning. Since women expect to take time out from the labor force for full-time work at home, they train for and later enter occupations that offer easy reentry and low depreciation of their skills and training while they are out of the labor force. Such occupations, of course, become predominantly female (Polachek, 1979, 1981a; Oppenheimer, 1970). (See the detailed discussion of this approach and evidence contrary to its assumptions and hypotheses in Corcoran et al., in this volume.)

Supply side arguments carry with them assumptions about people's education and training. Much formal training for work careers takes place early in a person's life, often before one starts full-time work because in part, as the human capitalist explains, early training provides a longer time over which to receive the returns to this training. Women's occupations are not necessarily low-skilled, but they are described as occupations in which a woman must bring her training with her to the job because her expected short tenure does not allow enough time to receive returns on her training there (Oppenheimer, 1970). An early choice of a typically female occupation, therefore, must be to some extent a choice about the type of training to get or the type of major to take in college (Polacheck, 1978). Training for a typically female job might preclude training for a typically male job; for example, when a woman decides or is advised to attend nursing school rather than medical school. Thus prepared, the woman lacks the credentials to enter a medical occupation atypical for her sex. Likewise, a young man

who does not take clerical courses in high school or vocational school may not be able to get a secretarial job. An early choice of training thus determines a person's later occupational career.

Labor Demand Explanations

Labor demand arguments say that the exclusion of women from traditionally male jobs, especially the ones that supposedly require continuous commitment, is largely a result of employers' and male workers' preferences, not women's choices. The internal labor markets' literature hypothesizes that on some career ladders that are protected from outside markets and for which workers receive on-the-job training, employers are unwilling to take a chance on losing their training investment by hiring members of high-risk groups; that is, members of groups known to be unstable workers (e.g., Doeringer and Piore, 1971; Edwards, 1979). Because of their propensity to marry and bear and raise children, women are considered one of these groups. On the basis of their group characteristics, then, all women might be screened from certain male jobs by what is known as statistical discrimination (Phelps, 1972).[2] Employers may also

---

[2] It is not necessary for the beliefs about certain groups to be true for statistical discrimination to occur (Spence, 1974; see also England, 1982a). If the supply of appropriate labor is great enough, and in the absence of other pressures, the employer will not be hurt even if the stereotypes about groups are objectively incorrect. At times, employers have even created the link between women's domestic roles and intermittent labor force participation, reinforcing stereotypes about women as workers. It is not that women have always chosen to leave the labor market when they marry or have children; it has also been the case that employers required that women who marry or have children leave their jobs. For example, secretaries, teachers, and flight attendants—the latter as late as 1972—have been required to leave their jobs when they marry (Davies, 1975; Cohn, 1982; see also Cook and Hayashi, 1980, on forces in contemporary Japanese firms pushing or encouraging women to leave the labor force at marriage or childbirth).

feel that on-the-job training is easier if the work force is homogeneous. Even for low-skilled jobs for which a long-term commitment is not expected, however, employers may hire on the basis of the sex appropriateness of the applicant to the sex type of the job (Levinson, 1975).

In addition, male workers in competition with female workers have excluded women from predominantly male training programs and jobs (see Baker, 1964; Hartmann, 1976). Such exclusion may be hidden in seemingly universal entrance requirements and hiring and promotion procedures (Roos and Reskin, in this volume).

Reinforcement of Sex Segregation

Once women have selected out of, or are excluded from, male occupations, some explanations go on to say, their tenure in typically female occupations further reduces their ability to change to a typically male occupation. In their typically female jobs, they get returns from the skills in which they have already invested; they do not have the chance to learn new skills necessary for male jobs; they may be isolated from information networks about typically male job openings (e.g., Roos and Reskin, in this volume); and therefore they do not have access to the male career ladders that provide better advancement than do female job ladders. As a result of few advancement opportunities and the demands of both a family and an outside job, women may indeed lack commitment to their jobs and decide to drop out of the labor force.

EXPLANATIONS OF MOBILITY

To begin to study mobility to and from a sex-typical occupation, rather than stopping with the conclusion of immobility, one must (1) examine more carefully the stereotypes of typically female and male jobs, (2) consider how supply side characteristics might change over a person's work life, and (3) consider changes in demand for certain kinds of labor.

Occupations and Sex Stereotyping

The contrast often made is between typically female white-collar occupations and typically male professions and crafts. One is led to forget the variation among typically male jobs and among typically female jobs. Some typically male jobs do not require much skill or continuity, although they may pay more than a predominantly female job (England and McLaughlin, 1979; England et al., 1982). Early decisions about future occupations and occupational training alone cannot account for the level of sex segregation one observes.

Not all female jobs are lower in their occupational rewards when compared with all male jobs, either. While female occupations pay less, on the average, than male occupations pay to either male or female incumbents, certain white-collar female occupations have relatively high status and relatively good working conditions. And while female occupations are described as giving little chance for advancement, some upward mobility may be possible. Men in these occupations are often the ones who take advantage of these possibilities. Oppenheimer (1970) has suggested that for some men of lower socioeconomic status, such female jobs may be seen as a move up, perhaps a step on the way to a managerial position. For example, men in teaching tend to end up disproportionately as principals and superintendents (Schmuck et al., 1981). In general, one finds that men in the female semiprofessions are overrepresented in administrative jobs (Grimm and Stern, 1974). (See also discussion in Sokoloff, 1980: 55-63.) In a case study of one firm that had encouraged people to move to jobs atypical for their gender, Schreiber (1979) found that men in clerical positions, in contrast with the women in those jobs, felt that these were jobs that would increase their chances to move into management. What is interesting about their perception is that it was not supported by the promotion records of men who had been clerical workers within the firm.

Individual Life Changes

Individuals' needs, employment behavior, and human capital can change over their lives. Not all men, for example, are highly committed to the work force over all their lives. Some are employed while still in school, although often in sex-typical occupations (Greenberger and Steinberg, 1983; Lewin-Epstein, 1981). Still, at this stage, a young man might end up in a typically female occupation that is convenient for him—e.g., the graduate student who is also a departmental secretary—and then change to a more typically male occupation after graduation.

Many women have fairly long periods of their lives when they are not involved with childrearing and when they would be suitable candidates for jobs that require a relatively long commitment (Kreps and Leaper, 1976). Schooling and training necessary to make an occupational change are possible later in life, as evidenced by the increasing numbers of women attending college at older ages (Heyns and Bird, 1982). Other changes in a woman's life circumstances could lead her to seek a job considered atypical for her. Many of the descriptions of women's careers implicitly place women in families where the husband provides the main economic support; in such a setting the woman can make her job decisions using criteria other than income maximization. With increasing divorce, inflation, and unemployment rates, however, more women find themselves without husbands or with husbands who do not earn enough, or anything, to support the family. Under such circumstances, women may decide they can no longer afford to remain in low-paying, though sex appropriate, jobs.

Changes in Labor Demand

Another source of individuals' mobility between sex-typical and atypical jobs is from changes in labor demand. A person may be able to fill an occupation usually held by the opposite sex, if the employer is experiencing a demand for labor in that occupation. For example, the feminization of clerical work and school teaching seems to have resulted from a scarcity of willing and suitably educated men (Davies, 1975; Strober and Tyack, 1980; Oppenheimer, 1970), although the women who entered these jobs usually were not moving from another job but from outside the labor force. World War II has already been mentioned as an example where women were suddenly brought into men's jobs. After World War II, of course, women were just as brusquely forced out of the labor force or into the usual female jobs (Anderson, 1981). Dramatic changes in demand, then, can bring about equally dramatic changes in the sex distribution of occupations, which strongly suggests the importance of demand for maintaining *and* changing occupational sex segregation.

Legislation can also affect labor demand and, as a result, movement from sex-typical to sex-atypical jobs. The enactment of the Equal Employment Opportunity (EEO) title of the 1964 Civil Rights Act, its expansion and strengthening in 1972, and Affirmative Action legislation may have permitted and encouraged at least some women to move to jobs that previously were closed to them. Beller (1982, and in this volume) did find dramatic decreases in occupational sex segregation in the 1970s and some links of this decrease to legislative enforcement of EEO.

At the same time, some movement back to sex-typical occupations may occur after individuals experience harassment by co-workers or difficulties in adjusting to work that was designed for the opposite sex (Schreiber, 1979; Gruber and Bjorn, 1982; Harlan and O'Farrell, 1982; Kanter, 1977; Roos and Reskin, in this volume).

The meaning of a move to a typical or atypical occupation might be quite different depending on whether the person is of a minority race. In the past, because of race discrimination in lower-level, male occupations, a black woman or man moving to a typically female occupation might find not only an increase in status, but also an increase in pay and a job more in line with her or his educational credentials. Many of the typical occupations for blacks, however, were sex typed as well as race typed; for example, private household workers were black women and porters were black men. Among blacks, therefore, one might still expect to see differences in occupational location and mobility by sex. It has been suggested that one result of the civil rights movement of the 1960s was the movement of some black males into higher level positions typically occupied by white males and the movement of black women into the lower-paying and lower authority positions typically filled by white women (Lewis, 1977; Jusenius, 1975; Malveaux, 1982). Analysis of mobility across sex-type boundaries needs to include differences related to race.

Why a person has either a sex-typical or sex-atypical occupation has received remarkably little investigation (see Polacheck, 1979, 1981b; England, 1982b; Jusenius, 1975; Daymont and Statham, 1981; Corcoran et al., in this volume; and Beller, 1982 for some of the exceptions to this statement). Even less has been studied regarding the extent and determinants of changes in occupational sex-type during the adult years. Some case studies (e.g., Schreiber, 1979; Kanter, 1977; McIlwee, 1982; Dressel and Petersen, 1982) provide interesting hints about what happens, but they do not generalize their findings to the occupational structure as a whole. Using national data, Jusenius (1975) and Corcoran et al. (in this volume) have shown that some black and white women move among male occupations; Corcoran and coworkers show that at least some black and white men change, as well. Both sets of authors make some initial analyses of the determinants of such change for women.

ORGANIZATION OF THE PAPER

This paper will examine both patterns and determinants of changes of occupational gender typicality by sex and race. The next section describes the data for the analysis. The third section shows the types of occupational mobility undertaken by women and men, black and white. The fourth section examines the individual and job-level determinants of a move to or out of a sex-atypical occupation. The final section summarizes the results and discusses their implications.

DATA

The data for this paper come from the January 1973 Current Population Survey (CPS) and its supplemental questionnaire that surveyed persons with new jobs since January 1972. Data were selected on out-of-school whites and blacks 20 to 50 years of age who had new employers at the time of the CPS and who had been employed at some time in the preceding 5 years.[3] The data set includes information on the respondents' previous jobs, their 1973 jobs, the way in which they spent time between jobs (if there was such a period), the reasons

---

[3] In January 1973, respondents were asked regarding each person in the CPS, "Was . . . doing the same kind of work a year ago, in January 1972?" The supplemental questionnaire was distributed to those over 16 who had new employers since January 1972 and who were not self-employed or working without pay in a family business in January 1973; the questionnaire asked about the previous job and about the job search. Although the question was meant to include persons who changed occupation or job with the same employer, almost all respondents seemed to interpret the question as referring to employer shifts. Of the 102,374 people about whom the January 1973 CPS inquired, only 326 were reported as changing jobs with the same employer, too few to include in the analysis here.

that they changed jobs, and such personal characteristics as marital status, age, and education. These data enable one to examine the job-changing process and the extent and determinants of changes in the sex composition of occupations held by individuals.

The timing of this survey on employer changers was fortunate, since January 1973 is a particularly interesting period in which to examine gender differences in job shifting. It was just after EEO legislation enforcement became stricter. It was also a time of recovery in the business cycle, when jobs may have been more available and the effectiveness of EEO legislation enhanced.

The availability of data on a relatively large sample of persons that changed employers during a particular period is also fortunate. Selecting only employer changes avoids confounding general inertia with the barriers to changing occupational type faced by movers. Of course, people can change jobs within the same employer. (Data on job shifters within a firm were not available from the CPS; see footnote 3.) One might expect, however, that the chances for changing from a sex-typical occupation to a sex-atypical occupation would be greatest across employers. Those changing jobs within the same firm might be more likely to continue along some job ladder rather than changing job ladders. Jusenius (1975) found that, among

white women aged 30 to 44 in 1967, about 50 percent of those who moved from an occupation predominantly of one sex to one predominantly of the other sex between 1967 and 1971 did so within a given firm. For black women, however, she found "changing type of occupation—either to or from a typical one—was much more likely to be accompanied by an employer change." Further, "these results are in part explained by the listing of occupational changes. . . . Among white women, there were those whose movement into an atypical occupation appeared to be an intrafirm promotion, from operative to foreman, for example. Among the black women, however, the atypical jobs into which women moved were considerably different from their previous, typical employment, from private household worker to operative, for example" (Jusenius, 1975:28).

There is considerable sex segregation within firms (Blau, 1977). Occupations that are atypical for a given sex in the labor market as a whole may be predominantly of that sex within a particular firm. Some of the intrafirm job changes that Jusenius labelled as changes in type of occupation may have actually been changes from one predominantly female (male) job to another predominantly female (male) job in that particular firm. While using data on employer changers does not solve the problem of possible inconsistency between the sex composition of an occupation as a whole and the sex composition for a given job, it does increase the chances that a change in occupational type represents a real change on the job. More will be said about this in the conclusions.

While there are advantages to using this particular sample, some important statistical problems are raised in limiting the study to those persons changing employers. In analyzing the outcomes of job changes across employers, one would like to be able to generalize these results to all potential job-shifters, including: (1) those persons who remained with their current employers from

---

Some of those with a new employer had never been employed before or had not been employed within the last 5 years. New labor force entrants will, by definition, not have had a previous job and so are not really job shifters. They are not included in the analysis. Further, the CPS supplemental questionnaire asked for detailed information about the job held previous to the January 1973 job only if it was one on which the respondent worked in 1968 or later. The data for the analysis presented in this paper are thus on those who had changed employer some time in the 5 years preceding January 1973. Previous job refers to that job immediately before the job in January 1973. For most people, this was a job held during 1972. For others, it may be separated from the January 1973 job by a period of up to 5 years out of the labor force or unemployed.

January 1972 until January 1973 but who might, if observed longer, change employers after January 1973; (2) those persons previously employed who were not in the labor force or who were unemployed and between jobs as of January 1973; and (3) those persons who did not have any previous job. Selecting only those persons for study who changed employers over a given period could bias coefficients estimated on the selected sample (Berk and Ray, 1982; Heckman, 1979; Barnow et al., 1980; Olsen, 1980). The author was not able to investigate all forms of selectivity in these data. The author did, however, use procedures described by Ray et al. (1981) to create a selectivity measure for moving from, as compared to staying with, an employer, 1972 through 1973. This measure was highly collinear with tenure on previous job for those who shifted jobs, not a surprising result given the decline of job mobility with tenure (Hall, 1980). Tenure on the job, then, differentiates those who changed employers from those who stayed with the same employer between January 1972 and January 1973. Since the correction proposed by Ray et al. (1981) is for an ordinary least squares model and this study used logits for much of the analysis, a direct measure of tenure on previous job to control for selectivity bias is used here rather than the derived selectivity measure.

The selection of those who change employers over those who remained with an employer is probably most significant for adult males, especially white adult males. For women, especially white women, the distinction between being in the labor force at all and not in the labor force can be equally important. The women in the sample *were* employed at a given time, January 1973. Only about 50 percent of all adult women are employed at a particular time. However, selecting on employment at any given time does not seem to bias cross-sectional analysis of women's occupational rewards and characteristics (Corcoran et al., in this volume; Fligstein and Wolf, 1978). They were also required to have had some *previous* job

in the last 5 years, perhaps thus selecting on those with more continuous labor force participation. At the same time, since this previous job could be one held at any time between 1968 and January 1973, the selectivity bias is probably less than if the requirement for inclusion in the analysis had been employment on two particular dates (Corcoran et al., in this volume).

DESCRIPTION OF OCCUPATIONAL SEX COMPOSITION AND EMPLOYER CHANGING

Table 4-1 describes the current and previous occupations of the sample in terms of the average percent male.[4] White males were most segregated on this measure: On the average, they held occupations composed of over 80 percent of the same sex. Black men were in somewhat less sex-segregated occupations. Women, both white and black, at the mean tended to be in occupations that were only 26 to 28 percent male (or, conversely, 74 to 72 percent female). As a result of changing employers, there was little change in average sex composition of occupations for any group.[5]

The overall low average change in percent

---

[4] In general, percent male was calculated for each 3-digit occupational code from the 1970 U.S. census. Ten large, miscellaneous groups of occupations (including clerical workers not specific and miscellaneous, managers and administrators not elsewhere classified, and inspectors n.e.c.) were further broken down by industry; see Spenner, 1977, for further details. Using the 1970 data to categorize occupations is problematical in that at least some occupations changed their sex composition between 1971 and 1974 (Beller, in this volume). It is not clear that such changes affect a large number of people. One should keep in mind, however, as discussed above, that just as individuals can change to occupations with different sex types, so whole occupations over time can change their sex composition and sex label.

[5] Since the CPS was a multistage rather than simple random sample, the significance levels in the tables are only approximate. Using the weights provided with the CPS, however, did not change the distribution of the dependent or independent variables.

TABLE 4-1   Description of Job Shifts and Occupational Sex Composition by Race and Sex: 1973 CPS Employer Changers

	Black Women	White Women	Black Men	White Men
Mean percent male of previous occupation	26.4	27.3	76.0	81.8
Mean percent male of 1973 occupation	28.9	27.3	76.6	82.1
Average change in percent male (percentage points)[a]	2.23	−.44	.86	.52
Correlation between percent male of previous and 1973 occupations[b]	.34	.32	.26	.29
N	185	2009	176	2358

[a] None of the changes is statistically significantly different from 0 at the .05 or .1 level.

[b] All correlations significantly different from 0 at the .05 level.

male might be interpreted as indicating little change of occupational sex type with a change of employer. This would be consistent with the representation of the labor market as sex-segregated and preventing any change to less sex-typical jobs by members of a given sex. Averages, though, can hide large changes in both directions, i.e., to and away from occupations with high proportions of the respondents' sex. As Table 4-1 also shows, there are surprisingly low correlations between the sex composition of the previous and the January 1973 occupations of the CPS employer changers, from a high of .34 for black women to a low of .26 for black men. Such low correlations suggest considerable change in occupational sex type with a change of employer, perhaps somewhat less so for women (black and white) than for men. One hypothesis to account for these results is that something is wrong with the data. Others (e.g., England, 1982b), though, have found similarly low correlations.

While lower than might have been expected, the correlations are positive. One can imagine that what is happening is that people are changing occupations within ranges of sex composition. For example, women could be shifting easily among occupations with anywhere from 0 to 30 percent male but be stuck at a hypothetical 30 percent male barrier. The image of the labor market is of barriers across which it is difficult to move (e.g., Sokoloff, 1980). One

would like, therefore, to go from a continuous measure of occupational sex composition to a categorical or ordinal measure of occupational sex-type or typicality.

While most occupations can be identified as male or female, the particular coding of occupations into these categories is somewhat arbitrary. In the remainder of this paper, occupations in which men are the majority (at least 51 percent of those in the occupation) will be labelled "male," "atypical for women," or "male dominant," while those with less than 51 percent male will be called "female," "atypical for men," or "not male dominated."[6]

Table 4-2 describes the employer changes of the 1973 CPS sample in terms of these categories. While there is considerable sex segregation, some people do move from or to sex-atypical jobs. Ten to 15 percent move from a sex-typical to a sex-atypical occupation with a change of employer; over 60 percent move back to a sex-typical one. While

---

[6] This categorization is similar to that used by Corcoran et al. (in this volume). The distribution of race and sex groups over the occupational percent male did not show any natural breaking points, but it was extremely skewed. The median percent male of the 1973 occupation was 16 for black women, 16 for white women, 87 for black men, and 93 for white men. Since most people are in the tails of the distributions, the exact points chosen to separate male from female occupations should have relatively little importance as long as they are somewhere in the middle of the distribution.

TABLE 4-2   Sex-type of 1973 Occupation by Sex-type of Previous Occupation by Race and Sex: 1973 CPS Employer Changers

	Black Women			White Women		
	Previous Occupation			Previous Occupation		
1973 Occupation[a]	Male-Dominated (%)	Not Male-Dominated (%)	Total (%)	Male-Dominated (%)	Not Male-Dominated (%)	Total (%)
Male-dominated	39.0	15.3	20.5	36.2	15.9	21.0
Not male-dominated	61.0	84.7	79.5	63.8	84.1	79.0
Total	100.0	100.0	100.0	100.0	100.0	100.0
N	41	144	185	503	1506	2009
%	22.2	77.8	100.0	25.0	75.0	100.0

	Black Men			White Men		
	Previous Occupation			Previous Occupation		
1973 Occupation	Male-Dominated (%)	Not Male-Dominated (%)	Total (%)	Male-Dominated (%)	Not Male-Dominated (%)	Total (%)
Male-dominated	86.5	62.9	81.8	90.2	71.6	88.4
Not male-dominated	13.5	37.1	18.2	9.8	28.4	11.6
Total	100.0	100.0	100.0	100.0	100.0	100.0
N	141	35	176	2136	222	2358
%	80.1	19.9	100.0	90.6	9.4	100.0

[a] Male-dominated occupations are those that are at least 51 percent male.

the flow is stronger in the direction of sex-typical occupations, at least at the level of census occupational codes, the barriers between male and female occupations are not impermeable.[7] In Table 4-2, results are generally consistent with other descriptions of occupational sex type by race. Black women as compared with white women, and black men as compared with white men, are somewhat more likely to be in female occupations, which is what Malveaux (1982) reports. Here, though, one does not see a greater tendency for black women than white women to move to female occupations. The mobility patterns of women by race are similar. Black men, on the other hand, show greater movement than white men out of male-dominated occupations and less movement to male occupations.

As Malveaux (1982) and others have emphasized, in making comparisons of sex type of occupations (and mobility between types) by race, one needs to keep in mind the race differences in occupation within the categories of male and female occupations. One way of understanding race and sex differences in mobility across or within occupational sex-type categories is by examining the outcomes of such mobility—i.e., the types of occupations where people work after a change. Table 4-3 shows these outcomes by race, sex, and sex type of 1973 occupation.

Typical occupations for the white women

---

[7] The movement across occupational sex types as defined here usually involves a relatively large change in the sex composition of a person's occupation; see Appendix A. (Results for blacks, not shown, are similar to those in Appendix A.) The majority of those who stay with an occupation labelled male or female hold occupations after their employer shift that are within 10 percentage points of the percent male of their previous occupation. A majority of those crossing the sex-type boundaries move to an occupation with a sex composition that differs by more than 50 percentage points from that of their previous occupation. Further, the direction of the change is as one would expect: Those women going from typical to atypical occupations, for example, are going to occupations that are considerably more male than their previous occupations.

job shifters are clerical occupations, although 13 percent end their employer changes as health workers or teachers and 19 percent as service workers. Atypical occupational outcomes for white women tend to be within the professional and managerial categories, though 16 percent are durable and nondurable goods operatives. While almost 40 percent of the black women who end up with sex-typical 1973 occupations are clerical workers, more of them as compared with white women have sex-typical blue-collar jobs—as operatives, nonhousehold service workers, and household workers. Black women's atypical occupations are roughly comparable to white women's atypical occupations.

Among white men, sex-typical occupational destinations are most often skilled and semiskilled blue collar. Almost one-quarter of those with male-dominated 1973 occupations have crafts occupations, while another one-fifth are operatives. Atypical occupations for white men after a job shift are in lower white-collar retail sales and clerical occupations, as well as in durable and nondurable operatives and service categories. For black men, both sex-typical and sex-atypical occupational outcomes tend to be lower skilled, as compared with the outcomes for white men. More of those with sex-typical destinations, as compared with white men (or women), are laborers or service workers. While 18 percent of the black men with sex-atypical outcomes are clerical workers and 12 percent are health care workers and teachers, another 35 percent are service workers.

Another approach to understanding race and sex differences in mobility across and within sex-type boundaries is to look at the outcomes of the mobility in terms of relative job rewards. Table 4-4 shows changes in status and wages by race and sex for different types of moves.

Consistent with Wolf and Rosenfeld's (1978) findings, all sex and race groups moving to a male-dominated occupation gained the most, or close to the most, in terms of

status, despite the greater proportion of white-collar jobs held by white women and black and white men who were in female occupations. Going to or even staying in male-dominated occupations, however, does not necessarily result in the greatest increases in wages. For white men, moving to a female occupation may not increase status, but it does increase wages more than any other type of move. For black women, those going to typically female occupations experience the greatest gains. Moving to a male-dominated occupation does provide greater wage increases for white women than other types of moves, but white women do not significantly gain in wages by going from one male occupation to another. The failure of male occupations to be wage growth occupations for women has been found elsewhere (Corcoran et al., in this volume; Jusenius, 1975; Rosenfeld, 1983). At the same time, those who stayed in male-dominated occupations as compared with others in their race/sex category have the highest 1973 wage levels.

Even among people changing employers, then, there is a considerable amount of sex segregation in both the origin and the destination occupations. At the same time, between 10 and 15 percent, depending on race and sex category, go from a sex-typical to a sex-atypical occupation with their employer move. A considerably larger proportion, 60 to over 70 percent, of those who previously had a sex-atypical occupation had a sex-typical one in 1973. The sex-type distribution and mobility across occupations differ between the sexes and between the races. Black women resemble white women in their distributions and mobility more than black men resemble white men. Yet even among women the characteristics of jobs labelled male or female and the consequences of mobility within and across categories differed by race. Such differences need to be kept in mind when interpreting sex and race differences and similarities in individuals moving to or between sex-atypical occupations, the subject of the next section.

TABLE 4-3   Occupational Destinations by Sex, Race, and Sex-type of 1973 Occupation: 1973 CPS Employer Changers

| 1973 Occupation | Black Women | | |
| | Occupational Destinations | | |
	Typical[b] (%)	Atypical (%)	Total
Engineer, physician, dentist	0	2.56	.54
Health worker, teacher (except college)	2.04	10.26	3.77
Engineering and science technicians	0	0	0
Other professional, salaried	1.36	17.95	4.84
Manager, salaried, manufacturing	0	0	0
Manager, other, salaried	0	7.69	1.61
Sales—retail	3.40	0	2.69
Sales—other	.68	2.56	1.08
Clerical	38.10	20.51	34.41
Crafts	0	7.69	1.62
Durable and nondurable goods operative	15.64	17.95	16.13
Other operative	2.04	10.25	3.76
Nonfarm labor	0	0	0
Private household worker	10.88	0	8.60
Service worker	25.85	2.56	20.97
Farmer, farm manager	0	0	0
Farm laborer, foreman	0	0	0
Total[a]	99.99	99.98	99.99
N	147	39	186
Percent white collar[c]	46	62	
	White Women		
Engineer, physician, dentist	0	.71	.15
Health worker, teacher (except college)	12.82	11.85	12.61
Engineering and science technicians	0	1.42	.30
Other professional, salaried	1.32	17.54	4.72
Manager, salaried, manufacturing	0	.71	.15
Manager, other, salaried	0	13.03	2.73
Sales—retail	5.40	1.18	4.52
Sales—other	0	6.64	1.39
Clerical	47.36	12.32	40.02
Crafts	.25	3.09	.85
Durable and nondurable goods operative	9.74	16.12	11.07
Other operative	1.76	5.45	2.54
Nonfarm labor	.06	4.26	.95
Private household worker	2.32	0	1.84
Service worker	18.98	4.97	16.04
Farmer, farm manager	0	0	0
Farm laborer, foreman	0	.71	.15
Total[a]	100.01	100.00	100.03
N	1596	422	2014
Percent white collar[c]	67	65	

   [a] Totals differ from 100 due to rounding.
   [b] A typical occupation is one that is male dominated (more than 50 percent male) for men and one that is not male dominated for women.
   [c] White-collar occupations are those in the major occupational categories of professional and technical, managerial and administrative, clerical, and sales.

TABLE 4-3   (Continued)

1973 Occupation	Black Men Occupational Destinations Typical[b] (%)	Atypical (%)	Total
Engineer, physician, dentist	.68	0	.55
Health worker, teacher (except college)	1.35	11.76	3.30
Engineering and science technicians	0	0	0
Other professional, salaried	7.43	2.94	6.59
Manager, salaried, manufacturing	1.35	0	1.10
Manager, other, salaried	5.41	0	4.40
Sales—retail	0	5.88	1.10
Sales—other	1.35	0	1.10
Clerical	4.05	17.65	6.59
Crafts	14.86	0	12.09
Durable and nondurable goods operative	10.81	23.52	13.18
Other operative	12.84	2.94	10.99
Nonfarm labor	22.30	0	18.14
Private household worker	0	0	0
Service worker	14.86	35.28	18.69
Farmer, farm manager	0	0	0
Farm laborer, foreman	2.70	0	2.20
Total[a]	99.99	99.97	100.02
N	148	34	182
Percent white collar[c]	22	38	

1973 Occupation	White Men Typical (%)	Atypical (%)	Total
Engineer, physician, dentist	3.09	0	2.73
Health worker, teacher (except college)	1.97	9.22	2.82
Engineering and science technicians	2.34	0	2.07
Other professionals, salaried	8.25	3.55	7.70
Manager, salaried, manufacturing	2.48	0	2.19
Manager, other salaried	9.14	0	8.07
Sales—retail	1.73	15.60	3.35
Sales—other	5.90	0	5.22
Clerical	3.98	23.05	6.21
Crafts	24.46	.71	21.69
Durable and nondurable goods operative	8.10	27.30	10.35
Other operative	12.93	3.19	11.80
Nonfarm labor	8.95	0	7.90
Private household worker	0	0	0
Service worker	5.00	17.38	6.48
Farmer, farm manager	.19	0	.17
Farm laborer, foreman	1.45	0	1.28
Total[a]	99.96	100.00	100.03
N	2134	282	2416
Percent white collar[c]	39	51	

[a] Totals differ from 100 due to rounding.

[b] A typical occupation is one that is male dominated (more than 50 percent male) for men and one that is not male dominated for women.

[c] White-collar occupations are those in the major occupational categories of professional and technical, managerial and administrative, clerical, and sales.

TABLE 4-4   Mean Status and Wage Changes With Employer Changes by Occupational Sex-type, Sex and Race: 1973 CPS Employer Changers

1973 Occupation	Black Women		White Women	
	Previous Occupation		Previous Occupation	
	Atypical	Typical	Atypical	Typical
Atypical				
Previous wage[a]	4.25	2.97	3.30	2.68
Current wage	3.84	3.70	3.54	3.10
Wage change	−.42	.73	.24	.41*
Previous SEI	53.7	32.3	48.0	39.6
Current SEI	60.4	39.3	48.9	46.4
SEI change	6.7†	7.0	.9	6.8*
Typical				
Previous wage	2.29	2.62	2.71	2.50
Current wage	3.30	2.59	2.54	2.83
Wage change	1.01*	−.03	−.16	.33*
Previous SEI	33.5	30.5	44.2	40.3
Current SEI	37.4	30.2	40.5	41.8
SEI change	3.9	−.3	−3.7*	1.6*

1973 Occupation	Black Men		White Men	
	Previous Occupation		Previous Occupation	
	Typical	Atypical	Typical	Atypical
Typical				
Previous Wage	3.54	2.98	3.98	2.75
Current wage	4.73	3.56	4.35	3.30
Wage change	1.18†	.59	.37*	.55*
Previous SEI	26.5	28.9	36.0	28.8
Current SEI	25.3	32.1	38.3	37.7
SEI change	−1.2	3.2	2.2*	8.9*
Atypical				
Previous wage	3.42	2.81	3.16	3.11
Current wage	3.39	2.77	4.01	3.40
Wage change	−.53	.25	.85†	.30
Previous SEI	27.7	22.7	32.7	27.8
Current SEI	30.0	25.9	33.9	30.0
SEI change	2.2	3.2	1.2	2.2

[a] All wages are expressed in 1972 dollars.
* Change significantly different from 0 at the .05 level.
† Change significantly different from 0 at the .1 level.

PREDICTING MOBILITY TO AND BETWEEN SEX-ATYPICAL OCCUPATIONS

In this paper occupations have been dichotomized into sex-typical (for men, occupations with a male majority; for women, occupations with ≤50 percent male) and sex-atypical jobs. Mobility between occupations for different race and sex categories was shown in Table 4-2 as the probabilities that either (1) persons who begin their employer change from a sex-typical occupation will end up in a sex-atypical one or (2) persons who start from a sex-atypical occupation will go to a sex-typical one. In this section the two kinds of probabilities are taken as the dependent variables, to be explained by a set of individual and job characteristics.[8]

Since the dependent variables are dichotomous, ordinary least squares is not an appropriate method of analysis. Logistic regression is used instead. The dependent variable with logit analysis is actually the logged odds of having one kind of occupational destination versus the other kind. This paper, however, will sometimes refer to effects of independent variables on the probability of being in an atypical occupation, since a simple transformation of the coefficients that does not change their signs does give the effect of the independent variable on the probability (see Hanushek and Jackson, 1977).

Independent Variables

While the various explanations of sex segregation usually focus on its extent and persistence rather than on individuals' mobility from or to sex-typed occupations, they do suggest what might affect mobility across occupational sex-type boundaries. For example, many labor supply explanations of why women are in female occupations emphasize sex differences in continuity, extensiveness, and intensity of employment. If such explanations are valid, then both women and men who have less continuous, extensive, or intense employment should be more likely to go to or stay in female occupations.

The variable *marital status* (presently married or not) used here indicates the extent of a woman's family responsibilities, since responsibilities accompanying marriage are often the reason for women's more intermittent and less intense employment (e.g., Sweet, 1973; Shaw, 1981). For women this variable would be expected, if anything, to decrease the probability of going to a sex-atypical occupation and to increase the probability of moving to a sex-typical one. For men, on the other hand, one would expect effects in the opposite direction, since responsibility to provide for a family has been described as part of men's motivation to remain continuously employed in good jobs (see Duncan et al., 1972; Rumberger and Carnoy, 1980; and Rosenfeld, 1980, for some evidence consistent with this view).[9]

For women, continuity of employment and extent of family responsibilities are also measured by whether a woman was *out of the labor force caring for her family* between her previous and 1973 job. Of course, it is possible that a woman reentering the labor force after a period of caring for a family is embarking on a fairly continuous work life; the data, however, do not give sufficient information on numbers or ages of children to predict this possibility. To the extent that there is statistically significant discrimination by sex and age, one would expect women who leave employment for family care to be

---

[8] An alternative to analyzing mobility across occupational categories would be to use as the dependent variable the distance moved, measured by the difference in percent male between the previous and the 1973 occupation. Percent male on the previous occupation could be included as one of the independent variables to control for the degree of sex segregation on the origin occupation. Such equations, however, are likely to violate the assumptions of ordinary least squares (OLS) regression. At least one of the independent variables (the lagged dependent variable) is usually correlated with the error term. OLS regression then gives biased and inconsistent estimates. The degree of bias may vary over groups, making comparisons risky. If one wants to keep the emphasis on mobility, and especially if the values on independent variables do not change (see Corcoran et al., in this volume), one can do little to correct this problem with data at only two times. (See Rosenfeld and Nielsen, 1984, for a discussion of this problem and of solutions when one has data over more than two times.)

[9] An alternative explanation of this evidence is that men who are more motivated, who remain employed, and who achieve higher occupational rewards, are also those who are motivated toward and successful at getting and remaining married. A preferable variable would be *changes in marital status* rather than simply marital status as of 1973. The CPS, however, did not give information on previous marital status.

less likely to move out of female occupations and more likely to move to them.[10] This variable is not included in models for men, since almost none of them had taken occupational leaves for care for a family.

Another kind of break in employment is *unemployment*, searching for a job—another of the independent variables. Such a period between jobs does not necessarily lead people to jobs that allow or encourage low labor force attachment; a period of searching for a job may be necessary to find a better job or one that is unusual for a person of a given gender.[11] Extent of attachment to a particular job is measured by whether a person had *more than two jobs in 1972*. (One generally would expect those with any jobs in 1972 to have at least two— one held previously and one held as of January 1973.) *Tenure on previous job* is in-

cluded, but its interpretation as an indicator of job attachment is complicated by its role as a measure of selectivity into the sample.

Intensity of employment is measured by whether the *previous and the 1973 job* were *full-time* (at least 35 hours a week). Women's occupations have been described as offering more flexibility in hours than typically male jobs. This flexibility, however, benefits employers by enabling them to pay lower wages, give fewer fringe benefits, and more easily hire and fire (see, for example, Sokoloff, 1980:106-107). Women are overrepresented among part-time workers, but they are also overrepresented among the involuntarily part-time (Barrett, 1979). To the extent that typically female occupations offer less than full-time employment, one might expect those—male or female—who seek or find full-time work after being employed part-time to be those who are also moving from female to male occupations. Conversely, those taking part-time employment may be going to a more typically female occupation. With cross-sectional data, Beller (1980, 1982) found some evidence to support this speculation. In general, though, the evidence for the effects of home responsibility, continuity, and extent of employment on the sex composition of women's—and in the case of Beller's research, on men's—occupations is weak (Beller, 1980, 1982; Corcoran et al., in this volume; Polachek, 1981b; England, 1982b; Daymont and Statham, 1981). One might expect similarly weak effects of these variables on mobility among occupations.

Cohort, age, and stage in the work career may all affect the nature of one's occupation. Older women and men may have sex-role attitudes that make them less willing than younger people to enter atypical occupations; they may also be less acceptable to employers as candidates for such occupations. Beller (in this volume) shows that younger age cohorts as compared with older ones are less sex-segregated. Young persons who are new to the labor market, however,

---

[10] Daymont and Statham (1981), who included number and various age groups of children in an analysis of middle-aged black and white women's occupational atypicality, did not find significant negative effects of children on sex-atypical occupation. Beller (1980, 1982), using data on a less restricted age range, likewise found that a large number of children did not significantly decrease the probability of a woman being in a male occupation.

[11] Length of time unemployed between jobs was dichotomized into no time and some time unemployed because the distribution was extremely skewed away from 0. The data contained a general measure of time not in the labor force between jobs, which was also positively skewed. This information was used to construct a variable representing whether persons had a period out of the labor force before their 1973 jobs (net of a period out for caring for a family by women). A third variable was created, indicating whether a job search had begun because a person left a previous job involuntarily, something that might be expected to modify the effects of having a period of unemployment. These three variables—*some unemployment between jobs, some time out of the labor force,* and an *involuntary job search*—were highly intercorrelated. Inclusion of them in various combinations showed no significant effects of an involuntary search or a period out of the labor force on subsequent job attachment, nor modification of the effect of a period of unemployment.

may not yet have learned about the possibility of atypical jobs (Malveaux, 1982). *Age* is included as a measure of both cohort and age per se, while whether a respondent was *in school in 1972* indicates stage in the work career. Many persons are employed while attending school (Lewin-Epstein, 1981); more persons have at least one period of employment or other activity between leaving high school and entering college. Thus, attendance in school the previous year and employment and out-of-school in 1973 do not necessarily mean that those persons have just entered the work force for the first time. At the same time, for men who have had a sex-atypical job while attending school, leaving school could mean acquiring a more sex-typical occupation.

Education has been shown to be a major determinant of occupational achievement, and is among the independent variables here. In general, though, occupations with more women do not have a less educated work force and do not require less education than those occupations with more men (England et al., 1982); this might lead one to hypothesize that education does not affect mobility between types of occupations. Research to date, however, hints at curvilinear effects of education: Both low and high levels of education increase the chances having an atypical occupation (Beller, 1980; Polachek, 1981b; Daymont and Statham, 1981). Those with the least education would "tend to apply for and obtain jobs that required less skill or training and among which transferability is relatively great. The atypical jobs for which they qualify would have as few skill requirements as the typical jobs they already held" (Jusenius, 1975:24). Jusenius found support for this idea among white middle-aged women: Those with fewer than 12 years of schooling as compared with those who had at least 12 years were more likely to go from typical to atypical occupations. At the other end of the spectrum, those with the credential of at least a college degree—as compared with those without a college

diploma—might be considered qualified to move into more traditionally male managerial or administrative positions or may have taken majors that prepared them explicitly for atypical careers.

Getting *additional education or training* could also influence whether a person moves to an atypical occupation. The CPS supplemental questionnaire asked respondents, "Did you take any occupational or educational training courses or programs during the time you were looking for work?" The response to this question is included with the independent variables. Relatively few people did have any training, which precluded coding the responses into general types of training. Training is a change in human capital; it allows one to change sex type of occupation only if one is trained for a sex-atypical occupation and if the training that the person took is accepted by employers. Job training programs often offer sex-stereotyped training that is not useful in getting a private sector job (see Roos and Reskin, in this volume; Waite and Berryman, in this volume). The CPS employer changers could have gotten their additional training from other than job programs (the source of the training is not specified), but if training was not aimed at sex-atypical work, it would not necessarily increase movement to or between sex-atypical jobs.

Since skills required by particular jobs limit mobility and since the relatively high status of some female jobs encourages mobility, *Specific Vocational Preparation* (SVP) required *for the previous occupation* and whether this occupation was *white collar* were also included among the independent variables. Especially among men, those who have white-collar jobs that require more skill could be those less likely to change their occupation, let alone the sex type of their occupation, across firms.

Region (South or not) is included as a control variable. In cross-sectional analysis of occupational atypicality, Daymont and Statham (1981) found black middle-aged women in the

TABLE 4-5   Logistic Regressions for Moving From a Sex-typical Occupation to a Sex-atypical Occupation by Sex and Race: 1973 CPS Employer Changers[a]

	Black Women (N = 138)	White Women (N = 1485)
Intercept	.45	−.96
Independent Variables		
Highest year of education completed[b]		
0-11	−1.08	.32
1-3 years of college	.002	.06
>3 years of college	2.80*	1.19**
Training while job seeking	.69	.14
Age		
20-29	−1.29	−.30
30-39	−1.11	−.28
Currently married	−.98	.06
In school in 1972	−3.70*	−.43
Taking care of a family before 1973 job	−1.94†	.02
>2 different jobs in 1972	.64	.43†
Some time unemployed before 1973 job	.26	.11
Going from		
part-time to full-time work	1.92**	.18
part-time to part-time work	2.08†	−.15
full-time to part-time work	.83	−.53*
SVP[c] of previous job	.28	−.05
Previous job white collar	−.19	−.06
Tenure on previous job[d]	−.34†	−.07
Region = South	.95	−.06
χ^2	32.0	51.4
df	18	18
p	.02	.00
D	.21	.03

* .01 < p ≤ .05.
** p ≤ .01.
† .05 < p < .10.
[a] A sex-typical occupation is one that is at least 51% male (for men) or less than 51% male (for women). Only those who were previously in a sex-typical occupation are included. The outcome variable = 0 if the 1973 occupation is sex-typical, = 1 if it is not.
[b] Dummy variables are coded 1 = Yes, 0 = No.

South less likely to be in sex-atypical occupations.

The independent variables thus include measures of employment continuity and intensity, changes in life cycle stage, age, education, training, and level of previous job. They do not, however, include labor demand variables, which will be discussed in the conclusions.

Results

Table 4-5 gives the results by race and sex for moving from a sex-typical occupation to a sex-atypical one. The coefficients show the effects of the independent variables on the logged odds of ending up in a sex-atypical rather than a sex-typical occupation. The chi-square statistic compares the estimated model with one including only the intercept, thus enabling one to calculate whether the estimated model as a whole is significant in predicting the outcome. The D statistic is equivalent to R^2 and measures the overall fit of the model (Harrell, 1980). Means and standard deviations for the variables are in Appendix B.

For all groups except white males, having

TABLE 4-5   (Continued)

	Black Men (N = 139)	White Men (N = 2105)
Intercept	−.73	−.88
Independent Variables		
Highest year of education completed[b]		
0-11	.20	−.22
1-3 years of college	1.05	.18
>3 years of college	3.75*	.11
Training while job seeking	1.13	.21
Age		
20-29	2.09†	.41
30-39	−.90	.33
Currently married	−.36	−.68**
In school in 1972	.93	−.16
Taking care of a family before 1972 job[e]	—	—
>2 different jobs in 1972	.49	.10
Some time unemployed before 1973 job	.24	.16
Going from		
part-time to full-time work	.17	.30
part-time to part-time work[e]	—	—
full-time to part-time work	1.37	.60*
SVP[c] of previous job	−.14	−.13**
Previous job white collar	−1.34	.26
Tenure on previous job[d]	−.17	−.09†
Region = South	.16	−.13
χ^2	30.02	71.7
df	16	16
p	.02	.00
D	.20	.03

  [c] SVP = Specific Vocational Training. From Temme's (1975) aggregation from the Dictionary of Occupational Titles (3rd ed.). 1 = short demonstration only, 10 = over 10 years of specific training required.

  [d] Tenure on previous job: 1 = less than 4 months; 2 = 4-6 months; 3 = 7-11 months; 4 = at least 1 year but less than 3; 5 = at least 3 years but less than 5; 6 = at least 5 years but less than 10; 7 = at least 10 years but less than 15; 8 = 15 or more years.

  [e] Not included for men because there were too few cases in this category to give a stable estimate.

more than 3 years of college (in contrast with some other level of educational attainment) increases the chances of going from a sex-typical to a sex-atypical occupation. Remember that for white women, their male-dominated and other occupations were about equally likely to be white collar, and for black women and men, sex-atypical occupations, as compared with sex-typical ones, were more likely to be white collar, and perhaps more likely to require college credentials. In contrast, then, with what Jusenius (1975) found in her cross-classification of education categories by type of occupation, the results here suggest that higher, rather than lower, educational levels enable one to break the sex-type barrier, unless one is a white male. For white men, education has no effect, although it is also true for them that those who hold typically female occupations are more likely to be in white-collar occupations.

For white men, skill level of their previous job is significant. The higher the skill level on their previous job, the less likely they are to go to an atypical job when they change employers. This result fits with the image of white men going to atypical jobs only if such moves are to better jobs, an image suggested by other authors (e.g., Oppenheimer, 1970), as well as by the average wage increase white men earn with a shift from male-dominated to other occupations (Table 4-4). Getting additional training or education while looking for a job has no effect for any race and sex group on chances for moving to an atypical occupation, perhaps because of the sex typing of such training.

For women and white men previously in sex-typical occupations, changes in amount of labor supplied had an effect on the type of occupational destination. Whites—men as well as women—who went from full-time to part-time work were also likely to be going to typically female occupations. Black women who went from part-time to full-time work (as compared with those with other patterns of hours) had an increased probability of going to occupations in which men were a majority.

It is not clear whether part-time employment represents involuntary underemployment or a choice to work less than full-time. For both white women and the relatively few white men who go to part-time employment, the move to part-time (and female) work could be due to (1) other opportunities closing (although whether the job search was involuntary did not change the size of the work intensity variables)—that is, the choice might be between part-time work and no work—or (2) white men and women might choose to take part-time employment, which is more readily available in typically female occupations, in order to combine employment with other activities.

One can speculate that black women are motivated by underemployment when they seek full-time work that is more often associated with typically male occupations than with typically female ones. White women going from part-time to full-time work could be those who have taken time out from a full-time work career to raise their families and now are reentering the labor force in a typically female occupation. The movement

from part-time to full-time employment thus has no effect on the sex type of their occupation.

For black men, the move from full-time to part-time work or part-time to full-time work has no effect on the sex type of their 1973 occupations. Black men tended to have both typical and atypical occupations that were lower in status and skill than other groups. For black men, even more than for black women, male and female jobs may be equally likely to require or provide less than full-time employment.

In trying to interpret the effect of a change in hours, one needs to keep in mind that part-time work is not simply redundant with female occupations: The correlation between percentage male of 1973 occupation and whether the job is full-time is only .14 for white men, .12 for black men, .05 for white women, and .06 for black women.

Human capital explanations for why women are in typically female jobs predict that being presently married and having taken time out for family care reduce the chances that a woman will move from a sex-typical to a sex-atypical occupation. If employers exercise statistical discrimination on the basis of more than sex alone—that is, to the extent that they see all married women or all women who have been out of the labor force as less committed to employment—one would also predict negative effects of these variables on going to an atypical occupation. The only effect of family responsibility, however, is for white men: They are less likely to change from a sex-typical to a sex-atypical occupation if they are married.

In this analysis of movement from a sex-typical occupation, significant effects of age or work career stage are present only for blacks, and only strongly for black women. Black women who were in school the previous year—and who tended to be younger—were less likely than others to leave female occupations (see also Malveaux, 1982). If opportunities in traditionally female occupations were just opening up to black women, one would not be surprised to find that those

TABLE 4-6 Logistic Regressions for Moving From a Sex-atypical Occupation to a Sex-typical Occupation by Sex: 1973 White CPS Employer Changers[a]

	White Women (N = 493)	White Men (N = 222)
Intercept	2.09†	2.20
Independent variables[b]		
Highest year of education completed		
0-11	−.66*	−.11
1-3 years of college	−.26	−1.11*
>3 years of college	−1.66**	−.53
Training while job seeking	.27	.60
Age		
20-29	.57†	.17
30-39	.31	1.14
Current married	.39	−.32
In school in 1972	.55	1.84**
Taking care of a family before 1973 job[c]	.24	—
>2 different jobs in 1972	.61†	.62
Some time unemployed before 1973 job	.04	.32
Going from		
part-time to full-time work	.18	−.22
part-time to part-time work[c]	.45	—
full-time to part-time work	1.04**	−.40
SVP of previous job	−.27**	−.09
Previous job white collar	.60*	.82†
Tenure on previous job	−.09	−.05
Region = South	−.13	.28
χ^2	86.7	29.3
df	18	16
p	.00	.02
D	.16	.13

† .05 < p < .10
* .01 < p ≤ .05
** p ≤ .01

[a] Only those whose previous occupation was sex-atypical are included. The outcome variable = 0 if the 1973 occupation is sex-atypical, = 1 if it is sex-typical.
[b] See Table 4-5 for coding.
[c] There were too few cases in this category to include men.

just leaving school were taking advantage of female occupations and keeping them. There is also a marginal negative effect of being under 30 on the chances that black men will stay with a male-dominated occupation. Since predominantly male occupations are the ones in which both black men and black women have the most to gain in terms of wage level, the younger blacks were at a disadvantage in the outcome location of their employer changes.

What about going the other way, from a sex-atypical to a sex-typical occupation? Table 4-6 presents the results for those who have

previous occupations that are sex-atypical. The coefficient estimates give the effects of the independent variables on the logged odds of ending the employer change in a sex-typical rather than a sex-atypical occupation. Table 4-6 does not include results for blacks, because of the small number of blacks who begin their job shifts from sex-atypical occupations. Means and standard deviations for the variables are in Appendix B.

Again, education helps predict the occupational outcome. Here one finds the curvilinear effect of education reported from cross-sectional analyses. Women with less than 12 years of schooling or more than 3 years of college are more likely to remain with a sex-atypical occupation than those with intermediate amounts of education. Further, the higher the specific skill preparation required on the previous job, the lower the odds that a woman will go to a sex-typical occupation with a change of employer.

As Table 4-5 showed, higher previous SVP also decreases the probability that white men will leave sex-typical occupations. Male occupations requiring higher skills or education may be especially likely to keep their incumbents even across employers, although women with lower education stay with their atypical occupations, too. For men who began their employer change from a typically female occupation, it is having only a few years of college, as compared with other levels of education, that inhibits movement to a sex-typical occupation. The interpretation may again have to do with credentials. If some women's occupations offer relatively good positions to men, one might have expected that those men who had filled higher-skilled and white-collar jobs and who had more than 3 years of education would also be less likely to move from a female to a male occupation. This does not seem to be the case. For white men, having held a white-collar occupation actually increased the chances of leaving a sex-atypical occupation, although this effect was of marginal statistical significance. If the managerial and administrative women's occupations do indeed offer men chances for promotion, perhaps men are moving to them in increasing numbers, resulting in occupations that are now more male, though considered female. For women, having a previous atypical occupation that was white collar, net of everything else, increases mobility to a sex-typical occupation.[12]

Some life cycle and age effects appear. Men who had sex-atypical occupations and were previously in school have greater odds of going to sex-typical occupations than those who were out of school in both 1972 and 1973. Younger women, as compared with older women, may have a somewhat greater tendency to stay with a sex-atypical occupation even across firms, although here the effect is only marginally significant.

While marital status and family related interruptions in labor force participation again have no significant effects on women's occupation-type mobility, changes in hours do. The women who go from full-time to part-time work are again more likely to move to typically female occupations.

Thus, as in the analysis of mobility from sex-typical occupations in Table 4-5, education, skill requirements, life cycle stage, and hours employed play a part in predicting who will move across sex-type boundaries, although the way in which these variables explain mobility is somewhat different here.

SUMMARY AND DISCUSSION

The labor market is extremely sex segregated. Some people, however, do move across the barriers built upon sex-typicality of occupations. This paper used data on 1972 to 1973 black and white employer changers to examine this phenomenon. At the level of 3-digit occupational codes, this study found that of those persons beginning a job shift

---

[12] In Table 4-6, the opposite signs for white women of whether the previous job was in a white-collar occupation and of its SVP look suspiciously like the result of multicollinearity. The correlation between whether the previous job was white collar and its SVP is moderately high—about .48 for white women. For black women and men it was approximately .43 and for white men, .34. When white-collar occupation for the previous job was dropped, the effect of SVP continued to be significantly negative for white women. When SVP was dropped, the effect of whether the previous job was white collar was positive, but not significant. For other groups and other kinds of mobility, including only SVP or only white collar did not change the results.

from a sex-typical occupation (defined in terms of whether the occupation had a male majority), 15 percent of both black and white women, 13 percent of black men, and 10 percent of white men moved to an occupation atypical for their sex. There was also a strong flow from atypical to typical occupations: Somewhat over 60 percent of women and black men made such a move, as well as over 70 percent of the white men. In general, the mobility patterns across sex types of occupations for black and white women resembled each other closely. Indeed, sex differentiated occupational locations and types of mobility to a much greater extent than did race. At the same time, there were race differences. Even among the women, the black women's female occupations were much less likely to be white collar ones than those held by white women, in part because of the overrepresentation of black women in typically female service occupations. Black women who were able to remain in predominantly male occupations actually had higher wage levels and status gains than white women in male occupations. Among men, blacks were more likely to be in or move to female occupations, although those who remained in predominantly male occupations received the greatest wage gains of any of the four race by sex groups. For black men, too, both the male and female occupations they held were relatively unlikely to be white-collar ones.

For neither white nor black women was there much support for the idea that extent of family responsibilities influences the chance to move from or to a sex-typical occupation. One could argue that this is because the variables measuring family responsibilities are not detailed enough. These results, however, are consistent with a number of other studies that show the effects of marriage and children on women's labor force participation but not on the status, income, or sex-type of the occupation women hold once they are in the labor force. Much of the lore about why women get lower wages

than men and about why they are in women's occupations focuses on women's roles within the home. For men, on the other hand, responsibilities for a family are usually ignored. Finding effects of family status for men but not for women suggests that our stereotypes about the interface of family and employment need to be reexamined with respect to both women and men.

Other variables, though, that indicate changing commitment to the labor force did have effects on the nature of women's and men's mobility between occupations with different sex types. Moving to part-time work was associated with moving to or staying with a typically female occupation for white women and men, while moving to a full-time job from one that had been part-time increased the probability of going to a typically male occupation for black women. Having been in school the previous year also increased the chances of moving to a sex-typical job for black women and white men previously in typically female occupations. As discussed in the preceding section, it is not possible to determine whether part-time employment represents a choice about how many hours to spend on market work versus other activities or whether it represents involuntary underemployment. For those persons who have demands on their time beyond employment, it would be possible, in some cases, to extend the range of jobs open to them through such options as flex-time.

Level of education influenced the types of occupation changes that persons made. Having more than 3 years of college, which in most cases would indicate having a college degree, made it more likely that women and black men would go from sex-typical to sex-atypical occupations and that white women would go from one atypical occupation to another. Unfortunately, the CPS did not give information on college major. It is not clear, therefore, whether it is the degree as a credential or the substance of the degree that enables someone to go to and stay with an atypical occupation. If demand is sex-segregated, then even having the training for an atypical occupation may not help the individual get the desired job; by virtue of gender, he or she will be considered inappropriate. If employers are pressured to desegregate the workplace, they may be more willing to hire people from other fields and train them on the job. With the decreasing sex segregation of college majors (Beller, in this volume; Heyns and Bird, 1982), it will be interesting to measure whether persons use such majors to follow atypical careers.[13]

White women and men who held male occupations that required more skill were more likely to stay with a typically male occupation when they changed employers. This effect, together with the effect of having a college education, suggests the attraction and retentive power of the higher-level male jobs. The effects of having less than a high school degree on a woman remaining with atypical occupations emphasize again the range of occupations that are predominantly male.

It is not skill and training alone that keep women out of male occupations. It could be that the less-educated women who stay in sex-atypical occupations are trapped in low-level jobs; they remain in these jobs because the pay is higher than that which they could earn elsewhere. Daymont and Stratham (1981) found that it is precisely among the blue-collar occupations, which often have lower educational requirements, that one finds an advantage to

being in a male-typed rather than a female-typed job.

The analysis did not present strong age effects, such as one might have expected from changes in the degree of sex segregation over cohorts (Beller, in this volume). It may be that both the strong movement back to sex-typical occupations and the failure to find age effects are the result of using data from a period when changes in the climate facilitating sex desegregation were just underway.

These analyses provide some insights into the nature of male and female typical jobs by race and sex and into the mechanisms by which persons change from an occupation of one sex type to one of another sex type. The explanatory power, however, of the independent variables taken together is low, as indicated by the D statistic. It is especially difficult to predict, for whites, who will leave a sex-typical for a sex-atypical occupation, at least using these individual and job-shifting characteristics as the independent variables. One reason for this could be that the individual and job-shifting variables were not detailed and extensive enough. Another reason could be that the factors that affect whether a person is in or moves to a sex-atypical occupation are outside the person. As already discussed, individual characteristics can seem to produce effects that, in reality, reflect outside forces. The demand for certain kinds of labor, e.g., the demand for women in atypical occupations, can work against even the strong sex role socialization that most of us receive. Kanter (1977), for example, recounts how within a given firm, management persuaded women against their initial resistance to move to more typically male positions. Within and among firms, employers vary in their encouragement of persons of the wrong sex to apply and be hired for jobs; this variation could explain whether an individual ends up in a sex-typical or atypical job. Once a person is hired into a sex-atypical job, whether that person stays with the job may depend

---

[13] Using data on female college graduates in 1961, Bielby (1978) showed that those who had sex-atypical college majors were more likely than other women to stay with sex-atypical careers. Conversely, Hearn and Olzak (1981) reported data on 1976 college seniors that showed women were actually more likely than men to study vocationally specific majors. The jobs for which these typically female majors were preparing them, however, were lower in status than those anticipated by typically male vocationally specific majors. Hearn and Olzak were not able to follow these seniors to see how closely the various majors predicted types of careers.

on management's efforts to curtail harassment and to adapt work conditions so that both men and women can continue employment there (Roos and Reskin, in this volume).

Such efforts at desegregating the workplace usually depend on whether it is profitable to make them. Legislation can make it unprofitable not to hire and retain a sex-integrated labor force by enacting direct monetary sanctions and by creating a climate in which expensive sex discrimination suits are possible. An unfavorable economy such as we have now, however, can redirect emphasis toward providing jobs and away from efforts to integrate jobs. While women may have a greater need to support their families now and may be more attracted to typically male jobs, competition for jobs increases the possibility of reverse discrimination charges by male and white workers, as well as informal efforts to exclude women from male occupational territory. Rapid changes in decreasing occupational sex segregation and improving sex role attitudes occurred in the 1970s; social scientists and policy makers need to monitor carefully what happens in the unfavorable economic climate of the early 1980s if these gains are to persist.

The dependent variables in this analysis were movements across occupation sex types that were created from the sex composition of 3-digit occupational codes. Information at the 3-digit census code level is generally the most detailed available for national samples. Sex segregation occurs within 3-digit codes. Firms are sex segregated (Blau, 1977), and within firms, women rarely work in the same jobs as men (Bielby and Baron, in this volume). It is not clear, then, that the women who move to male occupations or the men who move to female ones are really going to jobs shared with members of the opposite sex. One would hope that sensitivity to this level of measurement problem would lead more of those who design large surveys, especially longitudinal ones, to include questions on the sex composition of the respondents' specific jobs. The conditions on a person's job can be important in determining that person's rewards and motivation to stay with the job. O'Farrell and Harlan (in this volume) have urged that serious efforts be made to study sex segregation within organizations, where advancement and work conditions can be traced more precisely. The rewards of a given occupation over time may indeed depend on its overall sex composition, with those occupations dominated by women offering lower rewards than other aspects of the occupation would predict (England and McLaughlin, 1979). Future research needs to include not only the question of why individuals enter and stay with sex-typical as compared with sex-atypical occupations, but also the larger questions of why and how women, whose work is undervalued, have been excluded from the work that society values highly.

ACKNOWLEDGMENTS

The support of the Carolina Population Center and NSF grant DAR-79-1585 made this paper possible. I am grateful to referees and participants from the Workshop on Sex Segregation of Jobs (National Research Council, Washington, D.C., May 24-25, 1982) for comments on an earlier paper that informed the work on this one, to David Maume and Roberto Fernandez for merging the data, to Kenneth Spenner for providing the sex composition data, to François Nielsen and Kathy Ward for their advice, and especially to Barbara Reskin for her extensive and helpful suggestions.

APPENDIX A   Extent of Change in Percentage Male by Type of Occupation Change:
White 1973 CPS Employer Changers

	White Women			
	Type of Move[a] Typical to Typical (%)	Typical to Atypical (%)	Atypical to Typical (%)	Atypical to Atypical (%)
1973 percentage male-previous occupation percentage male =				
(1973 occupation greater % male)				
91 to 100	0	0	1.2	0
81 to 90	0	0	3.4	0
71 to 80	0	0	8.1	0
61 to 70	0	0	9.7	0
51 to 60	0	0	19.3	0
41 to 50	.9	0	22.7	.5
31 to 40	2.2	0	14.3	2.7
21 to 30	2.9	0	14.0	4.9
11 to 20	8.9	0	5.6	8.8
1 to 10	11.8	0	1.6	12.1
(No change) 0	42.4	0	0	34.1
(1973 occupation smaller % male)				
−1 to −10	13.1	2.1	0	13.2
−11 to −20	9.6	3.8	0	8.2
−21 to −30	4.7	5.0	0	10.4
−31 to −40	2.8	12.1	0	3.8
−41 to −50	.7	20.5	0	1.1
−51 to −60	0	20.9	0	0
−61 to −70	0	16.3	0	0
−71 to −80	0	12.1	0	0
−81 to −90	0	4.6	0	0
−91 to −99	0	2.5	0	0
Total[b]	100.0	99.9	99.9	99.8
N	1267	239	321	182

APPENDIX A   (Continued)

	White Men			
	Type of Move[a]			
	Typical to Typical (%)	Typical to Atypical (%)	Atypical to Typical (%)	Atypical to Atypical (%)
(1973 occupation greater % male)				
91 to 100	0	1.9	0	0
81 to 90	0	5.2	0	0
71 to 80	0	5.7	0	0
61 to 70	0	17.1	0	0
51 to 60	0	18.1	0	0
41 to 50	1.5	25.7	0	0
31 to 40	2.2	10.5	0	4.8
21 to 30	3.5	12.9	0	7.9
11 to 20	5.9	2.9	0	3.2
1 to 10	18.6	0	0	11.1
(No change) 0	31.1	0	0	47.6
(1973 occupation smaller % male)				
−1 to −10	18.6	0	.6	15.9
−11 to −20	7.4	0	2.5	1.6
−21 to −30	5.1	0	5.0	4.8
−31 to −40	4.9	0	10.7	3.2
−41 to −50	1.2	0	23.3	0
−51 to −60	0	0	21.4	0
−61 to −70	0	0	15.7	0
−71 to −80	0	0	11.3	0
−81 to −90	0	0	6.9	0
−91 to −99	0	0	2.5	0
Total[b]	100.0	100.0	99.9	100.1
N	1926	210	159	63

[a] A sex-typical occupation is one that is at least 51 percent male for men or less than 51 percent male for women.
[b] Totals differ from 100 due to rounding.

APPENDIX B   Means (and Standard Deviations) of Individual and Job-Shifting Characteristics by Race, Sex, and Typicality of Previous Occupation: 1973 CPS Employer Changers[a]

	Black Women		White Women		Black Men		White Men	
	Previous Occupation		Previous Occupation		Previous Occupation		Previous Occupation	
	Typical	Atypical	Typical	Atypical	Typical	Atypical	Typical	Atypical
Highest year of education completed[b]								
0-11	.29	.17	.16	.18	.44	.20	.23	.20
	(.46)	(.38)	(.36)	(.39)	(.50)	(.41)	(.42)	(.40)
1-3 years of college	.16	.17	.21	.17	.14	.11	.20	.26
	(.37)	(.38)	(.40)	(.38)	(.35)	(.32)	(.40)	(.44)
>3 years of college	.06	.20	.15	.22	.11	.14	.21	.25
	(.23)	(.40)	(.35)	(.41)	(.31)	(.36)	(.41)	(.43)
Training while job searching	.12	.17	.05	.06	.07	.11	.05	.04
	(.32)	(.38)	(.22)	(.24)	(.26)	(.32)	(.21)	(.20)
Age								
20-29	.63	.61	.63	.57	.56	.74	.60	.77
	(.48)	(.49)	(.48)	(.50)	(.50)	(.44)	(.49)	(.42)
30-39	.26	.27	.21	.25	.26	.14	.24	.13
	(.44)	(.45)	(.41)	(.43)	(.44)	(.36)	(.43)	(.34)
Currently married	.66	.59	.70	.71	.71	.74	.77	.63
	(.48)	(.50)	(.46)	(.46)	(.46)	(.44)	(.42)	(.48)
In school in 1972	.12	.12	.12	.13	.07	.09	.11	.24
	(.32)	(.33)	(.32)	(.34)	(.26)	(.28)	(.31)	(.43)
Taking care of a family before 1973 job	.23	.17	.28	.28	0	0	.002	0
	(.42)	(.38)	(.45)	(.45)	(0)	(0)	(.04)	(0)

>2 different jobs in 1972	.06	.07	.12	.13	.15	.20	.21	.18
	(.24)	(.26)	(.32)	(.34)	(.36)	(.41)	(.40)	(.39)
Some time unemployed before 1973 job	.20	.15	.08	.10	.14	.23	.16	.16
	(.40)	(.36)	(.27)	(.30)	(.35)	(.43)	(.36)	(.37)
Going from								
part-time to full-time work	.19	.10	.14	.16	.05	.17	.07	.17
	(.40)	(.30)	(.35)	(.37)	(.22)	(.38)	(.26)	(.38)
part-time to part-time work	.04	.07	.12	.12	.03	0	.02	.03
	(.20)	(.26)	(.33)	(.33)	(.17)	(0)	(.13)	(.16)
full-time to part-time work	.12	.10	.14	.11	.06	0	.04	.08
	(.32)	(.30)	(.34)	(.31)	(.25)	(0)	(.19)	(.27)
SVP of previous job	3.71	4.88	4.52	5.13	4.44	4.05	5.35	4.08
	(1.27)	(1.54)	(1.45)	(1.63)	(1.69)	(1.40)	(1.77)	(1.45)
Previous job white collar	.40	.63	.63	.69	.25	.26	.37	.40
	(.49)	(.49)	(.48)	(.46)	(.44)	(.45)	(.48)	(.49)
Tenure on previous job	3.34	3.56	3.04	3.13	3.32	2.88	3.19	3.07
	(1.86)	(1.34)	(1.66)	(1.74)	(1.92)	(1.87)	(1.82)	(1.78)
Region = South	.59	.56	.33	.33	.55	.57	.32	.27
	(.49)	(.50)	(.47)	(.47)	(.50)	(.50)	(.47)	(.45)
N[c]	144	41	1506	503	141	35	2136	223

[a] An atypical occupation is one held by a woman that is more than 50 percent male or one held by a man that is 50 percent male or less.

[b] See Tables 4-5 and 4-6 for coding of variables.

[c] Ns on which means are based vary somewhat across variables due to missing data.

REFERENCES

Anderson, Karen
1981   Wartime Women: Sex Roles, Family Relations, and the Status of Women during World War II. Westport, Conn.: Greenwood Press.

Baker, Elizabeth
1964   Technology and Women's Work. New York: Columbia University Press.

Barnow, Burt, Glen Cain, and Arthur Goldberger
1980   "Issues in the analysis of selectivity bias." In Ernst Stromsdorfer and George Farkas (eds.), Evaluation Studies Review Annual, Vol. 5. Beverly Hills, Calif.: Sage, pp. 43-59.

Barrett, Nancy S.
1979   "Women in the job market: Unemployment and work schedules." In Ralph E. Smith (ed.), The Subtle Revolution: Women at Work. Washington, D.C.: The Urban Institute, pp. 63-98.

Beller, Andrea
1980   "Occupational segregation by sex: Determinants and changes." Paper presented at the Population Association of America annual meeting, Denver, April 12.

1982   "Occupational segregation by sex: Determinants and changes." Journal of Human Resources 17:371-92.

Berk, Richard, and Subhash Ray
1982   "Selection biases in sociological data." Social Science Research 11:352-98.

Bielby, Denise
1978   "Career sex-atypicality and career involvement of college educated women: Baseline evidence from the 1960s." Sociology of Education 51:7-28.

Blau, Francine
1977   Equal Pay in the Office. Lexington, Mass.: Lexington Books.

Cohn, Samuel
1982   "Synthetic turnover: A reinterpretation of human capital models of occupational sex-typing." Unpublished manuscript. Department of Sociology, University of Wisconsin-Madison.

Cook, Alice, and Hiroko Hayashi
1980   Working Women in Japan. Ithaca, N.Y.: Cornell International Industrial and Labor Relations Report #10.

Davies, Margery
1975   "Women's place is at the typewriter: The feminization of the clerical labor force." In Richard Edwards, Michael Reich, and David Gordon (eds.), Labor Market Segmentation. Lexington, Mass.: D. C. Heath, pp. 279-95.

Daymont, Thomas, and Anne Statham
1981   "Occupational atypicality: Changes, causes, and consequences." In Lois Shaw (ed.), Dual Careers, Vol. 5. Columbus, Ohio: Center for Human Resources Research, Ohio State University, pp. 107-139.

Doeringer, Peter, and Michael Piore
1971   Internal Labor Markets and Manpower Analysis. Lexington, Mass.: D. C. Heath.

Dressel, Paula, and David Petersen
1982   "Becoming a male stripper: Recruitment, socialization, and ideological development." Work and Occupations 9:387-406.

Duncan, Otis Dudley, David L. Featherman, and Beverly Duncan
1972   Socioeconomic Background and Achievement. New York: Seminar Press.

Edwards, Richard
1979   Contested Terrain. New York: Basic Books.

England, Paula
1982a "Explanations of occupational sex segregation: An interdisciplinary review." Unpublished manuscript, University of Texas at Dallas, Department of Sociology and Political Economy.

1982b "The failure of human capital theory to explain occupational sex segregation." Journal of Human Resources 17:358-70.

England, Paula, Marilyn Chassie, and Linda McCormack
1982   "Skill demands and earnings in female and male occupations." Sociology and Social Research 66:147-68.

England, Paula, and Steven D. McLaughlin
1979   "Sex segregation of jobs and male-female income differentials." In Rodolfo Alvarez, Kenneth Lutterman, and Associates (eds.), Discrimination in Organizations. San Francisco: Jossey-Bass, pp. 189-213.

Fligstein, Neil, and Wendy Wolf
1978   "Sex similarities in occupational status attainment: Are the results due to the restriction of the sample to employed women?" Social Science Research 7:197-212.

Greenberger, Ellen, and Lawrence Steinberg
1983   "Sex differences in early labor force experience." Social Forces 62:467-86.

Grimm, James, and Robert Stern
1974   "Sex roles and internal labor market structures: The 'female' semi-professions." Social Problems 21:690-705.

Gruber, James, and Lars Bjorn
1982   "Blue-collar blues: The sexual harassment of women auto workers." Work and Occupations 9:271-98.

Hall, Robert E.
1980   "The importance of lifetime jobs in the U.S. economy." Cambridge, Mass.: National Bureau of Economic Research Working Paper #560.

Hanushek, Eric A., and John E. Jackson
1977   Statistical Methods for Social Scientists. New York: Academic Press.

Harlan, Sharon, and Brigid O'Farrell
1982   "After the pioneers: Prospects for women in nontraditional blue collar jobs." Work and Occupations 9:363-86.

Harrell, Frank
1980 "The LOGIST procedure." In SAS Supplemental Library User's Guide: 1980 Edition. Cary, N.C.: SAS Institute, Inc., pp. 83-102.

Hartmann, Heidi
1976 "Capitalism, patriarchy, and job segregation by sex." SIGNS 1:137-69.

Hearn, James, and Susan Olzak
1981 "The role of college major departments in the reproduction of sexual inequality." Sociology of Education 54:195-205.

Heckman, James
1979 "Sample selection bias as a specification error." Econometrica 47:153-61.

Heyns, Barbara, and Joyce A. Bird
1982 "Recent trends in the higher education of women." In Pamela Perun (ed.), The Undergraduate Woman: Issues in Educational Equity. Lexington, Mass.: Lexington Books, pp. 43-69.

Jusenius, Carol
1975 "Occupational change, 1967-71." In Dual Careers, Vol. 3. Columbus, Ohio.: Center for Human Resource Research, Ohio State University, pp. 21-35.

Kanter, Rosabeth Moss
1977 Men and Women of the Corporation. New York: Basic Books.

Kreps, Juanita, and R. John Leaper
1976 "Home work, market work, and the allocation of time." In Juanita Kreps (ed.), Women and the American Economy. Englewood Cliffs, N.J.: Prentice-Hall, pp. 61-81.

Levinson, Richard M.
1975 "Sex discrimination and employment practices: An experiment with unconventional job inquiries." Social Problems 22:533-43.

Lewin-Epstein, Noah
1981 Youth Employment During High School. Report to National Center for Education Statistics, U.S. Department of Education. Chicago: National Opinion Research Center.

Lewis, Diane
1977 "A response to inequality: Black women, racism and sexism." SIGNS 3:339-61.

Malveaux, Julianne
1982 "Recent trends in occupational segregation by race and sex." Paper presented at the Workshop on Job Segregation by Sex, National Academy of Sciences, Washington, D.C., May 24-25.

McIlwee, Judith
1982 "Work satisfaction among women in nontraditional occupations." Work and Occupations 9:299-336.

Olsen, Randall
1980 "A least squares correction for selectivity bias." Econometrica 48:1815-20.

Oppenheimer, Valerie
1970 The Female Labor Force in the United States: Demographic and Economic Factors Governing Its Growth and Changing Composition. Population Monograph Series, No. 5. Berkeley: University of California.

Phelps, Edmund
1972 "The statistical theory of racism and sexism." American Economic Review 62:659-61.

Polachek, Solomon
1978 "Sex differences in college major." Industrial and Labor Relations Review 31:498-508.

1979 "Occupational segregation among women: Theory, evidence, and a prognosis." In Cynthia Lloyd, Emily Andrews, and Curtis Gilroy (eds.), Women in the Labor Market. New York: Columbia University Press, pp. 137-57.

1981a "Occupational self-selection: A human capital approach to sex differences in occupational structure." Review of Economics and Statistics, pp. 60-69.

1981b "Occupational segregation: A defense of human capital predictions." Unpublished manuscript, University of North Carolina-Chapel Hill, Department of Economics.

Ray, Subhash, Richard Berk, and William Bielby
1981 "Correcting sample selection bias for bivariate logistic distribution of disturbances." Unpublished manuscript, University of California-Santa Barbara. Revision of a paper presented at the 1980 meeting of the American Statistical Association.

Rosenfeld, Rachel A.
1977 "Breaks in women's employment and labor market re-entry." Paper presented at the annual meetings of the Canadian Sociology and Anthropology Association, Fredericton, New Brunswick.

1980 "Race and sex differences in career dynamics." American Sociological Review 45:583-609.

1983 "Sex segregation and sectors: An analysis of gender differences in returns from employer changes." American Sociological Review 48:637-55.

Rosenfeld, Rachel A., and François Nielsen
1984 "Inequality and careers: A dynamic model of socioeconomic achievement." Sociological Methods and Research 12:279-321.

Rumberger, Russell, and Martin Carnoy
1980 "Segmentation in the U.S. labour market." Cambridge Journal of Economics 4:117-32.

Schmuck, Patricia, W. W. Charters, Jr., and Richard O. Carlson (eds.)
1981 Educational Policy and Management: Sex Differentials. New York: Academic Press.

Schreiber, Carol Tropp
1979 Changing Places: Men and Women in Transitional Occupations. Cambridge, Mass.: MIT Press.

Shaw, Lois
1981 "Causes of irregular employment patterns." In Lois Shaw (ed.), Dual Careers: A Decade of Changes in the Lives of Mature Women, Vol. 5. Columbus, Ohio: Center for Human Re-

source Research, Ohio State University, pp. 79-106.

Sokoloff, Natalie
1980   Between Money and Love: The Dialectics of Women's Home and Market Work. New York: Praeger.

Spence, Michael
1974   Market Signaling: Information Transfer in Hiring and Related Screening Processes. Cambridge, Mass.: Harvard University Press.

Spenner, Kenneth
1977   From Generation to Generation: The Transmission of Occupation. Unpublished Ph.D. thesis, University of Wisconsin-Madison.

Strober, Myra, and David Tyack
1980   "Why do women teach and men manage?" SIGNS 5:494-503.

Sweet, James A.
1973   Women in the Labor Force. New York: Seminar Press.

Temme, Lloyd
1975   Occupation: Meanings and Measurement. Washington, D.C.: Bureau of Social Science Research.

Wolf, Wendy, and Rachel A. Rosenfeld
1978   "Sex structure of occupations and job mobility." Social Forces 56:823-44.

5 Commentary

PAMELA STONE CAIN

Chapters 2, 3, and 4 view segregation from three different vantage points. Beller presents an analysis of aggregate occupational trends. Bielby and Baron explore the organization of jobs within firms. Rosenfeld looks at the occupational shifts of job changers. The resulting picture is a confusing one. Beller emphasizes the decline in segregation from 1960 to 1981, Rosenfeld the existence of significant (i.e., nontrivial) movement across the boundaries of sex-typed occupations. In contrast, Bielby and Baron highlight the finding that segregation is virtually complete across jobs and firms of widely varying characteristics. From their results, it appears that only about 10 percent of workers are employed in integrated job titles, and even in those jobs they often work at different sites or with different clients. Moreover, Bielby and Baron found no decline in job segregation over a period roughly comparable to the one studied by Beller.

How to reconcile these results? In part, the contradictions can be attributed to interpretation. Although the segregation index declined at an ever-increasing rate, Beller finds that the resulting level of segregation was still very high: in 1981 approximately 60 percent of workers of either sex would have had to change occupations in order to achieve identical male and female distributions. Indeed, over a 20-year period, the index dropped by only 5 percentage points.

Rosenfeld finds that over a 1- to 5-year period, 10 to 15 percent of the individuals in her sample of job changers moved from an occupation typical of their sex to one that was atypical; 60 to 70 percent moved from an atypical to a sex-typical occupation. Thus, over a relatively short period of time, only about 15 to 30 percent of job changers failed to cross the sex-typed boundary. These figures indicate a movement of individuals across segregated occupations that is not immediately obvious given the level and constancy of segregation indices for the aggregate distribution. These results, however, like those of Beller, are less cause for optimism when one realizes that fewer than 5 percent of the 1973 Current Population Survey sample changed jobs. Their behavior, then, represents a flux at the margin. Most workers were stayers not movers, and, judging from the other papers in Part I, they stayed in sex-typical jobs.

The inconsistency in results between Beller

and Rosenfeld, on one hand, and Bielby and Baron, on the other, is also attributable to different units of analysis. Beller's and Rosenfeld's use of relatively aggregated occupations underestimates the degree of segregation, given the considerable heterogeneity of jobs within even fairly detailed three-digit census categories. Beller and Rosenfeld recognize this but nonetheless adopt a more optimistic, "half full" interpretation of their results. In light of Bielby and Baron's findings and the considerations cited above, a "half empty" interpretation might be more in order.

This is not to deny that Beller and Rosenfeld found evidence of change, however incremental and slow-moving. Moreover, each found that sex-typed patterns were most yielding among younger workers. Both also found that the decline in segregation was concentrated among certain occupations, especially those in the professional, managerial, service, and health care sectors. Other sectors, particularly skilled crafts, appear to present formidable barriers to women's entry.

Although Bielby and Baron found little evidence of change, a case-by-case analysis of those companies that did move toward greater integration led them to tentatively identify several factors responsible for, or at least facilitative of, such change. High on their list are rapid growth in company size and technological changes. To a lesser extent, the presence of a sizable female work force was also helpful. Surprisingly, federal intervention in the form of contract compliance regulations during the early period appears to have had no impact on segregation. By enabling an empirical assessment of the correlates (if not the causes) of segregation, Bielby and Baron's unique firm-level focus contributes immensely to a better understanding of the overall downward trend in segregation that Beller documents.

Beller attributes the decline primarily to equal employment opportunity legislation and enforcement activities, citing the enactment of Title VII and the Equal Rights Act early in the period under study. Putting aside questions about using time-ordering as a basis for attributing cause, the credibility of this interpretation is undermined by what we know about the slowness and inefficiency of the enforcement process and by the limited scope of some federal enforcement efforts, especially contract compliance.

Bielby and Baron's cross-sectional and longitudinal analyses suggest that more important than regulatory efforts are larger structural changes in the economy that lead to the creation of new types of work, to new forms of work organization, and/or to changes in employee-employer relationships. They find less pronounced segregation in establishments engaged in nonmanual service work, with unspecialized job structures and an absence of formal bargaining agreements. Larger firms with well-structured internal labor markets as well as very small firms were extremely segregated.

Projecting these results and assuming that the factors Bielby and Baron identify are causes not correlates of segregation, there is reason to believe that segregation could decline as the national economy shifts from a manufacturing to a service base and the number of workers covered by collective bargaining drops. Countering these trends, however, are trends toward larger firm size and greater bureaucratization. Unfortunately, the main effects of each factor can be disentangled only in multivariate analyses and then only if the individual factors are not highly correlated with one another. Ultimately, it is the complex interplay of these factors that will determine the direction of segregation in the 1980s, and it is difficult to predict this outcome given our current level of understanding. Certainly, a continuation of the downward trend that Beller documents cannot be taken for granted, given the scenario that Bielby and Baron depict.

Confounding these structural changes that may affect segregation are the changes noted by Rosenfeld in women's family and household responsibilities, which have been brought on largely by inflation, unemployment, and divorce. As their paychecks become increasingly critical to household survival, women can even less afford, if indeed they ever could, "women's work."

Given that naturally occurring trends have opposing implications for segregation and that many previous interventions appear to have had little effect, what policy implications can be drawn from these papers? Bielby and Baron's contention is persuasive that, with such widespread segregation, any intervention is warranted. What, then, should be the focus of intervention? Beller views the sex composition of occupations as especially amenable to manipulation, presumably through the use of quotas and various affirmative action strategies. Enhancing the success of this strategy would be the changes in younger workers' job preferences that are already taking place.

Bielby and Baron's results suggest that the solution may not be straightforward. Fundamental forms of workplace organization appear to be in need of alteration if segregation is to abate. Some of the crucial factors they identify (e.g., firm size, degree of job differentiation, and unionization) are outside the scope of government intervention as typically conceived. If their analysis is correct, the greatest hope for future integration may lie not in the public policy domain but in the hands of workers themselves, through either more enlightened collective bargaining or other mechanisms of workplace democracy. The complex organization of the contemporary workplace appears to play a major role in maintaining segregation. This organization can perhaps be changed only from within.

Women moving into professional and managerial positions may be a catalyst in transforming the traditional organizational structures that have functioned so long to exclude them. As other papers in this volume suggest, however, change will not be accomplished easily or without resistance (see, for example, Roos and Reskin).

Turning to the research implications of these papers, Bielby and Baron's paper reminds us of the distinction between research questions and researchable questions. On the face of it, such guiding questions as "Why is there job segregation?" and "What causes it?" are plausible until it is recognized that the level of job segregation may not vary substantially. As a virtual constant, job segregation defies social science, as all our empirical methods determine cause and effect through covariation of variables. Thus, in the absence of variation, we cannot really "explain" segregation.

This predicament may direct us to explore phenomena that do vary to see what they can tell us about sex segregation. For example, particular occupations and jobs have changed sex type, i.e., are no longer mainly female or male. Newly emerging occupations such as computer programming, as Beller finds, are becoming rapidly identified with one sex. Bielby and Baron's work also points out that, although the level of segregation does not vary much from firm to firm, specific jobs may be female in one firm and male in another. These examples lead to interest in historical or comparative inquiries into the determinants of the sex composition of a job or job family.

A new research question dictates changes in methods. The importance of firms in Bielby and Baron's work establishes the importance of using jobs rather than occupations as the unit of analysis and the concomitant need for firm-specific data. This is not merely because the use of job data uncovers more segregation, but because job-level analysis picks up organizational context and variations in hiring and allocation that occupational-level analysis does not. Firms appear to exert a strong effect on occupations, and disregarding their context may obscure more than it illuminates. For example, it is difficult to know what the occupational shifts Rosenfeld measured represent, especially as we do not know whether they were voluntary or involuntary moves. Moreover, the high rate of movement across sex-typed occupations may be misleading. A move to a sex-atypical occupation is not necessarily a move to an integrated job.

Focusing on jobs, not occupations, raises problems of data availability. Few individual-level surveys have any information on respondents' jobs or firms. At firms themselves, it is often difficult to obtain cooperation and access. These problems point to the need for new data collection efforts to supplement existing surveys. More broadly, the difficulties Beller encountered in compiling a series of data on occupational segregation should alert us to the need for improved national statistical reporting systems that would enable us to monitor this critical indicator of sex equity. But prospects for better data at the national level are not encouraging, given the current political climate. The agency within the U.S. Department of Labor, for example, that collected the data Bielby and Baron used in their analysis has now been all but shut down.

Bielby and Baron's paper also underscores the need for new analytic strategies. Their survey analysis complements case studies by Rosabeth Moss Kanter (*Men and Women of the Corporation*, Basic Books,

New York, 1977) and others, and, in their careful attention to selected firms (outliers), they blend case study and survey methodologies. The richness of their analysis should settle the debate between those who advocate one method over another. Clearly we need both, especially in this area, because of the problems of obtaining valid survey data on jobs and firms from either workers or employers.

Finally, how do these studies enlighten the major debate of whether segregation is the result of employee choice or employer discrimination? These papers offer evidence for both positions. Within firms, Bielby and Baron document the existence of powerful mechanisms of control that would support an employer-side explanation. Among workers, Rosenfeld shows considerable circulation across sex-typed occupations. Moreover, she finds some evidence that male employees are making rational choices in their avoidance of lower-paying, female-dominated occupations as their family responsibilities increase. The question of cause—employee or employer—is undoubtedly too simply framed. The different levels of analysis and seemingly contradictory findings of these papers highlight the complexity of the etiology of job segregation.

6 Occupational Sex Segregation: Prospects for the 1980s

ANDREA H. BELLER *and*
KEE-OK KIM HAN

Occupational segregation declined 2 to 3 times as rapidly during the 1970s as during the 1960s (Beller, in this volume). While this is encouraging, segregation continues at a high level overall; as of 1981, 61.7 percent of women (or men) would still have to change occupations for the occupational distribution to become completely integrated by sex (Beller, in this volume). What prospects lie ahead for the remainder of this decade? To attempt to answer this question, we shall make several projections of occupational segregation to 1990. These projections are based on the trends in segregation analyzed and reported in Beller (in this volume).

The best measure of occupational segregation, the segregation index, is computed as follows:

$$S_t = \frac{1}{2}\sum_i \left| m_{it} - f_{it} \right|, \qquad (1)$$

where m_{it} is the percentage of the male labor force employed in occupation i in year t, and f_{it} is the percentage of the female labor force employed in occupation i in year t.

The index may take on a value between 0 and 100, where 0 represents perfect in-tegration and 100, complete segregation. The number tells the proportion of women (or of men) that would have to be redistributed among occupations for the occupational distribution to reach complete equality between the sexes.

ASSUMPTIONS, DATA, AND METHODOLOGY

In order to project the index of segregation, we need to know the projected distribution of employment across occupations and the projected sex composition within each occupation. Occupational employment projections for 1990, constructed by the Bureau of Labor Statistics (BLS), are published in Volume 2 of *The National Industry-Occupation Employment Matrix* (Department of Labor, BLS, 1981). These projections are based upon the bureau's intermediate labor force projections and assume a 4.5 percent unemployment rate in 1990. These projections are discussed further in Appendix A.

In constructing projections on the sex composition within occupations, we employ a number of techniques and entertain a variety of alternative assumptions. The basic assumption underlying most of these projections is that the sex composition of all occupations or of each occupation individually continues to change during the 1980s along the path established during the 1970s. The data on which we base our projections come from the Current Population Survey (CPS), collected monthly by the Bureau of the Census either from the March Annual Demographic File (ADF) or from the unpublished annual averages (AA) computed by BLS from the monthly data. First, we make three projections based upon information about the labor force as a whole, employing linear and logistic models. Then we make four projections based upon information for age cohorts; the equations are specified according to the linear spline model. All of these projections are based upon 255 3-digit census occupations.

Linear Group Labor Force Projection (P1)

First, as in Blau and Hendricks (1979), we assume that the sex composition in all occupations changes over time according to the same linear function. We estimate an equation in which the proportion of males in each occupation in 1981 is a linear function of the proportion of males in that occupation in 1972, of the percentage change in employment in that occupation over the period, and of the interaction between the proportion of males and the percentage change in employment. Using the AA data, the following equation is estimated:

$$p_{i,81} = \alpha + \beta p_{i,72} + \gamma \Delta E_{i,81-72} \\ + \delta(p_{i,72} * \Delta E_{i,81-72}) + e_i , \quad (2)$$

where $p_{i,t}$ is the percentage of males in occupation i in year t = 1972 or 1981, and $\Delta E_{i,81-72}$ is the percentage change in employment in occupation i between 1972 and 1981.

This model has a logical rationale. The proportion of males in an occupation depends on the initial proportion of males as well as on the growth in the occupation over the period. It is easier for women to enter growing occupations than to enter stable or declining ones. Moreover, the effect of the initial proportion on the present proportion might depend on the growth rate of the occupation. This model also has some drawbacks. Because it averages over all occupations, it will overestimate change in some occupations and underestimate change in others. Because it is linear rather than logistic, the projected values for the proportion of males could exceed 1.0 or be negative.

To eliminate the effects of averaging, in our two other labor force projections we assume that each occupation's sex composition is a function of time.

Linear Individual Labor Force Projection (P2)

First, we specify the percentage of males in each occupation as a linear function of time:

$$p_t = a + bt + e_t , \quad (3)$$

where t is 1,2,...11 for years = 1971 to 1974, 1977, and 1981.[1] But, since p_t is a fraction between 0 and 1, the linear function might not be a good model, particularly near the extremes.

----

[1] Eqs. (3) and (5) require a time series data set. Data for 1971 to 1974 and 1977 are from the Annual Demographic Files (ADF) of the monthly CPS, while 1981 data are from the unpublished BLS annual averages of the monthly CPS. The former are the only years for which we have the ADF, while the latter is the most recent year of data available. The AA data are somewhat more reliable statistically than are the monthly data. Eq. (2), which requires data only for the end points, is estimated with AA data alone, since we can remain within a single, statistically more reliable data set.

Logistic Individual Labor Force Projection (P3)

The logistic equation constrains the value of p_t to lie between 0 and 1:

$$p_t = \frac{e^{t'\beta}}{1 + e^{t'\beta}} , \qquad (4)$$

where β is a vector of parameters to be estimated, and t is the year as above. Eq. (4) can be rewritten in the "log odds ratio" form:

$$\ln \left(\frac{p_t}{1 - p_t} \right) = \beta t . \qquad (5)$$

This equation, which can be estimated by ordinary least squares (OLS), will have heteroscedastic residuals, increasing the standard errors; however, this is not important for purposes of prediction.[2]

A different approach to projecting the segregation of the work force in 1990 is to piece together information about population subgroups. Beller (in this volume) examined occupational segregation by work experience cohort and found that (1) new entrants into the labor market are less segregated than is the rest of the labor force, and (2) between 1971 and 1977, occupational segregation declined for the entering cohort as it aged and between entering cohorts. Changes in occupational segregation can be projected by cohort and aggregated to the labor force. In order to accomplish this, we need to know the age-sex specific composition of the civilian labor force in 1990; fortunately it has been projected by the BLS (Department of Labor, BLS, 1979). Since we do not have the additional data for 1990

needed to identify work experience cohorts, we make our projections based upon age cohorts. We project to 1990 the sex composition of individual occupations for each age group. Then we use the BLS projections on cohort size to aggregate over groups and to obtain the sex composition of each occupation for the labor force as a whole. Combining these with the BLS occupational employment projections, we compute the projected segregation index. The details of this approach are described in Appendix A.

The advantage of using these projection methods is that we can incorporate speculations about what might happen under alternative scenarios for such factors as federal efforts on affirmative action. The disadvantage is that projections for specified small subgroups of a population are likely to be less reliable than are projections for the whole population. We make four projections based upon age cohorts: conservative, moderate, moderately optimistic, and optimistic.[3] All cohort projections are based upon trends between 1971 and 1977 only; the latter is the most recent year for which we have the ADF data containing the demographic detail to identify age cohorts.

Conservative Age Cohort Projection (P5)

The conservative projection assumes that no further change occurs for a given cohort after 1977, partly because equal employment opportunity (EEO) efforts have slowed down. Each cohort maintains the same sex composition within occupations as it ages, and the youngest cohort (16 to 24 years of

---

[2] This equation should be modified to include an equation error, interpreted as a surrogate for omitted variables, in addition to the usual error term. We will assume that the variance of the equation error equals 0, as discussed in Medoff (1979). In his empirical results the estimates of the equation modified to include equation error were not much different from those that were not.

[3] The assumptions about behavior and policy underlying each of these projections do not generate the particular mathematical models we use. Rather the models postulate change as a linear function of time, since affirmative action policies and related behavior have changed over time. More complex mathematical models might also be consistent with the underlying assumptions about change.

age) has the same occupational sex composition in 1990 as in 1977:

$$p_{i,j+1}(1990) = p_{i,j}(1977), \qquad (6)$$

and

$$p_{i,1}(1990) = p_{i,1}(1977), \qquad (7)$$

where j is age cohorts 1 to 5, defined by the age groups in the 1990 BLS projections, shown in Appendix A.

The assumption of no further change for an individual cohort need not imply no change for the labor force as a whole as long as younger cohorts are less segregated than older ones are. As the labor force ages, younger, less segregated cohorts replace older, more segregated ones. Nonetheless, the assumption of no change for all cohorts after 1977 is quite conservative in light of the decline in segregation through 1981 shown by the aggregate labor force data (Beller, in this volume, Table 2-1). Thus, these conservative assumptions may be viewed as yielding a lower-bound estimate on the projected decline in the index of segregation during the 1980s.

Moderate Age Cohort Projection (P6)

The moderate projection is constructed under the assumption that the rate of change in the sex composition of occupations for the youngest (entering) cohort will be the same between 1977 and 1990 as it was between 1971 and 1977—a period of considerable change. We might expect this if youthful attitudes and aspirations have changed, but equal opportunity efforts subside so that, as it becomes older, the rest of the labor force remains as segregated as it was in 1977. This projection applies Eq. (6) to older cohorts and projects change for the youngest cohort according to a linear spline function estimated on 1971 and 1977 data. The linear spline allows different segments of a continuous linear function to have different slopes (Poirier, 1976). It is likely that the sex com-

position of highly male (more than 85 percent male) and highly female (less than 15 percent male) occupations will change at different rates than will occupations with sex compositions in between. We estimate the following equation:

$$p_{i,1}(1977) = \alpha_1 + \beta_1 p_{i,1}(1971) \\ + \gamma_1 F_{i,1}(1971) + \delta_1 M_{i,1}(1971) + u_1, \qquad (8)$$

where

$$F_{i,1} = 0.00 \text{ if } p_{i,1} = 0.15 \text{ to } 1.00,$$
$$F_{i,1} = 0.15 - p_{i,1} \text{ if } p_{i,1} < 0.15,$$

and

$$M_{i,1} = 0.00 \text{ if } p_{i,1} = 0.00 \text{ to } 0.85,$$
$$M_{i,1} = p_{i,1} - 0.85 \text{ if } p_{i,1} > 0.85.$$

This equation is estimated for a six-year period, 1971 to 1977, and thus can be used to predict the value of $p_{i,1}(1983)$ using 1977 data for the independent variables. The 1977-1983 growth rate in the proportion of males in occupation i for this cohort can then be used to predict $p_{i,1}(1990)$.

Optimistic and Moderately Optimistic Age Cohort Projections (P8 and P7)

The optimistic projection (P8) is constructed under the assumption that affirmative action, attitudes, and other factors continue to change during the 1980s at the same rate as during the 1970s. Actually, this is quite optimistic given what we already know about the Reagan administration's proposed cutbacks in affirmative action and de-emphasis on enforcement. Thus, we consider this to be an upper-bound estimate on how much change could occur under the best of circumstances. For P8, we assume that as each 1977 cohort ages to 1990 its rate of change in percentage of males in each occupation is the same as for the similar cohort as it aged between 1971 and 1977, and that the rate of change between entering cohorts in 1977 and 1990 is the same as between entering cohorts in 1971 and 1977. For these projections, we apply Eq. (8) to the youngest cohort and estimate the following equation for older cohorts:

$$p_{i,j+1}(1977) = \alpha_j + \beta_j p_{i,j}(1971) + \gamma_j F_{i,j}(1971) + \delta_j M_{i,j}(1971) + u_j . \quad (9)$$

If the mechanisms have been put into place, then Reagan's policies may succeed only in reducing but not in eliminating change. We consider it moderately optimistic (P7) to assume that the rate of change for each cohort during the 1980s is one-half the rate during the 1970s. The value of $p_{i,j+1}(1983)$ provides the moderately optimistic projection, P7, and

the value of $p_{i,j+1}(1990)$, the optimistic projection, P8.

PROJECTIONS OF OCCUPATIONAL SEGREGATION, 1981 TO 1990

Segregation indexes computed using BLS occupation projections and our linear projections on the sex composition of occupations for the labor force yield only a modest decline in occupational segregation between 1981 and 1990. As shown in Table 6-1, column 1, the segregation index is projected to decline by 1.69 percentage points to 59.97

TABLE 6-1 Actual and Projected Segregation Indexes, 1972, 1977, 1981, and 1990

Year	Unstandardized	Employment Standardized
1972	68.32	67.23
1977	64.15	64.02
1981	61.66	61.66
1990		
Labor force		
Linear-group (P1)	59.97	59.35
Linear-individual (P2)	60.37	59.51
Logistic-individual (P3)	56.06	55.20
Combined-individual (P4)	59.91	59.03
Age cohort		
Conservative (P5)	62.11	60.89
Moderate (P6)	57.29	56.02
Moderately optimistic (P7)	50.02	49.09
Optimistic (P8)	42.20	41.33

NOTES: P1 was computed based on the following equation for projecting percentage of males in occupation i:

$$p_{i,81} = \underset{(1.65)}{-.016} + \underset{(75.61)}{.970}\, p_{i,72} - \underset{(1.64)}{.036\Delta}\, E_{i,81-72} - \underset{(1.36)}{.042}\, (p_{i,72} * \Delta E_{i,81-72}) ,$$

$R^2 = .966$, N = 262, t-values in parentheses.

P2 and P3 were computed based upon separate linear or logistic equations for each occupation, respectively. P4 was computed by selecting the equation for each occupation with the highest R^2 if either functional form was significant; if neither was significant assuming the 1981 value. P5 assumes no further change after 1977 in the percentage of males in each occupation for each age cohort; P6 assumes no change for all but the youngest cohort, which experiences a linear change for all but the youngest cohort, which experiences a linear rate of change; P7 assumes a linear rate of change of percentage of males in each occuaption for each age cohort at one-half the rate during the 1970s; P8 assumes a linear rate of change at the same rate as during the 1970s. Employment standardized indexes are standardized to 1981 employment totals. Projected segregation indexes include only 255 occupations because the BLS employment projections were unavailable for 7 of the occupations included in the analysis of trends in Beller (in this volume).

SOURCES: Annual Demographic Files of Current Population Survey, 1972 to 1975 and 1978, computer tapes; and Bureau of Labor Statistics, annual averages of monthly Current Population Surveys, 1972, 1977, and 1981, unpublished tabulations.

or by 1.29 percentage points to 60.37 according to the linear-group (P1) and linear-individual (P2) projections, respectively. These projected rates of decline in the overall index are much slower than during the past decade. A logistic rate of growth (P3) in the sex composition of individual occupations combines with the BLS occupation projections to predict a decline in the segregation index from 61.66 in 1981 to 56.06 in 1990. This projected 5.6 percentage point decline is around 84 percent of the actual 6.66 percentage point decline between 1972 and 1981.

To decompose these changes, we standardize the projected segregation indexes to the 1981 occupational distribution.[4] Shown in column 2, the employment standardized segregation indexes lie slightly below the unstandardized indexes indicating that the occupational distribution is projected (by the BLS) to change slightly toward more segregated occupations between 1981 and 1990. This contrasts with the slight change in the occupational distribution toward less segregated occupations during the 1970s. The projected employment standardized segregation index based upon logistic trends (P3) declines by 6.46 percentage points during the 1980s to 55.20, or by more than the 5.57 percentage point decline in the standard- or by 1.29 percentage points to 60.37 ac-

cording to the linear-group (P1) and linearized index during the 1970s. Thus, according to logistic trends, changes in the sex composition of occupations toward a less segregated work force will be larger during the 1980s than during the 1970s; however, projected adverse changes in the occupational distribution will more than offset these more favorable changes in sex composition. From these data we conclude that projected changes in the sex composition of occupations during the 1980s based upon changes between 1971 and 1981 will decrease occupational segregation less than in the past in part because of opposing changes in the occupational distribution toward increased segregation.

However, these projections of occupational sex composition may be somewhat off, because they project the female share of the labor force in 1990 as higher than the BLS projects them (Department of Labor, BLS, 1979, Table 5, p. 7). The BLS projects the female share of the labor force to grow from 41.0 in 1977 to 45.5 in 1990, whereas P1 projects the female share (aggregated from occupational shares) to be 49.3 in 1990, P2 projects it to be 48.2, and P3 projects it to be 50.3. Since projections for a population (the labor force) tend to be more accurate than projections for a specified subset of that population (occupations), the BLS projections suggest that our own projections somewhat overestimate the female share of the labor force in 1990.[5]

What, then, do these projections tell us? The sex composition of some occupations changed so rapidly during the 1970s that the rate cannot be sustained during the 1980s on the basis of projected growth in the female labor force. For which subset of occupations will the female rate of entry decline during the 1980s? Will it decline further

---

[4] The employment standardized index of segregation is defined as follows:

$$S_{it}^* = \frac{1}{2}\sum_i \left| m_{it}^* - f_{it}^* \right|,$$

where

$$m_{it}^* = \frac{(M_{it}/T_{it})\,(T_{it-1})\,(100)}{\sum_i (M_{it}/T_{it})\,(T_{it-1})},$$

$$f_{it}^* = \frac{(F_{it}/T_{it})\,(T_{it-1})\,(100)}{\sum_i (F_{it}/T_{it})\,(T_{it-1})},$$

F_{it} is the number of females in occupation i in year t, M_{it} is the number of males in occupation i in year t, and T_{it} equals $F_{it} + M_{it}$ equals total employment in occupation i in year t.

[5] This difference may be somewhat mitigated by the fact that the BLS has consistently underestimated the growth rate of the female labor force (Lloyd and Niemi, 1979, p. 311, n. 19; Smith, 1977, p. 23).

in the large, traditionally female occupations so that not only will the proportion of the female labor force that is in them decline, but also the female proportion of these occupations will decline? If so, occupational segregation will decline more than is projected. Or will it decline in the traditionally male occupations to which access has been increased so recently? If so, occupational segregation will decline less than is projected. Obviously incentives can be created by public policy for movement in one direction or the other. If affirmative action continues to promote equal opportunity for women in nontraditional occupations, then traditionally female occupations will become relatively less attractive. If opportunities decline in nontraditional jobs, then female occupations will look relatively more attractive. As our experience during the 1970s suggests, federal policy can significantly affect occupational segregation (Beller, 1982a,b).

Each of these projection methods has advantages and disadvantages, and each makes projections that are quite reasonable for many individual occupations. The projected female percentages of P1 to P3, as well as the estimated annual linear trend of P2, are presented in Appendix B, Table B-1. As these data show, the logistic growth model, P3, does very well in capturing the acceleration or deceleration in the rate of change in percentage of females near the tails of the distribution; however, it overprojects the female share of the labor force the most. The linear-individual projection, P2, overprojects the female share the least. Since the truth probably lies somewhere in between, we construct a combined estimate. For each occupation we choose the individual equation with the highest R^2, where at least one is significant at the 10 percent level according to the F-statistic. Where neither the linear nor the logistic equation is significant, we assume that no change occurs in percent female between 1981 and 1990. As shown in Table B-1, while the majority of occu-

pations shows no significant trend in the percent female, more than one-fourth, 27.5 percent, shows a significant increase. These assumptions yield the combined-individual projection (P4) of the segregation index of 59.91, only slightly below P2.

MAJOR COMPONENTS OF PROJECTED CHANGE IN THE INDEX

Many of the trends toward decreasing segregation begun in the 1970s (Beller, in this volume) are projected to continue into the 1980s. However, counterbalancing these will be a major new source of increasing segregation. According to the P2 linear projections, a number of predominantly male crafts and operative and laborer occupations are projected to grow (some rapidly) and to account for increasing proportions of the male labor force during the 1980s. According to the P1 linear projections, if women take a larger share of the growth in these jobs as they did in the male occupations that grew rapidly during the 1970s, then these occupations may not increase overall segregation. Several traditionally female occupations are projected to continue to account for decreasing proportions of the female labor force, while some increase in segregation will result from the expansion of the predominantly female health services occupations.

According to P2, occupations projected to continue contributing to declines in the segregation index during the 1980s are elementary school teachers; telephone operators; cooks, except private household; child care workers, private household; and maids and servants, private household. Declines in the segregation index during the 1980s are projected from some new sources as well: secondary school teachers; managers and administrators, not elsewhere classified; bookkeepers; waiters; and hairdressers and cosmotologists. Also projected to decrease the segregation index during the 1980s are two female occupations—registered nurses and bank tellers—that increased it during the 1970s.

The occupation of miscellaneous clerical workers is projected to continue increasing the segregation index by a large amount. Also projected to increase the index during the 1980s is the rapidly growing secretarial occupation, which decreased it during the 1970s. Several female health services occupations are projected to grow and to become more segregated: health aides, nursing aides, and practical nurses.[6]

As mentioned before, the biggest change projected for the 1980s that will hinder further declines in occupational segregation is substantial growth in a number of highly male crafts and operative and laborer occupations. The following occupations, with the projected percentage of females in parentheses, will add a large amount to the 1990 segregation index if their female percentage grows during the 1980s at the same linear rate as during the 1970s: carpenters (3.0 percent); auto mechanics (0.7 percent); heavy-equipment mechanics (2.8 percent); welders and flame-cutters (5.3 percent); machine operatives, miscellaneous (27.7 percent); truck drivers (4.0 percent); and construction laborers (4.5 percent). Of these, women made significant inroads during the 1970s only into the occupations of carpenter, heavy-equipment mechanic, and truck driver. In all except machine operatives, the percentage of females is projected to grow between 1981 and 1990, but by nearly imperceptible amounts. However, growth in these occupations need not hinder declines in occupational segregation; if these male blue-collar occupations respond to growth in the same way as the male white-collar occupations did during the 1970s, allocating a higher share of new than of existing jobs

to women, the P1 projections show that the percentages of females could increase among carpenters (to 8.3 percent); auto mechanics (to 6.8 percent); heavy-equipment mechanics (to 9.4 percent); welders and flame-cutters (to 11.2 percent); machine operatives, miscellaneous (to 34.1 percent); truck drivers (to 9.2 percent); and construction laborers (to 9.1 percent). Increasing the rate at which women enter those blue-collar occupations that are projected to grow during the coming decade should be a major focus of any public policy designed to reduce occupational segregation.[7]

PROJECTIONS BASED ON AGE COHORTS

The four segregation indexes based upon projections of occupational sex composition within age cohorts vary considerably depending upon the assumptions. Based upon conservative assumptions, P5 projects only a slight decline in the index of segregation, from 64.15 in 1977 to 62.11 in 1990, slightly above the actual 1981 index. (The projected indexes for each age cohort, as well as the indexes for 1971 and 1977, appear in Appendix B, Table B-2.) Note that these conservative assumptions yield a projection only slightly above P1, P2, and P4. The conservative projection appears especially so in light of the actual 1981 segregation index.

Based upon moderate assumptions that further declines occur only for the youngest cohort after 1977, P6 projects a decline in the index of segregation to 57.29 in 1990, closest to the logistic projection, P3, of 56.06. (P6 projects a female share of the labor force of 48.3 percent in 1990.) While the linear spline equation predicts a substantial drop

---

[6] These occupations were identified on the basis of the linear trends for each individual occupation; they carry the assumption that the percentage of females during the 1980s follows the same trend as during the 1970s regardless of any changes in total occupational employment that might occur.

[7] Whether this projected growth in blue-collar jobs will be realized is questionable because of the present high unemployment rate contrasted with the 4.5 percentage rate embedded in the BLS occupation projections for 1990. Moreover, as Carey (1981, p. 42) points out, job growth in blue-collar occupations is more sensitive to the underlying assumptions of the projections than in other major occupational categories.

in segregation for the youngest cohort (see Table B-2), even changes of substantial magnitude restricted to a single cohort have a limited impact on the overall index. It would take many years of a continued influx of less segregated cohorts for the overall occupational distribution to show a major decline in segregation.

The moderately optimistic and the optimistic age cohort projections, P7 and P8, depart from the others in projecting a significant decline in the index of segregation during the 1980s. Based upon the assumption that the total change in percentage of males for each occupation as a cohort ages between 1977 and 1990 is the same as for the similar cohort between 1971 and 1977, i.e., one-half the rate of change, P7 projects the index of segregation overall to decline by 11.68 percentage points to 50.02 in 1990. P7 projects the female share of the labor force at 47 percent, which is close to the BLS projection of 45.5. Projection P8 is very optimistic and assumes that the rate of change in percentage of males by occupation for each cohort between 1977 and 1990 is the same as between 1971 and 1977 for the comparable cohort, i.e., double the total change. P8 predicts a rather substantial drop in the segregation index of nearly 20 points to 42.20 and projects a female share of the labor force just over 50 percent.

The age cohort projections differ from the labor force projections in their emphasis upon source of change. They assume that segregation is a characteristic of cohorts of individuals rather than of occupations or of the labor force. Thus, change is based more upon the characteristics of the supply side of the labor market than, as in the earlier projections, upon the demand side. If, on the one hand, segregation were primarily the result of the choices of each sex, then the optimistic projections suggest that occupational segregation could decline significantly during the 1980s. If, on the other hand, segregation were primarily the result of employer practices and other demand-side factors, modest further declines are predicted for the 1980s. The truth may well lie in between. In the next section, we focus on changes in the characteristics of the supply side of the professional labor market.

PROJECTIONS TO 1990 OF SEGREGATION AMONG PROFESSIONAL OCCUPATIONS BASED ON COLLEGE MAJORS

In our final set of projections on segregation among professional occupations we break with previous methodological patterns. So far we have projected trends in the sex composition of occupations either for the whole labor force or for a subgroup of that population. Here we use an aggregate time series regression framework in which the segregation indexes are variables. Since professional occupations generally require a college degree, segregation among professional occupations is hypothesized to be a function of segregation by college field of study among recent bachelor's degree recipients. As long as the sexes face equal opportunity in the job market, to the extent that a greater similarity arises in the educational preparation of men and women, segregation in professional occupations should decline. We have chosen to specify a relationship where segregation in professional occupations in year t is a function of segregation in college majors in year $t-3$, a lag of three years. While many of last year's college graduates fill this year's job vacancies, several previous years' graduates may also, especially where postgraduate education or training is involved.[8] We thus specify the following equation:

$$S_t^o = a + b\, S_{t-3}^m + e_t,\qquad (10)$$

where S^o is the index of segregation among

---

[8] We postulate a relationship for a single year, because the number of years for which we have comparable time series data is limited. If more years of data were available, a more complex distributed-lag model in which occupational segregation in year t was a function of several previous years of segregation among college graduates might be desirable.

professional occupations in year t, S^m_{t-3} is the index of segregation among bachelor's degree recipients by major field of study in year $t-3$, and t is 1974 to 1981.

The data on the size and sex composition of college majors are taken from the National Center for Education Statistics' (NCES, 1980) *Projections of Education Statistics to 1988-89*, and the data for professional occupations are from the published AA data (*Employment and Earnings*, various issues). The model and data are discussed in more detail in Appendix C.

First, we computed a time series of segregation indexes for college major among bachelor's degree recipients and for professional occupations, which appear in Table 6-2, columns (1) and (2), respectively. With these data we estimate Eq. (10); the estimated equation with t-values in parentheses is:[9]

$$S^o_t = 23.88 + 0.727\ S^m_{t-3}\ .$$
$$(23.50) \qquad (29.20) \qquad (11)$$
$$R^2 = 0.99,\ N = 8.$$

Initially we used the NCES projections of the number of female and male college graduates by field of study through 1989 (NCES, 1980, pp. 66-71) to compute projected segregation indexes for college majors, as shown in Table 6-2, column (3). In contrast to the increasingly rapid decline in segregation among college majors during the 1970s (column [1]), the NCES projections show a slight increase in segregation in 1979 and only a modest decline thereafter (column [3]). Then, using Eq. (11), we computed the projected segregation indexes for professional occupations, which appear in column (4). Likewise, the projected segre-

gation indexes for professional occupations increase (in 1982) and then decline very slowly thereafter. In fact, the projected segregation index for professional occupations of 48.36 in 1990 based on the NCES projections lies only slightly below the actual 1981 index—49.61. This value is slightly above one for professional occupations computed with the earlier combined-individual projection (P4), 47.05. We suspect from the distinct break in the series between 1978 and 1979 that the NCES projections underestimate the extent of change in the sex composition of college majors.[10]

Assuming that the number of majors by field has been correctly projected by NCES but that the sex composition has not, we estimate the trend in the sex composition for each college major as a linear function of time and then project it into the future. We estimate equations of the following form for each major field:

$$PF_t = \alpha + \beta t + e_t\ , \qquad (12)$$

where PF_t is the percentage of females among bachelor's degree recipients in a major field in year t, $t = 1969$ to 1978, and β is the estimated trend.

The estimated trends in percentage of females by major field of study are presented in Appendix B, Table B-3, along with the actual 1969 and 1978 values and the projected 1989 values. These estimates reveal two major trends among college students:

---

[9] We also estimated this equation for 1-, 2-, 4-, and 5-year lags, and found the explanatory power greatest for the 3-year lag. Given the linear trend in the data, a 3-year lag is approximately equivalent to a 5-year moving average.

[10] To check this we computed the actual segregation index among college fields of study of bachelor's degree recipients for 1979-1980 directly from data from *Earned Degrees Conferred 1979-80* (NCES, 1981). (The categories used for 1978-1979 data were not comparable with those published in the NCES projections volume.) The actual index for 1980 was 34.53, below that based upon NCES projections. While these data are not strictly comparable with earlier data, because the NCES supplemented the data from *Earned Degrees Conferred* with information from additional sources (NCES, 1980, p. 49), they are nevertheless suggestive.

TABLE 6-2   Actual and Projected Segregation Indexes for College Majors and Professional Occupations

Year	Actual		Projection I		Projection II		Projection III	
	College Majors (1)	Professional Occupations (2)	College Majors (3)	Professional Occupations (4)	College Majors (5)	Professional Occupations (6)	College Majors (7)	Professional Occupations (8)
1969	46.08							
1970	45.45							
1971	44.56							
1972	44.17	58.94						
1973	43.32							
1974	41.99	56.13						
1975	40.42	56.11						
1976	38.77	55.58						
1977	36.92	54.07						
1978	35.62	53.32						
1979		51.98	35.98		36.91		35.22	
1980	34.04	50.98	35.66		36.30		34.04	51.19
1981		49.61	35.54		35.67		32.85	50.33
1982			35.35	50.03	33.16	50.70	31.67	49.47
1983			35.33	49.79	34.18	50.26	30.48	48.61
1984			34.89	49.71	33.32	49.80	29.30	47.75
1985			34.46	49.57	32.47	49.43	28.12	46.89
1986			34.18	49.56	31.70	48.72	26.93	46.03
1987			33.69	49.23	30.97	48.09	25.75	45.17
1988			33.36	48.92	30.55	47.48	24.56	44.31
1989			32.94	48.72	30.43	46.92	23.38	43.45
1990				48.36		46.39		42.59

NOTES: Projection I is computed based on NCES projections of degree recipients by major field of study.

Projection II is computed based on projecting the previous linear trend (1969 to 1978) in the female proportion of degree recipients in each major field.

Projection III is computed based on projecting the previous linear trend (1969 to 1978) in the segregation index for college majors.

SOURCES: Cols. (1) (except 1980), (3), (5), and (7) are computed from NCES (1980, pp. 66-71).

Col. (1), 1980; NCES (1981, pp. 19-24).

Col. (2), 1974 to 1981 is computed from Department of Labor, BLS, *Employment and Earnings,* 1974 (March), 1975 (June), and 1976 through 1981 (January).

Col. (2), 1972 is computed from BLS unpublished annual averages.

(1) a decline in the percentage of females in nearly all traditionally female fields of study (public affairs and services, library sciences, letters, and education); and (2) an increase in the representation of women in all other fields. The largest upward trends are in the traditionally male disciplines of architecture (2.1 percent per year); agriculture and natural resources (2.5 percent per year); accounting (2.4 percent per year); business and management (2.0 percent per year); and computer and information sciences (1.5 per-

cent per year). In each of these fields, between 1969 and 1978, the number of women grew to around 25 percent of all majors; according to our projections, they will become 40 to 50 percent of these majors by 1989. The female proportion of psychology majors also grew by 1.9 percent per year during the 1970s. For such trends to continue the same conditions must prevail in the future as in the recent past, even at the higher number of female majors. That is, women must not encounter substantial resistance or increased discrimination as their numbers increase.[11]

Using these projections of sex composition by major, we recomputed the projected segregation indexes for college majors and, with Eq. (11), for professionals, and present them in columns (5) and (6) of Table 6-2, respectively. These projections show a rate of decline in the segregation index for college majors that seems more reasonable, although the level is even higher in the initial years than based upon the NCES projections. The index of segregation among college majors is projected to decline to 30.43 in 1989 and among professional occupations to 46.39 in 1990. Relating this value back to the projected indexes of segregation for professional occupations computed from previous methods, it lies between that of the combined-individual projection (P4), 47.05, and the projections of the linear-individual (P2), 45.26, and of the moderate-age cohort (P6), 45.43. Since there is strength in numbers, we feel confident that this is a reasonable moderate estimate: it projects a decline of around 3.2 percentage points in the segregation index for professional occupations between 1981 and 1990, or around one-third of the magnitude of decline between 1972 and 1981.

We can force the segregation index of college majors to decline after 1978, as we believe it did (see note 10), by estimating its historical trend and projecting it into the future. Under the assumption of a linear rate of decline in the index of segregation among college majors, estimated in an equation like (12), we obtain the projections in Table 6-2, column (7). From them we project the segregation indexes for professional occupations in column (8). This most liberal projection predicts an index of segregation for college majors of 23.38 in 1989 and for professional occupations of 42.59 in 1990.[12] This projection lies just above one computed from the logistic-individual projection (P3), 40.51. Thus, if we were to feed it back into the overall index, this most optimistic projection for professional occupations would be consistent with that of logistic trends, which project an overall decline in segregation during the 1980s slightly less than during the 1970s. Greater declines in segregation in professional occupations are predicted by the moderately optimistic projection (P7), 38.07, and by the optimistic projection (P8), 32.28.

It is hardly surprising that the optimistic projections predict greater declines than these projections because the optimistic projections assume changes in all cohorts, while these take account of changes just among new entrants. Thus, even with continued declines in segregation in the colleges (on the supply side), segregation among professional occupations would still decline less during the 1980s than during the 1970s and would still be substantial in 1990. At present rates of change, complete integration by sex among college fields of study (an index value of 0) would be attained in the year 2009, at which point (in the year 2012) the segregation index for professional occupations would equal 23.88; then, one-fourth of all women (men) would still have to change jobs to eliminate segregation. This result points to the fact that it is easier to change the flow

---

[11] According to Becker's (1971) theory of discrimination, they could encounter more discrimination as their numbers increased if they had to enter more discriminatory institutions, holding constant the level of discrimination. Increases in the numbers of women in traditionally male fields of study also probably results from their perception of improved job opportunities in related occupations. If such opportunities were to decline, say as a result of lesser efforts in affirmative action, a chain of responses could be set into motion whereby women would not increase their entry into traditionally male fields of study and would not increasingly prepare for traditionally male occupations.

---

[12] The index this method projects for 1980, 34.04, is quite close to the one computed from actual NCES data for 1980, 34.53 (see note 10 above).

of new workers than to change the stock of incumbent workers. Policies that promote affirmative action on the demand side could aid in bringing about such changes in occupational segregation, even among professionals.

That occupational segregation among professionals declined more than projected based on projected declines in segregation among college majors (compare 1980 and 1981 data in Table 6-2, columns [2] and [8]) is consistent with the explanation that, relative to young men, young women are quitting less than previously, due to enhanced opportunities for advancement.[13] In order for the segregation indexes to decline by more than is due to the influx of less segregated college graduates alone, less quitting must occur among women already in nontraditional professional occupations. This interpretation of the data is consistent with findings from our earlier study (Beller, in this volume) that show that declines in segregation were large not only among new entrants but also among those with a few years of previous work experience. It is quite logical that while entry positions are important, much advancement occurs in the subsequent early years of a career. Thus, these findings support our earlier findings, which suggest that the benefits from affirmative action have not been confined to new entrants but have been felt among recent entrants as well.[14]

---

[13] A recent study (Osterman, 1982) shows that affirmative action reduces female quitting. Further, Lloyd and Niemi (1979, p. 72) show that more and more women are remaining in the labor force, and thus experienced workers make up a larger proportion of the female labor force.

[14] An alternative explanation, suggested by a referee, is sex differences in the probability of college graduates moving into professional jobs. Since relative wages of many professional jobs have fallen, their increased integration could be the result of males moving into other occupations, such as business. While this explanation seems plausible, segregation declined among the managerial occupations as well.

CONCLUSION

Although significant declines in the occupational segregation of the sexes occurred during the 1970s, as measured by the index of segregation, projections from several methods predict only a modest further decline in the index during the 1980s. Although women are projected to continue entering the traditionally male professional and managerial occupations, they will also continue to enter the highly female clerical occupations, which are projected to grow by more than 2 million jobs. Also, women are not projected to enter several of the predominantly male crafts and operative and laborer occupations that are projected to grow considerably during the 1980s. Projected changes in the fields of study of female college graduates predict declines in segregation among professional occupations consistent with no more than moderate declines in the overall index of segregation. Only those projections that assume that *all cohorts* experience declines in segregation during the 1980s *at the same rate* as during the 1970s predict a large decline in the overall index of segregation. If these projections are correct, any significant decline in occupational segregation during the 1980s cannot be expected without major policy initiatives.

APPENDIX A   PROJECTIONS DATA AND METHODOLOGY

BLS Occupational Employment Projections

The BLS occupational employment projections that we use, which are based upon the classification system of the 1970 Census of Population, are not the most recent ones; however, the newer projections are based upon a different data matrix, which does not contain the same occupational categories (Department of Labor, BLS, 1981, p. 1).

Unlike the Census, the new Occupational Employment Statistics (OES) survey conducted by the BLS is a survey of jobs, not of people. Projections based on such a matrix avoid the problem of having to specify an unemployment rate, but the primary disadvantage is the lack of consistency with CPS data, which are based on a count of persons rather than of jobs. The first set of these new projections appears in Carey (1981).

As stated in the text of this paper, the BLS occupational employment projections used assume that a stable long-run unemployment rate close to 4.5 percent will be achieved by the mid-1980s. This seems exceptionally optimistic from the vantage point of the end of 1982 when, in September, the economy hit a high unemployment rate of 10.1 percent. How would an unemployment rate higher than 4.5 percent affect occupational employment projections for 1990? According to Carey (1981, p. 42), job growth in blue-collar occupations is more sensitive to the underlying assumptions than is job growth in other major occupational categories. The need for additional blue-collar workers is very much affected by the demand for manufactured goods as well as by changes in productivity. Job growth in the white-collar and service categories generally is less sensitive to the underlying assumptions than is blue-collar job growth. Most likely the employment estimates would overestimate the size of blue-collar occupational employment. This consideration should be kept in mind in examining the projections of occupational segregation, because many blue-collar occupations are highly male, and the larger they are the more they add to the index of segregation.

The BLS 1990 occupational employment projections "assume that the size, sex and age composition of the labor force will change as indicated by the intermediate labor force projections published by the BLS in *Employment Projections of the 1980's.*" We use those projections for our projections by age cohort. Since the occupation projections are based upon these labor force projections, they should be consistent with them.

Methodology of Projections Based on Age Cohorts

In order to make projections by age cohort, we need to know the sizes of age-sex cohorts for the projected year to supplement information on the projected occupational distribution and the projected sex composition of each occupation. Age-sex-specific projections on the size of the civilian labor force in 1990, created by the BLS, are presented in *Employment Projections for the 1980's*. They project the size of age cohorts, which we grouped into four categories: 16 to 24, 25 to 34, 35 to 44, and 45+. Unfortunately these categories cannot be transformed into cohorts based on potential labor market experience, which creates more meaningful and presumably more homogeneous groupings for labor force analyses. For example, the age group 16 to 24 contains a mixture of high school graduates already in their chosen field for several years and individuals who are still students and who work part time at jobs unrelated to their future occupations. In the analyses by experience cohorts presented in another paper, we excluded individuals with 0 years of potential work experience (defined as Age − Education − 6), hoping to eliminate students. Since we do not know the sizes of age-sex experience cohorts for the projected year, we must base our cohort projections on age rather than on work experience cohorts. Thus, we grouped our Annual Demographic File data for 1971 and 1977 into age cohorts. Segregation indexes by age cohort for 1971 and 1977 shown in Table B-2 differ from those by experience cohort (Beller, in this volume, Table 2-2). The youngest age cohort is more segregated than is the youngest experience cohort after exclusion of individuals with 0 years of potential experience.

To project what happened to a specific cohort as it aged over time, we aged each group backward to 1977 by subtracting 13 years. This yielded age groups in 1977 of 16 to 21, 22 to 31, and 32 to 41. We added the age group 42 + to complete the labor force. We also added the youngest complete cohort, 16 to 24 years of age, so that we could use it for the projections as well. Aging the groups backward by 6 years to 1971 yielded age groups 16 to 25, 26 to 35, and 36 to 45. We added the group 46 + and the youngest age cohort, 16 to 24. This construction can be diagrammed as follows:

Group	1971	1977	1990
		+6	+13
1	16-24 ——————→	16-24 ——————→	16-24
2	16-25 ↘	16-21 ↘	. . .
3	26-35 ↘	↗ 22-31 ↘	↗ 25-34
4	36-45 ↘	↗ 32-41 ↘	↗ 35-44
5	46 +	↗ 42 +	↗ 45 +

First, we must project the percentage of males in each occupation for each age group in 1990. To do this we choose three alternative assumptions, which allow for (1) no change between 1977 and 1990; (2) changes in the youngest cohort, group 1, only; and (3) changes in all cohorts. Changes are projected to occur at the same rate between 1977 and 1990 as a given group ages as the rate for the similar age group as it aged between 1971 and 1977. The methodology of these three projections (labeled conservative, moderate, and optimistic) is described in the text of this paper.

This method of projecting assumes that the sex composition of occupations is characteristic of the particular age cohort in question rather than of the labor force or the occupation. That is, it directs our attention to the characteristics of individuals, or the supply side of the labor market, more than do the projections based upon the whole labor force, which direct our attention more to the characteristics of employers, or the demand side. Of course, supply changes in response to perceived changes in demand. Women's aspirations change as they perceive reductions in the barriers to their entry into traditionally male occupations (Reskin and Hartmann, 1984).

Once we create projections of the percentage of males in each occupation by age group, we must combine them to create projections of the percentage of males in each occupation for the labor force as a whole. To obtain a labor force estimate from the cohort estimates, we use the BLS projections on the age-sex distribution of the labor force in 1990. We know the projected number of males, females, and total labor force for each age group. We also know from BLS projections the projected distribution of employment across occupations for the civilian labor force as a whole. We need to combine these two pieces of information to determine the occupational distribution of employment for each age group, and we must make assumptions to do this. The simplest assumption is that the occupational distribution is the same for each age group as it is for the labor force as a whole; this is equivalent to standardizing the employment distribution of each subgroup to the employment distribution of the whole. (Thus, looking ahead, when we use the projected sex composition within each occupation of each age group to compute segregation indexes, we will see differences in the indexes that are based upon differences in their occupational sex composition alone.) Another possible assumption is that each age group has the same occupational distribution of employment in 1990 as it did in 1977. This, too, is imperfect, because the occupational distribution is projected to change. Consequently we opted for the first approach.

We computed total employment, number of males, and number of females in occupation i in age group j in 1990 according to the following:

$$T_{ij} = \frac{E_i}{\sum_i E_i} \times T_j , \qquad (A1)$$

$$M_{ij}^n = T_{ij} \times p_{ij}^n , \qquad (A2)$$

$$F_{ij}^n = T_{ij} - M_{ij}^n , \qquad (A3)$$

where T_{ij} is total employment in occupation i for age group j, where $j = 1,\ldots,5$ as in the diagram above; E_i is total employment in occupation i, given by BLS projections; T_j is civilian labor force in age group j, given by BLS projections; p_{ij}^n is proportion male in occupation i for age group j according to cohort projection n, where $n = 1,2,3$; M_{ij}^n is the number of males in occupation i for age group j according to cohort projection

n; and F_{ij}^n is the number of females in occupation i for age group j according to cohort projection n.

These numbers are then aggregated over age groups to obtain the values for the civilian labor force in 1990:

$$M_i^n = \sum_j M_{ij}^n , \qquad (A4)$$

$$F_i^n = \sum_j F_{ij}^n , \qquad (A5)$$

$$p_i^n = \frac{M_i^n}{M_i^n + F_i^n} . \qquad (A6)$$

Using these projections of proportion of males by occupation and the BLS occupational employment projections for 1990, E_i, we compute four projected segregation indexes for 1990, P5 to P8.

TABLE B-1   Actual and Projected Proportion Female for Detailed Occupations

Occ. Code	Occupation Name	Actual 1972	1981	Annual Rate of Change*	Projected 1990 (P1)	(P2)	(P3)
I.	Proportion Female Increasing						
1	Accountants	.2171	.3850	.0152	.4291	.5239	.5476
3	Programmers, computer	.1989	.2941	.0093	.3247	.3822	.4113
10	Engineers, chemical	.0000	.0615	.0056	.1043	.0964	.4129
12	Engineers, electrical and electronic	.0105	.0378	.0028	.0817	.0594	.2666
13	Engineers, industrial	.0235	.1126	.0124	.1560	.2442	.6959
25	Foresters and conservationists	.0417	.1053	.0090	.1650	.1879	.7742
31	Lawyers	.0396	.1423	.0100	.1910	.2284	.3644
55	Researchers and analysts, operat. and sys.	.0991	.2551	.0188	.2741	.4188	.5883
56	Personnel and labor relations	.3097	.4977	.0133	.5342	.6028	.6063
64	Pharmacists	.1349	.2517	.0088	.3076	.3240	.3563
65	Physicians, medics, and osteopaths	.1006	.1376	.0030	.1909	.1620	.1681
85	NEC, health technicians	.5821	.5787	.0100	.6052	.6721	.6666
151	Technicians, chemical	.1169	.2574	.0155	.3022	.3965	.4874
152	Draftsmen	.0629	.1929	.0120	.2459	.2884	.3763
153	Technicians, elect. engineers	.0549	.1124	.0079	.1515	.1882	.3061
171	Operators, radio	.3514	.5738	.0380	.5988	.9790	.8860
192	Public relations	.2989	.4545	.0173	.5073	.5721	.5847
202	Officers and manag., bank	.1874	.3735	.0165	.4222	.5204	.5530
220	NEC, managers, office	.4190	.7024	.0233	.7300	.9356	.8628
222	NEC, pub. admin., office and admin.	.2006	.2900	.0057	.3100	.3414	.3496

NOTES: Column (P1) contains the linear-group projection, column (P2) contains the linear-individual projection, and column (P3) contains the logistic-individual projection. NEC = not elsewhere classified.

*Coefficient estimate on linear time trend in individual occupation projection, where estimate is significant.

TABLE B-1 (Continued)

Occ. Code	Occupation Name	Actual 1972	1981	Annual Rate of Change*	Projected 1990 (P1)	(P2)	(P3)
225	NEC, purchasing agents and buyers	.1326	.3038	.0135	.3426	.4148	.4648
231	Retail trade sales manag. and dept. heads	.2736	.4036	.0119	.4732	.5299	.5422
233	Sales manag., exc. ret. trade	.0292	.1362	.0105	.1944	.2242	.4391
245	NEC, manag. and admin.	.1214	.1966	.0080	.2424	.2724	.3049
260	Adv. agents and sales work	.2273	.4683	.0256	.5063	.7100	.7241
265	Ins. agents, brokers, and underwriters	.1179	.2363	.0128	.2867	.3508	.4173
266	Vendors and carriers, news	.2444	.2973	.0211	.3193	.4734	.6537
270	Agents and brokers, real est.	.3668	.5000	.0114	.5440	.5916	.5934
281	Sales rep., manuf. indust.	.0700	.2000	.0114	.2596	.2870	.3553
282	Sales rep., wholesale trade	.0460	.1199	.0071	.1681	.1837	.2506
301	Bank tellers	.8715	.9355	.0043	.9501	.9749	.9586
305	Bookkeepers	.8794	.9116	.0039	.9327	.9517	.9399
315	Dispatchers and starters, vehicle	.1628	.3805	.0249	.4065	.6186	.6883
323	Expediters and production controllers	.2308	.4096	.0113	.4561	.5056	.5159
331	Mail carriers, post office	.0667	.1548	.0090	.2026	.2444	.3091
333	Messengers and office helpers	.1410	.2766	.0202	.2934	.5129	.7250
343	Computer and peripheral equip. operators	.3776	.6407	.0290	.6596	.9335	.8555
360	Clerks, payroll, and timekeep.	.7174	.8097	.0135	.8367	.9446	.8965
361	Postal clerks	.2669	.3802	.0101	.4025	.4824	.4919
375	Clerks, statistical	.7090	.8006	.0090	.8364	.8913	.8667
381	Storekeepers and stock clerks	.2290	.3501	.0099	.3958	.4550	.4689
390	Agents, ticket station and express	.3178	.4722	.0188	.4941	.6625	.6732
412	Bulldozer operators	.0000	.0099	.0013	.1239	.0232	.1623
415	Carpenters	.0049	.0180	.0013	.0831	.0303	.0610
422	Compositors and typesetters	.1647	.3506	.0210	.3803	.5491	.6181
430	Electricians	.0043	.0168	.0012	.0720	.0255	.0496
441	NEC, blue-collar supervisors	.0701	.1134	.0033	.1606	.1434	.1562
455	Locomotive engineers	.0000	.0213	.0019	.0784	.0334	.1108
470	Air cond., heating, refrigeration	.0000	.0047	.0007	.0628	.0125	.0434
481	Mechanics, heavy equipment	.0070	.0179	.0012	.0936	.0285	.0472
482	Mechanics and install. appliance home	.0152	.0455	.0033	.1178	.0673	.2108
550	Structural metal workers	.0000	.0122	.0011	.0787	.0191	.0488
552	Teleph. install and repairers	.0194	.0982	.0076	.1378	.1684	.3495
554	Teleph. linemen and splicers	.0000	.0506	.0060	.0771	.1072	.8681
601	Asbestos and insulat. workers	.0000	.0377	.0056	.1000	.1037	.8507
631	Meat cutters, butchers, exc. manuf.	.0348	.0809	.0038	.1307	.1135	.1402
664	Shoemaking, machine operatives	.6184	.7260	.0122	.7223	.8539	.8248
666	Furnace tenders and stokers	.0123	.0128	.0012	.0507	.0201	.0527
703	Bus drivers	.3414	.4732	.0122	.5038	.6043	.6071
705	Delivery and route workers	.0247	.0856	.0057	.1420	.1393	.2172
715	Truck drivers	.0042	.0266	.0018	.0923	.0401	.0686
740	Animal caretakers, exc. farm	.4125	.5699	.0251	.6387	.8100	.7822
750	Carpenters' helpers	.0160	.0167	.0020	.1150	.0351	.3307
754	Garbage collectors	.0118	.0278	.0011	.1731	.0347	.0385
762	Stock handlers	.1687	.2479	.0093	.2911	.3267	.3530
764	Vehicle washers and equip. cleaners	.0909	.1576	.0042	.2149	.1920	.2017
785	Not specified laborers	.0396	.1122	.0073	.2181	.1778	.2881
903	Janitors and sextons	.1051	.1899	.0066	.2407	.2503	.2759
910	Bartenders	.2786	.4725	.0192	.5156	.6604	.6688

(Continued)

TABLE B-1 (Continued)

Occ. Code	Occupation Name	Actual 1972	1981	Annual Rate of Change*	Projected 1990 (P1)	(P2)	(P3)
932	Attendants, recreation and amuse.	.3120	.4477	.0155	.4814	.6146	.6230
962	Guards	.0461	.1366	.0086	.2062	.2017	.2936
II.	**Proportion Female Decreasing**						
141	Teach., adult ed.	.3768	.4267	−.0219	.4759	.2106	.2364
142	Teach., elem. ed.	.8505	.8359	−.0038	.8627	.8003	.7922
385	Telephone operators	.9668	.9302	−.0040	.9469	.8984	.8480
502	Millwrights	.0000	.0000	−.0029	.0594	.0000	.0000
624	Graders and sorters, manuf.	.7727	.6389	−.0162	.6869	.5119	.4772
822	Farm laborers, wage workers	.1535	.1594	−.0095	.1898	.0955	.1142
912	Cooks, exc. private household	.6236	.5228	−.0109	.5616	.4344	.4318
915	Waiters	.9173	.8967	−.0038	.9211	.8626	.8474
933	NEC, attendants, personal serv.	.6386	.5773	−.0117	.6077	.5135	.5096
III.	**Proportion Female—No Significant Trend**						
2	Architects	.0303	.0440	.0000	.1080	.0408	.0768
4	Syst. analysts, computer	.1081	.2584	.0000	.2993	.3121	.3266
6	Engineers, aero- and astro-.	.0000	.0122	.0000	.0467	.0124	.0245
11	Engineers, civil	.0065	.0164	.0000	.0652	.0251	.0963
14	Engineers, mechanical	.0000	.0243	.0000	.0652	.0396	.1713
23	NEC engineers	.0000	.0290	.0000	.0544	.0335	.0524
32	Librarians	.8278	.8580	.0000	.8745	.9020	.8914
44	Scientists, biological	.2778	.4035	.0000	.4609	.4525	.4563
45	Chemists	.1008	.2090	.0000	.2577	.2866	.3452
75	Nurses, registered	.9763	.9680	.0000	.9890	.9676	.9662
76	Therapists	.5826	.7049	.0000	.7271	.7781	.7675
80	Clinical lab. techs.	.7063	.7724	.0000	.7948	.7426	.7451
83	Radiologic techs.	.6618	.6863	.0000	.7299	.5765	.5681
86	Clergy	.0163	.0505	.0000	.0949	.0766	.0839
90	NEC, religious workers	.5745	.4717	.0000	.5276	.4281	.4380
91	Economists	.1176	.2484	.0000	.2927	.3620	.4014
93	Psychologists	.3800	.4870	.0000	.5349	.4369	.4373
100	Social workers	.5856	.6397	.0000	.6787	.5984	.5980
101	Recreation workers	.4457	.5798	.0000	.6288	.6511	.6487
140	Col. teach., not specified	.2703	.3788	.0000	.8194	.4974	.4971
143	Teach., pre- and kindergart.	.9681	.9833	.0000	1.0000	.9744	.9693
144	Teach., secondary sch.	.4964	.5136	.0000	.5289	.4933	.4932
145	NEC, teach., exc. col.	.7409	.7380	.0000	.7632	.7232	.7205
150	Technicians, ag. and biol., exc. health	.2927	.4400	.0000	.4794	.5386	.5551
161	Surveyors	.0141	.0114	.0000	.0563	.0188	.0743
162	NEC, techs., eng. and science	.1437	.2469	.0000	.2970	.3083	.3218
163	Pilots, airplane	.0000	.0125	.0000	.0769	.0152	.0278
174	Counselors, voca. and education	.5000	.5323	.0000	.5648	.5559	.5558
180	Athletes and kindred	.3077	.4351	.0000	.4610	.5434	.5495
183	Designers	.1909	.2953	.0000	.3242	.4180	.4384
184	Editors and reporters	.4110	.5050	.0000	.5465	.4908	.4901
185	Musicians and composers	.3058	.2535	.0000	.3232	.1960	.2062

NOTES: Column (P1) contains the linear-group projection, column (P2) contains the linear-individual projection, and column (P3) contains the logistic-individual projection. NEC = not elsewhere classified.

*Coefficient estimate on linear time trend in individual occupation projection, where estimate is significant.

TABLE B-1 (Continued)

Occ. Code	Occupation Name	Actual 1972	1981	Annual Rate of Change*	Projected 1990 (P1)	(P2)	(P3)
190	Painters and sculptors	.4264	.5121	.0000	.5424	.5559	.5558
191	Photographers	.1558	.2424	.0000	.2868	.1829	.1776
194	NEC, writers, artists, entertainers	.3333	.3853	.0000	.4272	.3115	.3171
195	Research, not specified	.2791	.3936	.0000	.4107	.4774	.4896
201	Assessors, controllers, treasurers	.3448	.5000	.0000	.5311	.6337	.6356
205	Buyer, whole. and retail	.3292	.4346	.0000	.4735	.5175	.5198
210	Manager, credit and collect	.2535	.3788	.0000	.4042	.4803	.4986
212	Administrators, health	.4746	.4954	.0000	.5442	.4941	.4937
215	Inspectors, exc. construct., pub. admin.	.0619	.1019	.0000	.1545	.2487	.3676
216	Manag. and superintendent, building admin.	.4265	.5063	.0000	.5572	.5134	.5134
223	Officials, lodges, soc. and unions	.1875	.2845	.0000	.3034	.3114	.3140
224	Mail super. and postmasters	.3409	.3636	.0000	.4121	.5071	.5347
230	Manager, rest., bar, cafeteria	.3239	.4045	.0000	.4356	.3893	.3893
235	Sch. admin., college	.2530	.3504	.0000	.3506	.3923	.4001
240	Sch. admin., sec. and clem.	.2624	.3668	.0000	.4010	.4255	.4313
262	Demonstrators	.9375	.9619	.0000	.9663	.9726	.9720
264	Hucksters and peddlers	.7304	.7964	.0000	.8295	.9441	.9106
271	Sales agent, stock and bond	.0990	.1667	.0000	.1915	.2186	.2461
283	Sales clerks, retail trade	.6887	.7130	.0000	.7504	.7298	.7302
284	Sales work, exc. clerks, retail	.1302	.1965	.0000	.2502	.2032	.2040
285	Sales work, service and construc.	.2941	.4304	.0000	.5146	.4648	.4654
303	Billing clerks	.8456	.8808	.0000	.9286	.9654	.9362
310	Cashiers	.8667	.8637	.0000	.8960	.8715	.8715
312	NEC, supervisors, clerical	.5779	.7073	.0000	.7469	.7731	.7631
313	Collectors, bill and account	.4833	.6444	.0000	.6740	.7942	.7702
314	Clerks, counter, exc. food	.7386	.7642	.0000	.8051	.7804	.7831
320	Enumerators and interviewers	.8205	.7544	.0000	.7842	.5988	.4914
321	NEC investigator and estimator	.4339	.5444	.0000	.5754	.5879	.5875
325	File clerks	.8493	.8371	.0000	.8619	.8068	.8027
326	Insur. adjusters, examiners, and investigators	.3519	.5753	.0000	.6189	.7291	.7181
330	Library attend. and assist.	.7518	.8255	.0000	.8600	.9261	.9012
332	Mail handlers, exc. post office	.4375	.4767	.0000	.5136	.4977	.4978
341	Bookkeep. and billing operators	.9130	.8936	.0000	.9329	.8085	.7311
345	Key punch operators	.8975	.9383	.0000	.9494	.9866	.9701
355	NEC, office machine operators	.6949	.6833	.0000	.7156	.5438	.4820
364	Receptionists	.9702	.9742	.0000	.9961	.9792	.9770
370	Secretaries, legal	.9908	.9888	.0000	1.0000	.9851	.9733
372	NEC, secretaries	.9909	.9914	.0000	1.0000	.9921	.9922
374	Clerks, shipping and receiving	.1486	.2272	.0000	.2734	.2667	.2769
376	Stenographers	.9040	.8611	.0000	.8790	.8164	.7413
382	Teacher aides	.8932	.9303	.0000	.9634	.9680	.9536
391	Typists	.9608	.9634	.0000	.9891	.9745	.9728
392	Weighers	.2791	.3421	.0000	.3996	.2969	.3035
394	Misc. clerical workers	.7513	.8200	.0000	.8716	.8911	.8778
402	Bakers	.2895	.4148	.0000	.4427	.4737	.4762
404	Boilermakers	.0000	.0000	.0000	.0840	.0000	.0010
405	Bookbinders	.6250	.5600	.0000	.6064	.5671	.5783
410	Brick- and stonemasons	.0059	.0000	.0000	.0842	.0000	.0002
413	Cabinetmakers	.0500	.0267	.0000	.0904	.0279	.0258

(Continued)

TABLE B-1   (Continued)

Occ. Code	Occupation Name	Actual 1972	Actual 1981	Annual Rate of Change*	Projected 1990 (P1)	(P2)	(P3)
652	Lathe and mill machine operatives	.0488	.0594	.0000	.1331	.0568	.0583
653	NEC, precision machine operatives	.1475	.1754	.0000	.2521	.0835	.0994
656	Punch and stamp press operatives	.2739	.3208	.0000	.4124	.3544	.3556
662	Sawyers	.0496	.0909	.0000	.1591	.1553	.6861
421	Cement and concrete finishers	.0127	.0000	.0000	.1030	.0000	.0010
424	Crane, derrick, hoist operators	.0467	.0070	.0000	.0941	.0124	.0068
425	Decorators and window dressers	.5977	.7222	.0000	.7627	.8934	.8542
433	Install. and repair elect. power lines	.0098	.0086	.0000	.0618	.0044	.0053
436	Excavat., grading, exc. bulldozer	.0000	.0062	.0000	.0740	.0113	.0315
452	NEC, inspectors	.0305	.0839	.0000	.1364	.1619	.2269
454	Job and die setters, metal	.0106	.0532	.0000	.1211	.0661	.0283
461	Machinists	.0054	.0388	.0000	.0861	.0769	.2243
471	Aircraft	.0000	.0325	.0000	.0916	.0414	.0486
472	Auto body repairers	.0000	.0098	.0000	.0675	.0217	.1132
473	Auto mechanics	.0058	.0058	.0000	.0685	.0068	.0066
475	Repairers, data process. machine	.0222	.0700	.0000	.1298	.0930	.2669
480	Farm implement	.0000	.0000	.0000	.0995	.0004	.0011
484	Office machine	.0000	.0400	.0000	.1086	.0481	.0456
485	Radio and television	.0081	.0367	.0000	.1216	.0406	.0501
503	Molders, metal	.0962	.1731	.0000	.2276	.1990	.2099
510	Painters, construct. and maintenance	.0188	.0575	.0000	.1149	.1114	.2060
522	Plumbers and pipe fitters	.0027	.0044	.0000	.0595	.0092	.0124
530	Printing press operator	.0563	.1091	.0000	.1595	.1350	.1699
534	Roofers and slaters	.0000	.0000	.0000	.0477	.0000	.0006
535	Sheetmetal workers and tinsmiths	.0139	.0397	.0000	.1069	.0577	.0911
545	Stationary engineers	.0105	.0165	.0000	.0639	.0316	.1634
551	Tailors	.3226	.4091	.0000	.5666	.5151	.5344
561	Tool and die makers	.0058	.0237	.0000	.0878	.0276	.0337
563	Upholsterers	.1364	.2222	.0000	.2612	.1425	.1499
575	NEC, craft and kindred workers	.0690	.1746	.0000	.2648	.4046	.6389
602	Assemblers	.4671	.5231	.0000	.5787	.5462	.5461
604	Bottling and can operatives	.3455	.4231	.0000	.4710	.4176	.4183
610	Checkers, examiners, inspec. manuf.	.4847	.5356	.0000	.5743	.5239	.5240
611	Clothing-ironers and pressers	.7683	.8067	.0000	.8334	.7846	.7831
612	NEC, cutting operatives	.2773	.3137	.0000	.3606	.3047	.3049
615	Drywall install. and lathers	.0120	.0127	.0000	.1034	.0272	.0790
621	Filers, sanders, polishers, buffers	.2213	.3186	.0000	.3614	.2806	.2813
622	Furnace tenders, smelters, pourers	.0429	.0323	.0000	.1058	.0965	.7333
623	Garage work and gas sta. attend.	.0458	.0559	.0000	.1048	.0797	.1100
625	Produce graders and packers, exc. fact. and farm	.7143	.7333	.0000	.7699	.8337	.8241
630	NEC, laundry and dry clean. opera.	.6970	.6614	.0000	.7044	.6600	.6594
633	Meat cutters, butchers-manuf.	.3258	.2917	.0000	.3297	.2832	.2832
634	Meat wrappers, retail trade	.9000	.8980	.0000	.9357	.8358	.7171
640	NEC, mine operatives	.0070	.0192	.0000	.0610	.0336	.1333
641	Mixing operatives	.0202	.0390	.0000	.0998	.0287	.0330
642	Oilers and greasers, exc. auto	.0435	.0526	.0000	.1189	.0719	.2183
643	Packers and wrappers, exc. meat and produce	.6090	.6339	.0000	.6827	.6354	.6352

NOTES: Column (P1) contains the linear-group projection, column (P2) contains the linear-individual projection, and column (P3) contains the logistic-individual projection. NEC = not elsewhere classified.

*Coefficient estimate on linear time trend in individual occupation projection, where estimate is significant.

TABLE B-1   (Continued)

Occ. Code	Occupation Name	Actual 1972	1981	Annual Rate of Change*	Projected 1990 (P1)	(P2)	(P3)
644	Painters, manufactured articles	.1461	.1667	.0000	.2314	.1469	.1458
645	Photographic process workers	.4691	.5177	.0000	.5679	.5503	.5501
650	Drill press operatives	.2267	.2500	.0000	.2936	.2607	.2618
651	Grinding machine operatives	.0538	.1119	.0000	.1499	.2038	.2699
663	Sewers and stitchers	.9583	.9603	.0000	.9908	.9558	.9565
665	Solderers	.7674	.7292	.0000	.7299	.6354	.6065
672	Spinners, twisters, and winders	.6071	.6735	.0000	.7174	.6720	.6727
674	NEC, textile operatives	.5282	.5520	.0000	.5959	.5060	.5056
680	Welders and flame-cutters	.0361	.0465	.0000	.1125	.0526	.0530
681	NEC, winding operatives	.4658	.4546	.0000	.5402	.5856	.5873
690	Machine operatives, misc. specified	.2814	.2913	.0000	.3408	.2769	.2773
692	Machine operatives, not specified	.2148	.2781	.0000	.3387	.3625	.3640
694	Misc. operatives	.3166	.3526	.0000	.3643	.3553	.3553
695	Not specified operatives	.3036	.3452	.0000	.4101	.4835	.4974
706	Fork lift and tow motor operatives	.0099	.0579	.0000	.1220	.0909	.2624
711	Parking attendants	.0303	.1000	.0000	.1922	.1283	.5642
712	RR brake operators and couplers	.0000	.0000	.0000	.0525	.0163	.0088
713	RR switch operators	.0000	.0000	.0000	.0553	.0175	.0092
714	Taxicab drivers and chauffeurs	.0904	.0932	.0000	.1361	.0902	.0936
751	Construction laborers, exc. carpenters' helpers	.0049	.0215	.0000	.0905	.0454	.0875
753	Freight and material handlers	.0604	.0966	.0000	.1544	.1106	.1139
755	Gardeners and groundskeepers, exc. farm	.0221	.0463	.0000	.1002	.0917	.1719
760	Longshore workers and stevedores	.0000	.0227	.0000	.0857	.0299	.0654
761	Timber cutting and logging	.0123	.0101	.0000	.0302	.0000	.0015
770	NEC, warehouse laborers	.0267	.0595	.0000	.0715	.0723	.0783
821	Farm supervisors	.0357	.0645	.0000	.1211	.1937	.2039
901	Cleaners, lodging quarters- exc.	.9786	.9657	.0000	1.0000	.9454	.9174
902	NEC, building interior cleaners	.5509	.5534	.0000	.5992	.5830	.5826
911	Waiters' assistants	.1367	.1982	.0000	.2802	.2882	.3110
913	Dishwashers	.3578	.2892	.0000	.3645	.3540	.3527
914	Food counter and fountain workers	.8208	.8370	.0000	.8752	.8788	.8709
916	NEC, food service workers, exc. private house.	.7377	.7342	.0000	.7723	.7387	.7391
921	Dental assistants	.9787	.9784	.0000	1.0000	.9761	.9840
922	Health aides, exc. nursing	.7973	.8454	.0000	.8932	.9321	.9084
925	Nursing aides, orderlies, attend.	.8344	.8665	.0000	.9034	.8682	.8698
926	Practical nurses	.9650	.9772	.0000	1.0000	.9652	.9131
942	Child care workers, exc. private	.9579	.9544	.0000	.9839	.9084	.8760
944	Hairdressers and cosmetologists	.9089	.8936	.0000	.9171	.8647	.8490
950	Housekeepers, exc. private house.	.7094	.6992	.0000	.7424	.6274	.6095
952	School monitors	.8750	.9722	.0000	.9962	1.0000	.9328
954	Welfare service aides	.8235	.8837	.0000	.9173	.9086	.9035
960	Crossing guards and bridge attend.	.6327	.6222	.0000	.6625	.5411	.5378
961	Firemen, fire protection	.0050	.0095	.0000	.0775	.0057	.0065
964	Police and detectives	.0264	.0557	.0000	.1125	.0856	.0987
965	Sheriffs and bailiffs	.0508	.0725	.0000	.1230	.1099	.3588
980	Child care workers, priv. house.	.9797	.9774	.0000	.9853	.9690	.9721
984	Private house cleaners and servants	.9719	.9519	.0000	.9700	.9395	.9320

TABLE B-2   Actual and Projected Segregation Indexes by Age Cohort, 1971 to 1990

| | 1971 | | | 1977 | | | Projected 1990 | | | | |
Group	Age	U	ES	Age	U	ES	Age	(P5)	(P6)	(P7)	(P8)
1	16-24	68.64	67.14	16-24	64.68	61.86	16-24	61.96	37.08	46.60	37.08
2	16-25	68.31	67.33	16-21	65.49	66.04	—	—	—	—	—
3	26-35	68.94	68.90	22-31	62.67	61.81	25-34	66.18	66.18	47.82	39.61
4	36-45	70.85	70.77	32-41	66.30	67.48	35-44	61.91	61.91	55.02	49.63
5	46+	68.62	69.16	42+	66.86	67.61	45+	68.19	68.19	58.17	48.90
Total	—	68.14	—	—	64.15	—	—	62.11	57.29	50.02	42.20

NOTES: The age groups are constructed so that each group can be followed as it ages over time. Thus, the difference between the 1971 and 1977 intervals is 6 years and between the 1977 and 1990 intervals, 13 years. U = unstandardized, and ES = standardized to the employment of the whole labor force in the given year.

SOURCES: 1971 and 1977: Current Population Survey, Annual Demographic Files, 1972 and 1978, computer tapes; 1990: Department of Labor, BLS (1979, Table 4, p. 5); Department of Labor, BLS (1981, Table 5, pp. 495-502).

TABLE B-3   Actual and Projected Proportion Female for College Majors, 1969 to 1989

| | Actual Percent Female | | | Projected Percent Female, 1989 |
| | 1969 | 1978 | Trend[a] | |
Field of Study	(1)	(2)	(3)	(4)
Social sciences	36.3	41.0	0.005	45.5
Psychology	42.9	58.8	0.019	79.4
Public affairs and services	71.6	49.4	−0.026	10.8
Library sciences	93.6	88.5	−0.003	87.4
Architecture and environmental design	4.3	23.7	0.021	47.0
Fine and applied arts	59.1	62.0	0.004	66.4
Foreign languages	73.1	75.9	0.003	79.7
Communications	42.2	46.9	0.007	51.0
Letters	63.4	57.1	−0.008	46.9
Mathematics and statistics	37.4	41.1	0.005	47.5
Computer and information sciences	13.0	25.7	0.015	40.7
Engineering	0.7	7.4	0.006	11.5
Engineering technologies	0.5	2.8	0.003	6.4
Physical sciences	13.6	21.3	0.009	30.4
Biological sciences	28.0	38.4	0.012	50.6
Agriculture and natural resources	3.8	24.6	0.025	50.1
Health care professions	76.9	80.5	0.004	84.0
Accounting	7.8	29.4	0.024	52.7
Business and management	9.1	26.4	0.020	45.4
Education	75.8	72.5	−0.004	67.2
Other	53.1	58.4	0.007	66.1
All fields	43.7	47.1	—	52.3[b]

[a] The trend value is the estimated coefficient on year in an OLS regression equation in which the percentage of females is regressed on time. All trend values are significant at the .05 level except communications, which is significant at .10 level.

[b] Computed from the projected sex composition for each major field.

SOURCE: NCES (1980, pp. 70-71).

APPENDIX C PROJECTIONS FOR PROFESSIONAL OCCUPATIONS BASED UPON COLLEGE MAJORS

The model used to project segregation among professional occupations based on segregation among college majors departs from the other models used in this paper. In this model the segregation index itself, rather than the sex composition of each occupation, becomes the data point. We chose this model because attempts to relate the sex composition of a professional occupation to that of a specific college major proved unsuccessful. Thus, we hypothesized that the overall degree of segregation among college graduates would affect the overall degree of segregation in professional occupations.

The data used for these projections for professional occupations are slightly different from the data used earlier in this paper. To obtain a continuous time series, data were taken from the published BLS AA data (*Employment and Earnings*, various issues). The female proportion of occupational employment was first published in 1974. Initially each published category represented an individual occupation or a combination of occupations having a minimum employment estimate of 150,000; the sex distribution was included only where the basis of the estimate was at least 15,000. By this criterion the sex distribution was not published for many detailed categories. Consequently to obtain comparable data over time, more aggregate categories of professional occupations were used in these analyses. Twenty-four separate categories were used for 1978 to 1981, 23 for 1975 to 1977, and 18 for 1974. We also used unpublished AA data for 1972 and used the same 24 categories as in 1978 to 1981. Thus, the segregation indexes used here differ slightly from the other ones reported in this paper, which include 59 disaggregated categories. For example, the segregation index for professional occupations based on the published aggregated data

is 49.61 in 1981, while that based on unpublished detailed data is 50.55. As is common, the aggregation tends to mask some segregation, but the effect here is small. It is even smaller in 1977, when the segregation index based on 23 aggregated categories is 54.07 and based on 59 detailed occupations is 54.35. The index based on unpublished aggregated data in 1972 is 58.94, while that based on detailed data is 59.44. Thus, the effect of this aggregation appears to be to somewhat overstate the decline in segregation in professional occupations during the 1970s.

ACKNOWLEDGMENTS

Discussions with Francine Blau, John Boyd, and Kenneth Stolarsky stimulated the development of ideas. Helpful comments on an earlier draft were provided by Marianne Ferber, Barbara Reskin, and several reviewers. Computational assistance by John Boyd and Alex Kwok is gratefully acknowledged.

REFERENCES

Becker, Gary S.
1971   *The Economics of Discrimination*. Chicago: University of Chicago Press.

Beller, Andrea H.
1982a   "The Impact of Equal Opportunity Policy on Sex Differentials in Earnings and Occupations." *American Economic Review, Papers and Proceedings* (May):171-75.
1982b   "Occupational Segregation by Sex: Determinants and Changes." *Journal of Human Resources* 17 (Summer):371-92.

Blau, Francine D., and Wallace E. Hendricks
1979   "Occupational Segregation by Sex: Trends and Prospects." *Journal of Human Resources* 14 (Spring):197-210.

Carey, Max L.
1981   "Occupational Employment Growth Through 1990." *Monthly Labor Review* 104(8):42-55.

Department of Labor, Bureau of Labor Statistics
1979   *Employment Projections for the 1980's*. Bulletin 2030. Washington, D.C.: U.S. Government Printing Office. June.
1981   *The National Industry-Occupation Employment Matrix, 1970, 1978 and Projected 1990*. Bulletin 2086, Vol. 2. Washington, D.C.: U.S.

Government Printing Office. April. *Employment and Earnings*. Various issues.

Lloyd, Cynthia, and Beth Niemi
1979   *The Economics of Sex Differentials*. New York: Columbia University Press.

Medoff, James L.
1979   "Layoffs and Alternatives Under Trade Unions in U.S. Manufacturing." *American Economic Review* 69 (June):380-95.

National Center for Education Statistics
1980   *Projections of Education Statistics to 1988-89*. By Martin M. Frankel and Debra E. Gerald. April.

1981   *Earned Degrees Conferred 1979-80*. September.

Osterman, Paul
1982   "Affirmative Action and Opportunity: A Study

of Female Quit Rates." Review of Economics and Statistics 64(4):604-12.

Poirier, Dale J.
1976   *The Econometrics of Structural Change, With Special Emphasis on Spline Functions*. Amsterdam: North-Holland.

Reskin, Barbara F., and Heidi I. Hartmann
1984   *Women's Work, Men's Work: Sex Segregation on the Job*. Washington, D.C.: National Academy Press.

Smith, Ralph E.
1977   "The Impact of Macroeconomic Conditions on Employment Opportunities for Women." Paper No. 6, prepared for U.S. Congress, Joint Economic Committee, 94th Cong., 2d sess.

Part II
Explaining Segregation:
Theoretical Perspectives
and Empirical Evidence

7 Occupational Segregation and Labor Market Discrimination

FRANCINE D. BLAU

The post-World War II period has witnessed a rapid growth in female labor force participation and a steady narrowing of sex differences in the extent of participation in work outside the home. In 1950, 86.8 percent of the (adult) male population participated in the labor force as compared with 33.9 percent of the (adult) female population (U.S. Dept. of Labor, ETA, 1981). By March 1982, 76.6 percent of males and 52.1 percent of females were labor force participants.[1] The large increase in participation rates of married women (with husband present) from 21.6 percent in 1950 to 51.0 percent in March 1981 (U.S. Dept. of Labor, BLS, 1982) was a major factor in the expansion of the female labor force.

These trends appear to have been accompanied by an increase in the labor force attachment of women. This is suggested by the marked rise in the labor force participation rates of married women (with husband present) with preschool-age children from 11.9 percent in 1950 to 47.8 percent in March 1981 (U.S. Dept. of Labor, BLS, November 1981). Further evidence of the increasing stability of women's participation is provided by the decrease in labor force turnover among women that has occurred over the last 20 years, particularly since the late 1960s (Lloyd and Niemi, 1979).[2] At the same time, the gap between men's and women's educational attainment (average

---

[1] Black women's participation rates have historically been considerably higher than those of white women, although the differential has declined in recent years. In 1955 the labor force participation rate of black and other nonwhite women was 46.1 percent in comparison with 34.5 percent for whites. By 1980 the participation rates were 53.4 and 51.3 percent for nonwhites and whites, respectively. The participation rates of black males have fallen more sharply than those of white males over this period. In 1955 the participation rate of both white and nonwhite males was about 85 percent; by 1980 the participation rates of whites and nonwhites were 78.3 and 70.8 percent, respectively (U.S. Dept. of Labor, BLS, 1980, 1981). These differing racial trends in participation rates are an important factor in evaluting the recent gains in black earnings noted below. See Brown (1981).

[2] Labor force turnover is measured by the ratio of the labor force experience rate (the percentage of women who were in the labor force at some time during the year) to the annual average labor force participation rate (the percentage of women who where in the labor force at any particular point in time or survey week).

years of schooling) has been eliminated (Lloyd and Niemi, 1979).

These dramatic shifts in the quantity and quality of labor supplied to the market by women do not appear to have been accompanied by a noticeable improvement in the relative economic status of women workers. In fact, the median earnings of year-round, full-time women workers as a percentage of men's fell from 63.9 to 60.2 between 1955 and 1981 (Lloyd and Niemi, 1979; U.S. Dept. of Commerce, 1982). Most of the decline had occurred by the early 1960s, and the earnings ratio has been roughly stable since then. The occupational distributions of men and women continue to differ significantly. A small movement toward greater similarity appears to have occurred between 1960 and 1970 based on census data (Blau and Hendricks, 1979). Some estimates suggest that the rate of decline in segregation may have accelerated between 1972 and 1981, although the magnitude of segregation remained substantial (Beller, this volume).[3] Throughout this period over 60 percent of the female (or male) labor force would have had to change jobs to eliminate the overrepresentation of women in certain occupations and their corresponding underrepresentation in others (Blau and Hendricks, 1979; Beller, this volume).

The precise role of labor market discrimination in producing these sex differentials in occupational distributions and earnings has been the subject of considerable debate among economists. In the first section we consider the explanations that have been of-

fered for sex differentials in employment patterns and earnings. We focus on the various neoclassical and institutional models of sex (and race) discrimination and on the alternative explanation provided by the human capital model, which emphasizes the voluntary choices of women. In the second section we first evaluate the empirical evidence on the degree of sex discrimination in the labor market, and then turn to an assessment of the role of employment segregation by sex in producing differential outcomes for men and women workers.

ECONOMIC EXPLANATIONS OF SEX DIFFERENTIALS IN OUTCOMES

Theories of Discrimination

While most of the discrimination models discussed here were developed to explain — or at least were illustrated in terms of — racial differences, we here apply them to sex differences. The foundation for the modern neoclassical analysis of labor market discrimination was laid by Becker (1957). For simplicity, it is assumed that male labor and female labor are perfect substitutes. That is, men and women are equally productive and thus deserving of equal wages in the absence of discrimination. Discriminatory tastes may exist in employers, coworkers, and/or customers.

Employers with "tastes for discrimination" against women will hire women workers only at a wage discount that is sufficiently large to compensate them for the disutility of employing women. Becker also showed that even if employers themselves have no tastes for discrimination against women, profit-maximizing behavior by employers may result in sex discrimination if employees or customers have such discriminatory tastes. Male employees with tastes for discrimination against women will work with them only at a wage premium that is sufficient to compensate them for the disutility of female

---

[3] Lloyd and Niemi (1979) find no change in the degree of segregation over this period using census data for 1970 and Current Population Survey (CPS) data for 1977. However, using comparable CPS data, Beller (in this volume) finds that segregation continued to decline over the 1970s. Full resolution of this disparity in results may await the availability of the 1980 census data. In any case both studies suggest that the magnitude of segregation remained quite high.

coworkers.[4] Customers with tastes for discrimination against women will buy products or services produced or sold by women only at a lower price. Intuitively we would expect this type of discrimination to be more important in sales or service occupations where face-to-face contact with the customer/client occurs. As a consequence of coworker or customer discrimination employers may, under certain circumstances, discount female wages to compensate for the higher costs (coworker discrimination) or lower revenues (customer discrimination) attendant upon employing women.

A definition of wage discrimination flowing from Becker's work has guided much of the empirical analysis of labor market discrimination. Wage discrimination (the market discrimination coefficient) may be defined as the difference between the actual ratio of male to female wages and the ratio that would exist in the absence of discrimination — assuming perfect substitutability, this would be wage parity (Becker, 1957, p. 126). In empirical work, where the wages of heterogeneous male and female labor are compared, this is approximated by the notion of pay differentials that are not accounted for by productivity differentials.

While the type of discrimination defined by Becker does not necessarily predict that occupational segregation by sex will occur, it may be made compatible with occupational segregation if we postulate that tastes for discrimination against women vary across occupational categories. The issue may be more one of socially appropriate roles than of the desire to maintain social distance that Becker emphasized. Employers may have no compunctions about hiring women as secretaries but may be reluctant to employ

them as pipefitters. Men may be willing to work with women in complementary (cooperative) or subordinate positions but dislike interacting with women as peers or superiors. Customers may be delighted to purchase nylons from female clerks but avoid women car salespersons or attorneys. These discriminatory tastes may be held independently of beliefs that women would be less productive than men in nontraditional pursuits. This latter possibility is considered under notions of statistical discrimination below.

While such reasoning makes Becker's model more compatible with the large magnitude of occupational segregation that we observe in the labor market, problems remain. First, as Blau and Jusenius (1976) point out, a high degree of segregation is still unlikely given (1) the wage flexibility generally assumed in neoclassical models and (2) the existence of a large *ceteris paribus* wage differential between men and women. (The empirical work considered below provides support for the existence of a substantial pay gap that is not accounted for by the productivity-related characteristics of men and women.) For example, let us consider the case in which discriminatory tastes reside in employers. Employers whose tastes for discrimination are so strong that they exceed the marketwide discrimination coefficient will not hire women. Employers who are exactly compensated for the disutility of hiring women by the market discrimination coefficient will be indifferent to whether they employ men or women and will presumably hire both. Employers with relatively weak tastes for discrimination — who are overcompensated by the marketwide discrimination coefficient — will hire only women. A high degree of occupational segregation by sex due to discrimination will not be observed unless most employers of workers in "male" jobs are in the first category, that is, unless most employers have such strong tastes for discrimination against women in male jobs that they are not sufficiently compensated by the large *ceteris paribus* pay dif-

---

[4] The notion of employee discrimination is developed by Bergmann and Darity (1981) in terms of productivity reductions due to employee hostility rather than of direct increases in costs due to compensating differentials.

ferentials that appear to exist between men and women. This seems to be unlikely.

Differences in tastes for discrimination among employers (employees, customers) can perhaps more plausibly produce sex segregation by firm in the Becker model (Arrow, 1973). That is, women would tend to be employed by less discriminatory employers who are overcompensated by the prevailing sex pay differential. A problem that arises here is the stability of this situation in the face of competitive forces (see below). Women may also, in this model, find better employment opportunities working with less discriminatory employees or selling to (serving) less discriminatory customers (clients).

Second, in the Becker model discriminatory pay differentials are in some sense the price paid by the discriminated group for associating with the discriminators. In general, differences between the two groups in factor endowments make such association profitable even in the face of discrimination. However, sufficient opportunities in a segregated context can eliminate the need for pay differentials. This may be illustrated by the case in which tastes for discrimination reside in coworkers. In the case of perfect substitutes, for example among workers in the same occupational category, complete sex segregation by firm is expected, since sexually integrated work forces are more costly (i.e., men must be paid a premium to work with women). The necessity for wage differences is obviated by such segregation, however, since men and women do not work together (and thus it is not necessary to compensate male workers for the disutility of working with women). Discriminatory pay differentials will arise in this case only if for some reason (e.g., costs of adjustment due to personnel investments in workers [Arrow, 1973]) complete segregation is not possible.[5]

From this perspective one may question why a high degree of occupational segregation by sex appears to be associated with large discriminatory pay differentials.

Even if discrimination is made compatible with occupational segregation in the Becker model, segregation does not play a causal role in generating the sex pay differential. Rather, both occupational and pay differentials are due to tastes for discrimination among employers, coworkers, and/or customers. Eliminating occupational segregation (were it possible to do so) would not eliminate the pay differential. Indeed, reducing segregation might require still further discounting of female wages, since it would necessitate women's making inroads into areas characterized by stronger discriminatory tastes on the part of employers, coworkers, and/or customers.

Bergmann (1974) has developed an analysis in the Becker tradition that gives a more central role to employment segregation. In Bergmann's "overcrowding" model,[6] discriminatory employer tastes result in the segregation of male and female labor into two sets of occupation. While such segregation need not result in sex pay differentials, differentials will occur if job opportunities (demand) in the female sector are small relative to the supply of female labor. Employers who do hire women will utilize the labor-intensive production techniques that their lower wages make profitable. Thus,

---

costs to change history matters. Given historically rising female participation rates, women, as relatively new entrants, may find males already in place in many sectors. However, women have always been heavily concentrated in a few female-dominated activities, even when they constituted a small proportion of the labor force. Assuming discrimination played a role in this segregation, it appears that the notion of the personnel investment tends to require both employer and employee discrimination. Further, once we have personnel investments men and women are no longer in fact equally productive, although they may be potentially equally productive (see below).

[6] See also Edgeworth (1922) and Fawcett (1918).

---

[5] Of course, one may wonder why men rather than women are the recipients of these personnel investments. As Arrow (1973) points out, where there are

in contrast to Becker's (1957) analysis, segregation may play a *causal* role in producing discriminatory pay differentials. Further, discrimination may cause both pay *and* productivity differentials between potentially equally productive male and female labor — women are less productive than men because, as a result of segregation and crowding, they have less capital to work with. The Bergmann formulation does not overcome the problem with the Becker model, noted earlier, that an extreme distribution of employer tastes is necessary to generate the high level of segregation we observe. However, while Bergmann postulated employer discrimination as the source of segregation, the overcrowding concept may be linked to any postulated reason for segregation. It is thus a persuasive explication of the wage consequences of segregation, regardless of its cause.

Another question that has been raised about the Becker analysis, particularly with regard to the case of employer discrimination, is the issue of the survival of discrimination in the long run under perfect competition (Arrow, 1973). Assuming that employer tastes for discrimination against women vary, the least discriminatory firms that hire the highest proportion of (lower-priced) female labor will have lower costs and thus higher profits. Capital will flow toward these firms, and, assuming constant returns to scale, only the least discriminatory (lowest-cost) firms will survive. The apparent persistence of sex (and race) discrimination in the labor market over time has given rise to additional analyses of discrimination, which we shall consider below. However, this criticism of the Becker model is a double-edged sword in that it creates skepticism among many economists that labor market discrimination is indeed responsible (in whole or part) for the observed sex differences in market outcomes. Perhaps the best developed alternative explanation is the human capital model considered in the next section.

One obvious solution to the problem raised above is that noncompetitive elements are responsible for the persistence of discrimination. Becker (1957) hypothesized that employer discrimination should, on average, be less in competitive industries than in monopolistic ones. In the case of sex discrimination the focus has tended to be on imperfections in the factor market rather than in the product market. Madden (1973) has developed Robinson's (1933) monopsony model to explain sex differences in wages. Monopsony describes the situation in which labor faces a single buyer. A price-discriminating monopsonist will pay female labor less if it is less elastically supplied to the firm than is male labor. Assuming that the supply curve of labor to the firm is positively sloped, the elasticity of labor supply to the firm is the percentage increase (decrease) in labor hours supplied to the firm in response to a given percentage increase (decrease) in the wage offered by the firm. A lower elasticity of labor supply for women thus means that the quantity of labor supplied by women to the firm is *less responsive* to wage changes than is the case for men.

The persuasiveness of this explanation for aggregate pay differentials by sex is unclear, a priori. One issue relates to Madden's (1973) argument that female labor is less elastically supplied to the firm. On the one hand, as Madden (1973, 1976) argues, such factors as occupational segregation and the power of male unions may limit women's alternatives and thus decrease their wage elasticity of supply to the firm, all else equal. Supply-side factors, such as the tendency for women to engage in less job search than men do or to seek jobs that are closer to home, could also contribute to this result. On the other hand, as Blau and Jusenius (1976) argue, the aggregate female labor supply curve (to the market) is more elastic than the male labor supply curve (to the market). This has consequences for the elasticity of supply to the firm in that home work provides a viable alternative for women at the margin of labor force participation.[7] Furthermore, if men are more likely than women to acquire firm-specific training, that would also lower their mobility relative to women. A second issue relates to the degree of monopsony that actually exists in the labor market. Pure monopsony (one buyer) in a labor market is undoubtedly quite rare. However, Madden (1973) argues that there are considerable monopsonistic elements in the labor market. This is an empirical issue deserving of more attention. Moreover, it is not clear that the case of few buyers of labor can be analyzed in the same way as can the case of one buyer.

It seems likely that the monopsony explanation is more applicable to specific occupations and labor markets than to the aggregate sex pay differential.[8] An ideal case might be the employed female (or male) Ph.D. with an employed Ph.D. spouse in a one-university town. Nonetheless, this theory does set up a mechanism by which occupational segregation may lower women's wages relative to men's — in this case by reducing women's options.

A second approach to explaining the long-run existence of discrimination is the notion of statistical discrimination (Phelps, 1972; Arrow, 1972a,b, 1973; Aigner and Cain, 1977). Statistical discrimination provides a motivation for discrimination that is compatible with profit-maximizing behavior on the part of employers. It stems from imperfect information and may take one of two forms.

First, employers may discriminate against women because of real or perceived average productivity or productivity-related behavioral differences between men and women. In this case sex is assumed to provide information regarding expected productivity. Aigner and Cain (1977) argue that economic discrimination does not exist if the employer's perception of the average sex difference is correct — since on average each group is paid in proportion to its productivity. However, they acknowledge as disquieting the result that at each ability level women will receive lower pay than men.[9] Others have called this discrimination in that the "individual is judged on the basis of the average characteristics of the group . . . to which he or she belongs rather than upon his or her own characteristics" (Thurow, 1975, p. 172).[10] Implicit in this view seems to be the assumption that other personal characteristics besides sex are readily available and that while the sex difference exists, on average it would not be present in a *ceteris paribus* comparison. If so, perhaps this might be more appropriately considered mistaken behavior on the part of employers. But, as Aigner and Cain (1977) point out, discrimination based on employers' mistaken beliefs is as unlikely (or even more unlikely) to persist over time in the face of competitive forces as is discrimination based on employer tastes. So the question of the persistence of discrimination in the long run remains.

---

[7] Women are more likely than men are to quit their jobs to leave the labor force, while men are more likely than women to quit to change jobs (Barnes and Jones, 1974).

[8] Some preliminary evidence in support of the monopsony view as an explanation for male-female wage differentials across urban areas, based on data for white males and white, never-married females, is presented by Cardwell and Rosenzweig (1980). Note that in restricting their analysis to never-married females they focus upon women with the lowest value of nonmarket time.

[9] This assumes that the variances of the measurement error and of the productivity indicator are the same for males and females.

[10] See also Blau and Jusenius (1976) and Piore (1971). Lewin and England (1982) argue that it is the explicit use of ascriptive characteristics like race or sex in personnel decisions that constitutes the discriminatory aspect of statistical discrimination, even when the employer perceptions are correct. From a normative perspective this is certainly correct, but it is not clear that it counters Aigner and Cain's (1977) argument that such behavior does not constitute economic discrimination.

Arrow's (1973, 1976) notion of perceptual equilibrium sheds some light on this issue. Arrow's model allows for the endogeneity of qualifications — workers become qualified by making some type of investment in themselves where the decision to invest depends on the gain from qualifying. In this case employers' perceptions of sex differences in qualifications may become self-confirming even when there is no intrinsic sex difference in ability or behavior. Multiple equilibria may result. For example, if employers' view of female job instability leads them to give women less training and to assign them to jobs where the cost of turnover is minimized, women may respond by exhibiting the unstable behavior employers expect. This in turn confirms employer perceptions. On the other hand, if employers believe women are stable workers, they will hire women into positions that are sufficiently rewarding to inhibit instability (Arrow, 1976).[11] Here, pay and productivity differences between potentially equally productive male and female workers that may persist in the long run can result from employers' in some sense erroneous beliefs. Viewing the matter somewhat differently, the employers' *ex post* "correct" assessment of sex differences in average productivity may be seen to result from their own discriminatory actions. Moreover, the resulting female sector may be subject to a Bergmann-type overcrowding problem, further reducing relative wages there.

A second type of statistical discrimination may occur even if the two sexes have equal average abilities or behavior. Risk-averse employers may discriminate against women if their ability or behavior is less reliably predicted by some indicator(s) than is men's (Phelps, 1972; Aigner and Cain, 1977). However, Aigner and Cain express doubts that risk aversion could cause discriminatory pay differentials of the magnitude obtained by

empirical studies (see below). As they note, dispersion in risk aversion among employers should result in the bidding up of women's wages, just as the existence of less discriminatory firms should erode discriminatory pay differentials in the Becker-type taste-for-discrimination model. Further, the existence of a large risk discount of women's wages should trigger a market for test instruments or indicators that are equally reliable for them.

At present neither the role of occupational segregation nor the issue of the persistence of discrimination in the long run appears to be satisfactorily understood at the theoretical level.[12] Perhaps the most promising notion advanced here is Arrow's idea of perceptual equilibrium, a kind of "vicious circle," or feedback theory of discrimination, which, as noted earlier, can accommodate and provide some rationale for occupational segregation.[13] The overcrowding concept can be appended to this model to imply a further reduction in wages due to segregation. A problem, however, is that this model cannot explain the sex segregation that appears to exist among jobs requiring similar amounts of skill, stability, etc. While this may not be a major component of occupational segregation, it is probably a nontrivial component.

Institutional models, such as the internal labor market analysis or the dual labor market model (Doeringer and Piore, 1971; Piore, 1971),[14] that give a more explicit role to occupations may be helpful here. Blau and Jusenius (1976) argue that the major contribution of such models is not to suggest

---

[11] See also Spence (1973, 1974).

[12] The latter point is emphasized in Darity's (1982) consideration of racial pay differentials.

[13] A number of other authors have emphasized the importance of feedback effects in analyzing sex pay and occupational differentials. See, e.g., Bergmann (1976), Blau (1977), Ferber and Lowry (1976), Strober (1976), Weiss and Gronau (1981).

[14] See also Cain (1976), Gordon (1972), and Wachter (1974).

new explanations for sex differentials in earnings and employment distributions but rather to elucidate the *linkage* between the two: to suggest why the same set of factors that produce earnings differentials is also likely to generate employment segregation. They argue that under the administered system of the internal labor market, the firm attaches wage rates to occupational categories rather than to individuals (see also Thurow, 1975). Under such circumstances the only way in which the firm can distinguish between men and women in terms of pay is to assign them to different job categories. Within occupational categories, institutional constraints mandate equal pay for equal work, except for relatively small distinctions based on seniority and/or merit considerations. Such group treatment of individuals will be most efficient (will result in the discarding of the least information) if occupational categories are as homogenous as possible. Thus, employers are likely to structure female jobs to fit the perceived average characteristics of women workers. This, in turn, influences women's behavior and productivity à la Arrow's perceptual equilibrium. Bergmann's overcrowding mechanism may further widen the pay differential between male and female jobs.

The Human Capital Alternative

Theories of discrimination are concerned with explaining occupational and pay differentials between (potentially) equally productive men and women. The aggregate figures cited earlier in fact compare heterogeneous male and female labor. Some or all of the observed occupation and pay differences may in fact be due to productivity differences between the sexes. The human capital model can provide a consistent explanation for occupation and pay differentials by sex in terms of the voluntary choices of women rather than of market discrimination against them. It then becomes an empirical question, albeit a difficult one, to determine which view is correct or what portion of the observed differences is accounted for by each explanation.

As developed by Mincer and Polachek (1974) and others, the human capital analysis calls attention to the traditional division of labor by sex within the family under which women can expect shorter and more discontinuous involvement in market work than can men. This reduces their long-run payoff to human capital investments, since they have a shorter work life over which to reap the returns. Similarly, employers will be reluctant to invest in firm-specific training for women workers. Thus, women may earn less than men both because of their lesser amount of labor market experience and because of the lower returns to experience they obtain (the latter reflecting their smaller investments per unit of time). Female earnings are further reduced by the depreciation of their stock of human capital during the time they spend out of the labor force.

The human capital model can also provide a theory of occupational choice to explain occupational segregation by sex (Polachek, 1976, 1979, 1981; Zellner, 1975; Landes, 1977). According to this view women will tend to avoid occupations requiring considerable investments in on-the-job training and having high rates of depreciation for time spent out of the labor force. Thus, we would expect predominantly female jobs to have relatively flat age-earnings profiles.

One problem with this analysis is that the sexual division of labor within the family is in turn influenced by the relative market rewards (wage rates) of husband and wife (Becker, 1965, 1973). This implies that labor market discrimination against women could influence their allocation of time between the home and the market and thus the amount and types of their human capital investments. From the standpoint of empirical work this means that analyses which treat such variables as experience and education as exogenous may underestimate the extent of labor market discrimination (Weiss and Gronau, 1981). Further, women's lower returns to experience may reflect employers' reluctance to provide opportunities for firm-specific training as well as their own voluntary decisions. In the latter case it would also be important to determine whether the employers' decisions are in fact justified by *ceteris paribus* sex differences in quit propensities.

EMPIRICAL FINDINGS

As indicated in the preceding section, there are alternative views as to how labor market discrimination might produce occupational and pay differences between men and women. Further, the human capital model provides an alternative explanation for sex differences in market outcomes that is consistent with voluntary decision making by women rather than with discrimination against them. For the most part empirical research has been focused on the question of whether or not labor market discrimination against women (and minorities) exists. Choosing among alternative models of discrimination and understanding the causes and consequences of employment segregation have received considerably less attention, particularly from economists.

In this section we first consider in some detail the question of whether or not discrimination exists. This is an important inquiry, since its resolution is necessary in order to determine the overall context in which employment segregation by sex takes place. There is no point in seeking to determine the role of segregation in producing discriminatory pay differentials by sex if in fact there is little evidence that such discriminatory differentials exist. Second, we explore the existing literature concerning the role of occupational segregation in producing pay differentials and, more briefly, some of what has been learned about the causes of such segregation.

Discrimination and Earnings

A crude test of the relative merits of the discrimination and human capital explanations for sex differences in earnings is provided by an examination of the time series trends in the sex pay differential. We first briefly consider this time series evidence, then move to a detailed discussion of the more sophisticated cross-sectional analyses of the extent of labor market discrimination. As noted in the introduction, there has actually been some deterioration in the relative earnings position of women since the mid-1950s. It has frequently and incorrectly been assumed that increases in the female labor force participation rate over time are indicative of declines in the average level of experience of women workers due to the impact of new entrants (*Economic Report of the President*, 1974). In fact, as Mincer (1979) explains, the female labor force grows not only through "widening" (increases in the flow of entrants or reentrants) but also through "deepening" (decreases in the flow of exiters). The impact on the average level of experience of female workers depends on the relative magnitude of these two flows. In addition, since labor force entry tends to be selective of female nonparticipants with higher levels of previous labor force experience, and labor force exit tends to be selective of female participants with lower levels of previous labor force experience, labor turnover does not dilute average experience levels as much as it might first appear (Blau, 1975, 1978).

Lloyd and Niemi (1979) present a variety of evidence indicating that the trend has been for women to remain in the labor force longer and more continuously and that entrants make up a decreasing proportion of the female labor force. They conclude that "it appears . . . the work experience differential between the sexes has narrowed in the past twenty years" (p. 133). Thus, female participation trends do not seem to be re-

sponsible for the widening pay gap. Moreover, they find that "over time, the gap between men's and women's educational
attainment has been eliminated and, among
young cohorts, it appears that women's propensity to enroll in college is roughly similar
to men's" (p. 146). Men and women do continue to differ sharply in fields of specialization, although some progress has recently
been made in this area as well (Baker, undated). Further, one may speculate that the
rising divorce rate has increased women's
incentives to invest in their labor-market-
related human capital.

While one would like better data, particularly on experience, it seems reasonable to
conclude that human capital factors do not
account for the widening pay gap between
men and women. This provides support for
the view that discrimination plays a role in
producing the differential. It is unlikely that
tastes for discrimination against women have
increased during this period. However, as
we have seen, little decline occurred in the
degree of sex segregation in employment
during that time. If increases in the demand
for labor in female jobs did not keep pace
with increases in the supply of female labor,
relative "crowding" in female jobs may have
worsened, exerting a downward pressure on
female wages *relative to* male wages. Increases in the real wages of women over the
period could have continued to induce increases in female labor force participation
ceteris paribus.

In addition, it may be argued that women
face substantial experience and training requirements in their efforts to move into high-
level male jobs (Freeman, 1973). This makes
it difficult for equal employment opportunity legislation to open the doors to such
jobs for older women. Further, younger
women may have had the opportunity to
incorporate new expectations of greater labor force attachment over their life cycles
into their human capital investment decisions to a greater extent than have older
women. It is true that younger women have

been increasing their earnings position relative to younger men. Between 1970 and
1981 the ratio of the median incomes of full-
time, year-round women workers to those
of men increased from 59 to 60 percent for
all women, but rose from 65 to 70 percent
among 25- to 34-year-olds (U.S. Dept. of
Commerce, 1980, 1982). Beller (this volume) also found that younger cohorts experienced greater declines in occupational
segregation than did the work force as a
whole. Thus far, however, the modest gains
by younger women do not provide overwhelming support for this view. Much will
depend on how this group fares in the next
few years. It is also important to point out
that if employers were willing to reevaluate
their traditional promotion ladders they might
find that many older women workers do have
the experience necessary for higher-level
positions.

During recent years, while women as a
group have made little progress in advancing their earnings positions relative to men,
black women have advanced relative to white
women. Black women's median (full-time,
year-round) incomes have increased from 69
percent of those of white women in 1964 to
90 percent in 1981. Black men have also
gained relative to white men. Their median
full-time, year-round incomes rose from 66
percent of those of white men in 1964 to 71
percent in 1981 (Lloyd and Niemi, 1979;
U.S. Dept. of Commerce, 1982). The gains
in the relative incomes of blacks are partially
due to substantial increases in their relative
educational attainment but cannot be fully
explained by that factor (Brown, 1982). They
may in part be due to the impact of equal
employment opportunity legislation. The
more rapid improvement in the relative income position of black women (compared
with white women) than of black men (compared with white men) may reflect the large
number of entry-level positions in many
typically female jobs, in comparison with
the higher experience and training requirements in typically male jobs discussed above.

We now turn to a review of studies that attempt to measure the extent of labor market discrimination explicitly. The general practice in empirically estimating the magnitude of labor market discrimination against a particular group, e.g., women, is to ascertain the proportion of the sex differential that is accounted for by differences in the productivity-related characteristics of male and female workers and to allocate the residual to discrimination. Discrimination may be measured by the coefficient on a sex dummy variable in an earnings regression equation, in which case the impact of the other explanatory variables on earnings is constrained to be the same for each sex group. More often, this constraint is relaxed by estimating separate earnings regressions for sex or race-sex groups. In this case the portion of the pay differential due to sex differences in the returns to a given set of characteristics (i.e., sex differences in coefficients, including the constant term) is attributed to discrimination; the portion of the pay differential that is due to sex differences in endowments of productivity-related characteristics (i.e., sex differences in the means of the independent variables) is attributed to nondiscriminatory factors (Blinder, 1973).

There are various problems with this "residual" approach to measuring labor market discrimination. Perhaps the most serious is the specification problem. On the one hand, conventional data sources do not allow for the measurement of all productivity-related characteristics. The absence of actual labor market experience from the data sets used in the early studies of sex discrimination is a prime example of an important omitted variable. Type (as opposed to amount) of schooling, which varies greatly between men and women, would be another example. If, on average, males are more favorably endowed with the characteristics measured by these omitted variables, the extent of labor market discrimination will be overestimated because of imperfect controls for these omitted factors. On the other hand, group differences with respect to some productivity-related characteristics may reflect the indirect effects of discrimination (Blinder, 1973). For example, as discussed earlier, women may be excluded from high-wage occupations because of their sex. Further, if the endogeneity of choice variables is taken into account, we see that labor market discrimination may discourage women's human capital accumulation or alter its type. Measured labor market discrimination is likely to be underestimated to the extent that such factors representing other dimensions of discrimination are controlled for.

A related problem is the interpretation of sex differences in the coefficients of earnings regressions. For example, a smaller coefficient on labor force experience for women may reflect their decisions to invest in less on-the-job training than men do, as proposed by human capital theorists, or discrimination on the part of employers resulting in less access to on-the-job training opportunities.[15] Similarly, sex differences in the returns related to marital status may reflect unmeasured differences in labor force attachment between married men and women (Polachek, 1975) or sex differences in employer treatment of marital status that is unrelated to productivity (e.g., the view that married men deserve higher salaries because they have families to support).

These problems of specification and interpretation of coefficients reflect a more fundamental problem. We would like to measure the extent of labor market discrimination—a demand-side phenomenon. But wages are influenced by both supply- and demand-side factors. The earnings functions that are typically estimated are essentially reduced-form equations, and thus their coefficients may reflect the influence

---

[15] Further, one may question the basic premise of the human capital model that upward-sloping experience-earnings profiles are indeed due to on-the-job training. See, e.g., Medoff and Abraham (1980, 1981).

of both supply and demand (Butler, 1981; Chiplin, 1981). Ideally, one would like to specify and estimate a structural model with separate supply and demand equations. No one has yet attempted to specify and estimate such a model on an economywide basis.

An additional problem with the earnings regression approach is that, while the theory specifies the measurement of discrimination in terms of pay differences that are not accounted for by productivity differences, the empirical work involves adjustment using proxies like education and experience for productivity. This gives rise to an errors-in-variable problem (Hashimoto and Kochin, 1980; Roberts, 1980). For simplicity, let us assume that the productivity proxies are measured so that they are positively related to earnings. Then it may be shown that if women have lower mean values of the productivity proxies than men have (as is generally the case), the coefficient on a sex dummy variable (female = 1) in an earnings regression is biased downward, giving an exaggerated estimate of the effect of discrimination (Hashimoto and Kochin, 1980).

Unfortunately, however, there is no obvious solution to this problem. Roberts (1980) suggests a procedure that he terms "reverse regression," in which the independent variable (e.g., education) is regressed on the dependent variable (e.g., earnings) and a sex dummy.[16] Such a procedure will produce unbiased coefficients only if the dependent variable is measured without error. But earnings as measured are only an imperfect indicator of permanent earnings capacity, which, one might argue, is the theoretically relevant variable (Hashimoto and Kochin, 1980). Moreover, measured earnings are only a proxy for the total rewards for the job, including fringes and the nonpecuniary benefits of the work (Madden, 1982). Hashimoto and Kochin (1980) suggest

performing the analysis on grouped data where the grouping criterion is independent of the measurement errors. But it may not be easy to meet this requirement (or to know whether or not one has met it), and, as they acknowledge, the results can be quite sensitive to one's choice of a criterion. Another classical approach to the errors-in-variable problem involves the use of instrumental variables. However, the specification of the appropriate instruments is difficult given the current state of theory and the availability of data (Kamalich and Polachek, 1982).

An additional problem in using conventionally estimated earnings regressions to measure discrimination most likely produces biases in the opposite direction, that is, leads us to underestimate discrimination. Regressions are generally estimated on the selected sample of labor force participants. But Gronau (1974) has argued that it is the wage *offers*, not the actual wages of males and females, that should be compared. The distribution of actual wages represents only that part of the offer distribution that is acceptable to job seekers.[17] Thus, according to Gronau, mean female wage offers will be overestimated by restriction of the sample to labor force participants.[18] He provides empirical evidence in support of this contention. Since male participation rates (particularly in the prime work ages) are still substantially higher than women's, it may be argued that data on men's wages are considerably less affected by selectivity bias.[19]

---

[16] See also Kamalich and Polachek (1982).

[17] See also Heckman (1974).

[18] Gronau has argued elsewhere (1973) that the value of time of housewives may be either higher or lower than the market wage of comparable employed women. If the former is true, it is not necessarily the case that restriction of the sample to labor force participants overstates women's wage offers. However, the empirical evidence he presents supports Gronau's (1974) contention. See also Cogan (1980).

[19] As noted earlier, black male participation rates are lower than those of whites. Thus, the same type of selectivity problem discussed in the text affects race comparisons among males.

Thus, observed wage differences between men and women will underestimate the "true" male-female wage-offer differential. On the other hand, over time male participation rates have been declining while female rates have been increasing (see above). Thus, we may be sweeping out more of the female offer distribution and less of the male offer distribution than was formerly done. This may be a partial explanation for our failure to observe a decline in the male-female pay gap over time.

Bearing these problems in mind, we consider the empirical work on sex discrimination. As noted earlier, most empirical work in this area has focused on the question of whether or not labor market discrimination exists and has attempted to estimate its magnitude. While there are still various unresolved problems in estimating the extent of labor market discrimination, it is not clear from our consideration of them that they result, on net, in overestimates or underestimates of discriminatory pay differentials. If the evidence suggests that there is labor market discrimination against women, then this will provide some motivation for considering the role played by sex segregation in employment in producing these discriminatory outcomes.

Not surprisingly, the estimate of the sex pay differential that is due to discrimination varies considerably depending on the group studied, data set employed, and variables controlled for. We shall focus our discussion on studies using national samples of individuals across a variety of occupations.[20] For the most part, the earlier studies of male-female pay differentials attributed a substantial portion of the sex pay differential to discrimination.[21] For example, using 1960 census data, Fuchs (1971) found that sex differences in individual characteristics could account for only 3 to 15 percent of the differential. Similarly, Oaxaca (1973a,b), using data from the 1967 Survey of Economic Opportunity, found that 80 percent of the pay differential between white men and white women and 94 percent of the differential between black men and black women could not be explained by productivity-related individual characteristics.[22]

As these authors were aware, their lack of data on actual labor force experience created an important omitted-variable problem.[23] The general procedure of estimating experience as the years elapsed since school completion, while fairly accurate for males, is much more questionable for females. In addition to their theoretical contributions noted earlier, Mincer and Polachek (1974) were the first to provide empirical estimates of the impact of labor force experience and time spent out of the labor force on the earnings of women using newly available longitudinal data. They analyzed retrospective work history data from the National Longitudinal Survey (NLS) of mature women aged 30 to 44 in 1967. Mincer and Polachek were able to account for 45 percent of the pay gap between white married men and women in that age group on the basis of human capital variables, including actual labor market experience and time spent out of the labor force. In arriving at this estimate, they were aware of the joint determination of earnings and experience and at-

_____

[20] For more detailed reviews of the empirical literature, including occupation-specific studies, see Kohen (1975), Lloyd and Niemi (1979), and Treiman and Hartmann (1981).

[21] The one exception was a study by Sanborn (1964); see below.

_____

[22] Oaxaca's results including controls for occupational and industrial characteristics are considered below. See also Gwartney and Stroup (1973), Sawhill (1973), and Blinder (1973). On the other hand, Darity and Myers (1980) found that while the structural equations for wages for white males and females were significantly different, they were not so in the case of black males and females.

[23] For an exception, see Suter and Miller (1973), who restricted their sample to women from the National Longitudinal Surveys in the 30- to 44-year age group who had worked continuously since school completion.

tempted to adjust for simultaneous equations bias by using a two-stage procedure. While Mincer and Polachek are to be commended for their awareness of the simultaneity problem, their application of the two-stage procedure in their exploratory study is far from thorough. For one thing, their specification of the determinants of lifetime labor supply (the proportion of years the respondent worked 6 months or more since school completion) includes an endogenous variable, number of children. For another, while lifetime experience is treated as endogenous, home time and job tenure (seniority) are entered into the earnings function as exogenous variables (Sandell and Shapiro, 1978; Mincer and Polachek, 1978).

That these problems are serious is suggested by their counterintuitive findings for the two-stage procedure. In the single-period context, economic theory would lead one to expect a positive relationship between labor force *participation* and own wage. An increase in the market wage available to a woman increases the opportunity cost of nonmarket activities for her. This encourages her to substitute market work for time spent on housework and leisure. However, in a multiperiod context this positive *substitution effect* could be outweighed by a negative *income effect*. The negative income effect arises from the fact that the increase in the wage obtained while the woman is working is like an increase in income. At higher-income levels she is expected to demand more of all goods from which she derives satisfaction, including leisure. She may thus consume more leisure over the life cycle by supplying less time to the market over the life cycle. Note that she must work some of the time for the income effect to come into play. The evidence suggests, however, that for married women's participation decisions the substitution effect dominates the income effect (where the latter is indicated by the response to changes in husband's income [Mincer, 1962]). Thus, women's labor supply is expected to be positively related to their wages.

This reasoning implies that the positive coefficient on experience in an ordinary least squares (OLS) earnings regression is biased upward. This is because some of the estimated positive impact of labor market experience on wages is really due to a positive effect of wages on experience (at higher wages, women supply more time to the market). Similarly, the negative coefficient on home time is biased upward in absolute value. This is because some of the estimated negative impact of home time on wages is really due to a negative effect of wages on home time (at higher wages, women spend less time out of the labor market). Correction for the simultaneous equations bias should thus reduce the size of both coefficients in absolute value. On the contrary, Mincer and Polachek (1974) find that, if anything, reestimation of the earnings function using two-stage least squares yields "larger positive coefficients for (total) experience and stronger negative coefficients for home time" (p. S99). Further, in estimating the proportion of the pay gap explained by the human capital variables, the actual mean levels of the variables are employed. Yet the heart of the endogeneity problem is that wage discrimination may have influenced the amount of human capital that women have accumulated. Thus, it is likely that Mincer and Polachek and analyses modeled on theirs overestimate the impact of the human capital variables on the sex pay differential. In light of this potential bias it is notable that Mincer and Polachek found that over half of the pay gap between white married men and women could not be explained by the human capital variables and was potentially due to discrimination.

Another issue that has been raised regarding Mincer and Polachek's (1974) findings is the generalizability of their results for the 30- to 44-year-old age group to the whole female population — as is necessary to draw inferences for the aggregate male-female pay gap. The work of Corcoran (1978, 1979) using a full age range from the 1976 Panel Study of Income Dynamics (PSID), suggests that their findings may not in fact be generalizable. She found that the wages of women aged 30 to 44 are much more strongly affected by labor force withdrawals than are those of the broader age range (Corcoran, 1979). Women in this 30-to 44-year age group are more likely than are women in general to have recently reentered the labor market after a prolonged period of nonparticipation. Corcoran suggests that her findings are consistent with the notion that women's wages are temporarily depressed by labor force withdrawals because of misinformation about job opportunities and/or about their own value as workers.[24]

In addition to providing work histories, the PSID data provide measures of labor force attachment (i.e., absenteeism due to own illness; absenteeism due to illness of others; self-imposed restrictions on work hours and/or job location; voluntary part-time work). For an unrestricted age group of women, Corcoran (1978) found that adjustments for schooling, work history, and labor force attachment accounted for 36 percent of the wage gap between white men and white women and 27 percent of the wage gap between white men and black women. In addition to the difference in age group, some of the difference between Corcoran's and Mincer and Polachek's findings with respect to the importance of the human capital variables may reflect a growing work force attachment of women over the period spanned by the 1967 NLS and the 1976 PSID (Mincer, 1979). These findings of large unexplained wage gaps for white and black women are impressive in light of Corcoran's detailed controls for productivity-related factors. In addition, since her findings are based on OLS estimates, she has not adjusted for the simultaneous equations bias

---

[24] Using longitudinal panel data from the NLS on the 30- to 44-year age group, Mincer and Ofek (1982) find direct evidence of rapid wage growth upon reentry. Unlike Corcoran (1979), however, they attribute it to the "repair" of previously eroded human capital.

discussed in reference to the Mincer and Polachek (1974) study. This suggests that, at least with regard to this consideration, she has underestimated the effect of labor market discrimination.

An additional issue raised by the human capital model is the interpretation of sex differences in returns to experience and marital status. For example, Mincer and Polachek (1974, p. S103) argue that

The association of lower [female] coefficients with lesser work experience is not fortuitious: a smaller fraction of time and energy is devoted to job advancement (training, learning, getting ahead) per unit of time by persons whose work attachment is lower. Hence, the 45 percent figure in the explanation of the gap by duration-of-work experience alone may be viewed as an understatement.

To what extent do sex differences in returns to experience and marriage reflect employer discrimination and to what extent do they reflect women's choices? While a definitive answer is not available, the evidence suggests that discrimination most likely plays a role.

With respect to returns to experience, a study by Duncan and Hoffman (1979) is particularly interesting. Using direct measures of on-the-job training from the 1976 PSID, they find that men and women receive about the same payoff to on-the-job training. However, "past years of work experience have a high payoff in training for men, especially white men, but have very little effect on the chances that women will receive training" (p. 601). They see their results as consistent with a view that firms have different promotion practices on the basis of sex (and race). Thus, the observed lower returns to experience of women may reflect to some extent employer discrimination in permitting women access to on-the-job training opportunities.

On the other hand, Sandell and Shapiro (1980), analyzing data from the NLS, have found that young white and black women who plan to work at age 35 have experience-wage profiles that "begin at a lower point and have a steeper (initial) slope than those of their 'no-work-plans' counterparts" (p. 343). Thus, some of the sex difference in work experience coefficients may reflect women's own investment decisions based on their work expectations. However, Sandall and Shapiro also find that the returns to job tenure (seniority), which they take as an indication of investment in firm-specific training, do not differ significantly between those who plan to work at age 35 and those who do not. This in turn suggests that part of the differential access to on-the-job training opportunities by sex implied by Duncan and Hoffman's findings may reflect the inability or the unwillingness of employers to distinguish between the committed and uncommitted group. As our previous discussion suggests, there is some difference of opinion as to whether such statistical discrimination would represent economic discrimination or not. However, it is likely to result in committed women getting less training and receiving lower returns to job tenure than do committed men.

In evaluating the implications of Sandell and Shapiro's findings for sex differences in earnings, it is instructive to consider Arrow's (1973) notion of perceptual equilibrium. Given the set of market opportunities she can reasonably expect and her expected value of nonmarket time, each young woman determines her work plans for age 35. Since women with given characteristics in the Sandell and Shapiro sample presumably face similar opportunities, the differences in their work plans probably reflect differences in their expected value of nonmarket time (perhaps due to differences in tastes). However, this does not preclude the possibility that, if confronted with a different set of market opportunities, substantially more of the women would be committed to market work. It is even possible that, given the male set of job opportunities (with similar returns to experience and job tenure), they would exhibit the same degree of labor force commitment as that of males.

With respect to worker and employer firm-specific training investment decisions, it is job (rather than labor force) stability that is the issue. Some evidence in favor of the Arrow notion in this case is provided by the findings of Blau and Kahn (1981), who used data on young men and young women from the NLS to analyze sex differences in quitting. They found that, all else equal (including job-related characteristics), white and black women were no more likely to quit their jobs than were men of the same race. They also found that a high proportion of the observed sex differential in quitting was associated with job rather than personal characteristics.[25] Similar findings were reported by Viscusi (1980) for a larger age range from the PSID.[26] Both Blau and Kahn and Viscusi found that, all else equal, blacks were less likely to quit their jobs than white workers of the same sex. Blau and Kahn also report some support for one of the models of statistical discrimination presented earlier in that female quits were found to be less accurately predicted than men's by the explanatory variables.[27] No basis for statistical discrimination was found in the case of race.

With respect to the interpretation of sex

---

[25] Job characteristics include current wage, long-run earnings opportunities associated with the job, collective bargaining coverage, and industry and occupation dummy variables.

[26] Ragan and Smith (1981) find that sex differences in *industry* turnover rates explain a substantial portion of the sex difference in earnings among individuals. However, as they acknowledge, since their data refer to the industry's history and not the individual's, their findings are consistent with the possibility that women are restricted to low wage/high turnover jobs (e.g., those requiring little specific training). Osterman (1979) found no sex differences in absenteeism, all else equal, for a sample of professional workers.

[27] While Osterman (1979) reports no basis for statistical discrimination on this ground, Kahn (1981) shows that Osterman does not employ the correct indicator of predictability. When the correct indicator is used, Kahn finds that women's absenteeism is less accurately predicted than men's.

differences in the returns to marital status, Hill (1979) uses explicit data on experience, human capital investment, and labor force attachment from the 1976 PSID to explore this issue further. She finds that, all else equal, marriage has strong positive wage effects for (white and black) men, while the effects of marriage on (white and black) women's wages are not significantly different from zero. Malkiel and Malkiel (1973) and Osterman (1979) report similar findings for the wage effects of marriage from studies of sex differences in the wages of professional workers, also including good controls for work experience and attachment. A supply-side explanation for these findings cannot be entirely ruled out: given the traditional division of labor within the home, married men may be more highly motivated or hardworking than single men with similar measured characteristics, while married women may be less highly motivated or hardworking than their single counterparts. But, as Osterman points out, how do we then explain the absence of a *negative* effect of marriage on the earnings of women? Moreover, Hill examined the effect of marital status and number of children on wages as more explicit controls for experience, human capital investments, and labor force attachment were added to the wage regressions. She finds that the wage effect of marital status among all race/sex groups remains quite stable and concludes that marital status does not serve as a proxy for these productivity-related factors. If marital status is not serving as a proxy for these obvious and important factors, it seems doubtful that it is serving as a proxy for more subtle traits like motivation. However, Hill does find that number of children is to some extent proxy for these factors. Both Osterman and Hill feel that employers may believe that married men deserve higher salaries because of their greater financial responsibilities. Given traditional views of men's and women's economic roles, they do not feel the same is true of married women. Such a difference

in treatment, if it exists, would have to be classed as discriminatory.

The evidence reviewed here strongly suggests that labor market discrimination does indeed play a role in producing the observed male-female pay differential. While it is difficult to pinpoint the exact portion of the sex pay gap due to discrimination, the findings suggest that over half of the differential cannot be explained by sex differences in productivity-related factors. Some considerations (e.g., omitted variables) suggest that this may be an overestimate of the magnitude of discrimination. On the other hand, other considerations (e.g., the impact of labor market discrimination on the incentives to acquire experience, training, etc.) suggest that it may be an underestimate. Thus, we are still left with fairly strong evidence of the importance of discrimination.

Occupational Segregation and Earnings

Having determined the overall labor market context in which employment segregation by sex takes place, we are now able to turn to a consideration of the empirical evidence regarding the role played by such segregation in producing pay differences and a consideration of some recent evidence on the causes of such segregation. According to the discrimination models considered earlier, segregation may work to lower women's earnings because of a lesser provision of on-the-job training and fewer incentives for worker stability in female jobs (Arrow's perceptual equilibrium model, institutional models) and/or because of overcrowding. While these notions suggest that it would be instructive to look at the relationship between earnings — particularly the discriminatory pay gap — and segregation, there are three major problems in arriving at an empirical estimate.

The first is a data problem. Most data sources, even detailed census data, tend to aggregate some male and female jobs into apparently integrated categories (Hartmann and Reskin, 1982). Further, insofar as men and women are segregated by firm within occupational categories, aggregation across firms will result in an underestimate of the extent to which men and women are in segregated work settings (Blau, 1977). The impact of both of these factors is revealed in a recent study by Bielby and Baron (this volume) of 393 California establishments. Using the employers' own job classifications, they found that 51 percent of the firms were completely sex-segregated with respect to job classification: no men and women shared the same job title. An additional 8 percent of the firms were single-sex establishments. The mean index of segregation of the remaining 41 percent of firms was 84.1. It has been found that the portion of the sex pay gap associated with occupational differences is larger, the finer the occupational categories employed (Treiman and Hartmann, 1981). Thus, it seems reasonable to conclude that aggregation problems result in an underestimate of the impact of employment segregation on the sex pay gap.

The second problem is more conceptual. The logical way to determine the impact of occupational characteristics or categories on pay, all else equal, is to control for sex or to look within sex groups. Yet it seems possible that the existence of overcrowding in female jobs may lower the wages of women in male jobs. Even when women work in male jobs their opportunity set may differ from that of their male coworkers: the lower-paying alternatives they face in the female sector may reduce their supply price to the firm. This is a potential wage spillover effect of overcrowding. Further, women may face discrimination in the male sector that lowers their relative wages there. Indeed, in Bergmann's original formulation of the overcrowding model it is the exclusion of women from male jobs due to discrimination that causes the overcrowding of the female sector. It makes intuitive sense that women remain concentrated in female jobs because they have little to gain by obtaining male jobs. Thus, measuring the impact of occu-

pation on pay by contrasting the wages of women in male and female jobs, *ceteris paribus*, may result in an underestimate. On the other hand, the internal labor market (institutional) model suggests that when women are able to obtain employment in male jobs within a firm, they should be paid at about the same rate as men. This implies that pay comparisons of women in male and female jobs can provide good estimates of the impact of occupation on wages. However, since data are generally aggregated over firms, women may earn less than men do in male jobs if they work for low-paying firms. Further, women may be segregated by job level within the same occupational category.

Judging the impact of occupation by comparing the wages of men in male and female jobs does not appear to be satisfactory either. A problem here is that men are not believed to be discriminated against in or excluded from male jobs, so the question arises as to why they are employed in the female sector. If it is because they have very strong nonpecuniary (nonmonetary) tastes for female jobs, then their wages may reflect a differential due to overcrowding. The pay differential between men in male and female jobs may also reflect overcrowding if bad luck, poor information, or job rationing in male jobs (e.g., due to unions) are responsible for the employment of men in female jobs. On the other hand, men may work in female jobs because they have found a niche there that pays comparably with what they could earn in male jobs, e.g., due to employment in a high-paying firm or at a high level in the occupation hierarchy. In that case a comparison of men's wages in male and female jobs will not reflect an overcrowding differential.

These two considerations suggest that empirical estimates may understate the contribution of employment segregation to the sex pay gap. A third point works in the opposite direction. Workers in higher-paying jobs (or firms) may have unobserved characteristics that are associated with higher productivity: what appear to be occupation effects on wages may actually be due to unobserved productivity differences among workers.

The union-impact literature suggests some fruitful alternative approaches for examining the impact of crowding, since many analogous problems arise in investigating that issue. For example, papers by Kahn (1980) and Flanagan (1976) suggest that one might look at the effect on the wages of men and women in male and female jobs of changes over time or of differences across labor markets, in the degree of crowding. This type of approach could provide an empirical estimate of the impact of crowding that takes spillover effects into account. The selectivity problem of comparing the wages of women (or of men) in male and female jobs might be overcome by using a technique developed by Lee (1978) in his investigation of the union-nonunion differential.

While existing studies may deal inadequately with the problems raised here, it is still instructive to review the findings in this area. Using data from the 1980 census, Treiman and Hartmann (1981) found that 35 to 39 percent of the earnings difference between men and women was associated with sex differences in the distribution of their employment among 479 detailed categories.[28] Occupational differences appear to be a significant factor in explaining the sex pay gap, even when other productivity-related factors are controlled for. For example, Oaxaca (1973a,b) found that the inclusion of controls for major occupation and industry and for class of worker increased the portion of the sex pay gap explained from 20 to 37 percent in the case of whites and from 6 to 39 percent in the case of blacks. In this case job characteristics accounted for some 20 to 35 percent of the discriminatory pay gap. Using 1950 census data, Sanborn (1964) was able to explain 43 percent

of the sex pay gap on the basis of controls for such factors as detailed occupation, age, and education.[29] The greater magnitude of the explained differential in the Sanborn study than in the studies of Fuchs (1971) and Oaxaca (1973a,b) cited earlier, in which occupational controls were not included, is an indication of the importance of occupational category in determining earnings. Further, using data from the 1974 PSID and the 1967 NLS, England (1981, 1982) found that, all else equal, the percentage of females in the occupation is significantly negatively related to female earnings.[30]

Table 7-1 illustrates the impact of occupational category within an individual firm — a large fiduciary institution.[31] In equation (1), only controls for sex and race are entered into the regression, thus providing an estimate of the gross or unadjusted sex-race differentials. Equation (2) includes controls for productivity-related individual characteristics but no controls for occupational characteristics. This

---

[28] See also Chiswick et al. (1974).

[29] Including adjustments for even more narrowly defined occupational categories from the BLS, as well as sex differences in turnover, absenteeism, and work experience, Sanborn (1964) was able to explain 71 percent of the pay gap. The problem with this portion of his analysis is that he most probably engaged in double counting. He assumed that the sex differences in age and education that prevailed within the census categories also prevailed within the more detailed BLS categories. Further, he adjusted within occupations for estimates of *aggregate* sex differences in turnover, absenteeism, and work experience. Leaving aside the issue of endogeneity, labor quality differences between men and women are likely to be considerably smaller within occupations than in the aggregate, since it is these traits that sort people into occupations. Indeed, in the presence of discrimination women may be more qualified than men in specific occupations. See Hamilton (1973) for some evidence consistent with the latter possibility.

[30] See also Roos (1981), Ferber and Lowry (1976), Cabral et al. (1981), Stevenson (1975), and Jusenius (1977).

[31] This analysis was part of the statistical evidence developed by Janice Madden and me in an employment discrimination case. Madden (1982) also provides a discussion and analysis of these data.

TABLE 7-1   Regression Analysis of the Salaries of Active Employees in 1978 (standard errors)

Independent Variables	(1)	(2)	(3)
Dependent Variable: Natural Log of Annual Salary			
Personal characteristics			
Female	-0.5659^a	-0.3236^a	-0.0785^a
	(0.0183)	(0.0151)	(0.0083)
Black	-0.3573^a	-0.1985^a	-0.0948^a
	(0.0243)	(0.0185)	(0.0092)
Other minority	-0.2091^a	-0.0943^a	-0.0459^a
	(0.0359)	(0.0267)	(0.0130)
Education (highest grade completed)	—	0.09410^a	0.0176^a
	—	(0.0035)	(0.0021)
Age (in years)	—	0.0512^a	0.0268^a
	—	(0.0042)	(0.0022)
Age (squared)	—	-0.00059^a	-0.00030^a
	—	(0.00005)	(0.00003)
Firm experience (in years)	—	0.0258^a	0.0088^a
	—	(0.0029)	(0.0014)
Firm experience (squared)	—	-0.00027^a	-0.00018^a
	—	(0.00010)	(0.00005)
Job characteristics			
Hay points	—	—	0.0007^a
	—	—	(0.00001)
Firm officer	—	—	0.3628^a
	—	—	(0.0132)
Other exempt	—	—	0.2332^a
	—	—	(0.0116)
Constant term	9.7748	7.1928	8.2253
R square	0.4156	0.6873	0.9294
F statistic	476.0479^a	550.1990^a	2145.5542^a
Number of employees	2012	2012	1806

^{a} Significant at the 1 percent level on a two-tailed test.

gives the total effect of discrimination (operating both through unequal pay for equal work and unequal access to higher-paying jobs). Discrimination is estimated to account for 57 percent of the gross pay differential in the case of women (controlling for race) and 45 to 56 percent of the gross pay differential in the case of blacks and other minorities (controlling for sex). Controlling for occupational characteristics in equation (3) gives us an estimate of pay differences between equally qualified male and female (black and white) workers in similar job categories. In this case the job characteristics include hay points — an employer evaluation of the value of the job to the firm — and two dummy variables indicating whether the individual is an officer of the firm or is in

another managerial or professional occupation (exempt from the Fair Labor Standards Act). A relatively small proportion of the discriminatory sex differential (controlling for race) — 24 percent $(-0.0785/-0.3236)$ — is due to pay differences within similar occupational categories. The remainder, 76 percent, is due to sex differences in distribution among occupational categories within the firm. Occupational differences explain somewhat less than half of the discriminatory pay gap in the case of blacks and other minorities (controlling for sex).

There are some problems with these specifications. For one thing age rather than actual labor market experience is used as an explanatory variable — due to data availability. (The firm experience variable does, however, measure actual firm experience.) However, the studies reviewed earlier strongly suggest that the discriminatory differential would persist even if we were able to control for actual labor market experience. For another, job grade (hay points) rather than occupational category is employed, making this similar to the type of investigation one would undertake in a study of the issue of comparable worth. But there are some advantages to the use of hay points as an overall measure of job level that cuts across male and female jobs. It overcomes one of the practical problems with efforts to ascertain the size of intraoccupational sex pay differentials: paucity of data on one sex group or another within a job category due to the very sex segregation by occupation that we seek to study.[32] These results support the notion that studies of the impact of occupation undertaken at the level of the firm and utilizing job categories more closely approximating the job titles used by the employer will reveal a greater impact of job category on wages than aggregate analyses.

The Causes of Occupational Segregation

As discussed earlier, the human capital model provides an explanation for occupational segregation by sex in terms of women's optimizing behavior, given the traditional division of labor by sex within the family. Polachek (1979, 1981) provides some support for this view when jobs are categorized according to variants of the census major occupational groups. The problem with his approach is that these major occupational categories combine predominantly male and predominantly female jobs (England, 1982). England (1981, 1982) explicitly examines whether women's earnings patterns in predominantly female and predominantly male occupations differ in the way predicted by the human capital model. She finds that the earnings of women in predominantly female occupations do not show lower rates of either depreciation or appreciation than do the earnings of women in occupations employing more males.[33] Further, she finds women who have discontinuous work histories are no more likely to be in predominantly female occupations than are women who have been employed more continuously. Indeed, since she finds that women earn less in female jobs at all levels of experience, she concludes that "the evidence does not support the contention of human capital theorists that women maximize lifetime earnings by choosing female occupations" (England, 1981, p. 18).

If we provisionally conclude that the human capital analysis of occupational choice discussed above does not explain occupational segregation, at least at the aggregate level, what does? Many potential candidates remain, ranging from premarket discrimination (e.g., by families through the socialization process, or by schools through the actions of teachers, guidance counselors, or admissions committees) to the exclusionary practices of employers (due to their own tastes, statistical discriminations, and/or the tastes of employees or customers). Clearly, considerable additional work needs to be done to narrow the field and/or to attach relative weights to these competing explanations.

Pay Differentials Within Occupations

The relatively flat earnings profiles of women in female jobs are consistent with

---

[32] Employer job evaluation schemes may, however, understate the relative value of predominantly female occupations (Treiman and Hartmann, 1981).

[33] See also Beller (1982). She finds that when one examines detailed (three-digit) census occupations, the evidence for the human capital model is mixed in that the expected signs on the labor supply variables are not always obtained. King (1977) finds little evidence of flatter age earnings profiles for women in female as compared with male professions.

the notion advanced in the institutional view and implied by Arrow's notion of perceptual equilibrium that employers would structure female jobs to fit the average perceived characteristics of women workers. However, the finding that women in male jobs also have relatively flat earnings profiles might at first appear inconsistent with the notion that the internal labor market mandates equal pay for equal work by sex. However, it should be noted that the census categories are aggregated across job levels and firms. Thus, firms may pay women and men in the same job category at roughly the same rate, but promote women more slowly.[34] Further, it may be that women and men in the same census job category are segregated by firm. Blau (1977) examines the extent of employment segregation by sex within occupational categories and its relationship to intraoccupational pay differentials within the context of an institutional model. Her findings suggest that pay differentials between men and women in the same occupational category may reflect hiring discrimination by firms.

Blau postulates that institutional and market forces determine a wage hierarchy of firms within the local labor market that is consistent across occupational categories. She argues that, while employer tastes for discrimination against women are fairly widespread, the ability to exercise them is constrained by the firm's position in the wage hierarchy. That position is determined by a variety of factors and cannot easily be altered to accommodate employer preferences regarding the sex composition of specific occupational categories. Thus, in each occupational category male workers are primarily sought by and attracted to the higher-wage establishments, while female workers for the most part find employment in the lower-paying firms, which, regardless of their preferences, are less able to compete for male labor.

Blau tests this model using unpublished 1970 wage data from the Bureau of Labor Statistics on extremely narrow, white-collar occupational categories (e.g., accounting clerk, class A) in three northeastern cities. She argues that within such narrow categories male and female labor is likely to be fairly homogeneous.[35] Blau finds that within occupations men and women are segregated by establishments to an extent in excess of what would be expected on the basis of chance. Within firms, occupational pay differences are found to be relatively small, and sex pay differentials within occupations are primarily due to differences in pay rates *among* (rather than *within*) firms.[36] Further, men tend to earn *less* when they work with women, which is counter to what we would expect on the basis of the Becker model if discriminatory tastes were located in employees.

Blau finds evidence of a wage hierarchy of firms that is consistent across occupations *and* sex groups. Controlling for occupational mix, the representation of women in the firm is found to be consistent across occupations and inversely related to the wage standing of the firm. Note that these findings also conflict with the Becker model. In the case of employee preferences it is not expected that men will earn more when they work with relatively fewer women. In the case of employer preferences it is not expected that the firms that hire relatively the

---

[34] Note that such a sex difference by job level would not support the human capital view in that it would not be economically rational for women to opt to take the lower-paid training positions, but not to reap the gains of moving up the job ladder. For findings suggesting that women have lower promotion probabilities, see Duncan and Hoffman (1979), Cabral et al. (1981), and Malkiel and Malkiel (1973).

[35] See footnote 29.

[36] For other studies reporting differences in the distribution of men and women by firm that are associated with pay differentials, see Buckley (1971), McNulty (1967), Bridges and Berk (1974), Talbert and Bose (1977), Allison (1976), and Dussault and Rose-Lizée (1980).

fewest women (presumably the most discriminatory firms) will pay women the highest wage rates.[37]

CONCLUSIONS

Various explanations have been offered for the pay and occupational differences between male and female workers. Some emphasize labor market discrimination, while others, most notably the human capital model, focus on the voluntary choices of women. A review of the empirical literature strongly suggests that, all else equal (including fairly refined measures of work experience and labor force attachment), women do earn less than men. This suggests that labor market discrimination does indeed play a role in producing the lower earnings of women. However, we lack a widely accepted economic theory of the role of occupational segregation in producing this differential and of the persistence of sex discrimination in the labor market over time in the face of competitive forces. Perhaps it is time now to devote less of our empirical efforts to ascertaining the existence of discrimination and more toward determining which model of discrimination is most consistent with the data and the mechanisms by which these discriminatory outcomes are produced. On the basis of the existing evidence it appears that sex segregation in employment is an important mechanism for producing sex differences in earnings and that the occupational differences between men and women do not seem to be consistent with optimizing behavior on the part of women. However, considerably more work is needed to understand the causes of sex differences in occupational distributions fully and to determine the role of such oc-

cupational differences in producing male-female pay differentials. One area of particular concern is the issue of the impact of crowding in female jobs on the wages of women in male jobs. Finally, the question of the indirect effects of discrimination on the qualifications of women (and minorities) is another area upon which future research could fruitfully be focused.

ACKNOWLEDGMENTS

Portions of this chapter draw on my work entitled "Discrimination Against Women: Theory and Evidence," in William A. Darity, Jr., ed., *Labor Economics: Modern Views* (Boston: Kluwer-Nijhoff, 1984). I am grateful to the publisher for granting permission for the reproduction of some of that material here.

I am grateful for the comments and suggestions of Barbara Reskin, William Darity, Jr., Katherine Abraham, Andrea Beller, Barbara Bergmann, Charles Brown, Paula England, Marianne Ferber, Claudia Goldin, Joan Huber, Robert Hutchens, Lawrence Kahn, Michael Reich, Harvey Rosen, and two anonymous referees. I am indebted to Susan Schwochan for excellent research assistance.

REFERENCES

Aigner, D. J., and G. C. Cain
1977   "Statistical Theories of Discrimination in Labor Markets," *Industrial and Labor Relations Review*, 30, 2 (Jan.) 175-187.

Allison, E. K.
1976   "Sex Linked Earnings Differentials in the Beauty Industry," *Journal of Human Resources*, 11, 3 (Summer) 383-390.

Arrow, K.
1972a   "Models of Job Discrimination," in A. H. Pascal, Ed., *Racial Discrimination in Economic Life* (Lexington, Mass: D. C. Heath and Co.) 83-102.

1972b   "Some Mathematical Models of Race in the Labor Market," in A. H. Pascal, Ed., *Racial Discrimination in Economic Life* (Lexington, Mass: D. C. Heath and Co.) 187-204.

1973   "The Theory of Discrimination," in O. Ashenfelter and A. Rees, Eds., *Discrimination in La-*

---

[37] Note that the comparisons made in the text between the results expected on the basis of the Becker and institutional models rest fairly heavily on the assumption that labor is fairly homogeneous within these detailed occupations. Otherwise, variations in labor quality might account for these interfirm differences in pay rates.

bor Markets (Princeton, New Jersey: Princeton University Press) 3-33.

1976 "Economic Dimensions of Occupational Segregation: Comment I," *Signs*, 1, 3, Part 2 (Spring), 233-237.

Baker, C. O.
Undated *Earned Degrees Conferred: An Examination of Recent Trends*, National Center for Education Statistics.

Barnes, W. F., and E. Jones
1974 "Differences in Male and Female Quitting," *Journal of Human Resources*, 9, 4 (Fall), 439-451.

Becker, G.
1957 *The Economics of Discrimination* (Chicago: University of Chicago Press).

1965 "A Theory of the Allocation of Time," *Economic Journal*, 75, 229 (Sept.), 493-517.

1973 "A Theory of Marriage," *Journal of Political Economy*, 81, 4 (July/Aug.), 813-846.

Beller, A. H.
1982 "Occupational Segregation by Sex: Determinants and Changes," *Journal of Human Resources*, 17, 3 (Summer), 371-392.

Bergmann, B. R.
1974 "Occupational Segregation, Wages and Profits When Employers Discriminate by Race or Sex," *Eastern Economic Journal*, 1 (Apr.-July) 103-110.

1976 "Reducing the Pervasiveness of Discrimination," in E. Ginzberg, Ed., *Jobs for Americans* (Englewood Cliffs, N.J.: Prentice Hall) 120-141.

Bergmann, B. R., and W. Darity, Jr.
1981 "Social Relations in the Workplace and Employer Discrimination," *Proceedings of the Thirty-Third Annual Meeting of the Industrial Relations Research Association*, University of Wisconsin, Madison, 155-162.

Blau, F. D.
1975 "Longitudinal Patterns of Female Labor Force Participation," in H. S. Parnes et al., *Dual Careers: A Longitudinal Analysis of the Labor Market Experience of Women*, V. 4 (Columbus, Ohio: Center for Human Resource Research, Ohio State University, Dec.), 27-55.

1977 *Equal Pay in the Office* (Lexington, Mass: D. C. Heath and Co.).

1978 "The Impact of the Unemployment Rate on Labor Force Entries and Exits," in *Women's Changing Roles at Home and on the Job*. A special report of the National Commission for Manpower Policy, Report No. 26 (Sept.), 263-286.

Blau, F. D., and W. E. Hendricks
1979 "Occupational Segregation by Sex: Trends and Prospects," *Journal of Human Resources*, 14, 2 (Spring), 197-210.

Blau, F. D., and C. L. Jusenius
1976 "Economists' Approaches to Sex Segregation

in the Labor Market: An Appraisal," *Signs: Journal of Women in Culture and Society*, 1, 3, Part 2 (Spring), 181-199.

Blau, F. D., and L. M. Kahn
1981 "Race and Sex Differences in Quits by Young Workers," *Industrial and Labor Relations Review*, 34, 4 (July) 563-577.

Blinder, A. S.
1973 "Wage Discrimination: Reduced Form and Structural Estimates," *Journal of Human Resources*, 8, 4 (Fall) 436-455.

Bridges, W. P., and R. A. Berk
1974 "Determinants of White-Collar Income: An Evaluation of Equal Pay for Equal Work," *Social Science Research*, 3, 3 (Sept.), 211-234.

Brown, C.
1981 "Black/White Earnings Ratios Since the Civil Rights Act of 1964: The Importance of Labor Market Drop-outs," *NBER Working Paper #617* (Jan.).

1982 "The Federal Attack on Labor Market Discrimination: The Mouse That Roared?" *Research in Labor Economics*, 5, 33-68.

Buckley, J. E.
1971 "Pay Differences Between Men and Women in the Same Job," *Monthly Labor Review*, 94, 11 (Nov.), 36-39.

Butler, R. J.
1982 "A Note on Estimating Wage Discrimination in the Labor Market," *Journal of Human Resources*, 17, 4 (Fall), 606-621.

Cabral, R., M. A. Ferber, and C. A. Green
1981 "Men and Women in Fiduciary Institutions: A Study of Sex Differences in Career Development," *Review of Economics and Statistics*, 63, 4 (Nov.) 573-580.

Cain, G.
1976 "The Challenge of Segmented Labor Market Theories to Orthodox Theory: A Survey," *Journal of Economic Literature*, 14, 4 (Dec.), 1215-1257.

Cardwell, L. A., and M. R. Rosenzweig
1980 "Economic Mobility, Monopsonistic Discrimination and Sex Differences in Wages," *Southern Economic Journal*, 46, 4, (Apr.), 1102-1117.

Chiplin, B.
1981 "An Alternative Approach to the Measurement of Sex Discrimination: An Illustration From University Entrance," *Economic Journal*, 91, 394 (Dec.), 988-997.

Chiswick, B. R., J. A. O'Neill, J. Fackler, and S. W. Polachek
1974 "The Effect of Occupation on Race and Sex Differences in Hourly Earnings," *Business and Economic Statistics Section Proceedings of the American Statistical Society*, 219-228.

Cogan, J.
1980 "Married Women's Labor Supply: A Comparison of Alternative Estimation Procedures," in J. P. Smith, Ed., *Female Labor Supply: The-*

ory and Estimation (Princeton, N.J.: Princeton University Press) 90-118.

Corcoran, M.
1978   "The Structure of Female Wages," *The American Economic Review*, papers and proceedings, 68, 2 (May), 165-170.

1979   "Work Experience, Labor Force Withdrawals and Women's Earnings: Empirical Results Using the 1976 Panel Study of Income Dynamics," in C. B. Lloyd, E. Andrews, and C. L. Gilroy, Eds., *Women in the Labor Market* (New York: Columbia University Press).

Darity, W. A., Jr.
1982   "The Human Capital Approach to Black-White Earnings Inequality: Some Unsettled Questions," *Journal of Human Resources*, 17, 1 (Winter), 72-93.

Darity, W. A., Jr., and S. Myers,
1980   "Changes in Black-White Income Inequality, 1968-1978: A Decade of Progress," *Review of Black Political Economy*, (Summer), 354-379.

Doeringer, P. B., and M. J. Piore
1971   *Internal Labor Markets and Manpower Analysis* (Lexington, Mass: D. C. Heath and Co.).

Duncan, G. J., and S. Hoffman
1979   "On-the-Job Training and Earnings Differences by Race and Sex," *Review of Economics and Statistics*, 61, 4 (Nov.), 594-603.

Dussault, G., and R. Rose-Lizée
1980   "La Discrimination à l'Égard des femmes et la Ségrégation sur les Marchés du Travail: Le Cas des Employés de Bureau à Montréal," in *La Discrimination à l'Égard des femmes sur le Marché du Travail*, Collection Tirés à Part, No. 25 (Québec: Université Laval) 475-504.

Economic Report of the President
1974   (Washington, D.C.: U.S. Govt. Printing Office, Feb.).

Edgeworth, F. Y.
1922   "Equal Pay to Men and Women for Equal Work," *Economic Journal*, 32 (Sept.) 431-457.

England, P.
1981   "Wage Appreciation and Depreciation: A Test of Neoclassical Economic Explanations of Occupational Sex Segregation," mimeo (Dec.).

1982   "The Failure of Human Capital Theory to Explain Occupational Sex Segregation," *Journal of Human Resources*, 17, 3 (Summer), 358-370.

Fawcett, M. G.
1918   "Equal Pay for Equal Work," *Economic Journal*, 28 (March), 1-6.

Ferber, M. A., and H. M. Lowry
1976   "The Sex Differential in Earnings: A Reappraisal," *Industrial and Labor Relations Review*, 29, 3 (Apr.), 377-387.

Flanagan, R. J.
1976   "Wage Interdependence in Unionized Labor Markets," *Brookings Papers on Economic Activity*, No. 3.

Freeman, R. B.
1973   "Changes in the Labor Market for Black Americans, 1948-1972," *Brookings Papers On Economic Activity*, 67-131.

Fuchs, V. R.
1971   "Differences in Hourly Earnings Between Men and Women," *Monthly Labor Review*, 94, 5 (May), 9-15.

Gordon, D. M.
1972   *Theories of Poverty and Underemployment* (Lexington, Mass: D. C. Heath and Co.).

Gronau, R.
1973   "The Intrafamily Allocation of Time: The Value of Housewives' Time," *American Economic Review*, 63, 4 (Sept.), 634-651.

1974   "Wage Comparisons — A Selectivity Bias," *Journal of Political Economy* 82, 6 (Nov./Dec.), 1119-1143.

Gwartney, J. D., and R. Stroup
1973   "Measurement of Employment Discrimination According to Sex," *Southern Economic Journal*, 39, 4 (Apr.), 575-587.

Hamilton, M. T.
1973   "Sex and Income Inequality Among the Employed," *Annals of the American Academy of Political and Social Sciences*, 409 (Sept.), 42-52.

Hartmann, H. I., and B. Reskin
1982   "Job Segregation: Trends and Prospects," paper presented at a Conference on Occupational Segregation, Ford Foundation, New York City, June.

Hashimoto, M., and L. Kochin
1980   "A Bias in the Statistical Estimation of the Effects of Discrimination," *Economic Inquiry*, 18 (July), 478-486.

Heckman, J. J.
1974   "Shadow Prices, Market Wages and Labor Supply," *Econometrica*, 42, 4 (July), 679-694.

Hill, M. S.
1979   "The Wage Effects of Marital Status and Children," *Journal of Human Resources*, 14, 4 (Fall), 579-594.

Jusenius, C. L.
1977   "The Influence of Work Experience, Skill Requirement, and Occupational Segregation on Women's Earnings," *Journal of Economics and Business*, 29, 2 (Winter), 107-115.

Kahn, L. M.
1980   "Union Spillover Effects on Unorganized Labor Markets," *Journal of Human Resources*, 15, 1 (Winter), 87-98

1981   "Sex Discrimination in Professional Employment: A Case Study — Comment," *Industrial and Labor Relations Review*, 34, 2 (Jan.), 273-275.

Kamalich, R. F., and S. W. Polachek
1982   "Discrimination: Fact or Fiction? An Examination Using an Alternative Approach," *Southern Economic Journal*, 49, 2 (Oct.).

King, A. G.
1977   "Is Occupational Segregation the Cause of the Flatter-Experience-Earnings Profiles of Women?" *Journal of Human Resources*, 12, 4 (Fall), 541-549.

Kohen, A. I., with S. C. Breinich, P. Shields
1975   "Women and the Economy: A Bibliography and a Review of the Literature on Sex Differentiation in the Labor Market," Center for Human Resource Research, College of Administrative Science, Ohio State University.

Landes, E. M.
1977   "Sex Differences in Wages and Employment: A Test of the Specific Capital Hypothesis," *Economic Inquiry*, 15, 4 (Oct.), 523-538.

Lee, L.
1978   "Unionism and Wage Rates: A Simultaneous Equations Model With Qualitative and Limited Dependent Variables," *International Economic Review*, 19 (June), 415-433.

Lewin P., and P. England
1982   "Reconceptualizing Statistical Discrimination," paper presented at the annual meetings of the Southwest Social Science Association, San Antonio, Tex., March.

Lloyd, C. B., and B. T. Niemi
1979   *The Economics of Sex Differentials*, (New York: Columbia University Press).

Madden, J. F.
1973   *The Economics of Sex Discrimination* (Lexington, Mass: D. C. Heath and Co.).

1976   "Economic Dimensions of Occupational Segregation: Comment III," *Signs*, 1, 3, Part 2 (Spring), 245-250.

1982   "The Measurement of Employment Discrimination: Reduced Forms, Reverse Regression, Comparable Worth and the Definition of Labor Markets," *Proceedings of the Social Statistics Section at the Annual Meeting of the American Statistical Association*, Cincinnati, Ohio, Aug.

Malkiel, B. G., and J. A. Malkiel
1973   "Male-Female Pay Differentials in Professional Employment," *American Economic Review*, 63, 4 (Sept.), 693-705.

McNulty, D. J.
1967   "Differences in Pay Between Men and Women Workers," *Monthly Labor Review*, 90 (Dec.), 40-43.

Medoff, J. L., and K. G. Abraham
1980   "Experience, Performance, and Earnings," *Quarterly Journal of Economics*, 95, (Dec.), 703-736.

1981   "Are Those Paid More Really More Productive? The Case of Experience," *Journal of Human Resources*, 16, 2 (Spring) 186-216.

Mincer, J.
1962   "Labor Force Participation of Married Women," in NBER, *Aspects of Labor Economics* (Princeton: Princeton University Press) 63-97.

1979   "Wage Differentials: Comment," in C. B. Lloyd, E. S. Andrews, and C. L. Gilroy, Eds., *Women in the Labor Market* (New York: Columbia University Press) 278-285.

Mincer, J., and H. Ofek
1982   "Interrupted Work Careers: Depreciation and Restoration of Human Capital," *Journal of Human Resources*, 17, 1 (Winter), 3-24.

Mincer, J., and S. Polachek
1974   "Family Investments in Human Capital: Earnings of Women," *Journal of Political Economy*, 82, 2 (Part 2) (March/Apr.), S76-S108.

1978   "An Exchange: Theory of Human Capital and the Earnings of Women: Women's Earnings Reexamined," *Journal of Human Resources*, 13, 1 (Winter), 118-134.

Oaxaca, R.
1973a   "Male-Female Wage Differentials in Urban Labor Markets," *International Economic Review*, 14, 3 (Oct.), 693-709.

1973b   "Sex Discrimination in Wages," in O. Ashenfelter and A. Rees, Eds., *Discrimination in Labor Markets* (Princeton, N. J.: Princeton University Press) 124-151.

Osterman, P.
1979   "Sex Discrimination in Professional Employment: A Case Study," *Industrial and Labor Relations Review*, 32, 4 (July), 451-464.

Phelps, E. S.
1972   "The Statistical Theory of Racism and Sexism," *American Economic Review*, 62, 4 (Sept), 659-661.

Piore, M. J.
1971   "The Dual Labor Market: Theory and Implications," in D. M. Gordon, Ed., *Problems in Political Economy: An Urban Perspective* (Lexington, Mass: D. C. Heath and Co.) 90-94.

Polachek, S. W.
1975   "Potential Biases in Measuring Male-Female Discrimination," *Journal of Human Resources*, 10, 2 (Spring), 205-229.

1976   "Occupational Segregation: An Alternative Hypothesis," *Journal of Contemporary Business*, 5, 1 (Winter), 1-12.

1979   "Occupational Segregation Among Women: Theory, Evidence, and A Prognosis," in C. B. Lloyd, E. S. and C. L. Gilroy, Eds., *Women in the Labor Market* (New York: Columbia University Press) 137-157.

1981   "Occupational Self-Selection: A Human Capital Approach to Sex Differences in Occupational Structure," *Review of Economics and Statistics*, 63, 1 (Feb.), 60-69.

Ragan, J. F., Jr., and S. P. Smith
1981   "The Impact of Differences in Turnover Rates on Male/Female Pay Differentials," *Journal of Human Resources*, 16, 3 (Summer), 343-365.

Roberts, H. V.
1980   "Statistical Biases in the Measurement of Employment Discrimination," in E. R. Livernash,

Ed., *Comparable Worth: Issues and Alternatives* (Washington, D.C.: Equal Employment Advisory Council) 173-196.

Robinson, J.
1933   *The Economics of Imperfect Competition* (London: Macmillan and Co., Ltd.).

Roos, P. A.
1981   "Sexual Stratification in the Workplace: Male-Female Differences in Economic Returns to Occupation," *Social Science Research*, 10, 3 (Sept.), 195-224.

Sanborn, H.
1964   "Pay Differences Between Men and Women," *Industrial and Labor Relations Review*, 17, 4 (July), 534-550.

Sandell, S. H., and D. Shapiro
1978   "An Exchange: Theory of Human Capital and the Earnings of Women: A Reexamination of the Evidence," *Journal of Human Resources*, 13, 1 (Winter), 103-117.

1980   "Work Expectations, Human Capital Accumulation, and the Wages of Young Women," *Journal of Human Resources*, 15, 3 (Summer), 335-353.

Sawhill, I. V.
1973   "The Economics of Discrimination Against Women: Some New Findings," *Journal of Human Resources*, 8, 3 (Summer), 383-396.

Spence, A. M.
1973   "Job Market Signaling," *Quarterly Journal of Economics*, 87, 3 (Aug.), 355-374.

1974   *Market Signaling* (Cambridge, Mass: Harvard University Press).

Stevenson, M. H.
1975   "Relative Wages and Sex Segregation by Occupation," C. Lloyd, Ed., *Sex, Discrimination, and the Division of Labor* (New York: Columbia University Press).

Strober, M. H.
1976   "Toward Dimorphics: A Summary Statement to the Conference on Occupational Segregation," *Signs*, 1, 3, Part 2 (Spring), 293-302.

Suter, L., and H. Miller
1973   "Income Differences Between Men and Career Women," *American Journal of Sociology*, 78, 4 (Jan.), 962-974.

Talbert, J., and C. E. Bose
1977   "Wage Attainment Processes: The Retail Clerk Case," *American Journal of Sociology*, 83, 2 (Sept.), 403-424.

Thurow, L. C.
1975   *Generating Inequality* (New York: Basic Books, Inc.).

Treiman, D. J., and H. I. Hartmann, Eds.
1981   *Women, Work, and Wages: Equal Pay for Jobs of Equal Value* (Washington, D.C.: National Academy Press).

U.S. Department of Commerce, Bureau of the Census
1980   *A Statistical Portrait of Women in the United States: 1978*, Current Population Reports, Special Studies, Series P-23, No. 100 (Feb.).

1982   *Money Income and Poverty Status of Families and Persons in the United States: 1981* (Advance Report), Current Population Reports Series P-60, No. 134 (Washington, D.C.: U.S. Government Printing Office, July).

U.S. Department of Labor, Bureau of Labor Statistics
1980   "Perspectives on Working Women," June.

1981   News Release 81-522 (Nov. 15).

1982   *Employment Earnings* (Apr.).

U.S. Department of Labor, Employment and Training Administration
1981   *Employment and Training Report of the President.*

Viscusi, W. K.
1980   "Sex Differences in Worker Quitting," *Review of Economics and Statistics*, 62, 3 (Aug.) 388-398.

Wachter, M.
1974   "Primary and Secondary Labor Markets: A Critique of the Dual Approach," *Brookings Papers on Economic Activity*, no. 3, 637-604.

Weiss, Y., and R. Gronau
1981   "Expected Interruptions in Labour Force Participation and Sex-Related Differences in Earnings Growth," *Review of Economic Studies*, 58 (Oct.), 607-619.

Zellner, H.
1975   "The Determinants of Occupational Segregation," in C. B. Lloyd, ed., *Sex, Discrimination and the Division of Labor* (New York: Columbia University Press) 125-145.

8 Toward a General Theory of Occupational Sex Segregation: The Case of Public School Teaching

MYRA H. STROBER

Occupational sex segregation has several interrelated dimensions. First, there is segregation between paid occupations and those that are unpaid—that is, the percentages of women and men in paid employment are unequal. In 1980 the civilian labor force participation rate for women over age 20 was 51 percent; for men it was 79 percent (*Monthly Labor Review*, 1981, 104:60). Second, there is segregation across occupations within paid employment: labor market segregation. The index of dissimilarity indicates that in 1977 about 64 percent of American men (or women) would have had to change their occupations in order to achieve equality in the gender distribution across occupations (see Lloyd and Niemi, 1979; Gross, 1968; Blau and Hendricks, 1979). In few occupations are women represented in accordance with their representation in the labor force as a whole. Third, within any single occupation, women and men are not distributed equally across the occupational hierarchy—that is, there is occupational stratification. Women are clustered at the lower levels, men at the upper levels. And this is often true even in occupations that are overwhelmingly female, such as teach-

ing and librarianship. Also, men spend less time on housework and child care than do women, and men engage in fewer different household tasks (Walker and Woods, 1976; Robinson, 1977; Stafford and Duncan, 1977).

Although this paper sometimes touches on issues of women's participation in the paid labor force and occupational stratification, its focus is on the second type of occupational segregation: segregation across occupations within paid employment. A theory of occupational segregation by gender within the labor market must deal with three central questions: (1) How does an occupation become primarily male or female? (2) Once an occupation is gender typed, what forces help keep it that way? (3) How do occupations change their gender designation?

TOWARD A GENERAL THEORY OF OCCUPATIONAL SEX SEGREGATION

Extant sociological and economic theories of occupational segregation by gender in the labor market stem from remarkably divergent world views and locate the causes of segregation in a variety of different actors with diverse motivations.[1] Status attainment theory in sociology and human capital theory in economics pinpoint women's own behavior as the primary cause of their segregation into occupations with low status and low pay. Women's own values, behaviors, aspirations, attitudes, sex-role expectations (status attainment theory), educational credentials, and interrupted work histories (human capital theory) are seen as the causes of their occupational designations and low pay rates.

The view that women's own behavior is central is clearly articulated by Matthaei (1982:194), who argues that job segregation exists because ". . . women wished to work in jobs done by women." Employment in women's work preserved women's sense of their femininity. Kessler-Harris's book (1982) on the history of wage-earning women in the United States, while less exclusively supply-side oriented, also stresses the role of women's choices in producing occupational segregations.

Economic theories of discrimination and statistical discrimination, on the other hand, locate the source of inequality of earnings and occupational distribution in employers and their "taste" for discrimination (discrimination theory) or their wish to minimize the risk associated with employing women (statistical discrimination theory). Discrimination theory, however, recognizes that the tastes of workers and customers may be important factors contributing to the formation of employers' tastes. The "overcrowding" explanation for occupational segregation builds on the theory of discrimination and points out that, as a result of employers' operationalizing their tastes for exclusion, women are crowded into certain occupations, and women's wages in those occupations are thereby depressed.

Although the world view of the dual labor market or internal labor market theories is much less oriented toward individual choice and market processes than is neoclassical economics, these theories also locate the source of occupational segregation in employer behavior. Employers create segments in the labor market, either to take advantage of profit opportunities (the view of the non-Marxist dual labor market theorists) or to prevent the development of worker solidarity (the view of the Marxists among the dual labor market theorists).

Feminists have viewed all of these theories as inadequate, largely because the theories have paid insufficient attention to the centrality of gender relations in the society at large. I have argued that, although the profit motive may explain employers' desires to augment the division of labor, it does not explain why that division turns into one based on gender (Strober and Best, 1979).[2] Hartmann (1976:138) has argued that to explain job segregation by gender one must examine patriarchy as well as capitalism. Hartmann defines patriarchy as "a set of social relations which has a material base and in which there are hierarchical relations between men, and solidarity among them, which enable them to control women. Patriarchy is thus the system of male oppression of women." In Hartmann's view, male capitalists and male workers oppress women. And Hartmann as well as Milkman (1980) point to the role of male worker organizations (i.e., trade unions) in initiating and

---

[1] Sociological theories and those of Marxist economists and feminists are reviewed in Sokoloff (1980); economic theories are reviewed in Blau and Jusenius (1976), Cain (1976), and Amsden (1980).

[2] Blau and Jusenius (1976) noted that "sex is an obvious basis for differentiation, due to employers' distaste for hiring women in male occupations and/or real or perceived quality differences between male and female labor" (pp. 192-193). But the unanswered question remains: Why do employers have a distaste for women, and why do they perceive them as being less qualified, or why are women "less qualified"?

maintaining occupational segregation by gender.[3]

In addition to these more formal theories of occupational segregation by gender, there are numerous explanations that seek to explain the gender designation of a job in terms of the job's characteristics. Oppenheimer (1970) has hypothesized that women fill those jobs that require relatively high levels of prejob, as opposed to on-the-job, training, such as nursing and teaching. There is also a rich folklore maintaining that women's jobs are those requiring dexterity or those that women traditionally performed in the home. None of these explanations provides a strong basis for a theory of gender segregation because for each hypothesis it is so easy to point to counterexamples. Why are certain occupations that require a great deal of prejob training, such as law and medicine, "reserved," in the United States, for men? If women are so dexterous, why are there so few female brain surgeons? If jobs that used to be, or are, performed in the home become women's jobs in the market, why are most chefs, bakers, and food servers men? Moreover, the difficulty with putting forth a theory of gender segregation based on the inherent characteristics of a job is that the analyst then finds it impossible to explain shifts in gender assignments or differences in the assignment of jobs in different countries. If the major reasons for a particular job assignment are the job's inherent characteristics, how can the gender assignment change while the inherent characteristics remain the same? Or, how can an occupation be assigned to one gender in one industrialized country but to the other gender elsewhere?

Neither the formal theories nor the ad hoc explanations offered thus far can answer the three major questions concerning the gen-

der designation of an occupation: its origin, its maintenance, and its change, if any. Yet each of the theories and many of the explanations contain threads of truth. What I have done is selected the strongest threads from each and woven them into a new theory. Orthodox adherents to various schools of thought may be uncomfortable in finding aspects of their theories woven into a new fabric, but I have purposely borrowed insights when their observations contributed to the overall explanation, without too much concern about the insights' ideological parentage. I call the theory "general" because it may be used to explain the origins, maintenance, and changes in the gender assignment of jobs in general, i.e., for all occupations.

My theory has two central tenets. It incorporates the concept of patriarchy, although I define patriarchy to make it applicable in a non-Marxist framework. My theory maintains that decisions concerning the gender assignment of jobs are made by men. In particular, I argue that, within the constraints laid down by race and class, it is male workers who decide which occupations they will inhabit. Male employers set wages and working conditions but, except when the job explicitly or implicitly requires female characteristics, male employers allow male workers to decide which jobs will be theirs. The remaining jobs are offered to women; if sufficient numbers of women do not wish to work in the job, the employer recruits immigrants. Sometimes new jobs appear to be "designed" for women, that is, it appears that men are not given "first dibs" on these jobs. In such cases, employers design the jobs for women and do not offer them to men first because they believe that most men would deem the jobs undesirable relative to existing ones.

The second key aspect of my theory is that, in deciding which new jobs to claim for themselves and which jobs to leave for women, male workers (again within the important constraints laid down by race and

---

[3] Rubery (1978), while not mainly interested in sex segregation, has also noted the importance of unions in perpetuating dual labor markets.

class) attempt to maximize their economic gain. They compare the wages, hours, and working conditions of the new job with those of existing jobs.[4] If the new job is superior, they claim it and move in; if not, the job becomes women's work. Thus, whether a particular job in a particular locale is initially male or female is a function of when the job came onto the market.

Suppose a technological or organizational change occurs and a new job develops. New plant and equipment are put into place and workers are to be hired. In the short run, in accordance with neoclassical assumptions, technology and capital are fixed. The employer estimates the product or service demand and determines the need for labor. Based on the existing wage structure of the firm or industry and the wages for similar jobs in the local labor market, he assigns a wage rate to the job and proceeds to advertise for workers.[5] If "qualified" men show up, they are hired. Qualifications, of course, may well be based on racial and class characteristics as well as on objective criteria.

Let's take up the case(s) where an insufficient number of men apply for the job. But first let's ask why male capitalists and/or managers give male workers first dibs on jobs. Why should employers use male workers for a particular job when they could hire female workers at a lower wage rate? Neoclassical theorists such as Arrow (1973) have responded to this question by citing various market rigidities that prevent profit maximization. Marxist dual labor market theorists such as Reich et al. (1973) have implicitly argued that capitalists are willing to sacrifice short-term profits for a long-run strategy that guards against the development of worker solidarity.

I have argued elsewhere (Strober, 1976:295) that ideology, i.e., "social, legal, cultural and economic conventions," including "subtle pressures from family, employees, customers and 'the community'," have enforced certain hiring taboos preventing employers from attempting to maximize profits. We need to move further and briefly define the concept of patriarchy, for it is patriarchy that is the source of these conventions and pressures. Based on Hartmann's work, I define patriarchy as a set of personal, social, and economic relationships that enable men to have power over women and the services they provide. This is a preliminary definition, and I am aware that it needs specificity and refinement.[6]

One reason for discussing the concept of patriarchy here is to demonstrate that male employers are not simply profit maximizers. They are simultaneously pursuing profit maximization and the maintenance of male privilege; that is, there is a tension between patriarchy and profit maximization. This tension is often latent; indeed, employers may not even be conscious of it. But the fact is that employers permit male workers to choose their jobs because employers want to maintain patriarchy. They recognize that if male privilege is threatened in the working class or among professionals or lower-level managers (by allowing women to have jobs that men want), upper-level managers, entrepreneurs, and capitalists would soon

---

[4] Blau (1977) points out that *within* an occupation, men tend to work in high-wage firms and women in low-wage firms. She argues that the high-wage employers are thus able to hire preferred workers—men.

[5] In this paper I refer to an employer as "he" because I believe that this designation reflects reality and, for purposes of explicating this theory, it is important to consider the gender of employers.

---

[6] It may be, as Whitehead (1979) has suggested, that patriarchy is not the best term to use to describe women's subordination in gender relations. Whitehead argues that the term *patriarchy* connotes the power of a husband over his wive(s), children, and property and is only one specific form of male dominance. She has also suggested that the term implies an unchanging, historically constant form of subordination. I use the term here mainly because it has been used in earlier work and do not mean for it to refer only to the relational aspects of gender, nor do I assume it to be historically constant.

find their own male privileges under siege. Male employers believe that they benefit from keeping women subordinate to and dependent on men in all classes of society, so that women need to be married to men and so that, because of their dependence, women will continue to provide children as well as domestic services for men. Male employers (as well as male workers) recognize that patriarchal relations must be maintained at the workplace if they are to remain unthreatened in the household. Thus, male managers are willing to sacrifice some potential profits by allowing men to choose the jobs they wish. Male managers are willing to trade off some profit opportunities to maintain the system of patriarchy.

Let us move to the question of how jobs are allocated by gender when an insufficient number of men apply for positions in a new occupation. The employer has several options: (1) raise the wage rate and try to attract (more) men; (2) hire women who apply and/or encourage (more) women to apply at the existing wage rate; (3) recruit male or female immigrants and hire them at the existing wage rate.[7]

The option exercised will depend first on how many men have already been hired. If, for example, a "significant" number of the positions have been filled by men, employers may prefer the first option: raising wages and attracting more men, for employers are unlikely to hire women to fill the remaining jobs in an occupation that men have claimed, even if men haven't filled all the job vacancies. To do so would erode the principles of patriarchy and male privilege. It might also violate societal taboos about the two sexes working together on certain jobs and/or might

interfere with male bonding.[8] However, some women might be hired, with the explicit or implicit understanding of both employer and employees that although hired they are nonetheless not full members of the "group." A sense of marginality might be conveyed through lower pay, ineligibility for promotion, or ineligibility for membership in the relevant union.[9]

Suppose, however, that few men apply for the new jobs at the existing wage rate. If the employer believes that an adequate supply of native male labor can be attracted from other industries or other parts of the country, he may raise the wage rate slightly to attract men. The employer will be more likely to do this if he believes that women may not be interested in holding the job, e.g., because holding such a job might violate existing norms and/or if he believes that native men would perform the job significantly better than either women or foreign workers. On the other hand, if financial constraints prevent him from raising wages, and he thinks women can perform the job adequately, he might try to hire women. If having women perform the job in question violates existing societal norms about which jobs are acceptable for women of a particular race or class, so that few women apply, the employer might engage in a campaign to alter those norms. If women's employment in the new occupation violates norms only moderately, the employer's efforts to change the norms would probably be successful and

---

[7] Of course, to options 2 and 3 could be added options specifying that the wage rate be lowered when recruiting women or immigrants. One could argue that during certain periods of our history the decision to recruit blacks was made on grounds similar to the decision to recruit immigrants.

[8] The issue of taboos against the sexes working together needs further investigation. For a discussion of male bonding, see Bradford et al. (1975).

[9] Meyers (1980) has detailed the exclusion of women from the teachers' union in France during the 1890s, when women were a minority of teachers. However, once women became the majority of teachers, the men remaining in the profession saw the need for gender cooperation and permitted women to join the union. Other examples of women's exclusion from unions are given in Hartmann (1976) and Milkman (1980).

women would be hired. Norms clearly can be changed, but, except during wartime or times of social revolution, they change fairly slowly. Thus, if according to existing norms a job is considered flagrantly unsuitable for women it is likely that, in the short run, ordinary campaigns to alter these norms would not bring forth an adequate supply of women workers. In such a situation the employer would begin to recruit workers from abroad.[10]

This discussion can be summarized by noting the conditions under which foreign men, or perhaps men from a native racial minority, would be recruited to fill a new occupation: (1) enough native majority men did not apply to fill an occupation; (2) financial constraints prevented the employer from raising the wage and/or the employer did not believe that native majority men would perform the job any better than women or foreign or minority men; and (3) employment of women in the occupation flagrantly violated existing norms. (A discussion of conditions under which foreign or minority women might be recruited goes beyond the scope of this initial sketch of the theory.)

Next comes the question of the development of the wage differential between women's and men's jobs. I have argued thus far that, if men do not apply for a new job at an existing wage rate and if employers do not decide to raise the wage rate in an effort to attract men from other areas in the nation or from other jobs, employers will offer the job to women at the same rate at which it was offered to men. Suppose then that a sufficient number of women apply and that all of the new job slots are filled at the posted wage rate. At this point, if we compare the wage rate earned by women in this job to the wage rate earned by the men who considered taking the job but decided not to,

we will find a wage differential, with men earning higher wages than women. After all, one of the reasons why the men declined the job in question was probably its low relative wage. Thus, within race and class categories, the fact that men have the first choice of occupations leads not only to occupational sex segregation but also to a gender wage differential. Patriarchy combined with men's desire to maximize their economic gain leads to higher relative wages for men.

As time passes and an occupation becomes solidly female, employers may lower the wage rate relative to others or fail to increase it as fast as others, thereby further increasing the gender wage differential. As noted earlier, when a wage rate is first set for a new occupation—when employers think that men will enter the occupation—the wage rate is set in accordance with the firm's or industry's internal wage structure and in accordance with wages for similar jobs in the local labor market. However, we may hypothesize that, once an occupation becomes a female occupation, employers will often lower its wage rate. First, the original wage rate, which was set in comparison to existing male wages, will be too high in comparison to the wages for other female jobs in the firm and in the local labor market.[11] Second, employers will see no reason to pay women male rates: women do not "need" the money as much as men, only men require a "family wage"—women need only enough income to support themselves—and women, because they are often geographically immobile and/or excluded from other higher-paying occupations have a less wage-elastic supply curve than men and therefore can be retained at a lower wage.

In the theory I have proposed, women's

---

[10] Alternatively, the employer might turn to a native racial minority.

[11] For a discussion of how firms' internal wage structures differ by gender and how job evaluation techniques cement these differences, see Treiman and Hartmann (1981).

job choices play a rather insignificant role. By and large, women move into only those jobs that men leave for them. Turning to the issues of stability and change in the gender assignment of occupations, we find that women's opportunities for choice are again overshadowed by men's actions. I do not want to argue that women make no choices at all. They do, and it is interesting to investigate their constrained choices and the circumstances under which some women are able to contribute to a modest breakdown of occupational segregation. However, like the origin of occupational segregation, the stability and change in that segregation is determined overwhelmingly by men's choices and men's behavior. In recent times, of course, equal employment opportunity legislation and affirmative action orders have served to increase women's choices and decrease the scope of men's exclusionary behavior. The following discussion, however, examines the dynamics of occupational segregation in the absence of legislation and executive and court orders.

Once a job has been inhabited by one gender or another, it becomes "typed" as male or female, and strong forces act to maintain its gender assignment. If men occupy an occupation, they might actively and collectively seek to keep women out, fearing that if women enter they will lower the earnings of the job by accepting lower wage rates or, if they are paid the same as men, diminish patriarchal hegemony. For although men act as individual maximizers in choosing their occupations, once they begin to work in an occupation and identify with it, they act collectively to maintain its gender designation. It is true, of course, that women will rarely choose to enter a male-typed occupation, fearing a diminution of their perceived femininity and thus a reduction of their prospects for marriage, which until recently was their primary avenue to economic gain. Women behave in this way primarily because they fear negative sanctions from men not because they have free choice

and are rejecting male occupations. When these negative sanctions disappear, e.g., during wartime, women more readily, and often enthusiastically, enter the higher-paid male occupations.

If an occupation is occupied by women, the barrier to integration is largely male behavior. Women put up no resistance to men entering "their" occupations, for they know that if more men enter both the prestige and earnings of the occupation are likely to rise. But men are reluctant to enter female occupations, primarily because of their low wages but also because they fear ridicule by other men and aspersions on their masculinity if they do.

If both genders initially take part in an occupation, call it X, eventually one of the two will come to dominate. Which gender achieves primacy in X depends on the attractiveness of alternative occupations for men. If, as time goes on, X is deskilled (i.e., requires lower skills) and wages fall, or if new occupations are created that men find more attractive economically, men will move out of X. On the other hand, if new and existing occupations come to be seen as less attractive economically than X, men will move into X. It is also possible that women will move to other occupations, in which case X may become an occupation for which foreign labor is recruited. One observes that, in the musical chairs of occupational shifts, there is a clear hierarchy of players: men get first choice of job opportunities. One is also impressed with the interdependence of occupational gender assignments. Whether a particular occupation remains gender typed or changes its gender assignment depends not only on its wages and working conditions but also on those in alternative occupations.

It seems to be that as occupations shift from one gender designation to another there are important "tipping" points. Once an occupation becomes significantly male (or female), it quickly tips and fairly soon thereafter becomes overwhelmingly male (or female). Just what percentage constitutes this tipping point probably varies by occupation and historical period.

The reasons for the existence of a tipping point are evident from our discussion of the forces that maintain the stability of an occupation's gender designation. Once it is clear that an occupation is significantly male, men actively prevent women from entering and women become reluctant to apply. By the same token, once it is clear that an occupation is significantly female, it will be shunned by men. In other words, the expectation that occupations will not be mixed but will be either male or female helps bring about the fulfillment of that expectation.

HOW TEACHING BECAME A FEMALE OCCUPATION

To what extent can my theory be applied to the case of public school teaching in the late nineteenth and early twentieth centuries? Statistics for the nation as a whole on the percentage of women teachers are unavailable for the years prior to 1870. In Massachusetts, which was at the vanguard of the movement of women into teaching, women made up 56 percent of the public school personnel in 1834 and 78 percent in 1860 (Vinovskis and Bernard, 1978). In Ohio, a more typical state with respect to women in teaching, women made up 39 percent of the teachers in 1840 and 46 percent in 1850 (Woody, 1929). For the United States as a whole, about 60 percent of all teachers were women in 1870. By 1900 the figure was up to 70 percent, and by 1920 it had reached a peak of 86 percent (U.S. Office of Education's Biennial Survey of Education for 1870, 1900, 1920).[12]

These figures conceal considerable variability by geographic region and rural/urban location. For example, in 1870, when women constituted 60 percent of all teachers nationwide, women made up less than half the teacher population in 26 states. In Washington, D.C., women made up 92 percent of the teachers in 1870, but in neighboring Virginia women filled only 35 percent of the teaching jobs.

Why did women come to constitute an increasingly larger percentage of teachers in the period from the mid-nineteenth century to the end of World War I? In the context of my theory outlined earlier, the question should be rephrased to read: why did men choose to leave the teaching profession during that period? We can begin by noting that the latter half of the nineteenth century witnessed a substantial increase in the demand for teachers as a result of population growth, increased commitment to universal education, and a desired decrease in the typical number of students in each class. For teaching to have remained a male profession, the percentage of all male workers engaged in teaching would have had to be increased.

Nonetheless, although demand for teachers was increasing, school boards were not willing to raise wages to attract male teachers. In fact, teachers, especially in rural areas, were paid very low wages, often on a par with those of common laborers. This may have resulted from a disinclination to set high tax rates and/or an ideological devaluation of education and teachers' roles. On the one hand, the educational requirements (literacy and a working knowledge of the three Rs) demanded of teachers at that time were modest by modern standards. On the other hand, school boards required a native-born middle-class appearance and behavior and good moral character. Nevertheless, it was virtually impossible to support a family with middle-class standards on a teacher's salary. Most men who taught school did so as a stepping stone to another career or on a part-time basis while pursuing other work. Most women who taught school were young

---

[12] The two major sources of statistics on teachers by gender are the annual and biennial reports of the U.S. Commissioner of Education and the decennial census reports.

and single with few financial responsibilities for others. Men often taught during the winter term, when the older boys were in attendance, while women were more likely to teach during the summer term.

During the latter half of the nineteenth century, although starting somewhat earlier in Massachusetts, teaching began to undergo a revolution in the organization of schools and schooling. The revolution began in urban areas and spread to the countryside. Schools became more formalized in three important ways. First, as schools grew in size, classes became graded, i.e., children were taught in groups divided by age. Second, once schools were large and graded, they were bureaucratized. A curriculum was developed for each grade, and a large number of school management functions were required. Third, as a result of a knowledge explosion, the growth of the middle class, and the increasing complexity of work, the high school evolved. Moreover, states began to regulate education, lengthening school terms and formally credentialling teachers. Teachers were often required to attend summer institutes to maintain their credentials.

These changes tended to make teaching less attractive to men. When teaching was a relatively casual occupation that could be engaged in for fairly short periods of time, it was attractive to men in a variety of circumstances. A farmer could easily combine teaching in the winter with caring for his farm during the rest of the year. A potential minister, politician, shopkeeper, or lawyer could teach for a short period of time to gain visibility within the community. However, once standards were raised for teacher certification and school terms were lengthened and combined into a continuous year, men began to drop out of teaching (Morain, 1974). In urban areas, where teaching was first formalized, and later in rural areas, most men found that the opportunity cost of teaching was simply too great. Even though annual salaries were higher once standards were

raised and the school term lengthened, the average teaching salary remained inadequate to support a family. Men also disliked losing their former classroom autonomy. And at the same time, and perhaps most importantly, attractive job opportunities were developing for men in business and in other professions.

As men left teaching, school boards turned more and more toward women. For a variety of reasons, women were ready to move into teaching. First, many young women possessed the required education. By the middle of the nineteenth century, women and men had virtually the same literacy rates, and girls were almost as likely to be attending school as were boys.[13] Second, young girls were moving increasingly into the paid work force. As the production of many goods and services moved out of the home and began to be supplied through the market, the domestic services of young women were less frequently needed by their parents. At first, young women did piecework in their own homes. They also worked as domestics in other people's homes. Finally, when New England mill owners sought young women to work in their factories, young women moved into these positions. But most other jobs were closed to women. Thus, although men were moving out of teaching because

---

[13] Lockridge (1974), using the ability to sign one's name on one's will as a measure of literacy, found that by 1850, except in the South, both men and women over the age of 20 were almost universally literate.

The causes of this silent revolution in girls' school attendance is an interesting topic in its own right, for in colonial times girls were generally excluded from district schools. Vinovskis and Bernard (1978) noted that in 1850 in New England about 80 percent of white males and about 75 percent of white females ages 5 to 19 attended school. Attendance rates for 1850 for both sexes and the ratio of female/male school attendance descends, however, as we move through the Middle Atlantic, North Central, South Central, and South Atlantic regions, respectively. In the South Atlantic, about 41 percent of white males and about 35 percent of white females ages 5 to 19 attended school.

the opportunity cost of remaining was too high, single young women with middle-class backgrounds found teaching an attractive alternative to other paid work or to remaining at home and assisting with domestic chores.

Young women might well have moved into teaching without any assistance from ideological campaigns. But perhaps to ensure women's interest in teaching or to make their entry more palatable to their parents, future husbands, and pupils, a major ideological crusade was waged in favor of women's entry into teaching. Advocates of women as teachers, such as Catharine Beecher, Mary Lyon, Zilpah Grant, Horace Mann, and Henry Barnard, argued that not only were women the ideal teachers of young children (because of their patience and nurturant qualities) but also that teaching was ideal preparation for motherhood. They also proclaimed the virtues of women's willingness to teach at lower wages than those required by men. Indeed the arguments in favor of women teaching were so compelling that one wonders how it was that any men remained in teaching. But a few did remain and at higher wages than those paid to women (Strober and Best, 1979).

Why didn't teaching become a completely female occupation? And why were the men who remained in teaching paid higher wages than women teachers? It is useful to answer these questions by looking separately at rural and urban labor markets.

In rural areas, one-room schoolhouses often persisted even after school terms were lengthened and credentialling was formalized at the state level. Women and men tended to do the same job, and the gender wage differential tended to be small, although invariably in men's favor. As already noted, prior to the lengthening of the school term, there had generally been two separate short terms, one in the winter and one in the summer. Men tended to teach in the winter term and had the older boys in their class. During the summer term, when men and older boys were engaged in farming,

women were generally the teachers. A myth grew that women had more difficulty than men in "handling" the older boys. Thus, it may be that in rural schools men received a pay premium for their supposed disciplinary abilities. It may also be that on the whole men had more experience in teaching and received a return on that experience.

In urban markets, however, the men who remained in teaching did not perform the same jobs as their female counterparts. The labor market for teachers in urban areas was highly stratified, and men had the higher-paying, more prestigious jobs: principals, vice-principals, and high school teachers. That management jobs were reserved for men even in an occupation that was overwhelmingly female is an important observation. It may be that school boards, which perceived women as impermanent members of the work force, believed they could decrease their management training costs by training only men for managerial positions. However, the fact is that even when women did maintain their attachment to the work force they were rarely trained or hired for management positions, thus suggesting that other considerations beyond training costs were operative in school boards' decisions. No doubt a desire for patriarchical hegemony at the local level was a factor in school boards' decision to hire male managers for schools and especially for the superintendency, a post that brought its incumbent into frequent contact with local male leaders in business and politics.

What quantitative evidence exists to support this theory? As any cliometrician has by now ascertained, it is not possible to provide a definitive empirical testing of the theory put forth here. The required data on alternative wage rates simply do not exist. There is, however, econometric evidence consistent with this theory.

In regressions designed to explain the cross-sectional variance in the percentage of women teachers in a sample of counties for 1850 and 1880, Strober and Lanford (1981) found that the length of the school year and the number of teachers per school—both measures of the relative formalization of school—were positive and significant determinants of the percentage of female teachers. At the same time, the female/male salary differential was found to be lower the greater the percentage of women in teaching (Strober and Lanford, 1981). In pooled cross-sectional regressions for the period 1870–1970, Lanford (as cited in Gordon, 1980) found support for the hypothesis that greater formalization of the educational system increased the proportion of female teachers. In a case study of school personnel in San Francisco in 1879, Strober and Best (1979) described their results as follows (p. 234):

Holding education and experience constant, sex played a significant role in determining the position and type of school of employment. We also concluded that education and experience were less important than position and type of school in explaining salary variation by sex and that, holding constant education, experience and position, a greater percentage of the F/M salary ratio stemmed from sex differentials in pay across types of schools than from sex differentials within types of schools.

Margo and Rotella (1981) found for the Houston school system in the 1892-1923 period that "although some of the prevalence of males in administrative posts and some of the size of the female/male salary differential is explained by differences in experience and education, maleness itself was a valued attribute in school personnel" (p. 20).

In the post-World War II period, teaching has maintained its gender designation, but the percentage of men in the profession has increased markedly. Moreover, women in teaching are no longer primarily young and unmarried. In 1978 about one-third of all teachers, elementary and secondary combined, were men. In high schools in 1978, men constituted slightly more than half of all teachers (54 percent), an increase of about 18 percentage points from the 1945-1946 fig-

ure of 36 percent. In elementary schools in 1978, men constituted about 17 percent of all teachers, an increase of about 11 percentage points from the 1945-1946 figure of 6 percent. The detailed reasons for this change remain to be explored (for a brief discussion, see Tyack and Strober, 1981). However, my theory suggests that men increasingly saw teaching as economically attractive (increased unionization has perhaps helped in this regard) and that, in accordance with the principle that men should have first choice in job opportunities, those responsible for teacher hiring were happy to readmit them to the profession.

CONCLUSION

In this paper I have sought to outline a new, general theory of occupational sex segregation. The theory suggests that occupational sex segregation as well as the female/male wage differential results from two major principles. First, although male employers set wages and working conditions, within the constraints set down by race and class, male employers allow male workers to decide which occupations they will inhabit. Second, in deciding which jobs to claim for themselves and which to leave for women, male workers, again within the constraints laid down by race and class, attempt to maximize their economic gain by comparing the economic package presented by any particular occupation with the economic packages offered by other occupations. Thus, occupations become male or female not because of their inherent characteristics but because of the interaction of patriarchy and male workers' utility maximization.

I have also used this general theory as a framework for explaining the changes in the gender composition of the teaching profession in the late nineteenth and early twentieth century. Stated most simply, teaching became a female occupation largely because men moved out of it. As schools and schooling became more formalized, teaching became less attractive to men while at the same time more lucrative job opportunities were developing for men in business and in other professions. Although the quantitative evidence summarized in the paper is consistent with the theory, it is difficult to obtain historical data that would provide a definitive test of the theory.

As noted earlier, recent changes in equal employment opportunity legislation and affirmative action orders have complicated the dynamics of occupational sex segregation. Clearly, future theoretical work will need to look carefully at these interventions. Based on what we have learned here, however, we predict that, in order to be successful in changing the gender assignment of jobs, any intervention strategy (such as equal employment opportunity efforts) would have to do more than merely attack hiring and promotion rules. It would have to concern itself with gender relations in society as a whole, because patriarchal ideology and supply and demand factors in the labor market are inextricably interwoven. It would appear that, unless there is widespread agreement on the virtues of breaking down patriarchal relations, male employers and male workers will find ample opportunities for frustrating the goals of governmental interventions in the job market.

ACKNOWLEDGMENTS

The following people provided helpful comments on the first draft of this paper: Alice Amsden, Francine Blau, Martin Carnoy, Regina Cortina, Heidi Hartmann, Henry Levin, Karen Oppenheim Mason, Aline Quester, Judith Steihm, Joan Talbert, Deborah Thresher, and David Tyack.

REFERENCES

Amsden, Alice H.
1980   Introduction. Pp. 11-38 in Alice H. Amsden, ed., *The Economics of Women and Work*. New York: St. Martin's Press.

Arrow, Kenneth
1973   The theory of discrimination. Pp. 3-33 in Orley Ashenfelter and Albert Rees, eds., *Discrimination in Labor Markets*. Princeton, N.J.: Princeton University Press.

Blau, Francine D.
1977   *Equal Pay in the Office*. Lexington, Mass.: D. C. Heath.

Blau, Francine D., and Wallace E. Hendricks
1979   Occupational segregation by sex: Trends and prospects. *Journal of Human Resources* 14:197-210.

Blau, Francine D., and Carol Jusenius
1976   Economists' approaches to sex segregation in the labor market: An appraisal. Pp. 181-199 in Martha Blaxall and Barbara B. Reagan, eds., *Women and the Workplace: The Implications of Occupational Segregation*. Chicago: University of Chicago Press.

Bradford, David L., Alice G. Sargent, and Melinda S. Sprague
1975   Executive man and woman: The issue of sexuality. P. 52 in Francine E. Gordon and Myra H. Strober, eds., *Bringing Women Into Management*. New York: McGraw-Hill.

Cain, Glen G.
1976   The challenge of segmented labor market theories to orthodox theory: A survey. *Journal of Economic Literature* 14:1215-1257.

Gordon, Audri
1980   A Dynamic Analysis of the Sexual Composition of Public School Teaching: 1870 to 1970. Unpublished Ph.D. dissertation, Stanford University.

Gross, Edward
1968   Plus ca change . . .? The sexual structure of occupations over time. *Social Problems* 16:198-208.

Hartmann, Heidi I.
1976   Capitalism, patriarchy, and job segregation by sex. Pp. 137-169 in Martha Blaxall and Barbara B. Reagan, eds., *Women and the Workplace: The Implications of Occupational Segregation*. Chicago: University of Chicago Press.

Kessler-Harris, Alice
1982   *Out to Work: A History of Wage-Earning Women in the United States*. New York: Oxford University Press.

Lloyd, Cynthia B., and Beth T. Niemi
1979   *The Economics of Sex Differentials*. New York: Columbia University Press.

Lockridge, Kenneth
1974   *Literacy in Colonial New England: An Enquiry Into the Social Context of Literacy in the Early Modern West*. New York: Norton.

Margo, Robert A., and Elyce J. Rotella
1981   Sex Differences in the Market for School Personnel: Houston, Texas, 1892-1923. Paper presented at the annual meeting of the Social Science History Association, Nashville, Tenn., October.

Matthaei, Julie A.
1982 *An Economic History of Women in America: Women's Work, The Sexual Division of Labor and the Development of Capitalism.* New York: Schocken Books.

Meyers, Peter V.
1980 From conflict to cooperation: Men and women teachers in the Belle Epoque. Pp. 493-505 in Donald N. Baker and Patrick J. Harrigan, eds., *The Making of Frenchmen.* Waterloo, Ontario: Historical Reflections Press.

Milkman, Ruth
1980 Organizing the sexual division of labor: Historical perspectives on "women's work" and the American labor movement. *Socialist Review* 49:95-150.

Morain, Thomas
1977 The Entry of Women Into the School Teacher Profession in Nineteenth Century Iowa. Unpublished paper, Iowa State University.

Oppenheimer, Valerie K.
1970 *The Female Labor Force in the United States: Demographic and Economic Factors Governing its Growth and Changing Composition.* Population Monograph Series, No. 5. Berkeley, Calif.: Institute of International Studies.

Reich, Michael, David M. Gordon, and Richard C. Edwards
1973 A theory of labor market segmentation. *American Economic Review* 63:359-365.

Robinson, John P.
1977 *How Americans Use Time.* New York: Praeger.

Rubery, Jill
1978 Structured labour markets, worker organization and low pay. *Cambridge Journal of Economics* 2:17-36.

Sokoloff, Natalie J.
1980 *Between Money and Love: The Dialectics of Women's Home and Market Work.* New York: Praeger.

Stafford, Frank, and Greg Duncan
1977 The Use of Time and Technology by Households in the United States. Working paper, Department of Economics, University of Michigan.

Strober, Myra H.
1976 Toward dimorphics: A summary statement to the conference on occupational segregation. P. 295 in Martha Blaxall and Barbara B. Reagan, eds., *Women and the Workplace: The Implications of Occupational Segregation.* Chicago: University of Chicago Press.

Strober, Myra H., and Laura Best
1979 The female/male salary differential in public schools: Some lessons from San Francisco, 1879. *Economic Inquiry* 17:217-236.

Strober, Myra H., and Audri Gordon Lanford
1981 The Percentage of Women in Public School Teaching: A Cross-Section Analysis, 1850-1880. Paper presented at the annual meeting of the Social Science History Association, Nashville, Tenn., October.

Strober, Myra H., and David Tyack
1980 Why do women teach and men manage? A report on research on schools. *Signs: Journal of Women in Culture and Society* 5:494-503.

Treiman, Donald J., and Heidi I. Hartmann, eds.
1981 *Women, Work, and Wages: Equal Pay for Jobs of Equal Value.* Washington, D.C.: National Academy Press.

Tyack, David B., and Myra H. Strober
1981 Jobs and gender: A history of the structuring of educational employment by sex. In Patricia Schmuck and W. W. Charters, eds., *Educational Policy and Management: Sex Differentials.* New York: Academic Press.

Vinovskis, Maris, and Richard M. Bernard
1978 Beyond Catherine Beecher: Female education in the antebellum period. *Signs: Journal of Women in Culture and Society* 3:856-869.

Walker, Katherine E., and Margaret E. Woods
1976 *Time Use: A Measure of Household Production of Family Goods and Services.* Washington, D.C.: Center for the Family of the American Home Economics Association.

Whitehead, Ann
1979 Some preliminary notes on the subordination of women. *IDS Bulletin* 10:10-13.

Woody, Thomas
1929 *A History of Women's Education in the United States.* New York: Science Press.

9 Commentary: Strober's Theory of Occupational Sex Segregation

KAREN OPPENHEIM MASON

As Francine Blau's review of the literature in Chapter 7 makes clear, neoclassical economists have had relatively little to tell us about the causes of sex segregation in the American economy. Economists have paid far more attention to the consequences of occupational sex segregation than to its causes and, as often as not, have attributed its existence to unspecified "tastes" or amorphous institutional factors outside the economy. Even when the nature of these tastes or institutional factors has been made concrete, the explanations offered have often failed to withstand the test of logic or empirical analysis.

In light of this, Myra Strober's attempted leap beyond the neoclassical in Chapter 8 is to be applauded. By explicitly recognizing that men exploit women and derive various advantages from doing so, Strober has sought to explain the existence and persistence of sex segregation in an economy that in many other ways may operate according to neoclassical market principles. Although Strober's attempt is not entirely successful, it is nonetheless valuable. Because her theory is straightforward and provocative, it provides an important stimulus to discussion and hence

to refining our ideas about the causes of occupational segregation. In what follows, then, I begin by criticizing Strober's theory. I then discuss sociological and economic ideas that, together with Strober's theory, help explain the job segregation of the sexes in the American economy.

Strober's theory lays the ultimate blame for occupational sex segregation on the patriarchal system in which men enjoy women's sexual, child-rearing, and domestic services in the household. The immediate blame for segregation, however, is laid on employers, most of whom are men. Employers are said to strive toward two goals (goals that Strober recognizes as potentially contradictory): (1) profit maximization and (2) enforcing the economic dependency of women on men. The latter is of interest to male employers because it provides the material base for the patriarchal system, i.e., it forces women to become dependent wives and mothers (employers are said to worry about maintaining women's dependency on men in social classes other than their own because threats to patriarchy in the working class may lead to threats to patriarchy within the managerial or capitalist class). In hiring workers for their establishments, employers are thus said to concern themselves not only with minimizing their wage bill (the usual neoclassical assumption) but also with minimizing the risk that women of a given race and class will earn more than the men of that race and class and consequently will no longer be dependent on them and forced to marry them.

How do employers meet the double goals of profit maximization and of ensuring women's dependency on men? They do so, Strober argues, by offering all new jobs first to men, at a wage determined by conditions in the local labor market. These jobs are offered to women only if men refuse to take them. Strober in turn argues that men's willingness to take particular jobs depends entirely on economic considerations: Unlike their bosses, male workers are strictly profit maximizers. Thus, if they can earn more money elsewhere, male workers will turn down the jobs that a particular employer offers them. The result is that the poorer-paying jobs are left for women, the better-paying jobs having been snatched up by men. Strober's theory thus suggests why there is a wage gap between the sexes as well as occupational sex segregation.

There are several points in Strober's theory with which I agree and for which there is fairly good empirical evidence. Women in this society are without question economically disadvantaged compared with men, and this situation is hardly an accident of history or nature. There are obvious ideological (Williams and Best, 1982), legal (Kanowitz, 1969), and informal mechanisms (Bernard, 1971:88-102) that maintain the system producing this disadvantage and that continue to do so even in the face of major protest movements. Most employers today are men and as men can be suspected of having a stake in the system of male privilege (Goode, 1982). There also are at least two fairly clear historical examples of occupational abandonment and succession— instances in which men left one line of work

when new and better-paying jobs opened up, leaving the old line of work to be filled by women: school teaching and clerical work (see Oppenheimer, 1970:77-79; Davies, 1982: 56-58).

Nevertheless, while containing sound elements, Strober's theory has several problems. Although it attempts to go beyond standard neoclassical assumptions, it retains enough of these assumptions to encounter one of the most serious problems that neoclassical explanations for sex discrimination tend to face, namely, the seemingly counterfactual prediction that sex segregation will gradually disappear. Moreover, whether Strober's theory can explain the extremely high levels of occupational sex segregation observed in our economy and preserved through decades of industrial change is unclear. And for the historical period for which it seems intended, Strober's theory is in several key respects surprisingly implausible. Finally, whether an entirely new theory of occupational sex segregation is needed is open to debate. Let me elaborate on each of these points.

THE PROBLEM OF THE DEMISE OF SEX SEGREGATION

As Blau (Chapter 7 in this volume) and others (e.g., Stevenson, 1978) have noted, most neoclassical theories of occupational segregation imply that it will gradually disappear because nondiscriminatory employers or firms will be at an economic advantage over other firms and will consequently experience greater growth. This implied disappearance of segregation is problematic, however, because occupational segregation has in fact remained firmly entrenched in our economy for over a century (Oppenheimer, 1970:64-77; Gross, 1968; Williams, 1979; Matthaei, 1982:187-232).

Strober's theory suffers the same problem. In an economy in which employers typically offer new jobs to men first, withholding them from women until such time as men have refused to take them, an employer who offers jobs to women first is likely to minimize his wage bill much more successfully than will discriminatory employers, because women's wages will have been driven downward by other employers' discriminatory practices. Over time, then, any employer whose desire for profits outweighs his desire for maintaining patriarchy is likely to undercut competing firms, thereby experiencing greater growth. The long-run implication is that such firms will succeed and discriminatory firms will fail, meaning that occupational sex segregation should gradually disappear.

THE PROBLEM OF EXTREME SEGREGATION

There is considerable evidence to suggest that the occupational segregation of the sexes in our economy is extreme. Studies of detailed occupations—which aggregate jobs and hence tend to underestimate the true extent of job segregation—show that at least two-thirds of male or female workers would have to switch occupational categories for the sexes to achieve identical occupational distributions (e.g., Williams, 1979). Moreover, studies conducted at the industry or firm level (e.g., Blau, 1977; Bielby and Baron, Chapter 3 in this volume) suggest an even higher level of segregation. To be plausible, then, a theory of job segregation must readily explain not only the existence of some sex segregation in our economy but also the existence of extreme segregation. A closer look at Strober's theory raises doubts on this score.

The basic tenets of Strober's theory can be interpreted in terms of a system of job and worker queues and their mapping onto each other within the labor market. In the simplest case, there is one job queue and one worker queue. In the job queue, jobs are ordered according to wage level, while in the worker queue, workers are ordered according to gender, and within gender categories, according to "qualifications." Employers and the market then function to create a one-to-one mapping between the two queues, with the best-qualified male worker getting the best-paying job and the best-qualified female worker getting a lower-paying job than any male worker.

Although this model implies the existence of job segregation between the sexes (or at least does so if we assume a tight connection between jobs and wage rates), the magnitude of the segregation implied will depend on where the divide between the sexes falls in the job queue. If the divide happens to coincide with the divide between two different jobs, there will be perfect segregation of the sexes. If it does not, however, there will be some degree of job integration, the precise degree depending on the number of positions in the job that straddles the divide between men and women in the worker queue (if there is a very large number of positions, a substantial portion of the work force may end up employed in the integrated job).[1]

To be sure, the notion that an entire labor market can be ordered into a single job and a single worker queue is unrealistic. Nevertheless, even if we imagine labor markets consisting of multiple job and worker queues, a mapping process of the kind described here seems likely to result in some degree of job integration, possibly far more integration than is in fact observed in our economy. Only if there are separate male and female job and worker queues, as some scholars believe

---

[1] Throughout this commentary, I distinguish between a *job*—which is a particular bundle of tasks assigned to individual workers in a given industry or firm—and a *position*, which represents one slot in a given job. There are certain jobs that involve only one position (e.g., President of the United States), but most jobs involve multiple positions. Hence, it is quite possible in the queue-matching system that Strober's theory implies for the divide between men and women within the worker queue to fall in the middle of a multipositioned job, thereby producing sexual integration of that particular job.

there are (e.g., Edwards, 1975), is the high level of segregation observed in our economy likely to occur. Thus, whether the basic tenets of Strober's theory necessarily imply the existence of high levels of job segregation is unclear.

Perhaps in recognition of this possibility, Strober supplements her theory's basic tenets with a set of ad hoc arguments about the actions both employers and male workers are likely to take once a job has become substantially but not entirely occupied by men. Strober argues that employers in this situation can pursue two courses. They can either fill the remaining positions with women workers, but pay them less than the male workers in the job in order to keep the women in an economically inferior position, or they can raise the job's wage level in order to try to attract men into the remaining positions.[2] While the first of these strategies will clearly maintain women's economic inferiority to men, it will not result in sexual segregation of the job. Thus, for her theory to imply a high level of job segregation, Strober must argue that employers will prefer the second strategy to the first.

Strober offers three reasons why employers might want to raise wages in order to make heavily male jobs entirely male. The first reason, which Strober states very cursorily, is that hiring women (even at an inferior wage) "would erode the principles of patriarchy and male privilege." It is unclear why the hiring of women at lower wages would erode patriarchy, since in Strober's theory the inferior earnings of women are apparently sufficient to maintain patriarchal relations. This first reason, then, is unconvincing.

Strober's second reason for suggesting that employers will prefer to hire men is that hiring women "might violate possible societal taboos about the two sexes working together on certain jobs." Although this is an intriguing suggestion, just how common such taboos are and whether they can explain the existence of high levels of segregation in the workplace is unclear.[3] Strober herself seems to think that the enforcement of such taboos is probably not the sole explanation for why employers prefer to hire men for jobs that are already heavily male; she describes the taboos as "possible" and pertaining only to "certain jobs." Moreover, whether job segregation and physical separation are necessarily coterminous is unclear. Indeed, it is probably just as common for workers in a given job to work at some distance from each other (e.g., parts inspectors who work in different locales within a plant) or for male and female workers in distinct jobs to work in close physical proximity to each other (e.g., a female secretary and her male boss) as it is for workers in the same job to work side by side while those in different jobs work apart from each other. Thus, although research into taboos against mixed-sex work groups would be useful (as Strober notes), the ability of these taboos to explain the high level of segregation observed in our economy seems doubtful.

Strober's final reason for suggesting that employers will fill an already largely male job with men is little more compelling than the first two reasons. It is that hiring women "would . . . interfere with male bonding." I am uncertain what "male bonding" is supposed to refer to (it smacks of reductionist

---

[2] There is actually a third option that I am ignoring here, only because it does not change Strober's theory materially—that is, that the employer's attempt to hire foreign or immigrant labor.

[3] The reason for the existence of these taboos is also not entirely clear. Presumably, a fear of illicit sexual relations is what motivates any desire to ensure that men and women do not work side by side. A desire on men's part to maintain social distance from their status inferiors (women), however, might be just as important. In this case, however, the functional—i.e., job—separation of the sexes would presumably be more important than would their physical separation; and male workers would be as concerned with maintaining patriarchy as with maximizing their economic gain (contrary to Strober's main theoretical tenets).

arguments about men's psychological "needs" or "masculine instincts," the existence of which is questionable). It is hard to believe that employers operating in a competitive and largely unregulated economy (the situation that Strober seems to be referring to) would deliberately raise their wage bill simply because hiring women might "interfere with male bonding."[4] Thus, in the final analysis, the willingness of employers to fill substantially male jobs with more expensive male workers rather than turning to cheaper female workers remains unclear.

If it is implausible that employers are the ones likely to ensure that high levels of job segregation exist, then in Strober's theory it must be male workers who do so (the only other possible creators of segregation are women, but in Strober's theory women are assumed to be powerless in the labor market). Strober's description of how male workers reinforce or increase segregation is as follows: Once an occupation has been "typed" as male (a process that seems to be inevitable, though for reasons Strober does not make clear), men "will actively and collectively seek to keep women out, fearing that if women enter, they will lower the earnings of the job by accepting lower wage rates or, if they are paid the same as men, diminish patriarchal hegemony."

It is unfortunate that Strober does not explicate these ideas further, since a number of questions remain unanswered. Why, for example, must male workers fear women's incursion into "their" occupations if employers are no less interested in ensuring women's economic inferiority than the male workers are? (Indeed, Strober initially implies that employers are more concerned

about preserving the sexual "purity" of occupations than the male workers are.) And what will male workers gain by preserving "patriarchal hegemony" (which is undefined but which I assume means monopolizing all the positions in a given job)? Male workers may, of course, fear that their boss's desire to earn profits will overcome his desire to bolster the patriarchal system, thereby leading him to replace male workers with less expensive female workers. But this possibility raises a more fundamental problem with Strober's theory, namely, how employers resolve the tension between the goals of profit maximization and maintaining patriarchy. In the end, then, Strober's attempts to ensure that her theory implies the existence of a high level of job segregation raise as many questions as they answer.

THE HISTORICAL CONTEXT

Although Strober does not spell out the precise historical period her theory is supposed to cover, it seems to pertain primarily to conditions in the mid to late nineteenth and early twentieth centuries, i.e., prior to any significant state intervention into the free market economy for the purpose of regulating employment conditions.[5] In this context, Strober's theory seems implausible in three respects. First, because the econ-

---

[4] It plausibly might do so were male workers to press for the exclusion of women through organized protests or political action (something that Strober later suggests they may indeed do). In this section of her argument, however, Strober is apparently concerned only with employers' own interests, not with the necessity of giving in to certain political pressures from male workers.

[5] This is certainly the period to which the example of school teaching pertains and is also the period during which much of the sex typing found in today's labor market was established (Oppenheimer, 1970:64-120; Snyder and Hudis, 1976). Moreover, Strober's concluding remarks about the impact of equal employment opportunity legislation suggest that state intervention in the free marketplace may change the terms of her theory (although only if that intervention takes particular forms). Finally, even if Strober intends her theory to be atemporal, it is important to recognize that the sex segregation of the economy has a history and that the processes influencing the economy can change over time. For all of these reasons, I have chosen to interpret Strober's theory as though it was primarily intended to describe late nineteenth and early twentieth century conditions, even if Strober herself did not have this explicitly in mind when creating the theory.

omy to which she refers was more highly competitive than is the monopoly economy of the twentieth century, the assumption that employers would be willing or able to forgo profits in the interests of maintaining domestic patriarchy seems especially open to question. One can envision firms relatively insulated from free market pressures making this choice, but it is much harder to envision small, struggling firms in the unregulated marketplace doing so.[6]

Also relatively difficult to accept in the nineteenth-century context is the notion that employers wishing to ensure that women earn less than men would bother with the complex procedure that Strober describes, i.e., offering jobs to men first, waiting to see if all positions are filled by men, etc. In the nineteenth century, there seems to have been little feeling that employed women deserved the same wages or job opportunities as men (Smuts, 1959:110-142; Kessler-Harris, 1981:54-70). Hence, a much easier strategy for the employer wishing to pay women less would have been to do just that: pay women less than men, regardless of the job. To be sure, in some situations this strategy might have required inventing separate job titles for women and men, so that the disparity in wages between the sexes could be masked or socially justified. But employers seem perfectly capable of inventing separate job titles or pay grades when they want to (e.g., Newman, 1976). Thus, even if we are willing to believe that nineteenth-century employers were interested in ensuring that women were paid less than men, whether they would have used the system Strober describes is questionable. Indeed, because a straightforward system of wage discrimi-

nation would have helped minimize some employers' wage bills, there is every reason to think employers would have preferred this approach to the "first dibs to men" approach that Strober outlines. Only with the creation of state-enforced regulations requiring equal pay for equal work does the approach Strober describes become more plausible.

A final point that is implausible in the nineteenth-century context is the idea that male employers would try to maintain women's economic inferiority in social classes other than their own. Strober's argument here is akin to a domino theory of political change. If working-class women are allowed to become economically independent from the men of their class and are consequently freed from the need to marry and serve them, then upper-class women might be inspired to follow their working-class sisters down the road to independence. Thus, even though most male employers would never seek to have their sons marry working-class women, they are said to be motivated to maintain gender inequality in the working class out of concern for their own position vis-à-vis upper-class women.

While there may be some validity to this idea in historical periods when feminist consciousness transcends class barriers, the idea seems implausible for the late nineteenth century, when most upper-class women apparently had little sense of identification with their working-class sisters or at best had a highly patronizing identification that made clear their own social superiority. Certainly, upper-class women in this period were willing to exploit the working-class women they hired as domestic servants, often treating them with little consideration or with the sense that the servant girl had much in common with the lady of the house (Katzman, 1978:158-173). Moreover, although nineteenth-century working-class women did not earn as much money as did working-class men, in some parts of the country these women worked in large numbers (Mason et

---

[6] It is interesting that the particular occupation Strober studies is found in the public sector and hence does not involve the same competitive forces that affect private sector employment. The assumption that employers are willing (and able) to forgo profits in order to help maintain patriarchy may be more realistic in the public sector than in the private one.

al., 1978). Yet despite this, upper-class women in these areas remained firmly devoted to the "cult of domesticity" and, by implication, to the patriarchal system. Working-class women's relative independence thus seems to have posed little threat to upper-class women's commitment to remaining ladies and hence economically dependent on their husbands.[7] This makes the idea that upper-class men would have cut into profits in order to ensure the economic inferiority of working-class women seem implausible.

FURTHER PROBLEMATIC ASSUMPTIONS

Strober's theory contains two other assumptions that are questionable. The first is that the wage gap was the only or by far the most important prop for the patriarchal system in the late nineteenth and early twentieth centuries. Although Strober nowhere states this assumption explicitly, it is implicit in her argument that, in order to maintain patriarchy, employers acted to ensure the existence of a wage gap. (If patriar-

---

[7] This is not surprising, since it was working-class women who tended to accept middle-class norms about a woman's place, rather than the reverse. Most evidence suggests that when women did go to work in the late nineteenth century, they justified doing so in terms of their future domestic roles or current family needs (Smuts, 1959; Matthaei, 1982; Kessler-Harris, 1981, 1982). In other words, the working-class girl who worked in a factory or went into service did not see herself as becoming independent from a potential husband (though she did sometimes see herself gaining partial independence from her family of origin). Rather, work for most working-class girls was an interlude between childhood and marriage, during which they helped support their families, increased their prospects for a "good" marriage by being able to afford a good wardrobe, or learned skills that were argued to be helpful to their future roles as housewives and mothers. It is, therefore, not surprising that upper-class women failed to become feminists in the face of high labor force participation rates among their working-class sisters; they already enjoyed the amenities to which these working-class women aspired.

chy could be maintained in other ways, why would employers cut into profits in order to offer jobs to men first?)

Although women's inferior earnings may have contributed to the patriarchal system in nineteenth-century society, there were other institutional factors that also did so. Among these were the laws and judicial precedents that made women the legal and political (as well as economic) inferiors of men (Kanowitz, 1969:35-93) and a host of norms, customs, and culturally transmitted beliefs that taught women to orient themselves exclusively toward careers as wives and mothers and to otherwise behave in a manner consistent with their label as the "weaker" sex (Kessler-Harris, 1982:49-53). These forces seem to have been no less important than the dismal wages and dead-end jobs available to women in convincing them that marriage and motherhood were the most satisfactory careers (Matthaei, 1982:101-140; Kessler-Harris, 1982:20-72, passim). Given this, whether upper-class men would have acted against their economic self-interests in order to produce a wage gap between working-class women and men seems questionable.

The other problematic assumption implicit in Strober's theory is that, in the context of the labor market, men were more interested in maintaining the domestic division of labor between the sexes than any other aspect of the patriarchal system, including the general male prerogative to control women and receive deference from them. True, even when acting as employers or as workers, men may have been interested in ensuring that women, as a class, were kept in an economically inferior position and hence forced to participate in a patriarchal family system. But it seems equally likely that, when acting as employers or workers, men were concerned about keeping women in their place on the job, i.e., ensuring that no woman would outrank or could give orders to a (native white) man.

To the extent this was true, it makes little

sense to think that employers offered all new jobs to men first. To be sure, if a job involved authority over other workers or, given the temporary nature of most women's work (Matthaei, 1982:195-196), required continuity of employment, then employers no doubt offered it to men. However, if a job was routine, easily learned, and neither required long-term employment nor involved control over other (male) workers, then employers had no reason not to offer it first to women (Matthaei, 1982:196). Indeed, there are historical cases in the textile and clothing industries, as well as in clerical and sales jobs, in which this appears to be exactly what happened (Kessler-Harris, 1982:142-179). This makes a theory that rests on the assumption that all new jobs are offered first to men untenable.

IS A NEW THEORY OF OCCUPATIONAL SEGREGATION BY SEX NEEDED?

Strober begins her paper by arguing that existing theories of sex segregation in the workplace are inadequate. None of these theories, she states, is "capable of answering the three major questions concerning the gender designation of an occupation: its origin, its maintenance, and its change, if any." Athough Strober is narrowly correct—no single theory in existence at the time her paper was written could adequately explain the origins and persistence of sex segregation in our economy—I am not convinced that a new theory of occupational segregation is needed. The old theories, although incomplete and not always systematic, nonetheless offer considerable insight into the segregation of the workplace, especially when considered together. Indeed, in my judgment, these "old" ideas more persuasively suggest why sex segregation is both extreme and enduring than does Strober's theory. To argue this claim, I will first review three of the most important ideas in the sociological, economic, and historical literatures about the origins or maintenance

of sex segregation and will then attempt an integration of these three ideas.

The first idea or set of ideas is the most amorphous, but it is also the most important. It is that an "ideology of gender" or normative/cultural system lies behind and guides both men's and women's behavior and in so doing tends to separate the roles and activities of the sexes, including their occupational roles (Reskin and Hartmann, 1984:Ch. 2; di Leonardo, 1982). Basic precepts in the American ideology of gender include (1) the assumption that the sexes are inherently different from each other in character, temperament, and capacity; (2) the specific perception that women are naturally suited to be mothers, soothers, supporters, and/or pets, while men are suited to be adventurers, leaders, fighters, and doers (Williams and Best, 1982); (3) the evaluation that the feminine is of lower prestige (less important) than the masculine and that for men to engage in feminine activities or pursuits is consequently highly stigmatizing (more so than for women to engage in masculine activities or pursuits, although that, too, is stigmatizing); and (4) the assumption that men have the right to control women and women have the obligation to acquiesce in this control (Collins, 1971).

Because gender is usually the first social identity learned by children, precepts such as these are strongly and often unconsciously cherished by both sexes. To the extent that this is true, such precepts are likely to shape virtually every decision made by women and men that affects the jobs into which they are recruited. This means that, once a set of occupations has been "typed" or labeled as appropriate for one sex only, these labels are likely to persist over time (unless revolutionary forces disturb them).

The fact that most individuals in society are socialized to an ideology of gender that emphasizes the oppositeness of the sexes may also help explain why occupations are sex-typed or labeled in the first place. If one's social respectability and sense of self-respect depend on behaving in a manner appropriate to one's gender (and inappropriate to the other gender), then working at jobs that members of the opposite sex work at may be degrading. Matthaei (1982:194) has argued that this was a critical influence on job segregation in the nineteenth century:

> Employment in a clearly masculine job, doing a job done by other men, fortified a man's sense of manhood; competition with these men to do the job well, or unification with them against the "big man," the employer, actively expressed and measured his manhood. . . . [On the other hand,] doing a job that women also performed expressed a man's similarity with the opposite sex, showed him to be womanly and feminine.
>
> Likewise, women wished to work in jobs done by women. A woman's femininity was already threatened by her presence in the labor force, the masculine sphere. . . . If a woman was forced to seek wages outside of the home she would seek jobs which were clearly woman's work.

In other words, individual men and women, in seeking work, may have created or contributed to their own segregation by avoiding employment in sexually integrated jobs. Other ways in which the ideology of gender may have influenced the occupational segregation of the sexes in the nineteenth and early to mid twentieth centuries are noted below.

The second idea that can help explain occupational sex segregation in our society is the concept of statistical discrimination. Because this concept is reviewed elsewhere in this volume (see Chapter 7), I will not attempt a full summary here. Suffice it to note that when employers pay for the training of workers, the perception that women are more likely than men to leave the labor force in order to marry or rear children may explain why employers are reluctant to hire women for these positions. Employers may also be reluctant to hire women for supervisory positions if they believe (as they are likely to) that this violates the natural order between the sexes or places women in positions for which they are inherently unsuited. The notion of statistical discrimination thus suggests how the ideology of gender—and the reality of most women's and men's lives— is likely to influence employers' behavior and thereby contribute to the sexual segregation of the work force. While it is clear that statistical discrimination cannot explain all forms of job segregation (e.g., that which occurs among unskilled workers doing equally heavy or light tasks), this concept nonetheless points to an important process likely to contribute to the segregation of male and female workers.

The final set of ideas relevant to understanding the sex segregation of the economy derives from Edna Bonacich's (1972) theory of the split labor market. The basic tenet of this theory, which was originally created to explain the existence of ethnic antagonism, is that there often are three significant classes in conflict within capitalist labor markets, not just the two that Marx identified: (1) the capitalists or employers, who are concerned with maximizing profits (a point on which Marxist and neoclassical economists seem to agree); (2) the high-priced "established" workers who, through political organization and struggle, have managed to wrest some degree of economic security from the capitalist class and who are interested in maintaining or improving this economic security; and (3) the low-priced workers, i.e., socially identifiable groups who, for a variety of reasons, are unable or unwilling to demand as high a wage as the established workers earn and whose primary concern is simply finding a job, rather than achieving a particular level of economic security.

In Bonacich's theory, there are three basic dynamics in the split labor market: (1) the capitalists try to minimize their wage bills and consequently try to replace high-priced labor with low-priced labor; (2) the low-priced workers try to find jobs; and (3) the high-priced workers struggle to protect themselves from the incursion of the low-priced workers. Bonacich argues that established

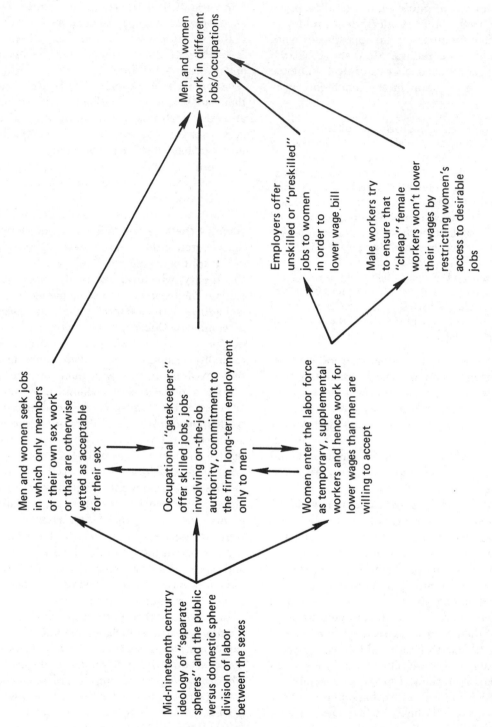

FIGURE 9-1 Schematic integration of ideas about the etiology of job segregation between the sexes.

workers use two strategies in attempting to protect themselves from the low-priced workers: exclusion and the creation of caste systems. In other words, established workers can either try to exclude low-priced labor from the labor market entirely (this is sometimes done via restrictive immigration laws) or they can try to restrict low-priced labor to a narrow range of poorly paid occupations in which they have little interest.

In the nineteenth century, women were low-priced workers compared with native white males. Women typically worked temporarily, before they were married, and usually worked as supplemental earners (in many occupations, including school teaching, the wages they earned were often insufficient to live on; Matthaei, 1982:187-232). For these reasons, women were usually willing to work for much lower wages than were men; they were also less frequently involved in labor actions (though there were notable instances in which women formed unions or participated in strikes; e.g., Dawley, 1976). While the "cheapness" of female labor did not always threaten male workers, there are well-documented cases in which it did and in which organized groups of male workers responded by attempting to ensure that their own jobs could not be taken over by women (e.g., by pressing for the passage of protective labor legislation; see Hartmann, 1976; Matthaei, 1982:217). One effect of this was to segregate women into certain poorly paid occupations that native white males were uninterested in. While the actions of male labor unions in response to the perceived threat of "cheap" female (and immigrant) labor cannot alone explain the occupational segregation of the sexes, it seems to have been one force that helped create and maintain this segregation.

Figure 9-1 depicts what I think is the most historically accurate and sociologically reasonable integration of these three sets of ideas. In the mid-nineteenth century—the period when women as well as men began entering wage work in large numbers—the ideology of women's and men's separate spheres was already well established (Kessler-Harris, 1982:20-72). For married adults the division of labor between the sexes matched this ideology, with women devoting themselves for most of their married lives to domestic work and men to work in the paid labor force. That this ideology and division of labor was already in place seems to have had three consequences. The first was that when young women and men sought work they tended to look for jobs that were known as women's or men's work, or, if the jobs were very new, that gave every indication of becoming women's or men's work (e.g., because the employer advertised for members of one sex only, as was typical in the nineteenth century). In other words, the first path through which the division of labor between the sexes and the ideology of separate spheres influenced the sexual segregation of the work force was by influencing young men's and women's own occupational choices (Matthaei, 1982:194).

Second, as the concept of statistical discrimination suggests, the ideology of separate spheres and the division of labor between the sexes also influenced the actions of various occupational "gatekeepers"— employers, schoolteachers, employment agencies, and the householders who hired domestic servants. One such influence may have been the one Strober emphasizes, namely, a tendency to favor men in the hiring process in order to maintain the primacy of wage work as part of the masculine sphere. However, occupational gatekeepers' prejudices probably had other effects on the occupational segregation of the sexes as well. Most important was a tendency to offer jobs to one sex only according to that sex's supposedly unique talents and traits or according to the structural position they were to occupy within the workplace. For example, in the period after the Civil War, women were preferred to men as domestic servants, partly because they could be hired for less money but also because they usually had prior experience. That they were normally supervised by a woman also meant that relationships between mistress and servant were much less strained than if the servant was a male (Matthaei, 1982:198).

Likewise, men were preferred for industrial jobs that involved on-the-job authority or that required a commitment to the firm or the establishment (Matthaei, 1982:196). Not only was it highly inappropriate for a woman to supervise others outside her own home, but also women typically worked only sporadically and usually quit altogether when they married. Consequently, they could not be expected to take on a responsible position that required considerable on-the-job training or at least employers were unwilling to offer them such jobs (most women may have been uninterested in them, too; see Matthaei, 1982:194). In various ways, then, the perceptions of the sexes that occupational gatekeepers developed during their socialization to the ideology of separate spheres— or by simply observing how most women and men in fact led their lives—led them to hire or direct members of each sex to the jobs that seemed appropriate for them.

The third influence of the sexual division of labor and ideology of separate spheres on the job segregation of the sexes was to cheapen the price of female labor compared with male labor. The fact that women were willing to work for less money than were most native white men can be seen as a direct outgrowth of the gender division of labor during this period of history. Because women viewed wage work as a temporary condition designed to help their families (or to pay for extras such as new clothes), they were willing to work for lower wages than were men, for whom work was a central, lifelong commitment (Matthaei, 1982:193-197). As Bonacich's theory and the historical record both suggest, this led organized groups of male workers to work for women's removal from certain jobs, something that no doubt contributed to the overall segregation of the sexes in the workplace.

The cheapness of female labor may also have contributed to the segregation of the sexes through another route. This was by encouraging employers to hire only women for jobs for which skills and on-the-job authority were minimal and the costs of labor turnover were also low. In other words, employers sought female workers not only because they perceived them to be inherently suited to particular kinds of work but also because women workers were inexpensive.[8] While it is impossible to gauge the impact this had on occupational segregation compared with the impact of male and female workers' own occupational choices and the choices of employers dictated by their perceptions of women's versus men's traits or patterns of employment, it seems clear that it contributed to the segregation of the sexes in the nineteenth and early to mid twentieth centuries.

In summary, several distinct processes stemming from the acceptance of a particular definition of masculine and feminine roles and temperaments in American society appear to underlie the segregation of the sexes within the workplace. If Matthaei (1982), Kessler-Harris (1982), and other historians are to be believed, women and men themselves helped create the segregation of the workplace by seeking jobs in which only their own sex worked. The tendency to choose a job labeled appropriate for one's own sex was exacerbated by the actions of employers and other occupational gatekeepers who, in keeping with the same precepts of masculine and feminine behaviors—and the real differences between women's and

---

[8] Marxist theorists also argue that employers hired men and women for different jobs as part of a strategy of labor market segmentation designed to keep the working class weak by creating divisions within it (e.g., Edwards, 1975). As Strober notes, while employers may indeed have used this strategy, why they chose gender as one of the bases on which to segment the labor market is not readily explained by their desires to weaken the power of the working class.

men's motives for working and patterns of employment—frequently sought workers of only one sex for particular jobs. Finally, organized groups of male workers further reinforced the segregation of the sexes by acting to ensure that women could not enter their occupations and thereby lower their wages. Because individual workers, employers, and organized groups of male workers all acted in ways that produced a separation of the sexes within the workplace, the extreme degree to which the American economy is sexually segregated should not be surprising. Nor should the incredibly slow speed at which sex segregation has changed over the past century (Williams, 1979).

The main implication of the views I have presented for the future of occupational segregation between the sexes is very similar to the point with which Strober ends her paper. Occupational segregation is unlikely to disappear or even lessen appreciably unless major revisions occur in our ideology of gender and the division of labor between the sexes. To be sure, some changes in gender ideology and in the male-female division of labor have occurred during the past four decades (e.g., Mason et al., 1976; Waite, 1981). And there are starting to be some noticeable changes in occupational segregation as well (see Chapter 2 in this volume), perhaps as a result of the ideological shifts. However, unless we give up our idea that men and women are inalienable opposites, more dissimilar than alike, we are unlikely to see the disappearance of occupational segregation between the sexes. Ultimately, job segregation is just a part of the generally separate (and unequal) lives that women and men in our society lead, and, unless the overall separateness is ended, the separateness within the occupational system is unlikely to end, either.

ACKNOWLEDGMENTS

I thank Barbara Reskin and Louise Tilly for their helpful comments on an earlier version of this paper and Madelon Weber and Mary Scott for their typing assistance.

REFERENCES AND BIBLIOGRAPHY

Bernard, Jessie
1971 Women and the Public Interest. Chicago: Aldine-Atherton.

Blau, Francine D.
1977 Equal Pay in the Office. Lexington, Mass.: Lexington Books.

Bonacich, Edna
1972 "A theory of ethnic antagonism: The split labor market." American Sociological Review 37:547-559.

Collins, Randall
1971 "A conflict theory of sexual stratification." Social Problems 19:3-21.

Davies, Margery W.
1982 Woman's Place Is at the Typewriter: Office Work and Office Workers, 1870-1930. Philadelphia: Temple University Press.

Dawley, Alan
1976 Class and Community: The Industrial Revolution in Lynn. Cambridge, Mass.: Harvard University Press.

de Leonardo, Micaela
1982 "Occupational segregation and cultural analysis." Washington, D.C.: Paper presented at the Workshop on Job Segregation by Sex, Committee on Women's Employment and Related Social Issues, National Research Council, May 25.

Edwards, Richard C.
1975 "The social relations of production in the firm and labor market structure." Pp. 3-26 in Richard C. Edwards, Michael Reich, and David M. Gordon, eds., Labor Market Segmentation. Lexington, Mass.: D. C. Heath.

Goode, William J.
1982 "Why men resist." Pp. 131-150 in Barrie Thorne with Marilyn Yalom, eds., Rethinking the Family: Some Feminist Questions. New York: Longman.

Gross, Edward
1968 "Plus ça change . . .? The sexual structure of occupations over time." Social Problems 16:198-208.

Hartmann, Heidi
1976 "Capitalism, patriarchy, and job segregation by sex." Pp. 137-169 in Martha Blaxall and Barbara Reagan, eds., Women and the Workplace: The Implications of Occupational Segregation. Chicago: University of Chicago Press.

Kanowitz, Leo
1969 Women and the Law: The Unfinished Revolution. Albuquerque: University of New Mexico Press.

Katzman, David M.
1978 Seven Days a Week: Women and Domestic

Service in Industrializing America. Urbana: University of Illinois Press.

Kessler-Harris, Alice
1981   Women Have Always Worked: A Historical Overview. Old Westbury, N.Y.: The Feminist Press.

1982   Out to Work: A History of Wage-Earning Women in the United States. New York: Oxford University Press.

Mason, Karen Oppenheim, John L. Czajka, and Sara Arber
1976   "Change in U.S. women's sex-role attitudes, 1964-1974." American Sociological Review 41 (August): 573-596.

Mason, Karen Oppenheim, Maris A. Vinovskis, and Tamara K. Hareven
1978   "Women's work and the life course in Essex County, Massachusetts, 1880." Pp. 187-216 in Tamara K. Hareven, ed., Transitions: The Family and the Life Course in Historical Perspective. New York: Academic Press.

Matthaei, Julie A.
1982   An Economic History of Women in America: Women's Work, the Sexual Division of Labor, and the Development of Capitalism. New York: Schocken Books.

Newman, Winn
1976   "The policy issues. Presentation III." Pp. 265-272 in Martha Blaxall and Barbara Reagan, eds., Women and the Workplace: The Implications of Occupational Segregation. Chicago: University of Chicago Press.

Oppenheimer, Valerie Kincade
1970   The Female Labor Force in the United States:

Demographic and Economic Factors Governing Its Growth and Changing Composition. Berkeley: University of California, Institute of International Studies, Population Monograph Series, No. 5.

Reskin, Barbara, and Heidi I. Hartmann, eds.
1984   Men's Work, Women's Work: Sex Segregation on the Job. Committee on Women's Employment and Related Social Issues. Washington, D.C.: National Academy Press.

Smuts, Robert W.
1959   Women and Work in America. New York: Columbia University Press.

Snyder, David, and Paula M. Hudis
1976   "Occupational income and the effects of minority competition and segregation: A reanalysis and some new evidence." American Sociological Review 41(April):209-234.

Stevenson, Mary Huff
1978   "Wage differences between men and women: Economic theories." Pp. 89-107 in Ann H. Stromberg and Shirley Harkess, eds., Women Working: Theories and Facts in Perspective. Palo Alto, Calif.: Mayfield Publishing Co.

Waite, Linda J.
1981   "U.S. women at work." Population Bulletin 36(2).

Williams, Gregory
1979   "The changing U.S. labor force and occupational differentiation by sex." Demography 16(February):73-87.

Williams, John E., and Deborah L. Best
1982   Measuring Sex Stereotypes: A Thirty-Nation Study. Beverly Hills, Calif.: Sage Publications.

10 Work Experience, Job Segregation, and Wages

MARY CORCORAN, GREG J. DUNCAN, *and*
MICHAEL PONZA

Women are a vital part of today's labor force, and work is clearly an important part of their lives. Women constituted more than two-fifths of the labor force in 1978, and almost 60 percent of all women aged 18 to 64 were employed in 1978. Almost all women work at some point in their lives, and their earnings are often necessary to ensure adequate family support. In 1978 nearly two-thirds of the women working were either presently unmarried or married to men earning less than $10,000 per year (in 1977).[1]

There is considerable evidence that men's and women's work participation patterns differ—with men working continuously after completing school and women moving in and out of the labor force to accommodate family and child-rearing duties. Women earn considerably less than men do. Since 1930 the median salary of full-time, full-year women workers has been about 60 percent of the median salary of men who work full time, full year. Women and men also have very different occupations. Treiman and Hartmann (1981) show that 70 percent of the men and 54 percent of the women in the labor force are concentrated in occupations dominated by their own sex. Unlike men, women are heavily concentrated in a few job categories—secretarial work, sales, teaching, nursing, and various service occupations.

The most prominent economic explanation linking labor supply patterns and wages is human capital theory.[2] Human capital itself is defined as worker skills or qualifications acquired through schooling or on-the-job training. An individual worker's stock of human capital can be increased by the process of investment. Investments have an opportunity cost (in terms of forgone earnings as well as of the direct costs of training) and a return (in the form of higher subsequent earnings). Human capital theory particu-

This paper was supported by a grant from the Alfred P. Sloan Foundation.

[1] These figures are taken from U.S. Department of Labor, Women's Bureau, *10 Facts on Women Workers*, Washington, D.C., August 1979.

[2] Human capital theory is quite similar to the functionalist theory of Davis and Moore. It has been argued that this theory underlies much of the empirical work in social stratification (see Horan, 1978).

171

larly emphasizes investment in formal schooling (Becker, 1975) and in on-the-job training (Mincer, 1974). Workers are presumed to choose freely among jobs with different amounts of training, and wages are presumed to reward past investments in education and training in a similar way for all workers.

In recent years human capital theory has been expanded to deal with the structure of female wages. Some of its proponents have argued that the sex division of labor within the home generates sex differences in patterns of investment in work-related human capital and that this in turn generates sex differences in wages and the sex segregation of occupations (Mincer and Polachek, 1974; Polachek, 1976, 1979, 1981; Mincer and Ofek, 1982). These arguments have focused particularly on sex differences in patterns of labor force participation.

This paper investigates human capital theory's predictions about the relationships between patterns of work, wages, and job segregation. The paper is in four major parts. The first summarizes human capital theoretical models. In the next section we use 13 years of data from the Panel Study of Income Dynamics (PSID) to describe and compare men's and women's patterns of work participation. These comparisons focus on aspects of lifetime work experience that are hypothesized to be important for women— duration of work and nonwork periods, the extent to which labor market experience involves part-time work, and the sex typing of experience (i.e., the extent to which past experience was in female-dominated occupations). The third section reviews past research on the extent to which different aspects of work experience influence wages and sex typing of a person's current job, and it also includes the results from our own analyses of these issues based on 13 years of PSID data. Finally, we discuss the theoretical and policy conclusions drawn from our reviews of past research and from our own research.

WORK HISTORY, WAGES, AND JOB SEGREGATION: THEORETICAL MODELS

Work Experience and Earnings

In the human capital model, investments in on-the-job training are considered to be critical determinants of wages (see Becker, 1975; Ben-Porath, 1967; Mincer, 1974; and Rosen, 1972). On-the-job training has a cost, since time spent in training is assumed to be time diverted from production, and production presumably determines earnings. On-the-job training also has a return in the form of higher later earnings. The following function describes this hypothetical relationship:

$$E_t = E_s + \sum_{i=0}^{t-1} rC_i = Y_t + C_t, \quad (1)$$

where E_t is earnings capacity in year t, E_s is earnings that would be received in the absence of any postschool training, C_i is the dollar cost of investments in human capital in the ith year, Y_t is earnings in the tth year, C_t is dollar cost of investments in the tth year, and r is rate of return to investments in human capital.

If we assume that total benefits of an investment increase as the payoff period increases and that the marginal costs of investments are upwardly sloping in a single time period, it can be shown that a profile of investment ratios (C_i/E_i) that are large at first and then decline over time maximizes the present value of expected lifetime earnings (see Ben-Porath, 1967). That is, the proportion of one's earnings capacity invested in on-the-job training will be high in the early years and then will decline rapidly.

The human capital model assumes that workers freely choose among a variety of jobs—each with a different combination of training and productive work. It generally views training and productive work as mutually exclusive activities, and, thus, according to the model, employers will pay less for jobs with training than for similar jobs that do not provide training. An implication of the model is that wages grow with experience because workers are acquiring additional skills as they increase their experience and so their wages grow not just because of seniority.

Labor Force Withdrawals and Wages

Mincer and Polachek (1974) extend the human capital model to account for the possible depreciation of human capital that may result from the discontinuity of women's work experience. They argue that during periods of labor force withdrawal for child-bearing and child-rearing, prolonged nonparticipation in the paid labor market can cause the skills acquired at school and work to become less valuable.

The following function adjusts the basic human capital wage model to account for depreciation or obsolescence effects:

$$E_t = E_s + \sum_{i=1}^{t-1} (rC_i - \delta_i E_i), \qquad (2)$$

where E_t, E_s, r, C_i are defined as in Eq. (1), δ_i is the depreciation rate of human capital in year i, and E_i is earnings capacity in year i.

The total benefits of investments in on-the-job training increase with the length of the payoff period but decline with the length of periods of nonparticipation that follow investments. This suggests that optimal investment patterns will differ depending on the continuity of market activities. Continuously employed workers should concentrate investments early in their careers. Workers who interrupt their work careers will defer investments in on-the-job training until they reenter the labor market after completing these activities so as to minimize the loss from depreciation. Since such workers have a shorter payoff period, their overall volume of investment should be lower than that of workers who remain continuously in the labor force.

Mincer and Ofek (1982) have since revised this initial model to account for "restoration" or "repair" of depreciated human capital. They argue that the "reconstruction of (previously eroded) occupational skills is more efficient than the construction of new human capital." That is, it costs less to repair human capital than to build it. This restoration phenomenon leads Mincer and Ofek to distinguish the short-run and long-run consequences of nonparticipation. In the short run (say, the first year following an interruption), one would expect sharply lower wages than those received just prior to the interruption, followed by a period of rapid wage growth during which human capital is restored. Thus, the long-run effects on wages of nonwork time may be considerably smaller than the short-run effects.

Since the empirical work of Mincer and Ofek and our own replication of it show that wage "rebound" following an interruption is an important phenomenon, it is useful to consider alternative explanations of it. Corcoran (1979) and Corcoran and Duncan (1979) suggest that time out may lead to a temporary reduction in wages because of temporary mismatches between worker skills and jobs. Women workers lack complete information about job opportunities when they do return to the labor force, and it takes time for them to discover jobs that are best matched to their skills. Employers also have imperfect information about the productivity of their new employees, and the learning process for them is time-consuming.[3] One

---

[3] Morgensen (1978), Jovanovic (1979), and Prescott and Visscher (1980), for example, explain that earnings rise with experience with a firm because firms learn about worker productivities in various jobs (instead of workers' acquiring skills through experience). This learning process results in the more senior workers being matched more accurately to jobs commensurate with their skills than less experienced workers. Better job matches allow the senior workers to exhibit higher productivity on average, and if the market rewards productivity, these differences may account for their higher average earnings.

common mechanism for this sorting process is to hire new workers in at low wages but then to promote them rapidly as they successfully complete their probationary periods. In neither of these cases are the workers "restoring" depreciated skills in the Mincer-Ofek sense. Wage increases accompany improved information of employees about their job opportunities or improved information of employers about the productivity of their employees.

Note that Mincer and Ofek have altered the original Mincer and Polachek model substantially. Since depreciated human capital can be restored, it no longer follows that intermittent workers will necessarily defer investments in on-the-job training until all interruptions are over. This decision will depend on the relative sizes of the depreciation and restoration effects.[4] Similarly, the relative sizes of these two effects will also determine the long-run wage costs of labor force withdrawals. If these long-run costs are small, then depreciation may account for little of the wage gap between men and women.

Part-Time Work Experience and Wages

Women are considerably more likely than men are to work in part-time jobs, a fact that may lead to considerable differences in the amount of on-the-job training women acquire and, therefore, in their relative wage growth. The most general human capital theories (Heckman, 1976; Blinder and Weiss,

1976) do not make unambiguous predictions about the effect of part-time work on human capital investment and wages, but there are reasons for believing that less training is acquired in part-time work than in full-time work. First, because part-time work means fewer hours in the labor market than full-time work does, women who expect to work part time in the future have a shorter expected work life and hence less incentive to invest in on-the-job training. In this case both the overall volume of investment and the rate of investment would be lower for those who plan to work part time than for those who plan to work full time. If current part-time work patterns are associated with the likelihood of future part-time work, then current part-time workers will be making fewer investments. Second, if employers suspect that part-time workers are more likely to leave than are full-time workers, they might restrict training opportunities in part-time work. Employers would be most likely to restrict opportunities for firm-specific training. Finally, just as it is argued that skills depreciate during periods of nonwork, skills could depreciate *more* (or appreciate less) during part-time work than during full-time work, since part-time work involves fewer hours of work (i.e., more hours of nonwork). The depreciation from nonuse would be greater if the nature of part-time work precluded workers from maintaining their market skills. If formal training is scheduled when part-time workers are not at work, then there will be less wage growth resulting from the acquisition of new skills for them.

Two sources of data with crude direct measures of on-the-job training do show a positive relationship between work hours and training. Duncan and Hoffman (1979) found with the 1976 wave of the PSID that adult workers aged 18 to 64 who worked less than 20 hours per week reported training periods attached to their jobs that were only about half as long as those of workers working between 40 and 50 hours. Stafford and Duncan

---

[4] A qualification suggested to us by Jacob Mincer is necessary here: For the intermittent worker, each interruption carries with it a positive probability of not returning to the labor market. Thus, the expected payoff period is diminished by more than the interruption each time it looms. So although wage loss due to depreciation can be made up, the intermittent worker's decision about whether and when to invest will depend jointly on the relative sizes of the depreciation and restoration effects and on the probability of returning to work.

(1979) found qualitatively similar, although less statistically significant, differences in training by labor supply for workers in the 1975-1976 Time Use Study.

Labor Force Withdrawals and Job Segregation: Human Capital Explanations

The 1974 *Economic Report of the President* speculated that sex differences in patterns of work participation may be the cause of the sex segregation of jobs. This line of reasoning has been extensively developed by Zellner (1975) and Polachek (1976, 1979, 1981).[5] Since Polachek's explanation subsumes Zellner's model, we will concentrate on his model in the following discussion. Polachek (1981) defines atrophy as the loss of earnings potential that occurs when skills are not continuously used. He shows that if the cost of labor force withdrawals (the atrophy rate) varies across occupations, and if lifetime labor force participation differs across individuals, then a worker will choose "that occupation which imposes the smallest penalty, given his desired lifetime participation." This model treats the "lifetime as a unit."[6] Thus, this model implicitly assumes that workers tend to work in the same sort of occupation throughout their lives or at least over long periods of time. Lifetime work participation is assumed to be exogenously determined, and atrophy rates are assumed to vary across occupations.

This model provides a human capital explanation for the sex segregation of the labor market. If work skills do atrophy during withdrawals from the labor force, then it is rational for women who expect to take time out from the labor force to work in fields where there is less chance of atrophy—i.e., in fields with low depreciation rates but also with low returns to experience. Thus, such women will experience less atrophy than will women who expect more continuous work participation. By selecting jobs that are easy to leave and reenter, women can thus more easily combine the dual demands of career and family. Polachek's model can explain sex segregation only if typically "female" jobs are those where there is the least atrophy. Note that if depreciated skills can be restored (as Mincer and Ofek argue), this weakens the force of Polachek's arguments.

Webster's defines atrophy as "a wasting away or progressive decline." Thus, the casual reader might assume that Polachek's atrophy rate is equivalent to Mincer and Polachek's depreciation rate. But atrophy, as defined by Polachek, picks up two things—depreciation (i.e., reduction in work skills due to nonuse) and forgone appreciation (i.e., the loss in expected earnings growth due to missing a year of work).[7]

Depreciation and the growth of earnings with experience are quite different processes. Depreciation implies that the level of work skills is lower following an interruption

---

[5] England (1981, 1982) provides an extensive discussion of these models. This section is informed by her work.

[6] Polachek notes that "this assumption can be relaxed by posing the problem within a dynamic control framework" but goes on to say that "even within such a framework the same conclusions hold for occupations chosen at a given stage of the life cycle" (Polachek, 1981, p. 64). Note that this relaxation still implies occupational immobility over a life-cycle stage.

[7] We are grateful to Siv Gustafson for first pointing out this distinction to us in a personal conversation in 1978. England (1981, 1982) is the first author who clearly makes this distinction in a published paper. England first referred to the loss in expected earnings growth as "forgone appreciation," and provides an excellent discussion of Polachek's models.

Zellner's explanation of the sex segregation of occupations rests solely on forgone appreciation. England (1981) points out: "Zellner assumes that occupations can be divided into those that offer high initial salaries and flat earnings profiles and into those with low initial salaries and steep earnings profiles. Women, because of their shorter expected work lives, will be more likely to maximize lifetime earnings in the occupations with high initial salaries and flat wage growth—i.e., in 'female' occupations."

than it was just prior to that interruption. If this earnings loss is long lasting, it is obvious why women who expect prolonged labor force withdrawals should enter fields with low depreciation rates. Polachek's model also implies that women who expect prolonged withdrawals should enter fields with high initial salaries but fairly flat earnings growth rates. This second decision only makes sense if we assume that, all else equal, jobs with high earnings growth pay less initially than jobs without such earnings growth. (England [1981] makes this point quite clearly.)

To summarize, Polachek provides an ingenious human capital explanation for job segregation. If Polachek's general model is correct, then women who anticipate prolonged nonwork time should work in fields with low atrophy rates and should experience less depreciation and less wage growth than do otherwise similar workers. Polachek's model also has several implications for the nature of typically female and male occupations. First, since women's choice of a "female" or "male" occupation reflects lifetime participation plans, we would expect that the sex typing of women's occupations change little over a prolonged period of time. In addition, we should find that depreciation and/or earnings growth will be lower in "female" occupations and that women who expect discontinuous careers will choose "female" rather than "male" occupations because discontinuity is penalized less. Because of this choice, women with discontinuous work careers will be concentrated in "female" occupations. Occupational immobility and low wage growth are also predicted by any job segregation model that presumes that women are locked into a set of female-dominated jobs that do not provide productivity-enhancing experience.

WOMEN'S WORK AND OCCUPATIONAL HISTORIES

The human capital models summarized above predict that women's low wages result from a low overall volume of work, inter-

mittent work participation, and part-time work. Most job segregation models, human capital or otherwise, implicitly assume considerable immobility between "female" and "male" jobs. As a first step toward testing these models, we use 13 years of data from the PSID to assess the accuracy of these descriptions of women's work behavior and occupational immobility.

Patterns of Labor Supply, 1967 to 1979

Every year PSID respondents report their own and their spouse's work hours. Corcoran et al. (in press) examined labor supply for adult men and women, aged 23 to 47 in the first year of the panel, who lived in their own households.[8] As expected, there were dramatic differences between the sexes in the frequency and regularity of work and in the extent of part-time or part-year work. Differences between the races were much less dramatic within the groups of men and women. Black women acquired more experience than white women did, while black men acquired less of it than did white men.

Between 70 and 80 percent of the two groups of women were absent from the labor force for at least 1 of the 13 years.[9] The

---

[8] In terms of the PSID sample, this group consists of all individuals who were household heads or wives in each of the 13 years. Eliminated from this analysis are children and the small group of other relatives of the household head (e.g., brother or sister). The lower age restriction was imposed to avoid sample selection problems associated with the decision to leave the parental home and form one's own household. The upper age restriction eliminated from the sample individuals who would have reached the early retirement age of 62 by the end of the panel period. The results are reported in Corcoran et al. (in press).

[9] We used 250 hours during a calendar year to define whether an individual was in or out of the labor force during that year, and we use 1,500 hours to separate part- from full-time workers. This procedure has its disadvantages. An individual with a 40-hour-per-week job who drops out of the labor force altogether for six months out of a calendar year will be classified as a part-time worker during that year without having a spell of nonwork. In one sense this individual was a

comparable fractions for white and black men were about 10 and 16 percent, respectively. Even when they did work, women were much less likely to work full time. Less than one-tenth of these adult women worked full-time during the entire 13-year period.

The total volume of work experience acquired by men was much higher than for women. On average, men worked in almost twice as many of the years as women did, in nearly twice as many weeks as women did, and for nearly three times as many hours as women did during this period.

The part-time nature of the work of women was highlighted when we examined hours worked per week and weeks worked per year during the work spells. The average work week of men exceeded 40 hours, amounting to 46 hours for white men and 43 hours for black men. In contrast, white and black women averaged 36 hours per week during work spells. Similar differences showed up in the number of weeks worked per year, with men averaging 47 weeks and women averaging 42 weeks. As a result, the total number of hours averaged by men during their work spells was almost twice as high as for women during their spells.

Patterns of Occupational Segregation, 1975 to 1979

Both Polachek's (1981) model and segmented labor market models assume little mobility between "male" and "female" occupations over a prolonged period of time. Yet England (1982) reports that the correlation between percent female in detailed census occupation coding of first job and percent female in detailed coding of 1967 job is only .39 for women aged 30 to 44 years in 1967. This suggests there may be considerable mobility between "male" and "female" job sectors.

We further tested this assumption of intersectoral immobility by calculating patterns of occupational segregation over the years 1975 to 1979. Our measure of occupational segregation is based on 2-digit occupation and 2-digit industry categories. Thus, it has the advantage of accounting for both occupational and industrial segmentation by sex.[10] We define a female-dominated job as an industry-occupation group with more than 50 percent women workers. Industry-occupation groups with less than 50 percent female workers are designated male-dominated jobs.

To investigate the dynamics of job segregation over the period from 1975 to 1979, we selected a sample of women aged 23 to 57 in 1975 who worked in the first and last years of that period and who may or may not have worked during the three years in between.[11] About 70 percent of white women workers held female-dominated jobs in 1975. If job segregation was completely rigid, then we would expect to observe that same fraction spending *all* of their working years in jobs dominated by women. Table 10-1 shows that this is clearly not the case. Only half of the white women spent all of their working years in the five years between 1975 and 1979 in jobs dominated by women. Less than one-sixth of these white women spent all of their working years in jobs dominated by men, *leaving more than one-third who switched job types at least once.* Switches between female- and male-dominated jobs for black women were almost as common—

---

full-time worker and in another sense this individual experienced a spell of nonwork during that year. Our measure considered part-time workers to be those either working a limited number of hours per week or those working during only part of the year. Our measure of nonwork spells required that such spells be long enough ·to take an individual away from work for virtually an entire year.

---

[10] Our procedure for determining whether a given job was "female-dominated" or "male-dominated" is detailed in Corcoran et al. (in press).

[11] As before, the sample consists of household heads and wives in this age range and thus excludes a small number of adults who are related to the head of the household in some other way.

TABLE 10-1   Dynamics of Occupational Segregation

	Subgroup					
	Women Who Worked at Least 250 Hours in 1975 and 1979			Men		
Occupational Change	White	Black	All	White	Black	All
Fraction spending *all* working years in female-dominated jobs[a]	.51 (871)	.61 (538)	.52 (1,409)	.07 (1,563)	.18 (606)	.08 (2,169)
Fraction spending *all* working years in male-dominated jobs	.15 (871)	.09 (538)	.14 (1,409)	.79 (1,563)	.67 (606)	.78 (2,169)
Fraction switching at least once in either direction	.34 (871)	.31 (538)	.34 (1,409)	.15 (1,563)	.18 (606)	.16 (2,169)
Fraction of those in female-dominated jobs initially who switched to male-dominated jobs	.31 (647)	.25 (423)	.30 (1,070)	.60 (207)	.37 (106)	.56 (313)
Fraction of those in male-dominated jobs initially who switched to female-dominated jobs	.44 (224)	.55 (115)	.45 (339)	.09 (1,300)	.13 (456)	.09 (1,756)

NOTES: Table reads: 51 percent of the 871 white women who worked at least 250 hours in 1975 and 1979 spent all of their working time in female-dominated jobs.

The number of observations is given in parentheses below each estimate.

[a] A job is designated as female dominated if the percentage of women comprising it is greater than or equal to 50. Otherwise it is designated as male dominated.

SOURCE: Panel Study of Income Dynamics.

31 percent of the black women were coded as switching from one type to the other.

These figures on the extent of switching between job types mix together both kinds of changes. A more relevant statistic on the issue of whether women who take female-dominated jobs remain in them is the fraction of women who began in female-dominated jobs and switched out of them. That fraction is 31 percent for white women and 25 percent for black women.

These figures on switches between job types deserve careful scrutiny. On the one hand, they are likely to understate the true amount of movement between job types because the time span over which such changes can be observed is limited to only five years.[12]

In addition, our classification procedure for identifying female- and male-dominated occupations is a crude one and undoubtedly misses some true switches that would be caught with a more refined set of occupational and industrial codes. On the other hand, errors in the coding of occupation and industry may create the appearance of a switch when in fact there was none.[13] It is impossible to say whether the net effect of these considerations is to increase or to decrease the estimated extent of switching be-

[12] Women who worked continuously in the same sector between 1975 and 1979 but switched in 1980 or had switched in 1974 are classified here as persistent residents in one sector. Also, while most of the women in this sample worked in every one of the five years,

some did not work in some of the middle three years, giving them fewer than five years in which a switch can be observed.

[13] Appendix Table B.1 in Corcoran et al. (in press) sheds some light on this by showing comparable mobility figures for the case when male-dominated jobs are defined as less than 40 percent female, and female-dominated jobs are defined as greater than 60 percent female. Less mobility is found with this more restrictive definition, but the extent of mobility is still substantial.

tween job sectors. However, it is almost certainly true that the extent of switching is substantial, a fact that is inconsistent with Polachek's assumption of occupational immobility and with any other labor market model based on rigid segmentation by sex. This result also suggests that analysts should be wary of using a woman's current occupation as a measure of her past occupational history.

WORK HISTORY AND WAGES: EMPIRICAL EVIDENCE

The Depreciation Effect

Empirical evidence on whether depreciation lowers wages consists mostly of cross-sectional data where earnings of different individuals with different work histories are compared, after statistical adjustment to make the individuals as similar as possible. This evidence has produced contradictory results about the size of the depreciation effect— i.e., about the extent to which wages decline with time out of the labor force once one controls experience and tenure. Mincer and Polachek (1974) reported that 1967 wages dropped by 1.2 percent per year out of work for white married women aged 30 to 44 with children. Sandell and Shapiro (1978) replicated the Mincer-Polachek analysis after correcting for coding errors in women's reports of employment behavior. They reported that wages declined only 0.4 percent per year of nonparticipation and that this effect was insignificant. Corcoran (1979) replicated the Mincer-Polachek analysis for a national sample of wives aged 30 to 44 with children, taken from the 1975 PSID and obtained similar results to those of Mincer and Polachek. But Corcoran (1979) and Corcoran and Duncan (1979) also reported that the decline in wages was much smaller (0.6 percent per year out of work) for working women in a broader age range (18 to 64 years). These results suggest that wages of married women aged 30 to 44 are more affected by labor force withdrawals than are wages of women in a broader age range.

A recent paper by Mincer and Ofek (1982) suggests that some of these inconsistencies in past research arise because cross-sectional analyses tend to confound the short-run and long-run effects of nonparticipation. Mincer and Ofek use eight years of National Longitudinal Survey (NLS) data to explore how time out of the labor force affected wage growth for a sample of women aged 30 to 44 in 1967 who were married sometime during 1967 to 1974. They found a large short-run loss in wages immediately following an interruption (ranging from 3.6 to 8.9 percent per year out of work), followed by a period of rapid wage growth. Estimates of long-run wage losses were moderae (0.4 to 1.1 percent per year out of work). A replication and extension of this analysis was conducted by Corcoran et al. (in press) using 13 years of information from the PSID. Short-run depreciation effects were estimated to range from 2.5 to 4.7 percent per year depending on the exact form of the model and on the definition of the sample when the age range was identical to the one used by Mincer and Ofek (30 to 44), and the effects were estimated to be similar in magnitude when the age range was extended to between 23 and 47 years. Long-run depreciation was estimated to be between 1.0 and 1.5 percent per year in the replication, with some of these coefficients not statistically significant at conventional levels.

This recent work reconciles the disparate estimates of depreciation. The past analyses of wage effects of withdrawals based on cross-sectional data are likely to pick up both short-run and long-run effects. Married working women aged 30 to 44 who have interrupted work are likely to have recently returned to the labor force, and so short-run effects may have a large weight in analyses run on this group (e.g., that of Mincer and Polachek, 1974). Analyses run on women in a broader age range (e.g., that of Corcoran, 1979; and that of Corcoran and Duncan, 1979) are likely to put more weight on the long-run effect and so will provide lower estimates of depreciation.

The Restoration Effect

In their original paper, Mincer and Polachek (1974) suggested that the optimal timing of investment in on-the-job training would differ depending on the continuity of market activities. In particular, workers who interrupt their work careers for nonmarket activities will defer investments in on-the-job training until they reenter the labor market after completing these activities so as to minimize the loss from depreciation. Mincer and Ofek (1982) have considerably revised this hypothesis by arguing that "depreciated" or "eroded" human capital can be cheaply and rapidly "restored" soon after labor market entry. They show that postinterruption wages grow at roughly 2.5 percent per year of experience, on average, and that growth rates in the first year following an interruption range from 5.8 to 6.4 percent per year depending on the exact specification of their model. This growth rapidly erases estimated short-term losses from the depreciation associated with short spells out of the labor force and is much larger than the wage growth of comparable continuous workers. They further demonstrate that growth in tenure accounts for less than half of this wage growth and interpret this to mean that the remainder is due to growth (repair) of general training.

The nature and causes of wage rebound following work interruptions are crucial elements in understanding the wage consequences and job choice of female labor supply patterns. If depreciation is quickly repaired, it no longer follows that intermittent workers will defer investments in on-the-job training until all interruptions are completed. Thus, the observation that the wages of women grow more slowly in the years following the completion of schooling because of the reduced incentives to invest in human capital may no longer hold. It also weakens the plausibility of the reasoning that

intermittent workers will concentrate in female jobs.

The Mincer and Ofek (1982) estimates of restoration came from the estimation of a cross-sectional wage equation. Corcoran et al. (in press) were able to use more complete information about the amount and sex typing of work experience before and after work interruptions and also estimated a wage-*change* equation—a specification with several statistical properties that make it preferred to a wage-*level* equation. Since this work has only recently been completed and addresses many of the important issues considered in this paper, we summarize our analysis here. Readers interested in the details are referred to Corcoran et al. (in press).

We selected the adult women in the PSID sample and used the 13 years of work history obtained for them. We developed our wage equation by identifying the first (F) and last (L) wage observation for all women who worked at least 2 of the 13 years.[14] A cross-sectional wage equation at time F would be of the form:

$$lnW_{iF} = \alpha_{0F} + \alpha_{1F}S_{iF} + \alpha_{2F}e_{0iF} + \alpha_{3F}h_{0iF} + \mu_F X_{iF} + \pi_F Z_{iF} + \theta_{iF}, \quad (3)$$

where W_{iF} is the wage rate of the ith individual in time F, α_{0F} is a constant in time F, S_{iF} is the education level of the ith individual in time F, e_{0iF} is years of work experience for the ith individual in time F, h_{0iF} is years of nonwork for the ith individual in time F, X_{iF} is a vector of *observed* productivity-related characteristics for the ith individual in time F, Z_{iF} is a vector of *unobservable* individual-specific productivity-related characteristics, workplace characteristics, and labor market differences for the ith individual in time F, and θ_{iF} is the

---

[14] Throughout this section we use 250 hours as the cutoff point to distinguish individuals in the labor force from those out of the labor force. The sensitivity of these results to change in this definition are detailed in Corcoran et al. (in press).

stochastic disturbance term for the ith individual in time F.

PSID information on the work history between F and L can be used to distinguish: e_L, years of work experience accumulated between F and L *since* the last completed interruption; e^*, years of work experience accumulated between F and L *prior to* the most recent completed interruption; h_L, years of nonwork between F and L *during* most recent completed interruption; and h^*, years of nonwork accumulated between F and L *prior to* most recent completed interruption.

The cross-sectional wage relationship at time L (allowing the parameters to change) is given by

$$lnW_{iL} = \alpha_{0L} + \alpha_{1L}S_{iL} +$$
$$\alpha_{2L}e_{0iF} + \alpha_{3L}h_{0iF} +$$
$$\alpha_4 e^*_i + \alpha_5 e_{Li} +$$
$$\alpha_6 h^*_i + \alpha_7 h_{Li} +$$
$$\mu_L X_{iL} + \pi_L Z_{iL} + \theta_{iL}. \quad (4)$$

The short-run depreciation and rebound effects are given by parameters α_7 and α_5, respectively. Subtracting Eq. (3) from Eq. (4), suppressing the subscript i, denoting changes from F to L as "Δ," and adding and subtracting $\alpha_{1L}S_F$, $\mu_L X_F$, and $\pi_L Z_F$ results in the following general equation for wage change:

$$\Delta lnW = \Delta_{a0} + \alpha_{1L}\Delta S +$$
$$\Delta\alpha_1 S_F + \Delta\alpha_2 e_{0F} +$$
$$\Delta\alpha_3 h_{0F} + \alpha_4 e^* + \alpha_5 e_L +$$
$$\alpha_6 h^* + \alpha_7 h_L + \mu_L \Delta X +$$
$$\Delta\mu X_F + \pi_L \Delta Z + \Delta\pi Z_F$$
$$+ \Delta\theta. \quad (5)$$

If one assumes that the cross-sectional *effects* of the explanatory variables are invariant between F and L and, further, that the *unmeasured* characteristics remain constant for the same individual, then the wage change equation simplifies to:

$$\Delta lnW = \alpha_{1L}\Delta S + \alpha_4 e^* + \alpha_5 e_L$$
$$+ \alpha_6 h^* + \alpha_7 h_L + \mu_L \Delta X + \Delta\theta \quad (6)$$

Although the dependent variable in Eq. (6) is wage *change* rather than wage *level*, the parameters on the experience variables ($\alpha_4 - \alpha_7$) correspond to the parameters in the cross-sectional Eq. (4). The key advantage to the change formulation is that estimates of these parameters are free from the statistical problems caused by retrospective reports and by unchanging, unmeasured variables correlated with the included (measured) explanatory variables. An additional advantage is that many more women meet the requirements of working at least 2 of the 13 years than work in a single year, and, therefore, selection bias problems are much less severe in estimating change Eq. (6) than in estimating a cross-sectional equation.[15]

Table 10-2, columns 1 and 2, shows estimates of wage-change Eq. (6), which is the longitudinal analogue to the Mincer-Ofek cross-sectional equation. The work segment following the most recent interruption (e_L) was entered quadratically to allow for a more rapid growth at first. Results show the estimated rate of wage growth immediately following the last interruption to be a little over 5 percent per year for white women and 8 percent for black women, with the rate of growth declining to zero after about 10 years for both groups, which is close to the maximum observed value for the e_L variable in the sample. Depreciation during the most recent interruption is estimated to be between 4 and 5 percent per year, so the initial wage rebound following an interruption more than makes up for the wages lost during a year out of the labor force.

Effects of Prospective Interruptions on Wage Growth

Since the profitability of investments is affected by the length of time over which

---

[15] See Corcoran et al. (in press) for more detailed discussions of the development of the wage-change equation and of selection bias adjustments.

TABLE 10-2   Basic Wage Growth Regression

Independent Variable	White	Black	White	Black
$h*$: years out of labor force prior to most recent	.016	−.016	.013	−.015
interruption	(.029)	(.030)	(.029)	(.030)
h_L: years out of labor force during most recent	−.038**	−.046**	−.035*	−.070**
interruption	(.013)	(.016)	(.015)	(.020)
$e*$: years in labor force prior to most recent reentry	.012†	.030**	.012	.023*
	(.007)	(.008)	(.009)	(.011)
e_L: years in labor force during most recent spell	.052*	.080**	.051†	.077*
	(.023)	(.026)	(.027)	(.032)
$e_L{}^2$	−.0027†	−.0041*	−.0025	−.0045*
	(.0016)	(.0019)	(.0015)	(.0022)
$NT79$: Did not work in 1979	—	—	−.017	−.124
	—	—	(.099)	(.103)
$NT79*h_L$	—	—	−.030	.059†
	—	—	(.029)	(.032)
$NT79*e_L$	—	—	.043	−.006
	—	—	(.056)	(.008)
$NT79*e_L{}^2$	—	—	−.0081	.0009
	—	—	(.0056)	(.0090)
R^2 (adjusted)	.021	.057	.024	.035
Number of observations	837	521	837	521

NOTE: Standard errors are in parentheses.
* Significant at .05 level.
** Significant at .01 level.
† Significant at .10 level.
SOURCE: Panel Study of Income Dynamics.

benefits are received, the human capital model predicts that otherwise identical workers will invest less if they anticipate labor market withdrawals than if they do not. This assumption is also implicit in Polachek's argument that workers who anticipate time out will choose occupations with low atrophy rates. Sandell and Shapiro (1980) test this proposition by estimating whether NLS women who expected to be out of the labor force at age 35 had flatter experience-earnings profiles before then than did women who expected to be working at age 35. Although most of their key parameter estimates are in the expected direction, none are significant at the 5 percent level for white or black women.

This hypothesis is an important one for the human capital model; it deserves testing in the context of the wage-change models developed here. Since we know which women in the PSID sample were not work-ing at the end of the 13-year period, we can test directly whether such workers' jobs provided them lower wage growth and lower depreciation. In contrast to the self-reported intentions of respondents used in the articles listed above, this procedure tests for the effects of actual labor force behavior in period $t + 1$ on wage profiles in period t. We did this by creating a dummy variable ($NT79$) for whether did not work in 1979, interacting this dummy with h_L, e_L, and e_L^2, and adding these four variables to the basic wage-change Eq. (6). The results of this analysis are reported in Table 10-3, columns 3 and 4. In general, white women who did not work in 1979 had the same wage increment for additional years of experience as women who did work in 1979 and similar wage loss with time out as did otherwise similar white women who were working in 1979. But one result for black women does conform with human capital predictions.

TABLE 10-3 Effects of Part-Time Work and Female-Dominated Work on Wage Growth

Independent Variable	White	Black	White	Black	White	Black
h^*: years out of labor force prior to most recent interruption	.023 (.029)	−.005 (.030)	.022 (.029)	−.026 (.029)	.021 (.029)	−.018 (.029)
h_L: years out of labor force during most recent interruption	−.034** (.013)	−.037* (.015)	−.035** (.013)	−.049** (.015)	−.036** (.013)	−.048* (.015)
Years of full-time e^*	.016* (.008)	.024* (.008)	.007 (.007)	.034** (.008)	.005 (.008)	.015 (.001)
Years of part-time e^*	.001 (.011)	.018 (.011)	−.002 (.011)	.023* (.011)	−.003 (.012)	.008 (.011)
Years of full-time e_L	.029** (.008)	.030** (.010)	.062** (.021)	.037 (.024)	— —	— —
(Years of full-time e_L)-squared	— —	— —	−.0036* (.0018)	−.008 (.0021)	— —	— —
Years of part-time e_L	−.001 (.010)	.017 (.013)	−.021 (.026)	.150* (.029)	— —	— —
(Years of part-time e_L)-squared	— —	— —	.0016 (.0025)	−.014** (.003)	— —	— —
Years of full-time e_L in male-dominated jobs	— —	— —	— —	— —	.026* (.012)	.008 (.016)
Years of part-time e_L in male-dominated jobs	— —	— —	— —	— —	−.009 (.019)	.024 (.028)
Years of full-time e_L in female-dominated jobs	— —	— —	— —	— —	.020* (.009)	.021* (.011)
Years of part-time e_L in female-dominated jobs	— —	— —	— —	— —	−.004 (.012)	−.003 (.014)
Number of cases	837	521	837	521	837	521
R^2 (adjusted)	.025	.049	.028	.096	.023	.044

* Significant at .05 level.
** Significant at .01 level.
SOURCE: Panel Study of Income Dynamics.

Black women who were not working in 1979 exhibited no wage loss during prior labor force withdrawals.[16] Their past wage return to experience, however, did not differ from that of otherwise similar black women who were working in 1979.

Part-Time Work Experience and Intermittency

Corcoran (1979) and Corcoran and Duncan (1979) included a retrospective measure of experience in a cross-sectional equation for a national sample of women. They report

[16] The depreciation estimate for black women who did not work in 1979 is the sum of the coefficient on h_L term (−.070) and the coefficient on the $NT79*h_L$ term (+.059).

that part-time work experience was significantly less valuable than full-time work experience.

Jones and Long (1979) used data from the NLS to estimate two cross-sectional wage equations that included interactions between work experience segments and whether the work was for part of a week. Although the signs of the coefficients they estimated were consistent with the hypothesis that part-time work leads to slower wage growth, only two of the 12 coefficients were statistically significant at conventional levels. Their measures of the part-time nature of the work segments were very rough, however, and may have biased some of the coefficient estimates.

Corcoran et al. (in press) also investigated the effects of part- and full-time work on the wage growth of women workers with some simple modifications to their basic wage-change equation. In Eq. (6), full- and part-time years in the e^* and e_L segments were not distinguished. Since the volume of work hours was ascertained for each of the 13 years under investigation, that information can be used to classify years of experience that involved part-time work (less than 1,500 hours) and full-time work (1,500 hours or more). Four variables were formed with this information: (1) the number of years of e^* that were part-time (e^*-part), (2) the number of years of e^* that were full-time (e^*-full), and (3) the number of years of e_L that were part-time (e_L-part), and (4) the number of years of e_L that were full-time (e_L-full). This decomposition of e^* and e_L yields the following equation:

$$\Delta lnW = \alpha_{1L}\Delta S + $$
$$\alpha_6 h^* + \alpha_7 h_L + $$
$$\alpha_8 e^*\text{-}part + $$
$$\alpha_9 e^*\text{-}full + $$
$$\alpha_{10} e_L\text{-}part + $$
$$\alpha_{11} e_L\text{-}full + $$
$$\mu_L \Delta X + \Delta \theta. \qquad (7)$$

As with the more basic measures of e^* and e_L, all four of these new variables are ob-

tained in each of the annual interviews and do not rely on retrospective reports by either women workers or their husbands.

The results of the estimation of the augmented wage-growth equation are shown in Table 10-2, columns 1 to 4. Full-time work does indeed appear to be associated with significant wage growth, while part-time work does not. When the two measures of e_L are entered linearly, the wage growth associated with full-time experience is positive and significant for both white and black women, while the wage growth associated with years of part-time work in the most recent spell of employment was insignificant for both groups of workers. With years of experience prior to the most recent spell of nonwork (e^*), the full-time work variables have larger coefficients than do the part-time variables, although these differences were not significant at conventional levels. A parabolic specification for the e_L measure gives expected results for white women—there is a parabolic rebound for full-time but not part-time work. For black women, there is parabolic wage rebound for part-time work—a puzzling result.

Sex Differences in Work History and the Sex-Based Wage Gap

Two sets of analysts have extensively examined the relationship between work history and the sex-based wage gap on a nationally representative sample of women. Mincer and Polachek (1974) estimated that sex differences in experience and time not working accounted for about 45 percent of the wage gap between employed married men and women aged 30 to 44 years in 1966. About half of this difference was due to the depreciation effect.[17] Corcoran and Duncan

---

[17] Mincer and Polachek used data from two different sources to make this comparison. This led to some inconsistencies between male and female variables. The sample of men was taken from the 1966 Survey of Economic Opportunity (SEO). This survey does not measure either work experience or tenure directly. Men

(1979), using a broader age range and a more extensive list of work history measures, found that sex differences in work history accounted for between one-third and two-fifths of the wage gap between working white men and working women aged 18 to 64 in 1975. This occurred largely because women had acquired less tenure and were more likely to have worked part time. The depreciation effect and intermittency did little to explain the wage gap between women and white men.

Work History and Occupational Segregation: Empirical Evidence

Polachek's (1981) argument implies that women choose "female" jobs because such jobs penalize discontinuous labor force participation less than "male" jobs do. This explanation presumes that there is immobility between occupations; that depreciation and/or wage growth are lower in "female" jobs than in "male" jobs and that women who expect discontinuous careers are concentrated in "female" jobs. We have already demonstrated that there is substantial mobility between "male" and "female" job sectors over a five-year period—a result that contradicts a basic assumption of Polachek's explanation.

The empirical evidence presented by Polachek for this argument is indirect. Polachek (1981) has shown that the probability of currently working in a given occupation (defined by 1-digit census categories) is affected by years out of the labor force and that the size of this effect differs by occupation. He has also demonstrated that the relationship between wage growth and years out of the labor force (home time) differs across occupations (i.e., occupations have different atrophy rates). He has further shown

that there is a negative correlation between the effect of years out of the labor force on the probability of working in an occupation and the atrophy rate in that occupation.

Even if we ignore the issue of mobility across occupations, Polachek's evidence does not unambiguously support his hypothesis. Take Polachek's first finding—that home time affects the probabilities of currently being in a particular occupation. This finding can only explain sex segregation of jobs if women with extensive home time were more likely to work in female-dominated occupations than were otherwise similar women without extensive home time. Polachek used his estimates of these effects to obtain a projected population-wide occupational distribution for women 30 to 44 if they had worked continuously since school completion. He reported that the proportion of women professionals and managers (currently male-dominated fields) would increase and that the proportion of women in household and service work (currently female-dominated fields) would decrease. On the other hand, his figures indicated an increase in the proportion of women employed in clerical work (a female-dominated field), a decrease in women employed in crafts (a male-dominated field), and a decrease in the proportion of women in sales (an integrated field). [18]

---

were assumed to have no interruptions. These two results are not inconsistent. In both cases, sex differences in work history explain a large but not major part of the sex-based wage gap. Sample differences likely account for differences in the importance of depreciation.

[18] Probably the best way to evaluate the quantitative importance of this evidence is to estimate the extent to which occupational sex segregation would be reduced if women's home time were zero—i.e., if men and women had the same work participation patterns. We estimated this by applying Duncan and Duncan's (1955) segregation index to Polachek's sample. This index measures "the minimum proportion of one group that would have to be shifted for its occupational distribution to be equal to that of the other." The segregation index for Polachek's sample is .50. Then we calculated this segregation index on the projected occupational distribution calculated by Polachek under the assumption that women worked continuously. If his theory is correct, occupational sex segregation should be considerably reduced. Under the assumption that women do not withdraw from the labor force, the segregation index is .48—a reduction of only 2 percent.

England (1982) investigated the effect of home time on sex typing of current occupation more directly. She reports that the sex composition of most recent occupation and the sex composition of first occupation were uncorrelated with the proportion of total time employed since school completion for white women aged 36 to 50 years in 1973.[19] This result does not suggest a strong link between labor force discontinuity and the sex typing of current or first job.

Now we turn to Polachek's second finding—that the detrimental wage effects of home time vary across occupations. He calculated this by regressing the difference between 1972 and 1967 wages on home time and other variables expected to affect wages. Unlike most economic studies of wage differentials based on the human capital model, Polachek examines dollar changes in wages rather than percentage changes. If all occupations had identical percentage wage decreases per year out of the labor force, Polachek would likely obtain differences in dollar wage change, with highly paid occupations showing greater decline. Indeed, in Polachek's analysis, dollar wage changes are most negative for professionals, craftspeople, and managers—the three highest-paid occupations.

In order to study wage change between 1967 and 1972, Polachek must restrict analysis to women who reported a wage in 1967 and in 1972. Thus, Polachek's sample is chosen on the basis of work behavior. This could possibly lead to selection bias problems when estimating effects of work behavior on wage change.[20]

A further problem is that Polachek's estimate of effects of home time will be dominated by short-run effects, since he restricts analysis to a five-year period and only examines the effects of withdrawals during that period. If lost skills were rapidly restored (as Mincer's and Ofek's [1982] and our results suggest), then Polachek's estimates will considerably exaggerate the lifetime costs of time out. Finally, note that Polachek's atrophy estimates pick up both depreciation and the forgone appreciation effects of fewer years of experience.

Even if Polachek's evidence that occupations differ in atrophy rates were correct, this would only explain sex segregation if there were less depreciation of skills and lower returns to experience in female-dominated occupations. England (1981, 1982) tested this assumption using both the NLS sample of mature women and a sample of women in a wider age range from the PSID. England's analyses have the two advantages of Polachek's analysis. She looks directly at the relationship between home time and sex typing of current job, and she examines depreciation and returns to experience separately. England regressed the natural logarithm of wages on experience, education, time out, and percent female in current occupation (coded at 3-digit census level), and tested for significant interactions between experience and percent female and between time out and percent female. She reports that neither the depreciation rate nor returns to experience were affected by percent female in current occupation. This is fairly strong evidence against Polachek's explanation.

Both Polachek's and England's empirical tests of the Polachek argument presume considerable immobility between occupa-

---

[19] England (1981) reports that Wolfe and Rosenfeld (1978) present some evidence that suggests a weak link between home time and sex composition of occupation.

[20] This sample selection bias is a general problem for analysts of women's wages. At any point in time only about half of all adult women are in the labor force. Restricting the sample to women who worked in two specific years as Polachek does eliminates even more

women from the sample. The wage-growth analysis of Corcoran et al. eliminates only about one-fifth of the sample, since it requires only that women work *at least* 2 of the 13 years under investigation. When we replicated our wage-change model for women who worked in 1975 and 1979, the results were inconsistent with results from the larger and less restricted sample.

tions over time. Whether their use of current occupation as a measure of occupational history is appropriate depends upon the validity of this presumption. As we have demonstrated, there is extensive mobility between "male" and "female" job categories. This in itself is inconsistent with Polachek's model. But it also suggests that the use of current occupation as a proxy for occupational history is inappropriate and may provide misleading information about whether job choice is conditioned by expectations about future work or whether experience garnered in "female" jobs results in lower wage growth and less depreciation than does experience garnered in "male" jobs.

We used the longitudinal nature of the PSID to develop more direct tests of the following two predictions of the human capital model:

1. Wage growth and depreciation are lower for work experience gathered in "female" jobs than in "male" jobs.

2. Women workers with extensive time out and frequent interruptions are more likely to have concentrated their work experience in "female" jobs.

We find virtually no support for the predictions.

To test the first proposition, we modified our basic wage-growth equation to include the sex typing of experience. In Eq. (7) we did not distinguish whether years in the e_L segment involved work in male-dominated or female-dominated jobs. Since both industry and occupation were reported for 9 of the 13 years under investigation, we could classify years in e_L that involved work in "female" and "male" jobs.[21] We combined

this with the information on work hours to create four new variables:

1. the number of years of e_L that were full-time in male-dominated jobs (e_L-*full-md*),

2. the numbers of years of e_L that were part-time in male-dominated jobs (e_L-*part-md*),

3. the number of years of e_L that were full-time in female-dominated jobs (e_L-*full-fd*), and

4. the numbers of years of e_L that were part-time in female-dominated jobs (e_L-*part-fd*).

This decomposition of e_L yields the following equation:

$$\Delta lnW = \alpha_{1L}\Delta S + \alpha_{10}e^*\text{-}part + \\ \alpha_{11}e^*\text{-}full + \\ \alpha_{14}e_L\text{-}full\text{-}md + \\ \alpha_{15}e_L\text{-}part\text{-}md + \\ \alpha_{16}e_L\text{-}full\text{-}fd + \\ \alpha_{17}e_L\text{-}part\text{-}fd. \quad (8)$$

As with the basic measures of e_L, these four new variables are obtained in each of the annual interviews and do not rely on retrospective reports by either women workers or their husbands. These variables also provide more complete measures of the extent to which work experience was acquired in "female" jobs than do measures of occupation that are taken at a single point in time.

The results of estimating Eq. (8), shown in Table 10-3, columns 5 and 6, provide little support for the argument that wage growth is much higher for male-dominated work than for female-dominated work, especially for white women. A much more important factor was whether the work performed in a

---

[21] Industry is coded into 2-digit categories for 1971 to 1979. Occupation is coded into 1-digit census categories for the years 1971 to 1974 and into 2-digit categories for all the years thereafter. For each occupation-industry subgroup, we calculated a measure of percent female. If there were more than 50 percent women in that subgroup, we called it a "female-dom-

inated" job. (See Corcoran et al., in press, for a more complete description of this procedure.) Since we only have measures of occupation and industry for the last 9 years of the study, we do not break experience in e^* (which tended to occur early on in 1967 to 1979) into "male" and "female" components.

particular kind of job was part time or full time. For white women a year of full-time, male-dominated work was associated with a 2.6 percent increase in hourly wages, while a year of full-time, female-dominated work was associated with a 1.9 percent increase in hourly wages. The differences between these two coefficients were not significant. For black women a year of female-dominated, full-time work was associated with a 2.1 percent increase in wages. This compares to a 0.8 percent increase for a year of full-time, male-dominated work. Again, the difference was not significant. Part-time work experience, whether in "male" or "female" jobs, had no significant effects on wages for either blacks or whites.[22]

We examined whether the sex typing of women's work experience affected the rate of depreciation during labor force withdrawals by interacting the two labor force withdrawal measures (h^* and h_L) with a measure of the average percent female in each woman's occupation-industry combination over the 13-year period. These interaction terms were always insignificant when added to the wage-change Eq. (8). This suggests that depreciation does not differ for "male" and "female" jobs.

The 13 years of PSID data allow a direct test of the second proposition—that workers who expect discontinuous labor force careers will concentrate in "female" jobs. If this hypothesis is correct, then the sex typing of work experience over the years 1967 to 1979 ought to be positively related to time out of the labor force in 1967 to 1979, intermittency of work participation in 1967 to 1979 (measured by number of labor force withdrawals), and whether working in 1979. Results of this exercise (see Corcoran et al., in press) confirm England's finding of no relationship between discontinuity of work

and sex typing of concurrent occupation. None of these three measures of labor force discontinuity over 1967 to 1979 had a significant, positive relation to the sex typing of work experience over that period.

SUMMARY AND CONCLUSIONS

The wage change models of Mincer and Ofek (1982) and those from our own work yield similar results. Women who drop out of the labor force have lower real wages when they return to work than they had when they left work. However, the period following the return is characterized by rapid wage growth, and the net loss in wages from dropping out is small. This result reconciles the apparently contradictory findings from cross-sectional studies about the size of the depreciation effect, because cross-sectional analyses pick up both short-run and long-run depreciation effects. Short-run effects are likely given more weight in an analysis of women aged 30 to 44 (a group likely to have recently completed labor force withdrawals) than in analyses run on women in a broader age range.

How does this empirical evidence affect our understanding of the process of female wage determination? The observed wage loss and rebound pattern is certainly consistent with the Mincer-Ofek story of human capital depreciation and restoration. This pattern is consistent with other stories as well—the job mismatch argument and the probationary period argument. We do not have the necessary data to disentangle these arguments. Regardless of the reason, the rapid rebound of wage losses after labor force withdrawals means that the wage losses associated with these withdrawals cannot explain much of the male/female wage gap.[23]

---

[22] The .0243 coefficient estimated for years of part-time, male-dominated work for black women appears to be out of line with the other results. This estimate is based on a small number of observations, as reflected in its large standard error.

[23] The fact that women work fewer years and more part-time years than men work does explain a substantial (one-third to two-fifths) part of the wage gap between men and women workers in a broad age range (Corcoran and Duncan, 1979). Note, however, that the bulk of the sex-based wage gap differences is still unexplained by male/female work history differences.

Women are often urged to choose part-time work rather than to stop work altogether to keep their "hands in." Our results provide little evidence that the wage consequences of these two alternatives differ. Part-time work experience is not rewarded for women—particularly for white women. And the long-run wage penalties due to labor force withdrawals are small. The decision whether to work full time or part time is considerably more important than is the choice between part-time work or no work. These part-time results, like the wage loss and rebound results, are consistent with several quite different labor market scenarios—a human capital model of lower training during part-time work, an imperfect information model, or an institutional model. Again, we do not have the necessary data to disentangle the competing explanations, since they each involve a different interpretation of the same employer behavior.

We also investigated the human capital models that explain job segregation as the result of women's discontinuous work history patterns. Such models emphasize two costs of discontinuous work participation: depreciation and forgone wage growth. The rapid restoration of wage losses in the period immediately following labor force withdrawals suggests that the first cost might be quite small. For these human capital explanations to hold, three things must occur: (1) there should be considerable immobility between "male" and "female" job sectors, (2) wage growth and depreciation should be lower for work in "female" jobs than for work in "male" jobs, and (3) women with discontinuous work careers will be more likely to choose "female" jobs than will women with continuous work careers.

We find little evidence for any of these propositions. First, there is considerable mobility between "male" and "female" job types. We did not find that either wage growth or depreciation varied significantly with the sex typing of work experience. These results are consistent with England's cross-sectional work. Finally, women with discontinuous work careers were no more likely to have worked at "female" jobs than were women with more continuous work experience.

These results also have implications for models of job segregation other than the human capital model. Many models of job segregation either implicitly or explicitly assume that there is rigid segmentation between "male" and "female" job sectors and that there are fewer promotion and/or training opportunities in the "female" job sector than in the "male" job sector. The analyses reviewed in this paper suggest these assumptions are likely wrong.

REFERENCES AND BIBLIOGRAPHY

Appelbaum, Eileen
1981   *Back to Work: Determinants of Women's Successful Re-entry.* Boston, Mass.: Auburn House Publishing Co.

Arrow, K.
1972   "Models of Job Discrimination." In *Racial Discrimination in Economic Life*, edited by A. H. Pascal, pp. 83-102. Lexington, Mass: D.C. Heath.
1976   "Economic Dimensions of Occupational Segregation: Comment I." *Signs*, 1, 3, Part 2 (Spring):233-237.

Beck, E.M., P.M. Horan, and C.M. Tolbert
1978   "Stratification in a Dual Economy: A Sectoral Model of Earnings Determination." *American Sociological Review* 43 (October):704-720.
1980a   "Industrial Segmentation and Labor Market Discrimination." *Social Problems* 28 (December):113-130.
1980b   "Reply to Hauser, 'Social Stratification in Industrial Society: Further Evidence for a Structural Alternative.'" *American Sociological Review* 45 (August):712-718.

Becker, G.S.
1957   *The Economics of Discrimination.* Chicago: University of Chicago Press.
1975   *Human Capital: A Theoretical and Empirical Analysis, With Special Reference to Education.* Second edition. New York: National Bureau of Economic Research.

Beller, A.H.
In   "Occupational Segregation by Sex: Determi-
press   nants and Changes." *Journal of Human Resources.*

Ben-Porath, Y.
1967   "The Production of Human Capital and the Life-Cycle of Earnings." *Journal of Political Economy* 75 (August):352-365.

Bergmann, B.R.
1974   "Occupational Segregation, Wages, and Profits When Employers Discriminate by Race or Sex." *Eastern Economic Journal* 1 (April–July):103-110.

Blau, F.D.
1977   *Equal Pay in the Office*. Lexington, Mass: D.C. Heath.

Blau, F.D., and C.L. Jusenius
1976   "Economists' Approaches to Sex Segregation in the Labor Market: An Appraisal." *Signs: Journal of Women in Culture and Society* 1, 3, Part 2 (Spring):181-199.

Blinder, A., and Y. Weiss
1976   "Human Capital and Labor Supply: A Synthesis." *Journal of Political Economy* 84(3):449-472.

Cain, G.
1976   "The Challenge of Segmented Labor Market Theories to Orthodox Theory: A Survey." *Journal of Economic Literature* 14, 4 (December):1251-1257.

Corcoran, M.
1978   "The Structure of Female Wages." *The American Economic Review* (papers and proceedings) 68, 2 (May):165-170.

1979   "Work Experience, Labor Force Withdrawals, and Women's Earnings: Empirical Results Using the 1976 Panel Study of Income Dynamics." In *Women in the Labor Market*, edited by C.B. Lloyd, E. Andrews, and C.L. Gilroy. New York: Columbia University Press.

Corcoran, M., and G.J. Duncan
1979   "Work History, Labor Force Attachment, and Earnings Differences Between the Races and Sexes." *Journal of Human Resources* 14, 1 (Winter):3-20.

Corcoran, M., G.J. Duncan, and M. Ponza
In   "Work Experience, Job Segregation, and
press   Wages." In *Five Thousand American Families—Patterns of Economic Progress*, edited by G.J. Duncan and J.M. Morgan. Ann Arbor: Institute for Social Research.

Doeringer, P.B., and M.J. Piore
1971   *Internal Labor Markets and Manpower Analysis*. Lexington, Mass: D. C. Heath.

Duncan, G.J., and S. Hoffman
1979   "On-the-Job Training and Earnings Differences by Race and Sex." *Review of Economics and Statistics* 61, 4 (November):594-603.

Duncan, O.D., and B. Duncan
1955   "A Methodological Analysis of Segregation Indexes." *American Sociological Review* 20 (April):210-217.

Edwards, R.
1979   *Contested Terrain: The Transformation of the Workplace in America*. New York: Basic Books.

England, P.
1981   "Wage Appreciation and Depreciation: A Test of Neoclassical Economic Explanations of Oc-cupational Sex Segregation." Mimeo, December.

1982   "The Failure of Human Capital Theory to Explain Occupational Sex Segregation." *Journal of Human Resources* (Spring).

Gronau, R.
1974   "Wage Comparisons—A Selectivity Bias." *Journal of Political Economy* 82, 6 (November/December):1119-1143.

Gwartney-Gibbs, P.
1981   *Married Women's Work Experience: Intermittency and Sex-Typed Occupations*. Ph.D. dissertation, University of Michigan.

Hanushek, E.A., and J.M. Quigley
1978   "Life-Cycle Earnings Capacity and the OJT Investment Model." Discussion Paper 7904. Rochester, N.Y.: Public Policy Program, University of Rochester.

Hauser, R.M.
1980   "Comment on Beck et al., ASR, October 1978, 'Stratification in a Dual Economy.'" *American Sociological Review* 45 (August):702-711.

Heckman, J.J.
1974   "Shadow Prices, Market Wages and Labor Supply." *Econometrica* 42, 4 (July):679-694.

1976   "A Life Cycle Model of Earnings, Learning, and Consumption." *Journal of Political Economy* 84(4):S11-S44.

Hill, M.S.
1979   "The Wage Effects of Marital Status and Children." *Journal of Human Resources* 14, 4 (Fall):579-594.

Horan, P.M.
1978   "Is Status Attainment Research Atheoretical?" *American Sociological Review* 43(August):334-341.

Jones, E.B., and J.E. Long
1979   "Part-Week Work and Human Capital Investment by Married Women." *Journal of Human Resources* 14(Fall):563-578.

Jovanovic, B.
1979   "Job Matching and the Theory of Turnover." *Journal of Political Economy* 87, 5, Part I (October):972-989.

Jusenius, C.L.
1977   "The Influence of Work Experience, Skill Requirement, and Occupational Segregation on Women's Earnings." *Journal of Economics and Business* 29, 2 (Winter):107-115.

Kahn, L.M.
1980   "Wage Growth and Endogenous Experience." *Industrial Relations* 19, 1 (Winter):50-63.

Landes, E.M.
1977   "Sex Differences in Wages and Employment: A Test of the Specific Capital Hypothesis." *Economic Inquiry* 15, 4 (October):523-538.

Lazear, E.
1976   "Age, Experience, and Wage Growth." *American Economic Review* (September):548-558.

Lloyd, C.B., and B.T. Niemi
1979   *The Economics of Sex Differentials.* New York: Columbia University Press.

Medoff, J., and K. Abraham
1981   "Are Those Paid More Really More Productive? The Case of Experience." *Journal of Human Resources* 16 (Spring).

Mincer, J.
1974   *Schooling Experience and Earnings.* New York: National Bureau of Economic Research.

Mincer, J., and H. Ofek
1982   "Interrupted Work Careers." *Journal of Human Resources* 16 (Winter).

Mincer, J., and S. Polachek
1974   "Family Investments in Human Capital: Earnings of Women." *Journal of Political Economy* 82, 2, Part 2 (March/April):S76-S108.

1978   "An Exchange: Theory of Human Capital and the Earnings of Women: Women's Earnings Reexamined." *Journal of Human Resources* 13, 1 (Winter):118-134.

Morgensen, D.
1978   "Specific Capital and Labor Turnover." *Bell Journal of Economics*, 2 (Autumn):572-586.

Oppenheimer, V.K.
1970   *The Female Labor Force in the United States: Demographic and Economic Factors Governing Its Growth and Changing Composition.* Westport, Conn.: Greenwood Press.

Piore, M.J.
1971   "The Dual Labor Market: Theory and Implications." In *Problems in Political Economy: An Urban Perspective*, edited by D.M. Gordon, pp. 90-94. Lexington, Mass.: D.C. Heath.

Polachek, S.W.
1976   "Occupational Segregation: An Alternative Hypothesis." *Journal of Contemporary Business* 5, 1:1-12.

1979   "Occupational Segregation Among Women: Theory, Evidence, and a Prognosis." *Women in the Labor Market*, edited by C.B. Lloyd, E.S. Andrews, and C.L. Gilroy. New York: Columbia University Press, pp. 137-157.

1981   "Occupational Self-Selection: A Human Capital Approach to Sex Differences in Occupational Structure." *Review of Economics and Statistics* 63, 1 (February):60-69.

Prescott, E., and M. Visscher
1980   "Organizational Capital." *Journal of Political Economy*, 88, 3 (June):446-461.

Rosen, S.
1972   "Learning and Experience in the Labor Market." *Journal of Human Resources* VII (Summer):326-342.

Sandell, S.H., and D. Shapiro
1978   "An Exchange: Theory of Human Capital and the Earnings of Women: A Reexamination of the Evidence." *Journal of Human Resources* 13, 1 (Winter):103-117.

1980   "Work Expectations, Human Capital Accumulation, and the Wages of Young Women." *Journal of Human Resources* 15, 3 (Summer):-335-353.

Stafford, F.P., and G.J. Duncan
1980   "The Use of Time and Technology by Households in the United States." In *Research in Labor Economics*, Vol. 3, edited by Ronald Ehrenberg. Greenwich, Conn.: JAI Press.

Treiman, D.J., and H.I. Hartmann, eds.
1981   *Women, Work, and Wages: Equal Pay for Jobs of Equal Value.* Washington, D.C.: National Academy Press.

Weiss, Y., and R. Gronau
1981   "Expected Interruptions in Labour Force Participation and Sex-Related Differences in Earnings Growth." *Review of Economic Studies* 58 (October):607-619.

Wolfe, W., and R. Rosenfeld
1978   "Sex Structure of Jobs and Job Mobility." *Social Forces* 56:823-844.

Zellner, H.
1975   "The Determinants of Occupational Segregation." In *Sex, Discrimination, and the Division of Labor*, edited by C.B. Lloyd. New York: Columbia University Press, pp. 125-145.

11 Sex Typing in Occupational Socialization

MARGARET MOONEY MARINI *and*
MARY C. BRINTON

The existence of sex segregation in the labor market is well documented (Gross, 1968; U.S. President's Council of Economic Advisors, 1973; Blau, 1977; Williams, 1976, 1979; U.S. Commission on Civil Rights, 1978; Blau and Hendricks, 1979). Women tend to be concentrated in a relatively small number of "female" occupations, whereas men are employed in a wider variety of "male" occupations. More than 40 percent of female workers are employed in the 10 occupations employing the largest number of women, whereas less than 20 percent of male workers are employed in the 10 occupations employing the largest number of men (U.S. Department of Labor, 1975). Women are overrepresented in clerical, sales, and service jobs; in a few professional and technical jobs (e.g., elementary and secondary school teacher, registered nurse, librarian, social worker, medical and dental technician); and in such jobs as machine operative, where they assemble or inspect goods, operate sewing and other machines, and work as packers and wrappers. Men are overrepresented in managerial, crafts, labor, and farm jobs and in most professional and technical jobs. Despite a substantial increase in the

labor force participation of women over the last several decades (Oppenheimer, 1970; U.S. Department of Labor, 1977), the amount of sex segregation in the labor market has decreased little (England, 1981a). As recently as 1976, more than two-thirds of one sex would have had to change occupations to make the occupational distributions of the two sexes equal (U.S. Commission on Civil Rights, 1978).

Three major types of explanations for sex segregation in the labor market have been advanced: (1) explanations focusing on employer demands, (2) explanations focusing on legal and institutional barriers within the workplace, and (3) explanations focusing on worker characteristics. The first two locate the source of sex segregation within the workplace. It has been hypothesized, for example, that exclusionary behavior by employers results in the overcrowding of women in a limited set of occupations and that this overcrowding reduces the wages of women in those occupations relative to the wages of the nonrestricted group of men (Bergmann, 1971, 1974). It has also been hypothesized that the structure of the labor market, which includes occupations filled

192

from external sources through the recruitment of new workers and occupations filled from internal sources through the promotion of in-house workers, creates institutional barriers in the process of job assignment and promotion that disadvantage women (Doeringer and Piore, 1971; Blau and Jusenius, 1976). Sex segregation in the labor market has been argued to occur at least in part as a result of "statistical discrimination," whereby individuals are judged on the basis of the perceived average characteristics of the group to which they belong (Thurow, 1975:170-81). Since, on the average, women are viewed as differing from men in their ability to perform certain types of jobs and in their attachment to the labor market, sex is used as a basis for "statistical discrimination" in the allocation of individuals to jobs.

In contrast to explanations of sex segregation that focus on the actions of employers and the structure of the labor market, a third set of explanations focuses on the characteristics of workers. These explanations attribute sex segregation to sex differences in individuals, including occupational preferences, skills, and other personal attributes. Women and men are hypothesized to be employed in different occupations because they choose different occupations and because they are differentially qualified for various types of jobs.

This paper examines the explanations for sex segregation that focus on the characteristics of workers entering the labor market. The first section outlines general theories of occupational choice and points to the need to consider sex-role socialization as an input to these theories. The second section presents evidence on the existence of sex differences prior to labor market entry in several areas relevant to occupational attainment, including occupational preferences, knowledge, values, skills, and dispositional traits. In the third section, we examine the socialization practices that appear to produce these sex differences prior to labor market entry, focusing primarily on socialization practices in the family and school but also considering messages conveyed by the mass media and employment experiences prior to leaving school. In the final section, we discuss the role that socialization can be interpreted to play in producing sex segregation in the labor market.

THEORIES OF OCCUPATIONAL CHOICE AND SEX-ROLE SOCIALIZATION

This section provides an overview of the theoretical bases on which sex differences in occupational orientation and job-relevant traits have been assumed to arise. We begin by outlining general theories of occupational choice that have emerged in various disciplines. Since the prediction of sex differences in outcomes using these theories requires prior knowledge that the two sexes differ on various inputs, we discuss theories of sex-role socialization. These latter theories, advanced primarily by psychologists, constitute the basis on which sex differences can be predicted by general theories of occupational choice.

Theories of Occupational Choice

General theories of occupational choice abound. Developmental theories such as those of Ginsberg et al. (1951) and Super (1953, 1957) describe the process of occupational selection in terms of general concepts of human development. Based on the principles of developmental psychology, occupational choices are viewed as developing gradually over time in a series of stages. Personality-based theories, such as Holland's (1959, 1966, 1973) typology theory, describe career orientations and preferences in terms of personality types. Still other psychological theories involve specific applications of general behavior theory. In Krumboltz's Social Learning Theory of Career Selection (Krumboltz et al., 1976; Mitchell et al., 1975), occupational decisions are viewed as an outcome of a lifelong series of learned responses. Other applications of general behavior theory focus more on information processing. The decision theories of Vroom (1964) and Kaldor and Zytowski (1969), for example, are concerned with the process of decision making based on the expected consequences of alternative decisions. The logic-flow theories of Hilton (1962) and Herchenson and Roth (1966) deal with the steps individuals go through in arriving at decisions. Sociological work on occupational choice, which has arisen out of the study of social stratification, focuses primarily on the status dimensions of occupations (e.g., Blau and Duncan, 1967; Sewell et al., 1969, 1970). Work by economists generally involves specific applications of general theories of utility maximization, particularly the theory of human capital, according to which occupational selection implies varying amounts of investment in human capital and affects returns on the investment (Becker, 1964).

In and of themselves, these general theories do not explain why males and females select different occupations. Unless the two sexes differ on the independent variables used as inputs to these theories, sex differences in occupational choice are not predicted. For example, unless the developmental experiences of the sexes differ, developmental and social learning theories of occupational choice do not predict sex differences in occupational selection. Similarly, unless the adult role expectations of the sexes differ, psychological and economic theories of decision making do not predict sex differences in occupational selection. In short, regardless of which general theory is used, the prediction of sex differences in outcomes requires the input of additional information that the sexes differ on variables predicting occupational choice.

Attempts to use general theories to understand why males and females select different occupations have actually been quite limited. The most extensive applications have been those of human capital theory. Under the assumption that individuals seek to maximize expected lifetime earnings, economists have used human capital theory to argue that sex differences in expected lifetime labor force participation produce sex differences in occupational choice. Specifically, Polachek (1976, 1979, 1981) has argued that sex segregation in the labor market arises because women's expectations of intermittency in employment cause them to choose occupations in which the amount of depreciation in earnings during periods of absence from the labor force is low. Zellner (1975), on the other hand, has argued that sex segregation arises because women's expectations of intermittency in employment cause them to choose occupations with high starting wages but low wage appreciation. In either case, it is implied that women tend to enter occupations that require few skills and provide little opportunity for increases in productivity through experience.

Critics of these neoclassical economic explanations of sex segregation have pointed to a number of theoretical problems. One is that both male and female occupations require differing amounts and types of skill. Women and men are employed in occupations of each skill type, and within each type some occupations are more often entered by women than by men. Women's lower expected lifetime labor force participation explains only the greater tendency of women to be in jobs requiring low skill, not the concentration of women in a small number of female occupations within each skill type (Blau and Jusenius, 1976). Within the human capital framework, the pattern of sex segregation existing in the labor market can be accounted for only by an extreme distribution of women's "tastes." Another problem is that the causal direction of the relationship between occupational outcomes and labor force attachment is ambiguous. Although it may be that those who anticipate being out of the labor force for a substantial amount of time initially select low-wage occupations, it may also be that those who spend a lot of time out of the labor force wind up in low-wage occupations as a result (Welch, 1979).

Recently, direct tests of the assumptions underlying human capital explanations have presented some disconfirming evidence. England (1982) shows that predominantly female occupations do not penalize inter-mittency less than male occupations and that women expecting fairly constant employ-ment are no more likely to choose male oc-cupations than women planning intermit-tent employment. England (1981b) further shows that women have higher lifetime earnings if they are employed in predomi-nantly male occupations, a finding that does not support the contention that women max-imize lifetime earnings by choosing female occupations. Given the lack of empirical support for human capital explanations of occupational segregation by sex, other ex-planations must be sought. It is possible that other general theories of occupational choice may be more successful than the human cap-ital approach in accounting for sex differ-ences in occupational outcomes, but these theories have not yet been applied to the study of sex differences.

Since all general theories of occupational choice require the existence of sex differ-ences on predictor variables in order to gen-erate predictions of sex differences in oc-cupational choice, we now turn to a discussion of theories of sex-role socialization. These theories provide a basis for understanding the developmental process by which most sex differences in behavior emerge.

Theories of Sex-Role Socialization

Theories of sex-role socialization explain the process by which individuals learn the behavior that a culture defines as appropri-ate for their sex. The theories differ pri-marily in the mechanism by which sex-typed behavior is hypothesized to be learned. Be-low we describe the major theories of sex-role socialization, including (1) social learn-ing theories, (2) cognitive developmental theories, (3) information processing theo-

ries, and (4) identification theories. After ex-amining the sex-role socialization *process*, we consider the *content* of what is trans-mitted via that process. That is, we examine the gender-linked behavior patterns that are learned and discuss the division of labor be-tween the sexes that constitutes the basis for many sex differences in behavior, atti-tudes, and personality.

Social Learning Theories Two basic learning processes, operant conditioning and observational learning, are at the heart of social learning theories. These theories are based primarily on a mechanistic model (Reese and Overton, 1970). Sex-typed be-havior is seen as resulting from the fact that reinforcement contingencies depend on the sex of the responder. That is, girls and boys are reinforced or punished for different kinds of behavior, and male and female models display different kinds of behavior. One ma-jor tenet of social learning theory is that sex-typed behavior need not be consistent across situations but depends on the social context in which it occurs. The bases of sex typing are viewed as arising in the social environ-ment, not the organism, so that relatively rapid changes can occur if learning condi-tions are altered. Sex-role learning is as-sumed to take place continuously, although the majority occurs during early childhood. Cognitive social learning theories use ad-ditional constructs to describe the internal mental processes that mediate learning, but cognitions play a secondary role, and sex typing is conceptualized primarily as a set of behavioral responses. An extensive dis-cussion of social learning theory is contained in Mischel (1970).

Cognitive Developmental Theories Cog-nitive developmental theories derive from Piaget's theoretical framework for under-standing child development. Unlike social learning theories, they are based primarily on an organismic model (Reese and Over-ton, 1970). Cognitive processes are viewed as ongoing processes of change. It is assumed that children play an active role in their own development, motivated by a desire for competence and mastery over their world. The child's concepts about masculinity, femininity, and sex appropriateness, rather than the child's sex-typed behavior, are at the core of sex typing. Such concepts or schema constitute organizing rubrics for the selection of information from the environment and for active processing of that input.

Developmental changes in sex typing are assumed to go hand in hand with general developmental changes in cognitive processes. To the extent that these changes are inherent in the organism, changes in sex typing are governed by maturational, internal variables in interaction with the social environment. Thus, these theories propose organismic as well as environmental influences on sex typing, and most therefore suggest some limits to the degree and rapidity with which sex typing can be changed (Huston, in press). Among the most prominent cognitive developmental theories are those proposed by Kolberg (1966), Block (1973), Pleck (1975), and Rebecca et al. (1976).

Information Processing Theories Theories of information processing schema are a hybrid set of theories based on information processing constructs (Huston, in press). They emphasize schemas as cognitive structures that guide and organize an individual's perception. The schemas are anticipatory mechanisms that cause an individual to search for certain information and to be ready to process it. Information inconsistent with the schema may be ignored or transformed. Models of sex typing based on information processing have been proposed recently by Bem (1981) and Martin and Halverson (1981). In these models sex stereotypes serve as schemas for organizing and structuring social information. Although schema theories are similar to cognitive developmental theories in focusing on cognitive processes that are active and constructive, they differ in that developmental processes are not em-

phasized as the source of schemas or the means of changing them. The cultural emphasis on gender rather than physical sex differences is what is seen as making gender salient.

Identification Theories Freudian psychoanalytical theory is the basis for all identification theories of sex-role learning. In classical Freudian theory, masculinity and femininity are acquired through a process of identification resulting from castration fear on the part of the male child and castration anxiety on the part of the female child. Although more recent theories of identification do not place as much emphasis on sexual motivation, identification with the same-sex parent continues to be viewed as an important basis for the development of permanent and global sex differences in personality. Patterns of behavior are assumed to be integrated, so that a child who is feminine in one situation is feminine in another. In recent years, classical theories of identification have fallen into disfavor, and theorists now emphasize parental identification less, viewing parents as one of many socializing influences (Huston, in press). However, there is little empirical evidence to support either the existence of identification or the contention that it accounts for sex-role learning (Parsons, 1978).

Some reformulations of psychoanalytic theory have been undertaken by feminists. These focus on envy of women's childbearing capacity and caretaking role as the reason for devaluation of the mother and of women in general (Horney, 1932; Klein, 1957; Lerner, 1974, 1978; Chodorow, 1978). Because the mother as primary caregiver is perceived as all powerful, men are hypothesized to develop envy, fear, and anger in a struggle to free themselves from her. According to Chodorow (1978), they generally come to see themselves as more distinct from others as a result. It is suggested that this basis for sex-role differentiation could be altered if the caretaking of young children were shared by males and females. Again, empirical evidence is lacking to support these reformulations as the basis for sex typing.

Next we consider the sex-typed *content* of what is transmitted via sex-role socialization. Although the division of labor between the sexes forms the basis for many sex differences in behavior, we present evidence to indicate that it alone does not account for all gender-based behavior patterns transmitted through socialization, including the segregation of women and men within the workplace.

Sex-Role Differentiation   Children learn the behavior that is appropriate for their sex via the process of sex-role socialization. Although this learning may occur in a variety of ways, the content of what is learned depends on the association of gender with particular types of behavior in the culture in which a child is raised. A gender-based division of labor exists to some extent in all societies and forms the basis for many of the sex differences in behavior, attitudes, and personality that are transmitted via socialization. In industrialized societies such as the United States, the sexual division of labor between the market and the home has important implications for the occupational orientation and preparation of the sexes prior to entry into the job market. For the most part, men are expected to support the family financially, and women take the major responsibility for home management, child care, and catering to the emotional needs of the family. This division of labor results in essential consistency between men's familial and occupational roles but produces conflict between the familial role of women and their participation in the labor market. Fulfillment of familial role responsibilities competes with work outside the home for the limited supply of a woman's time, energy, and emotional commitment.

Even the entry of increasing numbers of women into the labor force has not changed this fundamental division of labor. Changes in conceptions of the female role have resulted primarily in the need for choice re-

garding employment outside the home, a choice usually based on the decision of whether to add a new role to the traditional homemaker role rather than whether to substitute a new role for the old one (Poloma and Garland, 1971; Bahr, 1974; Vanek, 1974; Walker and Woods, 1976; Robinson, 1977; Berk and Berk, 1979). Because of the conflict between fulfillment of familial role responsibilities and work outside the home, women's investment in family roles negatively affects their labor force participation and employment in high-status occupations (Rossi, 1965; Sweet, 1973; Waite, 1976; Smith-Lovin and Tickamyer, 1978; Marini, 1980).

Differences in the occupational orientations and skills of the two sexes can be expected to arise as a consequence of the sex difference in consistency between familial and occupational roles. Women are more likely to view their work outside the home as a job than as a lifetime career and to choose jobs that permit better coordination of their responsibilities in the home with their employment (Rossi, 1965; Perucci, 1970). Because women are less likely to expect to work throughout their adult lives and to be the primary wage earners (Turner, 1964), their occupational interests focus less than men's on the monetary and status dimensions of jobs and tend to parallel their family functions, often involving an orientation toward helping others (Witty and Lehman, 1930; Singer and Stefflre, 1954; O'Hara, 1962; Lueptow, 1980; Herzog, 1982).[1] The sexual division of labor between the market and the home and its effect on the sex difference in consistency between

---

[1] It should be noted that the lower wages paid to women and typically associated with women's jobs are a cause as well as a result of women's orientation toward employment. Women may not seek to satisfy material ambitions through their own occupations because the incomes they can expect to receive are so low; however, because most women do not rely on their own occupations for full material support, they are not as likely to expect or demand higher wages.

familial and occupational roles may also be seen as promoting the development of different personality characteristics and abilities in the two sexes. Males are socialized to be assertive, authoritative, and competent in occupational skills, whereas females are socialized to be nurturant, deferent, and competent in domestic skills (Oetzel, 1966; Maccoby and Jacklin, 1974; Block, 1976; Tavris and Offir, 1977; Frieze et al., 1978).

The extent to which women's familial role responsibilities account for sex segregation in the labor market remains an open question. It can be argued that women's investment in family roles affects the probability of their employment in female-typed jobs for several reasons. First, women's investment in family roles may affect the status of the occupations they hold. Consequently, there may be a relationship between the status and sex type of occupations, with high-status occupations more often being traditionally male. Second, female jobs may have characteristics, such as greater flexibility of working hours, that make them easier to combine with family responsibilities. Third, women who invest relatively more in family roles may have traditional attitudes that cause them to select female occupations more often than male occupations.

Research bearing on the relationship between women's investment in family roles and the sex type of the jobs they hold suggests that the relationship differs depending on whether a woman has a college education. As indicated earlier, England (1982) found that women expecting constant employment (as measured by familial role status) were no more likely to choose male occupations than women planning intermittent employment. England's analysis was based on a sample covering the full range of variation in education. Analyzing a sample restricted to women who did not go to college, Hofferth (1980a) also found that marital status and children had no effect on the sex type of jobs held by women three, five, and ten years after high school. Research on samples of college-educated women, in contrast, has indicated that married women and women with a relatively large number of children are less likely to be employed in male occupations (Almquist and Angrist, 1970; Klemmack and Edwards, 1973; Bielby, 1978a; Brito and Jusenius, 1978; Daymont and Tsai, 1981). These findings suggest that a relationship between women's investment in family roles and the sex type of their occupations exists only at the upper end of the education distribution. Such a relationship is likely to arise because a relationship between the status and sex type of occupations exists at the upper end of the education distribution, where male occupations tend to be of higher status than female occupations. Women's fulfillment of traditional family responsibilities interferes with employment in high-status male occupations, which place heavier demands on their incumbents and are, therefore, less easy to combine with traditional family responsibilities.

The sexual division of labor between the home and the job market may, therefore, be seen as forming the basis for many sex differences in behavior that are transmitted via socialization, including sex differences in job-relevant skills and dispositional traits. However, this fundamental division of labor cannot account for all sex differences transmitted via socialization. Some sex differences, including the tendency for males and females to be employed in different occupations, have other origins. Regardless of its origins, gender-linked behavior is transmitted via sex-role socialization. Thus, because the occupational world is sex segregated, children learn to view some occupations as appropriate for their sex and others as inappropriate (Looft, 1971a,b; Schlossberg and Goodman, 1972; Siegel, 1973; Shepard and Hess, 1975; Heilman, 1979).

Biological Components of Sex Typing

Many theorists have proposed that sex differences in behavior are at least partially due to genetic, biochemical, and anatomical differences between the sexes. It is generally agreed that an either/or position concerning the effects of biology and socialization is too simplistic and that the important question focuses on the relative role of these two types of influences in determining sex-typed behavior. Although the role played by biology is unknown, evidence from three types of studies suggests that socialization rather than biology is the source of most sex differences in behavior, particularly those that are likely to have a bearing on occupational orientation and performance. First, studies of hermaphrodites, whose gender is biologically ambiguous, indicate that the gender according to which a child is reared is more important for the development of gender identity than genes or gonads (Money and Ehrhardt, 1972). Second, cross-cultural studies of sex-typed behavior indicate that many personality traits, activities, and occupations that are labeled feminine in one society are labeled masculine in another (Mead, 1935; McClelland, 1976; Tavris and Offir, 1977). Third, studies of sex differences in infancy, when the effects of culture are minimal, rarely find sex differences in behavior (Maccoby and Jacklin, 1974). Although it is difficult to document sex differences in infants for methodological reasons (Block, 1976)—and some biologically based sex differences do not emerge until later ages—the fact that sex differences are rarely found in infants does not support the view that sex differences are biologically determined (Maccoby and Jacklin, 1974; Frieze et al., 1978).

Not only is the role of biology in the determination of sex differences in various types of abilities and dispositional traits an open question, but the extent to which jobs that are thought to require sex-related traits actually do require those traits is unknown. Consequently, the extent to which biology may affect sex segregation in the labor market via its effects on the characteristics of workers is unknown. Since there is evidence to suggest that biology may play a small role in the determination of most sex differences, and since it seems likely that the extent to which one sex is better suited to perform sex-typed jobs has been greatly exaggerated, the role of biology in the determination of occupational segregation by sex is indeed likely to be small.

Summary

Theories used to predict occupational choice in various disciplines do not predict sex differences in occupational choice unless information that the sexes differ on variables used to make the prediction is available. Theories of sex-role socialization advanced within psychology constitute the primary basis on which sex differences in occupational orientation and job-relevant skills are viewed as arising over the early stages of the life course. These theories describe the process by which gender-linked behavior is learned. Biology also plays a role in the determination of some sex differences in behavior, but the fact that biologically based sex differences may have little bearing on occupational performance suggests that the effect of biology on occupational choice is small.

SEX DIFFERENCES IN OCCUPATIONAL ORIENTATION PRIOR TO LABOR FORCE ENTRY

As a result of sex-role socialization, sex differences in occupational orientation and preparation arise prior to entry into the labor market. This section examines the degree to which occupational aspirations and expectations prior to labor market entry are sex typed and considers the probable relationship between this sex typing and subsequent sex segregation in the labor market. We will also examine sex differences in knowledge of the occupational world and in occupational values held prior to labor market entry. Finally, we consider evidence bearing on the existence of sex differences in abilities, such as physical strength and verbal and quantitative skills, and in dispositional traits, such as aggressiveness, sociability, and self-confidence. It has been argued that all of these sex differences are determinants of sex segregation in the labor market. More specifically, it has been argued that women and men occupy different positions in the workplace because they choose different occupations and are differentially qualified for various types of jobs.

Occupational Aspirations and Expectations

Research on occupational aspirations and expectations held prior to labor market entry provides strong evidence that sex differences in occupational choice exist. Young women are more likely to choose typically "female" occupations, whereas young men are more likely to choose typically "male" occupations (Stephenson, 1957; Sewell and Ornstein, 1964; Douvan and Adelson, 1966; Werts, 1966; Astin and Panos, 1969; Marini and Greenberger, 1978; Harren et al., 1979; Herzog, 1982). To examine the degree of sex segregation in aspirations for the full range of the Census Bureau's detailed occupational categories, an index of segregation was calculated using data from the National Longitudinal Survey of Young Americans (NLS). These data were collected in 1979 from a nationally representative sample of youth ages 14 to 22 and are described in detail elsewhere. For a measure of occupational aspirations for age 35, the index of segregation was 61.0, indicating that 61 percent of one sex would have to change occupational aspirations to make the aspirations distributions of the two sexes equal. The degree of segregation in aspirations also was examined by age, but only a small change was observed over the age range studied.

Not only are the occupational choices of youth highly differentiated by sex, but the range of choices made by females is narrower than the range of choices made by males (Rodman et al., 1974; Marini and Greenberger, 1978). Further analysis of the 1979 NLS data indicated that 47.5 percent of young women aspired to the 10 occupations most often aspired to by women but that only 39.5 percent of young men aspired to the 10 occupations most often aspired to by men.

Previous research has shown that the occupational aspirations of males are also more highly sex typed than those of females (Marini and Greenberger, 1978). This finding is confirmed by analysis of the 1979 NLS data. We divided occupations into three sex-type categories on the basis of the percentage of female incumbents in the occupation. Occupations with less than 30 percent women were defined as male occupations; occupations with 30 to 59 percent women were defined as sex-neutral occupations, and occupations with 60 percent or more women were defined as female occupations. Based on this categorization, 86.3 percent of males aspired to male occupations, but only 4.1 percent aspired to female occupations. In contrast, 52.8 percent of females aspired to female occupations, and 34.5 percent aspired to male occupations. Similar percentages of each sex (9.6 percent of males and 12.7 percent of females) aspired to sex-neutral occupations. These sex differences in the distribution of aspirations by sex type indicate that females are considerably more likely than males to make cross-sex occupational choices.

Discrepancy Between Aspirations and Expectations By examining both occupational aspirations and expectations, some studies have attempted to sort out wishful aspirations from more realistic expectations, or plans (Burlin, 1976; Marini and Greenberger, 1978; Lueptow, 1981). Expectations are more likely to reflect perceptions of constraints such as limited opportunities, the sex type of the job, and personal qualifications. The discrepancy between aspirations and expectations therefore provides some indication of the degree to which individuals perceive that constraints may prevent realization of their aspirations. Studies of both aspirations and expectations uniformly indicate that there is greater sex typing of occupational expectations than of occupational aspirations.

The most detailed study comparing the sex typing of occupational aspirations and expectations was carried out by Marini and Greenberger (1978), based on data collected from a representative sample of eleventh-grade students in Pennsylvania in 1968. In this study there was virtually no difference between the mean percentage of women employed in occupations aspired to (17 percent) and expected (18 percent) by boys. However, the mean percentage of women employed in occupations expected by girls (75 percent) was significantly greater than the mean percentage of women employed in the occupations girls aspired to (66 percent). These findings indicate that the girls expected to enter occupations that, on the average, employed a higher proportion of women than those they aspired to.

Of respondents who aspired to occupations in which fewer than 50 percent of the incumbents were women (i.e., male-dominated occupations), a smaller percentage of the girls (52 percent) than the boys (94 percent) actually expected to enter an occupation of this type. Of respondents aspiring to occupations in which 50 percent or more of the incumbents were women (i.e., female-dominated occupations), the percentage of the boys (78 percent) expecting to enter a female-dominated occupation was almost as high as the percentage of the girls (85 percent). In addition, only about 3 percent of the girls who aspired to female-dominated occupations, in comparison with 22 percent of the boys, expected that they would instead enter male-dominated occupations. These findings indicate that the girls were more likely to shift their aspirations from male-dominated occupations to expecta-

tions in the female-dominated category than the boys were to shift their aspirations from the female-dominated category to expectations for male-dominated jobs. The girls, therefore, seemed to perceive the male-dominated jobs they aspired to as less accessible than the boys perceived the female-dominated jobs they aspired to. These findings suggest that the sex composition of an occupation influences the degree to which girls, but not boys, expect to realize their occupational aspirations.

Further support for the hypothesis that the sex type of an occupational aspiration influences the degree to which girls feel it can be realized is available in a survey by Burlin (1976) of adolescent girls in a Syracuse high school. She found that more than one-half of those with discrepant occupational aspirations and expectations attributed the discrepancy to the fact that the occupation aspired to was an "inappropriate occupation for a female." Data from a national sample of high school students collected in 1980 as part of the Monitoring the Future project also indicate that the girls surveyed more often perceived their sex as a barrier to fulfilling their occupational aspirations (Bachman et al., 1980). When asked to what extent they thought their sex would prevent them from getting the kind of work they would like to have, 87.9 percent of the males but only 66.4 percent of the females responded "not at all." Experimental research by Heilman (1979) provides further evidence that the sexual composition of an occupation influences the degree to which it is considered a viable career choice.

Relationship of Occupational Aspirations to Subsequent Occupational Behavior The degree of correspondence between occupational aspirations held prior to labor market entry and subsequent occupational attainments is indicative of the degree to which individuals realize their occupational aspirations. The occupational aspirations of high school students definitely play a role in the determination of adult occupational attainment, but the relationship between the sex type of occupational aspirations and the sex type of occupational attainments has not been estimated. This relationship is of interest because it would indicate the extent to which the sex segregation of occupational choices prior to labor market entry can account for the sex segregation in employment that is subsequently experienced by a cohort. To the extent that sex segregation in occupational choices exists prior to labor market entry, sex segregation in occupational outcomes cannot be attributed to the *direct* experience of sex discrimination in the labor market. However, as we will discuss, discriminatory practices and structural barriers within the labor market may generate a pattern of sex segregation that is maintained over time via socialization.

Most research on the relationship between occupational goals and attainments has focused on the overall degree of congruence between occupational aspirations and attainments, where congruence is defined as aspiring to and attaining an occupation in the same occupational category. The findings of such studies depend in part on the inclusiveness of the occupational categories used; the more inclusive the occupational categories, the greater the degree of congruence will appear to be. Variability among studies in the type of sample and the age at which respondents were initially studied also clouds the picture. Estimates of the degree of congruence between high school aspirations and subsequent occupational attainments range from about 50 percent (Schmidt and Rothney, 1955) to 80 percent (Porter, 1954) in studies done *6 months* after graduation from high school, to about 50 percent in a study of women done *5 years* after high school (Astin and Myint, 1971), to between 15 percent (Kohout and Rothney, 1964) and 25 percent (Kuvlesky and Bealer, 1967) in studies of men done *10 years* after high school. Conclusions about changes in congruence with time after high school

are difficult to draw, since studies done at different intervals are not comparable in the inclusiveness of the occupational categories used or in the type of sample studied.

The most readily interpretable estimates of the relationship between occupational aspirations and subsequent occupational attainments are available for the status of occupations, as measured by the Duncan Socioeconomic Index (SEI). Analyzing data from an 18-year follow-up study of Wisconsin high school seniors, Sewell et al. (1980) found correlations of .461 for females and .543 for males between the status level of the occupation aspired to in high school and the status of the first job held. Somewhat lower correlations of .342 for females and .491 for males were found between the status level of the occupation aspired to in high school and the status of the occupation held 18 years later.

In the absence of information on the relationship between the sex typing of occupational aspirations and the sex typing of occupational attainments for a sample of individuals studied while in high school and again some years later, it is of interest to compare measures of sex segregation in occupational aspirations for a national sample of youth with measures of sex segregation in occupational attainments for the adult population. Such a comparison permits a crude assessment of the extent to which sex segregation in occupational goals approximates sex segregation in employment. Measures of sex segregation in respondents' occupational aspirations for age 35 were calculated using the 1979 NLS and were then compared to measures of sex segregation in actual employment based on data from the U.S. census.

As indicated above, the index of sex segregation in occupational aspirations determined from the 1979 NLS over the full range of the Census Bureau's detailed occupational categories was 61.0. This figure can be compared to a figure of 66.1, measuring the degree of sex segregation in the labor

TABLE 11-1   Percentage Distribution of Occupational Aspirations and
Attainments by Sex

	Aspirations[a]		Attainments[b]	
Percentage of Female Incumbents	Females	Males	Females	Males
<30	34.6	86.5	12.5	78.0
30-59	12.6	9.4	17.6	14.7
≥60	52.8	4.1	69.9	7.3
Total	100.0	100.0	100.0	100.0
N	4,036	5,073	27,497,081	46,028,117

[a] Data from National Longitudinal Survey of Young Americans (NLS), 1979.

[b] Data from 1970 Census of Population, Vol. 2, pt. 7(a), Table 1.

market in 1976 for the same set of Census Bureau categories (U.S. Commission on Civil Rights, 1978). The comparison indicates that the aspirations of youth are almost as highly sex segregated as the occupations held by those currently employed.

It was observed earlier that the occupational aspirations of males are more highly sex typed than those of females. Analysis of the 1979 NLS data indicates that the mean percentage of males actually employed in occupations aspired to by young men is 87.9 percent, whereas the mean percentage of females employed in occupations aspired to by young women is 56.5 percent. These figures can be compared with ones calculated using 1970 census data, which describe the degree to which jobs actually held by women and men are sex typed.[2] The mean percentage of males employed in occupations held mostly by men in 1970 was 82.3; the mean percentage of females employed in occupations held mostly by women was 70.3. The jobs actually held by both men and women therefore have, on the average, a somewhat higher percentage of female incumbents than the jobs aspired to, but the difference between aspirations and attainments is greater for women than men.

The distribution of occupational aspirations and attainments by sex type is examined in greater detail in Table 11-1, which presents data on aspirations from the NLS and data on attainments from the 1970 census. Occupations are divided into three sex-type categories on the basis of the percentage of female incumbents in the occupation. It can be seen that the percentage of young women aspiring to typically male occupations (34.6 percent) is considerably greater than the percentage of women actually employed in those occupations in 1970 (12.5 percent). The percentage of young men aspiring to typically male occupations (86.5 percent) is also greater than the percentage of men employed in those occupations in 1970 (78.0). Again, however, the difference between aspirations and attainments is shown to be greater for women than men. It is difficult to interpret these differences. They may indicate that females aspiring to typically male occupations are, in fact, less likely than males aspiring to those occupations to realize their occupational goals. On the other hand, they may reflect an increased tendency on the part of younger women (the NLS sample) to seek entry into occupations that are currently male-dominated.

To conclude, our comparison of the sex typing of occupational aspirations and attainments indicates that the degree of sex segregation in aspirations is only slightly lower than the degree of sex segregation in employment. This overall similarity between the sex typing of occupational aspirations and attainments indicates that influences prior to labor market entry play an important role

---

[2] These figures were calculated from data reported in the 1970 Census of Population, Vol. 2, pt. 7(a), Table 1.

in the determination of occupational outcomes for individuals. However, young people of both sexes are more likely to aspire to typically male occupations than adults of the same sex are to be employed in those occupations, and this difference is greater for females than males. To understand more fully the relationship between the sex type of occupational aspirations and attainments, research on samples of individuals studied over time is needed. It is particularly important that such research be undertaken now, since social change is likely to be producing differences between cohorts.

Development Over the Early Stages of the Life Course Studies of the occupational aspirations of preadolescents (preschool and elementary school children) indicate that sex differentiation in occupational goals appears at an early age (Looft, 1971a,b; Siegel, 1973; Harris, 1974; Hewitt, 1975; Papalia and Tennent, 1975; Umstot, 1980). Children tend to look at activities, including work, in terms of sex-appropriate categories, viewing particular activities as appropriate only for males or only for females (Hartley and Klein, 1959; Schlossberg and Goodman, 1972; Tibbetts, 1975; Tavris and Offir, 1977:186; Cummings and Taebel, 1980; Umstot, 1980). Girls' occupational preferences are heavily concentrated in the occupations of teacher and nurse, which often account for 50 to 75 percent of their occupational choices (Clark, 1967; Looft, 1971a,b; Siegel, 1973; Hewitt, 1975). The range of options considered by girls is typically narrow, whereas boys' choices are dispersed among more occupations (Looft, 1971a; Siegel, 1973; Hewitt, 1975; Papalia and Tennent, 1975). Studies of the discrepancy between aspirations and expectations further indicate that girls are more likely than boys to expect to enter occupations that are sex typed to the same or a higher degree than their aspirations (Looft, 1971a:366; Papalia and Tennent, 1975).

Attempts to assess developmental changes in the sex typing of occupational choices with increasing age in any precise way have been few. Studies of the extent to which children look at work in terms of sex-appropriate categories indicate little change in occupational sex typing with age over the elementary school years (Hartley and Klein, 1959; Schlossberg and Goodman, 1972). Two recent studies, however, suggest that females may become slightly more liberal during the elementary years about the jobs they feel should be open to both males and females (Cummings and Taebel, 1980; Umstot, 1980). Such an increase in liberality would be consistent with other studies reporting somewhat less sex stereotyping of occupations in adolescence and early adulthood than at younger ages (Harmon, 1971; Shephard and Hess, 1975). There is also evidence that a sex difference emerges with age in the degree to which occupations are sex stereotyped, with females becoming more likely than males to view an occupation as appropriate for either sex (Shepard and Hess, 1975; Nieva and Gutek, 1981:12).

Our own analysis of sex typing in the occupational aspirations of youth between the ages of 14 and 22, based on the 1979 NLS, found a small decline in the sex typing of occupational aspirations over this age range. The index of segregation, indicating the percentage of one sex that would have to change occupational aspirations to make the aspiration distributions of the two sexes equal, was 67.6 for 14- and 15-year-olds and 61.5 for 20- to 22-year-olds. That only a small amount of change occurs over this age range is confirmed by the findings of two earlier studies. Based on analysis of the National Longitudinal Surveys of the Labor Market Experiences of Young Men and Young Women initiated in 1966 and 1968, respectively, Hofferth (1980a) found little change in the sex typing of occupations aspired to for age 35 from grade 9 through the first three years after high school. Similarly, in an analysis based on the 1973-1974 assessment of career and occupational development conducted by the National Assessment of Educational Progress, Gottfredson (1978) presents data showing little difference in the sex typing of occupational aspirations between 13-year-old and 17-year-old students.

Although there may be a small overall decline in the sex typing of occupational aspirations among youth, the occupational choices of college students have been found to become *more* sex typed over the college years (Davis, 1965; Astin and Panos, 1969; Hind and Wirth, 1969). Of entering freshmen planning careers in male occupations, women were more likely than men to switch to some other occupational choice during their undergraduate years. Women were also less likely to be recruited into a male occupation from some other field. In contrast, men were less likely to remain in or be recruited into a female field. This pattern of change was paralleled by a similar pattern of change in undergraduate majors. Men were more likely than women to remain in or shift to business, engineering, the physical sciences, and mathematics, whereas women were more likely to remain in or shift to majors in the arts, humanities, and education (Astin and Panos, 1969; Zinberg, 1974; Ernest, 1976).

It can be concluded, therefore, that sex differences in occupational aspirations appear at preschool ages and are maintained into adulthood. They may decrease slightly during late adolescence and early adulthood but have been found to increase during the college years. To accurately document the development of sex differences in occupational aspirations over the life course, however, will require longitudinal studies of cohorts over time, which have not yet been carried out.

Recent Historical Trends In the wake of the women's liberation movement, attitudes about the appropriate roles of women and men have been changing (Mason et al., 1976; Spitze and Huber, 1980; Thornton and Freedman, 1979). Part of this change involves a more favorable attitude toward the employment of married women. Within this climate of general attitude change, changes appear to be occurring in the sex segregation of occupational aspirations and plans among high school students. Studies examining such changes consistently indicate a decline in sex segregation, although the precise amount of decline is difficult to assess (Garrison, 1979; Lueptow, 1981; Herzog, 1982).

Studying the occupational goals of Wisconsin high school seniors in 1964 and 1975, Lueptow (1981) found that the percentage of girls planning to enter predominantly female occupations dropped from 79.7 percent in 1964 to 49.8 percent in 1975. This trend was offset somewhat by choices of a number of new sex-typed occupations in 1975. The overall drop in the proportion of females expecting to enter predominantly female occupations was, therefore, only 16.2 percent. Changes in the demographic composition of the schools studied between 1964 and 1975 and a low response rate in 1975, however, raise some question about the accuracy of these estimates.

Garrison (1979) examined changes in the sex segregation of occupational expectations among Virginia high school seniors between 1970 and 1976. Using a 7-category measure of expectations, he found that the index of segregation comparing the occupational distributions of the two sexes dropped from 43.6 in 1970 to 38.2 in 1976. Herzog (1982) examined changes in the sex segregation of occupational plans between 1976 and 1980 for national samples of high school seniors surveyed annually. Based on a 15-category measure of occupational expectations for age 30, she found that the index of segregation between male and female choices declined from 49.8 in 1976 to 36.3 in 1980. All three of these studies indicate declining sex segregation in the occupational goals of high school seniors, although estimates of the precise amount of decline in each study depend heavily on the way in which occupational goals are categorized. More detailed occupational classifications undoubtedly would indicate higher degrees of sex segregation and could affect the amount of change observed over time.

Occupational Knowledge

Given the narrower range of female occupational aspirations and the sex typing of both male and female choices, it is of interest to consider whether the two sexes differ in their knowledge of occupations. As indicated above, an understanding of what the adult world views as male and female jobs is acquired by children early in life, and the ability to identify occupations and describe them increases rapidly as children enter adolescence (DeFleur, 1963; Nelson, 1963).

Research indicates that neither boys nor girls are significantly superior in their ability to name and describe occupations (Nelson, 1963; O'Bryant et al., 1980), although sex differences do appear in children's assessments of different job dimensions. Boys seem to be more aware of the status and monetary rewards of jobs than are girls (DeFleur, 1963; O'Bryant et al., 1980) and to assimilate this information early. Girls do not become as aware of these dimensions until adolescence (O'Bryant et al., 1980).[3] In rating the importance of service provided to the community by an occupation, each sex gives higher ratings to occupations dominated by members of their own sex. Together, these studies indicate that although preadolescent males and females have comparable superficial knowledge of adult job roles—that is, they are able to identify roles and describe their duties—their sensitivity to the rewards associated with these roles (respect and status, money, a feeling of providing community service) may be conditioned by the values they learn to consider in choosing

an occupation. In other words, boys learn early to direct their attention to the status and monetary rewards of jobs, whereas girls pay more attention to altruistic concerns and personal fulfillment.

Three experimental studies that examine the effect of providing occupational information to children (Thompson and Parker, 1971; Barclay, 1974; Harris, 1974) indicate that knowledge alone plays a limited role in determining the occupational choices of young males and females. These studies indicate that, unless the presentation of jobs and career information includes examples of women in nontraditional roles or encourages discussion of sex-role stereotyping, the provision of information does little to heighten students' awareness of sex typing or to broaden their occupational aspirations to include jobs atypically held by their sex. Because there appears to be a relationship between the job-relevant information children process and the values they hold regarding occupations, we will now examine the evidence on sex differences in occupational values.

Occupational Values

Sex differences in the values placed on various dimensions of jobs have been documented across age groups in studies dating back to the 1930s. Witty and Lehman (1930) reported that, across ages ranging from 8 to 18 years, boys showed a consistently greater tendency than girls to aspire to jobs they judged to have high monetary returns. The public respect believed to be associated with jobs also played a larger role in the choices of boys than girls. Both of these differences increased with age, indicating that girls either increasingly looked to marriage as a means of obtaining financial support or became increasingly aware that many financially profitable and highly respected occupations were not open to them. More recently, O'Hara (1962) found financial rewards to be a stronger motivating force for elementary school boys

---

[3] O'Bryant et al. (1980) used the responses of college students as a standard by which to measure the accuracy of preadolescent responses. It is not known how well these college students' perceptions would correspond to those of a sample of older adults.

than for girls. Singer and Stefflre (1954) also found significant differences in the importance male and female high school seniors attached to job dimensions, with females attaching more weight to the amount of interest and opportunity to help people provided by jobs, and males attaching more value to jobs they saw as offering high monetary rewards, an opportunity to work more or less on one's own, and the chance to be the boss.

In the last few years, research has continued to document these sex differences in occupational values.[4] Studies attempting to assess recent changes in the job dimensions to which males and females attach significance have found surprisingly little convergence between the sexes during the 1970s (Lueptow, 1980; Herzog, 1982). Lueptow (1980) compared the occupational values of graduating seniors in 1961 and 1975 and found that at both time points males placed significantly greater value on status, money, freedom from supervision, and leadership than did females. Females valued working with people, helping others, using their abilities, and being creative more than males did. By 1975 there was some indication of increased male interest in working with people, but increased female interest in the stereotypically masculine-valued dimensions of money, status, freedom from supervision, and leadership was not evident. Herzog's (1982) analysis of data from the Monitoring the Future project replicated these differences for successive cohorts of high school seniors between 1975 and 1980. In addition, data collected from sophomores and seniors in a nationally representative sample of U.S. high schools as part of the High School and Beyond survey in 1980 indicate similar differences in male and female job values (Peng et al., 1981). These differences also were found in two other recent studies based on smaller, nonnationally representative samples (Brenner and Tomkiewicz, 1979; Tittle, 1981). Thus, despite some evidence of declining sex differences in the occupational plans of adolescents in the 1970s, which we discussed earlier, sex differences in occupational values persist.

Since the two sexes differ upon entry into the labor force not only in the attitudes, knowledge, and values they hold about occupations but also in the skills and personal-social attributes that affect access to occupations, we will consider evidence on the existence of sex differences in abilities and dispositional traits.

Abilities and Dispositional Traits

Evidence pertaining to sex differences in many abilities and dispositional traits has been reviewed recently by a number of psychologists (Oetzel, 1966; Maccoby and Jacklin, 1974; Block, 1976; Tavris and Offir, 1977; Frieze et al., 1978). Maccoby and Jacklin's (1974) extensive review of approximately 1,600 studies published, for the most part, between 1966 and 1973 has formed the basis for most later reviews, which expand upon it and, in some cases, reinterpret its findings (Block, 1976). In general, research to date permits few definitive conclusions to be drawn about the existence of sex differences, much less their origins (Block, 1976). There is some evidence to indicate the existence of sex differences favoring males in quantitative and spatial abilities and sex differences favoring females in verbal abilities (Terman and Tyler, 1954; Tyler, 1965; Oetzel, 1966; Dwyer, 1973; Maccoby and Jacklin, 1974; Block, 1976). However, although these differences appear rather consistently across studies, they are small. It has been estimated that in the large-sample studies reviewed by Maccoby and Jacklin (1974), sex accounted for only 1 to 2 percent of the

---

[4] A study of black inner-city high school students, however, found no significant differences between males and females in terms of valued job dimensions (Brief and Aldag, 1975), indicating that sex differences may not be uniform across racial groups.

variance in reading performance and 4 percent of the variance in mathematics performance (Plomin and Fock, 1981).

Sex differences in dispositional traits also have been documented, although the evidence pertaining to these traits is weaker. Among the most well documented sex differences is the tendency for males to be more aggressive than females (Maccoby and Jacklin, 1974; Block, 1976). There is also some evidence to indicate that males are more dominant, possessing a stronger, more potent self-concept; are more curious and explorative; more impulsive; and more active (Block, 1976). Other evidence suggests that females may be more fearful and timid, more susceptible to anxiety, less confident in task performance, and more likely to seek help and reassurance (Block, 1976). Females also appear to maintain closer proximity to friends than do males and to be influenced more by the social desirability of behavior (Block, 1976). No sex differences have been found in nurturance and maternal behaviors, such as helping and sharing, in general self-esteem, in achievement orientation, and in degree of auditory orientation (Maccoby and Jacklin, 1974; Block, 1976).

Research on sex differences in physical strength and ability has been reviewed less systematically but indicates substantial differences favoring males in upper body strength and smaller differences favoring males in leg strength (Wood, 1980). Females show somewhat greater tolerance for heat than do males and have more body fat, which gives them an advantage in some activities requiring endurance (Wood, 1980). Although it has not been replicated recently, early research indicated that boys possess greater speed and coordination of gross body movement (Maccoby and Jacklin, 1974). Girls are generally believed to have better manual dexterity than boys, but sex differences in dexterity depend on the task observed. Girls have been found to have somewhat better finger dexterity, but they do not have better overall manual dexterity (Maccoby and Jacklin, 1974).

In conclusion, there is evidence to indicate the existence of some sex differences in personality traits and abilities, but most appear to be small and, as discussed earlier, result primarily from sex-role socialization. That is, most appear to be learned and can be viewed as a *product* of differences in the expectations society holds for the two sexes rather than as a *cause* of those differences.

It has been argued that sex differences in personality traits and abilities form the basis for sex differences in occupational choice and, ultimately, for the allocation of males and females to different positions in the labor market. Although it is possible that sex differences, particularly in physical characteristics, are the basis for some occupational sorting by sex, the relevance of most stereotypically ascribed sex differences in personality and ability, including physical differences, to occupational performance remains unknown. That is, it is unknown to what extent jobs that are traditionally held by one sex and that are thought to require sex-related traits actually do. It seems likely that the extent to which one sex is better suited to perform sex-typed jobs has been greatly exaggerated. Because sex differences in personality traits and abilities are smaller than they are stereotypically ascribed to be and are of questionable relevance to the performance of most jobs, their role in the determination of sex segregation in the labor market is likely to be minimal.

Summary

Marked differences exist between males and females in occupational orientation. From very young ages, females aspire to and expect to enter typically female occupations, whereas males aspire to and expect to enter typically male occupations. These sex differences in occupational choice have an important bearing on subsequent sex segregation in the labor market, since the degree of sex segregation in occupational aspirations prior to labor market entry closely approximates the degree of sex segregation in the labor market. The sexes also differ in the importance they attach to various dimensions of jobs, with females valuing the intrinsic interest of a job and the opportunity it affords to work with and help others more than males do, and males valuing the extrinsic rewards of a job, including status, money, and power, more than females do. Although sex differences in abilities and dispositional traits exist prior to entry into the labor market, they are unlikely to play an important role in the determination of occupational segregation. Most differences are small and appear to result from, rather than cause, sex differences in occupational orientation. The relevance of sex differences in abilities and dispositional traits to occupational performance is also open to question, since it is unknown to what extent jobs that are traditionally held by one sex and that are thought to require sex-related traits actually require those traits.

DETERMINANTS OF SEX DIFFERENCES IN OCCUPATIONAL ORIENTATION

As discussed above, sex differences in occupational orientation and job-relevant traits can be seen as arising largely from the process of sex-role socialization, which begins at a child's birth. Messages about what is viewed as appropriate for the two sexes are conveyed in myriad ways and constitute the basis on which the two sexes learn to have different expectations about the roles they will fill and learn to behave differently. In this section, we examine some of the major sources of sex-role learning, focusing on factors that are likely to affect the development of sex differences in occupational orientation and preparation. Specifically, our review covers family influences, school influences, messages transmitted by the mass media, and early employment experiences.

Family Influences

The earliest and most pervasive influences on sex-role socialization arise within the family. Children not only interact with their parents earlier and more frequently than with other adults but they also have strong emotional ties to their parents that reinforce the effects of parental actions. Studies of modeling in laboratory settings suggest that parents are effective models for their children because they are the most nurturant and powerful people with whom a child interacts (Bandura and Huston, 1961; Bandura et al., 1963; Mischel and Grusec, 1966). In recent years, researchers have sought primarily to address two questions about parental effects on sex typing. First, do parents treat boys and girls differently? Second, do parents serve as role models for the adoption of nontraditional role behavior? Evidence pertaining to these questions is reviewed below.

Differential Treatment of Boys and Girls by Parents Based on a review of research focusing primarily on the sex typing of personal and social behaviors, Maccoby and Jacklin (1974) concluded that there were surprisingly few differences in parents' treatment of boys and girls. No differences were found in the total amount of interaction between parents and infants or in the amount and kind of verbal interaction. Based on observational studies, there was little evidence that children of the two sexes received different amounts of parental warmth or reinforcement for dependency. Similarly, there was no evidence that parents responded differently to aggression in boys and girls. However, boys were given more gross motor stimulation and were encouraged in physical activity more than girls were. Boys also received more praise and more punishment, particularly physical punishment. Likewise, boys received more pressure than girls not to engage in sex-inappropriate behavior. The fact that more differences in parental treatment of boys and girls were not documented may be attributable to limitations of the data base reviewed by Maccoby and Jacklin and to the procedures they used in drawing conclusions from the evidence (Block, 1976).

A more recent review of research by Huston (in press), focusing not only on the sex typing of personal and social behaviors but also on activities and interests, provides more evidence of differential treatment of the two sexes. Huston reviewed experimental studies in which the child's gender label was manipulated as well as observational studies of parents with their own children. She found evidence that boys and girls were encouraged in different types of play activities from infancy onward. Adults made sex-typed toy choices for children, offering dolls exclusively to children they believed to be girls. Gross motor activity was encouraged more in boys than in girls. Adults played more actively with male infants and responded more positively to physical activity in boys than in girls. In contrast, interpersonal play activity and dependent, affectionate behavior were more often encouraged in girls than in boys. Fathers emphasized sex-typed play activity more than mothers did and interacted with boys more than with girls. Like Maccoby and Jacklin (1974), Huston (in press) found little evidence that aggression provokes different parental responses for boys and girls. A considerable body of evidence, however, indicates that boys are given more opportunities to play away from home and, therefore, more freedom from adult supervision than are girls.

In addition to treating the sexes differently in terms of play activities, it has been well documented that parents have higher expectations for the adult achievement of their sons than of their daughters (Alexander and Eckland, 1974; Maccoby and Jacklin, 1974; Hauser et al., 1976; Hoffman, 1977; Marini, 1978a,b). Recent evidence indicates that parents also value mathematics achievement more in sons than in daughters and estimate the mathematics competence of sons to be higher than that of daughters (Fennema and Sherman, 1977; Fox et al., 1979). Observations of the teaching behaviors of

parents indicate that parents socialize achievement differently for boys and girls. Parents have higher expectations and demand more independence of boys, whereas they provide help more readily to girls and are more likely to focus on interpersonal aspects of the teaching situation (Huston, in press).

These sex differences in socialization, which are rooted in parents' general sex-role conceptions, can be expected to have long-term effects on the occupational behavior of the two sexes. Although the links between parents' socialization of personal and social behavior and occupational outcomes are indirect, childbearing practices that affect the acquisition of job-relevant skills and the development of occupational expectations bear on occupational choice. As we will discuss below, parents who display less traditional sex-role behavior, and who are therefore likely to hold less traditional sex-role attitudes, produce children whose occupational behavior is less differentiated along sex lines.

Parental Role Models The fact that mothers and fathers tend to be employed in different jobs outside the home, to perform different tasks within the home, and to have different interests and personal and social characteristics provides information to children about what is expected of women and men. A consistent finding of previous research is that children's sex-role attitudes are less traditionally stereotyped if the mother is employed outside the home than if she is not (Huston, in press). Maternal employment affects the sex-role attitudes of both sexes, but it affects the sex typing of personal and social attributes, interests, and activities almost exclusively for girls. Employed mothers have been found to be particularly attractive role models for their daughters, as evidenced by the fact that daughters of employed mothers more often want to be like their mothers and say they use their mothers as models (Hoffman, 1974; Miller, 1975). However, the effects of maternal employment may also arise because maternal employment is associated with other sex-role activities, personality characteristics, and child-rearing practices of parents.

Although there is considerable evidence to indicate that maternal employment fosters career salience among daughters, particularly if the mother has a positive attitude toward her employment (Beardslee and O'-Dowd, 1962; Siegel and Curtis, 1963; Douvan and Adelson, 1966; Hartley, 1966; White, 1967; Vogel et al., 1970; Almquist and Angrist, 1971; Baruch, 1972; Altman and Grossman, 1977; Hoffman and Nye, 1975; Bielby, 1978b; Kaufman and Richardson, 1982:22-27), there is less evidence that it affects the entry of daughters into traditionally male occupations. Studies of small, restricted samples of college students suggest that maternal employment increases the probability of entry into nontraditional fields by daughters (Almquist and Angrist, 1970; Almquist, 1974; Tangri, 1972; Klemmack and Edwards, 1973). However, studies of larger samples that are more representative of the U.S. college population find little or no positive effect of maternal employment on the entry of daughters into traditionally male occupations (Bielby, 1978a; Brito and Jusenius, 1978). It appears likely that the *type* of employment engaged in by the mother rather than her employment per se is the factor that influences entry into traditionally male occupations by daughters. Based on a study of high school students who did not go to college, Hofferth (1980a) found that for whites the sex type of the mother's occupation had a direct effect on the sex type of the daughter's occupation. This relationship may pertain over the full range of educational attainment, but it has not been investigated.

School Influences

The role of schools in promoting or inhibiting sex segregation in occupational goals is a multifaceted one. In this section we review research on a variety of socialization influences arising within the school, including the availability of same-sex role models, sex stereotyping in textbooks and educational material, the role of counselors in channeling students into careers, tracking and vocational education, and training in mathematics and science. We also consider evidence on the success of governmental intervention through legislation, such as Title IX, the Women's Educational Equity Act, and the 1976 Vocational Education Amendments.

Availability of Same-Sex Role Models   Although the importance of role models of one's own sex is a theme that implicitly runs through much of the research on sources of occupational socialization, empirical studies dealing with the processes involved in role modeling, particularly in the case of adolescents and young adults, are few. Douvan (1976) points to the prominent role of an older-woman model in biographies of women successful in such fields as politics and academics and suggests the advantages of womens' colleges in providing a broad array of female role models. In examining determinants of college females' occupational aspirations, Brito and Jusenius (1978) found that attendance at either a predominantly female or predominantly male college was associated with atypical aspirations. More direct evidence that same-sex role models may be salient to the educational and career choices of college students and to their career success is available. Basow and Howe (1979) indicate that college seniors reported their career choices to be significantly more affected by same-sex role models than by opposite-sex models. Tidball (1973) found that the number of women on the faculty at a college was a good predictor of the number of career women the school would produce. Fox (1974) found that the distribution of college males and females across fields of specialization closely mirrored the distribution of same-sex faculty, and the degree to which female students were concentrated in certain areas reflected the concentration of female faculty. Although prior socialization conditioning males and females to major in sex-appropriate fields was no doubt a factor influencing this concentration, the resemblance of students' choices to the pattern of faculty specialization was striking. Finally, career success has been linked to exposure to a same-sex mentor. In a study of psychology Ph.D.'s, Goldstein (1979) found that having had a same-sex adviser was significantly related to academic productivity (measured by number of publications) 4 years later. Although this result links career success to exposure to a same-sex mentor, attribution of a causal relationship is difficult because it is impossible to tell how the same students would have performed under the tutelage of an opposite-sex adviser. Taken as a whole, these studies indicate that same-sex role modeling influences occupational decision making, but more research is needed to further document the existence and nature of its effects.

Sex Stereotyping in Textbooks and Educational Materials   Sex bias in educational materials was recognized as a serious issue in the late 1960s, and several studies conducted in the early 1970s documented the existence of sex stereotyping, particularly in mathematics and science textbooks (Milnar, 1973; Rogers, 1975). With increasing public recognition of the problem and the passage of certain legislation, such as Title IX in 1972,[5] prohibiting the distribution of federal funds to schools that did not comply with sex-equity practices, biased representations of the sexes in educational materials were expected to decrease. However, textbooks published throughout the 1970s continued to portray the sexes in stereotypical roles.

---

[5] Legal judgment regarding the First Amendment and freedom of speech has since resulted in the exclusion of curriculum materials from coverage by Title IX.

Two groups of researchers, publishing comprehensive studies of sex stereotyping in elementary school textbooks in the mid-1970s, found pervasive evidence of sex bias. Weitzman and Rizzo's (1974) study of the illustrations in a sample of the most widely used textbooks revealed that males appeared in 69 percent of textbook illustrations, whereas females appeared in only 31 percent. These figures became more skewed the higher the grade level. The lopsided representation of the sexes was most apparent in the science field and least evident in social studies, a more feminine field. Whereas men were portrayed overall in more than 150 occupational roles, women appeared as housewives or, when working, in a narrowly circumscribed set of roles such as nurse, teacher, librarian, and sales clerk. Women on Words and Images (1975b), a New Jersey-based group of researchers and consultants, also assessed sex stereotyping in elementary school textbooks. They examined 134 readers (from 14 different publishers) in use in three suburban New Jersey school districts. Their findings on the portrayal of occupational stereotypes were as follows: (1) women were portrayed in stories and in illustrations in a total of 26 occupations, whereas men appeared in 147 different jobs; (2) aside from the role of doctor, women were universally portrayed in stereotypically feminine roles, such as cook, housekeeper, librarian, school nurse, teacher, and telephone operator; and (3) in terms of biographies, which can be viewed as important because they show adults in significant roles outside the home, there were 27 stories about 17 different women, compared with 119 stories about 88 men. The message conveyed by these depictions of adult males and females is that females have a narrow range of jobs to choose from and generally make less of a contribution to public life than do males.

Other investigators have examined sex stereotyping in textbooks used in particular subject areas. Stern (1976), in an examination of beginning and intermediate foreign language textbooks published between 1970 and 1974, found that both dialogues and photographs depicted a biased range of occupational roles for males and females and focused much more heavily on males' occupational aspirations than on those of females. Sex stereotyping in mathematics textbooks is particularly well documented. Kepner and Koehn (1977) evaluated 24 first-, fourth-, and seventh-grade mathematics texts put out by 8 major publishers between 1971 and 1975 to determine their representation of the sexes. They found that elementary mathematics texts tended to depict males in a greater variety of occupations than females, both in illustrations and in written problems, and that sex stereotyping of occupations was prevalent in these texts.

These researchers also examined three widely advertised mathematics textbooks published between 1975 and 1977. In these texts females were shown in a wider range of occupations than had been the case in previously published textbooks; in fact, women were shown as moving into typically male occupations, such as doctor, truck driver, and political candidate. However, males were not depicted in traditionally female occupations. Another study of sex bias in six widely used elementary mathematics textbook series published between 1970 and 1975 indicated that the two series published most recently showed more occupational role reversals for males and females than those published earlier in the decade (Steele, 1977).

Sex-role stereotypes are prevalent not only in textbooks but also in children's picture books. Studies by Weitzman et al. (1972) and Nilsen (1977) have demonstrated the predominance of male over female characters in books that were winners of the prestigious Caldecott Medal, awarded yearly to a book oriented toward preschool children. Nilsen documented an actual decline in the percentage of female characters during the 1950s and 1960s, from 46 percent in 1951-1955 to 26 percent in 1966-1970.

Unfortunately, little is known about the effects of sex-stereotyped educational materials on children's attitudes and, ultimately, on their occupational aspirations. Researchers have been guided by the assumption that reading materials do exert a pervasive influence on young readers' views and motivation, but the extent and permanence of such effects have generally not been investigated. Two exceptions are reports by Kimmel (1970) and Nilsen (1977) of experimental reading programs and short-term controlled experiments. Nilsen reports a direct correlation between the degree to which children classify activities as belonging in male and female domains and length of exposure to the Alpha One reading program, identified as presenting highly sex-stereotyped images to children. Kimmel reports on several experimental studies that appear to have an effect on children's stereotypical attitudes (in this case, of minorities) and concludes cautiously that books may play a significant role in conditioning children's attitudes, although the duration of the effect of specific books may not be long.

Counseling and Career Guidance   There is a large body of literature in the fields of educational and counseling psychology dealing with issues related to sex bias in career counseling. Although we can deal with this literature in only a cursory fashion here, we consider findings with implications for the career choices of women. The topics we touch on include counselor bias in assessment and counseling concerning women's career preferences, sex bias in occupational reference materials used for counseling purposes, and the importance of the counselor in effecting changes in females' occupational aspirations and outcomes.

Studies of counselors' attitudes and knowledge about women's careers suggest that counselors contribute to the sex stereotyping of occupations. A number of studies have documented the existence of traditional attitudes on the part of counselors regarding appropriate roles for women. In a much-cited experimental study, Thomas and Stewart (1971) found that counselors, regardless of their sex, perceived conforming career goals (such as home economist) as being significantly more appropriate for women than deviate career goals (such as engineer). This perception was correlated with counselors' level of experience; more experienced counselors perceived no statistically significant difference in the appropriateness of the goals. Female clients who purportedly held deviate goals were also judged to have a significantly greater need for counseling than those with conforming goals.

More recent studies have continued to indicate that school counselors have a restricted view of the occupations appropriate for women (Medvene and Collins, 1976) and suggest different occupational choices for intellectually gifted males and females (Donahue and Costar, 1977). In a study focusing on counselors' perceptions of the variables important in college students' career choices, counselors perceived women to be more influenced by such considerations as success avoidance, home-career conflict, and attitudes of the opposite sex than women reported themselves to be (Karpicke, 1980). Male counselors generally seemed to display somewhat more bias than female counselors, and at least one study suggests that school counselors may be more biased than other types of counselors, such as psychotherapists (Medvene and Collins, 1976).

In a study of the accuracy of counselors' knowledge of labor force issues relating to women, Bingham and House (1973) found that a sample of secondary school counselors demonstrated correct knowledge on only 12 of 25 items. On 7 of the items most frequently missed, significantly more female than male counselors responded correctly. Although the authors identified all items as factual, those missed more frequently by males than females seemed to be especially open to influence by attitudes. Examples included whether women need more employment alternatives, whether most women can perform the roles of worker and homemaker simultaneously in a satisfactory fashion, and whether women are discriminated against in employment practices.

Several researchers have examined career information materials published by private publishers and the federal government for their portrayal of occupational roles for males and females (Heshusius-Gilsdorf and Gilsdorf, 1975; Lauver et al., 1975). These studies indicate that women tend to be both underrepresented and portrayed in traditionally female occupations in illustrations and accompanying job descriptions. Males, on the other hand, tend to be portrayed in traditionally male occupations. Two popular and widely used career orientation textbook series put out by private publishers portrayed top-management, professional, and technical positions as being filled almost exclusively by men, and they portrayed extremely skewed sex ratios for traditionally sex-stereotyped jobs such as clerical workers; steward(esse)s; nurses; and construction, large machine, and repair workers (Heshusius-Gilsdorf and Gilsdorf, 1975). A study of the 1974-1975 *Occupational Outlook Handbook*, published by the U.S. Bureau of Labor Statistics, also found evidence of sex bias in career portrayal (Lauver et al., 1975), although a more recent study of the 1976-1977 edition reported substantial reduction in the amount of sex bias (Farmer and Backer, 1977).

In general, research on counselors' attitudes and knowledge, and on the career information materials they use, indicates that bias exists in the perceived appropriateness of a variety of occupational aspirations for women, in the roles women are assumed to fill in the labor market, and in the reasons perceived to lie behind career choices. Virtually every article in this area concludes with a recommendation that school counselors be required to receive exposure to statistics on female labor force participation and information on employer biases in various fields. The provision of accurate occupational information and training to alert school counselors to the possibility that their views may be sex biased is undoubtedly important. However, it should be recognized that little is known about the degree to which counselors actually influence students. Understandably, the counseling literature tends to attribute a strong role to counselors as possible agents of social change (Vetter, 1973; Verheyden-Hilliard, 1977). But studies that attempt to assess the impact of counseling on students are few. In one careful study of the effects of counseling on New York high school students, Rehberg and Hotchkiss (1972) found that nonschool influences such as socioeconomic status, intelligence, parental encouragement, and previously held educational expectations together exerted a much greater influence on students' educational expectations than their exposure to counseling. In another study of a small sample of high school students, Tittle (1981) found that only 27 percent of those surveyed reported having talked to a counselor about work possibilities.

Tracking and Vocational Education Empirical studies of tracking have typically focused on the determinants and implications of student placement in college and noncollege preparatory tracks rather than on specific vocational courses. However, the findings of these studies have some important implications that are generalizable to all types of tracking that segregate males and females and thereby affect their occupational orientations and outcomes. First, a review of the tracking literature by Rosenbaum (1980) underscores the degree to which students are labeled within the school and the community once they embark on a particular track, regardless of whether track placement is a result of their own free choice or counselor assignment (Cicourel and Kitsuse, 1963; Schafer and Olexa, 1971; Heyns, 1974; Rosenbaum, 1978). Second,

in the case of assignment to college and noncollege preparatory tracks, counselors' judgments of students' personalities often play a large role (Cicourel and Kitsuse, 1963), a finding that provides a disturbing complement to our discussion of counselor bias related to the sex of the student. Finally, students frequently are unaware of the implications of the tracks into which they have been guided or assigned, and frustration about plans for postsecondary education may result (Rosenbaum, 1980). Analyzing data from the National Longitudinal Survey of the High School Class of 1972, Rosenbaum (1980) showed that, for both males and females, the actual track had a greater influence on college attendance than did students' perceptions of the track to which they belonged. Misperceptions aside, therefore, track placement had an objective impact on educational outcomes.

Given the importance of tracking as a mechanism that sorts students into groups on the basis of presumed or stated abilities and preferences, the distribution of males and females in different vocational preparation tracks has potentially important consequences. Studies of the distribution of high school students across educational curricula in the late 1960s and early 1970s indicated that, when business and office programs were included in the definition of vocational education, 20 to 44 percent of senior girls were enrolled in vocational education programs (Grasso, 1980; Harnischfeger and Wiley, 1980; Hofferth, 1980b). Relatively few girls were enrolled in the vocational education track per se, since it tends to provide training for entry into blue-collar occupations. However, girls who did enroll in the vocational education track did not differ in ability from those in other noncollege preparatory tracks. In contrast, boys who enrolled in the vocational education track tended to be lower in ability than those in other noncollege preparatory tracks (Harnischfeger and Wiley, 1980). The overall distribution of females across vocationally oriented programs differs markedly from that of males, and there has been no substantial change in the sex typing of such programs between 1972 and 1978 (American Institutes for Research, 1980). Health, home economics, and business and office programs are enrolled in primarily by females (over 75 percent of those enrolled in 1972 and 1978 were females), and technical, agricultural, and trade and industrial programs are enrolled in primarily by males (over 75 percent of those enrolled in 1972 and 1978 were males). Only one program, retail sales, is enrolled in by approximately equal numbers of females and males (45 percent of those enrolled in 1972 and 42 percent of those enrolled in 1978 were females).

Since the purpose of vocationally oriented programs is to prepare students for particular types of occupations, it can be expected that the sex typing of such programs affects subsequent occupational segregation by sex. A study by Grasso (1980) of females who did not go to college, based on data from the National Longitudinal Survey of the Labor Market Experiences of Young Women collected in 1968 and 1972, indicated that girls in all curricula had highly sex-typed occupational aspirations but that those in business and office programs were the most traditional, with 69 percent aspiring to jobs that were 80 to 100 percent female. In accordance with their aspirations, female business and office program students were more likely than others to hold female-typical jobs 4 years later, with 65 percent holding jobs that were 80 to 100 percent female. Females who had been enrolled in vocational programs, where *vocational* refers to programs other than white-collar clerical programs, were less likely to hold female-typical jobs than those enrolled in business and office, general, and college preparatory programs. Another study of students who did not go to college by Hofferth (1980b), based on data from the National Longitudinal Surveys of the Labor Market Experiences of Young Men and

Young Women, collected in 1966 and 1968 and in three subsequent follow-ups, indicated that those enrolled in a vocational education track were less likely to be employed in female-typical jobs 10 years after high school than those enrolled in the general, commercial, and college preparatory tracks, which tend to prepare students for white-collar jobs.

Both the studies by Grasso (1980) and Hofferth (1980b), however, indicated that although females who had been enrolled in vocational programs were less likely to be employed in female-typed jobs, the jobs they held were *less* economically desirable than the jobs held by females who had been enrolled in business and office, general, and college preparatory programs. Grasso (1980) found that those enrolled in business and office programs had higher hourly wages (and yearly salaries) 4 years after high school than their peers enrolled in the general track. (Female vocational education enrollment was too low to permit examination of its effect on earnings.) Hofferth (1980b) found that those enrolled in a vocational education track received lower wages 10 years after high school than those enrolled in other programs. Black females enrolled in business and office programs maintained a wage advantage 10 years after high school compared with those enrolled in other programs, although white females did not. For females attending high school in the 1960s, therefore, enrollment in a vocational education track that prepares students for typically male blue-collar jobs did not result in employment in high-earning occupations. It is possible, however, that increased female enrollment in vocational education and greater awareness of discriminatory practices in male-typed blue-collar occupations could increase the number of women entering the more desirable blue-collar occupations and thereby produce earnings gains for women.

Planned interventions to decrease sex segregation in vocationally oriented programs have shown mixed results. Evenson and O'Neil (1978) reported on several projects in the 1970s that succeeded in markedly increasing female enrollment in trade and industrial courses. Components that seemed to be related to program success included attention to the training of teachers and counselors in ways of eliminating sex bias, provision of information and individual counseling to students, and the training of students to offer peer guidance. Programs focusing on change in both teachers and students offered the advantage of an approach that was well integrated. In contrast, Waite and Hudis (1980) reported on the more limited success shown by a number of programs. Although it is not possible to undertake a detailed comparison here, it appears that interventions concentrating on heightening student awareness of sex stereotyping do not result in altered occupational choices as much as do programs that also train school staff in issues of sex bias.

Training in Mathematics and Science An important difference in the formal education of the two sexes occurs in the area of training in mathematics and science. From high school onward, males take more advanced mathematics and science courses than females do (Ernest, 1976; Fennema and Sherman, 1977; Sherman and Fennema, 1977; Fox et al., 1979). This sex difference in technical training has important implications for sex segregation in the labor market since the poorer mathematics and science training of females prevents them from entering many traditionally male occupations. As discussed below, recent evidence suggests that sex differences in mathematics and science training arise not so much from sex differences in the ability to master these subjects or, at least in the case of mathematics, from sex differences in the appeal of the subject as from the labeling of these fields as male domains. Since the physical sciences and mathematics have traditionally been considered male subjects, and children are so-

cialized to view them as such, females are less likely than males to perceive training in science and mathematics as useful and to be confident of their ability in these subjects.

For the elementary school years, when the two sexes receive comparable training in mathematics and science, studies rarely report sex differences in aptitude or achievement in these areas (Fennema, 1974a; Maccoby and Jacklin, 1974; Fox et al., 1979). At the secondary and postsecondary school levels, sex differences in performance on standardized tests are evident (Maccoby and Jacklin, 1974), but studies have frequently failed to control for differential exposure to courses (Fox et al., 1979). Thus, the sex differences observed may be attributable to sex differences in motivation to study mathematics and the physical sciences rather than to sex differences in ability. Studies at the elementary and secondary school levels indicate that males do not report greater liking for mathematics than do females, nor do males show a greater preference for mathematics relative to other subjects (Stright, 1960; Aiken, 1970, 1976; Callahan, 1971; Ernest, 1976). Males do, however, show a greater preference for science at early grade levels (Ernest, 1976). At the postsecondary school level sex differences in attitudes toward both mathematics and science are evident (Dreger and Aiken, 1957; Aiken and Dreger, 1961; Aiken, 1970; Ernest, 1976).

It would appear that, at least at the secondary school level, sex differences in enrollment in mathematics courses arise not from different levels of interest in the subject but primarily from the two sexes' perceptions of mathematics as being differentially useful to them. Several studies indicate that perception of the future usefulness of mathematics is an important determinant of course enrollment in high school (Sherman and Fennema, 1977; see also Fox et al., 1979). Sex differences in the expressed usefulness of mathematics have been reported to occur as early as the seventh grade (Hilton and

Berglund, 1974; Fennema and Sherman, 1977; Sherman and Fennema, 1977). There is also evidence that girls are unaware of many of the uses of mathematics in careers other than strictly scientific ones (Fennema and Sherman, 1977). In addition, sex differences in enrollment in mathematics and science courses may also exist because the two sexes are not equally confident of their abilities in these areas. Such sex differences in self-confidence are well documented (Fox et al., 1979; Parelius, 1981, 1982). There is some evidence that these differences do not exist in elementary school (Ernest, 1976) but that they develop with age (Fennema, 1974b; Ernest, 1976; Fox et al., 1979). There is also evidence that they exist regardless of objective levels of performance. That is, even when girls get good grades in mathematics and exhibit higher achievement than boys, girls perceive themselves to be less competent (Fennema, 1974b; Fox et al., 1979).

Just as a variety of socialization agents are responsible for channeling the two sexes into different occupations, a variety of socialization agents teach children that mathematics and science are traditionally male domains. As noted earlier, there is evidence that parents value mathematics achievement more for their sons than for their daughters and that they estimate the mathematics competence of their sons to be higher than that of their daughters (Fennema and Sherman, 1977; Fox et al., 1979). There is also evidence that after the sixth grade both sexes get more help with mathematics homework from fathers than from mothers (Ernest, 1976). Learning experiences of this type within the home can be expected to affect the self-conceptions of male and female children in mathematics and their enrollment in such courses (Fox et al., 1979).

School teachers and counselors also convey messages to girls that may affect their self-confidence and interest in mathematics and science. There is evidence that teachers have different expectations for the two sexes in mathematics and science (Ernest, 1976;

Fox et al., 1979) and that they are particularly likely to interact more with males than females in mathematics and science classes (Levy, 1972; Good et al., 1973; Fox et al., 1979). A bad experience with a teacher is often the source of a very negative attitude toward mathematics (Ernest, 1976; Poffenberger and Norton, 1959), although having a good teacher also is often cited as a positive factor in the intellectual development of girls (Anderson, 1963; Ernest, 1976; Fox et al., 1979). When teachers recruit girls for mathematics programs and have high expectations for their performance, they can have decidedly positive effects (Fox et al., 1979). Mathematics and science teachers also generally provide better role models for boys than for girls from secondary school onward since most teachers of these subjects are male (Ernest, 1976). Although, as discussed above, it is unclear how much influence counselors have on students, there is considerable evidence to indicate that counselors have been a source of discouragement rather than encouragement to girls wanting to take advanced mathematics and science courses (Fox et al., 1979). Such sex stereotyping by counselors, however, may be declining (Engelhard et al., 1976).

Peer support for females interested in mathematics and science also has been lacking (Fox et al., 1979). Adolescents hold a more negative view of mathematically gifted girls than boys, and high school students, particularly males, view mathematics as a male domain (Ernest, 1976; Fennema and Sherman, 1977; Sherman and Fennema, 1977; Fox et al., 1979). Because the support of same-sex peers has been found to have a positive effect on the mathematics achievement of girls, it is possible that a critical mass (i.e., a particular sex ratio) may be needed to provide peer support for girls and to maintain an androgynous atmosphere in mathematics and science classes (Fox et al., 1979).

The evidence available on sex differences in mathematics and science training suggests that several types of interventions to increase female training in these areas may be helpful. Since sex differences in course enrollment have been found to arise at least in part from sex differences in the perceived usefulness of mathematics and science to one's future, earlier education and counseling programs that make females aware of career opportunities, and the courses necessary to prepare for them, may have a significant effect. Previous interventions suggest that role models are an important component of such programs (Fox et al., 1979). Increasing the amount of mathematics and science required as part of the basic school curriculum also may have a positive effect, since most sex differences in performance in mathematics and science and in attitudes toward these subjects emerge after it becomes possible for students to elect courses. Requiring more mathematics and science training at higher grade levels would reduce the sex gap in mathematics and science training and might improve the attitudes of girls toward these subjects (Fox et al., 1979:322). Other evidence that women planning to major in nontraditional fields show greater attrition from these fields during the college years (Astin and Panos, 1969; Zinberg, 1974; Ernest, 1976) suggests that provision of psychological support by peer advisers (e.g., other women in nontraditional majors) might slow the rate of attrition by women.

Legislation and Governmental Intervention Related to Education   Of the legislation designed to reduce sex discriminaton in employment and training, three pieces are particularly relevant to the occupational socialization of women prior to labor force entry: Title IX of the 1972 Educational Amendments, the Women's Educational Equity Act of 1974 and 1978, and the 1976 Vocational Education Amendments.

Title IX was passed by Congress in 1972 as part of the Educational Amendments, and final regulations for its implementation followed in 1975. Its significance lies not only in the fact that it prohibits discriminatory policies and practices in the treatment of workers in educational settings receiving federal funds but also in the fact that it is the first legislation to specifically protect students from sex discrimination. The domains of its coverage of students were originally interpreted broadly to include all activities affecting students within educational institutions and agencies receiving federal funds. It therefore covered admissions policies, access and treatment in curricular and extracurricular programs (including courses of study, career and course counseling, and extracurricular activities), and access to student financial awards. The Women's Educational Equity Act authorized funding at all educational levels for model educational programs of national, statewide, or general significance to eliminate sex stereotyping and promote educational equity for females. It thus provided administrative backup for sex-equity legislation prohibiting discrimination.

As a result of a 1984 Supreme Court decision in *Grove City* v. *Bell,* Title IX has been reinterpreted to pertain only to those activities within educational institutions that directly receive federal funds. This interpretation, if allowed to stand, would limit the jurisdiction of Title IX primarily to access to student financial aid. Even before the reinterpretation of Title IX, a report by the Project on Equal Education Rights (1978), part of the Legal Defense and Education Fund of the National Organization for Women, pointed to some of the difficulties and red tape in the implementation and enforcement of Title IX. A 1981 report by the National Advisory Council on Women's Educational Programs (which was established by the 1974 Women's Educational Equity Act), however, suggests that there has been much progress toward the goals of Title IX, although the report offers little in the way of hard evidence on the impact of Title IX.

The percentages of degrees earned by women and the enrollment of women in professional schools do indicate significant changes over the past decade, although their relationship to the implementation of legislation is unknown. The percentage of bachelor's degrees awarded to women increased from 44 percent in 1971-1972 to 55 percent in 1979-1980. Comparable figures for master's degrees were 41 and 50 percent; for doctoral degrees, 16 and 30 percent; and for first professional degrees, 6 and 25 percent. Percentage increases in the enrollment of women in professional schools during 1972-1981 are particularly impressive: dental schools, 1,011 percent; law schools, 337 percent; medical schools, 296 percent; and veterinary schools, 120 percent (National Advisory Council on Women's Educational Programs, 1981).

These data indicate important changes in the extent and ways in which women are participating in higher education. A study by Beller (1981) sheds some light on changes in the actual advantages that education is providing for women in terms of entrance into traditionally male occupations (defined as occupations in which the male share of employment exceeds the male share of the experienced civilian labor force by at least 5 percentage points). She found that, in 1967, increases in years of education resulted in greater access to male occupations at about twice the rate for men as for women but that by 1977 this differential had narrowed substantially for those with a college education or more. Equal employment policies were credited with these gains for college-educated women during the decade. Efforts to achieve equality of opportunity did not appear to have increased access to male occupations for those women with 12 or fewer years of education, however.

The 1976 Vocational Education Amendments (VEA 1976) were intended to provide a basis for the development of programs to eliminate sex bias, discrimination, and stereotyping and to promote equal access of the sexes to vocational education. Assessment of whether the implementation of VEA 1976 has accomplished more equitable access to

and benefit from vocational education programs by women is aided by a 1980 report of the National Advisory Council on Vocational Education and the National Advisory Council on Women's Educational Programs. This report presents a detailed analysis of enrollment data from 15 states that together accounted for 55 percent of the national enrollment in high school, postsecondary, and adult vocational education programs.

Vocationally oriented programs showed a large overall increase in enrollment of 44 percent between 1972 and 1978, while the increase in the number of women enrolled was even more dramatic — 60 percent over the 6-year period. The percentage of women enrolled in traditional programs[6] decreased slightly (from 65 to 56 percent), and the percentage of women in mixed programs and nontraditional programs increased by 6 and 4 percent, respectively. The increases in women's enrollment in nontraditional programs occurred in courses without a strong masculine image, such as drafting, graphic arts, and law enforcement, rather than in machine shop and construction.

Examination of data for states suggests some identifiable determinants of changes in enrollments. Specifically, the greatest increases in women's enrollment in nontraditional programs occurred in states where detailed plans were formulated, involving specific goals and timetables. The more scrutiny to which schools were subjected by the state, the more action was taken. Schools that were particularly active in attempting to redress skewed ratios of males and females in vocational areas were those with higher nontraditional enrollments of women to begin with. A further finding was that significantly greater increases in women's

---

[6] Traditional vocational education programs were defined as those made up of at least 75.1 percent women in 1972; mixed programs were made up of 25.1 to 75.0 percent women; and nontraditional programs had enrollments of 0.0 to 25.0 percent women.

enrollment in nontraditional programs occurred at the postsecondary and adult education levels than in high schools. This finding is consistent with the lack of change cited earlier in our discussion of tracking and vocational education in high schools.

Several conclusions can be drawn about the effectiveness of federal legislation in providing a more sex-equitable environment in the schools. First, as demonstrated by the differential success of various states' implementation of VEA 1976, the provision of federal funds coupled with a broad commitment will not effect change. Rather, active attention to the monitoring of schools and, in particular, the administration of pre- and inservice courses for teachers and counselors seem to be important. Special attention needs to be focused on secondary schools, where students are influenced to make decisions that will have significant ramifications for whether they continue on to college, receive postsecondary vocational education, or immediately enter the job market. Second, the provision of female role models in courses with a male or a "mixed" image and of male role models in courses with a female image may be a way to encourage both sexes to consider broader career options (Rieder, 1977). Third, state programs that were the most successful in diverting high female enrollments in traditional courses to less traditional specialities had established a broad base of support for women who took this route, by setting up orientation programs and providing connections with potential employers. This type of comprehensive planning, including follow-up support for students making nontraditional choices, appears to be successful in changing sex ratios (Evenson and O'Neil, 1978).

Mass Media Effects: Television Portrayal of Male and Female Occupational Roles

In recent years, a good deal of attention has been directed to the influence of the mass media, particularly television, on the development of attitudes and behavior patterns in children. In examining the portrayal of males and females in the media, we limit our discussion to the role of television as the principal medium by which the content and importance of male and female roles are communicated to children (Schramm et al., 1961). There have also been studies of the portrayal of males and females in newspaper stories (Foreit et al., 1980), nonfictional magazine pieces (Hatch and Hatch, 1958; Clark and Esposito, 1966), magazine fiction (Franzwa, 1975), and other media sources.

Many studies have indicated that males are disproportionately represented on television, whether the framework be prime-time television programs, children's programs, or commercials (Courtney and Whipple, 1974; Sternglanz and Serbin, 1974; Tedesco, 1974; Women on Words and Images, 1975a; Nolan et al., 1977). When sex differences in the frequencies of responses made by characters are assessed, males dominate the verbal and nonverbal action (Downes and Gowan, 1980). With respect to occupational representation, an early study (DeFleur, 1964) found that less than 20 percent of the occupational roles depicted were filled by women. More recent studies conducted in the mid-1970s also indicate narrowness and sex stereotyping in the roles assigned to women. In a study of prime-time television programs receiving high Neilsen ratings in 1973, Women on Words and Images (1975a) found that the range of occupations was nearly twice as broad for major male characters as for major female characters (although it was not clear whether the number of characters was held constant when such a comparison was made) and that there was little occupational overlap between the sexes. Findings were even more extreme in the case of commercials. In another study of prime-time programs, Kaniuga et al. (1974) found that among the women depicted as workers the most common occupational roles were those of secretary, nurse, and educator, and in only 10 percent of the cases were the working women married. Especially noticeable, therefore, was the predominance of white-collar employment for women and the implication that it was not common to combine work outside the home with marriage and family responsibilities.

Most studies of sex-role stereotyping on television have involved content analysis and have not attempted to examine actual effects on children. Frueh and McGhee (1975), however, examined the relationship between the amount of time children spent watching television and their identification with traditional sex roles. They found that high amounts of television viewing were associated with stronger traditional sex-role development and that the relationship between television viewing and sex-role attitudes existed across sexes and age groups (kindergarten, grades 2, 4, and 6). The degree to which actual occupational choices are conditioned by exposure to television remains unknown. But given the predominance of television as a media form for children and its role as a source of information about the world, especially prior to the development of reading skills and prior to entrance into the adult working world, it is likely to have a significant impact.

Early Work Experiences

A variety of groups, such as the President's Science Advisory Committee, the National Panel on High Schools and Adolescent Education, and the Carnegie Council on Policy Studies in Higher Education, have advocated the participation of teenagers in the work force as a means of helping them develop skills and attitudes that will facilitate a smoother transition into full-time adult work roles (Lewin-Epstein, 1981). Research on the employment experiences of youth prior to high school graduation is sparse, but two recent studies provide data portraying a sex-segregated occupational world for adolescents that closely mirrors the adult work world (Lewin-Epstein, 1981; Greenberger and Steinberg, 1983). These studies indicate that females are somewhat less likely to be employed than males and that when they are employed they tend to work fewer hours per week. The distribution of students across jobs is also significantly different for the two sexes. Thus, even when work is a secondary activity and both sexes are employed in low-skill nonspecialized jobs, as is the case in the adolescent years, job segregation by sex emerges.

In addition, as in the adult work world, adolescent females earn lower hourly wages than males, a pattern that holds across job categories, ethnic groups (whites, blacks, Hispanics), and high school grade levels. Hourly wages for adolescents are positively related to the degree to which a job is dominated by males, again mirroring the adult occupational environment. Based on data from the High School and Beyond survey of sophomores and seniors in a national sample of U.S. high schools in 1980, Lewin-Epstein (1981) found that sex was the most important determinant of wages earned by teenagers. He also found that the sex difference in actual wages was somewhat greater than the sex difference in reservation wages, as measured by the lowest hourly wage students said they would accept in high school. He argued that this pattern might help account for the lower labor force participation of females, since females may have greater difficulty than males in meeting their wage expectations in the job market. Together, sex differences in labor force participation, type of work experience, and earnings during adolescence are indicative of yet another way in which adolescent males and females develop different orientations toward the adult world of work.

Summary

Of the socializing influences in the lives of children and adolescents that are likely to produce sex differences in occupational orientation and preparation prior to entry into the adult work force, the earliest and most pervasive ones arise within the family, where mothers and fathers not only provide information as role models and teachers but also treat male and female children differently. School influences reinforce the effects of family socialization. Among these are the greater availability of same-sex role models for males across a variety of fields at higher levels of education, sex typing in the presentation of occupational roles in textbooks and other educational materials, sex bias in the attitudes and knowledge of guidance counselors regarding the appropriateness of various occupations for males and females, sex segregation in different vocational education programs, and sex differences in training in mathematics and science. Sex typing in the portrayal of occupational roles in the mass media provides another source of information about the adult occupational world, as do sex differences in the actual employment experiences of adolescents prior to leaving school. It is difficult, if not impossible, to estimate the effect of any single socializing influence on the development of sex differences in occupational orientation and job-relevant skills. However, it is clear that, collectively, they teach children to aspire to and prepare for different occupational roles in adulthoood.

SOCIALIZATION AS AN EXPLANATION OF SEX SEGREGATION IN THE LABOR MARKET

Since the purpose of this paper is to examine sex differences in occupational orientation and preparation prior to entry into the labor market as an outgrowth of the process of socialization and to consider the effects of these differences on subsequent sex segregation in the labor market, we will conclude by discussing the role of socialization as a *cause* of occupational segregation by sex. In attempting to understand the importance of socialization as a determinant of sex segregation in the labor market, it is reasonable to ask how important sex differ-

ences are in the characteristics of workers prior to entry into the labor market, compared to the actions of employers and other legal and institutional barriers in the workplace, in accounting for sex segregation in the labor market. This question cannot be answered, however, because it does not distinguish between the operation of two distinct, but related, processes: one at the micro level and one at the macro level.

At the micro, or individual, level, it is possible to examine the relative effects of different types of influences on the occupational outcomes of individuals in one or more cohorts. Socialization is a process that operates at the micro level, since it is the process by which individuals come to learn about the world in which they live and to understand what is considered appropriate and acceptable behavior for them. In a society in which adult roles are differentiated by sex and where the labor market is highly sex segregated, females and males develop different expectations of their adult work lives and the jobs appropriate for them via sex-role socialization. The effect of socializaton prior to entry into the labor market on the occupational outcomes of individuals can be examined by addressing the question: How important are sex differences in occupational orientation and preparation prior to entry into the labor market (which arise primarily as a result of socialization) compared to subsequent labor market experiences (which are attributable at least in part to the actions of employers and other legal and institutional barriers) in accounting for the sex-segregated pattern of employment for individuals in particular cohorts? On the basis of the evidence we have presented on the degree to which sex segregation in occupational aspirations approximates sex segregation in employment, socialization prior to entry into the labor market appears to be an important determinant of occupational outcomes for individuals, although the extent to which preemployment differences in worker characteristics account for subsequent sex segregation in the labor market remains to be estimated precisely using longitudinal data.

Because socialization prior to entry into the labor market appears to play a large role in the determination of occupational outcomes for individuals, is it reasonable to conclude that it is an important determinant of sex segregation in the labor market? Only if one is referring to its predictive power in accounting for the occupational outcomes of individuals. Socialization cannot explain why a sex-segregated labor market emerged, why each sex is allocated to particular types of occupations, and why the sex typing of occupations changes in particular ways over time. These characteristics of the labor market are outcomes of macro-level processes in which such factors as the supply and demand for particular types of workers, the structure of work organizations, cultural beliefs and practices, legal arrangements, and the actions of employers play a dominant role. To explain the existence of sex segregation in the labor market, it is necessary to address the question: Why did sex segregation in the labor market emerge and take the particular form it did? The answer to this question is to be found by analyzing variation at the macro level, including differences among organizations and societies and changes in these structures over time. Thus, although the maintenance of a sex-segregated labor market and changes in the pattern of segregation over time occur via the actions of individuals at the micro level, the origins, or causes, of sex segregation cannot be understood through analysis of micro-level processes such as socialization. Socialization is a process whereby prevailing cultural practices are transmitted to new generations, and as such it plays an important role in the determination of outcomes for individuals. However, the content of what is transmitted via socialization is determined by factors operating at the macro level.

Understanding that socialization is essentially a transmission process has implications for the conclusions to be drawn from our findings regarding interventions for change in sex segregation in the labor market. Although our findings indicate that socialization plays an important role in the determination of occupational outcomes for individuals, it should not be inferred that interventions for change should focus primarily on socialization practices. Because socialization is a process whereby existing cultural practices, including employment patterns, are transmitted, a reduction of sex segregation in employment affects what is transmitted via socialization and thereby ultimately reduces sex differences in occupational orientation and preparation. Interventions directed at changes in employment practices and in laws that affect sex segregation therefore can bring about both immediate change in employment patterns and eventual change in the messages about the occupational world that are conveyed to new generations.

Throughout our discussion of socializing influences, we have commented on interventions that might be undertaken to change socialization practices. Such changes are needed, and would undoubtedly effect some change in the occupational orientations and preparation of the two sexes. However, changes in socialization practices must go hand in hand with changes in employment practices. Because the actions of employers and the structure of work organizations are known to affect sex segregation, a reduction of sex differences in occupational orientation would not necessarily produce a concomitant reduction of sex differences in employment patterns. Moreover, for a major reduction of sex differences in occupational orientation to occur, a major reduction of sex segregation in the labor market is necessary, since existing employment patterns affect what is learned via socialization. That is, children and young adults must observe less sex-segregated employment patterns prior to labor force entry if sex differences in occupational aspirations and expectations are to be significantly reduced.

REFERENCES

Aiken, L.R., Jr.
1970 "Attitudes toward mathematics." Review of Educational Research 40:551-96.

1976 "Update on attitudes and other affective variables in learning mathematics." Review of Educational Research 46:293-311.

Aiken, L.R., Jr., and R.M. Dreger
1961 "The effect of attitudes on performance in mathematics." Journal of Educational Psychology 52:19-24.

Alexander, K.L., and B.K. Eckland
1974 "Sex differences in the educational attainment process." American Sociological Review 39:668-82.

Almquist, E.M.
1974 "Sex stereotypes in occupational choice: The case of college women." Journal of Vocational Behavior 5:13-21.

Almquist, E.M., and S.S. Angrist
1970 "Career salience and atypicality of occupational choice among college women." Journal of Marriage and the Family 32:242-49.

1971 "Role model influences on college women's career aspirations." Merrill-Palmer Quarterly 17:-263-79.

Altman, S.L., and F.K. Grossman
1977 "Women's career plans and maternal employment." Psychology of Women Quarterly 1:365-76.

American Institutes for Research
1980 "Enrollment and staffing patterns in vocational education." Pp. 27-78 in Education, Sex Equity and Occupational Stereotyping. Washington, D.C.: National Commission for Employment Policy.

Anderson, K.E.
1963 "A comparative study of student self ratings on the influence of inspirational teachers in science and mathematics in the development of intellectual curiosity, persistence and a questioning attitude." Science Education 47:429-37.

Astin, A.W., and R.J. Panos
1969 The Educational and Vocational Development of College Students. Washington, D.C.: American Council on Education.

Astin, H.S., and T. Myint
1971 "Career development and stability of young women during the post high school years." Journal of Counseling Psychology 18:369-93.

Bachman, J.G., L.D. Johnston, and P.M. O'Malley
1980 Monitoring the Future: Questionnaire Re-
sponses From the Nation's High School Seniors. Ann Arbor, Mich.: Institute for Social Research, University of Michigan.

Bahr, S.J.
1974 "Effects on power and division of labor in the family." Pp. 167-85 in L.W. Hoffman and F.I. Nye (eds.), Working Mothers. San Francisco: Jossey-Bass.

Bandura, A., and A.C. Huston
1961 "Identification as a process of incidental learning." Journal of Abnormal and Social Psychology 63:311-18.

Bandura, A., D. Ross, and S.A. Ross
1963 "A comparative test of the status envy, social power, and secondary reinforcement theories of identificatory learning." Journal of Abnormal and Social Psychology 67:527-34.

Barclay, L.K.
1974 "The emergence of vocational expectations in preschool children." Journal of Vocational Behavior 4:1-14.

Baruch, G.K.
1972 "Maternal influences upon college women's attitudes towards women and work." Developmental Psychology 6:32-7.

Basow, S.A., and K.G. Howe
1979 "Model influence on career choices of college students." Vocational Guidance Quarterly 27:239-43.

Beardslee, D.C., and D.D. O'Dowd
1962 "Students and the occupational world." In N. Sanford (ed.), The American College. New York: Wiley.

Becker, G.S.
1964 Human Capital. New York: National Bureau of Economic Research.

Beller, A.H.
1981 "The impact of education on entry into nontraditional occupations." Revised version of paper presented at the Econometric Society meetings, Denver, Colorado, September 1980.

Bem, S.L.
1981 "Gender schema theory: A cognitive account of sex typing." Psychological Review 88:354-64.

Bergmann, B.R.
1971 "The effect on white incomes of discrimination in employment." Journal of Political Economy 79:294-313.

1974 "Occupational segregation, wages and profits when employers' discriminate by race or sex." Eastern Economic Journal 1:103-10.

Berk, R.A., and S.F. Berk
1979 Labor and Leisure at Home. Beverly Hills, Calif.: Sage.

Bielby, D.D.V.
1978a "Career sex-atypicality and career involvement of college educated women: Baseline evidence from the 1960's." Sociology of Education 51:7-28.

1978b "Maternal unemployment and socioeconomic
       status as factors in daughters' career salience:
       Some substantive refinements." Sex Roles 4:249-
       65.

Bingham, W., and E. House
1973   "Counselors view women and work: Accuracy
       of information." Vocational Guidance Quar-
       terly 21:262-68.

Blau, F.
1977   Equal Pay in the Office. Lexington, Mass.:
       Lexington.

Blau, F., and W. Hendricks
1979   "Occupational segregation by sex: Trends and
       prospects." Journal of Human Resources 12:197-
       210.

Blau, F., and C.L. Jusenius
1976   "Economists' approaches to sex segregation in
       the labor market: An appraisal." Pp. 181-99 in
       M. Blaxall and B. Reagan (eds.), Women in
       the Workplace: The Implications of Occupa-
       tional Segregation. Chicago: University of Chi-
       cago Press.

Blau, P.M., and O.D. Duncan
1967   The American Occupational Structure. New
       York: Wiley.

Block, J.H.
1973   "Conceptions of sex role: Some cross-cultural
       and longitudinal perspectives." American Psy-
       chologist 28:512-26.

1976   "Issues, problems, and pitfalls in assessing sex
       differences: A critical review of 'The Psychol-
       ogy of Sex Differences.'" Merrill-Palmer
       Quarterly 22:283-308.

Brenner, O.C., and J. Tomkiewicz
1979   "Job orientation of males and females: Are sex
       differences declining?" Personnel Psychology
       32:741-50.

Brief, A.P., and L.J. Aldag
1975   "Male-female differences in occupational atti-
       tudes within minority groups." Journal of Vo-
       cational Behavior 6:305-14.

Brito, P.K., and C.L. Jusenius
1978   "Sex segregation in the labor market: An anal-
       ysis of young college women's occupational
       preferences." Pp. 57-75 in F.L. Mott (ed.),
       Women, Work, and Family: Dimensions of
       Change in American Society. Lexington, Mass.:
       Lexington.

Burlin, F.
1976   "Sex-role stereotyping: Occupational aspira-
       tions of female high school students." The School
       Counselor 24:102-8.

Callahan, W.J.
1971   "Adolescent attitudes toward mathematics."
       Mathematics Teacher 64:751-55.

Chodorow, N.
1978   The Reproduction of Mothering: Psychoanal-
       ysis and the Sociology of Gender. Berkeley:
       University of California Press.

Cicourel, A.V., and J. Kitsuse
1963   The Educational Decision-Makers. Indianap-
       olis: Bobbs-Merrill.

Clark, E.T.
1967   "Influence of sex and social class on occupa-
       tional preference and perception." Personnel
       and Guidance Journal 45:440-44.

Clarke, P., and V. Esposito
1966   "A study of occupational advice for women in
       magazines." Journalism Quarterly 43:477-85.

Courtney, A.E., and T.W. Whipple
1974   "Women in TV commercials." Journal of Com-
       munication 24:110-18.

Cummings, S., and D. Taebel
1980   "Sexual inequality and the reproduction of con-
       sciousness: An analysis of sex-role stereotyping
       among children." Sex Roles 6:631-44.

Davis, J.A.
1965   Undergraduate Career Decisions. Chicago: Al-
       dine.

Daymont, T.N., and P.L. Tsai
1981   "Sex inequality in the labor market: A multi-
       disciplinary approach." Paper presented at the
       American Sociological Association's Annual
       Meeting, Toronto, Ontario, Canada, August.

DeFleur, M.L.
1963   "Children's knowledge of occupational roles and
       prestige: Preliminary report." Psychological
       Reports 13:760.

1964   "Occupational roles as portrayed on televi-
       sion." Public Opinion Quarterly 28:57-74.

Doeringer, P.B., and M.J. Piore
1971   Internal Labor Markets and Manpower Anal-
       ysis. Lexington, Mass.: D.C. Heath.

Donahue, T.J., and J.W. Costar
1977   "Counselor discrimination against young women
       in career selection." Journal of Counseling Psy-
       chology 24:481-86.

Downes, A.C., and D.C. Gowan
1980   "Sex differences in reinforcement and punish-
       ment on prime-time television." Sex Roles
       6:683-94.

Douvan, E.
1976   "The role of models in women's professional
       development." Psychology of Women Quar-
       terly 1:5-20.

Douvan, E., and J. Adelson
1966   The Adolescent Experience. New York: Wiley.

Dreger, R.M., and L.R. Aiken, Jr.
1957   "The identification of number anxiety in a col-
       lege population." Journal of Educational Psy-
       chology 48:344-51.

Dwyer, C.A.
1973   "Sex differences in reading: An evaluation and
       a critique of current methods." Review of Ed-
       ucational Research 43:455-61.

Engelhard, P.A., K.O. Jones, and R.R. Stiggens
1976   "Trends in counselor attitudes about women's
       roles." Journal of Counseling Psychology 23:365-
       72.

England, P.
1981a "Assessing trends in occupational sex segre-
       gation, 1900-1976." Pp. 273-95 in I. Berg (ed.),

Sociological Perspectives on Labor Markets. New York: Academic Press.

1981b "Wage appreciation and depreciation: A test of neoclassical explanations of occupational sex segregation." Paper presented at the annual meeting of the American Sociological Association, August 1981.

1982 "The failure of human capital theory to explain occupational sex segregation." Journal of Human Resources 17:358-70.

Ernest, J.
1976 Mathematics and Sex. Santa Barbara: Mathematics Department, University of California.

Evenson, J.S., and M.I. O'Neill
1978 Current Perspectives on the Role of Career Education in Combatting Occupational Sex-Role Stereotyping. Washington, D.C.: National Institute of Education.

Farmer, H.S., and T.E. Backer
1977 New Career Options for Women: A Counselor's Sourcebook. New York: Human Sciences Press.

Fennema, E.
1974a "Mathematics learning and the sexes: A review." Journal for Research in Mathematics Education 5:126-39.

1974b "Sex differences in mathematics learning: Why???" The Elementary School Journal 75:183-90.

Fennema, E., and J. Sherman
1977 "Sex related differences in mathematics achievements, spatial visualization and affective factors." American Educational Research Journal 14:51-71.

Foreit, K.G., T. Agar, J. Byers, J. Larue, H. Lokey, M. Pallazini, M. Patterson, and L. Smith
1980 "Sex bias in the newspaper treatment of male-centered and female-centered news stories." Sex Roles 6:475-80.

Fox, G.L.
1974 "Some observations and data on the availability of same-sex role models as a factor in undergraduate career choice." Sociological Focus 7:15-30.

Fox, L.H., D. Tobin, and L. Brody
1979 "Sex role socialization and achievement in mathematics." Pp. 303-32 in M.A. Wittig and A.C. Peterson (eds.), Sex-Related Differences in Cognitive Functioning: Developmental Issues. New York: Academic Press.

Franzwa, H.H.
1975 "Female roles in women's magazine fiction, 1940-1970." Pp. 42-53 in R.K. Unger and F.L. Denmark (eds.), Women: Dependent or Independent Variable? New York: Psychological Dimensions, Inc.

Frieze, I.H., J.E. Parsons, P.B. Johnson, D.N. Ruble, G.L. Zellman
1978 Women and Sex Roles: A Social Psychological Perspective. New York: W.W. Norton.

Frueh, T., and P.C. McGhee
1975 "Traditional sex-role developments and amount of time spent watching television." Developmental Psychology 1:109.

Garrison, H.H.
1979 "Gender differences in the career aspirations of recent cohorts of high school seniors." Social Problems 27:170-85.

Ginsberg, E., S.W. Ginsberg, S. Axelrod, and J.L. Herma
1951 Occupational Choice: An Approach to a General Theory. New York: Columbia University Press.

Goldstein, E.
1979 "Effect of same-sex and cross-sex role models on the subsequent academic productivity of scholars." American Psychologist 34:407-10.

Good, T.L., J.N. Sikes, and J.E. Brophy
1973 "Effects of teacher sex and student sex on classroom interaction." Journal of Educational Psychology 65:74-87.

Gottfredson, L.S.
1978 "Race and sex differences in occupational aspirations: Their development and consequences for occupational segregation." Report No. 254, Center for Social Organization of Schools, Johns Hopkins University.

Grasso, J.
1980 "The effects of school curriculum on young women." Pp. 79-114 in Education, Sex Equity and Occupational Stereotyping. Washington, D.C.: National Commission for Employment Policy.

Greenberger, E., and L.D. Steinberg
1983 "Sex differences in early labor force experience: Harbinger of things to come." Social Forces 62:467-86.

Gross, E.
1968 "Plus ca change . . .? The sexual structure of occupations over time." Social Problems 16:198-208.

Harmon, L.W.
1971 "The childhood and adolescent career plans of college women." Journal of Vocational Behavior 1:45-56.

Harnischfeger, A., and D.E. Wiley
1980 "High school tracking and vocational stereotyping: Means of socioeconomic placement." In Education, Sex Equity and Occupational Stereotyping. Washington, D.C.: National Commission for Employment Policy.

Harren, V.A., R.A. Kass, H.E.A. Tinsley, and J.R. Moreland
1979 "Influences of gender, sex-role attitudes, and cognitive complexity on gender-dominant career choices." Journal of Counseling Psychology 26:227-34.

Harris, S.R.
1974 "Sex typing in girls' career choices: A challenge to counselors." Vocational Guidance Quarterly 23:128-33.

Hartley, R.E.
1966 "A developmental view of female sex-role identification." In B.J. Biddle and J. Thomas (eds.),

Role Theory: Concepts and Research. New York: Wiley.

Hartley, R., and A. Klein
1959   "Sex-role concepts among elementary school age girls." Journal of Marriage and the Family 20:59-64.

Hatch, M.G., and D.L. Hatch
1958   "Problems of married working women as presented by three popular working women's magazines." Social Forces 37:148-53.

Hauser, R.M., W.H. Sewell, and D.F. Alwin
1976   "High school effects on achievement." Pp. 309-41 in W.H. Sewell, R.M. Hauser, and D.L. Featherman (eds.), Schooling and Achievement in American Society. New York: Academic Press.

Heilman, M.E.
1979   "High school students' occupational interest as a function of projected sex ratios in male-dominated occupations." Journal of Applied Psychology 64:275-79.

Hershenson, D.B., and R.M. Roth
1966   "A decisional process model." Journal of Counseling Psychology 13:368-70.

Herzog, A.R.
1982   "High school seniors' occupational plans and values: Trends in sex differences 1976 through 1980." Sociology of Education 55:1-13.

Heshusius-Gilsdorf, L.F., and D.L. Gilsdorf
1975   "Girls are females, boys are males: A content analysis of career materials." Personnel and Guidance Journal 54:207-11.

Hewitt, L.S.
1975   "Age and sex differences in the vocational aspirations of elementary school children." Journal of Social Psychology 96:173-77.

Heyns, B.
1974   "Social selection and stratification within schools." American Journal of Sociology 78:1434-51.

Hilton, T.L.
1962   "Career decision-making." Journal of Counseling Psychology 9:291-98.

Hilton, T.L., and G.W. Berglund
1974   "Sex differences in mathematics achievement: A longitudinal study." Journal of Educational Research 67:231-371.

Hind, R.R., and T.E. Wirth
1969   "The effect of university experience on occupational choice among undergraduates." Sociology of Education 42:50-70.

Hofferth, S.L.
1980a   "High school experience in the attainment process of non-college boys and girls: When and why do their paths diverge?" Working Paper 1303-01, The Urban Institute, Washington, D.C.

1980b   "Long-term labor market effects of vocational education on young women." In Education, Sex Equity and Occupational Stereotyping. Washington, D.C.: National Commission for Employment Policy.

Hoffman, L.W.
1974   "Effects on child." Pp. 126-68 in L.W. Hoffman and F.I. Nye (eds.), Working Mothers. San Francisco: Jossey-Bass.

1977   "Changes in family roles, socialization, and sex differences." American Psychologist 32:644-57.

Hoffman, L.W., and F.I. Nye
1975   Working Mothers. San Francisco: Jossey-Bass.

Holland, J.L.
1959   "A theory of vocational choice." Journal of Counseling Psychology 6:35-45.

1966   The Psychology of Vocational Choice: A Theory of Personality Types and Model Environments. Waltham, Mass.: Blaisdel.

1973   Making Vocational Choices: A Theory of Careers. Englewood Cliffs, N.J.: Prentice-Hall.

Horney, K.
1932   "The dread of women." International Journal of Psychoanalysis 13:348-60.

Huston, A.C.
In
press   "Sex-typing." In P.H. Mussen (ed.), Carmichael's Manual of Child Psychology, 4th ed. New York: Wiley.

Kaldor, D.R., and D.G. Zytowski
1969   "A maximizing model of occupational decision-making." Personnel and Guidance Journal 47:781-88.

Kaniuga, N., T. Scott, and E. Gade
1974   "Working women portrayed on evening television programs." Vocational Guidance Quarterly 23:134-37.

Karpicke, S.
1980   "Perceived and real sex differences in college students' career planning." Journal of Counseling Psychology 27:240-45.

Kaufman, D.R., and B.L. Richardson
1982   Achievement and Women: Challenging the Assumptions. New York: Free Press.

Kepner, H.S., and L.R. Koehn
1977   "Sex roles in mathematics: A study of sex stereotypes in elementary mathematics texts." The Arithmetic Teacher 24:379-85.

Kimmel, E.A.
1970   "Can children's books change children's values?" Educational Leadership 28:209-14.

Klein, M.
1957   Envy and Gratitude. New York: Basic Books.

Klemmack, D.L., and J.N. Edwards
1973   "Women's acquisition of stereotyped occupational aspirations." Sociology and Social Research 57:510-25.

Kohout, V.A., and J.W.M. Rothney
1964   "A longitudinal study of vocational preferences." American Educational Research Journal 1:10-21.

Kolberg, L.
1966   "A cognitive-developmental analysis of children's sex-role concepts and attitudes." Pp. 82-172 in E.E. Maccoby (ed.), The Development of Sex Differences. Stanford, Calif.: Stanford University Press.

Krumboltz, J.D., A.M. Mitchell, and G.B. Jones
1976   "A social learning theory of career selection." Counseling Psychologist 6:71-80.

Kuvlesky, W.P., and R.C. Bealer
1967   "The relevance of adolescents' occupational aspirations for subsequent job attainments." Rural Sociology 32:290-301.

Lauver, P.J., R.M. Gastellum, and M. Sheehey
1975   "Bias in OOH illustrations?" Vocational Guidance Quarterly 23:335-40.

Lerner, H.E.
1974   "Early origins of envy and devaluation of women: Implications for sex role stereotypes." Bulletin of the Menninger Clinic 38:538-53.

1978   "Adoptive and pathogenic aspects of sex-role stereotypes: Implications for parenting and psychotherapy." American Journal of Psychiatry 135:48-52.

Levy, B.
1972   "Sex role socialization in schools." Today's Education 61:9,27-29.

Lewin-Epstein, N.
1981   Youth Employment During High School. Report prepared for the National Center for Education Statistics under contract OE-300-78-0208 with the U.S. Department of Education. Chicago: National Opinion Research Center.

Looft, W.R.
1971a   "Sex differences in the expression of vocational aspirations by elementary school children." Developmental Psychology 5:366.

1971b   "Vocational aspirations of second-grade girls." Psychological Reports 28:241-42.

Lueptow, L.B.
1980   "Social change and sex-role change in adolescent orientations toward life, work, and achievement: 1964-1975." Social Psychology Quarterly 43:48-59.

1981   "Sex-typing and change in the occupational choices of high school seniors: 1964-1975." Sociology of Education 54:16-24.

Maccoby, E.E., and C.N. Jacklin
1974   The Psychology of Sex Differences. Stanford, Calif.: Stanford University Press.

Marini, M.M.
1978a   "Sex differences in the determination of adolescent aspirations: A review of research." Sex Roles 4:723-53.

1978b   "The transition to adulthood: Sex differences in educational attainment and age at marriage." American Sociological Review 43:483-507.

1980   "Sex differences in the process of occupational attainment: A closer look." Social Science Research 9:307-61.

Marini, M.M., and E. Greenberger
1978   "Sex differences in occupational aspirations and expectations." Sociology of Work and Occupations 5:147-78.

Martin, C.L., and C.F. Halverson, Jr.
1981   "A schematic processing model of sex typing and stereotyping in children." Child Development 52:1119-34.

Mason, K.O., J.L. Czajka, and S. Arber
1976   "Change in U.S. women's sex role attitudes, 1964-1974." American Sociological Review 41:573-96.

McClelland, D.C.
1976   Power: The Inner Experience. New York: Halsted.

Mead, M.
1935   Sex and Temperament in Three Primitive Societies. New York: Dell.

Medvene, A.M., and A.M. Collins
1976   "Occupational prestige and appropriateness: The views of mental health specialists." Journal of Vocational Behavior 9:63-71.

Miller, S.M.
1975   "Effects of maternal employment on sex role perception, interests, and self-esteem in kindergarten girls." Developmental Psychology 11:405-6.

Milnar, J.
1973   "Sex Stereotyping in Mathematics and Science Textbooks for Elementary and Junior High Schools." Pp. 56-59 in Report on Sex Bias in the Public Schools. New York: Education Committee, New York chapter of the National Organization for Women.

Mischel, W.
1970   "Sex typing and socialization." Pp. 3-72 in P.H. Mussen (ed.), Carmichael's Manual of Child Psychology, 3d ed., Vol. 2. New York: Wiley.

Mischel, W., and J. Grusec
1966   "Determinants of the rehearsal and transmission of neutral and aversive behaviors." Journal of Personality and Social Psychology 3:197-205.

Mitchell, A.M., G.B. Jones, and J.D. Krumboltz (eds.)
1975   A Social Learning Theory of Career Decision Making. Palo Alto, Calif.: American Institute for Research.

Money, J., and A.A. Ehrhardt
1972   Man and Woman, Boy and Girl. Baltimore: Johns Hopkins University Press.

National Advisory Council on Vocational Education and National Advisory Council on Women's Educational Programs
1980   Increasing Sex Equity: The Impact of the 1976 Vocational Education Amendments on Sex Equity in Vocational Education. Washington, D.C.: U.S. Department of Education.

National Advisory Council on Women's Educational Programs
1981   Title IX: The Half Full, Half Empty Glass. Washington, D.C.: U.S. Government Printing Office.

Nelson, R.C.
1963   "Knowledge and interests concerning sixteen occupations among elementary and secondary school students." Educational and Psychological Measurement 23:741-54.

Nieva, V.F., and B.A. Gutek
1981   Women and Work: A Psychological Perspec-
        tive. New York: Praeger.

Nilsen, A.P.
1977   "Sexism in children's books and elementary
        teaching materials." Pp. 161-80 in A.P. Nilsen,
        H. Bosmajian, H.L. Gershuny, and J.P. Stan-
        ley (eds.), Sexism and Language. Urbana, Ill.:
        National Council of Teachers of English.

Nolan, J.D., J.P. Galst, and M.A. White
1977   "Sex bias on children's television programs."
        Journal of Psychology 96:197-204.

O'Bryant, S.L., M.E. Durrett, and J.W. Pennebaker
1980   "Sex differences in knowledge of occupational
        dimensions across four age levels." Sex Roles
        6:331-37.

Oetzel, R.M.
1966   "Annotated bibliography." Pp. 223-51 in E.E.
        Maccoby (ed.), The Development of Sex Dif-
        ferences. Stanford, Calif.: Stanford University
        Press.

O'Hara, R.P.
1962   "The roots of careers." Elementary School
        Journal 62:277-80.

Oppenheimer, V.
1970   The Female Labor Force in the United States.
        Population Monograph Series, No. 5. Berke-
        ley: University of California.

Papalia, D.T., and S.S. Tennent
1975   "Vocational aspirations in preschoolers: A man-
        ifestation of early sex role stereotyping." Sex
        Roles 1:197-99.

Parelius, A.P.
1981   "Gender differences in past achievement, self-
        concept, and orientation toward mathematics,
        science, and engineering among college fresh-
        men." Paper presented at the American So-
        ciological Association's Annual Meeting, To-
        ronto, Ontario, Canada, August.

1982   "Recruitment to mathematics, science, and en-
        gineering: Gender differences and similarities
        in the experiences of college freshmen." Paper
        presented at the American Sociological Asso-
        ciation's Annual Meeeting, San Francisco, Cal-
        ifornia, September.

Parsons, J.E.
1978   "Classic theories of sex-role socialization." Pp.
        95-113 in I. Frieze, J. Parsons, P. Johnson, D.
        Ruble, and G. Zellman (eds.), Women and Sex
        Roles. New York: Norton.

Peng, S.S., W.B. Fetters, and A.J. Kolstad
1981   High School and Beyond: A Capsule Descrip-
        tion of High School Students. Washington,
        D.C.: National Center for Education Statistics.

Perrucci, C.C.
1970   "Minority status and the pursuit of professional
        careers." Social Forces 49:245-59.

Pleck, J.H.
1975   "Masculinity-femininity: Current and alterna-
        tive paradigms." Sex Roles 1:161-78.

Plomin, R., and T.T. Foch
1981   "Sex differences and individual differences."
        Child Development 52:386-88.

Poffenberger, T.M., and D.A. Norton
1959   "Factors in the formation of attitudes toward
        mathematics." Journal of Educational Re-
        search 52:171-76.

Polachek, S.W.
1976   "Occupational segregation: An alternative hy-
        pothesis." Journal of Contemporary Business
        5:1-12.

1979   "Occupational segregation among women:
        Theory, evidence and a prognosis." Pp. 137-
        57 in C.B. Lloyd, E.S. Andrews, and C.L.
        Gilroy (eds.), Women in the Labor Market.
        New York: Columbia University Press.

1981   "Occupational self-selection: A human capital
        approach to sex differences in occupational
        structure." Review of Economics and Statistics
        63:60-69.

Poloma, M.M., and T.N. Garland
1971   "The myth of the egalitarian family: Familial
        roles and the professionally employed wife."
        Pp. 741-61 in A. Theodore (ed.), The Profes-
        sional Woman. Cambridge, Mass.: Schenk-
        man.

Porter, R.J.
1954   "Predicting vocational plans of high school sen-
        ior boys." Personnel and Guidance Journal
        33:215-18.

Project on Equal Education Rights
1978   Stalled at the Start: Government Action on Sex
        Bias in the Schools. Washington, D.C.: Na-
        tional Organization for Women Legal Defense
        and Education Fund.

Rebecca, M., R. Hefner, and B. Oleshansky
1976   "A model of sex-role transcendance." Journal
        of Social Issues 32:197-206.

Reese, H.W., and W.F. Overton
1970   "Models of development and theories of de-
        velopment." Pp. 115-45 in L.R. Goulet and
        P.B. Baltes (eds.), Life-Span Developmental
        Psychology: Research and Theory. New York:
        Academic Press.

Rehberg, R.A., and L. Hotchkiss
1972   "Educational decision-makers: The school
        guidance counselor and social mobility." So-
        ciology of Education 45:339-61.

Rieder, C.H.
1977   "Work, women and vocational education."
        American Education 13:27-32.

Robinson, J.
1977   How Americans Use Time: A Social-Psycho-
        logical Analysis. New York: Praeger.

Rodman, H., P. Voydanoff, and A.E. Lovejoy
1974   "The range of aspirations: A new approach."
        Social Problems 22:184-98.

Rogers, M.A.
1975   "A different look at word problems — even
        mathematics texts are sexist." Mathematics
        Teacher 68:305-7.

Rosenbaum, J.C.
1978   "The structure of opportunity in school." Social Forces 57:234-56.
1980   "Track misperception and frustrated college plans: An analysis of the effects of tracks and track perceptions in the National Longitudinal Survey." Sociology of Education 53:74-88.

Rossi, A.S.
1965   "Barriers to the career choice of engineering, medicine, or science among American women." Pp. 51-127 in J.A. Mattfeld and C.G. Van Aken (eds.), Women and the Scientific Professions. Cambridge, Mass.: MIT Press.

Schafer, W.E., and C. Olexa
1971   Tracking and Opportunity. Scranton, Pa.: Chandler.

Schmidt, J.L., and J.W. Rothney
1955   "Variability of vocational choices of high school students." Personnel and Guidance Journal 34:142-46.

Schlossberg, N.K., and J. Goodman
1972   "A woman's place: Children's sex stereotyping of occupations." Vocational Guidance Quarterly 20:266-70.

Schramm, W., J. Lyle, and E.B. Parker
1961   Television in the Lives of Our Children. Stanford, Calif.: Stanford University Press.

Sewell, W.H., and A.M. Ornstein
1964   "Community of residence and occupational choice." American Journal of Sociology 70:551-63.

Sewell, W.H., A.O. Haller, and A. Portes
1969   "The educational and early occupational attainment process." American Sociological Review 34:82-92.

Sewell, W.H., A.O. Haller, and G. Ohlendorf
1970   "The educational and early occupational attainment process: Replications and revisions." American Sociological Review 35:1014-27.

Sewell, W.H., R.M. Hauser, and W.C. Wolf
1980   "Sex, schooling, and occupational status." American Journal of Sociology 86:551-83.

Shepard, W.O., and D.T. Hess
1975   "Attitudes in four age groups toward sex role division in adult occupations and activities." Journal of Vocational Behavior 6:27-39.

Sherman, J., and Fennema, E.
1977   "The study of mathematics by high school girls and boys: Related variables." American Educational Research Journal 14:159-68.

Siegel, C.L.F.
1973   "Sex differences in the occupational choices of second graders." Journal of Vocational Behavior 3:15-19.

Siegel, E., and E.A. Curtis
1963   "Familial correlates of orientation toward future employment among college women." Journal of Educational Psychology 54:33-37.

Singer, S.L., and B. Stefflre
1954   "Sex differences in job values and desires." Personnel and Guidance Journal 32:483-84.

Smith-Lovin, L., and A.R. Tickamyer
1978   "Nonrecursive models of labor force participation, fertility behavior, and sex role attitudes." American Sociological Review 43:541-57.

Spitze, G., and J. Huber
1980   "Changing attitudes towards women's nonfamily roles: 1938 to 1978." Sociology of Work and Occupations 7:317-35.

Steele, B.
1977   "Sexism in math texts." Edcentric (Spring/Summer):17-19, 60.

Stephenson, R.M.
1957   "Mobility orientation and stratification of 1,000 ninth graders." American Sociological Review 22:204-12.

Stern, R.H.
1976   "Review article: Sexism in foreign language textbooks." Foreign Language Annals 9:294-99.

Sternglanz, S.H., and L.A. Serbin
1974   "Sex role stereotyping in children's television programs." Developmental Psychology 10:710-15.

Stright, V.N.
1960   "A study of the attitudes toward arithmetic of students and teachers in the third, fourth and sixth grades." The Arithmetic Teacher 7:280-86.

Super, D.E.
1953   "A theory of vocational development." The American Psychologist 8:185-90.
1957   The Psychology of Careers: An Introduction to Vocational Development. New York: Harper.

Sweet, J.A.
1973   Women in the Labor Force. New York: Seminar Press.

Tangri, S.S.
1972   "Determinants of occupational role innovation among college women." Journal of Social Issues 28:177-99.

Tavris, C., and C. Offir
1977   The Longest War: Sex Differences in Perspective. New York: Harcourt Brace Jovanovich.

Tedesco, N.S.
1974   "Patterns in prime time." Journal of Communication 24:119-24.

Terman, L.M., and L.E. Tyler
1954   "Psychological sex differences." Pp. 1064-1114 in L. Carmichael (ed.), Manual of Child Psychology, 2d ed. New York: Wiley.

Thomas, A.H., and N.R. Stewart
1971   "Counselor response to female clients with deviate and conforming career goals." Journal of Counseling Psychology 18:352-57.

Thompson, C.L., and J.L. Parker
1971   "Fifth graders view the work world scene." Elementary School Guidance and Counseling 54:281-88.

Thornton, A., and D. Freedman
1979   "Changes in the sex role attitudes of women,
        1962-1977: Evidence from a panel study."
        American Sociological Review 44:831-42.

Thurow, L.
1975   Generating Inequality. New York: Basic.

Tibbetts, S.L.
1975   "Sex-role stereotyping in the lower grades: Part
        of the solution." Journal of Vocational Behavior
        6:255-61.

Tidball, M.E.
1973   "Perspective on academic women and affirm-
        ative action." Educational Record 54:130-35.

Tittle, C.K.
1981   Careers and Family: Sex Roles and Adolescent
        Life Plans. Beverly Hills, Calif.: Sage.

Turner, R.H.
1964   "Some aspects of women's ambition." Ameri-
        can Journal of Sociology 70:271-85.

Tyler, L.E.
1965   The Psychology of Human Differences. New
        York: Appleton-Century-Crofts.

Umstot, M.E.
1980   "Occupational sex-role liberality of third-,
        fourth-, fifth-, and seventh-grade females." Sex
        Roles 6:611-18.

U.S. Commission on Civil Rights
1978   Social Indicators of Equality for Minorities and
        Women. Washington, D.C.: U.S. Govern-
        ment Printing Office.

U.S. Department of Labor, Bureau of Labor Statistics
1977   United States Working Women: A Databook.
        Washington, D.C.: U.S. Government Printing
        Office.

U.S. Department of Labor, Women's Bureau
1975   1975 Handbook on Women Workers, Bulletin
        297. Washington, D.C.: U.S. Government
        Printing Office.

U.S. President's Council of Economic Advisors
1973   Economic Report of the President. Washing-
        ton, D.C.: U.S. Government Printing Office.

Vanek, J.E.
1974   "Time spent in housework." Scientific Amer-
        ican 231:116-20.

Verheyden-Hilliard, M.E.
1977   "Counseling: Potential superbomb against sex-
        ism." American Education (April):12-15.

Vetter, L.
1973   "Career counseling for women." Counseling
        Psychologist 4:54-67.

Vogel, S.R., I.K. Broverman, D.M. Broverman, F.E.
Clarkson, and P.S. Rosenkrantz
1970   "Maternal employment and perception of sex
        roles among college students." Developmental
        Psychology 3:384-91.

Vroom, V.H.
1964   Work and Motivation. New York: Wiley.

Waite, L.J.
1976   "Working wives: 1940-1960." American Soci-
        ological Review 41:65-80.

Waite, L.J., and P.M. Hudis
1980   The Development and Maintenance of a Seg-
        regated Labor Force: Review, Synthesis, Cri-
        tique of Recent Research. Report prepared for
        the National Commission for Employment Pol-
        icy.

Walker, K.E., and M.E. Woods
1976   Time Use: A Measure of Household Produc-
        tion of Family Goods and Services. Washing-
        ton, D.C.: Center for the Family, American
        Home Economics Association.

Weitzman, L.J., and D. Rizzo
1974   Biased Textbooks: A Research Perspective.
        Washington, D.C.: The Resource Center on
        Sex Roles in Education, National Foundation
        for the Improvement of Education.

Weitzman, L.J., D. Eifler, E. Hokada, and C. Ross
1972   "Sex role socialization in picture books for pre-
        school children." American Journal of Sociol-
        ogy 77:1125-50.

Welch, F.
1979   "Comment." Pp. 168-70 in C.B. Lloyd, E.S.
        Andrews, and C.L. Gilroy (eds.), Women in
        the Labor Market. New York: Columbia Uni-
        versity Press.

Werts, C.E.
1966   "Social class and initial career choice of college
        freshmen." Sociology of Education 39:74-85.

White, K.
1967   "Social background variables related to career
        commitment of women teachers." Personnel
        and Guidance Journal 45:649-52.

Williams, G.
1976   "Trends in occupational differentiation by sex."
        Sociology of Work and Occupations 3:38-62.

1979   "The changing U.S. labor force and occupa-
        tional differentiation by sex." Demography
        16:73-88.

Witty, P.A., and H.C. Lehman
1930   "Some factors which influence the child's choice
        of occupations." Elementary School Journal
        31:285-91.

Women on Words and Images
1975a   Channeling Children: Sex Stereotyping in
        Prime-Time TV. Princeton, N.J.: Women on
        Words and Images.

1975b   Dick and Jane as Victims: Sex Stereotyping in
        Children's Readers. Princeton, N.J.: Women
        on Words and Images.

Wood, P.S.
1980   "Sex differences in sports." New York Times
        Magazine, May 18:30-33, 38, 98-104.

Zellner, H.
1975   "The determinants of occupational segrega-
        tion." Pp. 125-45 in C.B. Lloyd (ed.), Sex,
        Discrimination, and the Division of Labor. New
        York: Columbia University Press.

Zinberg, D.
1974   "When the future becomes the present." In
        R.B. Kundsin (ed.), Women and Success: The
        Anatomy of Achievement. New York: William
        Morrow.

12 Commentary

WENDY C. WOLF

In Chapter 11, Marini and Brinton provide a very good review of the literature on the multitude of factors that influence the occupational choice of girls prior to entrance into the labor market. My perspective is that the goal of such a paper should be to identify the most critical or most powerful forces that influence girls' job choices, decide which of these are amenable to policy intervention, and discuss what strategies are effective to intervene in these processes. In light of that goal, a few general comments are in order.

The forces that impinge on job choice for girls are many, strong, and cumulative. Their cumulativeness is important to remember when considering points of intervention. If one intervenes early in a girl's life, there are myriad other forces that act on her before she gets to the point of making a job choice. Changing one aspect of the system rarely has, or for that matter should be expected to have, marked impact on the ultimate job choice. For example, we know that textbooks affect girls in some way. So do counselors. But changing one textbook, or textbooks in one course, or changing counselors in one school in one year, is not likely to have a significant impact on girls' occupa-

tional choices. Many have tried small experiments to change one aspect of a girl's educational experience—lo and behold, they don't find any impact. This is not very surprising. Even if there is an intervention in one or two areas, there are always other factors that in fact reinforce occupational choices that are sex typed or views about appropriate roles for girls.

The second point relates to the issue of premarket versus market forces. It may be a fallacy to neatly separate all forces into two types. There are a number of ways that the labor market feeds back information to young girls about appropriate roles for females. It is important, therefore, not to make such a rigid distinction.

One area of special importance in Marini and Brinton's review relates to the math/science issue in high school. Despite recent news articles suggesting that the difference in math/science ability between girls and boys may be due to girls' lack of testosterone, there is evidence that girls and boys with comparable levels of achievement in math and science at the end of the eighth grade take different amounts of math and science in high school. Enrollment in high school math and science courses has fairly substantial consequences on the kinds of job choices that are made at later points. This is one area in which concrete steps can be taken to allow girls to make schooling choices that will not limit their access to jobs later.

Generally, the cumulativeness of forces makes me a bit skeptical about the success of any one intervention, especially if it is too distant from the time of the actual job choice. The closer to the time of job choice that the intervention is made, the more likely it is to change the job aspirations of girls.

What prompts a statement such as this? Looking at a number of nontraditional programs for women makes it clear that one can stimulate the demand for such programs. If told about the advantages and disadvantages of men's jobs, women with high income needs, who are older, who have been out in the labor force, or who have been in traditionally female jobs that are low paying will respond with interest. At least enough persons will respond to fill openings. The demand for nontraditional work can be stimulated. This may be one of the reasons that, looking at college students or young girls, one doesn't observe much of a change over time in sex-typed occupational aspirations. Once women have been working for a while and have had some negative experiences, they are more willing to entertain nontraditional career options than at younger ages, when peer group pressures are important forces reinforcing traditionally female aspirations.

There is anecdotal evidence (and we need more concrete empirical evidence) that at least for women with high income needs, one can stimulate the demand for nontraditional training and employment, despite years of socialization. Nevertheless, there is variation in aspirations for nontraditional occupational choices (and the ability to stimulate them). Older women tend to be more likely to have such aspirations, and Hispanics less, than black and white women. In short, there is some promise, despite the evidence that high school girls are likely to be disinterested in nontraditional careers.

One final comment is in order. It is a shame that we, as researchers and policy makers, often focus so much on individual factors that affect individual women and their choices and neglect employers and how they, through subtle and some not so subtle mechanisms, influence occupational sex segregation.

This neglect occurs for a number of reasons. First, it is easier to study women than it is to study employers. Second, in a peculiar way, it is felt that we may have more control or effect on individuals than we do on institutions and businesses. It should be obvious that individual factors and often individual forces are but one part of the spectrum. There are numerous factors related to behaviors of employment that affect women once they enter the labor force. And, in fact, there are labor market factors that influence their choices prior to entry into the labor market.

13 Institutional Factors Contributing to Sex Segregation in the Workplace

PATRICIA A. ROOS *and*

BARBARA F. RESKIN

Researchers have frequently attempted to explain sex segregation in the workplace by invoking either workers' or employers' preferences. In economic terms, the former emphasizes the characteristics and choices of the labor supply; the latter claims gender discrimination in the labor market. Research guided by each perspective has shed light on the causes of the unequal distributions of the sexes across occupations, but neither workers' nor employers' preferences systematically assess how the organization of labor markets and the way work is carried out within establishments constrain the sexes' occupational outcomes. As Granovetter (1981) persuasively argued, to understand the operation of the labor market, one must examine the processes through which jobs and workers are matched. Scott (1981:186) directs our attention to internal (or *organizational*) processes and workplace mechanisms that result in people being recruited, allocated, and retained in particular jobs. Their work and others (e.g., Kanter, 1977; Kelley, 1981) focus on both formal and informal processes existing within the workplace that constrain the free operation of the labor market.

The effect of informal processes on women's employment prospects has been the topic of much work in recent years (e.g., Epstein, 1970a, 1975; Coser and Rokoff, 1971; Kanter, 1977). For example, women's exclusion from or marginality in work groups, which often extends into nonworking hours (Martin, 1980), has been found to impair their performance on the job (Kanter, 1977; Schafran, 1981). Women may also lack access to necessary information or be overlooked by senior people who could facilitate their career advancement (Epstein, 1970a). Sometimes coworkers try to sabotage women's entry into positions men customarily hold by harassing them or refusing to provide help or instruction (O'Farrell and Harlan, this volume). Such informal barriers have been found to hamper women's employment prospects in such diverse occupations as blue-collar jobs (Walshok, 1981a; Harlan and O'Farrell, 1982), police forces (Martin, 1980), forestry (Enarson, 1980), construction (U.S. Department of Labor, Employment Standards Administration, 1981), law (Epstein, 1981), medicine (Freidson, 1970), science (Reskin, 1978), and management (Kanter, 1977).

In contrast to these informal processes,

the segregative effects of formal barriers that are *institutionalized* in labor markets and firms' personnel practices have been investigated less thoroughly. The effects of these institutional mechanisms constitute the focus of this paper. We define institutionalized factors as those that are either embedded in or stem from the formal procedures or rules of firms and other labor market entities. These processes include recruitment and job assignment practices, promotion systems, administrative regulations regarding job transfers, stipulations regarding participation in training programs, and barriers to information about certain labor market opportunities. Some factors, such as seniority systems, are by-products of administrative procedures established for other purposes. Others represent deliberate segregative practices in keeping with laws no longer on the books (as in the assignment of men to "heavy" work and women to "light" work; Bielby and Baron, this volume). In this paper, we examine how these institutionalized mechanisms within establishments, and other organized entities in labor markets such as unions and federally administered training programs, contribute to sex segregation by limiting the access of workers of one sex to certain occupations and channeling them into others. The emphasis in this paper is on institutionalized barriers to women's employment in sex-atypical jobs (e.g., construction and police work). Of course, occupational sex segregation is also maintained in part by institutional barriers limiting men's employment in female-typical jobs (e.g., secretarial and nursing) and mechanisms fostering both sexes' employment in sex-typical occupations (e.g., women in clerical or librarian jobs and men in engineering or firefighting work), and we discuss these processes, albeit less extensively. The barriers we consider occur at four points: preemployment training, job access and assignment, job mobility, and retention.

Most of the mechanisms that affect access to training, job assignment, and mobility occur within labor markets, and our discussion considers relevant labor market theories. In synthesizing these theories, we draw heavily on Althauser and Kalleberg's (1981) conceptual analysis of firms, occupations, and labor market structure, although we deviate from their nomenclature and distinctions to highlight what is relevant for our purposes. It is useful first to distinguish between external and internal labor markets. External labor markets include traditional, competitive markets through which employers fill entry-level jobs on ladders and other jobs that are not on ladders (including Althauser and Kalleberg's "secondary labor market"). The entry-level and job assignment barriers we identify occur in this market.

Internal labor markets, according to Althauser and Kalleberg (p. 130), have three defining characteristics: a job ladder exists, entrance is restricted to the lowest level, and movement up the ladder is accompanied by the progressive acquisition of job-related skills and knowledge. The barriers to mobility we identify reside primarily in firms' internal labor markets. Althauser and Kalleberg distinguish "firm internal labor markets" from "occupational internal labor markets" and "occupational labor markets," the last of which lacks the internal labor market characteristics described above. Individuals in the latter two markets have specialized skills and knowledge, acquired through extensive education or training accompanied by practice, which may culminate in licensing, certification, or registration. Although these occupational markets may exist within firms, they often span several enterprises, and mobility among firms is common. The occupational labor market is relevant here because it is the locus of institutionalized rules or policies restricting access to training.

Institutional barriers to the retention of workers in sex-atypical jobs tend not to be located in labor markets as commonly conceived but in the way that tasks are organized or in the informal organization of the workplace. Finally, some constraints on the sexes' free access to jobs operate outside labor markets in other institutional arrangements (examples include communication networks and child care facilities). We should note that these functions could be institutionalized within labor markets (including the workplace) to expand women's occupational options. (Kanter, 1977, offers some useful strategies along these lines.)

We note at the outset that because the practices we consider are institutionalized their effect is net of employers' intentions and workers' preferences. However, they neither emerged nor exist in a vacuum, independent of social or cultural factors that define certain kinds of jobs as appropriate for one sex only. Widely held, deep-seated stereotypes about differences between the sexes and assumptions about their proper roles provide an often invisible foundation for many of these organizational practices and encourage sex "traditional" decisions by individuals in the labor market (Reskin and Hartmann, 1984). In sum, these institutionalized factors have a life of their own in terms of their segregative consequences. However, they persist in part because they are reinforced by sex-role norms and cultural beliefs that shape the preferences of employers, workers, and consumers.

INSTITUTIONAL BARRIERS TO JOB TRAINING

For many occupations, workers acquire the necessary skills on the job, and barriers to training for women in sex-atypical jobs reside primarily in the resistance of male coworkers. However, many occupations that exist in what Althauser and Kalleberg (1981: 134) call "occupational labor markets," require substantial preemployment training. Here training has the same function as "port of entry" positions in internal labor markets in providing access to a job ladder. The training that permits entry into occupational

labor markets is available in a variety of settings. High schools offer some vocationally specific classes, and other courses (for example, on electronic equipment repair or bartending) are available commercially to anyone who can afford the tuition. The higher education system selects and trains persons for most professional occupations. Sex discrimination in training, along with institutional barriers that discourage women's participation in "male" professions, has been thoroughly addressed elsewhere (Epstein, 1970a,b; Theodore, 1971; Hochschild, 1975).[1] In comparison, the effects of formal vocational and technical training programs operated individually or cooperatively by unions, employers, and public agencies have received less attention. Because such training is the route to — and indeed is sometimes requisite for — many predominantly male occupations, we first consider institutional barriers in such training.

Apprenticeship Programs

Apprenticeship programs are an important avenue for entry into skilled blue-collar jobs, especially those in union-dominated occupations and industries (since apprenticeship is often the simplest way to enter a union; Briggs, 1981). These programs provide a formal mechanism whereby skilled workers pass on their knowledge to new workers through classroom and on-the-job training. Such programs are seldom available to women. Despite progress in the number of occupations in which women are now apprenticed (up from 17.5 percent in 1973 to 44.4 percent in 1977), in 1978 women constituted only 2.6 percent of the more than 250,000 apprentices registered with the U.S. Department of Labor (Ullman and

---

[1] We do not consider training that takes place in public schools and institutions of higher education. For an analysis of the impact of educational institutions on sex segregation, see Marini and Brinton, in this volume.

Deaux, 1981).[2] In addition to their small numbers, women are located disproportionately in certain apprenticeship categories: they constituted 54 percent of the barber and beautician apprentices in 1975 but only 6 percent of craft-worker apprentices (O'Farrell, 1982) and 1.9 percent of construction apprentices (Ullman and Deaux, 1981; Briggs, 1979:225-226).

The presence of women is rare in apprenticeship programs because they are less likely than men to learn about openings, to meet their requirements, and to be selected. Information about apprenticeship programs, usually transmitted by friends or relatives (Sexton, 1977), outreach programs, and publicity, is less likely to reach women who seldom belong to the networks in which such information is circulated (Waite and Hudis, 1981). Even in the female-dominated occupation of hairdressing, Allison (1976:390) found that women were less likely than men to have semiinformal apprenticeships, which were associated with subsequent employment in better shops and at higher wages. The few women who had been apprentices had male relatives in the industry and thus presumably were better informed about their availability and/or value.

Many labor-management agreements stipulate that apprenticeship openings be advertised only within the plant, where few women have worked. Moreover, they may be posted in areas inaccessible to women employees such as men's restrooms (Briggs, 1974:13). When unions go outside the plant to recruit, they might consult high school industrial arts teachers, who are unlikely to nominate female candidates since only a small number of women take such courses.[3]

Often apprenticeship requirements are harder for women to meet. The upper age limit (as low as 24 to 27 in some trades) is the most significant obstacle for women, given the typical timing of child-bearing. Because of their socialization, few young women even consider skilled blue-collar work before they have spent several years in sex-traditional jobs, at which point economic exigencies often force them to seek better-paying work (Kane and Miller, 1981:90; Waite and Hudis, 1981; Walshok, 1981a; O'Farrell, 1982).

Apprenticeship programs are geared to young unmarried men who can sustain unpaid work or low wages and the uncertainty of immediate employment. These conditions constitute particular obstacles for economically disadvantaged women, who are likely to have families to support. In the construction trades, for example, high application or union induction fees and the long wait between application and acceptance are hardships for women with dependents and may deter them from seeking apprenticeships (U.S. Department of Labor, Employment Standards Administration, 1981; Walshok, 1981a).

Women who apply are at a disadvantage in the selection process. Unions practice nepotism or require sponsorship by a member in awarding apprenticeships (Simmons et al., 1975:119; U.S. Department of Labor, Employment Standards Administration, 1981). In the construction industry, for example, where unions often have absolute control over the certification and supply of labor, labor unions have been particularly resistant to accommodating women. As a consequence, women must generally rely on outreach agencies to place them in jobs or cer-

---

[2] This figure is even smaller than the number of women workers in craft jobs — in 1978, 5.6 percent of craft workers were women (Ullman and Deaux, 1981).

[3] One recent study of New York City's vocational education system found that of 21 job-training high schools 12 were primarily male and 5 were primarily female. The 5 predominantly female schools were train-

ing their students for traditionally lower-paid employment than the predominantly male schools. The study cited sex-biased admission tests, guidance counselors steering students to sex-typical fields, and male antagonism to female students in traditionally male fields as the primary explanations for the large sex difference in vocational training (*New York Times*, 1983).

tification programs in the construction trades. For example, one study found that women who had not been apprentices were aided by family ties in gaining access to the construction trades (U.S. Department of Labor, Employment Standards Administration, 1981:34, 41).

Another factor hampering women's selection into apprenticeships is that they are unlikely to have completed vocationally relevant programs in high school and are often unfamiliar with the tools, procedures, and terminology used in blue-collar work. The current unstable nature of the economy undoubtedly works against women being accepted in apprenticeship programs, since the availability of apprenticeships declines with rising unemployment (Briggs, 1979).[4]

The structure of apprenticeship programs hinders women's ability to complete them and find craft jobs. Many female apprentices whom Walshok (1981b:177) interviewed complained that they lacked the opportunity for hands-on experience and that hostile journeymen prevented their learning necessary skills. Some (*New York Times*, 1982b) argue that unions may provide "separate and unequal" apprenticeship training for workers who are not white males. One example led the New York State Division of Human Rights to find a construction union local guilty of unlawful discrimination for requiring nonwhite apprentices to work more than twice as long as whites to reach journeyman status. Moreover, nonwhite trainees had obsolete textbooks and were denied a fifth year of classroom training. Whether the same inadequate training also affects women's apprenticeship experience requires investigation.

Several experimental programs have been

developed to address the problems facing women apprentices. Walshok (1981b) claimed that "competency-based testing" of apprentices in a pilot program at General Motors offered apprentices feedback on expectations and performance, while reassuring journeymen that standards had not been reduced for women and minority apprentices. Instituting placement services has also proved essential for women, who often encounter discrimination from employers (U.S. Department of Labor, Employment Standards Administration, 1981:33; Walshok, 1981a). Preapprenticeship training in certain construction programs enhances women apprentices' chances for success. In addition, efforts to match female apprentices with journeymen can reduce friction on the job and thus contribute to more effective training (U.S. Department of Labor, Employment Standards Administration, 1981:57).

However, apprenticeship is not the primary entry channel into the trades. Even in the unionized sector, which represents 40 percent of the industrial work force, only one-fifth of workers enter trades through apprenticeship programs (U.S. Department of Labor, Employment Standards Administration, 1981:23). We now turn to other paths by which workers enter jobs.

Federal Job Training Programs

The federal government sponsors training programs to provide an avenue for unskilled, economically disadvantaged workers to move into more skilled blue-collar work. Recent investigations of the effects of these federal programs on women (Harlan, 1980, 1981; Berryman and Chow, 1981; Wolf, 1981; U.S. Commission on Civil Rights, 1981; Waite and Berryman, this volume) indicate sex inequality in training, employment, occupational placement, and wages.

The Comprehensive Employment and Training Act (CETA), enacted in 1975 and amended in 1976 and 1978, is the largest federal program designed to increase the

---

[4] O'Farrell and Harlan (this volume), for example, found evidence that women are more likely to make progress at integrating traditionally male employment in rapidly expanding firms than in companies experiencing retrenchment.

employability and earnings of the disadvantaged (U.S. Commission on Civil Rights, 1981:28-29). As paraphrased by Wolf (1981:87), the amended law recommends that CETA sponsors:

. . . overcome sex stereotyping and artificial barriers to employment . . . [presumably] by attempting to (1) expose women to nontraditional career options, and (2) overcome additional barriers to the employment of women (such as child care, transportation to work).

Despite the fact that the law requires prime sponsors to include eligible groups equitably, other regulations favor other groups such as Vietnam veterans or youth (Wolf, 1981:109). As a result, in 1977 women were underrepresented in CETA programs relative to their numbers in the eligible populations (National Commission on Manpower Policy, as cited in U.S. Commission on Civil Rights, 1981:29). More important here are the segregative implications of their uneven participation in individual programs. For example, women were less likely to be assigned public service jobs or on-the-job training (which more often leads to unsubsidized jobs) and more likely to be in classroom training — usually preparation for clerical jobs (Harlan, 1980; O'-Neill and Braun, 1981:102; Wolf, 1981:94). In fiscal year 1980, for example, 56 percent of those in classroom training were female, compared with 36 percent of those in on-the-job training programs (Bendick, 1982:259). In addition, while CETA women expressed increasing interest in nontraditional jobs between 1976 and 1978, their placement in such jobs dropped (Wolf, 1981:98).

Several features of federally sponsored training programs impede women's access to nontraditional jobs. First, these programs put priority on quick, low-cost placement in order to reduce welfare dependency, which does little to ensure long-run financial independence. This emphasis on placing the most "job-ready" individuals encourages placing women in traditionally female em-

ployment.[5] Second, CETA programs are targeted to families rather than to individuals and to the single person within the family who has "primary" support responsibility. These features of the CETA legislation hinder the participation of married women because any man in the home is assumed to bear the support obligations for the family (Harlan, 1981:37). Third, veterans' preference policies reduce women's participation in CETA. Prior to 1978, this preference was explicit: President Carter directed that 35 percent of those assigned to public service employment be Vietnam veterans. Although this directive was rescinded, some claim the preference persists (Wolf, 1981:109). Fourth, while the CETA authorization empowers prime sponsors to provide support services (such as child care and transportation costs) to those otherwise unable to participate, the standard in-program evaluation of a high ratio of trainees to expenditures discouraged sponsors from using funds in this way (U.S. Commission on Civil Rights, 1981:30-32; Wolf, 1981).

INSTITUTIONAL FACTORS ASSOCIATED
WITH ACCESS TO SEX-TYPICAL AND
SEX-ATYPICAL JOBS

This section considers the institutional factors affecting women's access to entry-level jobs, particularly barriers to sex-atypical jobs. Typically these barriers reside in external labor markets through which entry-level positions are filled. They are of two types: firm-based limitations for certain kinds of jobs and restrictions on women's access to certain occupational labor markets. Several firm-based limitations restrict the sexes'

---

[5] This problem affects all workers. Schiller (1980:197) noted the general tendency of federally sponsored job-training programs to "cream" the most job-ready program applicants for job placement, thus enhancing program success ratios at the expense of the most needy job seekers.

access to sex-atypical entry-level jobs, including employers' and workers' preferences and beliefs, entrance requirements, and organizational practices regarding job assignment. Except when they are institutionalized in personnel practices, employers' discriminatory preferences fall outside the scope of our essay. However, we mention their manifestation in statistical discrimination because of their special importance in excluding women from entry-level positions. In employment, statistical discrimination involves treating individuals based on beliefs about group differences in relevant characteristics (Phelps, 1972). With respect to women it is most often manifest in employers' reluctance to hire *any* woman for jobs that require appreciable on-the-job training, because they believe many young women leave the labor force to have children. As a result, newly hired females are often assigned to low-skilled dead-end jobs (Grinker et al., 1970). Because transferring across internal labor markets is very difficult, if not impossible (see the next section), statistical discrimination has long-lasting implications for women's occupational outcomes.

With regard to the second barrier, two processes restrict the occupational labor markets in which women can seek jobs. The first we have already discussed — mechanisms limiting their chance to train for certain occupations. Women also lack access to selected labor markets because they have insufficient information about their very existence. Few methods of job recruitment are fully public; state employment services and classified advertisements in mass circulation newspapers are notable exceptions. Instead, personal ties through which job seekers learn of possible job opportunities and employers of possible applicants are important in determining who is hired at the entry level. Below we show how sex-segregated personal networks foster sex-typed occupational outcomes. Because these mechanisms

differ for blue- and white-collar workers, we discuss them separately.

Blue-Collar Workers

Access to Information Regarding Job Opportunities Women are unlikely to learn about predominantly male blue-collar jobs for several reasons. First, the common assumption that women are not interested in craft employment is reflected in brochures and publicity oriented toward men (Stevenson, 1977; Briggs, 1981). Such materials generate little response from women. In an ingenious study to determine the impact of such materials, Bem and Bem (1973) found that sex-biased wording in job advertisements and the placement of ads in sex-segregated newspaper columns discouraged women's interest in traditionally male jobs: only 5 percent of the women surveyed expressed interest in linemen and framemen jobs when they were written in sex-biased language, but 25 percent were interested when the language was sex-neutral, and 45 percent expressed interest when the ad was written to appeal specifically to women.

Traditionally, blue-collar employees in the crafts have been recruited from secondary schools and through employee referrals, methods unlikely to elicit female recruits (Golladay and Wulfsberg, 1981:78). To the extent that employers rely on employee referrals, new recruits will tend to reproduce the existing sex-segregated work force.[6] This is especially true in certain industries such as construction, where referral and hiring are often accomplished via nepotism and word of mouth recruitment (U.S. Department of Labor, Employment Standards Administration, 1981:22).

---

[6] Harkess (1980) found that employers often hold their employees responsible for the job candidates they nominate, so even unbiased workers may hesitate before taking the risk of recommending someone whose sex or race does not match the work group.

Employers' reliance on traditional recruitment techniques reflects their belief that a homogeneous labor force will facilitate the transfer of craft knowledge via on-the-job training (Stevenson, 1977). Whether or not they are right, the practice perpetuates sex segregation. In general, to the extent that the recruitment process involves parties who hold sex-typed notions about who should hold certain jobs — whether they be recruiters, training program administrators, current employees, or job seekers — formal mechanisms such as outreach programs are necessary to ensure that women are trained and recruited. As we noted with respect to apprenticeship programs, information about most typically male jobs is circulated in all-male informal networks. For example, a 1966 study by Sheppard and Belitsky (as cited in Folk, 1968) noted that 77 percent of the blue-collar workers surveyed found their jobs through friends and relatives. In our discussion of access to information about white-collar jobs (see below), we consider in more detail the segregative implications of informal networks and review several empirical studies.

Employers often claim that they cannot comply with federally mandated affirmative action requirements because the pool of eligible women is too small (U.S. Department of Labor, Employment Standards Administration, 1981), while women interested in nontraditional jobs contend that there are too few openings to accommodate all those seeking blue-collar employment (Westley, 1982). Kane and Miller (1981:88) argued that both views are accurate: while the number of women who want to participate in outreach programs and the number of employers requesting referrals have increased, the resources for training have remained constant. As a consequence, the supply of trained women these programs are able to produce is severely limited.

Special programs often succeed in placing women in nontraditional jobs. For example,

40 percent of the women in nontraditional blue-collar occupations whom Walshok (1981a) interviewed had direct contact with special recruitment and counseling agencies that were specifically designed to link interested women with job opportunities in nontraditional fields. Almost none of these women found their jobs through advertisements. Thus, while men can be recruited through existing recruitment channels, placing women in heavily male jobs appears to require specialized intermediary placement agencies or other outreach efforts.[7]

Employer Practices Regarding Entrance Requirements Several kinds of rules or requirements employers impose restrict women's access to a variety of jobs. While instituted to help returning veterans, veterans' preference rules also limit women's access to several occupations that have been labeled male. For example, 65 percent of the government agencies surveyed gave some form of preference to veterans in selecting police officers, an occupation women have had considerable difficulty entering (Eisenberg et al., 1974, as cited in Martin, 1980:47). By restricting competition, veterans' preference rules serve the latent function of reserving such occupations for men. Interestingly, some states have exempted traditionally female occupations from veterans' preference (*Personnel Administration of Massachusetts* v. *Feeney, 1979*), so these policies do not increase male access to traditionally female occupations. Despite their segregative effect, the Supreme Court allowed veterans' preference rules to stand in its 1979 decision in *Feeney.*

For much of this century, protective labor laws ruled out many occupations to women and provided an excuse to employers who

---

[7] See U.S. Department of Labor, Employment Standards Administration (1981:32), for how this method of recruitment operates in the construction industry.

did not want to hire women for other jobs. Under the regulations interpreting Title VII of the 1964 Civil Rights Act, such laws cannot be applied to only one sex. Recently, however, employers in some industries (e.g., rubber, lead, metal, and chemical) have refused to employ women of child-bearing age in jobs that expose them to toxic substances (e.g., lead, vinyl chloride, carbon disulfide, pesticides), rather than develop standards that would protect both male and female workers. Bell (1979) and Wright (1979) pointed out that employers ignore toxic hazards in traditionally female jobs (e.g., operating room nurses' exposure to waste anaesthetic gases, beauticians' to hydrocarbon hairspray propellants, flight attendants' to above-average levels of radiation).

In *Grigg* v. *Duke Power Company* (1971), the Supreme Court construed Title VII of the 1964 Civil Rights Act to prohibit job requirements that disproportionately exclude members of protected groups unless they were demonstrably job related. This ruling was applied in 1975 to strike down the height and physical agility requirements that barred nearly all women from being police officers in San Francisco (Gates, 1976; Martin, 1980:44). Reflecting the lag between court rulings and changes in practices, many police departments continue to use height and agility requirements, with the result that women are underrepresented among those eligible to apply for positions (Martin, 1980:47). A maximum-age restriction for police recruits adversely affects women's chances to become police officers for the same reasons it limits their participation in apprenticeship programs.

Access to traditionally male jobs is also impaired by what Newman (1976:272) characterized as "sex bias in machinery design." Because of sex differences in physical size, some women may find it difficult to use machines designed for men. Similarly, machinery used in traditionally female employment (such as fine work requiring finger dexterity) may inhibit men's employment. Employers have sometimes claimed that the cost of adapting machinery for women is prohibitive. This problem is highlighted in the military. In discussing the costs of redesigning special clothing and equipment to accommodate the increasing the number of women in the Armed Forces, Binkin and Bach (1977:54) noted:

In particular, the assignment of women to traditionally-male occupations could require extensive changes. . . . In a number of critical dimensions — weight, stature, sitting height, . . . the average woman measures significantly less than the average man.[8]

Organizational Practices Regarding Job Assignment In establishments with only a few occupations, decisions regarding hiring and job assignment may be one and the same. However, for large establishments that are continuously hiring for a variety of occupations, it helps to examine separately the factors associated with the kinds of jobs to which workers are assigned — the focus of this section. Sex differences in initial job assignments reflect sex stereotypes about appropriate work roles for men and women. Certain jobs have been historically sex typed as male or female (Oppenheimer, 1968). Sex typing persists in part because men and women learn to "prefer" jobs that society deems appropriate for their sex. However, the persistence of occupational sex segregation cannot be reduced to sex differences in employees' preferences. In the case of initial job assignments, employers' organi-

---

[8] In the same vein, military authorities have argued that the number of women who can be assimilated into the Armed Forces is limited by the cost of adapting living and working facilities for their use. For example, the Department of Navy has estimated that the total cost for adapting all active Navy ships would range from $96 to $132 million, depending on how many women needed to be accommodated (Binkin and Bach, 1977:54).

zational practices contribute to the perpetuation of sex segregation, and these institutional practices reflect, and are reinforced by, societal norms.[9]

Based on their sex, workers are often assigned to so-called light or heavy work. These initial assignments are often due less to job content than to stereotypical notions about what kinds of work are compatible with female and male workers' alleged strengths and weaknesses. For example, lifting one heavy object a day has justified restricting a job to males. Under *Griggs* (1971), Alabama height and weight minima for prison guards that excluded almost all women were struck down (*Dothard* v. *Rawlinson*, 1977).[10] Formal policies assigning women to light work would probably not survive legal challenge, but litigation — always expensive and slow — is not a viable option for many women.

Even women who are employed in such nontraditional sectors as the military typically work in what are traditionally female jobs outside the military. Considering how this comes about is instructive. After the 1970 decision to end the draft, the U.S. Department of Defense began to increase the number of women in the Armed Forces. Within four years, the proportion of women had more than doubled to approximately 5 percent of all Armed Forces personnel (Binkin and Bach, 1977:14). Prior to 1972 only 35 percent of the military's occupa-

tional specialties were open to women; currently, all but combat-related assignments (about 42 percent of all enlisted *positions* in the Armed Forces in 1977) are available to women (p. 17).[11] Although the percentage of women working in male sex-typed military specialties (e.g., infantry, electronic equipment repair) increased from 9 percent in 1972 to 40 percent in 1976 (p. 19), most women in the military still work as medical and dental specialists and administrative specialists and clerks.

The U.S. General Accounting Office (1976) identified three reasons for the persistence of sex-segregated occupational assignments in the military. First, women lack information regarding the full range of job opportunities. For example, over half of the female Army recruits interviewed in 1974 reported that their recruiters had not informed them of various assignments for which they were eligible (a comparable percentage was not provided for men; p. 10). Second, many women reportedly preferred administrative or medical jobs, perhaps because young women who choose military careers may wish to avoid being doubly unusual in selecting specialties with few or no women. In addition, because military pay is determined by rank and time in service (and not by occupation), women lack the financial incentive to pursue jobs that in civilian life are both higher paying and held predominantly by men.

Third, and most important, women are automatically excluded from both combat-related occupational specialties and positions set aside for men who return to the United States from male-only overseas and sea-duty jobs (estimated to be another 9 percent of all enlisted positions, yielding a total

---

[9] While certain jobs have been historically labeled male or female, this does not mean that jobs never change their sex type. Clerical jobs, for example, have shifted from a male to a female sex type (Tilly and Scott, 1978:157), as has public school teaching (Tyack and Strober, 1981). Carter and Carter (1981) argued, with respect to the professions at least, that this shifting of sex types derives from the deskilling of occupations and that women entering jobs previously identified as men's employment move into the most routinized sectors of these occupations.

[10] The Supreme Court, however, permitted the state to deny women jobs as prison guards in male maximum-security prisons where their safety was allegedly in jeopardy.

[11] The definition of combat-related occupations has recently been broadened to include 23 additional military occupational specialties. The U.S. Army currently bars women from a total of 61 (or 17 percent) of its job specialties (*New York Times*, 1982a).

of 51 percent of positions not open to women; Office of the Assistant Secretary of Defense, 1977:Table 11).[12] Each of the services has additional restrictions on the entry of women that further limit women's job options. Thus, according to the U.S. General Accounting Office report, while nearly all military occupational specialties were open to women, once all restrictive factors were taken into account, only 26 percent of all enlisted positions were available to them.[13] Not only do these restrictions inhibit job access at the entry level, but they also limit women's later mobility, since combat and other male-only jobs are the main route to upward mobility in the military.

White-Collar Workers

Sex differences in access to information and recruiting networks, entrance restrictions, and the allocation of men and women to sex-typical entry-level jobs also contribute to sex segregation among white-collar workers.

Access to Information and Recruitment Networks Occupational sex segregation persists in white-collar jobs in part because information networks are sex segregated.

Granovetter (1974) explored the role of personal contacts in securing employment among professional, technical, and managerial workers. He concluded that the key to the process by which a worker with certain characteristics gets "matched" to a particular job lies in large measure in the dynamic process whereby job information flows through informal personal networks. Those outside networks (e.g., young labor force entrants, recent immigrants) must rely on formal means of finding employment, such as intermediary agencies. With respect to sex segregation, the questions of interest are whether the sexes have equal access to personal networks, whether they are equally likely to use them, and whether networks are equally effective for women and men.

In holding most professional and managerial jobs, men enjoy personal and work associations that facilitate learning of other opportunities in those fields. Women, concentrated in clerical and service jobs, normally find themselves outside that network. Instead they share information with same-sex friends and coworkers. Thus, men's and women's positions in the occupational structure themselves contribute to continued sex segregation in occupational allocation. Several network studies elucidate these sex differences. Langlois (1977:Table 1) found, for a small sample of government workers, that men were slightly more likely than females to secure their initial employment via personal contacts, while women more often acquired their jobs through direct application. Moreover, sex differences in the use of personal contacts were largest in the two occupational categories with the fewest women (administrative workers and laborers/service workers).

Ensel and Lin (1982:8) found that men were more likely than females to have used personal contacts in their *initial* employment search, whereas women were more likely to have relied on formal job-search methods. Interestingly, although each sex relied predominantly on same-sex contacts

---

[12] This total estimate varies by military service. In 1977 the percentage of all positions unavailable to women because of a combat restriction was 50 percent in the Army, 60 percent in the Navy, 7 percent in the Air Force, and 73 percent in the Marine Corps (calculated from Office of the Assistant Secretary of Defense, 1977:Table 11).

[13] This varies substantially by military service. In the Army only 8 percent of all positions were available to women, compared with 8, 76, and 5 percent for the Navy, Air Force, and Marine Corps, respectively. The greater proportion of open jobs in the Air Force was due to the small number (7 percent) of all positions that are classified as combat related (all figures calculated from Office of the Assistant Secretary of Defense, 1977:Table 11). These figures are from 1977. As noted in note 11, the estimates for the Army will be reduced with the new restriction in the number of specialties open to women.

in searching for their jobs, men were less likely to use cross-sex contacts, which would reduce their chances of learning about job opportunities in female-dominated occupations. (Of course, they may have refrained from consulting female informants because they did not want low-paying female jobs.) Finally, women who found high-status jobs were more likely than men to have used mere acquaintances and indirect contacts ("weak ties") with males. This finding is consistent with the conventional wisdom that women who want to progress in their careers in male occupations need men's help either as sponsors or at least as intermediaries (Hennig and Jardim, 1977).

Caplette (1981:176) found that identical percentages of male and female employees in a variety of publishing settings used personal contacts to break into the book publishing field. However, men relied more on same-sex contacts than did women. Because men hold the more prestigious jobs in publishing, as in other industries, male contacts are likely to be more useful. Here too the women relied more on formal job search methods: they were twice as likely as men to have used intermediary agencies and half as likely as men to have "knocked on doors" to secure their first job in publishing.

Taken in sum, these studies suggest that the use of personal contacts in securing initial employment is more effective for men, which may explain men's greater propensity to use them. This difference reflects both the sex-stratified occupational structure and employers' conservatism in hiring.

Entrance Restrictions Employers' entrance requirements operate somewhat differently in white- than blue-collar occupations because of the different nature of the jobs for which entry is sought. In blue-collar jobs they often consist of formal rules (such as veterans' preference, for example), whereas restrictions on white-collar entry operate more subtly. Hiring decisions, especially those for prestigious professional and

managerial occupations, often involve subjective evaluations of whether the applicant will "fit in." While the problem of fitting in also contributes to women's underrepresentation in craft and other blue-collar employment (Martin, 1980; Walshok, 1981a), hiring an "outsider" for a prestigious white-collar occupation has greater organizational implications, given the higher levels of uncertainty in these jobs as well as their greater rewards (Kanter, 1977). Because workers in these occupations have more control over their work, organizational elites must ensure that those hired will not disrupt the ongoing work or challenge the nature of the organization. They do this by hiring those whose socialization and backgrounds resemble those of members of the organization and by fostering unobtrusive controls that structure people's work attitudes and behavior (Perrow, 1979:152; Smith and Grenier, 1982).[14] Finally, firms with highly structured internal labor markets face more serious potential consequences of a hiring error. As a result, except during periods of labor shortage, employers may prefer to err by failing to hire a qualified worker rather than hiring an unqualified worker (Stevenson, 1977).[15] Apparently, qualified applicants whose personal characteristics make them suspect are particularly likely to fall victim to such decision strategies.

Sexton (1977:26) argued that the use of highly subjective evaluations unrelated to job content tends to favor hiring men for jobs they customarily hold (see also Epstein, 1975). There is also limited evidence that subjective evaluations based on interviews

---

[14] Perrow (1979:152) labeled these unobtrusive controls "premise-setting." While premise controls are not a direct example of *entrance* restrictions, by structuring people's behaviors and attitudes once they are hired they help ensure that any recruits with "deviant" backgrounds (e.g., women or members of minority groups) are kept "in line" within the organization.

[15] The caution exercised by academic tenure committees often illustrates this principle.

are detrimental to women seeking sex-atypical employment.[16]

Finally, nepotism rules are also important in restricting women's access to white-collar employment; the traditional exclusion of women from teaching at universities that employ their husbands (although no longer the case in most universities) is an obvious example. A recent example appeared in a news story in a national news magazine in which the chairman of a major corporation was quoted as remarking that "we have a policy at this company that we don't hire wives" (Newsweek, 1982a,b). In a letter to the editor, he corrected himself saying that the policy applied to spouses of corporate officers, not wives in general. However, in reality women have probably borne most of the brunt of such rules.[17]

Organizational Practices Regarding Job Assignment While sex segregation in entry-level occupations has been well documented, our understanding of the processes whereby differential allocation occurs is largely speculative. Two recent case studies provide insights into how workers have traditionally been assigned to jobs: Caplette's (1981) study of the publishing industry and Epstein's (1981) study of the male-dominated legal profession. Although Caplette investigated an entire *industry* (which includes management, sales, editorial, and clerical occupations) and Epstein an *occupation*, similar processes apparently operated to allocate men and women to sex-typical employment in both settings. We should note that, while the processes Caplette and Epstein document still prevail, they are nevertheless changing in the direction of the relaxation of sex typing.

Although publishing, which is one-half to two-thirds female, is viewed as a women's business, it has always been controlled by men (Caplette, 1981:71). Having entered book publishing in increasing numbers in recent years, women are still concentrated in advertising and publicity, art design, production, and editing children's books and manuscripts (p. 75). Men dominate marketing, sales, and management. Sex typing becomes even more apparent when these specialties are broken down further: women predominate as manuscript editors, editorial assistants, design directors, and secretaries; men are editors, publishers, sales representatives, and marketing directors. Differences in background and credentials could not account for these sex differences (p. 155). Women traditionally entered publishing through secretarial jobs, whereas men entered as sales representatives or editorial assistants. College textbook publishing illustrates the general pattern of sex differences in initial job assignment. According to Caplette (p. 205), those in the field tacitly understand that sales, particularly the college traveler job, is *the* route to upward mobility: approximately two-thirds of the men began their careers in this position but only 9 percent of the women did so, all of whom were hired in a single year. Women were automatically excluded from these positions, on the assumption that the extensive traveling required would conflict with their

---

[16] Dubeck (1979) found that gender affected how interviewees for jobs in management were evaluated. Among applicants whom interviewers considered qualified, men were significantly more likely to be recommended for a job. Dubeck suggested that being "qualified" is determined differently for men and women. She found that the four most important factors affecting the decision to hire males were (in order) an evaluation of their qualifications, leadership experience, interest in the job, and academic performance. In contrast, the most important factors for women were job interest, academic performance, race, and qualifications. Thus, the criteria for evaluating female and male applicants were ranked differently. Dubeck (p. 97) concluded that the primacy of job interest (i.e., whether the applicant was rated as interested in the job) over qualifications for female applicants reflects employer concern about female career orientation.

[17] The Supreme Court declined to consider this issue in refusing to review a decision by the 7th U.S. Circuit Court of Appeals that found Libby-Owens-Fords' nepotism policy to be job related.

present or future domestic responsibilities (p. 208).

Epstein (1981) also found sex typing in lawyers' entry-level positions. First, a large number of women lawyers work for the government: in 1970, 37 percent did, compared with 19 percent of the men. By 1977 the percentage of women lawyers working for the government had decreased to 22 percent, compared with 17 percent for men (Epstein, 1981:112). Second, women lawyers are overrepresented in certain specialties (including trusts and estates, domestic relations, and tax law) and in particular types of jobs (research, writing of briefs, and providing legal assistance). Not surprisingly, these specialties and positions rank lower than those in which men are concentrated. Third, women have generally been accepted in *nonpublic* positions but not in the more public corporate and litigation specialties. Epstein's (p. 107) interviews revealed that firms were reluctant to hire women because they feared clients' reactions. Women were also considered not tough enough for negotiations and less able to participate in the camaraderie between lawyer and client. In sum, specialty assignments for lawyers reflected the norms governing the sex appropriateness of jobs. This is due both to self-selection of women into jobs in which they are accepted and to employer biases that derive from sex-role stereotypes.

INSTITUTIONAL FACTORS AFFECTING MOBILITY INTO SEX-TYPICAL AND SEX-ATYPICAL JOBS

The recognition that workers' mobility opportunities are governed by internal labor markets that exist within firms or occupations (or both; Althauser and Kalleberg, 1981) is critical for identifying institutional barriers to women's mobility into and advancement within sex-atypical jobs. Internal labor market theory identifies the job ladder as the primary path by which workers improve

their occupational status. It is only for entry-level positions that workers must compete in a relatively open labor market. Following labor market entry, job shifts — both horizontal and vertical — are restricted largely by the job family in which a worker is located. An establishment's internal labor market primarily consists of its promotion practices that define mobility opportunities across and up job ladders. These may be firm, union, or civil service rules about controlling movement across jobs. Several researchers (e.g., Stevenson, 1977; Osterman, 1979; Harlan and Weiss, 1981; O'Farrell and Harlan, this volume) have noted the role that internal labor markets play in limiting women's mobility into and advancement in traditionally male jobs. Internal labor markets do not rob personnel officers and supervisors of all discretion in employment decisions. Both conventional and statistical sex discrimination still occur, although they are more likely to occur with respect to promotion, where merit is often a legitimate consideration, than in layoff decisions, where seniority usually governs (Althauser and Kalleberg, 1981). However, discrimination may be less common than at the entry level. First, to the extent that hiring at the entry level is segregative, job groups will already be relatively homogeneous with respect to gender. Second, insofar as job ladders structurally constrain promotion decisions, they should override biases of individuals. In this section we focus on how seniority systems constrain mobility into sex-atypical jobs. We then examine how the organization of two particular promotion systems contributes to sex segregation.

Seniority Systems and Mobility Opportunities

Seniority systems consist of formal rules within organizations in which a worker's length of employment must be given weight by decision makers in promotions, transfers, layoffs, and benefits. Along with procedures regulating job posting and bumping and bidding rights, seniority systems structure workers' mobility prospects. These formalized procedures ensure a stable work force and transferability of skills from senior to new employees, while providing workers with job security by protecting them against being replaced by younger workers (Stevenson, 1977). However, they also limit minorities' and women's access to many jobs (Kelley, 1981). Recent court decisions (*U.S.* v. *Teamsters et al.*, 1977; *American Tobacco Company* v. *Patterson*, 1982) have permitted seniority systems as long as they were not adopted with discriminatory intent, despite their demonstrated segregative effect.

Organizations vary in the units across which a seniority system operates. They can govern an entire plant, a department, or a job sequence. In job sequence systems the seniority unit is a cluster of occupationally related jobs that represents a skill ladder even if the jobs are in different departments (e.g., all painters in a firm may constitute one seniority unit). When paired with restrictions or penalties for transferring across units, more narrowly defined seniority systems are problematic for women because they constitute a barrier to mobility for those outside the department or job family.[18] Workers transferring across seniority units may lose their seniority and are vulnerable to layoffs (Kelley, 1981:5). In keeping with narrow seniority units, rules may limit job bidding to members of the unit and job openings may be posted only in the department or work areas frequented by workers in the job sequence. Hence, outsiders lack information about such jobs. Another practice that

hampers the mobility prospects of those outside the seniority unit includes ambiguous eligibility requirements for transfers. Adopting plantwide seniority systems would eliminate much of their disparate adverse impact on women and minorities in one-union firms, but, where employers have collective bargaining agreements with more than one union, opportunities for mobility can remain limited (Steinberg and Cook, 1981:69).

Kelley's (1981) study of an electric products manufacturing company (an industry that traditionally employs a substantial number of women) illustrates that seniority reform alone is not necessarily sufficient to enhance women's mobility prospects. All workers in the plant were subject to one collective bargaining agreement and seniority was plantwide. In 1967 prohibitions against transferring across seniority units were lifted and plantwide bidding and posting procedures established. Yet 9 years later, despite the absence of exclusionary language in the collective bargaining agreement and a strong seniority clause that should have ensured that seniority would govern transfers and upgrading, few cross-system transfers had occurred. Sixty percent of recent openings that could have been filled by transfers were filled by new hires, mostly white men. While some men helped integrate the plant by moving into some traditionally female fields, this did not enhance women's opportunities. Men continued to be concentrated in restrictive high-wage job ladders with few workers. Thus, continued discrimination in hiring undermined formal reorganization efforts, suggesting that a more active set of reforms would be needed to reduce occupational segregation by sex (for documentation of this point, see O'Farrell and Harlan, this volume). As the Conference Board (Shaeffer and Lynton, 1979) survey implied, the right to transfer laterally must be accompanied by mechanisms to publicize job openings, encourage and prepare women to pursue them, and provide support for those

---

[18] Of course, more narrowly defined seniority systems are preferable for incumbents of high-wage units, since they insulate jobs from the competition of other workers.

women who transfer into traditionally male jobs.[19]

The Structuring of Opportunity: Other Organizational Practices

O'Farrell's (1980) case study of a local union in a large Northeastern industrial plant illustrates ways other than seniority systems that mobility opportunities are structured for blue-collar jobs. Employment in O'Farrell's plant was highly segmented: of the two company plants the union local represented, the smaller plant was historically female dominated, while the more modern plant was male dominated. The two plants remained sex segregated partly because jobs were posted separately *within* each. Furthermore, jobs that opened up when a worker changed jobs within the plant were not posted but instead were filled at the managers' discretion. Thus, workers were unaware of opportunities available in the other plant. Even if they learned of transfer opportunities, workers lacked cross-plant bidding rights. Given the greater number of jobs in the larger mostly male plant, the detrimental effects of posting and bidding restrictions fell primarily on the mostly female workers at the smaller plant. Treating the two sex-segregated plants as separate organizational entities ensured the persistence of sex segregation.

Recent studies of state civil service employment focused on structural barriers in white-collar jobs. Here researchers examined "career" or promotion ladders associated with particular entry-level jobs. Workers in certain entry-level jobs were "on the

mobility track," while others had to shift "tracks" to move up.

A case study of promotion under New York State's civil service system by the New York State Commission on Management and Productivity in the Public Sector (1977) showed how career ladders perpetuate sex segregation. Women and minority workers, concentrated in the lowest-level jobs with short career ladders, had few advancement opportunities. Of the 43 different career ladders, women generally filled the low-floor/low-ceiling ladders, while men predominated in the higher, longer ladders (p. 30).

In a similar study in four other New York State agencies, Peterson-Hardt and Perlman (1979) found that in over 90 percent of the career ladders, the incumbents were at least 60 percent one sex.[20] Moreover, in all four agencies, female-dominated career ladders began at lower entry levels and offered fewer opportunities for advancement: fewer than 14 percent of the female ladders ranged into high civil service grades, compared with 31 to 41 percent of the male ladders, depending on the agency (p. 57). Not only were women in New York State government more likely than men to be on truncated ladders — in essentially dead-end jobs — but their job ladders were also harder to climb because the educational and experience requirements for promotion were harder to satisfy than in male-dominated career ladders (p. 78). Smith's (1979) findings replicate these results. In 13 job "chains" with at least three steps, high-opportunity chains (defined as those in which at least 15 percent of the jobs were at or above the entry man-

---

[19] The Conference Board report also revealed that plantwide seniority had not been successful in moving women into higher-skilled blue-collar jobs in some companies, where blue-collar women workers who had accumulated enough seniority bid into clerical jobs where they preferred to remain (Shaeffer and Lynton, 1979:70). Mobility may also have been limited by more informal

barriers, expected opposition from coworkers or workers' sense of achievement at having escaped blue-collar origins.

[20] Since women comprised about 45 percent of the civil service work force in New York in 1977, the results would have been more useful had the researchers set a higher value to define sex-dominated jobs.

agerial level) were filled predominantly by men, while low-opportunity job chains were held mainly by women.

Research currently under way at the Center for Women in Government (Ratner, 1981; Haignere et al., 1981) extends that of Peterson-Hardt and Perlman (1979) by investigating the differential impact of personnel practices on women's and minorities' prospects for promotion to management positions. In New York State government, promotion involves several steps: setting criteria for eligibility to compete for the promotion, a competitive examination, and selecting the successful candidate from the top three who pass the exam (Ratner, 1981:3). Eligibility is limited to employees in "feeder" jobs specified in the job posting. Although women made up 53 percent of all state employees in 1979, they constituted only 12 percent of those in designated feeder jobs for management positions. Female and male applicants for the New York management jobs were equally likely to pass the exam, and, when women got into the three-person pool, their chances of being chosen were good. However, the consequence of basing eligibility on a feeder system composed of jobs held disproportionately by men was that over 70 percent of the three-person pools were all male. This system ensured that men would hold almost all managerial jobs — which was the case.

In less bureaucratized promotion systems, recommendations play a larger role than the formal procedures we have described above. This too can contribute to sex segregation because female clerical jobs are more likely than male jobs to provide direct services to one's immediate supervisor (a reflection of the institutionalization of women in helper or assistant roles; Epstein, 1976:191). Because supervisors may be reluctant to recommend very effective assistants for promotion, relying on supervisors' recommendations of candidates for promotion from clerical to managerial jobs may undermine organizational efforts to promote women (Kanter, 1977; Shaeffer and Lynton, 1979).

Informal networks in the workplace also differentially affect the sexes' mobility prospects. Epstein (1970a,b, 1975, 1976) has identified several informal mechanisms that restrict women's mobility prospects: women are likely to be less connected to communication networks, less involved in sponsor-protege relationships, and less likely to have access to the clublike relationships characteristic of many of the professions. (While Epstein concentrated on the professions, the logic of her argument holds for blue-collar occupations as well.) Kaufman (1978) found that female professors (especially those who were not married) had fewer males in their collegial networks than did their male colleagues. Because men dominate the upper levels of academe, women had less access to those in authority positions. Contrary to these results, Strober (1982:32) found no significant sex differences in access to mentorships for a sample of Stanford MBAs four years after graduation. Strober's study and that of Harlan and Weiss (1981) suggest that more investigation is needed to provide a definitive answer on the role of mentorship in female and male mobility.

Some companies have restructured their internal labor markets to increase women's employment opportunities, partly in response to federal enforcement efforts (Shaeffer and Lynton, 1979:34; O'Farrell and Harlan, this volume). Changes include developing strategies by employers, support groups, and managers to make job openings known to women and minorities; analyzing jobs to retain only those qualifications that are truly necessary; enacting safeguards against managers' biases for fair evaluation of candidates; and monitoring the promotion process. In recognition of the fact that existing career ladders curtail women's chances for mobility, some firms have analyzed and revised job families to create new career lines for women into managerial positions.

INSTITUTIONAL MECHANISMS ASSOCIATED WITH RETAINING WORKERS IN SEX-ATYPICAL JOBS

This section focuses on institutionalized features of the workplace that affect the retention of workers employed in sex-atypical jobs. Since most workers are in sex-typical jobs, institutionalized factors that facilitate the retention of workers in these jobs are probably more important in maintaining sex segregation. For example, the availability of part-time clerical work enables women to combine paid employment with child-rearing, thus contributing to the highly segregative character of clerical employment. The compatibility of short working days and free summers with child-rearing attracts mothers to public school teaching. That these same features are accompanied by smaller salaries is likely to discourage the retention of men. Many mechanisms that encourage workers to remain in sex-typed jobs have evolved hand in hand with the development of these jobs and may have been influenced by workers' sex. Unfortunately, space constraints preclude examining them here. With respect to sex-atypical jobs, we note two recent studies that show a considerable amount of mobility by workers of both sexes into and out of sex-atypical jobs: Rosenfeld (this volume), and Jacobs (1983). Obviously, segregation results from both entry barriers to sex-atypical jobs and mechanisms that discourage workers who hold such jobs from remaining in them. We have considered some of these factors in describing the mechanisms associated with *access to* sex-atypical jobs and will return only to those that affect retention differently.

Recruitment Practices and Information About Jobs

A recent study of women in nontraditional jobs in 10 public utility companies suggested that recruitment methods strongly affect retention. Meyer and Lee (1978) interviewed 164 women, and their supervisors, peers, and subordinates, regarding the effectiveness of special programs devised to move women into nontraditional jobs. The interviews suggested that informing female applicants about the characteristics of jobs for which they were applying reduced turnover. Nowhere is this more evident than in the comparison of the typical experiences of professional/managerial and blue-collar workers. Women selected for professional and managerial jobs usually underwent extensive screening, whereas program administrators often had to persuade blue-collar women to apply for traditionally male jobs. The dropout rate for women recruited for blue-collar jobs in this manner was very high, especially in jobs that required heavy physical labor or had undesirable working conditions (p. 17). Shaeffer and Lynton (1979) also found that the more information firms provided women entering traditionally male blue-collar jobs, the higher the retention rates. Particularly useful were clear descriptions of job demands, slides, tours, opportunities to talk with workers (especially female workers), and a chance to try out various aspects of the job. See O'Farrell and Harlan (in this volume), for additional recruitment practices found to be successful in retaining women in nontraditional jobs.

Training

Training — both prior to beginning a nontraditional job and on the job — may be the most important determinant of retention. The study of women in public utilities cited above as well as two surveys of women in construction stressed the value of special pretraining for women entering traditionally male blue-collar jobs (Meyer and Lee, 1978:18; U.S. Department of Labor, Employment Standards Administration, 1981; Westley, 1982). By exposing women to the tools and techniques with which most men become familiar while young, pretraining puts women on a more equal footing with new male recruits (see O'Farrell and Harlan in this volume for additional evidence on this point).

Walshok's (1981a) interviews with women in nontraditional blue-collar employment indicated that unstructured on-the-job training in which apprentices depend on a single journeyman is problematic for women, since it makes them vulnerable to their trainers' biases. Some formal on-the-job training enhances the chance that women will obtain necessary skills. But Walshok also stressed the importance of hands-on experience during formal training. Women whose preemployment training in male occupations included actual work experience were more likely to find jobs, to learn how to perform them well, and to succeed in them.

Organizational Mechanisms That Influence Women's Retention in Sex-Atypical Jobs

Certain organizational arrangements facilitate women's success in nontraditional jobs. Of particular importance are commitment by top management to improve women's employment opportunities (Shaeffer and Lynton, 1979:21) and a full-time equal employment opportunity staff (Meyer and Lee, 1978:4). O'Farrell (1980:124) identified lack of organizational support as an important barrier to women's employment in nontraditional work: missing at the industrial plant she studied were any special recruitment programs to inform women about the nature and advantages of nontraditional jobs, transition programs to ease the shift into nontraditional employment, and support on the job for women experiencing difficulty.

Other organizational practices, which cannot be thoroughly examined here because of space constraints, foster or hinder women's retention in sex-atypical jobs. Pregnancy leave, opportunities for flextime or part-time work, and child care can make jobs more accessible to women, whereas required shift work, overtime, and extensive travel may discourage women from staying in certain jobs.

The Role of Unions While unions can facilitate women's entry into nontraditional employment, they can negatively affect women's retention (O'Farrell, 1980; Newman and Wilson, 1981; Steinberg and Cook, 1981). Lack of female leadership may limit the effectiveness of unions. Programs that would enhance women's retention in jobs (such as child care) are more expensive than the bread-and-butter issues unions have traditionally addressed (Steinberg and Cook, 1981:63). Women as a group are only one constituency of unions and, given their underrepresentation in leadership positions, not a particularly powerful or vocal one. Without female leadership to press for such programs, they are often bargained away in negotiated agreements.

Lack of Standards for Entry Lack of specified standards for job performance has limited women's ability to perform on the job and, hence, their retention in blue-collar jobs. The U.S. General Accounting Office (1976) found that some women in traditionally male military jobs had been assigned to jobs for which they were not physically suited, and their lack of strength contributed to their inability to complete required tasks. The report recommended that the military services develop physical and operational standards required for job performance as well as measures of men's and women's ability to satisfy established standards. Of course, the danger of instituting such standards is that they may be used to keep *all* women out of traditionally male employment rather than to ensure that only those men and women physically suited to the job will be hired.

Seniority We considered seniority systems in some detail earlier in our discussion of mobility. Here we simply stress that seniority systems organized for units smaller than an entire plant have predictable negative consequences for women's retention. Department or job sequence systems render women who transfer to male jobs in different seniority units vulnerable to layoffs in an economic downturn.[21] Steinberg and Cook (1981:68) noted that seniority systems also inhibit women's retention by reducing the likelihood that work-sharing systems might be implemented as an alternative to layoffs. When narrowly structured seniority systems are used to determine shift assignments and overtime allocation, as in the steel industry, women with low seniority who are assigned to night shifts or required to work overtime may have to quit if they cannot arrange adequate child care (Walshok, 1981a). Seniority systems that guarantee bumping rights in the case of layoffs — including the right to bump back into sex-traditional jobs they left — may facilitate women's willingness to enter and their retention in sex-atypical employment. Not only are their jobs more secure in the event of an economic downturn, but women gain expertise in more jobs in the plant, thereby enhancing their future job prospects.

Organization of Work and the Workplace

When only a few women work in a group and male coworkers are not supportive, the amount of interdependence necessary to accomplish a task is important. Some of the women Walshok (1981a) interviewed indicated that male coworkers' unwillingness to work with them on multiperson tasks hampered their ability to complete their own job duties and ultimately discouraged them. Although the resistance of male coworkers is not an "institutionalized" barrier, it comes

into play when work is organized such that women's ability to do their jobs depends on male cooperation. By assigning women jobs they can do alone or by providing female work partners, organizations can retain women working in nontraditional jobs (Shaeffer and Lynton, 1979; Walshok, 1981a).[22]

Some intrinsic aspects of the work itself, the tools, and the typical division of labor also influence the success and retention of women working in nontraditional blue-collar jobs. With training, women can learn how to use unfamiliar tools, but, as we noted above, equipment and tool design may occasionally interfere with successful job performance. Pioneers in nontraditional jobs have found it difficult to obtain proper work clothes (*Business Week*, 1978:90). At AT&T, for example, the higher accident rate of women in outdoor jobs spurred the company to introduce lighter-weight and more mobile equipment. Bales and White (1981) of the Coal Employment Project found that over one-half of their sample of women miners feared for their safety because of improperly fitting protective equipment. Boots and hard hats were too large, and oversized gloves got stuck in moving machinery.

Studies of women in forestry, mining, construction, and other outdoor jobs (Enarson, 1980; Bales and White, 1981; U.S. Department of Labor, Employment Standards Administration, 1981; Walshok, 1981a) have pointed out the very real problem that access to adequate sanitary facilities presents. The absence of such facilities for

---

[21] Of course, newly hired women from the outside will also lack seniority regardless of the structure of the seniority system. For them it is seniority per se and not the type of seniority that threatens their retention.

[22] Blalock (1962) has argued that minorities will encounter less discrimination in occupations with a high division of labor, where the group output depends on each worker's performance. There is some evidence that this may also be true in science (Hagstrom, 1965). This should hold for women in nontraditional jobs insofar as their jobs are necessary to complete a group product and no male can substitute for them, but probably neither condition holds very often in most blue-collar settings where several workers do the same job.

women exposes them to health risks and sexual harassment (see Enarson, 1980; and White et al., 1981). While costly (Bethlehem Steel spent over $10 million to outfit its mills, shipyards, and mines with women's lockers, restrooms, and showers over a 5-year period; *Business Week*, 1978:90), these facilities are essential for making traditionally male blue-collar jobs accessible to many women.

INSTITUTIONAL FACTORS OUTSIDE THE WORKPLACE

The focus of this paper is on institutionalized factors that exist within the workplace. However, many factors outside the workplace affect women's occupational and advancement prospects indirectly by affecting their labor force participation.

The lack of adequate child care affects women's access to and retention in jobs. The recognition that inadequate child care constitutes a barrier to women's employment is recent, at least among lawmakers. Not until 1978 did Congress, in an amendment to Title VII of the 1964 Civil Rights Act (U.S. Commission on Civil Rights, 1981:5), specifically recognize that women's childbearing role constrained their educational and employment opportunities. Inadequate child care affects women's employment options in several ways: (1) by limiting their entry into the labor force; (2) by restricting their participation in federally sponsored education and training programs; (3) by reducing the amount of time they can devote to their jobs and encouraging their retention in part-time jobs; (4) by restricting their ability to work certain shifts; (5) by preventing them from being able to take advantage of training for more demanding jobs for which they are qualified; and (6) by constraining their participation in jobs that require traveling. It probably also contributes to women's lesser participation in union activities and ultimately union leadership.

Surveys have indicated how inadequate

child care arrangements limit women's employment prospects. Shortlidge (as cited in U.S. Commission on Civil Rights, 1981:10) estimated that approximately 20 percent of currently nonemployed women do not work because of unsatisfactory child care arrangements. Presser and Baldwin (1980) reported a similar figure: 17 percent of nonemployed women would look for work if satisfactory child care were available and 16 percent of currently employed women would work more hours given suitable and reasonably priced child care.

It has been suggested that inadequate child care may contribute to higher accident rates among women assembly line workers. Cuthbertson (as cited in U.S. Commission on Civil Rights, 1981:12) suggested that stress is a significant factor in industrial accidents, and worry about inadequate child care may contribute to stress. However, more research is needed before we can accept this contention.

Federal laws contribute to sex segregation by affecting women's labor force participation. Income tax laws discourage secondary family earners — usually women — from entering the labor force, since additional earnings are taxed at a progressively steeper rate (Blumberg, 1979; Gordon, 1979a).[23] Social security laws have a similar effect, since dual-earner families get a lower return to their social security investment than do single-earner couples, and married women are often entitled to higher benefits as their husbands' dependents than as retired workers in their own right (Blumberg, 1979; Gordon, 1979b). The federal policies underlying these laws discourage women's continuous labor force attachment, which in turn has a strong negative impact on their access to high-wage employment and mobility opportunities.

---

[23] The effect of income tax laws has recently (tax year 1982) been ameliorated by a special tax deduction designed to reduce the so-called marriage penalty.

Finally, economic factors also reduce women's opportunity to go into business for themselves. One barrier to entrepreneurship among women is difficulty in obtaining financing. Financial institutions prefer to support larger and less risky enterprises, and women are prone to start small businesses in low-profit, labor-intensive industries (U.S. Department of Commerce, 1978:5).

CONCLUSION

This paper reviews workplace mechanisms that act as barriers to women's employment in traditionally male jobs. These mechanisms, institutionalized in the labor market and in firms' personnel practices, are less well understood and less studied than those factors more often cited as explanations for occupational sex segregation: characteristics and choices of the labor supply, on the one hand, and gender discrimination by employers, on the other. Using internal labor market theory as our theoretical framework, we argue that such workplace mechanisms act as barriers to women's employment prospects at four points in the job allocation process: preemployment training, access and assignment to jobs, mobility, and retention.

Investigating barriers to women's job opportunities that are institutionalized in the labor market and the organization of work is valuable in identifying useful areas for future inquiry and essential for developing intervention strategies. Empirical studies that document sex differences in access to employment information, the allocation of the sexes to "sex-appropriate" employment, the sexes' differential location in job clusters, barriers to women's access to entry-level positions on high-prestige job ladders, and so forth will help us better understand how internal labor markets operate and how they might be modified to work to women's advantage. Our analysis also suggests the kinds of organizational changes that might reduce

segregation. As the paper by O'Farrell and Harlan (in this volume) shows, many of the mechanisms that we identify as barriers have been manipulated by organizations attempting to improve women's employment opportunities. What remains to be explored more fully is what functions these institutional mechanisms serve within organizations and labor markets and for whom.

Edwards (1975, as cited in Tolbert, 1982) noted that when bureaucratic control emerged in labor markets at the beginning of the century, large firms could no longer personally manage employees. In response, they instituted administrative regulations regarding qualifications for employment, wages, criteria for promotion, and so forth. In unionized industries, many of these procedures became union as well as company policy. At that time, the exclusionary implications for women of bureaucratic procedures were not viewed as problematic in light of prevailing social values. By the time law and social opinions challenged their discriminatory effects, resistance to modifying long-established personnel procedures would be expected from those with a stake in their administration. For example, seniority systems and other job ladders that structure promotion opportunities are economically advantageous to both employers and workers well positioned in firms' internal labor markets. Fuller analysis of other functions these segregative mechanisms fulfill is necessary to devise nondiscriminatory alternatives.

ACKNOWLEDGMENTS

This paper was supported in part by a UAP Faculty Research Fellowship and Grant-in-Aid (#431-7531-A), 1982 from the State University of New York at Stony Brook. We would like to thank the following people for their helpful comments on earlier versions: Lee Clarke, Carolyn Ellis, Cynthia Epstein, Meryl Fingrutd, Arne Kalleberg, Maryellen

Kelley, Edward Royce, Jo Shuchat, Robert Smith, Glenn Yago, and members of the Sociology Workshop at SUNY, Stony Brook.

REFERENCES

Allison, Elizabeth K.
1976   "Sex-linked earnings differentials in the beauty industry." Journal of Human Resources 11 (Summer):383-90.

Althauser, Robert P., and Arne L. Kalleberg
1981   "Firms, occupations, and the structure of labor markets: a conceptual analysis." Pp. 119-49 in Ivar Berg (ed.), Sociological Perspectives on Labor Markets. New York: Academic Press.

Bales, Jeanne, and Connie White
1981   "Personal protective equipment in the mining industry: a survey of women miners." Unpublished paper, Coal Employment Project, Oak Ridge, Tenn.

Bell, Carolyn
1979   "Implementing safety and health regulations for women in the workplace." Feminist Studies 5(Summer):286-301.

Bem, Sandra L., and Daryl J. Bem
1973   "Does sex-biased job advertising 'aid and abet' sex discrimination." Journal of Applied Social Psychology 3(1):6-18.

Bendick, Marc
1982   "Employment, training, and economic development." Pp. 247-69 in John L. Palmer and Isabel V. Sawhill (eds.), The Reagan Experiment: An Examination of Economic and Social Policies Under the Reagan Administration. Washington, D.C.: The Urban Institute Press.

Berryman, Sue E., and Winston K. Chow
1981   CETA: Is It Equitable for Women? Rand Note, N-1683-NCEP. Santa Monica: The Rand Corp.

Binkin, Martin, and Shirley J. Bach
1977   Women and the Military. Washington, D.C.: The Brookings Institution.

Blalock, Hubert M.
1962   "Occupational discrimination: some theoretical propositions." Social Problems 9(Winter):240-47.

Blumberg, Grace G.
1979   "Federal income tax and social security law." In Ann Foote Cahn (ed.), Women in the U.S. Labor Force. New York: Praeger.

Briggs, Norma
1974   Women in Apprenticeship — Why Not? Manpower Research Monograph, No. 33. Washington, D.C.: U.S. Government Printing Office.

1979   "Apprenticeship." Pp. 225-33 in Ann Foote Cahn (ed.), Women in the U.S. Labor Force. New York: Praeger.

1981   "Overcoming barriers to successful entry and retention of women in traditionally male skilled blue-collar trades in Wisconsin." Pp. 106-31 in Vernon M. Briggs, Jr., and Felician Foltman (eds.), Apprenticeship Research: Emerging Findings and Future Trends. Ithaca, N.Y.: New York State School of Industrial Relations.

Business Week
1978   "The hardships that blue-collar women face." Vol. 87, August 14, 88-90.

Caplette, Michele K.
1981   Women in Book Publishing: A Study of Careers and Organizations. Ph.D. dissertation, State University of New York, Stony Brook.

Carter, Michael J., and Susan Boslego Carter
1981   "Women's recent progress in the professions or, women get a ticket to ride after the gravy train has left the station." Feminist Studies 7(Fall):477-504.

Coser, Rose L., and Gerald Rokoff
1971   "Women in the occupational world: social disruption and conflict." Social Problems 18(Spring):535-54.

Dubeck, Paula J.
1979   "Sexism in recruiting management personnel for a manufacturing firm." Pp. 88-99 in Rodolfo Alvarez, Kenneth G. Lutterman, and Associates (eds.), Discrimination in Organizations. San Francisco: Jossey-Bass.

Enarson, Elaine
1980   "Sexual relations of production: women in the U.S. Forest Service." Paper presented at the annual meetings of the Pacific Sociological Association.

Ensel, Walter M., and Nan Lin
1982   "Social resources and strength of ties: gender differences in status attainment." Paper presented at the annual meetings of the American Sociological Association, Toronto, August 1981.

Epstein, Cynthia F.
1970a   Woman's Place: Options and Limits in Professional Careers. Berkeley: University of California Press.

1970b   "Encountering the male establishment: sex-status limits on women's careers in the professions." American Journal of Sociology 75(2):965-82.

1975   "Institutional barriers: what keeps women out of the executive suite?" Pp. 7-21 in Francine E. Gordon and Myra H. Strober (eds.), Bringing Women Into Management. New York: McGraw-Hill.

1976   "Sex role stereotyping, occupations and social exchange." Women's Studies 3:185-94.

1981   Women in Law. New York: Basic Books.

Folk, Hugh
1968   "The problem of youth unemployment." Pp. 76-107 in Princeton Manpower Symposium, The Transition From School to Work. Princeton, N.J.: Industrial Relations Section, Princeton University.

Freidson, Eliot
1970   Profession of Medicine. New York: Harper & Row.

Gates, Margaret
1976   "Occupational segregation and the law." Signs 1:3(Part 2, Spring):335-41.

Golladay, Mary A., and Rolf M. Wulfsberg
1981   The Condition of Vocational Education. Washington, D.C.: U.S. Government Printing Office.

Gordon, Nancy M.
1979a   "Institutional responses: the federal income tax system." Pp. 201-21 in Ralph E. Smith (ed.), The Subtle Revolution: Women at Work. Washington, D.C.: The Urban Institute Press.

1979b   "Institutional responses: the social security system." Pp. 223-55 in Ralph E. Smith (ed.), The Subtle Revolution: Women at Work. Washington, D.C.: The Urban Institute Press.

Granovetter, Mark S.
1974   Getting a Job: A Study of Contacts and Careers. Cambridge, Mass.: Harvard University Press.

1981   "Toward a sociological theory of income differences." Pp. 11-47 in Ivar Berg (ed.), Sociological Perspectives on Labor Markets. New York: Academic Press.

Grinker, William J., Donald D. Cooke, and Arthur W. Kirsch.
1970   Climbing the Job Ladder: A Study of Employee Advancement in Eleven Industries. New York: E. F. Shelley and Co.

Hagstrom, W. O.
1965   The Scientific Community. New York: Basic Books.

Haignere, Lois V., Cynthia H. Chertos, and Ronnie J. Steinberg
1981   "Managerial promotions in the public sector: the impact of eligibility requirements on women and minorities." Albany: Center for Women in Government, State University of New York.

Harkess, Shirley
1980   "Hiring women and blacks in entry-level manufacturing jobs in a southern city: particularism and affirmative action." Paper presented at the annual meetings of the Society for the Study of Social Problems, New York.

Harlan, Sharon L.
1980   "Sex differences in access to federal employment and training resources under CETA: an overview." Working Paper No. 58, Center for Research on Women, Wellesley College, Wellesley, Mass.

1981   "The social context of employment choice: women in CETA." New England Sociologist 3(1):32-45.

Harlan, Sharon L., and Brigid O'Farrell
1982   "After the pioneers: prospects for women in nontraditional blue collar jobs." Work and Occupations 9(August):363-86.

Harlan, Anne, and Carol Weiss
1981   Moving Up: Women in Managerial Careers. Final report. Working Paper No. 86, Center for Research on Women, Wellesley College, Wellesley, Mass.

Hennig, M., and A. Jardim
1977   The Managerial Woman. New York: Anchor Press.

Hochschild, Arlie R
1975   "Inside the clockwork of male careers." Pp. 47-80 in Florence Howe (ed.), Women and the Power to Change. New York: McGraw-Hill.

Jacobs, Jerry
1983   The Sex Segregation of Occupations and Women's Career Patterns. Ph.D. dissertation, Harvard University.

Kane, Roslyn D., and Jill Miller
1981   "Women and apprenticeship: a study of programs designed to facilitate women's participation in the skilled trades." Pp. 83-105 in Vernon M. Briggs, Jr., and Felician Foltman (eds.), Apprenticeship Research: Emerging Findings and Future Trends. Ithaca, N.Y.: New York State School of Industrial Relations.

Kanter, Rosabeth M.
1977   Men and Women of the Corporation. New York: Harper & Row.

Kaufman, Debra R.
1978   "Associational ties in academe: some male and female differences." Sex Roles 4:9-21.

Kelley, Maryellen R.
1981   "Legal and empirical issues in determining when seniority systems discriminate." Unpublished paper. Alfred P. Sloan School of Management, Massachusetts Institute of Technology.

Langlois, Simon
1977   "Les réseaux personnels et la diffusion des informations sur les emplois." Recherches Sociographiques 2:213-45.

Martin, Susan E.
1980   Breaking and Entering: Policewomen on Patrol. Berkeley: University of California Press.

Meyer, Herbert H., and Mary Dean Lee
1978   Women in Traditionally Male Jobs: The Experiences of Ten Public Utility Companies. Washington, D.C.: U.S. Government Printing Office.

New York State Commission on Management and Productivity in the Public Sector
1977   Job Promotion Under New York State's Civil Service System: A Case Study of the Office of General Services. New York: Commission on Management and Productivity in the Public Sector.

New York Times
1982a   "Army to enlist more women but in limited job categories." August 29.

1982b   "Labor's enemy: labor." September 5.

1983   "Desex schooling for jobs." March 9.

Newman, Winn
1976 "Combatting occupational segregation: presentation III." Pp. 265-72 in Martha Blaxall and Barbara Reagan (eds.), Women and the Workplace: The Implications of Occupational Segregation. Chicago: University of Chicago Press.

Newman, Winn, and Carole W. Wilson
1981 "The union role in affirmative action." Labor Law Journal (June):323-42.

Newsweek
1982a "Did Bill and Mary blunder?" October 11:94.
1982b "Hiring spouses." November 29:6.

O'Farrell, Brigid
1980 "Women and nontraditional blue collar jobs: a case study of local I." Report prepared for the Employment and Training Administration, U.S. Department of Labor.
1982 "Women and nontraditional blue collar jobs in the 1980s: an overview." Pp. 135-65 in Phyllis A. Wallace (ed.), Women in the Workplace. Boston, Mass.: Auburn.

Office of the Assistant Secretary of Defense
1977 Use of Women in the Military. Washington, D.C.: Office of the Assistant Secretary of Defense.

O'Neill, June, and Rachel Braun
1981 "Women and the labor market: a survey of issues and policies in the United States." Washington, D.C.: The Urban Institute Press.

Oppenheimer, Valerie K.
1968 "The sex-labeling of jobs." Industrial Relations 7(May):219-34.

Osterman, Paul
1979 "Sex discrimination in professional employment: a case study." Industrial and Labor Relations Review 32 (July):451-64.

Perrow, Charles
1979 Complex Organizations: A Critical Essay, 2d ed. Glenview, Ill.: Scott, Foresman and Co.

Peterson-Hardt, Sandra, and Nancy D. Perlman
1979 "Sex segregated career ladders in New York state government: a structural analysis of inequality in employment." Albany: Center for Women in Government, State University of New York, Albany.

Phelps, Edmund S.
1972 "The statistical theory of racism and sexism." American Economic Review 62 (September):659-66.

Presser, Harriet B., and Wendy Baldwin
1980 "Child care as a constraint on employment: prevalence, correlates, and bearing on the work and fertility nexus." American Journal of Sociology 85(March):1202-13.

Ratner, Ronnie Steinberg
1981 "Barriers to advancement: promotion of women and minorities into managerial positions in New York state government." Albany: Center for Women in Government, State University of New York, Albany.

Reskin, Barbara F.
1978 "Sex differentiation in the social organization of science." Sociological Inquiry 48(3/4):6-36.

Reskin, Barbara F., and Heidi I. Hartmann (eds.)
1984 Women's Work, Men's Work: Sex Segregation on the Job. Washington, D.C.: National Academy Press.

Schafran, Lynn Hecht
1981 Removing Financial Support From Private Clubs That Discriminate Against Women. New York: Women and Foundations Corporate Philanthropy.

Schiller, Bradley R.
1980 The Economics of Poverty and Discrimination, 3d ed. Englewood Cliffs, N.J.: Prentice-Hall.

Scott, W. Richard
1981 Organizations: Rational, Natural, and Open Systems. Englewood Cliffs, N.J.: Prentice-Hall.

Sexton, Patricia C.
1977 Women and Work. Washington, D.C.: U.S. Government Printing Office.

Shaeffer, Ruth Gilbert, and Edith F. Lynton
1979 Corporate Experiences in Improving Women's Job Opportunities. Report No. 755. New York: The Conference Board.

Simmons, Adele, Ann Freedman, Margaret Dunkle, and Francine Blau
1975 Exploitation From Nine to Five. Report of the Twentieth Century Fund Task Force on Women and Employment. Lexington, Mass.: Lexington Books.

Smith, Catherine Begnoche
1979 "Influence of internal opportunity structure and sex of worker on turnover patterns." Administrative Science Quarterly 24(September):362-81.

Smith, Howard L., and Mary Grenier
1982 "Sources of organizational power for women: overcoming structural obstacles." Sex Roles 8:733-46.

Steinberg, Ronnie, and Alice Cook
1981 "Women, unions, and equal employment opportunity." Working Paper 3, Center for Women in Government, State University of New York, Albany.

Stevenson, Mary H.
1977 "Internal labor markets and the employment of women in complex organizations." Center for Research on Women, Wellesley College, Wellesley, Mass.

Strober, Myra
1982 "The MBA: same passport to success for women and men?" Pp. 25-44 in Phyllis A. Wallace (ed.), Women in the Workplace. Boston, Mass.: Auburn.

Theodore, Athena
1971 The Professional Woman. Cambridge, Mass.: Schenkman.

Tilly, Louise A., and Joan W. Scott
1978 Women, Work, and Family. New York: Holt, Rinehart & Winston.

Tolbert, Charles M., Jr.
1982   "Industrial segmentation and men's career mo-
        bility." American Sociological Review
        47(August):457-77.

Tyack, David B., and Myra H. Strober
1981   "Jobs and gender: a history of the structuring
        of educational employment by sex." Pp. 131-
        52 in Patricia Schmuck and W. W. Charters
        (eds.), Educational Policy and Management:
        Sex Differentials. New York: Academic Press.

Ullman, Joseph C., and Kay K. Deaux
1981   "Recent efforts to increase female participation
        in apprenticeships in the basic steel industry
        in the midwest." Pp. 133-49 in Vernon M.
        Briggs, Jr., and Felician Foltman (eds.), Ap-
        prenticeship Research: Emerging Findings and
        Future Trends. Ithaca, N.Y.: New York State
        School of Industrial Relations.

U.S. Commission on Civil Rights
1981   Child Care and Equal Opportunity for Women.
        Washington, D.C.: U.S. Commission on Civil
        Rights.

U.S. Department of Commerce, Office of the Secretary
1978   The Bottom Line: Unequal Enterprise in
        America. Report of the President's Inter-
        agency Task Force on Women Business Own-
        ers. Washington, D.C.: U.S. Department of
        Commerce.

U.S. Department of Labor, Employment Standards
Administration
1981   Participation of Females in Construction Trades.
        Washington, D.C.: U.S. Department of La-
        bor, Employment Standards Administration.

U.S. General Accounting Office
1976   Job Opportunities for Women in the Military:
        Progress and Problems. Washington, D.C.: U.S.
        General Accounting Office.

Waite, Linda J., and Paula M. Hudis
1981   "The development and maintenance of a seg-
        regated labor force: review, synthesis, critique
        of recent research." Prepared for the National
        Commission for Employment Policy, Wash-
        ington, D.C.

Walshok, Mary L.
1981a   Blue-Collar Women: Pioneers on the Male
        Frontier. Garden City, N.Y.: Anchor.

1981b   "Some innovations in industrial apprenticeship
        at General Motors: locally developed compe-
        tency-based training as a tool for affirmative
        action." Pp. 174-82 in Vernon M. Briggs, Jr.,
        and Felician Foltman (eds.), Apprenticeship
        Research: Emerging Findings and Future
        Trends. Ithaca, N.Y.: New York State School
        of Industrial Relations.

Westley, Laurie A.
1982   A Territorial Issue: A Study of Women in the
        Construction Trades. Washington, D.C.: Wider
        Opportunities for Women.

White, Connie, Barbara Angle, and Marat Moore
1981   "Sexual harassment in the coal industry: a sur-
        vey of women miners." Unpublished paper,
        Coal Employment Project, Oak Ridge, Tenn.

Wolf, Wendy C.
1981   "The experience of women in federally spon-
        sored employment and training programs." Pp.
        87-130 in National Commission for Employ-
        ment Policy (ed.), Increasing the Earnings of
        Disadvantaged Women. Washington, D.C.:
        National Commission for Employment Policy.

Wright, Michael J.
1979   "Reproductive hazards and 'protective' dis-
        crimination." Feminist Studies 5 (Sum-
        mer):302-9.

14 Commentary: The Need to Study the Transformation of Job Structures

MARYELLEN R. KELLEY

Research undertaken within an institutional framework attempts to explain labor market outcomes for different race and sex groups (e.g., relative wages, unemployment rates, and occupational status) as a function of the efforts of trade unions, professional associations, and employers to control the employment relationship. The arrangements that shape the work situations of different groups have been described by John Dunlop (1958) as a "web of rules," both formal and informal, that *structure* employment opportunities and *allocate* workers to different segments of the labor market.[1]

In Chapter 13, Roos and Reskin have shown that the phenomenon of sex-segregated work can be analyzed, at least in part, as a function of this *regulating* of labor market operations. They discuss institutional arrangements that have been found to restrict women's entry into the higher-paying, more stable jobs typically held by men. In so doing, the authors have focused on only one set of practices that regulate labor market opera-

tions: those that pertain to the allocation of workers to different kinds of employment opportunities. Within that general category, their analysis is further limited to rules that act as artificial barriers to the movement of women out of the so-called female domain of work into male-typed jobs. While their efforts to identify all the exclusionary practices that have been uncovered by researchers in recent years in the areas of recruitment, hiring, initial job assignment, training, promotion, and intrafirm transfer are valuable, I think this is an insufficient view of the problem. The problem encompasses the whole literature, and therefore my remarks should be taken to be constructive and mainly directed toward *future* research—both conceptual and empirical.

First, I discuss some of the limitations of the studies to which Roos and Reskin refer. I then offer a brief criticism of the conceptual framework they themselves use in discussing the institutional arrangements that promote a sex-divided workplace.

It is difficult to draw any general conclusions about the relative importance of the many specific practices described by the authors in explaining patterns of sex segrega-

---

[1] For a recent presentation of segmented labor market theory, see Gordon et al. (1982).

tion in employment. This is because the research to which they refer is exploratory, its purpose being to *identify* different practices and to show how they act as barriers to the integration of women into male-typed jobs. For the most part, the research consists of case studies of particular establishments or small sample surveys of individuals from selected occupational groups. Some of the practices the authors describe are well-known and blatant examples of deliberate sex bias. But the more obvious barriers may not be the major impediment to the integration of women into male-typed jobs. There is a need for research that, in a systematic fashion, examines the incidence of certain practices within and across industries, occupational groups, and locales.

I recognize that it is extremely difficult to do such research. It requires the cooperation of managers and union officials, who may not want to have a researcher look too closely at the inequities in their practices. Even so, such research is needed to dispel whatever misconceptions we may have about the relative importance of one or another kind of arrangement. Making checklists of "source of bias" is not enough—certainly not if we ultimately care about formulating an effective policy and strategy for change that will result in the improvement of the economic position of large numbers of women.

One problem with lists is that they are static. Organizational rules and the institutional arrangements of labor markets change over time—including exclusionary practices. Thus, for example, arbitrary and sex-biased entry requirements to union-controlled apprenticeship programs in the building trades were once effective barriers to women's employment in the construction industry because the unions acted as "employment intermediaries between their members and contractors" through hiring-hall arrangements (Glover and Marshall, 1977:26). As a consequence of the increasing importance of the *nonunion* sector in the construction industry during the 1970s, the apprenticeship programs and hiring halls of the building trades are no longer effective methods for controlling entry to construction jobs, for either men or women (Mills, 1980).

Another problem with lists is that they tend to imply that at least some increase in equal treatment would be gained by the removal of any one of these barriers, holding the others constant. But in any sort of complex work situation, that is unlikely. Rules interact. Let me illustrate by criticizing an aspect of my own recent work (Kelley, 1982). In the case of complex seniority systems, the absence (or even removal) of rules that penalize mobility across sex-segregated job ladders may not signal (or lead to) a meaningful change or improvement in the opportunities for women to be promoted into male-typed jobs, if the rules governing the selection of eligible workers permit the employer to hire from the outside (rather than strictly promote from within) or if those higher-paid jobs simply are not expanding.

This leads me to my major concern with the conceptual framework within which Roos and Reskin have placed their discussion of how the regulation of labor market operations promotes sex segregation. They have focused on those arrangements that inhibit the integration of women into the male domain of work. Research on racial stratification tends to do the same thing: "White" jobs are the norm and the object of inquiry; the problem is seen as one of how to reduce the barriers to entry to those jobs for people who are not white. This association of an institutionalist analysis almost exclusively with rules that restrict competition within labor markets reflects an implicit theoretical assumption: that the regulation of labor market operations is primarily the result of efforts of formally organized groups of workers (in trade unions or professional associations) to protect (or "shelter") themselves from competition with each other, from different groups within the membership or from non-members. There are, however, two other areas of regulation that this perspective neglects. Both entail looking at the active, self-interested roles of personnel managers, industrial engineers, and strategic corporate planners in structuring the employment relationship. I have in mind rules that channel women into same-sex employment opportunities in the first place, together with those that govern the creation of new, explicitly "female" jobs.[2]

There are a number of examples of research examining how men are channelled into what are thought to be appropriate career paths, but little research has been done to investigate that question for women. Osterman's recent study (1980) of the early work experience of young men is the kind of research that needs to be done on young women. In that study, Osterman examines the function of certain small-sized establishments in the secondary labor market in providing training and experience for entry into large organizations with characteristically primary-sector jobs. Such linkages between young women's early work experiences (by type of employer) and their future career paths within the so-called traditional domain of female-typed work need to be investigated to discover if there exist typical "feeder" systems for regulating the flow of young women into labor market segments in which women predominate and to understand in what ways they are similar to or different from those that seem to apply to young men.

Roos and Reskin's focus on barriers gives short shrift to those practices that structure the employment opportunities facing women—e.g., job design, wage setting for individual jobs, and location decisions promulgated unilaterally by managers. Instead,

these structures are taken as given. Like so many writers concerned about the problem of sex-segregated work, these authors treat the problem of the sex-typing of jobs almost as if it were a fact of nature. That is, because the sexual division of labor in some form is evident in all societies, regardless of their social or economic structures, and because sex differences in treatment have a long history in this country, it is assumed that the separation of the sexes in the workplace today has been a constant for a long period of time and is ultimately exogenously determined by social and cultural forces outside the employment relationship. To Roos and Reskin, "traditional" sets of jobs are readily identifiable as invariantly male or female. These distinctions are so apparent and thought to be so enduring over time that the authors do not feel that they even need to tell us what they mean by the categorization "traditionally male" or "traditionally female."

Besides the implication that the competition between men and women is more important than the conflict between workers and the managers who administer employment systems, Roos and Reskin's depiction of rigidly sex-segregated spheres of work ignores the great _changes_ in technology and the occupational structure of the U.S. economy that have taken place over the past 80 years and the _shifts_ in the domains of women's work that have occurred at the same time.[3] Because affirmative action policy prescriptions motivate their analysis, the authors are concerned almost exclusively with the set of practices by which people are _processed_ through a given structure of jobs

---

[2] There is yet another approach, which Roos and Reskin ignore altogether: the radical feminist literature that focuses not so much on competition or other processes within markets for wage labor as on the relationship of such markets to nonmarket institutions, notably patriarchical relations in the household and the linkages between paid and unpaid work. For examples of each, see Hartmann (1979) and Power (1983).

[3] For an exposition of the relationship between technological change and the growth of employment opportunities for women in the twentieth century, see Baker (1964). For a less benign view on how the introduction of new work methods and machinery has affected the task structure of jobs and the demand for different kinds of workers, see Braverman (1974) and Edwards (1979). For a study that describes the changing sexual division of labor within new areas of work, see Kraft (1979).

and the reward systems to which they are attached. The importance of job design criteria, job evaluation practices, and the location of work in maintaining sex segregation is hardly considered. But in fact we have evidence that new jobs are often designed and valued explicitly in relation to the gender of the work force expected to be recruited to fill those positions. For example, according to one recent study on work organization and the location decisions of managers, branch offices were located in communities in which large numbers of married women could be expected to be in need of employment (because of high unemployment among male heads of households). Their labor market choices were also constrained by geographic immobility and child care responsibilities (Teegarden, 1983). Barbara Ehrenreich's most recent monograph (Fuentes and Ehrenreich, 1983) is one of a growing number of feminist studies of the ways in which electronics firms search the globe for locations where they will be able to continue to organize assembly work around the use of extremely low-paid young women.

By limiting the analysis to only those rules that act as barriers to or constraints on women's movement into and out of different types of work, the analyst can account only for differences in the ways in which women and men are processed through a *given* structure of jobs and system of rewards. To explain how jobs become sex-typed or indeed, even resegregated, after having been integrated, we need also to take into account how the structure of work changes, i.e., how managers bundle tasks into jobs and how those jobs are then linked to particular reward systems and opportunity structures.

REFERENCES

Baker, Elizabeth Faulkner
1964   *Technology and Women's Work*. New York: Columbia University Press.
Braverman, Harry
1974   *Labor and Monopoly Capital: The Degradation of Work in the Twentieth Century*. New York: Monthly Review Press.
Dunlop, John
1958   *Industrial Relations Systems*. New York: Holt.
Edwards, Richard
1979   *Contested Terrain: The Transformation of the Workplace in the Twentieth Century*. New York: Basic Books.
Fuentes, Annette, and Barbara Ehrenreich
1983   *Women in the Global Factory*. New York: Institute for New Communications.
Glover, Robert W., and Ray Marshall
1977   The response of unions in the construction industry to antidiscrimination efforts. In Leonard J. Hausman et al., eds., *Equal Rights and Industrial Relations*. Madison, Wis.: Industrial Relations Research Association.
Gordon, David M., Richard Edwards, and Michael Reich
1982   *Segmented Work, Divided Workers*. Cambridge, Eng.: Cambridge University Press.
Hartmann, Heidi I.
1979   Capitalism, patriarchy and job segregation by sex. In Zillah Eisenstein, ed., *Capitalist Patriarchy and the Case for Socialist Feminism*. New York: Monthly Review Press.
Kelley, Maryellen R.
1982   Discrimination in seniority systems: A case study. *Industrial and Labor Relations Review* 36(1):40-55.
Kraft, Philip
1979   The industrialization of computer programming: From programming to "software production." Pp. 1-17 in Andrew Zimbalist, ed., *Case Studies on the Labor Process*. New York: Monthly Review Press.
Mills, D. Quinn
1980   Construction. Pp. 49-78 in Gerald D. Somers, ed., *Collective Bargaining: Contemporary American Experience*. Madison, Wis.: Industrial Relations Research Association.
Osterman, Paul
1980   *Getting Started: The Youth Labor Market*. Cambridge, Mass.: MIT Press.
Power, Marilyn
1983   From home production to wage labor: Women as a reserve army of labor. *Review of Radical Political Economy* 15(1):71-91.
Teegarden, Suzanne
1983   Women's Labor and Changes in the Occupational Structure in the Office Industry: A Case Study of an Insurance Company. Unpublished master's thesis, Department of City and Regional Planning, University of California, Berkeley.

Part III
Reducing Segregation:
The Effectiveness
of Interventions

15 Job Integration Strategies: Today's Programs and Tomorrow's Needs

BRIGID O'FARRELL *and*
SHARON L. HARLAN

Scores of private employers, including large corporations such as AT&T, General Electric, and Ford, have experimented with programs to reduce sex segregation in their work forces.[1] Primarily in response to federal equal employment opportunity (EEO) enforcement activities and pressure from women desiring expanded opportunities, some of these firms have successfully increased the number of women in nontraditional jobs, i.e., jobs predominately held by men. By studying the experiences of these companies, we hope to learn what interventions have been successful and how they can be more effective in the future.

This corporate perspective on job integration is important because the extremely slow progress reflected in national statistics masks both progress and problems in the industries and firms where enforcement efforts have been targeted.[2] The experiences

---

[1] It is not possible to identify or even to enumerate all the American companies that have actively tried to facilitate job integration. Although there has been no systematic data collection, we estimate that the number is quite large based on the number of company experiences discussed in this paper and on other literature designed to help firms meet affirmative action requirements (e.g., Pfeiffer and Walshok, 1981; Farley, 1979; Hall and Albrecht, 1979; Stead, 1978; Larwood, 1977; Cunningham, 1976; Foxley, 1976; Purcell, 1976; Gordon and Strober, 1975; Iacobelli and Muczyk, 1975; Hollander, 1975; Jongeword and Scott, 1973). The activities of the Equal Employment Opportunity Commission also provide an index of corporate activity in this area. The Commission reported that it is monitoring 20 major affirmative action agreements (personal communication, 1982). In fiscal 1981 it settled 16,730 charges of employment discrimination and filed 368 lawsuits under Title VII of the 1964 Civil Rights Act as amended. These included charges based on race,

national origin, and religion as well as sex. In the same year EEOC reported receiving 47,454 new charges of discrimination under Title VII (including 2,462 filed concurrently under age discrimination or equal pay acts). Because there are multiple bases (e.g., race, sex) and issues (e.g., hiring, discharge), the Commission analyzed a total of 77,802 charges against private employers, 37,703 or 48 percent of which involved charges of sex discrimination (U.S. Equal Employment Opportunity Commission, 1982).

[2] In part this is due to the inadequacy of available data discussed in papers from this and other conferences (C. Brown, 1981; Wallace and LaMond, 1977). For example, the census data are not current enough, occupational codes and EEO-1 categories are too broad, the U.S. Department of Labor's Establishment Survey does not include sex (Bergmann, 1980; Barrett, 1978), and none of these studies controls for program interventions.

---

of these firms, reflected primarily through case studies and corporate surveys, are the focus of this paper. More specifically, the focus is on two important policy questions posed by the Committee on Women's Employment. First, what kinds of interventions are likely to succeed or fail in reducing sex segregation in the workplace? Second, under what conditions are the chances for success enhanced or impaired?

The first section of this paper discusses two important issues in research on corporate job integration policies: establishing an analytic framework to identify separate dimensions of change in corporate equal employment policy and assessing the quality of available data. The second and third sections address the committee's concern with successful intervention programs. We analyze case examples of strategies used by companies to recruit, hire, and train women for nontraditional entry-level jobs and identify the sources of problems encountered in promoting women. The fourth section addresses the committee's question about social and economic conditions that influence success. Several examples are given of how external business conditions, internal management structure, and union involvement affect the likelihood of reducing job segregation in a firm. In the final section we offer recommendations for what the federal government and private sector employers and unions can do to increase the effectiveness of programs for job integration.

RESEARCH ISSUES

Some research has been undertaken during the past 10 years to assess the impact and to evaluate the effectiveness of federal laws and corporate policies aimed at reducing occupational segregation. The joint evolution of federal and corporate policies over time has led to two important developments which bear directly on the analysis presented here: (1) an evaluation framework based on the experiences of companies that have made institutional changes to accomplish job integration and (2) a body of research consisting of case studies and corporate surveys that enhances the understanding and interpretation of national employment data and complements statistical analyses of company compliance with EEO laws.

The Evaluation Framework

Firms that have entered the postpioneer era of job integration are the subject of this paper. Postpioneer companies have agreed to initiate organizational changes that facilitate the entry of more than token numbers of women into nontraditional jobs and to take an active role in their recruitment, hiring, and training. In contrast, firms in the pioneer era have not undertaken such changes and may be trying to discourage women from following the lead of a few exceptional pioneers who have gained access to men's jobs through personal initiative.[3]

---

[3] *Pioneer* is a term commonly used to describe the first women in nontraditional jobs (e.g., Walshok, 1981), and several studies have documented the experiences of these women. Much less is known about the progress and problems of women who came after the pioneers. Epstein (1981) made a distinction between old and new women of the law but did not tie it to organizational changes within firms. Our review of the research, however, indicates that a pattern of transition from the pioneer to the postpioneer era of institutional change is typical of many firms. For example, in our own longitudinal study of a large manufacturing firm, the Harbor Company (Harlan and O'Farrell, 1982), we distinguished between these two fundamentally different phases. During the pioneer era, from the late 1960s to the late 1970s, a few women of extraordinary initiative recognized discriminatory practices and pressed their demands in light of the federal civil rights legislation. However, the hostility they faced from management and male coworkers and the isolation they experienced prevented most women from following their lead. The postpioneer era began in 1978 when the company and the federal government signed an affirmative action agreement. This second phase of job integration within the firm has been characterized by the hiring of a relatively large number of white women into entry-level jobs previously reserved for men and a reassessment of company training programs. Priscilla Douglas and Maryellen Kelley contributed to our early thinking about this pioneer/postpioneer distinction.

Postpioneer companies are not necessarily typical of most U.S. firms, but they are the ones from which we can learn about the effects of intervention strategies.

Research and program accounts of job integration processes suggest that the watershed in a firm's transition to the postpioneer era corresponds with some sort of federal pressure.[4] The evidence available does not enable us to quantify the amount of job integration resulting from enforcement activities, but it does indicate that the federal presence is a significant motivator of companies' efforts in this regard. In many instances it is because of direct federal intervention in sex discrimination complaints against large companies, e.g., the court-ordered consent decree of AT&T (Wallace, 1976; Northrup and Larson, 1979). Less well documented is the indirect effect on companies anticipating federal action, e.g., voluntary acceptance of the steel industry consent decree by the aluminum industry (Ichniowsky, 1983). In all of the studies we reviewed, awareness of the federal laws and regulations and their related financial costs were cited by managers and workers as important factors stimulating change.

The consent decrees resulting from court settlements of discrimination complaints and the federal affirmative action guidelines for employers (U.S. Equal Employment Opportunity Commission, 1974; 41 *Code of Federal Regulations* § 60-2, 1979) have taken a comprehensive approach to identifying issues and developing intervention strategies. Among the most important problems addressed are the establishment of mechanisms for integrating individuals into sex-atypical jobs (including the controversial procedures establishing goals and timetables), upgrading women's jobs, changing personnel systems and benefits for all employees, and the development of procedures for monitoring the terms of the agreement. They have also specified intervention at four critical points in the employment process for nonmanagement and management employees: recruitment, hiring, training, and promotion. These parameters of the postpioneer agreements establish our analytic framework.[5]

Quality of the Data

We have reviewed and compared many case examples of firms' experiences based on company self-reports in publicly available sources, original research on single firms or corporate employers done by social scientists, and surveys that compare a large number of employers primarily from the perspective of personnel directors. These data differ greatly in quality and degree of completeness.

The principal strengths of the data rest on their ability to show a unique perspective on the process of change, thus complementing and enriching the analysis of national data on occupational segregation. First, in contrast to the slow rate of change portrayed in the national data, our analysis shows more variation across and within companies, which permits a more accurate identification of both progress and problems. At AT&T, for example, while total employment increased by only 1,270 between 1973 and 1979, the number of women in the officials and managers category increased by 15,364,

---

[4] Companies could undertake program interventions voluntarily or as a result of pressure from other external sources. Thus, in theory we do not equate the postpioneer era with federal intervention, but in practice we have not identified any companies where the two did not coincide.

[5] For the purpose of this paper we accept the definition of equal employment opportunity that has been legislated by Congress and promulgated in the regulations of federal enforcement agencies, and we deal only with program interventions that fall within those parameters. We believe, however, that this definition should be expanded to specifically recognize womens' child-bearing role and the barriers to EEO created by current employment practices that do not recognize parental responsibilities (see U.S. Commission on Civil Rights, 1981).

or 5,000 more than the increase for men (Northrup and Larson, 1979).

Second, the perceptions of managers and workers about the effectiveness of federal equal employment policy in reducing job segregation within companies is often much more optimistic than analyses of economic impact based on national data. For example, managers report that goals and timetables are critical management tools for achieving greater job integration. Evaluation research in the construction trades (Kane and Miller, 1981) and the maritime industry (Marshall et al., 1978) show that they produce substantial change. The psychological importance of national EEO laws in encouraging women to press their demands for better jobs was evidenced in our research at the Harbor Company (O'Farrell, 1980a; Harlan and O'Farrell, 1982).

The principal weaknesses of the data lie in their selectivity and uneven quality, which derive from the fact that available data consist mainly of what companies choose to put in the public domain, limiting the objectivity, comprehensiveness, and comparability for both legal and competitive reasons. Several of the best reviews and case studies are illustrative of the data limitations. Shaeffer and Lynton's (1979) study of 265 companies and McLane's (1980) interviews in 42 companies are both based on personnel department surveys and interviews, and neither systematically compares company programs nor relates program initiatives to quantifiable measures of change. Each has a selection bias, since Shaeffer and Lynton surveyed only large corporations and McLane reviewed only data on managers.

Case studies such as those by Meyer and Lee (1978) on public utilities, Northrup and Larson (1979) on AT&T, Deaux and Ullman (1983) on steel companies, or Harlan and O'Farrell (1982) on Harbor Company are designed to cover only one company or several firms in the same industry. Thus, they do not offer a comparative view of program implementation or change. Since they are done in cooperation either with management or with a union, none offers a truly balanced assessment of problems and progress based on the views of managers and workers. Most of these studies also provide limited analysis of quantitative data, and, although all of the case study companies were targets of federal enforcement activity, most of the research does not systematically focus on the impact of federal regulations on organizational change. Studies by Northrup and Larson (1979) and Ichniowski (1983) suggest there is considerable data available from consent decrees in the public domain, but it is expensive to copy and often difficult to use. There has been little public or private interest in supporting more comprehensive analysis of the compliance data.

Finally, in addition to focusing mostly on large companies acting under government pressure, we are reporting almost exclusively on the experiences of white women. There is very little information about minority women, but available research, primarily in the nonmanagement sector, suggests that they are moving to factory and clerical jobs traditionally held by white women (Reubens and Reubens, 1979; Douglas, 1981; Malveaux, 1982). Thus, the negative effects of race and sex are compounded for both hiring and promotion of minority women.

STRATEGIES: MOVING WOMEN INTO ENTRY-LEVEL JOBS

Most of the successful intervention programs dealt with changes in company recruitment, hiring, and training programs for entry-level jobs. The framework for these programs was established as an employer obligation in affirmative action programs and supported to some extent by federal programs such as the Comprehensive Employment and Training Act (CETA). Gradually employers have begun to reach the increasing number of qualified or qualifiable women interested in and available to try nontraditional positions in both blue-collar (O'Farrell and Harlan, 1982; O'Farrell, 1982; Kane and Miller, 1981; Walshok, 1981; Schreiber, 1979) and white-collar occupations (McLane, 1980; Shaeffer and Lynton, 1979).[6]

There are still many women who do not seek nontraditional jobs (Hoffman and Reid, 1981; Barrett, 1980) and many institutional barriers remain (Roos and Reskin, this volume), but stereotypes about women's work behavior and motivation are gradually being discredited (Crowley et al., 1973; Kanter, 1977; Feldberg and Glenn, 1979; Heidrick and Struggles, Inc., 1979; O'Farrell and Harlan, 1982). EEO policies that increase women's job choices are being incorporated into personnel procedures, and there is a growing acceptance of these policies by corporate managers. In two recent surveys of managers the majority reported that equal employment was a major concern (Heidrick and Struggles, Inc., 1977) and that corporate executives support the guidelines of the U.S. Equal Employment Opportunity Commission for affirmative action (Barnhill-Hayes, 1979). In the Barnhill-Hayes survey the majority of executive respondents said that affirmative action had not resulted in a decline in employee productivity. The importance of EEO to business practice is further evidenced at the Harvard Business School, where over 80 of the cases in the Case Clearing House now address equal employment and affirmative action issues.

When turned into action, management concern and support have concentrated on integrating entry-level blue-collar and management jobs by expanding recruitment re-

sources, reevaluating job requirements in relation to job content, and developing or supplementing training programs. Programs have been developed to overcome sex differences in early socialization, education, and training and thus reduce sex segregation in initial job assignments.

Recruitment: External and Internal Outreach

An issue faced by many firms is how to expand traditional recruiting sources and methods to reach women. A successful strategy appears to combine very active recruiting with greatly expanded external and internal recruitment sources (Shuchat et al., 1981; Shaeffer and Lynton, 1979). In screening and selecting women for new jobs, employers must also provide sufficient information to enable women to make informed choices and must elicit sufficient information from the women to determine if they can perform the necessary tasks. Increased selectivity based on job-relevant criteria may result in fewer new hires but more long-term success (Meyer and Lee, 1978; McLane, 1980).

To expand external recruiting sources for blue-collar jobs, companies must go beyond high school shop classes, trade schools, and the military services, which traditionally supply young men. Skilled-trades training programs, funded primarily through federal government programs, such as the Comprehensive Education and Training Act (CETA) outreach and training program for women in apprenticeship, have been an important resource for company recruiters (Kane and Miller, 1981; Ullman and Deaux, 1981). One Midwestern steel company responded to the 1974 industry consent decree by establishing a training school for motor inspectors that could provide a source of craft-trained women and minorities. In each class half the students were plant employees and half were CETA referrals. Approximately two-thirds of the 106 female motor

---

[6] We have not fully reviewed the literature on supply, but the future supply of women for technical and managerial positions is encouraging given the steady increases in the number of women in engineering, chemistry, and business programs (Vetter et al., 1982; Strober, 1982). For example, the General Motors Institute (engineering) enrolled no women until 1965, and now 28 percent of the student body is female (McLane, 1980).

inspectors and millwrights were recruited from outside the firm through CETA, but no female applicants were recruited from trade schools (Ullman and Deaux, 1981).

Companies that have done successful recruiting recommend reaching out specifically to rural women and physical education majors because of a general interest in and experience with physically demanding work and to women in blue-collar community organizations because of their general familiarity with blue-collar jobs (Shaeffer and Lynton, 1979). There is also growing evidence that women interested in nontraditional blue-collar jobs are more likely to be in their late twenties and thirties rather than recent high school graduates (O'Farrell, 1982; Kane and Miller, 1981; U.S. Dept. of Labor, 1978). This suggests reaching out to currently employed women or to older women now reentering the work force.

For entry-level management positions, expanded external recruitment may involve going to more colleges in different geographic regions or initiating recruitment programs at women's colleges (Shaeffer and Lynton, 1979). Nontraditional methods for recruiting higher-level managers include searching in the public sector and on the East and West coasts (especially New York). Retaining a consultant or search firm that specializes in recruiting women or specifying that the recruiter be a woman are also effective (McLane, 1980). An example of a model long-term recruiting system for technical fields involving universities and companies is the Program for Increasing Minority Engineering Graduates (PIMEG) described by Hayes (1980).

Women already employed by a company in traditional female clerical and factory jobs are an important source of candidates for nontraditional jobs in the skilled trades and management. Internal intervention programs for white- and blue-collar jobs require opening access systems to women, which may include establishing job posting procedures or changing seniority systems (Roos and Reskin, this volume; Steinberg and Cook,

1981; Shaeffer and Lynton, 1979).[7] For example, many unionized firms traditionally have departmental seniority systems under which years of service in a department entitle workers to promotion opportunities during prosperous times and to protection from layoffs during slow periods. Workers cannot, however, move between departments without losing seniority, possibly some pay, and other benefits related to seniority. If women have to give up seniority, they are less likely to move when jobs in traditionally male departments are opened to them regardless of other incentives such as higher pay or bonuses. When a large company in the Northeast initiated a transfer program based on company rather than departmental seniority, women were able for the first time to bid on craft jobs without loss of seniority. Three years later, 101 women, almost all the women in one of the craft jobs, had transferred from other departments in the company, bringing from 1 to over 20 years of company service (O'Farrell and Harlan, 1982).

Changes in formal seniority provisions appear to be an important first step in opening nontraditional jobs to women currently employed in firms. Additional incentives may be needed, however, to encourage women (or minorities or white men) to transfer from one department to another (Ichniowski, 1983; Kelley, 1982; Shaeffer and Lynton, 1979). In the steel industry's consent decree, for example, rate retention (or "red circling") was used as an incentive (available to all workers) for transferring from one department to another under the new plant seniority system. If the rate of pay for those transferring to an entry-level job in a new department was lower than their current rate of pay, they could keep their current rate of pay in the new department for a 2-year

---

[7] Seniority and EEO laws have been the subject of a series of court cases and consent decrees during the last 15 years. For a review of the issues, see Ichniowski (1983), Kelley (1982), and Wallace and Driscoll (1981).

period. In other words, a woman would not have to take a cut in pay to enter a department with much better long-term opportunities previously reserved for men. The agreement also included a 45-day trial period during which transfers could return to their former jobs without any penalties (Ichniowski, 1983).[8]

The *Teamsters* decision of 1977 greatly reduced the legal pressure on companies and unions to change seniority systems. Under the Supreme Court's ruling, seniority systems are considered bona fide or legal if there was no intent to discriminate even though the system may perpetuate the effects of previous discrimination (Kelley, 1982; Wallace and Driscoll, 1981). Changes in seniority systems, however, remain an important intervention strategy to reduce occupational segregation by race or sex.

Opening career opportunities in management to current office workers may involve less formal procedures than changing seniority systems established through collective bargaining agreements, but it is nonetheless reported to "take a lot of effort and a close critical look at the company's inner workings." The personnel director of a major bank outlined the following internal mechanisms in use at the bank to facilitate the upgrading of office workers: a computerized skills data bank; identification of employees with satisfactory records remaining in grade beyond the average time spans; companywide internal searches; job posting of exempt positions; a system for employee transfer and promotion requests; a hotline for employees who believe they are in dead-end jobs or are being held back; a liberal, well-publicized tuition-refund program; analysis of job families to create new career paths; individual career counseling on request; and group career counseling (Shaeffer and Lynton, 1979:52-53).

Both external and internal recruitment require aggressive methods. This may involve using newspapers, school and community groups, company bulletins, meetings, job fairs, etc. (Shuchat et al., 1981) as well as providing more information about job content. Many women are unfamiliar with nontraditional work. Some companies have reported the need for clear job descriptions that include information on training and promotion opportunities, hours, pay, and pressures. Companies have found it effective to involve women already doing the work in interviews or presentations. It was often important, particularly for internal recruits, to have trial periods during which women can go back to their previous jobs without loss if the nontraditional job was not acceptable. Tours of the work environment, some hands-on experience, and use of media presentations seemed particularly useful for blue-collar jobs (Kane and Miller, 1981; Walshok, 1981; McLane, 1980; Shaeffer and Lynton, 1979).

More careful recruitment and screening may also reduce employee turnover, furthering the long-term goal of job integration. Meyer and Lee (1978) found that women were much less carefully screened for blue-collar jobs than for white-collar jobs and that the turnover rates for blue-collar jobs were higher. McLane (1980) reported similar examples comparing entry-level and higher-level management. Companies reported conducting much more extensive screening for higher-level jobs and better retention rates than for entry-level management jobs.

---

[8] Seniority systems are often complex and extensive changes may yield only limited results. For example, AT&T adopted company but not systemwide seniority that did not address the regional difference in opportunities for blue-collar workers generally recognized in the management job structure. In the steel industry, plant seniority represented an expansion of opportunities that the union had tried and been unable to achieve through collective bargaining. Women in the clerical and service jobs were still excluded, however, leaving them with limited opportunities (Kleiman and Frankel, 1975). Company seniority was in place at Harbor Company but was limited to specific geographic locations that were not changed by the affirmative action agreement. This left sex-segregated plants with different advancement opportunities intact (Harlan and O'Farrell, 1982).

Companies surveyed by Shaeffer and Lynton (1979) also reported that job analysis is crucial to increasing the number of women in nontraditional jobs of all kinds. Job analysis means reevaluating the current qualifications required for a job in light of the actual job content. Establishing the actual skills and personal experiences necessary for adequate job performance can expand the range of jobs for women by identifying common domains of skills across seemingly unrelated jobs and by recognizing past related experiences. For example, a restaurant chain recruiting recent college graduates for first-line supervisory positions was unsuccessful because many of the women were unable to meet the demands of the work and were too inexperienced to manage a work crew. Subsequent management discussions led line managers to revise the job qualifications by replacing the college degree requirement with knowledge of the food industry (e.g., restaurant work), retail experience (with customer contact), or other experiences related to supervisory ability (e.g., teaching or home economics) (Shaeffer and Lynton, 1979).

Training: Skills and Information

Training is an established part of affirmative action programs. Two innovative examples are the multimillion-dollar training fund for women employees established by Bank America in lieu of back pay awards and the 1978 General Electric Agreement that provided more than $500,000 to train managers to implement the affirmative action agreement. Among conventional training programs, the evidence suggests that special skills training for women in blue-collar jobs and substantive information training for all employees, especially managers, on EEO laws and related company policies are most important in integrating women into nontraditional jobs. At the management level, women do not need special training programs but instead need access to existing training for men. There is considerable disagreement about the effectiveness of related programs to develop awareness, mentors, and networks.

The basic competence of women to do nontraditional jobs affects their initial acceptance and the ultimate pace of integration. Introducing unqualified women into nontraditional jobs reinforces male workers' stereotypes about women and strengthens resistance to their integration (McLane, 1980; Meyer and Lee, 1978; O'Farrell, 1977). Because of sex differences in educational background and experience, women entering blue-collar jobs need additional training in such areas as tool familiarization and basic electronics. In general, they have not learned basic craft skills in high school shop courses, trade schools, the military service, or just from "tinkering around cars with their fathers." Companies surveyed by Shaeffer and Lynton (1979) found that their ability to provide training was critical to opening these jobs. Preplacement training and supplementary courses available during on-the-job training or between formal training sessions have been tried successfully. In the Meyer and Lee study, training directors frequently reported that (formal) training programs for craft jobs assumed that all of the trainees had mechanical interests and experience. Therefore, terminology such as *open-end wrench, hexnut,* or *right-hand thread* was used without considering that many women were unfamiliar with such terms and were likely to be at a decided disadvantage. To overcome these difficulties, some companies designed special vestibule training for women. These special programs were said to have two advantages: helping to acquaint women with unfamiliar tasks in a more protective climate and helping women perform better on the job, thus increasing their acceptance by male coworkers and access to on-the-job training (Meyer and Lee, 1978:18).

Instructors may reassess and adjust their on-going training courses to incorporate teaching more basic concepts and skills, or they may develop formal courses to teach what had previously been taught informally by senior craftsmen or foremen (O'Farrell, 1977; Ullman and Deaux, 1981). Equipment modifications may also be necessary for blue-collar women (Meyer and Lee, 1978; Northrup and Larson, 1979). For example, the Bell System's equipment for pole climbers (gloves, shoes, climbing apparatus) was all specifically designed for men. Early failure to modify the equipment contributed to higher accident rates for women. Shuchat et al. (1981) found that many men also benefit from these sorts of changes.

Comparing the experience of nontraditional female employees in 10 utility companies, Meyer and Lee (1978) found that women in blue-collar jobs needed job-specific training but that women in white-collar jobs did not. Special training is generally not considered necessary for women in management positions and is perceived by some as detrimental, either by providing women with services not available to men or by exaggerating any sex differences (Shaeffer and Lynton, 1979; McLane, 1980). It is necessary, however, to identify the critical, formal and informal sources of male training and to make sure that women are integrated. Formal classroom training for executives, specific patterns of job rotation, and assignment to particular jobs or supervisors are examples of such training. (Barriers to managerial training are discussed more fully in the next section.)

Providing information about EEO issues is another important area. In a 1973 study, Lyle commented on the appalling lack of information available to line managers about EEO matters, and there is increasing awareness that laws and company policies are not automatically known or understood throughout an organization. Manager preparation was frequently mentioned in the Shaeffer and Lynton (1979) study as an activity critical to successful implementation of EEO policies. The purpose of the preparation is to explain the organization's overall EEO obligations and the basic responsibility of line managers. It is essential that the information go to all employees at every level and in every location. For example, Continental Illinois Bank used a series of brief film clips highlighting a variety of work-related problems to remind people of potentially discriminatory actions. Managers were cautioned, for example, not to assume that a woman being considered for a promotion would not be free to travel (McLane, 1980).

Companies suggested holding meetings and issuing publications to keep the staff up-to-date on changes in the law and their organizational implications. They reported that internal communications are improved if provisions are made for opponents of EEO to voice their concerns (McLane, 1980). The development of information programs was also recommended for union officials, especially shop stewards, but there are few models to follow (O'Farrell, 1980b; Shaeffer and Lynton, 1979).

Training resources have also been allocated to programs that focus on changing attitudes and interpersonal relationships often involving the development of mentors and networks. Both the corporate and the research communities are divided on the usefulness of such programs in general and on the effectiveness of company-sponsored programs in particular (L. Brown, 1981; McLane, 1980; Shaeffer and Lynton, 1979). Even to some who accept the idea that mentors and networks are important elements in achieving success, company-sponsored networks seemed to be artificial constructions that may not produce the essential conditions—trust, shared beliefs, commonality of interests—that foster the growth of these personal relationships (McLane, 1980). Such programs may benefit women in some companies, but they do not appear to be a high priority among intervention strategies.

PROBLEMS: PROMOTING WOMEN TO HIGHLY SKILLED AND EXECUTIVE-LEVEL POSITIONS

In companies where women have been hired for entry-level management and blue-collar positions, there are no guarantees that they will progress to the higher-paying, more skilled positions. In fact, it appears that when solutions to recruitment, hiring, and training problems begin to work (i.e., there are more women in the organization), more complex problems arise. Promotion, defined as individual mobility through lines of progression in internal (firm) labor markets, is emerging as a critical issue in the 1980s for firms in the postpioneer era.

Doeringer and Piore (1971) identified limited job progression lines, administrative regulations for job upgrading systems, and lack of training as mechanisms that perpetuate discrimination within firms. Based on several recent studies, Roos and Reskin (this volume) have described specific examples of how these institutional barriers block traditionally male promotion paths and prevent women from advancing in organizations. Although affirmative action agreements (especially consent decrees) have tried to anticipate some difficulties by imposing changes on internal mobility structures, the evidence suggests that these alterations have been too few and too limited to provide long-term relief from job segregation.

Looking to the future, we believe that the promotion problems of both women and men will be compounded by the growing number of women in entry-level nontraditional jobs, the low advancement opportunities in some job progression lines, the limited number of higher-level jobs, and low turnover. Successful job integration efforts ultimately mean finding solutions to two related questions: How can the newly integrated entry-level positions be kept from resegregating and becoming new female "ghettos"? How can opportunities for women and men be expanded to facilitate advancement into the highest-paying, prestigious positions?

Variations in Opportunity Structures

Most research on occupational segregation emphasizes that traditionally female jobs have very limited opportunities for advancement, but the nontraditional job ladders women are entering also vary in the degree of opportunity they offer. In fact, the advancement potential of women in low-opportunity nontraditional jobs may be no greater than their counterparts' in traditionally female jobs. Several studies have found limited opportunities in management and professional categories, for example, in legal or personnel departments (Strober, 1982; Harlan and Weiss, 1981, 1982; Epstein, 1981; Rosenbaum, 1979; Swanson and Milward, 1979; Kanter, 1977, 1979) and in the blue-collar categories of laborer or maintenance work (Deaux, in press; Schreiber, 1979; Harlan and O'Farrell, 1982). Reubens and Reubens (1979) and Briggs (1981) have suggested that newly hired women are becoming the majority in some of these traditionally male jobs.

Studies by Kelley (1982) and Harlan and O'Farrell (1982) illustrate the diversity among nontraditional job ladders. Nontraditional jobs, like traditional women's jobs, vary in entry-level wage (floor), top wage (ceiling), number of jobs within job progression ladders (range), and number of people (density)—thus providing very different promotion opportunities (Kelley, 1982).

The Harbor Company (O'Farrell, 1980a; Harlan and O'Farrell, 1982) provides a detailed example of women disproportionately entering traditionally male jobs with limited opportunities and the potential for resegregation. During a period of rapid hiring (40 percent of the work force had been hired in the previous 5 years), women's opportunities were improved in the short run. By 1980, 9 percent of the blue-collar work force was female, and 66 percent of these women had been hired since the EEO agreement with the government was signed in 1978. However, no precautions were taken to recruit and train women at different levels in the organization.

Relative to newly hired men, newly hired women of both races were disproportionately represented in jobs at the bottom of the job hierarchy. Hierarchies at the Harbor Company were organized into 8 predominately male job families that connect hundreds of blue-collar classifications based on similarities in work tasks and increasing skill levels. Women's chances for moving up were lower than men's because they had been disproportionately hired into the job families with the lowest ceiling rates and the fewest number of highly skilled jobs. Newly hired men were also placed in jobs above them in the hierarchy, effectively closing off those potential opportunities as well. Advancement opportunities were further limited for women by a recession, during which hiring stopped and layoffs were threatened. The result may be a bottleneck where women newly hired in nontraditional jobs find themselves stuck in jobs that increasingly become traditional for women.

An important question that bears on future promotion opportunities is how women's first nontraditional job assignment is determined by the company. Research at the Harbor Company suggests that there are differences in the education, training, and previous experience of female and male applicants that may partially account for the assignment of most women to low-opportunity job ladders. For example, men were more likely than women to have trade school experience that qualified them for entry-level positions in the skilled trades. On the other hand, many of the women interviewees believed that the company selectively placed women and minorities in the least-skilled jobs regardless of qualifications, and they gave specific and convincing examples of how this was done. The Harbor Company's personnel department evidently used unsystematic screening procedures with little analysis of job ladders.

In searching for ways to increase women's access to job ladders with greater opportunities for advancement, we should not overlook highly skilled clerical jobs that have traditionally been closed to women. In their

comparison of the 1960 and 1970 census data, Reubens and Reubens (1979) found that women had made the greatest breakthrough in male-intensive occupations in the clerical field: insurance adjuster, postal clerk, dispatcher, production controller, ticket agent. The skills required for these jobs are related to those used in traditional female jobs, such as filing, report writing, and customer contact. In addition, qualifications for the two sets of jobs are not distinguished by education, training, or physical characteristics. Despite these similarities, the women pioneers at the Harbor Company (O'Farrell, 1980a) found that it was just as difficult to enter the higher-skilled clerical jobs as it was to enter the traditionally male factory jobs. After the first women succeeded, however, others in the lowest-level clerical jobs (and some in factory jobs) aspired to the relatively small number of traditionally male clerical jobs such as production clerk. In fact, by 1980 that job was almost half female. Without any intervention on the part of the company (and none was in evidence), it appeared that these clerical jobs, similar to the entry-level factory jobs, were likely to become predominately female.[9]

Assessing Qualifications and Potential for Promotion

A second set of issues concerns the criteria and methods used to select individuals for promotion and layoff and how these are

---

[9] The future of wage rates in both the entry-level factory and high-level clerical jobs at Harbor Company is provisional. In both cases the wages are relatively high and better than what was available to women before. It seems unlikely that there would be any attempt to lower the wages in these job categories. However, whether these jobs keep pace with the overall wage increases in the skilled, predominately male jobs must be carefully monitored. Preston (1978) found that in New England the wages of teachers did not go down when women entered the field in large numbers; they just did not continue to increase at the pace of men's jobs.

applied to women. To ensure upward mobility for women, companies and unions must examine the ramifications of collective bargaining agreements for job advancement, reassess their current management qualifying procedures, and expand opportunities for all workers.

Individual qualifications and seniority are two standard criteria used by managers in selecting candidates for promotion opportunities. Although the ways in which these criteria are applied may vary greatly from company to company and across levels of the occupational hierarchy, the basic principles are deeply ingrained in industrial relations and are often formalized in collective bargaining agreements. It is not surprising, then, that one of the most controversial provisions of the AT&T consent decree concerned changes in the use of qualifications and seniority to determine job advancement. Under AT&T's agreement, certain circumstances permitted a less-senior but basically qualified member of a protected group to be promoted over more-senior, more-qualified white men in order to meet affirmative action goals. Although disaggregated statistics by sex and race are not available, AT&T reports that the override provision was used a total of 35,479 times for blue-collar workers during the 6 years of the consent decree. There are no statistics covering instances where management personnel were passed over by less-senior, less-qualified employees, but personnel executives interviewed by Northrup and Larson (1979) testified that it happened regularly. After the first year of the consent decree, AT&T achieved between 90 and 99 percent of its targets for hiring and promoting women and minorities, and the override provision appears to have contributed to that success. Loomis (1979) and Northrup and Larson (1979) feel that the AT&T data actually underrepresent the impact of the override. They estimate that it was used in close to 25 percent of all promotions during the 6-year period.

Seniority systems may reinforce the limited opportunities and bottlenecks described previously. Changes in seniority systems (discussed in the recruitment section) that facilitate the advancement of women from traditional to entry-level nontraditional jobs also facilitate advancement within the nontraditional job categories.

Another issue of particular concern to aspiring women managers is access to company programs that develop and measure personal qualifications for upper management.[10] A survey of 2,000 members of the American Management Association (AMA) found that 70 percent of the employers used formal programs to assess managerial potential in their employees (McLane, 1980; Burrows, 1978). Yet many companies apparently denied women access to these programs. Fifty-eight percent of the AMA respondents considered only a limited number of women qualified for development, 12 percent did not admit any women, and only 9 percent specifically recruited women for developmental activities.

Managers alleged that women's lack of education, experience, motivation, and career commitment were the principal reasons why they did not recruit women. AT&T's experience with its extensive management assessment center, however, contradicts these stereotypes about women workers. Once women were allowed to participate in the Center, they performed equally with men, and assessment results correlated with later management progress for men and women (Moses and Boehm, 1975).

Access to existing programs is one barrier for women, but absence of development

---

[10] Extensive procedures have been developed for test validation. Companies must establish that any tests they use are both job related and free of racial, ethnic, or sex bias (*Guidelines on Employee Selection Procedures*, 29 CFR §1607, 1970; U.S. Equal Employment Opportunity Commission, 1974). For a discussion of testing at AT&T, see the chapters by Ash and by Lopez in Wallace (1976).

programs in many companies is a serious concern for other women as well as men. Harlan and Weiss's (1981) study of managers in retail companies that had no formal programs for developing managerial potential found that the majority of women and men had unfocused career plans and did not initiate training or development activities. A battery of psychological tests showed few significant sex differences in level of motivation or aspirations. The authors concluded that both women and men need more career development activities, including assessing and measuring skills and competencies, career planning, and supervisory training. The need for better career development for men and women has been further documented by Kanter (1977, 1980) and Fernandez (1981).

Given the resistance of management and unions to changing general qualification and seniority rules and the courts' support of bona fide seniority systems, it is unlikely that firms will adopt interventions like the AT&T override or change seniority systems without strong government pressure and continued litigation. The issue of modifying existing systems to accommodate women and minorities, however, raises important questions about how promotion systems worked for white men in the past. For example, Medoff and Abraham (1980, 1981) have questioned the assumption that the more productive workers are rewarded. They found that earnings were positively related to experience but not to rated job performance for white male managers in two major companies. The definition and use of qualifications should be carefully examined within each firm to discover how the system might be improved for all employees.

CONDITIONS: MANAGING INTERVENTION STRATEGIES

The momentum for job integration will be sustained by the pressure of large numbers of women with heightened expectations continuing to enter the labor force in the 1980s and 1990s. The pace of change and the level of effort required to implement it, however, will vary with selected business conditions and the internal management practices of postpioneer-era firms. This section examines recent evidence that suggests how these two sets of factors operate singly and in combination to affect the degree of sex segregation in the workplace. First, it is widely recognized that national and industry-specific economic conditions are related to the rate of job integration. Norton (1981) has argued persuasively that future affirmative action efforts will be more effective if employers coordinate their planning with trends in labor force composition, regional changes in economic opportunities, and technological innovation. Second, program interventions implemented under corporate affirmative action plans, such as those discussed above, are major organizational changes that require sound management to be effective.

Business Conditions

Two studies that compared national data on industries and occupations have shown that rates of job integration are positively associated with growth in total industry employment and female participation in the work force. Shaeffer and Lynton's (1979) study of large corporations indicated that the increase in women's employment was greater for each nontraditional occupational category in the industries that experienced greater increases in total employment between 1970 and 1975. Similarly, Reubens and Reubens' (1979) analysis of census data for occupational categories in 1960 and 1970 showed that women made greater gains in nontraditional occupations where men were also increasing in number. They concluded that "the fortunes of men and women ride in tandem, and for both sexes the white-collar and higher paid occupations have shown the greatest expansion" (p. 123). Shaeffer and Lynton also found that the increase in women's nontraditional employment was proportionately greater in relatively female-intensive industries. They proposed several plausible and interrelated explanations, including a higher average employment growth rate in female-intensive industries between 1970 and 1975, a larger pool of women available in those industries, managements' experience working with women in a wider variety of jobs, the less technical nature of the jobs, and women's familiarity with industry working conditions.

It is not always the case, however, that employment growth and a female-intensive work force will reduce negative stereotypes of women in an industry. For example, in a study of female and male managers in two retail firms, Harlan and Weiss (1981) found that the level of perceived sex bias was higher in the firm with a faster growth rate and a larger increase in the proportion of women managers between 1974 and 1979. This period of high growth, a 46 percent increase in women managers, was followed by a sharp business decline and a period of economic instability that increased the anxiety of male managers about promotion opportunities. Although progress in increasing the number of women managers was slower in the second firm, a 20 percent increase in women managers, it was based on moderate growth followed by a period of business stability. Harlan and Weiss concluded that the higher level of sex bias in the first company could have been caused by uncertainty in the economic environment and that it could ultimately result in poorer future job opportunities for women managers despite their rapid short-term progress.

Economic recession, especially in male-intensive industries such as steel, has the anticipated negative effect. It quickly halts or eliminates recent progress in hiring and promoting women. Deaux and Ullman (1983) report that fewer women were employed in the steel industry in 1983 than before the 1974 consent decree. This was due to seniority-based layoffs and the closing of entire plants where all workers lost their jobs. The conflict between seniority-based layoffs and affirmative action efforts should eventually be resolved by the Supreme Court. Unions, in the meantime, have made several alternative proposals for changing seniority rules that would lessen the disproportionate economic impact of layoffs on recently hired women and minority workers, but few have been implemented.[11]

Economic growth in the Sunbelt and loss of job opportunities in the Northeast have important implications for future strategies to reduce job segregation (Norton, 1981). Northrup and Larson's (1979) analysis of the results of the AT&T consent decree showed that the southwestern and western regions of the company accounted for 38 to 50 percent of the new openings in each of five major nontraditional occupational categories between 1973 and 1979. These two regions alone accounted for more than half the new female entrants to a nontraditional job that had been particularly difficult to integrate, and they reported more successful recruitment of Hispanic workers and managers than any other region. The shift in AT&T employment to the Sunbelt is expected to be even greater in the future. Thus, despite the bleak employment picture in many parts of the country, geographical var-

---

[11] The United Auto Workers Union has proposed extending indefinitely the time that minorities and women are laid off (and thus eligible for recall as well as benefits such as insurance and vested vacation pay) rather than limiting it to the equivalent time they were actually employed. When discrimination in hiring has occurred, the UAW recommends front pay, that is full wages and benefits for minorities and women while laid off. Incentives for voluntary early retirement are another possible program. An alternative approach is the recent California unemployment insurance law, which allows workers to reduce their work week to three or four days and collect unemployment benefits for the remaining workdays (*UAW Administrative Letter*, 1975, 1976; Steinberg and Cook, 1981). These and other alternatives are in need of further research and discussion, which should be given high priority by unions, employers, and the government.

iations offer some promise for increased integration on a regional basis.

Rapid technological changes have very important long-term implications for job integration, particularly in telecommunications and other industries where automation is reducing the total number of jobs while creating new jobs requiring new skills. New female "ghettos" are developing as a result of women moving into declining occupations traditionally held by men (Hacker, 1979; Reubens and Reubens, 1979). Reubens and Reubens found that, although women made greater gains in jobs that were also expanding for men, the increase of women in 27 of 53 nontraditional occupations between 1960 and 1970 was due to slow growth or decline in the number of men in those jobs. An occupational shift of this type often reflects the displacement of skilled men by semi-skilled or unskilled women due to technological innovations.

Data presented by Hacker (1979) and Northrup and Larson (1979) suggest that the simultaneous occurrence of technological changes and affirmative action efforts at AT&T will gradually lead to some traditionally male jobs becoming newly segregated into a smaller number of less-skilled jobs for women. Hacker (p. 550) described the movement of women into traditionally male craft jobs that were becoming obsolete even as the affirmative action agreement was being implemented:

As women learned to climb poles, AT&T was shifting to microwave and laser (Fiber Optic) transmission systems. As women learned to install telephones, "clip and take" customer installation and phone stores were markedly reducing the need for installers. Framework is a semi-skilled job where women have made the greatest inroads. Framework is slated for total automation. . . . [E]lectric switching systems can virtually eliminate most switchwork and all framework. Framework went from 20 percent female in 1972 to 32 percent in 1973.

It remains to be seen whether the new technological jobs developing in high-tech industries will be integrated. The AT&T example supports the need for further inquiry into the consequences of technological change for female employment in particular industries. More broadly, it stresses the urgency for managers to treat technological innovations and affirmative action efforts as planned interventions in the firm that must be more closely coordinated if job resegregation is to be avoided.

Management Practice

During the 1970s EEO-related issues gradually moved from the domain of minor personnel officials to the level of corporate policy set by top management and carried out by line managers. Corporate managers and government officials rate an effective internal administrative structure for setting policy and carrying out programs as extremely important to success in integrating jobs (U.S. Equal Employment Opportunity Commission, 1974; Stead, 1978; Gordon and Strober, 1975; Meyer and Lee, 1978; Shaeffer and Lynton, 1979; McLane, 1980). Five components of this structure include top-level commitment, line responsibility, centralized accounting and control, resource allocation, and union involvement.

Despite the rapidly changing image of corporate presidents from rugged entrepreneurs to committee members, job integration appears to be an area where the individual chief executive officer (CEO) can and does make a difference. Since the average tenure of CEOs is only about 6 years, however, continued commitment cannot be taken for granted. Commitment of the CEO, regardless of the motivation, is crucial to the success of intervention programs and can be demonstrated in several ways. Strong policy statements are an initial step, but they must be followed by the allocation of resources (staff, money, facilities), the direct review of results, reports to the board of directors, and concrete examples set by hiring women into the highest levels of the organization. For example, in his initial address as chief executive of Equitable Life Assurance in 1975, Coy Eklund commented on the desirability of advancing women in the organization, and the following month he hosted a summit conference of women from throughout the company. An advisory panel of women meets on a regular basis with the chief executive, and affirmative action goals are part of the executive appraisal process. Although the company traditionally had 1 female officer, there now are nearly 30, and 4 women serve on Equitable's Board of Directors (McLane, 1980).

Top-level policy is ultimately carried out by line managers. In their very early assessments of affirmative action plans, Lyle (1973) and Heard (1975) noted the lack of involvement by line managers and the heavy concentration of responsibility for meeting goals on personnel staffs. Line managers should be involved in planning the goals and programs they will be responsible for implementing. Most of the authors recommending line responsibility for affirmative action, however, have not realistically addressed the problems of gaining managers' support (Wallace and LaMonde, 1977; Meyer and Lee, 1978). AT&T provides an example where the line supervisors' powers were curtailed as part of the affirmative action agreement. The personnel office had the power to override the decisions of line managers by holding up promotions, vetoing promotion and hiring decisions, and intervening in disciplinary matters involving women and minorities. Managers at the lower end of the hierarchy may feel more immediately threatened by affirmative action efforts and consequently be less supportive (Meyer and Lee, 1978). For example, O'-Farrell (1977) found that foremen acquired an increased workload (which was unrecognized and uncompensated for by the company) because women were hired without adequate training. At the same time, women were being promoted above the first-line supervisors who were training them.

One midwestern company seems to have succeeded in transferring responsibility to line managers. The first 3 years of the affirmative action program were conducted as a personnel department activity. Progess was minimal until the CEO delegated responsibility to line managers, down to the first line supervisor. Those who did not meet objectives got smaller bonuses. "We now have 45 women department managers, compared with one when the program started. . . . [L]ine management was the turning point" (McLane, 1980:23). Providing incentives is an important motivation, and several companies in the McLane study reported tieing performance to bonuses. The importance of line involvement in successfully implementing other kinds of organizational change is well documented (Whyte, 1969). Failure to enlist the support of foremen and other managers directly responsible for business operations has undoubtedly slowed the progress of job integration.

There is a fine balance, however, between line responsibility and centralized management and control, as demonstrated by the AT&T case. Managers reported that both are very important. Two critical components in maintaining the balance are the person heading the EEO program and the data management system. According to McLane (1980), the EEO post is now regarded by managers as a very demanding job requiring knowledge of the legal regulatory process, quantitative skills for increasingly complex analysis of the work force, and the ability to work with a variety of individuals both internal and external to the organization.

Accurate information about current employees and projections of future needs is essential for the EEO director's effectiveness. Approximately two-thirds of the companies in the Shaeffer and Lynton (1979) study reported establishing overall results-oriented management planning and control systems for affirmative action, and fully one-third of those said it was the single most successful EEO action they had taken. Procedures for setting goals and measuring progress have become increasingly sophisticated. General Electric has experimented with a series of mathematical models to develop realistic EEO goals (Hayes, 1980). Churchill and Shrank (1976) have developed a flow model that requires management to identify job ladders, measure the current race and sex mix of employees, specify a desired hiring mix for minorities and women, and develop promotion probabilities based on anticipated hiring and turnover rates. All of these efforts have generated more realistic estimates of the amount of time needed to change a firm's employment profile, particularly given the low turnover in the highest-rated management and blue-collar jobs.

Underlying the success or failure of intervention strategies is the allocation of corporate resources. The best strategy will fail if it is not sufficiently supported. Meyer and Lee (1978) found that the public utility companies had different patterns of resource allocation for different types of jobs. Some companies placed the major thrust on professional and managerial positions, while others balanced their efforts between blue- and white-collar areas. No company, however, reported giving a major priority to integrating blue-collar jobs, and they directly linked this difference in priority to successful results. Of the companies surveyed that employed blue-collar workers, fewer than 10 percent placed their primary emphasis on the blue-collar area compared with 44 percent that placed primary emphasis on the professional and managerial jobs. Correspondingly, far less success was reported in the entry-level, semiskilled, and skilled blue-collar jobs. It appears that more progress has been made for women in management than for women in blue-collar jobs, at least in part because more company effort and resources have been allocated to integrating management jobs.

Finally, an important part of the administrative structure affecting job integration in unionized firms is the collective bargaining agreement. Developing or changing wage structures, job posting and bidding procedures, seniority systems, training programs, job qualifications, and dispute-resolution procedures are subjects of collective bargaining as well as affirmative action efforts (Wesman, 1982; Newman and Wilson, 1981; Steinberg and Cook, 1981; Wallace and Driscoll, 1981; O'Farrell, 1980b; Ratner, 1980; The Women's Labor Project, 1980; Leshin, 1979; Hausman et al., 1977; Stone and Baderschneider, 1974).

Under Title VII, unions, like employers, are prohibited from discriminatory practices. Unions are held responsible with employers for discrimination caused by provisions in collective bargaining agreements, and the union duty of fair representation in grievance handling is well established (Steinberg and Cook, 1981; Wallace and Driscoll, 1981). Newman and Wilson (1981) articulated several ways in which government agencies not only do not cooperate with unions but, in fact, also discourage unions from pursuing charges of discrimination by their members.

Unions, however, like employers, have responded diversely to government enforcement activities. Unfortunately, little attention has been paid to the role of labor unions in facilitating intervention programs (Wesman, 1982; Wallace and Driscoll, 1981; O'Farrell, 1980b). Most research on unions and equal employment opportunity policy has focused on the discriminatory behavior of unions toward black workers and the resulting legal developments (Wallace and Driscoll, 1981). This in part reflects federal policy, holding unions equally responsible with employers for discrimination (O'Farrell, 1980b; Steinberg and Cook, 1981).

Changes in federal policy toward unions were initiated in the late 1970s. In 1980 the U.S. Equal Employment Opportunity Commission developed a policy recognizing and encouraging the efforts of unions in the area of equal employment opportunity policy. At the same time, the U.S. Department of Labor proposed changes in the guidelines of the Office of Federal Contract Compliance Programs (OFCCP) that would have broadened union participation. For example, unions would be notified if a compliance review was to take place in a company where the unions are party to a collective bargaining agreement. Currently, however, the Commission's policy has not been implemented, and the proposed regulation changes have been withdrawn.

Yet union officers and staff are potentially as important for integrating nonmanagement jobs as are CEOs and line managers. Recent studies have found women to be generally satisfied with their unions (Kochan, 1979) and to have positive attitudes toward local union policies and practices (Bohlander and Cook, 1982). In O'Farrell's (1980a) study of one union local, women respondents were generally satisfied with the union, and even dissatisfied women felt that they needed the union to represent their positions to management. Women identified such issues as job upgrading and maternity leave that they thought the union should bargain on, and they used union procedures such as filing grievances, voting in elections, and establishing a union women's committee.

At both the national and local levels, this particular union had been excluded from affirmative action negotiations between the company and the government despite a strong record supporting EEO programs and policies, including filing sex discrimination suits on behalf of women workers. Union officials and women members were unhappy with the national affirmative action agreement, and this led to 3 more years of litigation by the union on behalf of its women members. Ultimately, these activities resulted in a stronger affirmative action program.

The experiences in European countries (Ratner, 1980) and research in the United States (Steinberg and Cook, 1981; O'Farrell, 1980b) have recommended a much stronger EEO role for unions in the future. Newman and Wilson (1981) argued that because of their knowledge of plant practices and access to employer information unions could take a more active role in identifying discriminatory practices, informing workers about their rights, providing financial and legal assistance, and offering moral support. Newman and Wilson also concluded that discrimination cannot be corrected exclusively through collective bargaining and called for increased government-union collaboration.

CONCLUSIONS AND RECOMMENDATIONS

This review of intervention programs began by distinguishing between the pioneer and postpioneer eras. We then focused on the current postpioneer era during which companies make formal agreements and commit resources to redress the institutional causes of job segregation. But many companies, or their departments, remain in the pioneer era. They have no women in certain jobs or departments, and pioneer women are filing complaints of discrimination. The pioneer and postpioneer eras exist simultaneously, and a continued federal presence is likely to be necessary for some time to initiate and keep companies actively recruiting, hiring, and training women for nontraditional entry-level jobs. At the same time, new initiatives by the government, companies, and unions are needed to meet the challenges presented by barriers to women's advancement in nontraditional jobs.

There are 10 key findings from our analysis that bear further consideration and scrutiny in future evaluations of corporate intervention strategies.

1. Federal EEO laws have been important in producing substantial changes in the work forces of targeted firms. There is a growing acceptance of EEO principles by corporate managers and a demonstrated psychological impact on women's willingness and ability to press their demands for nontraditional jobs.

2. Most of the successful corporate intervention strategies for increasing job integration have been in the areas of recruit-

ing, hiring, and training women for previously all-male entry-level jobs.

3. An effective recruitment strategy combines active external recruitment from nontraditional sources with innovative internal recruitment efforts that usually involve changes in company seniority systems. Careful screening of applicants results in lower turnover, which furthers the long-term goal of job integration.

4. Preplacement training and supplementary courses for women in blue-collar jobs are effective in overcoming women's lack of technical education and experience, in helping them to perform better on the job, and in increasing their acceptance by male coworkers.

5. Special training for women in managerial positions is generally not necessary, but women need to be integrated into the formal and informal sources of training traditionally available to men.

6. The exclusive focus on integrating men's jobs is not a sufficient long-term strategy for reducing job segregation—the evidence suggests that it may provide only a temporary solution. The increasing number of women being hired into entry-level jobs, combined with bottlenecks in promotion opportunities, may lead to resegregation of the lowest-paying, least-prestigious men's jobs, resulting in new female "ghettos."

7. The most effective strategies to ensure that women have equal promotion opportunities in an organization are to make initial job assignments that place women on career paths with high opportunities for advancement, to make temporary modifications in qualifications and seniority provisions to meet affirmative action goals, and to develop methods for individual qualification assessment and career planning that increase opportunities for men and women.

8. To increase the chances for ultimate success in reducing job segregation, companies should implement their intervention programs in areas of projected corporate growth and in coordination with long-term plans for technological innovation.

9. An effective internal administrative structure for planning EEO policy and implementing intervention programs is essential for ultimate success in job integration. The important elements of administrative effectiveness are commitment from top executives and line managers (which can be facilitated by staff EEO training), a skillful EEO manager, an accurate data management system, and allocation of sufficient corporate resources for implementation and monitoring.

10. In firms with collective bargaining agreements, the cooperation of union staff and officers in eliminating barriers to job integration (e.g., changes in job posting, outreach, qualification assessment, training and seniority systems) is essential for achieving a strong and effective EEO policy.

There is little doubt that the policies of the Reagan administration are negatively affecting progress on reducing job segregation. Lack of leadership at the U.S. Equal Employment Opportunity Commission and the U.S. Department of Labor, proposed changes in guidelines for federal contractors, and reduced commitment to employment and training programs diminish the pressure and resources for change. Current economic policies and high unemployment limit new opportunities and affect recent gains. These concluding recommendations attempt to address the realities of today within the context of the long-term goal of achieving equal employment opportunity for women and men. Future programs and policies should include the following:

• federal support for the development of alternative EEO monitoring systems, the involvement of labor unions in EEO negotiations, and upgrading women's jobs;
• federal support for skills training, information dissemination, and leadership development;
• corporate improvement of human resource planning;
• union programs to develop women leaders and to identify EEO problems;

• joint union and company initiatives to improve the terms of collective bargaining agreements for women workers; and

• cooperatively planned and executed longitudinal comparative research by the government, companies, unions, and researchers.

Federal Equal Employment Opportunity Policy

Federal enforcement activities have had a positive effect on reducing sex segregation within the work force of some firms, yet the government cannot and indeed shouldn't supervise employment practices within firms. Rather, federal policy must strengthen the incentives for change at the firm level, and there are at least three areas where the U.S. Equal Employment Opportunity Commission and the Office of Federal Contract Compliance Programs need to initiate action: monitoring, union involvement, and integrating traditionally women's jobs.

A targeted monitoring plan, similar to the existing targeted enforcement plan (U.S. Equal Employment Opportunity Commission, 1982), should be developed and implemented by the Commission. A limited number of companies could be identified, based on carefully developed selection criteria, and comparative analysis could be conducted to reduce and refine the type of data needed to measure compliance, to develop technical assistance materials for a wide range of firms, and to improve the process of establishing goals and timetables.

At a minimum, enforcement agencies should facilitate the active involvement of labor unions in efforts to reduce job segregation. The Commission should reaffirm and implement its 1980 policy statement that recognizes and encourages the voluntary efforts of unions in the area of equal employment opportunity. Unions should be brought into negotiations that affect collective bargaining agreements, and women members should be included on committees that de-

velop or implement agreements at the national and local levels. The U.S. Department of Labor should revise the OFCCP Guidelines, under consideration since 1981 (*Federal Register*, 1981), to require notification of unions when compliance reviews are conducted in firms with collective bargaining agreements and to enable their voluntary cooperation.

Company experiences in the postpioneer era suggest that integrating entry-level traditionally male jobs is an important but limited approach. Reducing sex segregation will require integrating women's jobs as well. The Commission should continue to develop current strategies for integrating women's jobs: establishing goals and timetables (e.g., the AT&T consent decree); limited upgrading (e.g., the GE consent decree), and pursuing affirmative action negotiations in the area of equal pay for work of comparable worth. Upgrading women's jobs not only improves working conditions for women but also will facilitate the increase of men into these jobs.

Federal Training and Education Policy

An important issue for reducing job segregation involves how much outreach and training are needed and who should pay for it—women, employers, or government. The burden is currently on women and employers. Government subsidy for skills training and worker education is lower in the United States than in almost any other industrial country (Woodcock, 1977). Yet the few government programs for integrating women into nontraditional jobs have been somewhat successful and need to be continued and expanded. Congress should increase the funding for federal training subsidies, maintain targeting for women and women's programs, and emphasize training for nontraditional jobs. The U.S. Department of Labor should disseminate information about successful techniques used by public and private organizations to train and recruit women for nontraditional jobs and should act on proposals to increase financial incentives (e.g., tax exemptions) for employers to develop and expand apprenticeship training with targeting for women. Finally, federally aided programs for worker education and leadership training in EEO policy could be initiated, for example, through subsidies to community colleges and land-grant institutions.

Management and Union Initiatives

Managers reported that EEO policies have had a positive effect on improving overall personnel policies and procedures. Affirmative action must now move beyond formalizing, clarifying, and modifying existing procedures to developing new and innovative practices that result in and are part of larger organizational changes. Corporations and business schools should expand their research and development programs for exempt and nonexempt employees in the following areas: systematic career development and training, performance appraisal systems, improved communication and information sharing, job redesign, job rotation, decentralization of decision making, and the planning and implementation of technological changes.

To adequately represent women, unions must undertake internal affirmative actions such as increased support for leadership training for women members, developing EEO training for union officers, appointing and hiring women in staff positions, encouraging women to run for union office, and requesting and analyzing EEO compliance data now available through recent court decisions. Collective bargaining between management and labor should include the following subjects with specific concern for their impact on women and minority workers: job posting and bidding procedures, seniority systems, grievance procedures, job redesign, introduction of technological changes, job evaluation and comparable worth, and nontraditional job training.

Research Agenda

All of the current EEO policies, programs, and proposed new initiatives are in need of more information. To measure the effectiveness of program interventions on reducing job segregation, it is essential to have longitudinal analysis of employee advancement within firms coupled with information about the changes in firm activities and procedures (Kanter, 1979; Rosenbaum, 1979). How important is initial job assignment? Do existing training programs make a difference in career advancement? How can we identify formal and informal opportunity structures in the organization? How do these factors interact with the education and training individuals bring to the job or acquire on the job? What are the effects of external economic factors?

All of these questions can be systematically addressed within an organization that has reasonably accurate, computerized personnel files. The methodological issues are complex, however, and few organizations have the internal capabilities to design and carry out such a comprehensive evaluation that would enable them to effectively intervene in the mobility patterns of the organization. There are also serious legal and competitive constraints on such analysis. The necessary research might best be done through a cooperative effort jointly funded and implemented by government, companies, unions, and researchers.

ACKNOWLEDGMENTS

We would like to thank the committee and workshop participants for their helpful comments, especially Barbara Bergmann, Alice Ilchman, and Barbara Reskin.

REFERENCES

Alvarez, Rodolfo, Kenneth G. Lutterman, and Associates
1979   *Discrimination in Organizations.* San Francisco: Jossey-Bass.

Ash, Philip
1976   "The Testing Issue." Pp. 203-216 in Wallace
        (ed.), *Equal Employment Opportunity and the
        AT&T Case.* Cambridge, Mass.: MIT Press.

Barnhill-Hayes
1979   *Employer Attitudes Toward Affirmative Ac-
        tion.* Milwaukee, Wis.: Barnhill-Hayes. Re-
        ported in Linda K. Brown, "The Woman Man-
        ager in the United States: A Research Analysis
        and Bibliography." Washington, D.C.: Busi-
        ness and Professional Women's Foundation,
        1981.

Barrett, Nancy
1978   "Data Needs for Evaluating the Labor Market
        Status of Women." Census Bureau Conference
        on Issues in Federal Statistical Needs Relating
        To Women. Washington, D.C.: U.S. Census
        Bureau.

1979   "Women in the Job Market: Occupations,
        Earnings, and Career Opportunities." Pp. 31-
        62 in Ralph E. Smith, *The Subtle Revolution.*
        Washington, D.C.: The Urban Institute.

Bergmann, Barbara R.
1980   "The Contribution of Labor Market Data in
        Combating Employment Discrimination." Pp.
        443-457 in Ronnie Ratner (ed.), *Equal Em-
        ployment Policy for Women.* Philadelphia:
        Temple University Press.

Bohlander, George W., and Suzanne Cook
1982   "Women Unionists: Attitudes Toward Local
        Union Policies." *Labor Studies Journal* Vol. 7
        No. 2 (Fall), pp. 142-157.

Briggs, Norma
1979   "Apprenticeship." Pp. 225-236 in Cahn (ed.).
        Women in the U.S. Labor Force. New York:
        Praeger.

1981   "Overcoming Barriers to Successful Entry and
        Retention of Women in Traditionally Male
        Skilled Blue-Collar Trades in Wisconsin." Pp.
        106-132 in Briggs and Foltman (eds.), *Appren-
        ticeship Research.* Ithaca, N.Y.: ILR Publica-
        tions Div., Cornell University, 1981.

Briggs, Vernon B., and Felician F. Foltman (eds.)
1981   *Aprenticeship Research: Emerging Findings and
        Future Trends.* Ithaca, N.Y.: ILR Publications
        Division, Cornell University.

Brown, Charles
1981   "The Impact of Federal Equal Opportunity
        Policies: What We Do and Do Not Know."
        Rockefeller Foundation Conference on Equal
        Employment Opportunity. New York: Rock-
        efeller Foundation.

Brown, Linda K.
1981   "The Woman Manager in the United States:
        A Research Analysis and Bibliography." Wash-
        ington, D.C.: Business and Professional Wom-
        en's Foundation.

Burrows, Martha G.
1978   *Developing Women Managers: What Needs to
        Be Done?* New York: American Management
        Associations, 1978. Reported in Helen J.

McLane, *Selecting, Developing and Retaining
Women Executives.* New York: Van Nostrand
Reinhold Co., 1980.

Cahn, Ann F. (ed.)
1979   *Women in the U.S. Labor Force.* New York:
        Praeger.

Churchill, Neil C., and John K. Shrank
1976   "Affirmative Action and Guilt-Edged Goals."
        Harvard Business Review March-April, pp. 111-
        116.

Crowley, Joan E., Teresa E. Levitan, and Robert P.
Quinn
1973   "Facts and Fiction About American Working
        Women." In Robert P. Quinn et al., *The 1969-
        70 Survey of Working Conditions* (Final Re-
        port). Washington, D.C.: Employment Stand-
        ards Administration, U.S. Department of La-
        bor.

Cunningham, John
1976   "Avoiding Common Pitfalls in Affirmative Ac-
        tion Programs." *Personnel Journal* March, pp.
        125-128.

Deaux, Kay K.
In   "Blue Collar Barriers." *American Behavioral
press   Scientist.*

Deaux, Kay K., and Joseph C. Ullman
In   "Hard-Hatted Women: Reflections on Blue-
press   Collar Employment." In J. Bernardin (ed.),
        Women in the Workforce. New York: Praeger.

1983   *Women of Steel: Female Blue-Collar Workers
        in the Basic Steel Industry.* New York: Prae-
        ger.

Doeringer, Peter B., and Michael J. Piore
1971   *Internal Labor Markets and Manpower Anal-
        ysis.* Lexington, Mass.: D.C. Heath.

Douglas, Priscilla H.
1981   "Black Working Women." Doctoral disserta-
        tion, Graduate School of Education, Harvard
        University.

Epstein, Cynthia F.
1981   *Women in Law.* New York: Basic Books.

Farley, Jennie
1979   *Affirmative Action and the Woman Worker:
        Guidelines for Personnel Management.* New
        York: AMACOM.

Federal Register
1981   Vol. 46, No. 164, "Proposed Rules," August
        25.

Feldberg, Roslyn L., and Evelyn N. Glenn
1979   "Male and Female: Job Versus Gender Models
        in the Sociology of Work." *Social Problems* Vol.
        26, pp. 524-538.

Fernandez, John P.
1981   *Racism and Sexism in Corporate Life: Chang-
        ing Values in American Business.* Lexington,
        Mass.: Lexington Books.

Foxley, Cecilia H.
1976   *Locating, Recruiting and Employing Women:
        An Equal Opportunity Approach.* Garrett Park,
        Md.: Garrett Park Press.

Gordon, Francine, and Myra Strober (eds.)
1975   Bringing Women into Business. New York: McGraw-Hill.

Hacker, Sally L.
1979   "Sex Stratification, Technological and Organizational Change: A Longitudinal Case Study of AT&T." Social Problems Vol. 26, pp. 539-557.

Hall, Francine S., and Maryann H. Albrecht
1979   The Management of Affirmative Action. Santa Monica, Calif.: Goodyear Publishing Co.

Harlan, Sharon L., and Brigid O'Farrell
1982   "After the Pioneers: Prospects for Women in Nontraditional Blue-Collar Jobs." Work and Occupations Vol. 9, No. 3 (August) pp. 363-386.

Harlan, Anne, and Carol L. Weiss
1981   Moving Up: Women in Managerial Careers (Final Report). Center for Research on Women, Wellesley College.

1982   "Sex Differences in Factors Affecting Managerial Career Advancement." Pp. 59-100 in Wallace (ed.), Women in the Workplace. Boston: Auburn House.

Hausman, Leonard J., et al. (eds.)
1977   Equal Rights and Industrial Relations. Madison, Wis.: Industrial Relations Research Association.

Hayes, Harold P.
1980   Realism in EEO. New York: John Wiley & Sons.

Heard, Jamie
1975   "Availability and Use of Information on Corporate Equal Employment Programs." Washington, D.C.: Investor Responsibility Research Center, Inc.

Heidrick and Struggles, Inc.
1977   Profile of a Chief Personnel Officer. Reported in Helen J. McLane, Selecting, Developing and Retaining Women Executives. New York: Van Nostrand Reinhold, 1980.

1979   Profile of a Woman Officer. Reported in Helen J. McLane, Selecting, Developing and Retaining Women Executives. New York: Van Nostrand Reinhold, 1980.

Hoffmann, Carl, and John S. Reid
1981   "Sex Discrimination?—The XYZ Affair." The Public Interest No. 62 (Winter), pp. 21-39.

Hollander, James
1975   "A Step-by-Step Guide to Corporate Affirmative Action." Business and Society Review (Fall), pp. 67-73.

Iacobelli, John L., and Jan P. Muczyk
1975   "Overlooked Talent Sources and Corporate Strategies for Affirmative Action." Personnel Journal (November), pp. 575-578.

Ichniowski, Casey
1983   "Have Angels Done More? The Steel Industry Consent Decree." Industrial and Labor Relations Review Vol. 36, No. 2 (January), pp. 182-198.

Jongeword, Dorothy, Dru Scott, et al.
1973   Affirmative Action for Women, A Practical Guide. Reading, Mass.: Addison-Wesley.

Kane, Roslyn D., and Jill Miller
1981   "Women and Apprenticeship: A Study of Programs Designed to Facilitate Women's Participation in the Skilled Trades." Pp. 83-105 in Briggs and Foltman (eds.) Apprenticeship Research: Emerging Findings and Future Trends. Ithaca, N.Y.: ILR Publications Division, Cornell University.

Kanter, Rosabeth M.
1977   Men and Women of the Corporation. New York: Basic Books.

1979   "Differential Access to Opportunity and Power." Pp. 52-68 in Alvarez et al. (eds.), Discrimination in Organizations. San Francisco: Jossey-Bass.

1980   "The Impact of Organization Structure: Models and Methods for Change." Pp. 311-327 in Ratner (ed.), Equal Employment Policy for Women: Strategies for Implementation in the United States, Canada and Western Europe. Philadelphia: Temple University Press.

Kelley, Maryellen
1982   "Discrimination in Seniority Systems: A Case Study." Industrial and Labor Relations Review Vol. 36, No. 1 (October), pp. 40-55.

Kleiman, Bernard, and Carl B. Frankel
1975   "Seniority Remedies Under Title VII: The Steel Consent Decree—A Union Perspective." 28th Annual Conference on Labor. New York: New York University.

Kochan, Thomas A.
1979   "How American Workers View Labor Unions." Monthly Labor Review (April), pp. 23-31.

Larwood, Laurie
1977   Women in Management. Lexington, Mass.: Lexington Books.

Leshin, Geraldine
1979   Equal Employment Opportunity and Affirmative Action in Labor Management Relations, A Primer. Los Angeles: Institute of Industrial Relations, University of California.

Loomis, Carol J.
1979   "AT&T in the Throes of Equal Employment." Fortune (January 15).

Lopez, Felix
1976   "The Bell System's Non-Management Personnel Selection Strategy." Pp. 217-242 in Wallace (ed.), Equal Employment Opportunity and the AT&T Case. Cambridge, Mass.: MIT Press.

Lyle, Jerolyn R.
1973   Affirmative Action Programs for Women: A Survey of Innovative Programs. Washington, D.C.: U.S. Equal Employment Opportunity Commission.

Malveaux, Julianne
1982   "Recent Trends in Occupational Segregation by Race and Sex." National Research Council,

Workshop on Occupational Segregation by Race and Sex.

Marshall, Ray, L. Knapp, M. Liggett, and R. Glover
1978   *Employment Discrimination: The Impact of Legal and Administrative Remedies.* Austin: University of Texas.

McLane, Helen J.
1980   *Selecting, Developing and Retaining Women Executives: A Corporate Strategy for the Eighties.* New York: Van Nostrand Reinhold Co.

Medoff, James L., and Katharine G. Abraham
1980   "Experience, Performance, and Earnings." *The Quarterly Journal of Economics* Vol. XCV, No. 4 (December), pp. 703-736.

1981   "Are Those Paid More Really More Productive? The Case of Experience." *The Journal of Human Resources* Vol. XVI, 2, pp. 186-216.

Meyer, Herbert, and Mary D. Lee
1978   *Women in Traditionally Male Jobs: The Experience of Ten Public Utility Companies* (R&D Monograph No. 65). Washington, D.C.: Employment and Training Administration, U.S. Department of Labor.

Moses, Joseph L., and Virginia R. Boehm
1975   "Relationship of Assessment-Center Performance to Management Progress of Women," *Journal of Applied Psychology* Vol. 60, No. 4.

Newman, Winn, and Carole W. Wilson
1981   "The Union Role in Affirmative Action." *Labor Law Journal* (June), pp. 323-342.

Northrup, Herbert R., and John A. Larson
1979   *The Impact of the AT&T-EEO Consent Decree.* Labor Relations and Public Policy Series No. 20. Philadelphia: Industrial Research Unit, The Wharton School, University of Pennsylvania.

Norton, Eleanor Holmes
1981   "Affirmative Action and Labor Force Trends." Rockefeller Foundation Conference on Equal Employment Opportunity. New York: Rockefeller Foundation.

O'Farrell, Brigid
1977   "Affirmative Action for Women in Craft Jobs: Change in the Small Industrial Work Group" (Working Paper). Wellesley, Mass.: Center for Research on Women, Wellesley College.

1980a   Women and Nontraditional Jobs: A Case Study of Local I (Final Report). Washington, D.C.: Employment and Training Administration, U.S. Department of Labor.

1980b   "Equal Employment Opportunity, Women and Unions: An Industrial Union Alternative." (Working Paper No. 54). Wellesley, Mass.: Center for Research on Women, Wellesley College.

1982   "Women and Nontraditional Blue-Collar Jobs in the 1980s: An Overview." Pp. 135-166 in Wallace (ed.), *Women in the Workplace.* Boston: Auburn House.

O'Farrell, Brigid, and Sharon L. Harlan
1982   "Craftworkers and Clerks: The Effect of Male Coworker Hostility on Women's Satisfaction with Nontraditional Jobs." *Social Problems* Vol. 29, No. 3 (February), pp. 252-265.

Pfeiffer, Donald, and Mary L. Walshok
1981   "Some Innovations in Industrial Apprenticeship at General Motors: Locally Developed Competency-Based Training as a Tool for Affirmative Action." Pp. 173-184 in Briggs and Foltman (eds.), *Apprenticeship Research: Emerging Findings and Future Trends.* Ithaca, N.Y.: ILR Publications Division, Cornell University.

Preston, Joan
1978   Presentation on Women and Teaching in New England. Wellesley, Mass.: Center for Research on Women, Wellesley College.

Purcell, Theodore V.
1976   "How G.E. Measures Managers in Fair Employment." In *Equal Opportunity in Business.* Harvard Business Review (Reprint Series No. 21132), pp. 102-107.

Ratner, Ronnie (ed.)
1980   *Equal Employment Policy for Women: Strategies for Implementation in the United States, Canada and Western Europe.* Philadelphia: Temple University Press.

Reubens, B.G., and E.P. Reubens
1979   "Women Workers, Nontraditional Occupations and Full Employment." Pp. 103-126 in Cahn (ed.), *Women in the U.S. Labor Force.* New York: Praeger.

Rosenbaum, James E.
1979   "Career Paths and Advancement Opportunities." Pp. 69-87 in Alvarez et al. (eds.), *Discrimination in Organizations.* San Francisco: Jossey-Bass.

Schreiber, Carol T.
1979   *Changing Places: Men and Women in Transitional Occupations.* Cambridge, Mass.: MIT Press.

Shaeffer, Ruth G.
1980   *Nondiscrimination in Employment and Beyond* (Report No. 782). New York: The Conference Board.

Shaeffer, Ruth G., and Edith F. Lynton
1979   *Corporate Experiences in Improving Women's Job Opportunities* (Report No. 755). New York: The Conference Board.

Shuchat, Jo, with Gerii Guinier and Aileen Douglas
1981   *The Nuts and Bolts of NTO: A Handbook for Recruitment, Training, Support Services, and Placement of Women in Nontraditional Occupations.* Cambridge, Mass.: Technical Education Research Centers.

Stead, B.
1978   *Women in Management.* Englewood Cliffs, N.J.: Prentice-Hall.

Steinberg, Ronnie, and Alice Cook
1981   "Women, Unions and Equal Employment Opportunity" (Working Paper No. 3). Albany, N.Y.: Center for Women in Government, State University of New York.

Stone, Morris, and Earl R. Baderschneider (eds.)
1974   *Arbitration of Discrimination Grievances, A Case Book*. New York: American Arbitration Association.

Strober, M.H.
1982   "The MBA: Same Passport to Success for Women and Men?" Pp. 25-44 in Wallace (ed.), *Women in the Workplace*. Boston: Auburn House.

Swanson, Cheryl, and H. Brinton Milward
1979   "The Impact of Organizational Structure, Technology and Professionalism on the Policy of Affirmative Action." Pp. 41-56 in Marian L. Palley and Michael B. Preston (eds.), *Race, Sex and Policy Problems*. Lexington, Mass.: Lexington Books.

The Women's Labor Project
1980   *A Guide to Collective Bargaining Solutions for Workplace Problems That Particularly Affect Women*. San Francisco: San Francisco Bay Area National Lawyers Guild.

UAW Administrative Letter
1975   Vol. 27, No. 3, August 12.
1976   Vol. 28, No. 7, July 14.

Ullman, Joseph C., and Kay K. Deaux
1981   "Recent Efforts to Increase Female Participation in Apprenticeship in the Basic Steel Industry in the Midwest." Pp. 133-140 in Briggs and Foltman (eds.), *Apprenticeship Research*. Ithaca, N.Y.: ILR Publications Div., Cornell University.

U.S. Commission on Civil Rights
1981   *Child Care and Equal Opportunity for Women*. Clearinghouse Publication No. 67, June.

U.S. Department of Labor
1978   "Women's Guide to Apprenticeship" (Office of the Secretary, Women's Bureau). Washington, D.C.: U.S. Government Printing Office.

U.S. Equal Employment Opportunity Commission
1974   *Affirmative Action and Equal Employment, A Guidebook for Employers, Vols. 1 & 2*. Washington, D.C.: U.S. Equal Employment Opportunity Commission.
1980   "Title VII and Collective Bargaining: Proposal and Resolution to Encourage Voluntary Efforts." Washington, D.C.: U.S. Equal Employment Opportunity Commission, April.
1982   *16th Annual Report, FY 1981*. Washington, D.C.: U.S. Equal Employment Opportunity Commission.

Vetter, B., E. Babco, and S. Jensen-Fisher
1982   "Professional Women and Minorities: A Manpower Data Resource Service." Washington, D.C.: Scientific Manpower Commission (AAAS). Reported in *Women Today*, Vol. 12, No. 8, April 18, 1982.

Wallace, Phyllis A. (ed.)
1976   *Equal Employment Opportunity and the AT&T Case*. Cambridge, Mass.: MIT Press.
1982   *Women in the Workplace*. Boston: Auburn House.

Wallace, Phyllis A., and James W. Driscoll
1981   "Social Issues in Collective Bargaining." Pp. 199-254 in Jack Stieber et al. (eds.). *U.S. Industrial Relations 1950-1980: A Critical Assessment*. Madison, Wis.: Industrial Relations Research Association.

Wallace, Phyllis A., and Annette M. LaMond (ed.)
1977   *Women, Minorities and Employment Discrimination*. Lexington, Mass.: Lexington Books.

Walshok, Mary L.
1981   *Blue Collar Women: Pioneers on the Male Frontier*. Garden City, N.Y.: Anchor Books.

Wesman, Elizabeth C.
1982   "Public Policies at Loggerheads: The Effect of Equal Employment Opportunity Legislation on Unions." Doctoral dissertation, Cornell University, Ithaca, N.Y.

Whyte, William F.
1969   *Organizational Behavior*. Homewood, Ill.: Richard D. Irwin Inc. and the Dorsey Press.

Woodcock, Leonard
1977   "Call for a Coalition to Establish a National Extension Service." *Labor Studies Journal* Vol. 1, No. 3 (Winter), pp. 281-285.

16 Occupational Desegregation in CETA Programs

LINDA J. WAITE *and*
SUE E. BERRYMAN

This paper examines the occupational distributions in the Comprehensive Employment and Training Act (CETA) and the wage implications of these distributions for men and women of different racial and ethnic origins. Our data come from two separate projects on CETA, both conducted for the National Commission on Employment Policy. One (Berryman et al., 1981) assessed the nature and equity of men's and women's experiences in CETA, a substantial part of the study being devoted to CETA's occupational desegregation record for women. The second (Berryman and Waite, 1982) assessed ethnic and racial differences in CETA experiences, focusing on whites, blacks, and Hispanics and on Hispanic subgroups.

CETA's occupational desegregation record for women is important for several reasons. First, one of CETA's legislated purposes is to improve the economic prospects of its clients. As we know, substantially more female than male occupations pay poverty-level wages (Sawhill, 1976). Persistent occupational segregation parallels the persistent male-female wage differential, and differences in male and female occupational distributions account for over a quarter of the wage differential (Chiswick et al., 1974). Even when labor force attachment is controlled, women also have much flatter lifetime earnings profiles than do men (Sawhill, 1973). Theoretical arguments (Wolf and Rosenfeld, 1978) and fragmentary evidence (Barrett, 1979) implicate occupational segregation in these profile differences. Male but not female occupations seem associated with career paths that carry wage advancement with experience.

Second, poverty in the United States is becoming increasingly female poverty, primarily as the result of the rising number of female-headed households and the relationship between households of this kind and poverty.[1] Thus, from the economic perspective, the issue of occupations and wages for women is not transitory.

---

[1] From 1969 to 1979 the percentage of female-headed households of all races increased by a third. For whites and Hispanics the increase was about 25 percent; for blacks, over 40 percent. Although the chances that a household of this kind was poor declined slightly over the decade, in 1979 they were still very high: 30 percent for all races and almost 50 percent for black female-headed households (Bureau of the Census, 1981).

Third, CETA has represented a major federal lever for affecting occupational desegregation for women and women's wages. From FY 1974 to FY 1980, 19 million individuals entered CETA in job training or employment capacities, somewhat fewer than half of these being women. Thus, over time CETA has had the potential for affecting the occupational preferences and skills of large numbers of women.

Finally, CETA flows from early federal manpower programs of the 1960s and can be expected to affect future federal training and employment programs. Thus, even if CETA is virtually dismantled under the Reagan administration, its occupational desegregation record for women is of more than historic interest. As we show later, women's occupational options in CETA are affected by how CETA is structured and by how men and women are funneled through this structure. Our experience with CETA has implications for designing future programs that would increase women's exposure to occupations currently held mostly by men.

The paper has five sections. The first briefly describes CETA's legal structure — its titles, their legislated purposes, and eligibility rules. The second describes the data base used in the two studies that underlie this paper. The third shows how the CETA title under which individuals enter CETA and their CETA activity (e.g., work experience) affect their occupational options. The fourth documents CETA's occupational desegregation record for white, black, and Hispanic women; and the final section shows the wage consequences of women's occupational distributions in CETA.

DESCRIPTION OF CETA TITLES AND ELIGIBILITY REQUIREMENTS

For reasons of simplicity and of data restrictions, we deal only with CETA Titles I, II, and VI.[2] The major services available under these titles were basic skills, job training, and jobs, although, as we describe later, not all services are available in all titles. For example, basic skills and job training are essentially restricted to Title I. The purposes of the jobs also vary by title. Most Title I jobs, called work experience, are income transfer jobs[3] that are not intended as a bridge to unsubsidized employment. Jobs in Titles II and VI, known as public service employment (PSE) jobs, are expected to lead to unsubsidized employment, although the economic environments in which these jobs are offered presumably vary. Title II jobs are available in areas with high, structural unemployment; Title VI jobs, in areas with short-term, cyclical unemployment.[4]

The eligibility by title varied, although, as we discuss below, titles overlapped in their eligibility requirements. All of the titles had eligibility criteria of economic disadvantage, underemployment, or unemployment. For Title I, eligibility was restricted to those economically disadvantaged or unemployed or underemployed.[5]

---

[2] These are the title numbers before the 1978 reauthorization of CETA; they correspond to the postreauthorization numbers of IIB, IID, and VI. This paper does not discuss Title III because most slots in this title (Title IIIA or the Summer Youth Program) are jobs of short duration, intended as a mechanism of income transfer, and without a training component.

[3] By "income transfer jobs" we mean jobs used primarily as a means of allocating money to people, not as bridges to private or public sector jobs unsubsidized by CETA.

[4] Title II was targeted on regions with lingering unemployment. Title VI was designed to reduce the presumably short-term unemployment associated with the recession of the mid-1970s. However, as Mirengoff and Rindler (1978) observe, the unemployment rate used to define an area's eligibility for Title II was surpassed in most places by that used to define an area's eligibility for Title VI funds. Thus, de facto the distinction between the two titles was eliminated.

[5] To receive one of the small number of PSE jobs in Title I the individual had to be unemployed or underemployed.

For Title II, individuals had to reside in areas of substantial unemployment. They also had to be unemployed for at least 30 days prior to application *or* underemployed.

Before January 1977 individuals were eligible for Title VI if they had been unemployed for 30 days, or if they resided in an area with excessive unemployment and had been underemployed or unemployed for at least 15 days. After January 1977 the eligibility rules became more complicated. However, in general, individuals could enter if they were (1) unemployed or underemployed; or (2) a member of an economically disadvantaged family *and* either a member of an Aid to Families With Dependent Children (AFDC) family, *or* unemployed and an unemployment insurance recipient, *or* unemployed and ineligible for unemployment insurance, *or* unemployed and an insurance exhaustee.

DATA

Continuous Longitudinal Manpower Survey (CLMS)

Both studies on which this paper is based used Continuous Longitudinal Manpower Survey (CLMS) data. The Bureau of the Census has conducted the CLMS quarterly since January 1975, sampling respondents from the previous quarter's new enrollees in CETA. Respondents are sampled from four CETA functional activities: public service employment, employability development, direct referrals,[6] and youth work experience (including summer programs).

The CLMS has two main objectives. First, it is designed to obtain characteristics of the CETA participants and the services they received, thus providing data not available from

the usual sources, the prime sponsor[7] reporting system. Second, the CLMS is intended to measure the effect of CETA programs on participants, including earnings and labor force status.[8]

The CLMS comprises an initial intake interview, an activity record, and several other interviews during and after the CETA enrollment. In the initial interview, the CLMS determines what CETA service the enrollee received (e.g., public service employment) and, if the service was a job or job training, the enrollee's occupation and wages. The CLMS also obtains information on the enrollee's attitudes toward manpower programs and services received, what service and occupation the enrollee wanted from CETA, his or her trade or vocational training before entering CETA, veteran status, marital status, number of dependents, family composition, receipt of government transfer payments (food stamps, subsidized housing, AFDC, Supplemental Security Income, unemployment benefits, and other public assistance), the enrollee's employment/schooling history in the previous year, wages or salary in the last year, and personal and family income by source. The CLMS contains information on the highest grade or year of regular school the enrollee attended, whether that grade had been com-

---

[6] In a direct referral, CETA refers the individual to a job vacancy. The individual does not receive any other CETA services and does not necessarily get the job to which he or she is referred.

[7] The federal government administers decentralized CETA programs through administrative units called prime sponsors. Federal funds for these programs are allocated to the prime sponsors. State, county, or local governments can be prime sponsors if they govern a minimum population of 100,000. State governments tend to become prime sponsors for governmental units within the state that do not meet the minimum population requirement.

[8] The CLMS—sponsored by the Employment and Training Administration—samples mainly decentralized CETA programs, i.e., programs operated by CETA prime sponsors. Thus, special-purpose programs such as the Job Corps (Title IV, reauthorized as Title IVB), Young Adult Conservation Corps (Title VIII), and several Title III (reauthorized as various Title IV) programs are not included in the CLMS file.

pleted by the time of CETA enrollment, and whether the enrollee had a high school equivalency certificate or General Educational Development (GED) certificate. Our analysis relies especially on detailed data on the enrollee's ethnic origin or descent and on whether the enrollee was limited in the amount or type of work he or she could do because of problems in speaking English. We use all of this information in various sections of our analysis, either as dependent or as independent variables.

In our analyses we use only data from the initial questionnaire and activity record, since our purpose is to assess the services provided within CETA and not to assess the impact of CETA services on later outcomes. We included all CETA enrollees surveyed by the CLMS during the period October 1975 through September 1978 in order to (1) maximize the period covered by our analyses and (2) maximize the number of cases available for analysis.[9] In each quarter the CLMS sampled between 3,500 and 4,000 CETA enrollees and completed initial interviews with 3,300 to 3,600. To have sufficient numbers of observations for race/ethnic groups by sex we pooled information for all quarters in the October 1975 to September 1978 or March 1979 time period (Barrett, 1979). Pooling observations across time periods provides large sample sizes that allow us considerable flexibility in the types of analyses we do and that allow us to dis-

aggregate the sample by sex and race/ethnicity. For the October 1975 to March 1979 period, the CLMS contains approximately 42,000 initial interviews.

Analytic Strategy

We assessed the impact of race and ethnicity on enrollees' experience in CETA in two ways.[10] First, we estimated a general linear model of each CETA outcome separately for men and women in which we controlled for all characteristics of the enrollee and the enrollment that were relevant for CETA assignment.[11] This model included a series of dummy variables for race/ethnicity: white, black, and Hispanic. Second, we performed an analysis of covariance for each CETA outcome in which we tested for difference between race/ethnic groups in the slope coefficients in the model.

CETA AS A SYSTEM OF OPPORTUNITIES

We can think of CETA as a system for distributing opportunities of several kinds: (1) participation in CETA; (2) a CETA service or activity — basic education, job training in a classroom setting, on-the-job training, work experience, and public service employment; (3) an occupation for those in jobs or job training; and (4) a CETA wage for those in jobs or job training. Since this paper focuses on CETA's contribution to occupational desegregation for women, CETA occupations are the resource of primary concern. However, to interpret the data on oc-

---

[9] We begin with October 1975 because the CLMS did not record CETA title until the second quarter of FY 1976 (October 1975). The sample for the multivariate analysis ends with March 1979 because CETA was reauthorized in October 1978 and regulations governing the revised act were released to prime sponsors in April 1979. Since those enrolled in CETA in the third and fourth quarters of 1979 entered under revised guidelines, the data for these quarters are not completely comparable with early data, and we eliminated them to ensure comparability. The sample for the crosstabular analysis ends with September 1979 because data to this date only were available at the time this analysis was done (Berryman et al., 1981).

[10] We follow census definitions; persons of Hispanic origin may be of either race. We divide enrollees into whites (non-Hispanic), blacks (non-Hispanic), and Hispanics of both races. We omit those of other races who are not Hispanic.

[11] These included age, marital status, poverty status, labor force experience, educational attainment, desired CETA services, and problems with the English language—all at the time of enrollment, plus, for males, veteran status.

cupations it is important to understand the process by which a CETA participant is assigned an occupation, either in the form of a job or job training.

An individual enters CETA under a title and a CETA activity that is authorized for that title. If the activity is job training or a job, the individual is assigned to an occupation and receives a wage in connection with it. Eligibility rules determine if an individual can enter CETA, and under what title he or she may enter. Although these rules vary for different CETA titles, individuals can be eligible for more than one title, giving CETA prime sponsors some discretion in their title assignments.

Titles affect CETA service or activity assignments in that not all CETA services are available in all titles. Titles II and VI consist only of public service employment (PSE) jobs, and almost all of these jobs occur in these two titles. Title I consists primarily of basic education, job training in a classroom setting, on-the-job training (OJT), and work

experience activities, and these services occur only in Title I. In sum, Titles II and VI imply a public service job; Title I, a basic education, job training, or work experience activity. If a CETA participant is only eligible for Titles II or III, his or her CETA activity is determined. If the participant is only eligible for Title I, his or her activity options are constrained but not determined.

As Table 16-1 shows, each CETA service has a different occupational distribution and therefore different occupational assignment probabilities. All of the occupations available in CETA are available in each of the services, but the occupational emphases differ for each CETA service. Relative to the distributions for the other services, classroom training has the highest percentage of clerical openings; on-the-job training, the highest percentages of crafts and operatives options; work experience, the highest percentage of service jobs; and public service employment, the highest percentages of professional/technical and laborer jobs.

TABLE 16-1   CETA's FY 1976-FY 1979 Occupational Structure by CETA Activity (percent)

Occupational Category[a]	CETA's Occupational Structure				
	All CETA Activities	Classroom Training	OJT	Work Experience	Public Service Employment
Professional/technical	10.7	6.9	4.9	6.7	15.8
Managerial/administrative	2.3	0.4	2.9	0.9	3.6
Sales workers	1.0	1.2	3.7	0.9	0.3
Clerical	27.2	38.0	16.3	32.1	23.5
Crafts	12.0	20.3	21.5	6.7	10.3
Operatives	7.5	14.9	28.0	4.2	2.1
Transportation equipment operatives	2.7	1.2	3.6	2.1	3.3
Laborers	15.2	1.2	8.6	13.8	22.0
Service	21.5	15.8	10.4	32.8	19.0
Total[b]	100.0	100.0	100.0	100.0	100.0
N (000)	2,770	389	319	790	1,272

[a] These are the 1-digit census occupational categories. They exclude three categories that do not occur in the CETA occupational structure: Farmers and Farm Managers, Farm Laborers and Supervisors, and Private Household Workers.

[b] Columns may not add to 100 due to rounding.

SOURCE: Table 31, Berryman and Waite (1982), p. 79.

The process by which a CETA participant is assigned an occupation varies across time for any given CETA office and across CETA offices at any given time. Any specific occupational assignment reflects several factors: (1) the participant's title eligibility and the subsequent activity and occupational constraints that are associated with each title; (2) the participant's activity and occupational needs and preferences; (3) the activity and occupational vacancies available at any given time as a function of the local labor market, the CETA office's efforts to develop particular opportunities, and the amount of federal money then available for different CETA titles; and (4) judgments by CETA assignment personnel about what kinds of occupations are appropriate for what kinds of people.

Our analyses show that in FY 1976 to FY 1978, relative to their eligibility, women 18 to 65 years of age were underrepresented in all CETA titles for all three fiscal years except Title I in FY 1978. The underrepresentation varied from 64 to 87 percent, depending on fiscal year and title. Thus, women did not receive CETA resources, including occupational experiences, at rates commensurate with their eligibility. The discrepancy between eligibility and participation was greater for Titles II and VI than for Title I.[12]

When we looked at how female and male CETA participants distributed across titles, a logistic regression showed that relative to men with the same placement-relevant characteristics (see note 11), women were more likely to enter CETA under Title I and less likely to enter CETA under Titles II and VI. Thus, they were more likely than

were men to receive basic education, job training, and work experience services and less likely to get public service jobs.

Although sex affected title assignment, Berryman and Waite (1982) found few effects — and no important effects — of race/ethnicity on the CETA title under which enrollees enter CETA. Whites of both sexes entered CETA under Titles I and II slightly more often than did blacks or Hispanics with similar characteristics. But these differences never exceeded about 3 percentage points and, although statistically significant, were hardly substantively so.

As noted, Title I consists of several CETA services: basic education in a classroom, job training in a classroom setting, OJT, work experience, and a small number of PSE jobs. Again, multivariate analyses showed that race and ethnicity had no or only trivial effects on assignment to CETA services. However, relative to males in Title I, women in this title were placed more frequently in classroom training and work experience jobs and less frequently in OJT and PSE jobs. Although the percentages declined across fiscal years, even in FY 1978 *a third of all women in CETA* were in Title I classroom training.

Thus, relative to men's occupational options, women's options were more apt to be those associated with classroom training and work experience. They were less apt to be those associated with OJT and PSE jobs.

We would like to use multivariate analyses to assess CETA's occupational sex segregation for racial and ethnic groups. However, Berryman et al. (1981) did not conduct multivariate analyses of occupational segregation by sex and race and ethnicity. Berryman and Waite (1982) conduct multivariate analyses separately by sex and by race and ethnicity and have no direct measure of the sex composition of occupations for these groups. The occupational measure used in Berryman and Waite was occupational status, a measure that does not directly bear on occupational segregation. However, we

---

[12] Available eligibility estimates for this time period are by sex and by race and other ethnicity separately. Thus, we cannot assess racial and ethnic differences in women's CETA participation, relative to eligibility. We can note that, relative to eligibility, whites are underrepresented and blacks are overrepresented in all three titles, and Hispanics are overrepresented in Title I and underrepresented in Titles II and IV.

can use our multivariate results for the effects of race and ethnicity on CETA title, CETA service, occupational status, and CETA wages to draw tentative inferences about these effects on occupational segregation in CETA by race and ethnicity.

We have already noted that there are few, if any, effects of race and ethnicity on CETA title and service assignments. Our analyses of the impact of race/ethnicity on the occupational status of CETA jobs and job training showed mixed results. As Table 16-2 shows, we found no differences among white, black, and Hispanic males in status of job training, but we found lower occupational status for white and black than for Hispanic females, net of other characteristics. For job status we found lower scores for whites and blacks of both sexes than for Hispanics. As before, the differences tended to be statistically significant but substantively unimportant. The largest coefficient for race/ethnic groups appeared for black females in occupational status of job training and equaled 5 points on a 100-point scale, the Duncan Socioeconomic Index.

Our results for race/ethnic differences in CETA wages, shown in Table 16-3, rein-

TABLE 16-2   Effects of Race and Ethnicity on Occupational Status of CETA Job Training and CETA Job

Unstandardized Regression Coefficients, Net of Social, Economic, and Demographic Characteristics of the CETA Entrant[a]

	Males	Females
Job training		
White	.5086	-3.3100^b
Black	.5447	-3.9040^b
Job		
White	-2.4285^b	-3.3197^b
Black	-2.7244^b	-4.9859^b

[a] These characteristics are listed in note 11 of this paper.

^{b} $p < .05$. This indicates effects that would appear by chance less than 5 times out of every 100 analyses.

SOURCE: Tables 42 and 43, Berryman and Waite (1982), pp. 97 and 99.

TABLE 16-3   Effects of Race and Ethnicity on Hourly Wage of CETA Job Training and CETA Job

Unstandardized Regression Coefficients, Net of Social, Economic, and Demographic Characteristics of the CETA Entrant[a]

	Males	Females
Job Training		
White	.0001	$-.0225$
Black	$-.0149$	$-.0555^b$
Job		
White	.0065	$-.0149^b$
Black	$-.0396^b$	$-.0285^b$

[a] These characteristics are listed in note 11 of this paper.

^{b} $p < .05$. This indicates effects that would appear by chance less than 5 times out of every 100 analyses.

SOURCE: Tables 46 and 47, Berryman and Waite (1982), pp. 105 and 107.

forced the conclusions we reached for occupational status. Table 16-2 presents results of the regression of the Duncan Socioeconomic Index of CETA job training or CETA job on assignment-relevant characteristics (see note 11) of the individual. Since these models omit the variable for the "Hispanic" race/ethnicity category, the coefficients show the deviation of white and black occupational status from that for Hispanics, controlling for the other characteristics of the enrollee. Among males in job training, we found no differences in wages, but among males in jobs, black males received wages 4 percent lower than those of Hispanic and white males with comparable characteristics. For females, we found very small differences — on the order of 1 or 2 percent — but those that did exist favored Hispanics.

The analyses of covariance allowed us to test the hypothesis that the process which determines CETA occupational status and wages depends on race/ethnicity. We found evidence of some rather minor differences. These analyses showed different effects of the variables in the models for race/ethnic groups on occupational status of CETA job training for males but not for females and for status of CETA jobs for both males and females. But few sizable differences appeared in individual coefficients in any of these models.

In sum, when we considered males and females separately, we found small or no effects of race/ethnicity on CETA title, activity, occupational status, or wages. The differences that existed tended to favor Hispanics over blacks and whites. These results suggest that, given an appropriate measure of occupational segregation, we would have found that the process of occupational segregation did not depend on race and ethnicity.

The remainder of this paper focuses on CETA's occupational distribution and its wage implications by sex, without regard to race or ethnicity. The conclusions from our multivariate analysis of the impact of race/ethnicity on CETA experiences argue for this approach. In addition, analysis of two sexes and three racial/ethnic groups becomes too cumbersome for the resulting small gain in analytic detail.

OCCUPATIONAL DESEGREGATION IN CETA

Since FY 1974 millions of adult women have participated in CETA. In connection with the reauthorization of CETA in October 1978, CETA regulations directed state and local CETA administrators to reduce sex stereotyping in employment and training. We only had data for October 1975 to September 1978 for these analyses. Thus, we can only describe CETA's occupational segregation record prior to the introduction of the desegregation directive and cannot assess CETA's responses to this directive.

At the same time, even prior to CETA's 1978 reauthorization, CETA — especially Title I — was expected to improve the economic prospects of its clients. Since female-dominated occupations command lower wages than those of mixed and male-dominated occupations, it is reasonable to look for evidence that CETA tried to train and employ women in mixed and male occupations.

In describing CETA's occupational desegregation record, we use the CETA's definitions. In a *male-dominated* occupation females constitute less than 25 percent of that occupation's labor force; in a *mixed* occupation, 25 to 74 percent; and in a *female-dominated* occupation, 75 percent or more.

Table 16-4 shows the distribution of CETA jobholders among male, female, and mixed CETA jobs by sex and race. For FY 1976 to FY 1978, although only about 10 percent of the women in CETA jobs (work experience or PSE jobs) worked in male-dominated jobs, CETA placed about 25 percent in mixed occupations. Data published elsewhere show that CETA's occupational desegregation record for jobholders improved across the three fiscal years, the percentage of adult

TABLE 16-4 Distribution of FY 1976-FY 1978 CETA Jobholders by Sex Composition of Occupation and Sex (percent)

| Sex Composition of Occupation | Sex and Race/Ethnicity | | | | | | | |
| | Female | | | | Male | | | |
	Total	White	Black	Hispanic	Total	White	Black	Hispanic
Male-dominated	10.8	10.9	11.9	6.2	71.1	71.4	70.3	70.1
Female-dominated	64.1	62.8	64.4	74.4	8.3	8.0	8.2	11.0
Mixed	25.1	26.3	23.7	19.4	20.7	20.6	21.4	18.9
Total	100.0	100.0	100.0	100.0	100.0	100.0	100.0	100.0
N	401,176	256,073	115,261	29,842	605,484	407,838	150,568	47,078

SOURCE: Table 9, Berryman et al. (1981), p. 31.

TABLE 16-5   Distribution of FY 1976-FY 1978 CETA Trainees by Sex Composition of Occupation and Sex (percent)

Sex Composition of Occupation	Sex and Race/Ethnicity							
	Female				Male			
	Total	White	Black	Hispanic	Total	White	Black	Hispanic
Male-dominated	11.6	12.6	9.5	9.1	65.9	68.1	63.3	57.1
Female-dominated	49.3	46.2	55.8	55.8	4.1	3.0	6.8	6.5
Mixed	39.1	41.2	34.7	35.1	30.1	28.9	30.0	36.4
Total	100.0	100.0	100.0	100.0	100.0	100.0	100.0	100.0
N	56,264	38,030	13,359	13,792	104,828	74,169	16,867	4,875

SOURCE: Table 11, Berryman et al. (1981), p. 38.

women employed in male-dominated CETA jobs increasing from 7 to almost 12, the percentage in female-dominated CETA jobs decreasing from 68 to 62, and the percentage in mixed jobs remaining stable (Berryman et al., 1981). Adult females showed slightly more distributional change across time than that for adult males, but neither sex showed large changes.

CETA's occupational desegregation record in job training may be a better test of its desegregation success than is its record for jobholders. Since clients in job training presumably lack human capital in any specific occupation, CETA's occupational assignments should be less constrained by clients' prior occupational investments. More importantly, training can provide women with skills and credentials to enter male-dominated occupations.

Table 16-5 shows the distribution of those in CETA job training among male-dominated, female-dominated, and mixed occupations. Although CETA trained about the same percentage of women in male-dominated occupations as it employed in those occupations, it did train higher percentages in mixed occupations, reducing the percentage in female-dominated occupations to a little under 50 percent.

As the data in Table 16-1 suggest and data published elsewhere (Berryman et al., 1981) show, where training occurs (in a classroom or on the job) is clearly related to the sex

composition of the occupation in which the person is trained. As noted earlier, the causal relationships between activity and occupational assignments vary: an activity assignment may precede an occupational assignment, or vice versa, and in some cases both may be simultaneously determined by a third factor, such as title eligibility. Without addressing causality, we can note that women in classroom training were 60 percent more likely to be trained in a sex-typical occupation and about 60 percent less likely to be trained in a mixed occupation than were women in on-the-job training. Although classroom training assignments reduced female chances of being trained in a male-dominated occupation, the effects were not as great for this as for the other two occupational types.

The data reveal that women in on-the-job training were more likely to be trained in mixed and male-dominated occupations primarily as a function of OJT's occupational mix. OJT contains much larger proportions of male-dominated and mixed occupations than does classroom training. Although women were substantially overrepresented in the female-dominated occupations in OJT, the smaller numbers of female-dominated occupational slots in OJT produced some occupational desegregation. These data indicate that if CETA increases women's OJT participation, it should simultaneously increase occupational desegregation for women.

TABLE 16-6 Occupation of Last Pre-CETA Job by Occupation of CETA Job for Males and Females (FY 1976-FY 1978) (percent)

| Occupation of CETA Job | Occupation in Pre-CETA Job | | | | | |
| | Female | | | Male | | |
	Male-Dominated	Female-Dominated	Mixed	Male-Dominated	Female-Dominated	Mixed
Male-dominated job	37.6	6.8	9.9	84.0	39.4	54.0
Female-dominated job	43.4	75.8	44.8	4.2	37.2	7.6
Mixed job	19.0	17.4	45.3	11.9	23.4	38.4
Total	100.0	100.0	100.0	100.0	100.0	100.0
N (000)	24	138	83	279	27	114

SOURCE: Tables 13 and 14, Berryman et al. (1981), pp. 36-37.

Table 16-6 shows whether adult female and male CETA jobholders stayed in the same occupational type as their last pre-CETA job or moved to a new one. Thus, this table shows how much CETA changed participants' occupational patterns.

About 75 percent of adult females in female-dominated pre-CETA jobs entered female-dominated CETA jobs. Of those who moved out of female-dominated pre-CETA jobs, more than two-thirds entered mixed CETA jobs.

CETA retained less than 40 percent of adult females whose pre-CETA job was in a male-dominated occupation in their pre-CETA occupational type and placed more than 40 percent in female occupations. For females who had pre-CETA mixed jobs, CETA retained 45 percent in the same occupational type and placed more than 40 percent in female-dominated occupations.

Adult males had patterns similar but not identical to those of their female counterparts; where CETA assignment altered occupation it tended to move both males and females to occupations dominated by the same sex. A smaller percent of males than of females shifted out of sex-typical pre-CETA jobs (16 and 24 percent, respectively). Males shifted out of sex-atypical pre-CETA jobs at almost the same rate as that of females; they shifted out of mixed occupations at somewhat higher rates.

In sum, CETA changed the occupational type of proportionately more females than of males who had pre-CETA occupations typical for their sex. For those with pre-CETA mixed occupations or occupations atypical for their sex, CETA retained the same or a higher percentage of females than of males in CETA occupations of the same type. However, CETA shifted only one-quarter of those females in female-dominated pre-CETA occupations into mixed or male-dominated occupations. It did not retain even half of those women in pre-CETA mixed or sex-atypical occupations in occupations of the same type and placed most of the changers in female-dominated occupations, not mixed or male-dominated occupations.

Finally, we can ask about CETA's record in meeting clients' occupational preferences, as expressed in terms of its sex composition.[13] The data on occupational preferences should be treated with caution. Participants answered the preference question after they had enrolled in CETA, and most had been assigned to an occupation. Their responses may be biased in the direction of their postenrollment occupational

---

[13] The occupational preference data came from questions on the CLMS that asked: "Did you want a certain kind of (job/job training) when you visited the manpower office?" [If Yes] "What was the (job/job training) that you wanted?"

TABLE 16-7   Distribution of Desired Occupation by Obtained Occupation for Male and Female CETA Jobholders (FY 1976-FY 1978) (percent)

| Occupation of CETA Job | Desired Occupation | | | | | |
| | Female | | | Male | | |
	Male-Dominated	Female-Dominated	Mixed	Male-Dominated	Female-Dominated	Mixed
Male-dominated job	41.6	6.1	9.7	84.6	31.9	50.1
Female-dominated job	40.5	77.9	43.4	4.2	43.9	7.6
Mixed job	17.9	16.0	46.8	11.3	24.2	42.3
Total	100.0	100.0	100.0	100.0	100.0	100.0
N (000)	22	140	81	253	26	104

SOURCE: Table 17, Berryman et al. (1981), p. 42.

assignments. If they had no pre-enrollment preferences, they may have responded to this question by naming their assigned CETA occupation. If they were assigned to an occupation different from their preference, they may have accommodated to the discrepancy by modifying their original preference. Both of these potential biases would produce overestimates of the match between preferred and actual assignment. As such, our data on the match between preferred and actual occupational assignments represent the *maximum* responsiveness of CETA to clients' preferences.

In each fiscal year more than half of the adult female respondents indicated that they had had occupational preferences at the time of CETA entry.[14] For those women who expressed preferences, a small but increasing proportion wanted male-dominated jobs across time (5 percent to 10 percent). An increasing proportion (from 26 percent to 35 percent) wanted mixed jobs, and a declining majority (from 69 percent in FY 1976 to 55 percent in FY 1978) wanted jobs in female-dominated occupations.

Table 16-7 shows the CETA occupational distribution of adult females relative to their preferences at CETA entry. Fewer than half of the females who wanted male-dominated

---

[14] The percentages were 65, 57, and 59 for FY 1976, FY 1977, and FY 1978, respectively.

or mixed jobs got them. Of the females who wanted and failed to get sex-atypical jobs, 69 percent ended up in female-dominated jobs. Similarly, of the females who wanted but did not get mixed jobs, 82 percent ended up in female jobs. More than 75 percent of the women who wanted female jobs got them; and of those who failed to get desired female jobs, almost three-quarters got mixed, not male, jobs.

In sum, from FY 1976 to FY 1978 CETA employed or trained fewer than half of its female participants in male-dominated or mixed occupations. The percentages increased across fiscal years and were higher in on-the-job training than in CETA's classroom training or job services. Relative to their representation in the particular CETA service, females in on-the-job training were much more likely to be assigned to female-dominated occupations than were females in classroom training. OJT's better occupational desegregation record was attributable to the small number of female occupational slots in that activity. For women whose pre-CETA job had been a male or mixed occupation, CETA employed fewer than half in occupations of the same sex-composition type, shifting almost half of the "movers" into female occupations. For women whose pre-CETA job had been a female-dominated occupation, CETA shifted 25 percent to a mixed or male occupation — primarily to the former. Finally, for women who had occupational preferences at CETA entry, the match between preferred and actual CETA occupation was much higher for those with preferences for female-dominated jobs than for those with preferences for male or mixed jobs.

WAGE IMPLICATIONS OF CETA OCCUPATIONS

The low wages of female-dominated occupations are one of the primary reasons for trying to desegregate occupations for women. From this perspective wages are the critical basis for judging women's occupational experiences in CETA. We examine their wages during CETA and the wages paid in the labor force as a whole for the CETA occupation in which they trained or were employed.

In-CETA Wages

We assess sex differences in the CETA wage implications of female CETA occupational assignments in three ways: by 1-digit census occupational codes, the CETA service, and the sex-typicality of the occupation.

Table 16-8 shows the real average hourly CETA wage by sex for the 1-digit census occupational codes. Without exception males earn higher hourly wages than do females in the same occupational category.[15]

Table 16-9 shows the real average hourly wage by sex and CETA activity. Both sex and CETA activity affect CETA wages. If we look at wages by sex for the same CETA activity, males again get systematically higher wages than do females. The effects of CETA activity are the same for males and females — and, as data published elsewhere show, for whites, blacks, and Hispanics

TABLE 16-8   Average Hourly Wage of CETA Occupations by Sex (FY 1976-FY 1979) (constant dollars)

Occupation	N (000)	Males	N (000)	Females
Professional/ technical	(136)	3.56	(133)	3.39
Managerial/ administrative	(39)	3.78	(21)	3.56
Sales workers	(11)	3.24	(12)	2.49
Clerical	(98)	3.05	(537)	2.69
Crafts	(249)	3.25	(20)	2.72
Operatives	(121)	3.19	(43)	2.67
Transportation equipment operatives	(63)	3.04	(7)	2.75
Laborers	(380)	2.97	(32)	2.71
Service	(326)	2.86	(217)	2.54
Average	(1,422)	3.10	(1,023)	2.76

SOURCE: Table 37, Berryman and Waite (1982), p. 89.

(Berryman and Waite, 1982). As the last column of Table 16-9 shows, the rank order of wages by CETA activity is: public service employment > on-the-job training > work experience > classroom training. We noted earlier that females are more apt than males are to be funneled into Title I. Once in Title I, they are more apt than males are to be funneled into classroom training and work experience activities. Thus, a much larger percentage of CETA females than of CETA males are in the two activities (work experience and classroom training) that receive the lowest CETA wages.

Table 16-10 shows that women in CETA training and in CETA jobs received lower wages than men did in each of the three sex-composition occupational categories (Berryman et al., 1981). The wage difference between the sexes was greatest for the female-dominated occupations, less and about the same size in the male-dominated and mixed occupations.

Women in CETA job training received somewhat lower hourly wages if they trained in a female-dominated occupation than if they trained in either a male-dominated or mixed

---

[15] The large sample sizes make tests of significance relatively uninformative. We examine wages for differences large enough to be significant substantively.

TABLE 16-9   Average Hourly Wage by CETA Activity and Sex (FY 1976-FY 1979)
(constant dollars)

CETA Activity	N (000)	Males	N (000)	Females	N (000)	Total
Classroom training	(210)	2.23	(297)	2.06	(507)	2.13
OJT	(207)	3.22	(109)	2.70	(316)	3.04
Work experience	(398)	2.51	(400)	2.38	(797)	2.45
Public service employment	(794)	3.30	(476)	3.09	(1,270)	3.24

SOURCE: Table 44, Berryman and Waite (1982), p. 102.

occupation. However, training in a female-dominated occupation did not reduce the wages of men relative to the wages of those training in male-dominated and mixed occupations.

Women in CETA jobs received the lowest wage rates in female-dominated occupations and the highest in mixed occupations. Although men in CETA jobs also received the highest wage rates in mixed occupations, working in a female occupation did not depress their wages relative to the wages associated with male occupations.

However we categorize CETA occupations—by census code, CETA activity, or sex-typicality—within each category women's wages were on average about 90 percent of the men's wages. It is not clear how to judge this wage record. Although the average difference between male and female wages in CETA was small, men consistently

made higher wages than women did, and for two reasons the smallness of the difference between them may be less impressive than it initially appears. First, CETA wages were subject to floors and ceilings, thus compressing the wage range for both sexes. Second, however we categorize CETA occupations, participants in the same CETA activity or CETA occupation were probably more homogeneous even on unmeasured characteristics that affect wages than were members of an occupation in the general labor force.

Post-CETA Wages

We do not know the relationship between the occupation of the CETA job or job training and that of participants' post-CETA jobs. However, if CETA clients train or work in occupations whose counterparts in the labor

TABLE 16-10   Average Hourly Wage for CETA Trainees and CETA Jobholders by Sex
Typicality of Occupation (FY 1976-FY 1978) (constant dollars)

CETA Activity/Sex Typicality of Occupation	Male Total	White	Black	Hispanic	Female Total	White	Black	Hispanic
Trainees								
Male-dominated	3.63	3.66	3.61	3.46	3.00	3.04	2.96	2.82
Female-dominated	3.52	3.64	3.39	3.46	2.79	2.77	2.78	2.93
Mixed	3.32	3.37	3.19	3.25	2.89	2.88	2.94	2.94
N (000)	103	70	16	13	56	37	13	5
Job Holders								
Male-dominated	3.34	3.43	3.11	3.25	3.12	3.21	2.95	3.18
Female-dominated	3.34	3.41	3.25	3.10	2.90	2.94	2.84	2.79
Mixed	3.53	3.60	3.36	3.42	3.35	3.39	3.18	3.45
N (000)	609	396	145	46	407	251	112	29

SOURCE: Tables 20 and 21, Berryman et al. (1981), pp. 50-51.

TABLE 16-11 FY 1976-FY 1979 CETA Occupational Distribution by Sex and CETA Activity and the 1979 Unemployment Rates and Median Wages of Occupations in the Unsubsidized Sector

Occupational Category[a]	Males		Females		Unsubsidized Sector	
	CETA Training (percent)	CETA Job (percent)	CETA Training (percent)	CETA Job (percent)	1979 Unemployment Rates[b]	1979 Median Weekly Earnings[c] (Full-time Wage and Salary Workers) (dollars)
Professional/ technical	5.6	10.8	6.4	14.4	2.4	316
Managerial/ administrative	2.0	2.8	1.0	2.2	2.1	349
Sales workers	2.5	0.3	2.1	0.8	3.9	254
Clerical	6.1	7.2	53.3	53.5	4.6	195
Crafts	35.5	14.4	4.3	1.4	4.5	303
Operatives	28.7	4.0	11.9	1.4	8.4	211
Transportation equipment operatives	4.0	4.4	0.3	0.7	5.4	272
Laborers	7.7	30.1	1.0	3.5	10.8	206
Service	7.9	25.9	19.6	22.1	7.3	164
Total or average	100.0	100.0	100.0	100.0	5.8	244
N	375,246	1,189,725	332,945	872,307		

[a] These are the 1-digit census occupational categories. They exclude three categories that do not occur in the CETA occupational structure: Farmers and Farm Managers, Farm Laborers and Supervisors, and Private Household Workers.

[b] From Table A-23, Department of Labor (1980), p. 257.

[c] From Table 704, Bureau of the Census (1980), p. 424.

market as a whole have high unemployment rates, they should have less chance of capitalizing on their CETA occupational experience. If the labor market counterparts of their CETA occupations have low wages and CETA clients obtain a post-CETA job in the same occupation as their CETA occupation, their wages will be low.

Table 16-11 shows how CETA males and females distributed across the 1-digit census occupational codes by CETA service (training and jobs). It also shows the 1979 unemployment rates and median weekly earnings for these occupations in the labor market as a whole. The occupations with the highest 1979 unemployment rates were the operative, laborer, and service occupations; those with the lowest median weekly wage rates were the clerical, operative, laborer, and service occupations.

Females in CETA job training had about the same occupational distribution as that of females in CETA jobs. About 75 percent of the women in each of these activities fell into two occupations: clerical and service, both with low wages rates in the labor market as a whole. The service occupation also had relatively higher unemployment rates.

Males in CETA job training had different occupational distributions than those of males in CETA jobs. Of those in CETA jobs, more than 50 percent fell into two occupations: laborer and service, both with low wage rates and relatively high unemployment rates. For males in CETA job training, almost two-thirds fell into two different occupations: crafts and operatives. The former had a moderate unemployment rate and relatively high wage rate; the latter, a relatively high unemployment rate and low wage rate.

Thus, from FY 1976 to FY 1979 CETA employed most women in occupations with low wages in the labor market as a whole. CETA did not use training to alter the proportion of women in occupations offering relatively little economic security. CETA employed most men in two of the least economically secure occupations with relatively low median wages and high annual employment rates. However, CETA used training to reduce the percentage of men in the four low-wage occupations from two-thirds to one-half.

Conclusion

Training or working in male-dominated or mixed occupations gave women higher CETA wages than those from training or working in female-dominated occupations. However, CETA wages were consistently lower for women than for men in the same census occupation, in the same CETA service, or in the same sex-composition category.

Of those in CETA jobs, CETA employed 80 percent of the women and 67 percent of the men in the four occupations whose unsubsidized counterparts had the lowest wages and/or high unemployment rates. For those in CETA training, CETA did not alter the percentage of women in lower wage occupations, but reduced the percentage of men in these occupations from 67 to 50 percent.

However we judge CETA's occupational desegregation record, the bottom line of that record for women — their CETA wages and post-CETA economic prospects — is not impressive.

SUMMARY AND POLICY IMPLICATIONS

The analyses reported in this paper are useful as baseline information about women and CETA for the three years *prior* to CETA's 1978 reauthorization. We found that, relative to their eligibility for CETA, women were underrepresented in CETA's Titles I, II, and VI for all three fiscal years except in

Title I for FY 1978. When we controlled on variables that should affect title and activity assignments, we found women overrepresented in training activities, especially in classroom training relative to OJT, and in income-transfer jobs relative to jobs designed to lead to permanent, unsubsidized employment.

For all three years, female CETA participants were concentrated in female-dominated occupations, although the concentration was less among CETA job trainees than among CETA jobholders. CETA placed only about 40 percent of the women whose last pre-CETA occupation had been male-dominated *or* who had expressed a preference at CETA entry for a male-dominated occupation. In both cases, for those not placed in a male-dominated occupation, about two-thirds were placed in sex-typical occupations.

However we categorized the CETA occupation, within each category women's wages were about 90 percent of men's wages. Although the wage difference between men and women was not large, it was consistent, and for reasons discussed earlier in this paper, the smallness of the difference may be less impressive than it appears. In terms of their post-CETA prospects, about three-fourths of the women in CETA jobs *and* in CETA job training were employed or trained in occupations that paid low wages in the general labor market: service and clerical occupations.

The policy implications of these data are not clear for three major reasons:

1. In connection with CETA's reauthorization, CETA prime sponsors were directed to reduce occupational sex segregation in CETA. Our analyses provide a baseline for assessing CETA's response to that directive but not its current occupational status.

2. One of the reasons for desegregating CETA occupations was to improve women's post-CETA wages. At this juncture we lack

analyses that show that being trained or employed in male-dominated CETA occupations positively affects women's post-CETA economic outcomes. If the effects are negative for reasons substantially beyond the control of CETA, trade-offs between these two policy objectives — reduced occupational sex segregation and economic self-sufficiency — have to be made.

3. The male-dominated occupations for which most female CETA participants will be eligible are blue-collar occupations. Structural changes in the American economy — and the occupational consequences of these changes — imply that we need to re-examine what occupations — sex-typical or atypical — best equip CETA participants for economic self-sufficiency.

The avowed purpose of job programs, including CETA, is to improve the prospects of those who lack the skills to obtain acceptable employment on their own. This means getting people jobs at decent wages. Moving women into jobs currently filled predominately by men is desirable to the extent that it serves this purpose. But a number of factors may decrease the utility of occupational desegregation as a means to the ends espoused by job programs. First, most women eligible to participate in job programs could enter white-collar occupations only through stereotypically female jobs such as clerical work. The male-dominated jobs potentially available to them tend to be blue collar, primarily service, operative and, perhaps, crafts jobs. Many of these occupations show high rates of unemployment currently, and women seeking to enter them would face competition from large numbers of men. Second, the structural changes now taking place in the economy make unskilled and semiskilled blue-collar jobs especially susceptible to technical obsolescence. Third, little empirical evidence exists on the success of occupational integration as a mechanism for improving the employment prospects of women. For these reasons, we argue

that job programs for women should carefully assess their goals and the ways in which the sex composition of the occupation affects the chances of achieving those goals.

REFERENCES

Barrett, Nancy S.
1979 "Women in the Job Market: Occupations, Earnings, and Career Opportunities." P. 39 in Ralph E. Smith, ed., *The Subtle Revolution*. Washington, D.C.: The Urban Institute Press.

Berryman, Sue E., and Linda J. Waite
1982 *Hispanics and CETA: Issues of Access, Distribution, and Equity*. Unpublished working paper, Rand Corporation, Santa Monica, Calif.

Berryman, Sue E., Winston K. Chow, and Robert M. Bell
1981 *CETA: Is It Equitable for Women?* N-1683-NCEP. Santa Monica, Calif.: Rand Corporation.

Bureau of the Census
1980 *Statistical Abstract of the United States: 1980* (101st ed.) Washington, D.C.: U.S. Government Printing Office.
1981 Current Population Reports, Series P-20, No. 363. *Population Profile of the United States, 1980*. Washington, D.C.: U.S. Department of Commerce. Available from the U.S. Superintendent of Documents, U.S. Government Printing Office.

Chiswick, Barry, J. Fackler, June O'Neill, and Solomon Polacheck
1974 "The Effect of Occupation on Race and Sex Differences in Hourly Earnings." Pp. 219-228 in *Proceedings of the American Statistical Association*. Washington, D.C.: American Statistical Association.

Department of Labor
1980 *Employment and Training Report of the President*. Washington, D.C.

Mirengoff, William, and Lester Rindler
1978 *CETA: Manpower Programs Under Local Control*. Washington, D.C.: National Academy of Sciences.

Sawhill, Isabel V.
1973 "The Economics of Discrimination Against Women: Some New Findings." *Journal of Human Resources* 8: 383-396.
1976 "Discrimination and Poverty Among Women Who Head Families." Pp. 201-211 in Martha Blaxall and Barbara Reagan, eds., *Women and the Workplace*. Chicago: University of Chicago Press.

Wolf, Wendy C., and Rachel Rosenfeld
1978 "Sex Structure of Occupations and Job Mobility." *Social Forces* 56(3):823-844.

17 Commentary

WENDY C. WOLF

The paper by Waite and Berryman deals with the Comprehensive Employment and Training Act (CETA) system and its record in providing access to nontraditional jobs. CETA represented a potential area of federal intervention but also a potential force that may have perpetuated sex-segregated job choice. It also represented a system in which there had been considerable effort during the last decade to improve services to women and, in fact, to improve nontraditional options for women. When inspecting this system, one could look at the record—that is, have the kinds of services improved (i.e., offering nontraditional options)? What is the impact of this system itself on women and men?

Before commenting on this paper, it is critical to consider a little history. In 1978 there were considerable changes in the CETA legislation to make it more responsive to the needs of women, both in terms of serving them in numbers relative to their proportion in the eligible population and in trying to increase their nontraditional options. Unfortunately, the data used by Berryman and Waite came from the pre-1978 period. So they are looking at the CETA system prior

to the time that this "new" legislation took effect. The relevant question to be answered is, therefore, how was CETA doing *before* this additional emphasis was put on services to women.

Another critical point to consider is that Berryman and Waite often mention public service employment (PSE). PSE has been out of vogue for a while. For this reason, the focus of my comments is on classroom training, on-the-job training, and adult work experience.

Even prior to the 1978 amendments, which were designed to encourage the expansion of nontraditional opportunities for women, there were slightly increasing proportions of women moving into nontraditional jobs within CETA and into nontraditional training, despite the fact that, within CETA, the overall proportion of women being exposed to nontraditional options was not high. But the CETA system was not keeping pace with women's changing aspirations. An inspection of the aspirations of women for nontraditional work reveals they were rising at a faster rate than was the opening up of nontraditional career options within CETA. It is interesting to note that the aspirations among women for nontraditional work were growing (which I think is very divergent from the evidence Marini and Brinton present in Chapter 11 about high school girls) but that the whole system wasn't changing fast enough to accommodate these changes.

Berryman and Waite show the relationship between aspiration and the type of service received. Of the women who had traditionally female aspirations, 77 percent were placed in female-typed jobs; of those with male aspirations, 41.5 percent were placed in male-typed jobs, and 40 percent into female-typed jobs; of those with "mixed" aspirations, 46.8 percent were placed in mixed occupations, and 43 percent into female-typed occupations. This suggests that if one enters the CETA system with nontraditional aspirations, one is likely to get funneled into female-typed jobs anyway.

The Berryman and Waite paper makes a big deal about wages—I am less likely to be so excited about this issue. The National Research Council's Committee on Evaluation of Employment and Training Programs once produced a table showing male-female differences in wages in CETA. It showed that women earned 90 percent of what men earned in CETA. This is a bit misleading, however, in part due to the fact that within CETA there was a floor and a ceiling on wages, thus little variation.

I have one minor caution about Berryman and Waite's analysis. They talk about assignment either to on-the-job training or classroom training and how that increases or decreases one's likelihood of being in or getting into a sex-typed job. One has to be careful about assuming directionality between the two. The fact is that clerical training occurs in the classroom. So if a CETA participant is going into clerical training, he or she is assigned to classroom training. So I don't really think that you can treat one as exogenous and one as endogenous. They are jointly determined.

This paper shows some potential for change in the CETA system, especially since it was done in the preamendment days. It also shows that the CETA system has helped perpetuate the status quo in terms of occupational segregation.

It is important to realize that Berryman and Waite describe CETA before the 1978 amendments. From 1978 to 1983, specific language was added to the law to encourage sex equity and the movement of women into nontraditional jobs. It should be noted that in the new Job Training Partnership Act, very little proscriptive language is included to help legislate fair and equitable treatment for women.

18 Concluding Remarks

FRANCINE D. BLAU

Employment segregation by sex is one of the most persistent and pervasive characteristics of the labor market. The papers in this volume help us to understand the dimensions of such segregation, its fundamental causes, and its consequences for women's economic status. They also shed some light on the effectiveness of policy interventions.

In Chapter 2, Andrea Beller gives us the heartening news that, on the basis of analysis of Current Population Survey data, the tendency of men and women to be segregated by occupation declined noticeably over the 1970s, particularly among younger women. Moreover, this decline was at a rate nearly three times that of the extremely small decline that occurred during the 1960s. We must remember, however, that the magnitude of segregation remains high. Furthermore, although women increased their share of many traditionally male managerial and professional occupations during the 1970s, this was not the case for heavily male craft and operative jobs.

In Chapter 3 Bielby and Baron demonstrate that estimates of the magnitude of sex segregation in employment are extremely sensitive to the level of aggregation of the data. Even detailed (three-digit) census occupational categories group some typically male and some typically female jobs into apparently integrated categories. To the extent that men and women workers in the same occupational categories are segregated by firm, aggregation across firms will result in an underestimate of the magnitude of sex segregation in employment. Using establishment-level data and defining segregation in terms of the employer's own job categories, Bielby and Baron find a striking pattern of complete sex segregation by occupation at the establishment level for a majority of firms (including some single-sex enterprises) and an extremely high level of segregation for the others. Their work raises the question of whether estimates of trends in the magnitude of occupational segregation based on such microdata might differ from Beller's estimates on the basis of aggregate data. Less than a quarter of the firms in Bielby and Baron's longitudinal sample experienced any declines in the degree of occupational sex segregation during the late 1960s and early 1970s.

These are the contours of occupational

segregation by sex in the U.S. labor market. In assessing the significance of occupational segregation, we must know more about its causes and consequences. From a policy perspective, an understanding of the consequences is crucial for assessing how important a problem it is, while an analysis of its causes helps us determine the most effective tools for attacking it.

The studies I reviewed in Chapter 7 suggest that occupational segregation does reduce the earnings of women, although there are considerable problems in precisely estimating the magnitude of this effect. A particular problem is that overcrowding in the female sector may adversely affect women's wages in the male sector as well. This imparts a downward bias to estimates of the wage consequences of segregation based on comparisons of women's wages in female and male occupations. It is also important to point out that the focus on earnings does not take into account the possibly negative nonpecuniary consequences of sex segregation in employment for women. Intuitively one feels that occupational segregation reinforces cultural notions that men and women differ fundamentally in capabilities, preferences, and social and economic roles.

Our appraisal of the seriousness of the problem of occupational segregation may depend in part on the ease with which women are able to move between the male and female sectors. The studies in Chapters 4 and 10 do find some movement of women from predominantly female to predominantly male jobs and vice versa. In Chapter 4, Rosenfeld found that such changes in the sex labels of occupations were experienced by about one-third of women job changers over a one-year period, while in Chapter 10 Corcoran, Duncan, and Ponza found that about one-third of all employed women made such shifts over a five-year period. These findings suggest that the male and female sectors ought not to be viewed as watertight compartments, but they do not in my opinion greatly

mitigate our concern over the issue of occupational sex segregation. First, the magnitude of movement is fairly small—that is, most women workers did not change the sex label of their jobs over the periods analyzed. Moreover, it is difficult to judge the magnitude of the probability of such moves in the abstract. We need to know more about the desire for such moves on the part of workers and how easy it is for women relative to men to move out of (generally lower-paying) female jobs into (generally higher-paying) male jobs. It is instructive in this regard that both studies find the probability of a man moving from a predominantly female to a predominantly male job to be considerably higher than the probability of a woman making such a move. Furthermore, women whose previous jobs were predominantly male were much more likely to change the sex label of their jobs than women whose previous jobs were predominantly female. Second, Bielby and Baron's findings raise the question of how much of what appear to be shifts in the sex labels of jobs as measured by aggregate data actually entails changes in the sex label of the individual's job at the establishment level.

The causes of occupational segregation are often classified in terms of supply- versus demand-side factors. The major supply-side explanations considered in this volume are sex-role socialization and the human capital model. In Chapter 11, Marini and Brinton describe how the socialization process influences the occupational orientation of men and women as well as the role they see market work playing in their lives. It is the latter difference between men and women that is emphasized by the human capital explanation critiqued by Corcoran et al. According to this view, because women anticipate shorter and less continuous work lives than men, it will be in their economic self-interest to choose female occupations, which require smaller human capital investments and have lower wage penalties for time spent out of the labor force. Their own research and that of others summarized by Corcoran et al. does not tend to support the human capital model. In particular, women with discontinuous work careers appear to be no more likely to work at female jobs than women with more continuous work experience. Nor did their findings suggest that the selection of female jobs is consistent with a strategy of maximizing lifetime income, given shorter, more disrupted work lives.

On the demand side, I point out in Chapter 7 that employers may be motivated to exclude women from particular jobs because of the belief that they would be less stable or productive workers than men. Even if not initially correct, such views can become self-fulfilling prophesies if women are then given fewer incentives than men to become stable, productive workers. Roos and Reskin in Chapter 13 emphasize institutional factors in their review of a variety of barriers to female employment in traditionally male jobs at four points in the job allocation process: pre-employment training, access and assignment to jobs, mobility, and retention. The operation of these barriers does not rely on conscious, overt discriminatory acts on the part of employers. Rather, the everyday operation of the system works against female employment in traditionally male jobs. A clearer understanding of the functions these institutional mechanisms serve is of long-run importance in devising effective strategies to remove these obstacles to women's advancement.

While the papers in this volume do not endeavor to fully evaluate the impact of federal government intervention in this area, an interesting view emerges of what such an evaluation would entail. A variety of ways in which the government potentially influences women's economic status are identified. Some of these effects are positive and some are negative. An overall assessment of the government's impact would necessitate identifying the net effect of all its many policies and programs. This point may be il-

lustrated by a discussion of the impact of a few government policies. On one hand, as Roos and Reskin point out, governmental income tax and social security policy tend to discourage female labor force participation. To the extent that the human capital explanation has merit, the resulting decrease in women's work lives would increase the likelihood of their entering traditionally female jobs. Furthermore, while government training programs provide an opportunity for intervention to reduce segregation by training individuals for sex-atypical jobs, Waite and Berryman's research suggests in Chapter 16 that occupational training under the Comprehensive Employment and Training Act (CETA) is sex segregated to a great extent.

On the other hand, of course, the government administers an impressive array of antidiscrimination legislation and regulations. There is some debate over the effectiveness of these activities, and it is undoubtedly difficult to measure governmental impact in this area. But it is significant that O'Farrell and Harlan report in Chapter 15 that governmental pressure was an important factor promoting change within some firms. They also find that the employment growth of firms provides opportunities for integration and thus also facilitates change. The government's macroeconomic policies and their impact on overall business conditions are therefore another way in which government may have an effect on the employment opportunities of women—the quality of jobs obtained as well as the probability of finding a job at all.

While all movements toward occupational integration should be welcome, it is important to realize that the movement of women into male jobs does not always bring women significantly closer to economic parity with men. For one thing, occupational sex segregation may be replaced by female enclaves at the lower levels of male job ladders—a process O'Farrell and Harlan term *resegregation*. For another, O'Farrell and

Harlan note that women may gain access to male jobs just as they are becoming technologically obsolete. Indeed, Strober argues in Chapter 8 that, in general, women are restricted to the leftovers, the jobs that men do not want.

Sex segregation in employment remains a pervasive feature of the labor market and a major cause of women's lower earnings. While sex differences in socialization and the voluntary choices that women make in their selection of jobs may play a role in producing sex segregation in employment, labor market discrimination is undoubtedly also a major factor. Such discrimination is deeply entrenched: Within the workplace, a myriad of institutional mechanisms work to perpetuate segregation of work along sex lines without requiring overt, conscious acts of discrimination on the part of employers. While some government policies work to reduce sex segregation in employment, others actually help perpetuate it. Thus, change will not be easy—yet such change is essential if we are to move substantially closer to the goal of economic parity between women and men in the labor market.